FEAR WITHOUT FRONTIERS:
HORROR CINEMA ACROSS THE GLOBE

First edition published July 2003
by FAB Press

FAB Press
Grange Suite
Surrey Place
Godalming
GU7 1EY
England, U.K.

www.fabpress.com

Text copyright © 2003 Steven Jay Schneider and individual contributors.

Design and layout by Harvey Fenton.

Front cover design by Deborah Bacci, Chris Charlston and Harvey Fenton.

This Volume copyright © FAB Press 2003
World Rights Reserved.
No part of this book may be reproduced or transmitted in any form or by any means, electronic or mechanical, including photocopying, recording, or by any information storage and retrieval system, without the prior written permission of the Publisher.

Copyright of illustrations is the property of the production or distribution companies concerned. These illustrations are reproduced here in the spirit of publicity, and whilst every effort has been made to trace the copyright owners, the editor and publishers apologise for any omissions and will undertake to make any appropriate changes in future editions of this book if necessary.

Front cover illustration:
Maa ki Shakti (aka *Ammoru*) (India).

Back cover illustrations:
top right: *Khooni Panja* (India), middle left: *Exorcismo Negro* (Brazil), bottom right: *Seytan* (Turkey)

Frontispiece illustration:
Dany Carrel discovers the secret of the stone women in the shadows of the Mill tower,
Mill of the Stone Women (Italy).

Contents page illustration:
Promotional montage for Sohail Shaikh's *Ab Kya Hoga* (India).

A CIP catalogue record for this book is available from the British Library

ISBN 1 903254 15 9

Fear Without Frontiers
Horror Cinema Across the Globe

edited by
Steven Jay Schneider

Contents

Preface — Kim Newman ... 7

Introduction — Steven Jay Schneider ... 11

PART I: ARTISTS, ACTORS, AUTEURS

Madmen, visionaries and freaks: the films of Alejandro Jodorowsky ... 15
- Pam Keesey

Coffin Joe and José Mojica Marins: strange men for strange times ... 27
- André Barcinski

Return of the phantom: Maxu Weibang's *Midnight Song* ... 39
- David Robinson

Enfant terrible: the terrorful, wonderful world of Anthony Wong ... 45
- Lisa Odham Stokes & Michael Hoover

The rain beneath the earth: an interview with Nonzee Nimibutr ... 61
- Mitch Davis

Cinema of the doomed: the tragic horror of Paul Naschy ... 69
- Todd Tjersland

Sex and death, Cuban style: the dark vision of Jorge Molina ... 81
- Ruth Goldberg; followed by an interview with the director, "Testing Molina," by Steven Jay Schneider

PART II: FILMS, SERIES, CYCLES

Fantasmas del cine Mexicano: the 1930s horror film cycle of Mexico ... 93
- Gary D. Rhodes

The cosmic mill of Wolfgang Preiss: Giorgio Ferroni's *Mill of the Stone Women* ... 105
- David Del Valle

The "lost" horror film series: the Edgar Wallace *krimis* ... 111
- Ken Hanke

The exotic pontianaks ... 125
- Jan Uhde & Yvonne Uhde

Playing with genre: defining the Italian *giallo* ... 135
- Gary Needham

The Italian zombie film: from derivation to invention ... 161
- Donato Totaro

Austrian psycho killers & home invaders: the horror-thrillers *Angst* & *Funny Games* ... 175
- Jürgen Felix & Marcus Stiglegger

PART III: GENRE HISTORIES AND STUDIES

Coming of age: the South Korean horror film — 185
- Art Black

Between appropriation and innovation: Turkish horror cinema — 205
- Kaya Özkaracalar

Witches, spells and politics: the horror films of Indonesia — 219
- Stephen Gladwin

The unreliable narrator: subversive storytelling in Polish horror cinema — 231
- Nathaniel Thompson

The Beast from Bollywood: a history of the Indian horror film — 243
- Pete Tombs

In a climate of terror: the Filipino monster movie — 255
- Mauro Feria Tumbocon, Jr.

French revolution: the secret history of Gallic horror movies — 265
- David Kalat

PART IV: CASE STUDY - JAPANESE HORROR CINEMA

Pain threshhold: the cinema of Takashi Miike — 285
- Rob Daniel & Dave Wood; followed by an interview with the director, "When cynicism becomes art," by Julien Fonfrède

The Japanese horror film series: *Ring* and *Eko Eko Azarak* — 295
- Ramie Tateishi

The urban techno-alienation of Sion Sono's *Suicide Club* — 305
- Travis Crawford

Notes on contributors — 312

Index — 314

Preface

Kim Newman

Of all screen genres, only the western and the musical were invented and developed primarily or even exclusively in the USA.[1] And yet, in almost all cases, the dominant strains of any given genre, identifying cycles and stand-alone individual masterworks, are American: the gangster film, the melodrama, the war movie, the romantic comedy, science fiction. Only the martial arts movie grew up away from Hollywood, a non-American alternative to the western.

The mainstream of the horror film is American, though the defining cycle of the 1930s, commenced at Universal Studios by Tod Browning's *Dracula* and James Whale's *Frankenstein* (both 1931), is a synthesis of Hollywood industrial production methods with a primarily (though not exclusively) British literary tradition (Bram Stoker, Mary Shelley, R.L. Stevenson) and the expressionist visual techniques coined by the run of silent horror films from Germany. Many of the key personnel in the first American horror boom, often employed by Universal Pictures and then taken up by competitor studios eager to get in on the act, came from the United Kingdom (James Whale, Boris Karloff, Claude Rains, Charles Laughton, Colin Clive, Lionel Atwill) or had experience in the German film industry (Bela Lugosi, Karl Freund, Edgar G. Ulmer, Paul Leni, Curt Siodmak, Peter Lorre, Michael Curtiz). The death of home-grown macabre icon Lon Chaney[2] after the completion of his only talkie (*The Unholy Three*, 1930) meant that for Americans horror would speak with a European accent, whether the sly Anglo-Indian lisp of Karloff or the drawled Hungarian cadences of Lugosi.

Aside from the persistent run of films (*Murders in the Rue Morgue*, 1932; *The Black Cat*, 1934) drawn from the works of Edgar Allan Poe - who half-aspired to a European sensibility even as he incarnated the first great stereotype of American letters, the alcoholic newspaperman - most of the subjects of early American horror films were European. Chaney's greatest grotesque characters were French, in *The Hunchback of Notre Dame* (1923) and *The Phantom of the Opera* (1925), while 1930s monsters hailed from that imaginary Mittel Europa which is always "Transylvania" whether or not it is actually supposed to be Czechoslovakia (*Mark of the Vampire*, 1935) or the made-up "Kleinschloss" (*The Vampire Bat*, 1933), Haiti (*White Zombie*, 1932), the South Seas (*King Kong*, 1933), Ancient Egypt (*The Mummy*, 1932), fogbound London (*Dr. Jekyll and Mr Hyde*, 1932, *The Lodger*, 1944), Paris (*Mad Love*, 1935) or the Far East (*The Mask of Fu Manchu*, 1932). Some films even doubled the alienation effect by bringing monsters from remote locales to a contemporary London that still seemed mid-Victorian by Yankee standards, as witness the Transylvanian visitors of *Dracula* and *Dracula's Daughter* (1936), and the Tibetan curse of *The WereWolf of London* (1935). Even the odd American-set horror, like Warner Brothers' *Dr. X* (1932) and *Mystery of the Wax Museum* (1933), took pains to establish a "European" feel, casting Englishman Lionel Atwill as foreign-sounding madmen (Dr. Xavier, Ivan Igor) who menace all-American Fay Wray and handing directing chores over to the versatile Hungarian Michael Curtiz, who deftly laid Technicolor expressionist touches over the typical Warners US big city feel. The Curtiz films make something of the disjunction between mad science experiments or bodies encased in wax and fast-talking, cynical reporters who joke

[1] Nevertheless, the western owes a great deal to the pre-cinematic traditions of bandit tales found in every culture in the world and the musical to many European varieties of theatre-with-music.

[2] Chaney was never quite the horror star Forrest J. Ackerman would like him to have been. His career range, taking in pirates in *Treasure Island* (1920) to the drill instructor of *Go Tell the Marines* (1927), marks him out to be as much a precursor of chameleon character actor stars like Alec Guinness and Peter Sellers as it does a monster man like Karloff or Lugosi.

about Prohibition and snarl their copy down the telephone like refugees from *The Front Page* (1931).

The 'Universal' style of horror stayed in vogue for fifteen years, modified a little by the arrival of a new American horror star in the doggily unlikely Lon Chaney, Jr. - his most successful vehicle, *The Wolf Man* (1941), casts him as a Yankee who goes back to his roots in a backlot Wales and mingles with all manner of Brits and gypsies, accepting the script's curse via a bite from Bela Lugosi that also suggests a curse of typecasting being passed on. In the 1940s, the most invigorating new cycle came from the Russian-born Val Lewton, whose first features were directed by the Frenchman Jacques Tourneur (*Cat People*, 1942; *I Walked With a Zombie*, 1943; *The Leopard Man*, 1943) and set in the Americas[3] but who called in American directors Mark Robson and Robert Wise even as his films cast Karloff and looked to Greece (*Isle of the Dead*, 1945), Scotland (*The Body Snatcher*, 1945) or London (*Bedlam*, 1946). In the 1950s, a fresh approach to horror was established by *The Thing From Another World* (1951), which at once looked further afield than Romania for its monster but emphasised the very Americanness of its human characters and combined gothic shadows with the fast pace and tough dialogue associated with its supposed producer, Howard Hawks. The gothic came back via England's Hammer Films (their breakthrough feature was *The Curse of Frankenstein*, 1957) and the most completely American cycle of horror emerged in Roger Corman's series of Poe-derived films starring the effete but non-European Vincent Price (commencing with *The Fall of the House of Usher*, 1960).

Independent American filmmakers like George A. Romero (*Night of the Living Dead*, 1968), Wes Craven (*The Last House on the Left*, 1972), Larry Cohen (*It's Alive!*, 1975), the Canadian David Cronenberg (*Shivers*, 1976), John Carpenter (*Halloween*, 1978) and Tobe Hooper (*The Texas Chain Saw Massacre*, 1974) might have rebelled against the conventions of the Universal-Hammer-Hollywood style when they set out to make committed, extreme, gruesome, genuinely scary, politically provocative horror films, but they nevertheless constituted a mutation of the mainstream. From the low-budget zombie, slasher and venereal mutant movies that invigorated American horror in the 1970s rose entire cycles, including the larger-budgeted Devil movies that followed *Rosemary's Baby* (1968) and *The Exorcist* (1973), which came to dominate the genre in ways still being felt. Almost all the auteurs cited above have made films based on the works of Stephen King,[4] who became the default American horror writer after Poe (H.P. Lovecraft never quite took pole position) and represents the most monolithically American face the genre has ever had. They have also all worked through their combination of debt to tradition and desire to escape from it by making revisionary vampire movies: Cronenberg's *Rabid* (1978), Romero's *Martin* (1978), Hooper's *Salem's Lot* (1979), Cohen's *A Return to Salem's Lot* (1986), Craven's *A Vampire in Brooklyn* (1995), Carpenter's *Vampires* (1999).

The figure of the vampire has come to stand for the horror film as the figure of the cowboy does for the western, and a handy way of encapsulating the horror film in any culture is to examine its vampire movies. Vampire movies have been made in Turkey (*Drakula Istanbul'da*, 1953), India (*Bandh Darwaza*, 1990), Hong Kong (the *Mr.*

---

[3] Though all are foreign-tinged: *Cat People* is about a Serbian curse, *I Walked with a Zombie* concerns Caribbean voodoo and *The Leopard Man* transfers a novel set in South America to New Mexico.

[4] Hooper's *Salem's Lot* (1979), Cronenberg's *The Dead Zone* (1983), Carpenter's *Christine* (1983), Cohen's *A Return to Salem's Lot* (1986), Romero's *The Dark Half* (1993). Craven's *A Nightmare on Elm Street* (1984) is heavily King-influenced.

Vampire series), Italy (*L'ultima preda del vampiro/Playgirls and the Vampire*, 1960), Spain (*El gran amor del Conde Dracula/Dracula's Great Love*, 1972), France (*Le frisson des vampires/Sex and the Vampire*, 1970), Germany (*Der fluch der grunen augen/Cave of the Living Dead*, 1963), Korea (*Wolnyoui Han*, 1980), the Philippines (*The Vampire People*, 1966), South Africa (*Pure Blood*, 2001), Greece (*Dracula Tan Exarchia*, 1983), Taiwan (*Elusive Song of the Vampire*, 1987), Denmark (*Dracula's Ring*, 1978), Malaysia (*Pontianak*, 1956), Belgium (*Le rouge aux levres/Daughters of Darkness*, 1971), Argentina (*Sangre de Virgenes*, 1968), Brazil (*As sete vampiras/7 Vampires*, 1985), Cuba (*¡Vampiros en la Habana!/Vampires in Havana*, 1985), Mexico (*El vampiro/The Vampire*, 1958), Japan (*Chi o Suu Me/Lake of Dracula*, 1971), the Netherlands (*Bloedverwanten/Blood Relations*, 1977), Australia (*Thirst*, 1979) and the former Soviet Union (*Pyuschye Krovy/Blood-Suckers*, 1991) - and though it took a surprisingly long time (discounting US-backed efforts like the *Subspecies* films), even Romania has gotten in on the act, with the 2002 release of *Vlad nemuritorul/Dracula the Impaler*.

In each case, the elements come from English-language horror literature and film, with the archetypal figure of the cloaked Dracula reincarnated in a local context and set among conventions drawn from specific lore. Obviously, in vampire movies made in non-Christian countries, the monster is not repelled by the cross - but might shrink from a statue of the Buddha or the aum symbol. Frequently, the fanged blood-drinker of Hollywood and Hammer is commingled with whatever variant features in national myth, like the hopping, mummy-look jiangshi of Chinese films. Occasionally, there seems even to be a deliberate setting of different horror traditions against each other, for satirical purpose in *¡Vampiros en la Habana!*, in which languidly decadent European vampires and aggressively capitalist American gangster vampires are both put in their places by a revolutionary Cuban half-breed; or just to lever in a contrast, as in *As sete vampiras*, whose cloaked Count-type turns out to be innocent of vampire murders actually committed by a blood-sucking plant, or the several recent Hong Kong films that take a cue from Hammer's *The Legend of the Seven Golden Vampires* (1973) by mixing Transylvanian-style vampires with their hopping Chinese cousins.

The first important studies of the history of the horror film, by Carlos Clarens (*An Illustrated History of the Horror Film*, 1967) and Ivan Butler (*The Horror Film*, 1967), made the development of genre a story, conceding its roots with Méliès in France and the Expressionists in Germany but then following an Anglo-American narrative with very occasional diversions like the Italianate horrors of Mario Bava. Since the 1960s, this has been the accepted and natural way of looking at genre - until recently for the very practical reason that most commentators writing in English had probably seen every American or British horror film ever made but only a scattering of genre movies from other territories. It was a simple matter to dismiss, say, the Mexican gothic cycle of the late 1950s and early 1960s by ridiculing the likes of *El Santo contra las mujeres vampiro* (*Samson vs. the Vampire Women*, 1961), or to shudder at the "ineptitude" of Jesus Franco on the strength of an hour-long cut-down of *La comtesse noire* (*Female Vampire*, 1973). Of course, the French magazine *Midi-Minuit Fantastique* was more open to films from non-Anglophone cultures, and Gallic enthusiasm for Bava was caught by British critics frustrated at the censor-imposed withholding of *La maschera del demonio* (*The Mask of Satan*, 1960) from the United Kingdom even as AIP was hammering out Americanised versions of his films for kiddie matinees.

It is possible that English-language releases did no favours. To this day, there is an oppressive tendency on the part of American writers when discussing 'foreign' horror films to use slapdash American release titles - listing *La maschera* as *Black Sunday*, or even to colonise Brazil's major horror icon by tagging Jose Mojica Marins's alter ego "Coffin Joe" rather than Zé do Caixão, as if a character as strange and specifically resonant could be processed at Ellis Island and repackaged as a samba Freddy Krueger. To a certain breed of camp-follower, the poor dubbing is essential to appreciation of films that can therefore be sneered at for their technical ineptitude and recycled for contemptible horror host shows, cut into with pathetic jokes and contextualised as trash. It's an especial irony that this unearned superiority is achieved in the process of Americanisation in that the bad dubbing was usually done Stateside - the average Mexican horror movie is lit, art-directed, photographed and edited to a high standard,[5] and the adoption of different

[5] As is made especially obvious by those scrambled versions made by Jerry Warren, who would transform *La Momia Azteca* (1957) and *La Casa del Terror* (1960) into *Attack of the Mayan Mummy* (1964) and *Face of the Screaming Werewolf* (1965) by intercutting footage from the original with new material shot with flat lighting, locked-down camera, non-existent art direction and endless pointless dialogue.

preface

(though not necessarily worse) styles of acting is a cultural variant rather than a failing. Bela Lugosi and Robert Englund are no more high-mimesis in their line readings than German Robles or Marins. The worst type of colonialism comes in the practice of remaking foreign horror films to suit a notional American audience, with the incidental effect of insulting the original audience when Hollywood exports their versions of *Godzilla* (1998), *Diabolique* (1996) or *The Vanishing* (1993) back to Japan, France and the Netherlands. Low-budget American attempts at Italian-style zombies (*Shock Waves*, 1977) or HK-ish hopping vampires (*The Jitters*, 1988) aren't usually up to much either.

Aside from the odd article on figures like Dario Argento, Mario Bava, Jean Rollin or Paul Naschy, and the occasional round-up of the monster movie scenes in Spain or Italy, little serious writing on non-English language horror was available until the publication in 1986 of the first edition of Phil Hardy's *Film Encyclopedia: Horror* volume, from Aurum in the UK and Overlook in the US.[6] Often erroneously thought to be entirely written by its editor, the Hardy volume gives at least equal space to horror films from around the world as it does to the more familiar British and American product, showcasing thoughtful, informed pieces from unsung experts Paul Willeman, Tom Milne and Verina Glaessner. The real importance of the Hardy encyclopedia may be in its tone: not academic, but also not crippled by the Michael Medved 'Golden Turkey' approach that has made so much writing on cinema in general, and horror cinema in particular, irrelevant, witless, wilfully ignorant and irritating. Compiled well before the wide availability of most of the films it mentions on video when even researching basic credits resembled a trip into a lost continent, the first edition of the book had more than its share of errors but also more than its share of first-time-in-print coverage. For instance, Willeman's entries on Franco cleared the way for a more thoroughgoing reassessment of this filmmaker's work, while the openness of the project encouraged later writers like Pete Tombs (*Immoral Tales*, 1995, *Mondo Macabro*, 1997), Steve Thrower (editor of the indispensable *Eyeball* magazine) and Tim Lucas (of *Video Watchdog*) to search even further afield and open up the horror subcultures of many lands.

Fear Without Frontiers is not an entry-level book. It is assumed that the reader will already have a working knowledge of mainstream horror and be open to alternative possibilities, even purposes, of the genre. It does not pretend to be a complete overview of non-Anglo-American horror, focusing instead on a clutch of specific creators or countries, asking always what horror might mean in this particular context, what are the local factors that may have shaped these films (and which might be obscure to an overseas audience) and what relationship they might have to the great ongoing tradition. It is an inverse snobbery to claim that anybody's horror is somehow "better" than anybody else's, and there's no point in using Lucio Fulci as a club to batter Wes Craven. The high amazement factor found in many films discussed here comes as much from unfamiliarity as from genuine worth: watching one Indian, Malaysian or Hong Kong horror picture is a revelation,[7] but ploughing through fifty will reveal conventions and clichés as prevalent and ultimately limiting as those that obtain in the American slasher film. There is also something faintly trainspotterish about those who prize foreign films for levels of gore, sexual violence or general depravity they feel US movies are not delivering. If that's your only interest in cinema, then form an internet newsgroup and swap lists of ten favourite eyeball-gouges with similarly sad fellows - this book will have little to say to you.

"Foreignness" is an essential component of horror - to meet a monster, it must come to you (like Dracula emigrating from Transylvania) or you must go to it (like the Mummy, waiting in an Egyptian tomb). Here, we are considering the possibility that you might yourself be foreign.[8] Some things (death, darkness, being alone) frighten us all; others (flying severed heads, Godzilla, the golem) are culturally specific. In this book, we're interested in the second category. Now, let's meet some interesting people.

Kim Newman
London, 2003

---

[6] An honourable exception is Barrie Pattison's *The Seal of Dracula* (1975), with its excellent round-ups of vampire movies from Spain, the Philippines, Italy, Mexico and France.

[7] The Asian specialist critic Tony Rayns has pointed out that the English-language title used for the export of Ching Siu-Tung's *Qian Nu You Hun* (1987), *A Chinese Ghost Story*, seemed to mislead a lot of reviewers into believing that this was the first film of its kind rather than a summation of years of genre activity, as if critics were to consider, say, Terence Fisher's *Frankenstein Must Be Destroyed* (1967) without acknowledging that the Hammer horror cycle was ten years and several dozen films old by then.

[8] Perhaps surprisingly, there are few scary Americans in world horror to stand as the equivalents of the sinister Yanks who crop up in spaghetti westerns (like Lou Castel in *¿Quien sabe?* / *A Bullet for the General*, 1967), though monstrous Brits like Dr. Jekyll and Jack the Ripper are familiar figures in continental horror movies, some of which are set in a pretend-London (the German *Die Toten augen von London* / *Dead Eyes of London*, 1961, the Spanish *Dr. Jekyll y el hombre lobo* / *Dr Jekyll and the Werewolf*, 1971, the Swiss *Jack the Ripper*, 1976) as bizarre to English audiences as the Paris of *Mad Love* (1936) or *Theatre of Death* (1967) must seem to the French.

Introduction

Steven Jay Schneider

Despite the occasional ebb of popular interest (followed by the inevitable flow), throughout the history of cinema the horror genre has proven itself perhaps the most profitable of all those competing for play time in theatres across the US and UK. But as even a brief look at the line-ups of recent film festivals and conventions makes apparent, the United States and Britain are by no means the only countries to develop, produce and promote cinematic tales of terror. Horror films serve as dark playgrounds for the embodiment and dramatisation of both universally felt anxieties and culturally specific fears in a whole slew of other nations and regions as well.

With the rise of the internet and the increased availability of previously unseen (sometimes unheard of) titles on video and DVD over the past ten years, both fans and scholars - not to imply the existence of a dichotomy where one really doesn't exist - have become increasingly familiar with the passionate and perverse horror directors, films and stars to come out of such countries as Italy, Japan, Spain, Germany and Hong Kong. But still not enough are aware of the fact that the genre's geographic borders stretch from Turkey to Thailand, from France to the Philippines, from Chile to Czechoslovakia to Cuba, and beyond. That significant, or at least noteworthy, horror film output comes from areas as diverse as Singapore, Mexico, India, Austria, Korea, Brazil and Poland. That classics of the genre like *Dracula* (1931), *Psycho* (1960), *The Exorcist* (1973) and *The Silence of the Lambs* (1990) have exerted nearly as profound an influence on cinematic traditions abroad as at home, and, conversely, that recent Hollywood productions such as *The Vanishing* (1993), *Vanilla Sky* (2001), *Insomnia* (2002) and *Ring* (2002) are themselves remakes of foreign horror films and thrillers.

What do horror films from other parts of the globe look like, and sound like? What are their particular conventions, their stylistic trademarks, and their sources of inspiration? Who are their major auteurs, actors and monstrous antagonists? And what are the dynamics of cross-cultural horror exchange? In the pages that follow, a collection of experts on horror cinema from around the world occupy themselves with all of these questions, and others besides, attempting to answer them through a productive and entertaining mix of historical background, comparative analysis and close readings of particular films, cycles, series and subgenres. Interspersed throughout the book are interviews and conversations with key players in contemporary world horror cinema, from innovative writer-directors such as Nonzee Nimibutr (Thailand), Jorge Molina (Cuba), Takashi Miike (Japan) and Sion Sono (also Japan) to award-winning Hong Kong "Category III" superstar Anthony Wong.

In his Preface to this collection, horror novelist, critic and scholar Kim Newman has done a wonderful job of setting the global stage for what is to come. All that remains by way of introduction is a brief note about the policy of selection employed herein. The editor's working definition of "horror" was left intentionally broad, not because it was felt that *any* candidate film from *any* country should count as a member of the horror genre in some conventional, Western-oriented sense of the term, but that, at this still-early stage of world horror cinema study, it's a lot safer - and much more fun - to be too *inclusive* rather

introduction

than too *exclusive*. Of course limitations of space made it impossible to devote a chapter to *every* country with a horror film tradition, and my admittedly lame excuse for leaving out relevant material on such English-speaking nations as Australia, New Zealand, South Africa and Canada, not to mention the United States and Britain, is that the book's original title (quickly discarded by the publisher) was *The Subtitles That Dripped Blood!* (I said it was a lame excuse...) This just means that, in the best horror movie tradition, *Fear Without Frontiers* needs a sequel - or maybe three, depending on the box-office returns.

acknowledgements

Any edited collection is the product of intense and sustained collaboration behind the scenes as well as between the covers, and the present volume is no exception. I would like to extend my sincerest thanks to all the usual suspects, without whose assistance, guidance and support this project would not have come together anywhere near as well as it has - in particular Jane Bacci, Lucas Balbo (artschiv@wanadoo.fr), Dennis Bartok, Adam Buck, Kelly Burkhardt (TLA Releasing), Nigel Burrell, Renata Clark, Ian Conrich, DiRT, Rogelio Agrasánchez Jr. and Xochitl Fernandez de Agrasánchez at the Agrasánchez Film Archive (www.agrasfilms.com), Roger Garcia, Ruth Goldberg, Susanne Groh, Andrew James Horton, Kier-La Janisse-Wood, David Kalat, David Kerekes, *Kinoeye*, Bill Knight, Edith Kramer, Frank Lafond, Mirek Lipinski, Xavier Mendik, Martin and Tom Mes, Jorge Molina, Marc Morris, Thomas Weisser, Tony Williams and Masa Yoshikawa.

Special thanks are due to my publisher, Harvey Fenton at FAB Press, who also undertook all the design, layout and production co-ordination duties, and to Francis Brewster for his sterling efforts at the proofing and indexing stage. Hearty thanks are also due to all of the *Fear Without Frontiers* contributors; to the students who took my classes on horror cinema (even when that wasn't what they signed up for) at Tufts University, New York University, U.C. Berkeley and CUNY-Staten Island; and to my veeeerrrrrry understanding family and friends, especially Elyse, Stuart, Pammy, Owen, Suzie, Max and Erin. And above all, thank you to Katheryn Winnick (my little Beelzebub) for hanging in there through thick, thin and everything in between.

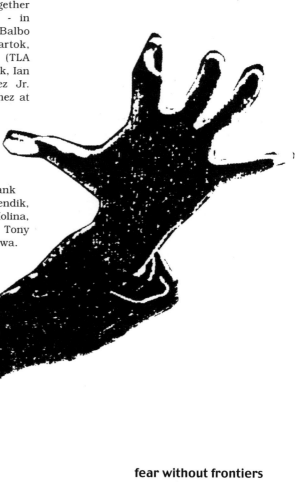

Part One:
Artists, Actors, Auteurs

Madmen, visionaries and freaks: the films of Alejandro Jodorowsky   15
- Pam Keesey

Coffin Joe and José Mojica Marins: strange men for strange times   27
- André Barcinski

Return of the phantom: Maxu Weibang's *Midnight Song*   39
- David Robinson

Enfant terrible: the terrorful, wonderful world of Anthony Wong   45
- Lisa Odham Stokes & Michael Hoover

The rain beneath the earth: an interview with Nonzee Nimibutr   61
- Mitch Davis

Cinema of the doomed: the tragic horror of Paul Naschy   69
- Todd Tjersland

Sex and death, Cuban style: the dark vision of Jorge Molina   81
- Ruth Goldberg; followed by an interview with the director, "Testing Molina," by Steven Jay Schneider

artists, actors, auteurs

Madmen, visionaries and freaks: the films of Alejandro Jodorowsky

Pam Keesey

Alejandro Jodorowsky is a director who defies categorisation. With a career that has spanned nearly 50 years, including musical theatre, street theatre, mime, the circus, comic books, esoteric philosophy and the Tarot in addition to his work in film, it is hard to imagine that there is anything Jodorowsky hasn't done. Jodorowsky's films, like Jodorowsky himself, also defy any easy classification. Drawing from surrealism, science fiction, Zen Buddhism, classic Hollywood and Mexican urban life, just to name a few of his many influences, Jodorowsky's films have inspired widely divergent critical assessments. While many critics have found his films horrifying - bloody, violent, excessive and grotesque - Jodorowsky's name is not one many viewers associate with the horror genre. Yet in 1989, after a ten-year absence from the silver screen, Jodorowsky resurfaced with the release of *Santa Sangre*, a smart, elegant and stylish horror film produced by Claudio Argento, brother of Italian horror director Dario Argento. *Santa Sangre* is perhaps Jodorowsky's most mature, most polished work, exhibiting his many talents, interests and influences, as well as his remarkable skill as a storyteller and visual artist.

When Jodorowsky showed up in New York in 1970 with *El Topo* under his arm, he had every reason to think that he was on the verge of international success. After all, his film *Fando y Lis* (1968) garnered worldwide attention when the Mexican government banned the film. Weeks before the premiere, the Mexican police clashed with student protestors, leaving hundreds of young people dead or wounded. Reporters from all over the world who were in Mexico to cover the 1968 Summer Olympics covered the massacre. When *Fando y Lis* was released, viewers saw it as an allegory for the country's political climate. The film inspired riots, and the government, concerned that it might inspire further civil unrest, banned the film altogether. The Acapulco Film Festival, where the film was being shown, closed early that year.

In *Fando y Lis*, based on a street play written by Jodorowsky's long-time friend and collaborator, Fernando Arrabal, Fando (Sergio Klainer) and his wheelchair-bound girlfriend Lis (Diana Mariscal) journey through urban rubble to find the mystical city of Tar. As they proceed, they encounter a variety of people who dance in the midst of corruption and decay. At one point, a middle-class gentleman draws blood from Lis's arm into a glass and then drinks it. While not an overtly political film, *Fando y Lis* touched a nerve among youth who found themselves out of step not only with their parents and their generation, but also with the middle-class establishment. They felt betrayed by the government, the police and the army, who showed themselves capable of bloodshed when faced with the voice of youthful opposition.

Fando y Lis would not be the first of Jodorowsky's pictures to engender controversy. In fact, controversy would become one of Jodorowsky's chief trademarks in the film industry. His controversial nature, as well as his controversial content, may partly explain why Jodorowsky hasn't made more films. It also helps to explain why Jodorowsky's films remain fresh, innovative and challenging. Say what you will about Alejandro Jodorowsky, but one thing is certain: he is not just another Hollywood director.

opposite:
Santa Sangre

Chile/Mexico

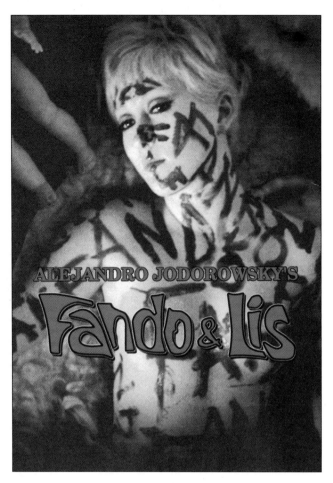

above:
Considered lost for 30 years, **Fando y Lis** was released on DVD by Fantoma in 1999.

[1] Wilmington, M. (1990) "Jodorowsky Looks At Himself And Uncovers 'Santa Sangre'." *Los Angeles Times* Home Edition (April 14), 4.

The early years

Although Jodorowsky transcends any nation-state boundaries, he was born in 1930 in Iquique, Chile, the son of Russian immigrants. As a child, he didn't fit in, and turned to books and movies for companionship. In an interview with the *Los Angeles Times*, Jodorowsky reminisced, "All my life...movies was [sic] the most important thing. I was very solitary boy: immigrant, white, with a big nose... The movies were the only friend I could have. I loved Erich Von Stroheim, *The Cabinet of Dr. Caligari*, *Frankenstein* and Charles Laughton in *The Hunchback of Notre Dame*."[1]

It wasn't long before his family left the small, seaside town of Iquique and moved to Santiago. There, Jodorowsky's interest in the arts blossomed. He worked with the circus, and began performing as a mime. He became involved with street theatre, and in 1955 left for France, where he studied with Marcel Marceau. His work in France also included a stint directing and producing Maurice Chevalier, who was making his comeback at the Alhambra Theatre. While in France, Jodorowsky made his first film, a mime production of Thomas Mann's *The Severed Heads*, which included an introduction by Jean Cocteau. Jodorowsky became increasingly involved with the French surrealists, and was heavily influenced by Antonin Artaud and his Theatre of Cruelty. Artaud rejected traditional Western notions of theatre in favour of a theatre that would "make itself the equal of life" and in which "[themes] will be cosmic, universal, and interpreted according to the most ancient texts." According to Artaud, a Theatre of Cruelty was to be "bloody and inhuman" in order to exorcise the viewer's repressed impulses, a philosophy Jodorowsky would take to heart.

By 1960, Jodorowsky was travelling back and forth between Paris and Mexico City. Along with Fernando Arrabal and Roland Topor, Jodorowsky founded the surrealist review *SNOB*, and *Producciones Pánicas* - the Panic Movement. The Panic Movement took its name from the Greek *pan*, meaning "all" or "everything." The Panic Movement embraced all things social, cultural and political. Drawing on Artaud's Theatre of Cruelty, the Panic Movement also included the burgeoning popular culture of the 60s, including science fiction, comic books and rock-'n-roll. *Producciones Pánicas* first major production was "Sacramental Melodrama" (1965), a four-hour play that premiered at the Paris Festival of Free Expression and included Jodorowsky in motorcycle leathers slitting the throats of geese, smashing plates, dancing with a cow's head and castrating a rabbi.

While in Mexico, Jodorowsky started a weekly comic strip (*Fábulas Pánicas*, or Panic Fables), directed over one hundred plays and made his second film, *Fando y Lis*. [One of the other avant-garde artists involved in the production, Juan López Moctezuma, would go on to direct such horror cheapies as *Dr. Tarr's Torture Dungeon* (1972) and *Mary, Mary, Bloody Mary* (1976).] *Fando y Lis* has been frequently, and unfavourably, compared to Fellini's *Satyricon* (1969). Although the two films contain many visual and narrative similarities, and despite the fact that Jodorowsky has often been accused of imitating the Italian director, *Fando y Lis* was released a full year before Fellini's.

Quite aware that his next film, *El Topo*, would get short shrift (if, that is, Mexican authorities would allow it to be shown at all), Jodorowsky decided to leave Mexico for

Alejandro Jodorowsky

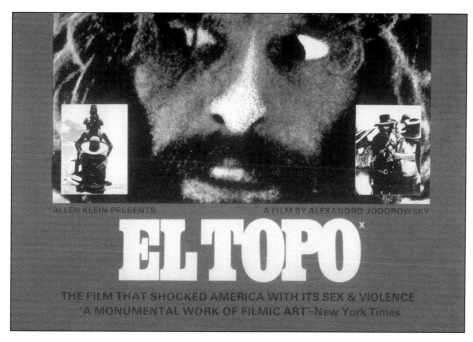

left:
UK theatrical poster

his film's premiere. Jodorowsky thus made his way to the heart of counter-cultural activity: New York City. While it has been argued that Jodorowsky's timing was off, showing up at the waning of the "Movement" characterised by counter-culture art icons such as John Lennon and Yoko Ono, Paul Morrissey and Michael Sarne, he nevertheless found a ready audience for his avant-garde mystical western. ("I tried making a western", Jodorowsky has said, "and wound up with an eastern.")

In December of 1970, Jonas Mekas, a leading figure in the world of alternative and independent cinema, was organising one of his periodic avant-garde film festivals at a rundown theatre in Manhattan called the Elgin. Mekas chose to premiere Jodorowsky's film, showing it the same nights as the three devoted to the films of John Lennon and Yoko Ono. *El Topo* would only be shown at midnight, Mekas announced, because it was a film that was too "heavy" to be shown at any other time. *El Topo*'s run was extended, playing continuously seven nights a week from its debut on 18 December 1970 through the end of June 1971. While *El Topo* didn't exactly launch Jodorowsky's career, it did launch the phenomenon of the "midnight movie", a marketing and exhibition phenomenon that continues to lure audiences to specialty, cult and horror films to the present day.

Jodorowsky wrote, directed, scored and was the star of *El Topo*, which may, in part, explain the frequent description of the film as narcissistic. With an opening scene reminiscent of a spaghetti western, Jodorowsky also draws on surrealism, Buddhism, Zen, nihilism and good old-fashioned morality plays in structure and narrative, a story Jodorowsky has described as a "quest for sainthood." Drawing from a variety of mystical, religious and occult texts, the story is less important than the meaning. While there is a thread of a plot, the pursuit of meaning is really the main force behind the film. *El Topo* has four acts: "Genesis", "Prophets", "Psalms" and "Apocalypse." The film plays as a multicultural, multi-denominational tale of enlightenment. In the beginning of the film, El Topo ("the Mole" in English, played by Jodorowsky) claims that he is God. As a result of his journey, he learns humility and, in the end, realises that he is not a god, but a man.

Mixing sex, violence, sadomasochism and a variety of marginalised characters, including prostitutes, dwarves, armless and legless men (in one of the more interesting visual plays that are characteristic of Jodorowsky, a man with no arms carries on his back a man with no legs), *El Topo* elicited a variety of reactions. In the *Village Voice*, Glenn O'Brien waxed poetic about the meaning and symbolism of the film: "It's midnight mass at the Elgin... They've come to see the light - and the screen before them is illumined by an abstract landscape of desert and sky - and the ritual begins again... Jodorowsky is here to confess; the young audience is here for communion."[2]

[2] Quoted in Hoberman, J. and J. Rosenbaum, *Midnight Movies* (1983). New York: Harper & Row, 94.

Chile/Mexico

The *New York Times*'s Vincent Canby, however, had a considerably different reaction: "Has *El Topo* really rendered film criticism superfluous, or is it spawning a kind of fascistic film criticism that hopes to strong-arm the opposition with suggestions of reflected ineptitude and confused minds? I'd hazard the guess that a certain amount of the pro-criticism and of the pro-audience reaction generally is itself the result of calculated intellectual intimidation within the film itself..."[3]

Despite mixed reaction to *El Topo*, the New York art scene welcomed Jodorowsky with open arms. Former Beatles manager Allen Klein agreed to represent him, and Jodorowsky started work on his next feature, *The Holy Mountain* (1973). Where *El Topo* was an avant-garde spaghetti western, *Holy Mountain* might be regarded as a surrealist science-fiction film. With the heavy philosophy of *El Topo* and the visual appeal of *Barbarella* (1968), *Holy Mountain* was also a "head trip" movie, a genre described by commentator Danny Peary as "films that are confusing but mentally stimulating."[4]

At one point, Jodorowsky was under contract to direct the adaptation for Frank Herbert's acclaimed science-fiction novel *Dune* - a film, it is worth noting, that may just be one of those great "might-have-beens", featuring such legends as Gloria Swanson, Orson Welles and Salvador Dali - a job that would later be handed over to another alternative film director with a cult following, *Eraserhead* (1977)'s David Lynch.

Jodorowsky's collaboration with Klein did not go well, resulting in Klein retaining rights to both *El Topo* and *Holy Mountain*, placing stipulations on the showing of the two films that kept them out of distribution for years. Jodorowsky then moved permanently to France. He remained active - among other things producing comic books, including the highly successful *Moebius* series and a restored version of the *Tarot of Marseilles* - although he fell into relative obscurity in the U.S. in the years following *Holy Mountain*. Jodorowsky also continued to make films throughout the years, including *Tusk* (1978), *Santa Sangre* (1989) and in 1990, *The Rainbow Thief* (1990) - Jodorowsky's most commercial film, starring Christopher Lee, Omar Sharif and Peter O'Toole.

Jodorowsky has disowned both *Tusk* and *The Rainbow Thief*. *Tusk*, a movie about elephants and elephant hunting, was made in India. The producer, Jodorowsky claims, pocketed most of the production budget, leaving him to finish the film with minimal resources. *The Rainbow Thief*, on the other hand, was well financed. However, Jodorowsky ran into a different set of problems with the producers. Produced by Alexander Salkind, the producer of *Superman* (1978), and written by Berta Dominguez, Salkind's wife, Jodorowsky was asked to make the film with two conditions: no violence, and complete respect for the script.

The demands of "keeping to the script" - and a personality conflict with Peter

right:
Jodorowsky took the lead role in his 1973 epic **The Holy Mountain**.

[3] Canby, V. (1972) "Is *El Topo* a Con?" In *Film 71/72: An Anthology*. Simon & Schuster: New York. www.hotweird.com/jodorowsky/canby.html. Accessed 5 December 2001.

[4] Peary, D. (1981) "*El Topo*." In *Cult Movies*. New York: Dell Publishing, Co. www.hotweird.com/jodorowsky/peary.html. Accessed 5 December 2001.

Alejandro Jodorowsky

O'Toole - left a bad taste in Jodorowsky's mouth. Jodorowsky summarises his conflict with the producer in a rather amusing anecdote pertaining to the sewer rat: "For instance, in this film I'm doing now, a person is living with a rat, and they [the producers] say, "This picture is too expensive." I ask, "Why?" and they tell me they need to make an artificial rat to do everything the script is saying. And I say "But you're crazy, we'll use a real rat and we'll follow what the rat does!" "Oh, you'll improvise?" They're horrified! Sure I'll improvise, the rat will improvise! I'll shoot what the rat does and change the script to fit! They went crazy - it took me two days to convince them not to use an artificial rat."[5]

While *The Rainbow Thief* may not be Jodorowsky's favourite project, it still carries the unmistakable stamp of the director. Christopher Lee stars as Uncle Rudolf, a wealthy, aristocratic eccentric worthy of Buñuel who lavishes his dogs with love and caviar, but feeds his dinner guest giant bones. One evening, in an orgy with local prostitutes, Uncle Rudolf slips into a coma. His nephew, Prince Meleagre (Peter O'Toole) - equally eccentric, but more reclusive than his uncle - retreats to the sewers to await his uncle's death and his inheritance. The thief Dima (Omar Sharif), looking forward to his share of the wealth, cares for the prince - Meleagre's only connection to the world above. In his role as caretaker, Dima learns that there is more to life than money. Like so many Jodorowsky films, *The Rainbow Thief* is a tale of enlightenment and redemption.

Santa Sangre

In between *Tusk* and *The Rainbow Thief*, Jodorowsky made *Santa Sangre* (1989), arguably his most successful film. Jodorowsky had been working on the screenplay for *Santa Sangre* for six years when Claudio Argento approached him about collaborating on a project. Jodorowsky asked Argento to consider his script for *Santa Sangre*. Argento agreed, and Jodorowsky accepted an unusually modest fee in order to maintain complete artistic control over the production. The result is a stunning work that reflects Jodorowsky's many passions and influences, from favourite childhood movies and mime to mysticism, repression and redemption.

Santa Sangre is loosely based on a real person, the Mexican serial killer Goyo Cardenas. While living with his mother, Cardenas murdered several women, and

above: Santa Sangre.

buried them all in his garden. Then, one day, he called the police, telling them everything, including where to find the bodies. After his trial, Cardenas was institutionalised. He was released ten years later, with no recollection of his past misdeeds. He studied, became a writer and lawyer, married and had two children. He became a contributing member of society, a "sweet man" in Jodorowsky's words. It was as though his past belonged to an entirely different person. "[Reality] was not real for him", Jodorowsky comments, "[reality was] a fairy tale."[6]

Jodorowsky embellished the essential truths of Goyo Cardenas's life, making the killer's fairy tale reality the centre of the story. The result is a film that is part thriller, part fantasy, part surreal and part homage to some of the greatest directors of suspense and horror films of the 20th century.

Jodorowsky's son Axel plays Fénix (Spanish for "Phoenix", the mythological bird that self-immolates, only to rise again from its own ashes), a young man who believes himself to be an eagle, who has been confined to a mental hospital as a result of the traumatic events of his childhood. Jodorowsky tells the story of Fénix's past in an elaborate flashback sequence which begins with the circus coming to town. The circus is the "Circo del Gringo" and the town is Mexico City. The Gringo is Orgo (Guy Stockwell), proprietor of the small circus and Fénix's father.[7] Fénix's friend Aladin (Jesús Juárez), the "World's Smallest Elephant Trainer", asks Fénix why his father drinks all the time. "My mother says he killed a woman in America", he responds. But all is quickly forgotten when Aladin and Fénix go to see "the new act", a voluptuous but mean-

[5] Interview with Alejandro Jodorowsky, "Wrapped in Salamander Cloth, He Played House." *Forced Exposure* #17: www.hotweird.com/jodorowsky/forced.html. Accessed 5 December 2001.

[6] *Ibid.*

[7] The young Fénix is played by another of Jodorowsky's sons, Adan.

Chile/Mexico

above:
The once-censored bleeding elephant scene from **Santa Sangre**.

spirited tattooed woman (Thelma Tixou, billed only as "The Tattooed Woman"), and Alma (Faviola Elenka Tapia), a young deaf mute who has been trained as a tight-rope walker whose name means "Soul." Orgo is also interested in the act, particularly the tattooed woman. Orgo seduces her by sliding her up against a target and throwing knives at her.

Fénix's mother, Concha (Blanca Guerra), is an aerialist who is also a very religious woman. While her husband is under the big top with the tattooed woman, Concha is defending a small local church, a shrine to her favourite saint, from the onslaught of developers and the disinterest of the institutionalised church. The saint is an uncanonised school girl whose arms were cut off by attackers who then raped her and left her to die in a pool of her own blood, the "Holy Blood" of the title. The Bishop refuses to protect the church, proclaiming the folk religion a sacrilege and a heresy, a reflection of Jodorowsky's distrust of established religion and the institution of the Church.

Concha returns to the circus and finds her husband with the tattooed woman. Outraged, she attacks him, but Orgo hypnotises her with the sound of his voice and the glint of his knife as he waves it in front of her eyes. Having calmed her down, Orgo takes her behind the animal cages, where Fénix catches a glimpse of them in a torrid and unsentimental sex act. At the point of climax, Fénix's attention is torn away from the sight of his parents when he hears the elephant trumpeting. The creature is dying, blood flowing from his trunk in an unmistakable (and typically "Jodorowskian") allusion to an ejaculating phallus. But the allusion is passing, the death of the elephant foreshadowing all of the deaths to come.

In one of the more memorable sequences in the film, a sombre, yet carnivalesque, funeral procession ensues. The gargantuan coffin is led to the outskirts of town, to the gorge that separates the city from the slums. The elephant is sent to his final resting place at the bottom of the gorge, and hordes of hungry people from the shantytown descend upon the coffin, dividing the carcass among themselves. According to Jodorowsky, elephants are "the image of Christ", and the people eating the elephant symbolic of communion. While the scene may have religious overtones for Jodorowsky, the most striking image is one of poverty and political powerlessness, harkening back to *Fando y Lis*.

The night of the funeral, Concha finds Orgo in bed with the tattooed woman. She threatens the woman, and throws acid on Orgo's groin. In pain and enraged, Orgo cuts off both of Concha's arms at the shoulder, leaving her to die in a pool of her own blood before slitting his own throat and putting himself out of his misery. The tattooed woman and Alma flee, and Fénix is left locked in the trailer, crying as his life crumbles around him. End of flashback.

Fénix is on his way to the movies with a number of young men with Down syndrome when a pimp (Teo Jodorowsky) intercepts them and takes them to the red light district rather than the theatre. It is in the red light district that Fénix sees the tattooed woman, waking him from his fantasy and returning him to human, rather than eagle, consciousness.

The next morning, Fénix hears his armless mother calling to him from the street below. Delighted to see her once again, he climbs through the window to join her, leaving the institution behind. That night, the tattooed woman is brutally murdered in a scene reminiscent of the shower scene in Alfred Hitchcock's *Psycho* (1960). In the morning, Alma, the young deaf woman who has been living with the tattooed woman since they left the circus, finds the bloody remains of the mutilated body.

Fénix, who has donned the magician's tuxedo, cloak and top hat of his childhood, is reunited with Aladin, once the "World's Smallest Elephant Trainer" turned shoe-shine boy. He takes Aladin with him to a theatre where he and his mother form "Concha and Her Magic Hands." Her hands, of course, are not her own, but Fénix's. Dressed in a gown made for two, Fénix's arms become his mothers as she performs "The Creation of the Universe", a mime-style performance inspired, the credits inform us, by a similar work by Marcel Marceau.

The beauty of the performance is the way in which Concha and Fénix work together, Fénix's hands moving in time with Concha's expressions and responses, clearly two bodies but behaving as one. The strength of these two performances allows for the suspension of disbelief, letting the viewer experience the illusion of Fénix's arms becoming his mother's, to the point where Concha has far more control over Fénix's actions - the way he uses his hands and his arms - than he himself does. This is especially important given the scene that follows.

Another performer at the theatre, the exotic dancer/stripper Rubi (Gloria Contreras), has become infatuated with Fénix. His hands fascinate her. Rubi arranges to meet Fénix at the theatre later that night. When Fénix arrives, he is wearing a sequined circus masters suit identical to the one his father wore. He tells Rubi that he will throw knives at her, and when she voices her concern that she will be afraid, Fénix comforts her by saying, "I will hypnotise you." She succumbs, and he begins throwing his knives, visualising the tattooed woman as he saw her that day under the big top while his father threw knives at her. Concha walks in on them, horrified by what she sees. "You know what you have to do", she tells Fénix. "I am ordering you - my hands and my arms - to kill her." And he does.

The next morning, Fénix and Concha awake in the same bed, Fénix instinctively reaching to scratch Concha's belly as if it were his own. His clothes are fashioned to complement Concha's, his sleeves an extension of her dress. At breakfast, Concha eyes a poster of *The Invisible Man* (1933) hanging in the kitchen. "Without me you are nothing. No one sees you and no one notices you, just like your stupid hero", she says, gesturing toward the poster.

Fénix is plagued by hallucinations, moments during which Jodorowsky is able to return to the striking and surreal images of his street theatre days. In one scene, Fénix sees chickens pecking away at Concha's severed arms while Fénix, as Christ, dodges hens falling from the sky. Jodorowsky has been quoted as saying, "The Virgin Mary is a chicken."[8] If the Virgin Mary is indeed a chicken, and the chickens are raining down on Christ, this image raises the question, did Christ suffer at the hands of his mother the way Fénix suffers?

Fénix wants nothing more than to be invisible. Alone in his room, under a poster of James Whale's 1933 classic and watching the film, he sits in a rocking chair, his head wrapped in bandages, mimicking every move Claude Rains makes as the transparent anti-hero of the film. Complete with a laboratory set-up straight out of the movie, Fénix attempts to make his own invisibility serum, but to no avail. Fénix removes his bandages in sequence with the Invisible Man's unmasking in the film, but underneath his bandages, the face of Fénix remains.

Santa Sangre offers tribute not only to American popular culture through

[8] Loud, L. (1990) "The Virgin Mary is a Chicken." *American Film* 15.6 (March), 80.

right:
Jodorowsky's son Axel in the central role of Fénix in **Santa Sangre**.

Universal classics, but also to Mexican popular culture with its reference to masked Mexican wrestling. Fénix becomes infatuated with, and brings home, a woman who might just be a match for his overbearing mother: a transsexual masked wrestler ("the World's Strongest Woman") named for Mexico's most famous wrestling superhero, El Santo ("The Saint").

But The Saint proves to be no match for Concha. Indeed, it is only Alma, the deaf mute who has followed Concha and Fénix since the night her guardian, the tattooed woman, was killed, who is able to challenge Concha. Dressed in tightrope walker's mourning clothes, she arrives at the scene and, by her very presence, helps Fénix find redemption.

Alejandro Jodorowsky

Jodorowsky's tribute to the father of freaks

The carnivalesque features of Jodorowsky's films have drawn comparisons to Federico Fellini, and Fénix's dependence upon his mother (which involves her control over Fénix's behaviour, urging him as she does to kill the young women who arouse him) have inspired more than a few comparisons to *Psycho*. One reviewer described *Santa Sangre* as resembling a "Buñuel remake" of the classic Hitchcock film.[9] Of course, there is an homage to James Whale's *The Invisible Man*, and Jodorowsky himself has acknowledged a tribute to George Romero's *Night of the Living Dead* (1968). Both of these tributes - to Whale and Romero - are described by Jodorowsky as inverting what has become the traditional horror image, horror effectively becoming *anti*-horror: "Yes, there's *The Invisible Man*, and the Zombie scene is from Romero. I made some echoes, but I played with them, In *Night of the Living Dead* they were terrible persons coming back from the dead, and here they are beautiful women. It is anti-terror. In *The Invisible Man*, he became and he suffered because he was invisible. Here he takes off his bandages and suffers because he doesn't like himself as a criminal. So here I am playing with horror, and at the same time I am making anti-horror."[10]

Like the tender music that accompanies the most discomfiting scenes in the film, the juxtaposition of horror with beauty is the Romantic vision of the sublime, of terrible beauty. Jodorowsky clearly sees *Santa Sangre* as a romantic film, a film as much about the power of redemption - and the redemptive power of love - as it is about horror, murder or despair.

More evident, however, than the influences of Buñuel, Fellini, Romero, Hitchcock or even Whale is the influence of Tod Browning, director of the legendary 1932 film, *Freaks*. Populated with a variety of side-show talents, including Johnny Eck, the "half-boy" whose body ends just below his rib cage, Pete Robinson ("The Human Skeleton") and Olga Roderick, a "traditional" bearded lady, *Freaks*, it is worth noting, is the film that followed *El Topo* in the midnight slot at New York's Elgin Theatre. Browning and Jodorowsky clearly have similar sensibilities, finding people with handicaps and/or deformities of various kinds interesting, even beautiful. "Normal people are monstrous", according to Jodorowsky, "because they are so similar. For me, difference is what is Art... [Nature] has a big imagination."[11]

The film Browning is most famous for - *Dracula* (1931), starring Bela Lugosi - is considered by many Browning aficionados to be one of his weakest works. *Freaks*, on the other hand, was one of the director's pet projects. Loosely based on a short story entitled "Spurs", *Freaks* is the tale of a circus midget named Hans (Harry Earles) who falls in love with a "big" trapeze artist (Venus, played by Olga Baclanova). Venus agrees to marry Hans, believing that midgets have a shorter life span than "normal" people. Hans's inheritance makes the union all the more appealing, ensuring that upon his death, Venus and her lover, Hercules the strong man (Henry Victor), will live happily ever after.

At their wedding feast, Venus is welcomed into the family of freaks as they chant, "We accept her, we accept her...." Venus, overwhelmed and disgusted, responds by yelling "Dirty - slimy - freaks! Make me one of you, will you?" Offended, the freaks take her at her word. Her lover is castrated, and Venus mutilated. The last we see of her, she is a misshapen chicken woman, nestled into a sideshow booth of her very own.

Merrill Pye, the art director on *Freaks*, recalled the first showing of the film: "Halfway through the preview, a lot of people got up and ran out. They didn't walk out. They *ran* out."[12] MGM attempted to market the film as a compassionate human story, and Tod Browning as a great humanist. Nonetheless, *Freaks* was pulled from circulation just months after it was released in the U.S.

Despite being described as "loathsome, obscene, grotesque and bizarre", *Freaks* found a following in Europe, especially among the surrealists. The numerous films in which Browning teamed with Lon Chaney, Sr. (the so-called "Man of a Thousand Faces") were, as film historian David J. Skal has noted, particularly popular in France, where many saw in these pictures the legacy of German Expressionism. In 1956, French critic Louis Seguin described Browning as "one of the greatest directors who ever lived... [Far] superior to men like John Ford or Hitchcock" (quoted in Skal, 221).

Jodorowsky, who was in France in the mid-to-late 50s and may have read these critical assessments of the director, also thinks highly of Browning and his films: "The only picture I liked all the actors in was *Freaks*... All of the actors in that film

---

[9] Jay Carr of the Boston Globe, quoted in the movie trailer for *Santa Sangre*: http://us.imdb.com/Trailers?0098253&3322&28. Accessed 5 December 2001.

[10] Jodorowsky, "Wrapped in Salamander Cloth, He Played House."

[11] *Ibid*.

[12] Quoted in Skal, D. J. and E. Savada (1995) *Dark Carnival: The Secret World of Tod Browning, Hollywood's Master of the Macabre*. Anchor Books: New York, 174.

opposite:
Rare German poster for Jodorowsky's **The Holy Mountain**.

were good. My favourite was the man who has no legs or arms. That was a good actor to me. That's one I remember very, very well. I like Tod Browning a lot. He is like a father to me. I think maybe I'm a reincarnation of Tod Browning. Who knows?"[13]

If *Santa Sangre* is any indication, Jodorowsky might very well *be* Browning reborn. The two directors have much more in common than a fondness for people with physical deformities. Browning, like Jodorowsky, ran away to join the circus as a young man, and his love of circuses, carnivals and sideshows would continue to creep into his work long after he'd left the Midway. After a brief stint in Vaudeville, Browning was introduced to D.W. Griffith, and began his career in film as one of the primary actors on the Biograph Studio roster. When Griffith left Biograph, Browning went with him. It wasn't long before Browning moved from being in front of the camera to working behind it. Browning became a master of this silent medium, directing dozens of film before the advent of sound.

Santa Sangre bears a striking resemblance to *The Unknown* (1927), one of Browning's best films. Originally titled *Alonzo the Armless*, *The Unknown* is, like many Browning films, set in the circus. Lon Chaney is the armless Alonzo, a knife-thrower and sharpshooter who handles both blades and bullets with his bare feet. His aim is so precise that he is able to disrobe his beautiful assistant, Nanon (played by a very young Joan Crawford), by severing the stays of her garment. Alonzo is in love with Nanon. Nanon, who has a deep-seated fear of men and their arms (presumably the result of an earlier sexual trauma), is fond of Alonzo precisely because he is armless.

Alonzo, however, harbours a secret identity known only to his dwarf assistant, Cojo (John George). Alonzo is a criminal on the run, and is using the circus to hide from the police. Alonzo also has arms that he keeps hidden by having them laced into a tight leather corset (an actual corset that Chaney used as part of his costume for the film). Although he does have normal arms, Alonzo is possessed of a second thumb on one hand, making his six-fingered imprint a link to his criminal past. The corset, however, has kept his true identity hidden from both the police and from his circus colleagues.

Alonzo's attention to Nanon infuriates her father Zanzi (Nick De Ruiz), the owner of the circus. Alonzo, temporarily freed from his corset and angered by the prohibition Zanzi has placed on his relationship, kills him, leaving his signature six-fingered print on the man's neck. Unable to ever reveal his true identity to his beloved Nanon, Alonzo blackmails a surgeon to remove his arms, making him the man of Nanon's dreams.

Nanon, however, has other plans. When Alonzo returns from recuperating from his surgery, he discovers that Nanon has fallen in love with, and is engaged to, the strong man, Malabar the Mighty (Norman Kerry). Infuriated, Alonzo plans to sabotage Nanon and Malabar's new act: a pair of white stallions on treadmills is whipped into frenzy by a scantily clad Nanon while Malabar restrains them. Alonzo attempts to sabotage the treadmills, hoping that their breakdown will rip Malabar's arms from their sockets. Instead, Alonzo falls onto the treadmill himself, and is trampled to death by the horses' beating hooves.

It is not merely the circus, the knife throwing, the beautiful assistant, the armless killer, nor the midget sidekick that links Browning's *The Unknown* to Jodorowsky's *Santa Sangre*. It is a shared aesthetic, a dark, brooding atmosphere that is as compelling as it is disturbing. Just as significant, however, is the difference between the two films and the two filmmakers: Jodorowsky's story is one of love, hope and redemption while Browning's is one of vengeance, despair and retribution.

Jodorowsky, like Browning before him, has always had a bold vision for his films and treasures; above all else, the freedom to pursue his artistic inclinations. Jodorowsky is an iconoclast: he defies the conventions of Hollywood cinema, holding the industry's measure of success with a certain disdain. It is ironic, then, that *Santa Sangre*, the film that most encapsulates the director's passion for life, love and theatre, is also the film that has been most well received by the critics. *Santa Sangre* both celebrates and defies Hollywood, invoking Browning, Whale and Hitchcock while being made completely outside of the studio system. It also celebrates and defies the tropes of traditional horror films, relying as much on love and compassion as it does on blood and violence to communicate with the audience. *Santa Sangre* is a unique and refreshing film that celebrates Jodorowsky's vision of the universe, a world where madmen are visionaries, freaks are a balancing force and horror is the path to enlightenment.

[13] LaBine, J. (1996) Interview with Alejandro Jodorowsky. *Fad* 36. www.hotweird.com/jodorowsky/fadinterview.html. Accessed 5 December 2001.

Alejandro Jodorowsky

horror cinema across the globe

artists, actors, auteurs

Coffin Joe and José Mojica Marins: strange men for strange times

André Barcinski

The word most commonly associated with José Mojica Marins is "strange." In 1968, he shot a film entitled *The Strange World of Zé do Caixão*; that same year, he starred in a television show with the same name. And when he ran for Congress in Brazil in 1982, his slogan was "a strange man for strange times."

Marins's films are strange indeed, a mix of gothic horror and Third World barbarism, Expressionism and Surrealism, Catholic guilt and Nietzschean nihilism. He single-handedly invented a Brazilian horror genre and created the country's most famous movie character, an evil gravedigger called Zé do Caixão (or "Coffin Joe", as he is known in the U.S. and in Europe).

But if Marins's *films* are strange, his life is even stranger. In his case, fact is indeed stranger than fiction. At the age of thirteen, José Mojica Marins was expelled from Catholic school after shooting a film called *Judgement Day*, in which aliens attacked the Earth in flying saucers and killed priests. Before his sixteenth birthday, Marins had shot twenty short films and founded his own "movie studio" in a chicken barn. At seventeen, he had to interrupt his first feature film due to the tragic deaths of three (!) actresses. By the age of eighteen, he was running his own acting school. In the 1960s, he directed five of Brazil's biggest box-office hits, had his own TV show, his own comic book, and recorded a samba album. He directed westerns, comedies, musicals, porn flicks, and shot the first ever love scene between a woman and a dog in Brazil. He was a partner in a funeral parlour, had his own line of Coffin Joe cosmetics, a shampoo, and even a Coffin Joe sugarcane liquor. He ran for Congress, was thrown in jail, founded his own church, and had seven children with five different women. He was also the most censored filmmaker in Brazilian history, and the country's only true independent filmmaker.

To fully understand what makes José Mojica Marins such a special character though, it is necessary, first of all, to know where he came from.

Tracing roots

Marins was born in São Paulo, Brazil, on (appropriately enough) Friday the 13th of March 1936, the son of Spanish immigrants. His father, Antonio, was the manager of a small movie theatre, and made some extra money on weekends bullfighting in small arenas in São Paulo. His mother, Carmen, was a housewife and, according to testimony, a great tango singer and dancer. For the first 18 years of Marins's life, the family lived in the back of the movie theatre managed by Antonio. It was a small, 200-seat theatre in Vila Anastácio, a working-class neighbourhood surrounded by factories.

Vila Anastácio was called the "Tower of Babel", because of the large numbers of immigrants from different countries. There were families from Spain, Portugal, Russia, Poland, Hungary, Lithuania, Italy, Romania, and even Africa, who had come to Brazil escaping the horrors of the Second World War. Many arrived in Vila Anastácio not speaking a word of Portuguese. Marins remembers visiting friend's houses and not understanding anything anybody said.

Each group of immigrants had its own social clubs. But they also mingled with their neighbours and absorbed their

opposite:
José Mojica Marins in the role of his lifelong alter-ego Zé do Caixão ("Coffin Joe").

above:
Brazillian 'Coffin Joe' comic books, testament to the iconic status of Marins's creation in his homeland.

customs and traditions. Thus, Vila Anastácio became a joyous mess: Italians and Hungarians attended Polish parties; Lithuanians spent their Sundays at Spanish bullfights. Marins's best friend, José Andrusiac, was Lithuanian. To make things a little bit more confusing, Vila Anastácio also had a large black community.

The neighbourhood was a deeply religious place. Blacks had their macumba temples, where people would dance and sing to the beat of the drums. There were Hungarian gypsies and Romanian fortune-tellers. Marins was particularly struck by the macumba ritual, with its party atmosphere of live percussion and dancing. He remembers being totally shocked the first time he saw a macumba priestess incarnating an evil spirit: "She started dancing, then she threw herself on the ground and her body started shaking. Suddenly everything stopped. She stood up, and her face was transformed, she looked like someone else. When she opened her mouth, her voice had changed too. She sounded like a big man."[1]

Marins was an impressionable child, and the mystic atmosphere of Vila Anastácio certainly appealed to him. When he was eight, he witnessed an incredible event that would change his life: he saw a dead man open his eyes and stand up in the middle of his own wake. The "dead" guy was the owner of a grocery shop, and had actually suffered a cataleptic attack. Although hard to believe, this really happened, as proven by several articles in local papers and by the testimony of dozens of people in Vila Anastácio. Marins never forgot the image. Almost forty years later, he recreated that incredible event in the film *The End of Man* (1971).

But the supernatural was not Marins's only interest. He was also obsessed by movies. The theatre where his family lived showed Brazilian comedies and all kinds of American films. On weekends, there was a matinee showing cartoons and serials such as *Buck Rogers*. Marins spent the greater part of his childhood inside the theatre, watching everything he could. He recalls being particularly impressed by a medical documentary about venereal diseases, shown as part as a government prevention campaign ("It was scarier than any film I had seen!"). He also loved the Universal horror films, and worshipped Bela Lugosi and Boris Karloff.

While all his friends were riding bikes and playing soccer, Marins was staging plays and drawing comic books. He was suspended from school after throwing a lizard on a classmate during a play. "Well, it was supposed to be a scary scene", he remembers almost sixty years later, "but the girl was a terrible actress and she wasn't convincing at all. So I had caught this small lizard and kept it in a box, just in case I needed something to scare the girl."

On his tenth birthday, Marins got an 8 mm camera. Two years later, his father gave him a 16 mm camera. Marins immediately started experimenting with his new

right:
At Midnight I Will Take Your Soul.

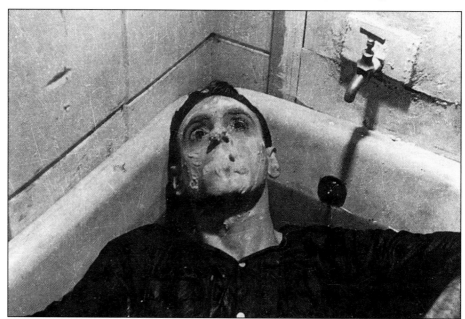

[1] All quotes from José Mojica Marins come from personal correspondence with the author.

José Mojica Marins

above:
Strange Hostel of Naked Pleasures.

toys, shooting dozens of short films. Although most of this material has disappeared forever, what remains provides a fascinating glimpse into the mind of a very gifted and creative child. Marins tried everything: he even drew directly on the film, scratching the emulsion and creating very weird images. For his *Judgement Day*, he shot scenes of the sky in Vila Anastácio and subsequently drew spaceships attacking the neighbourhood. Most impressive is *Bloody Kingdom*, an adventure story set in the Arab countries in which Marins plays a sultan with magic powers. Marins would show these films in circuses and amusement parks, sometimes dubbing the dialogue live through a microphone. The small amount he made from these films was immediately invested in other ones. Between 1949 and 1952, he made over thirty films in all.

Midnight strikes

Marins career as a horror director began in 1963, when he shot *À Meia-Noite Levarei Sua Alma* (*At Midnight I Will Take Your Soul*). It was his third professional feature, after the western *A Sina do Aventureiro* (*The Adventurer's Fate*, 1958) and the juvenile drama *Meu Destino em Tuas Mãos* (*My Destiny in Your Hands*, 1961). At that time, no one had done a horror film in Brazil, and Marins thought the genre would be totally unacceptable to Brazilian audiences. He had originally planned on shooting a juvenile delinquency police story entitled *Geração Maldita* (*Cursed Generation*), and started selecting actors from among the students in an acting school he had opened up. His financial situation was critical at the time. Worse, his womanizing had led to major problems: Marins was married but had several affairs. One of his girlfriends at the time got pregnant, and was forcing him to leave his wife. Debt collectors knocked on his door every day, and his landlord was threatening to evict the acting school from the building.

below:
At Midnight I Will Take Your Soul.

Brazil

above:
Marins proudly displays the trademark Coffin Joe finger-nails.

All of this pressure finally got to him. One night, Marins had a terrible nightmare. He dreamed he was being dragged to a cemetery by a faceless creature, all dressed in black. The monster carried him to the graveyard and stopped next to an open grave. The tombstone read "JOSÉ MOJICA MARINS." He could see the date of his birth: 1936. There was another number there too- probably the year of his death-but Marins closed his eyes. He didn't want to know when he was going to die.

The nightmare was like a spark that fired his imagination. In one afternoon, he wrote the draft of a horror story. Then he called a meeting with his pupils and announced that they were abandoning the police film and were going to shoot a horror film instead. Needless to say, the reaction was the worst possible. Unable to find a single actor that would take on the main role, Marins decided to play it himself. He assembled a crew, bought thirteen cans of negative (130 minutes of film!) and, in a mere thirteen days, shot *At Midnight I Will Take Your Soul*.

It is very hard to believe that *At Midnight I Will Take Your Soul* was even released at the time. Brazil was - and still is - the biggest Catholic country in the world. Even by today's standards, the film is incredibly blasphemous and violent. To imagine that anyone would shoot a film like this in 1963 is truly unbelievable.

The story is set in a very poor town in upstate São Paulo. The locals are terrorized by an evil gravedigger named Zé do Caixão (Coffin Joe). Dressed in black, with a cloak, a top hat, and five-inch fingernails, he insults and humiliates the locals, mocking their religious beliefs and their provincial manners. Zé do Caixão's dream is to have a child. Because his own wife, Lenita, is barren, he kills her by dropping a huge tarantula (real, of course) on her body, after tying her to a bed and taping her mouth so she that isn't able to scream. He proceeds in his quest for the "perfect woman", raping Terezinha, the wife of his best friend, after drowning the guy in a bathtub. Some friendship! Terezinha hangs herself, but not before she has cursed Zé do Caixão and promised to come back from the dead in order to claim his soul.

The film was very violent, but what really shocked Brazilian audiences was Zé's blasphemy. In one now famous sequence, Zé eats a big piece of lamb while watching the Holy Friday procession passing beneath his window. Any good Catholic knows that you're not supposed to eat meat on a Holy Friday, much less offer a piece of lamb to the priest, like Zé does, before laughing mischievously at the holy man. In another outrageous sequence, Zé points to a crucifix and says, "What should we believe in? A symbol? An invisible force created by ignorance?"

The film's two biggest inspirations were Universal horror flicks and 1950s EC comic books, particularly *Tales from the Crypt*. Like the comic books Marins read as a child, *At Midnight I Will Take Your Soul* starts with a host "introducing" the story, in this case a gypsy woman with large eyes and a scary voice. Clutching a skull, she stares at the camera and speaks directly to the audience: "I wish you all a very

fear without frontiers

unpleasant evening, my friends... After this film, if you have to cross dark alleys all by yourself, there's still time... Go home! Don't watch this film!" Then a bell rings midnight... "Too late... You didn't believe me...so stick around...and suffer! Because...at midnight I will take your soul!"

Visually, the film seems taken directly from the pages of comic books. The black and white photography is highly contrasted, and the lighting totally Expressionistic, with rays of light cutting through the pitch black scenery. Despite his financial problems, Marins was able to put together a very talented crew, which included a number of professionals who worked at big studios in Brazil. Therefore, the cinematography (by Italian Giorgio Attili, who became a lifelong Marins collaborator) is extremely accomplished, as is the editing (by Luiz Elias) as well. The cast, however, consisted of amateur actors chosen from amongst Marins's students.

At Midnight I Will Take Your Soul was a huge box-office hit, but Marins didn't see a dime of it. To finance the film, he had convinced his father to sell the family's house and car. A couple of weeks before the film's release, Marins sold the rights to producer Ilídio Simões for half of what he had spent in the production. This was only the first of many examples of his incompetence as a businessman, a flaw that would plague him throughout his entire career. Marins used to walk around in downtown São Paulo counting the number of people in line to buy tickets for his film, and say to his friends, "I just want to know how much money I lost!" It was a lot of money: *At Midnight I Will Take Your Soul* was shown for sixteen months in São Paulo.

Even though he was broke, Marins had become a very famous man. Coffin Joe turned into a phenomenon, a cultural icon in Brazil. The film's impact was felt everywhere. A chain of car retailers started using the title in a publicity campaign: "At Midnight I Will Take Your Best Offer and Sell You a Brand New Volkswagen." Even mothers started invoking the name of Coffin Joe, to control their unruly sons: "If you don't behave, I'll call Coffin Joe to get you!" The success of *At Midnight* started attracting some film producers. Augusto de Cervantes, who, like Marins, was from a Spanish family, but who, unlike Marins, was a very smart businessman, hired him to direct the sequel to *At Midnight I Will Take Your Soul*. The title of the sequel: *Esta Noite Encarnarei no Teu Cadaver* (*This Night I Will Possess Your Corpse*).

A successful sequel

This Night was a much larger production than *At Midnight*, with a bigger budget and even some professional actors. At that time, Marins had moved his film school to an abandoned synagogue in São Paulo. All the sets for the film, including a forest, a lake, and Coffin Joe's mansion, were built either inside the synagogue or in the backyard. The story is a follow-up to the first film: Coffin Joe continues his quest for the woman that will bear him the "perfect child." With the help of a hunchbacked assistant named Bruno (Jose Lobo), he kidnaps six women and

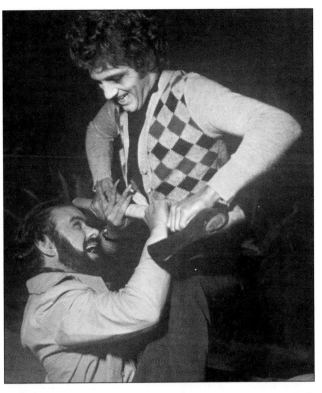

above:
Battling away in **Exorcismo Negro**.

left:
At Midnight I Will Take Your Soul.

Brazil

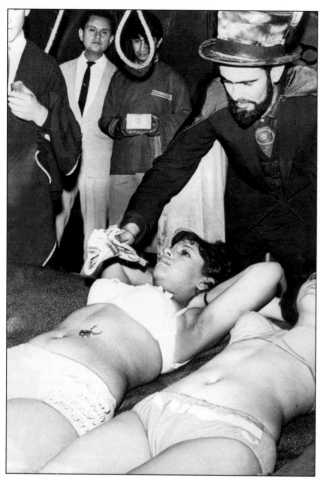

above:
Marins is famous for auditioning potential female co-stars by testing their ability to tolerate all manner of insects and reptiles crawling on their bodies.

submits them to several "tests of bravery", which include attacks by dozens of tarantulas and snakes.

Marins wanted to do a film even more shocking than the first one, thus the idea of using real snakes and spiders. With that in mind, he started auditioning actors for the parts. The examination included some very repulsive examples of method acting: candidates were asked to lick snakes, caress tarantulas, and kiss frogs. These auditions made the front pages of all the newspapers in São Paulo. When asked why he was overseeing such bizarre tests, Marins answered, "Well, I have to be sure that my actors will be able to fulfil their duties when the time comes. If an actress has to do a scene in which she will be covered by snakes, I can't run the risk of hiring someone that will quit as soon as she sees the serpents."

The filming of *This Night I Will Possess Your Corpse* makes for one of the most bizarre chapters in Brazilian cinema. For two months, Marins, his crew, and his cast - which included eighty tarantulas and sixty snakes - were locked inside the synagogue. The scenes with the spiders were the most difficult to shoot. At the end of each take, some trembling assistants would collect the tarantulas and put them into a huge box. Often, some of the spiders would disappear, only to be found - sometimes days later - inside one of the actor's shoes or locker. At one point, after two huge tarantulas were found in a bakery next door, almost killing the poor baker of a heart attack, the shooting of *This Night* was interrupted by police.

A crucial scene in this film was the recreation of the dream that originally inspired Marins to create Coffin Joe. In this sequence, Coffin Joe is dragged by a faceless creature to a cemetery and then taken to hell. In order to increase the impact of the scene, Marins decided to shoot the hell sequence in colour, while the rest of the film was in black and white. Marins's vision of hell is unique and disturbing: instead of fire, there is plenty of snow (made of popcorn); the walls are decorated by human heads, arms, legs, and torsos, all moving independently in a macabre ballet. The human body parts were real, of course. The actors were literally plastered on the walls, hung up like decoration pieces.

This Night was an even bigger success in Brazil than *At Midnight*. Although it is impossible to know the exact number of tickets sold because of the precarious system of box-office accounting at the time, it is widely accepted that the film was seen by an estimated audience of six or seven million, which would make it one the Top 10 biggest box-office hits in Brazilian history.

The release of *This Night I Will Possess Your Corpse*, in 1967, marked Marins's apogee in Brazil. In the following three years, he would become the country's most famous filmmaker. In that same year, he started a TV show called *Além, Muito Além do Além* (*Beyond, Far Beyond the Beyond*), a *Twilight Zone*-type weekly show with horror stories that became the number one show in its time slot, attracting more viewers than all of the other channels combined. In 1968, he was hired by TV Tupi, a very prestigious network, to host another show, *O Estranho Mundo de Zé do Caixão* (*The Strange World of Coffin Joe*). But *This Night I Will Possess Your Corpse* also marked the beginning of Marins's problems with the Censorship Board, a fight that would eventually threaten to destroy his career.

José Mojica Marins

Censorship blues

Censorship existed in Brazil since the 1930s, but things got much worse after the military coup in 1964, and especially after the Institutional Act 5, created at the end of 1968, which closed Congress and extended the powers of the Censorship Board. Many Brazilian filmmakers had a hard time with Censorship, but no one suffered more than Mojica. Starting in 1967, all of his horror films would either be cut to shreds or else prohibited entirely. By 1970, over 60% of every frame he had shot was banned from Brazilian screens.

The first of his films to suffer at the hands of the censors was *This Night I Will Possess Your Corpse*. Not only was the film cut by twenty minutes, but the ending was changed too. In the original ending, Coffin Joe is shot by the locals he had been terrorizing. Moments before disappearing into the filthy waters of a swamp, he screams: "God doesn't exist! I'll be back and I will kill all of you!" One of the heads of the Censorship Board, Augusto da Costa, demanded changes, and Marins was instructed to dub the dialogue, transforming Coffin Joe into a pious man. In the new version of the ending, Coffin Joe says: "God! Yes, God is the truth! I believe in your powers, master! Save me!" To make sure that the changes would be made, Costa even wrote the dialogue himself (a copy of the handwritten text can be found in the Brazilian National Archives in Brasília). Costa was a pretty famous man in Brazil. Before getting a position on the Censorship Board, he was a defender with the Brazilian national soccer team that lost the 1950 World Cup to Uruguay in front of 200,000 people in Maracanã stadium.

The problems with *This Night I Will Possess Your Corpse* started worrying film and TV producers, and Marins was having difficulty in securing financing for his next projects. It was a bizarre situation: Brazil's most famous filmmaker couldn't get money for a new film because everyone was afraid of putting resources into a project only to have it banned by the censors upon completion. Marins's next two features - *Trilogia de Terror* (*Trilogy of Terror*) and *O Estranho Mundo de Zé do Caixão* (*The Strange World of Coffin Joe*), both made in 1968 - were film adaptations of short stories he had shot for TV. The first one was split between three directors - Marins, Ozualdo Candeias, and Luis Sergio Person - while Marins directed all three episodes of the second one.

above:
Marins directing himself in the role of a rapist who ends up suffering rough justice in **Perversão**.

left:
The Strange World of Coffin Joe.

horror cinema across the globe

Marins's episode in *Trilogy of Terror*, entitled *Pesadelo Macabro* (*Macabre Nightmare*), is one of his best works, the chilling story of a man who has a premonition that he will be buried alive. When the poor man wakes up and sees that he has, in fact, been buried, he screams in agony. But there is no sound at all inside his coffin. Marins cuts from outdoor scenes in the cemetery, with the mourners crying loudly, to close-ups of the desperate man screaming for his life - but not being heard.

The Strange World of Coffin Joe consists of three short stories. The first one, *O Fabricante de Bonecas* (*The Doll Maker*), is a straight-up horror tale about a doll maker who uses real human eyes in his puppets. The second episode, *Tara* (*Obsession*), is an experiment in filmmaking, shot with no dialogues, about a homeless man who is so infatuated with a rich girl that he breaks into her crypt, after she is murdered, in order to possess her dead body. The third episode, *Ideologia* (*Ideology*), is Marins's most violent piece of work. He plays Professor Oaxiac Odez (Coffin Joe spelled backwards!), a specialist in human behaviour who believes that instinct always prevails over reason. Challenged by a pompous journalist to prove his theory, Odez invites the man and his wife to visit his mansion. When the couple arrive in Odez's house, they are greeted by the host and taken to a small theatre, were they are forced to watch the most horrific burlesque show ever performed: a man is hung upside down and eaten alive by a bunch of cannibals; another has needles stuck in his neck; an old man eats molten lead. Everything is shot in close-ups, with no recourse to cuts. Marins used real circus artists for these scenes, and the effect is brutal.

After the "show", Odez and his assistants imprison the couple in separate cages. They are locked up for a whole week, with no food or water. In the end, both are nothing more than animals. When Odez stabs the journalist in the neck with a knife, the latter man's wife, dying of thirst, drinks her own husband's blood. "My theory is proven!" screams Odez, "Instinct has triumphed!" The episode concludes with a cannibal banquet in which Odez and his assistants eat the couple, whose severed heads are served on a silver platter. This was not the kind of thing censors at

below:
The Strange World of Coffin Joe.

José Mojica Marins

above:
Hallucinations of a Deranged Mind.

the time wanted to see. One of them went so far as to ask for Marins's arrest. The film was cut by over thirty minutes, and all three episodes had their endings deleted. Marins was also forced to change the conclusion of the third episode. The Censorship Board decided that Oaxiac Odez should die in the end. Unable to scrape together enough funds to shoot another ending, Marins used a creative - though not very honest - solution: he borrowed a copy of an old Egyptian war film starring Omar Sharif, which included a huge explosion scene, and added that sequence to the end of *The Strange World of Coffin Joe*, in order to give the impression that Odez was killed in the blast.

If Marins's problems with the Censorship Board weren't enough, another blow to his career came towards the end of 1969, when the government created Embrafilme, a State-financed company that would control Brazilian cinema. The relationship between Embrafilme and the Brazilian filmmakers, especially those from the so-called "Cinema Novo" movement - directors such as Glauber Rocha, Carlos Diegues, Nelson Pereira dos Santos, and many others who claimed to have created a "revolutionary" and popular cinema, inspired by the French Nouvelle Vague and Italian neorealism - still hasn't been studied enough in Brazil, in large part because it was a disgraceful alliance. These filmmakers began controlling Embrafilme, and had their films financed by the State. Or, in plain English, by the military dictatorship.

Embrafilme was a nest of corruption and shady deal making. A small group of filmmakers received all of the available money, while the rest of the country had to deal with the absurd laws created by the bureaucrats. Their idea was simple: Brazilian cinema should be protected at all costs. This included forcing theatre owners to show Brazilian films at least 100 days of the year (the number reached 140 days per year in 1980), and obligating theatres to show Brazilian short films before each foreign feature, paying 5% of the box-office take to the producer of the short film.

Theatres, especially the smaller ones, started closing. In the first fifteen years of Embrafilme's reign, Brazil lost three theatres per week. In 1969, there were 3,500 screens in the country. By 1984, that number would be reduced to 1,553. The number of tickets sold annually dropped from 300 million in 1970 to 90 million in 1984. The protectionist laws created by

above:
Inferno Carnal.

below:
Perversão.

Embrafilme (and approved by the Cinema Novo gang) effectively destroyed Brazilian independent cinema, created a hyper-inflation in movie budgets, annihilated small neighbourhood theatres, and obliterated 60% of Brazil's existing movie screens. Embrafilme made it impossible for an independent filmmaker like José Mojica Marins, who never received a penny from the State, to survive. And it literally bankrupted the Marins family: in 1970, the theatre that Antonio Marins had managed for over thirty years closed down.

The final nail in Marins's professional coffin came in 1970, when his film O Despertar da Besta (*Awakening of the Beast*) was banned outright. *Awakening* was Marins's most personal project, a horror-exploitation story about drug subculture and urban violence. Marins had the idea for the movie after witnessing a pregnant prostitute being beaten and killed by police officers. This horrific scene made such an impression on him that he decided to shoot a film involving police officers, drug dealers, prostitutes, perverts, and every seedy character he could think of. Unable to find a single producer that would put up money for his project, Marins did everything he could to scrape together funds for the film: he threw parties to collect money, and sold everything he had; several filmmakers donated cans of negative. All of the interior shots were done in Marins's two-room office in downtown São Paulo.

The film, created by Marins but written by his brilliant screenwriter, Rubens Francisco Lucchetti, starts inside a TV show, in which a psychologist is talking to a panel of "experts" about the effects of drug use. To illustrate his theory, the doctor begins describing some very bizarre stories: a girl is brought by a bunch of wild-eyed hippies to an orgy, where she takes drugs and is raped by a Moses lookalike... with Moses's staff! Another woman is shown injecting drugs into her foot, while five horny and sweaty men stare at her doing it.

José Mojica Marins

The doctor then starts describing an experiment he did with four drug addicts. He gives each one of them large doses of LSD, and takes them to a room decorated with a huge Coffin Joe poster. Inspired by the sight of Coffin Joe, all four subjects begin hallucinating. Several people consider the "trip sequence" in *Awakening of the Beast* Marins's crowing achievement. In his groundbreaking book *Mondo Macabro*, Pete Tombs writes:

"The half hour showing the quartet's visions contains some of the strangest and most powerful images ever put onto celluloid. Far from the high-tech, computer generated fantasies of Hollywood, these visions are much more raw and more disturbing. Marins makes a positive advantage of his low budget to create effects that few art directors would dare to even dream of. In one scene, a man is menaced by strange, fleshy faces that appear to be closing in on him. Gradually it becomes obvious that these "faces" are in fact a row of human arses, with features painted onto them, including moustaches and top hats. The natural reaction would be to laugh, but the hellish context of the scene makes the trick almost unbearably bizarre. The sense of fear and isolation that these scenes create is quite terrifying. Like a powerful drug, the film can be only taken in small doses and is difficult to watch more than once. It may be Marins's best film. It's definitely his strangest. ...It's certainly the closest thing to a genuine acid trip ever put on film."[2]

Marins had huge expectations for this film, but not surprisingly, the Censorship Board thought different. *Awakening of the Beast* was banned. One censor even wrote: "I strongly suggest burning the negatives of this film." To this day, Marins's best film has never been released commercially in Brazil.

After the prohibition of *Awakening*, Marins never again shot a film over which he had complete artistic control. He started working as a director-for-hire, doing comedies, sex flicks, and adventure stories. He directed some interesting films, such as *Finis Hominis* (*The End of Man*, 1971), an ironic take on the exploration of faith, about a prophet who walks in São Paulo doing miracles. But his films never reached the level of intensity and brutal beauty he achieved in such classics as *At Midnight I Will Take Your Soul*, *This Night I Will Possess Your Corpse*, and *Awakening of the Beast*.

Hard times, and a new beginning

From the mid-70s to the mid 90s, Marins's life was hell. Barred from doing the horror films he loved so much, his work declined in quality and he began to have some very serious drinking problems. Unable to make money in movies, he appealed to all kinds of tricks: in 1980, he founded a church, but went bankrupt a couple of months later. In 1982, Marins ran for Congress, promising to help filmmakers, garbagemen, gravediggers, and prostitutes. "These are people that nobody likes, but everyone needs", he declared. Probably the low point of his life was a speech he made during a political rally in São Paulo, attended by 15,000 people. Completely drunk, Marins addressed the crowd: "My people, the beast is coming! The beast will arrive here and take the milk away from our children! And there is only one person who can deal with this hideous monster, and that's me, Coffin Joe!" He was not elected.

In the 1980s, Marins started shooting hardcore sex films, the only job he could get at the time. Even in the xxx genre, he was an innovator: in *24 Horas de Sexo Ardente* (*24 Hours of Explicit Sex*, 1984), he directed the first love scene between a woman and a dog ever shot in Brazil. The film was a monster box-office hit, but Marins had chosen to be paid a salary instead of a percentage of the profits, and so received only a small fraction of what he could have made.

In 1993, when everything looked very grim for Marins, a Seattle-based video company called Something Weird put out a dozen of his films. Little by little, his talent started to get discovered by American and European horror fans, and rediscovered in Brazil (where Marins was already considered a has-been). In the following years, he travelled to the United States, Spain, The Netherlands, Italy, France, Portugal, and Argentina. Zé do Caixão became Coffin Joe, and Marins's career was resurrected.

In 2001, Fantoma Films released Marins's three best films - *At Midnight I Will Take Your Soul*, *This Night I Will Possess Your Corpse*, and *Awakening of the Beast* - on DVD. And there's more to come: riding on the wave of his new respectability, not to mention a small financial stability, Marins is preparing a new feature film, *Os Demônios* (*The Demons*). This film is probably the most important one in Marins's career, for it represents a new beginning for Brazil's horrormeister, the country's most radical and idiosyncratic artist.

above:
The End of Man.

[2] Tombs, P. (1998) *Mondo Macabro: Weird & Wonderful Cinema Around the World*. New York: St. Martin's Griffin, 123-24.

below:
A recent portrait of José Mojica Marins.

artists, actors, auteurs

Return of the phantom: Maxu Weibang's *Midnight Song**

David Robinson

Even though it may be forgivable to mislay the odd *Phantom of the Opera* here and there, given the number of versions and variants, that can hardly explain or excuse the half-century eclipse of Maxu Weibang's *Midnight Song* (*Yeban gesheng*), made at United China Pictures in Shanghai in 1936. The film (and its 1941 sequel) surfaced in Europe in 1999 at the Udine Far East Film Festival, to be revealed as arguably the most fascinating and creative of all interpretations of Gaston Leroux's horrid tale. Along with the film comes the rediscovery of the dark, original talent of actor-director-designer Maxu, a name which figures in none of the authorized histories of Chinese film, though Stephen Teo's recent *Hong Kong Cinema, The Extra Dimensions* discusses the filmmaker's later career in the former colony.

Very little is known about Maxu's life. He was born in 1905 in Hangzhou, in Zhejiang Province. His parents died when he was young, which is said to be the reason why he added his wife's family name Ma to his original name of Xu. He graduated from the Shanghai School of Fine Arts and after a period as an assistant teacher, was taken on by the Mingxing Studios. Like Alfred Hitchcock, he progressed from designing title cards to full-fledged art direction.

He soon gave up designing for acting, playing his first role in Zhang Shichuan's *The Marriage Trap* (*You hun*, 1924) at age 19. An unidentified critic writing in 1942 recalled that his talent as an actor "lay in his extraordinary ability to embody the character he was playing, using every word and action to express complex moods. None of his peers could match his portrayal of a character's deepest emotions... Maxu Weibang would go to tremendous pains to think through even the tiniest gesture, to find the best way to move people, and in doing so to add to the power of a film. His style of working was to be consistently sincere and honest."

The same writer described him as "a kind, tolerant-looking man with a long, angular face." He had an exceptionally large forehead: "From time to time he would play an artist or scholar, not just because of their closeness to his own nature, but also because he naturally looked the part: an artist with a somewhat scholarly demeanour."

At 21, Maxu had the opportunity to direct his first film, *The Love Freak* (*Qing chang guairen*, 1926) - apparently not a great success - at the Langhua Film Company. Returning to Mingxing when Langhua closed down, he was assistant director on *Love and Gold* (*Aiqing yu huangjin*, 1926), directed by Zhang Shichuan, for whom he had worked several times as an actor. He was definitively established as a director in his own right in 1928, and the titles of at least five further silent films are recorded: *Freak in the Night* (*Helye guairen*, 1928); *Devil Incarnate* (*Hunshi mowang*, 1929); *The Cry of Apes in a Deserted Valley* (*Kong gu yuan sheng*, 1930); *Pear Blossom in the Storm* (*Baoyu lihua*, 1934); and *Prison of Love* (*Ai yu*, 1934).

Of these the only film known to survive, *The Cry of Apes in a Deserted Valley*, appeared at a recent Pordenone Festival. It is a pretty silly thriller in which Lily, the beautiful daughter of an engineering works manager, is apparently carried off by a gorilla. Investigation reveals that Lily's captor is in fact a man disguised

* A version of this essay first appeared in *Film Quarterly* 53.2 (Winter 1999-2000) and appears here with kind permission of the author. © 2000 by the Regents of the University of California.

opposite:
Song Danping and his lover Li Xiaoxia, as portrayed by Jin Shan and Hu Ping in **Midnight Song** (aka **Song at Midnight**).

horror cinema across the globe 39

China

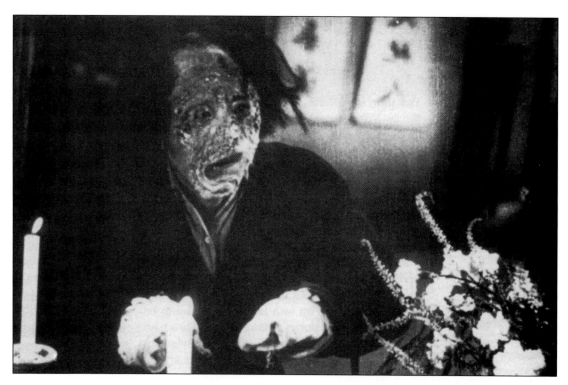

above:
In Maxu Weibang's films the face and its disfigurement are central concerns. **Midnight Song**'s hero, Song Danping becomes physically deformed.

below:
Song Danping before he became the "phantom", seen in a picture taken when he was a famous actor.

as a gorilla who is abducting young girls to be sold for rejuvenation experiments. (In the late 1920s rejuvenation and "monkey-glands" provided the same kind of thrill for tabloid-science as Viagra does today.) For all the shortcomings of the plot, the characters are vividly developed, and the villain's underground lair is quite a stylish piece of design. Moreover, the 25-year-old Maxu, lean and handsome in a sinister way, appears as an actor, playing a lurking, mysterious stranger who in the last reel turns out to be the great detective who finally brings the gorilla-man to justice.

After a first experiment with sound, *A Goose Alights on the Wintry River* (*Han jiang luo yan*, 1935), Maxu made his undoubted masterpiece, *Midnight Song*. The film opens in Old Dark House-style with the arrival of a bedraggled touring opera company at a dilapidated theatre guarded by a crazy, cackling old hunchback caretaker. They learn that the theatre has been empty and crumbling since the apparent death there of the great opera star Song Danping, ten years before.

The company clean up the theatre and embark on rehearsals, but the young star has trouble with his songs and stays behind to rehearse after the rest have left. Alone in the theatre, he is alarmed to hear a beautiful voice, which guides him through his song. It is of course Song Danping, who thereupon appears in person to relate his story in flashback. He was in love with the daughter of a rich and powerful feudal lord, who punished him for this presumption by having him beaten and horribly disfigured. Since then he has hidden in the theatre, waiting for a singer who can take over his artistic mantle. The young newcomer is chosen, and entrusted with the manuscript of Song Danping's operatic *chef d'oeuvre*. He is also required to be envoy to Song Danping's former love, Li Xiaoxia, whose mind has broken from sorrow.

The major departure from Leroux and other film adaptations is that the Phantom is the unequivocal protagonist, and wholly benevolent, even though at the end he becomes the instrument of killing his old malefactor when the feudal lord menaces the young singer and his fiancée. This is in marked contrast to the conventions of Western horror films, which invariably marginalize their monsters, however sympathetic, generally pivoting the plot on a decorative romantic duo.

In Leroux, the Phantom's protégée is a female singer, and the Phantom is provoked to lethal sexual jealousy of her fiancée. Maxu develops much more complex and ambiguous relationships by making the protégé male. The hallucinating Li Xiaoxia believes the young man to be Song Danping himself, and fascination and delight begin to heal her tormented mind. Song Danping is perfectly content to place the young man in this beneficent role of surrogate, and his distress when he discovers that the young man has a fiancée is a kind of jealousy on behalf of Li Xiaoxia, a strange and subtle anxiety about the boy's commitment to his go-between role.

The expressionist settings, presumably the work of Maxu himself, are richly atmospheric. Clearly he had seen the James Whale films, but the German Expressionists are still quite evidently a much stronger influence on the lighting, use of shadows, and sinister chiaroscuro. Maxu is a master of mise-en-scene and suspense: most notable is the scene when the bandages are finally removed from the Phantom, whose head is out of shot, below the frame line. The doctor slowly unwinds the bandages as Song Danping's loving mother and sister watch with eager expectation, and the spectator waits with growing anxiety, anticipating the shock of the exposure of the face - which indeed sends them reeling across the room.

Other factors enrich the film. Maxu was, by all accounts, a highly politicized person, deeply and personally affected - to a degree of permanent melancholy - by China's decades of trauma. (The film was released in February 1937, only months before the Japanese bombing of Shanghai effectively closed down film production there.) Song Danping is portrayed as a fugitive revolutionary, using the theatre as sanctuary, and the characterization of the evil feudal lord has clear references to the chaotic political struggles of the 1920s.

Part of the film's huge success on its first release was due to the songs, at least one of which has remained a favourite long after the film itself has been forgotten. The lyrics were by Tian Han (a left-wing writer who at the time was under house arrest by

left:
Song is trapped in a burning tower:
Midnight Song.

the Kuomintang), who also helped revise the script to strengthen its nationalist and anti-feudal sentiments. At Tian's suggestion, the composer was Xian Xinghai, who deliberately combined elements of popular and folk song with idioms of both Western and traditional Chinese opera.

The incidental music is another matter, and a cause for some anxiety for modern European viewers. It is a compilation in the manner of a silent film score, recklessly juxtaposing popular classics, from "Night on Bare Mountain" to "Orpheus in the Underworld," Handel's "Largo" and "Rhapsody in Blue." It is not easy for the contemporary spectator to make the adjustment necessary to gauge the effect of these (essentially skilfully chosen) melodies upon a Chinese public, to whom in 1937 they were still quite unfamiliar.

The film's enormous commercial success launched the star career of its leading actor Jin Shan, created a long-lasting vogue for horror films, and firmly typed Maxu as a genre director. His next four films included *Tales of a Corpse-Ridden Old House* (*Gu wu Xing shi ji*, 1938)

below:
The Phantom.

China

above:
At the end of **Midnight Song II**, Song's lover Li Xiaoxia has become blind, sparing her the sight of Song's skull-like visage.

right:
Midnight Song II's Mad Doctor (Hong Jingling), the villain who destroys Song's face.

and *Leper Woman* (*Mafeng nü*, 1939). Then in 1941 he decided, or was pressed, to make a sequel to *Midnight Song*.

Even if *Midnight Song II* (*Yeban gesheng xuji*), with an entirely new cast, has not the quality of its predecessor, it is still the work of an artist of exceptional fantasy and visual gifts. It opens with the funeral of the young singer's fiancée, shot by the evil lord at the climax of the original film. After the funeral the singer leaves the opera troupe - whom we see being harassed by unidentified occupation troops - to go and fight with the Nationalist army. Meanwhile, the wandering Song Danping is reunited with his little sister, now grown up. In the flashbacks to which Maxu was by this time chronically addicted, Song Danping relates his story. At the end of the original *Midnight Song*, he was last seen trapped at the top of a tower, which had been fired by an angry mob. He explains that he had leapt into the sea below and been rescued by sailors.

More bizarrely, he recounts how his appearance, though still monstrous, has been changed in the meantime. This sequence gives an insight into Maxu's obsessive visual preoccupations. From the sketchy biographical information available, we learn that he was passionate in his study of makeup, and would spend hours trying out different opera makeups on his own face. It is tempting to guess that between 1937 and 1941 he had seen Rupert Julian's 1925 version of *The Phantom of the Opera*, and had preferred Lon Chaney's death's-head makeup to the rather more scrofulous face he had designed for Midnight Song. To justify making this change without breaching the story logic linking the two films, he devised a strange subplot in which the Phantom is taken up by a crazy old doctor who rushes about like La Fee Carabosse, with a goblin nose, vampire teeth, and Quasimodo hump. The doctor and his assistants perform an elaborate operation in a Frankenstein-like laboratory. The hands come out all right, but when the face is unwrapped, the doctor's assistants recoil at the disaster: far from improved, the face has been transformed to the Lon Chaney pattern.

Maxu introduces another outrageous narrative convenience later in the film. Song Danping's tragic lover Li Xiaoxia has lain sick and delirious in her bed throughout the film, and in the final reel suffers the additional affliction of blindness. It is at this moment that the young singer reappears with his Nationalist troops, to rout the invaders and effect a meeting between the two one-time lovers. Now blind, the lady of course remains blissfully unaware of the disfigurement of her long-lost love, and dies happy, while the Phantom, precluding all further sequels, takes his life with a poisoned dart purloined from the crazy old doctor. The film ends, as it began, with a funeral - this time a double one. The manipulation may be blatant, but it works infallibly: there were few dry eyes at the Udine screening.

Despite such evident mechanics (not to speak of the music, which this time adds the "Pathetique" to the repertory), Maxu's soaring imagination and vision remain supreme. In *Midnight Song II* the influence of James Whale is more apparent: a scene where the Phantom comes upon a crowd of villagers listening to a professional storyteller has something of the look of

Maxu Weibang

above:
The Mad Doctor's laboratory in **Midnight Song II**, complete with live nude models posed as statues.

Hollywood Transylvania, but this, and some exotic mountain scenes, apparently done on location, have a grandeur and painterly style that the Universal stages could not rival. Nor is there anything in Whale to match Maxu's moments of romantic madness, which rather bring to mind the Buñuel of *Abismos de Pasion*.

In his eight remaining years in Shanghai, Maxu made ten more films, and in 1949 moved to Hong Kong, where he was to make twelve more. Of all this output, his first Hong Kong production appears to be the only film at present available for viewing, although the others may still be lingering in video catalogues. *The Haunted House* or *A Maid's Bitter Story* (*Quionglou hen*, 1949) (regarded by Stephen Teo as Maxu's "Hong Kong masterpiece") intermittently retrieves the old fantasy and expressionist imagery, and there is a throwback to *Midnight Song* in the story of a tyrannical old parent (an Emil Jannings-style performance) who disfigures the disapproved lover of his daughter, driving her to suicide. Facial disfigurement clearly remained a special preoccupation: it had also featured in *Autumn Begonia* (*Qiu haitang*, 2 parts, 1943), which for Julien Carbon represents Maxu's unqualified masterpiece. Although his career seems to have declined following the commercial failure of the high-budget *The Haunted House* and his subsequent three-year withdrawal from production, Maxu continued to work regularly (on films whose titles admittedly included *Resurrected Rose* and *Booze, Boobs and Bucks*) from 1954 to 1961, when he died after being knocked down by a car.

Not everyone forgot *Midnight Song*. In 1962, Maxu's former assistant Yuen Chiufeng remade it for Shaw Brothers, as *Mid-Nightmare* - this time to feature a woman star, Le Ti. In 1995, Ronny Yu directed a new version as a vehicle for Leslie Cheung, with the title *The Phantom Lover*. It is a spectacularly lavish and handsome production, though one yearns for Maxu's eerie chiaroscuro, and the story does not benefit from the over-elaboration involving the heroine's forced betrothal. Most fatally, the operatic Romeo and Juliet that is supposed to be Song Danping's masterwork sounds as if it was concocted of numbers rejected from Cliff Richards's Heathcliff. It is a far, far cry from the haunting songs of Xian Xinghai.

artists, actors, auteurs

Enfant terrible: the terrorful, wonderful world of Anthony Wong

Lisa Odham Stokes & Michael Hoover

Asking fans of Hong Kong cinema to name their favourite Anthony Wong character brings an array of responses. There's his performance as the "bunman" in *The Untold Story* (1993), a brutal murderer who serves the remains of his victims to restaurant diners. Then there's the trucker Tong in *The Underground Banker* (1993), striking back against a local triad boss who exploited his wife and tormented his family. There's also the deadly virus carrier on a mission to kill in *Ebola Syndrome* (1996). And the police detective possessed by an evil force bent on destroying the world in *Armageddon* (1997). Not to mention the depraved, disfigured, and greedy Mister Kim who controls Hong Kong's fresh water supply in *The Executioners* (1993). These are among the myriad hyperbolic roles that have earned wonderful Wong his reputation as an irascible figure in the Hong Kong film industry.

Born in 1961 to a Chinese mother and British father, Wong says the latter "left when I was very young and my family was very poor. I grew up with a Chinese family and I went to a Chinese school. At that time, being poor and being mixed led to many problems. They treated you like a monster."[1] After finishing school, he went through a series of low income, working-class jobs. Wong began formal acting training at the age of twenty-one and upon graduation from Hong Kong's Academy of Performing Arts spent much of the late 1980s in front of television cameras. The actor gained attention in movie circles for his 1992 performances in John Woo's *Hard-Boiled* (as gangster Johnny Wong) and Alex Law's *Now You See Love, Now You Don't* (as Chow Yun-fat's loyal and humorous friend), receiving a Hong Kong Best Supporting Actor nomination for the latter. Wong followed up that success by winning Hong Kong's 1993 Best Actor award for his aforementioned performance in *The Untold Story*.

Ever busy, Anthony Wong has appeared in over 100 films since his big-screen debut in 1985. He has directed two feature films, *New Tenant* (1995) and *Top Banana Club* (1996), and has also released two CDs of self-penned music (*Underdog Rock* and *Useless is Useful*). Meanwhile, the actor has since won a second Hong Kong Best Actor award for his portrayal of a police detective traversing the line between "good and bad" in *Beast Cops* (1998). Of the numerous roles he's played, Wong indicates that he's partial to the mild-mannered insurance agent turned killer of taxi cab drivers in *Taxi Hunter* (1993) saying "I think it is my best piece of work because that role involves a humanized character, it involves diversification and is layered." The actor also favours his *Cop Image* (1994) performance; Wong plays a traffic monitor who dreams of being a super-cop in the tradition of the characters played by the likes of Chow Yun-fat and Danny Lee whose movie posters adorn his walls.

Sex, horror and cannibalism: hardcore Hong Kong

Hong Kong filmmaker Ronny Yu, commenting on the inevitable return of Great Britain's colonial possession to Mainland China, has said that "Hong Kong is the only place in the world where you were told as a kid, by 1997 your lifestyle might end."[2] As the 1970s closed, almost two decades before the hand-over, nervous residents and corporate planners in the

[1] Anthony Wong, personal interview, 2 July 2000. All Anthony Wong quotations are either this or one of the following sources: personal correspondence, 6 May 1999, personal correspondence, 2 May 2001.

[2] Ronny Yu, personal interview, 17 October 1998. All Yu quotations are this source.

opposite:
Anthony Wong in **The Executioners**.

territory could already be seen and heard. The colony began an irrevocable change following Chinese Premier Deng Xiaoping's 1979 visit, in which he articulated for the first time the mantra "one country, two systems." British Prime Minister Margaret Thatcher's 1982 trip failed to persuade Chinese leaders that Britain should have some official capacity in Hong Kong after 1997. And the 1984 Sino-British Joint Declaration establishing the terms under which "the return" would occur did not include residents of the colony. As Yu, best known in the West for 1998's *Bride of Chucky*, indicates, "Everybody trying to do something, either making money or making a name, before the deadline... if I can find a way to jump from A to C, I don't care about the in between... I have no time; I don't want to know. That's why the Hong Kong film pace is so frenetic...the audience is like that. Their daily life is like that."

While spectacle and speed in both camera and footwork are Hong Kong cinema trademarks in the West, the movies themselves run the gamut. Gangster and martial arts pictures by no means comprise the whole of the territory's film industry that once ranked first in the world in per capita production, second to the United States in film export, and third in the world in terms of the number of films made per year.[3] Lightweight comedies and meditative dramas are regularly served fare, as is the horror genre with its free mixture of Western movie motifs and Chinese literature. A film censorship ordinance permitting more nudity and sex in films was enacted in 1988. According to David Bordwell, the new rating systems law "had the effect of creating a safety zone hospitable to exploitation items."[4]

The result has been widespread production of Category III films (for persons aged eighteen and above only). The equivalent U.S. classification would be NC-17 (no one under seventeen admitted); few Hollywood releases have received this rating since it was introduced in 1990. Since many theatre chains refuse to show NC-17 productions, films such as *Basic Instinct* (1992) are re-cut in order to receive the Motion Picture Association of America's R-rating (no one under seventeen admitted without an adult). In contrast, 39% of films (662 out of 1,697) approved for 1997 public exhibition in Hong Kong received a Category III classification, almost twice the number (336) that received a Category I (suitable for all ages) rating. Another 17% (296) were classified as Category IIA (not suitable for children) and 24% (403) were assigned a Category IIB (not suitable for young persons and children) classification.[5] Two years later, when 1,408 films were approved for public screening, 405 (29%) were classified as Category III, 294 (21%) as Category I, 274 (19%) as Category IIA, 435 (31%) as Category IIB.[6] Categories I, IIA, and IIB are advisory, while Category III is enforced by law.

Censorship of Hong Kong cinema for political reasons was a long-standing practice given Britain's prohibition of anti-colonial messages from the industry's outset. In 1928, the chief censor remarked to the local American General Consul that his responsibility was to sustain British eminence in a "small settlement of white men on the fringe of a huge empire of Asiatics."[7] That same year, a United Artists representative in Hong Kong indicated that proscribed topics included "armed conflict between Chinese and whites" and depiction of "white women in indecorous garb or positions or situations which would tend to discredit our womenfolk with the Chinese."[8] Officially, however, political state censorship of Hong Kong films dates to 1953.[9] More than twenty films were subject to film board cuts and demands for changes between 1974 and 1988 when the "liberalized" code went into effect, including Akira Kurosawa's Soviet-financed *Dersu Uzala* (1975) which was considered anti-Chinese. The most notable locally-produced example was Tsui Hark's *Dangerous Encounter of the First Kind* (1980), an unrelentingly violent urban-realist, anti-colonial rant. The 1988 system, which remains on the books, specifically addresses potential harm to relations with other countries. Obviously intended to placate Mainland China, this concern has also been useful in mollifying Southeast Asian financiers and governments, upon which the Hong Kong film industry has depended for investments and markets. Quite simply, Hong Kong censors are more likely to prohibit social and political material than they are to forbid films containing sex and violence.

The first Category III films to gain notoriety were sexploitation flicks such as *Erotic Ghost Story* (1990), *Robotrix* (1991), and *Naked Killer* (1992). Often campy, such films sold soft-core porn containing scenes with exposed women's breasts, simulated copulation, and intimate relations between women. Some trucked in graphic violence, generally linking brutality and sex, both in terms of rape as well as rape-revenge.[10]

---

[3] "Film Entertainment Services", www.info.gov.hk (8 July 1997).

[4] Bordwell, D. (2000) *Planet Hong Kong: Popular Cinema and the Art of Entertainment*. Cambridge: Harvard University Press, 155.

[5] "Film Classification in Hong Kong", www.info.gov.hk (9 November 1998).

[6] "Film Classification in Hong Kong", www.info.gov.hk (13 March 2001).

[7] Shohat, E. and R. Stam (1994) *Unthinking Eurocentrism: Multiculturalism and the Media*. London: Routledge, 112.

[8] Ibid.

[9] Cheuk-to, L. (Summer 1989) "Political Censorship: The Fatal Blow", *Cinemaya* 4, 44-45.

[10] Actor Karen Mok deplores the retrograde trend of 1990s "rape films requiring little budget and production" that manufacture as well as mirror the ideological notion that men both desire to, and in fact do, violently control women. Karen Mok, personal correspondence, November 18, 1998.

Anthony Wong

But even as the Cat III rating was becoming identified with more explicit cinematic sexuality in the early 1990s, a horrific type of film was about to burst onto the then-colony's theatre screens. Termed "Hardcore Hong Kong" by William S. Wilson, these films revolve around serial killer characters frequently based on ostensible real-life murderers engaging in torture, mutilation, cannibalism and necrophilia.[11] According to filmmaker Herman Yau, who has directed several such films, "Cat III movies are not considered mainstream most of the time. Sometimes, they become mainstream for a certain (usually short) period of time if we have one with a very good box office. The theatres that show Cat III movies are mostly the same as those that show other movies, but some theatres refuse to show Cat III movies because they think that showing such movies will ruin their image as 'high class' theatres."[12]

Dr. Lamb (1992), the story of a deranged cab driver (Simon Yam) who rapes and dismembers young women, takes photographs of his gruesome acts, and then stashes body parts in his home, ushered in this sub-genre, termed the "horror/crime" film by Jeff Beres.[13] The film was the directorial debut of popular actor Danny Lee who also plays an earnest cop in the mould for which he is well known. *Dr. Lamb* explains the main character's behaviour and the film's misogyny as the outcome of absent motherly love: it is the woman who's to blame. Moreover, in what would become stock-in trade "horror/crime" Hong Kong filmmaking, *Dr. Lamb* expresses both repugnant cruelty and repulsively dark humour, the latter serving to add to viewer discomfort. Screenwriter Law Kam-fai and director Lee also establish the terrain that similar films would negotiate, that of a working person caught in the Hobbesian-like environment of Hong Kong's competitive "cutthroat" capitalism. No minimum wage, no official poverty line, no full employment policy, and a minimal social safety net.

The movie (and subgenre) appeared as a side effect of the territory's cultural crisis. Three years after the 1989 Tiananmen Square massacre, Hong Kongers were still scrambling for foreign passports, standing in long lines outside of foreign consulates, and calling for abrogation of the 1984 Joint Declaration. Upwards of 50,000 people per year (out of a total population of 6,500,000) were emigrating from the territory in light of the events on the Mainland. Not surprisingly, the professional-managerial stratum constituted the largest percentage of those able to leave. As Ronald Skeldon notes, references at the time to Hong Kong émigrés as "yacht people" were not entirely inaccurate.[14] Moving to overseas enclaves or travelling between home and enclave were less feasible options for the working class. In the midst of transition to a service economy that would eliminate 400,000 manufacturing jobs, working people in Hong Kong confronted potential abandonment by footloose industries looking elsewhere for cheaper labour. Moreover, as public housing construction slowed, numbers of low-income people found themselves in danger of being priced out of affordable residences by rent inflation following the elimination of rate controls for all old private buildings.

Simon Yam's performance in *Dr. Lamb* was but one of more than 100 movies the actor made between 1989 and 1998, many of them low-budget Cat III productions in which he was alternately typecast as a gigolo or a lunatic. Among the latter roles were his portrayals of a savage home invading stalker in *Insanity* and a ruthless tormenting ex-soldier in *Run and Kill*, both 1993; having been accused of signing onto such flicks solely for the money, the actor says, "I've tried lots of roles. I understand that I am only interpreting. I've done research in order to

above:
Run and Kill, a typical Cat III film.

[11] Wilson, W.S. (13 March 2001) "Hardcore Hong Kong", *Video Junkie*, www.vidjunkie.com. Several Western critics have made comparisons to *Henry: Portrait of a Serial Killer*, John McNaughton's 1986 film about Texas mass murderer Henry Lee Lucas that is based on a real-life story and that features scenes of graphic violence.

[12] Herman Yau, personal correspondence, 13 May 2001. All Herman Yau quotations are either this or the following source: personal correspondence, 12 March 2001.

[13] Beres, J. (July 2000) "Horror in Crime Films", *Horrorwood Webzine*. www.horror-wood.com/crime.htm (13 March 2001).

[14] Skeldon, R. (Winter 1990-91) "Emigration and the Future of Hong Kong", *Public Affairs* 63, 507.

[15] Simon Yam, personal correspondence, 24 December 1998.

[16] Marx, K. (1967) *Capital* vol. 1. New York: International Publishers, 763.

interpret the character successfully in every single movie."[15] But if Yam was the "guy who started it all" so far as Hong Kong splatter films are concerned, it was fellow actor and colleague Anthony Wong who came to embody the cinematic psychopath.

**Telling tales:
cooking up *The Untold Story***

Many Western fans' introduction to Anthony Wong was through his portrayal of the greedy, power-hungry Johnny Wong in *Hard-Boiled*. While Wong's character is like other villains in that he disregards human life, the gangster's decadent lifestyle of expensive clothes, chauffeured luxury cars, and fashionable clubs is far removed from the later "blue collar" roles for which the actor would become known. In *Hard-Boiled*, Wong's mania is that of the capitalist who, as Marx puts it, "always kills many."[16] Ironic in retrospect is that at the time Woo included a second villain because he feared that Anthony Wong couldn't entirely carry the "heavy" role set against Chow Yun-fat and Tony Leung Chiu-wai. Another prologue to the actor's work would be the sex crazed three-headed demon Wu-tung he plays in *Erotic Ghost Story 2* (1991), a Cat III film of the numerous "naked women" kind. Clearly hamstrung by the limitations of a character who, buried under a weighty costume, mostly grunts and groans, Wong appears full-frontally nude in one scene that serves as a self-referential comment on his view that Hong Kong's mainstream suppresses actors' freedom and creativity. In another instance, the perverse Wu-tung, making carnal with a woman's severed sex organs, offers viewers a glimpse of the terrorful Anthony Wong screen persona to come.

Wong found his *metier* and his best collaborator when he starred in Herman Yau's 1993 'true-crime' drama *The Untold Story* (a.k.a. *Bunman)*, based on a case, as Yau recalls, that happened in Hong Kong in 1978. The actor plays Wong Chi-hang, a fry cook accused of hacking his restaurant-owner boss and the boss's family to death and serving the remains as 'human pork buns.' Director Yau says, "I don't know whether it is true or not. At the time, many newspapers and magazines said the flesh of the victims was made into buns and were sold in the restaurant. I did not notice that newspapers retracted that part. I remember that they all treated it as big news and exaggerated it very much. Actually, the 'human pork buns' might just be a rumour. I don't think that people chose to believe the reporting. You know, when people who had eaten buns sold by the restaurant read about it, it was enough for them to feel sick even if the possibility of the reporting to be true was only one percent."

Yau's research for the film included a visit to Macau, and numerous interviews with an inmate who had shared a cell with the notorious "bunman" from whom he learned about his behaviour and personality. He also met with reporters who covered the story. With the facts he gathered the director used his imagination to construct the characterization. Actor Wong worked from an actual photograph of the criminal to imitate his face. *The Untold Story* cost HK$5.19 million (approximately US$600,000). According to Yau, "the shooting schedule was nineteen days of 12 hour shoots plus one month post-production for editing, dubbing, music, mixing, colour correction, etc." Grossing HK$15.8

million (about US$2 million) during its initial three week run in theatres, the film was a commercial success.

What sets Yau's Cat III movie apart from many others is its arty camera work and editing in relation to story and character development. Having worked in the Hong Kong industry for many years as a cinematographer, he has the experience and expertise to visualize and get what he wants. Yau cites R. W. Fassbinder, David Lynch, and Roman Polanski as directors he admires. Of his almost two- decade friendship with actor Anthony Wong, the filmmaker says, "He acted in my film when I was a film student. I think he is a very talented actor, maybe the best contemporary actor of our time. He is very creative and always adds his own characteristics." With their collaboration in *The Untold Story*, Anthony Wong became the most notorious screen villain in the Asian market.

The Untold Story, even before its opening credits, reveals a world askew. A bird's eye view of circa 1978 Hong Kong's crowded tenements swoops and dips 360 degrees to establish the lead character's environment and his place within it. No successful business people inhabit this landscape far removed from the high-walled private homes, luxury hotels, and indoor malls that have made the city-state one of the contemporary world's capitalist showcases. Rather, poor labourers, sole proprietors, and street people dwell in a landscape of sweatshops, storefronts, and shantytowns of unrelieved squalor, with too many people for too little land.**17**

The establishing shot is followed by a vicious crime in which Wong Chi-hang (aka Chan Chi-leung) brutally murders a man by hitting him over the head with a chair and banging his head into the wall while arguing over money as they gamble at mahjongg. Next he pours gasoline on him and sets him afire. Yau's unusual camera work and Wong's facial expressions and delivery as a money-obsessed, crazed character amplifies the horror. By dutching the camera, oblique angling makes this a confused and almost indecipherable world. In contrast to the big picture of the aerial shot, here everything's cramped and fetishized. We don't see whole bodies, only close up fragments - hands, arms at frame's edge, standing legs seen from beneath a table - a portent of the body parts to appear later. And the blurring effect of step printing photography eerily creates a strobe-like effect as if we are physically being taken on an acid trip into dread. Yau describes the scene as "kind of a flashback, so I wanted the images to be different from normal in some ways. I shot with twelve frames per second for that scene and I believe step printing can create a tempo inside the shots."

Jump ahead eight years to a beach in Macau where children discover severed limbs and stinking body parts wrapped in a shopping bag resembling the Union Jack. The police called to the scene are made squeamish by the rancid odour; one officer rips a finger from evidence that he is collecting. Danny Lee, the film's producer, playing a less-than-by-the-books captain, arrives to supervise his investigative unit with a prostitute in tow, the first of several instances showing Lee in the company of hookers. Unsurprisingly, the lone woman detective is constantly subjected to the sexism of her male counterparts, whose routines alternate between disparaging her small breasts and making vulgar comments about her being "butch."

above:
The Untold Story.

17 Nowhere is social class polarity in Hong Kong more evident than in residential patterns. Much of the population lives on less than five percent of the land in the crowded towns of Victoria and Kowloon.

Hong Kong

above:
Anthony Wong in award-winning form: **The Untold Story**.

The bumbling and incompetent cops ostensibly serve as comic relief. During a surveillance scene, for example, they neglect to sort through the trash that Wong has thrown out and are forced to dive into a sanitation truck in a futile attempt to sort through his garbage.

Wong Chi-hang's "makeover" following the murder of his boss Cheng Lam gives him close-cropped hair, big thick nerdy eyeglasses, and a new identity card. Assuming "ownership" of the Eight Immortals restaurant that specializes in barbecue pork buns, he unsuccessfully tries to convince a lawyer to transfer the business deed to his name, lying that he paid the previous proprietor who then left the country with his family. Meanwhile, the Macau police have received a letter asking that they look into the disappearance of Cheng Lam. Detectives pay Wong a visit, whereupon he repeats the story that he bought the business from Cheng while denying any knowledge of the latter's disappearance. The "kindly" Wong feeds them "really delicious" BBQ pork buns; in fact, he sends some to share with their co-workers back at headquarters. Unbeknown to the cops, of course, the buns are filled with human flesh, not the chicken or pork over which they argue.

The pork bun "delicacy" is the result of *The Untold Story's* second grisly act; accused of cheating at mah-jongg by the butcher that he has hired, Wong stabs the employee in the eye with a receipt holder. Then, inflicting numerous blows to the head with a ladle, the miscreant bludgeons the defenceless man to death. Wong's hyper-mania, evident in his face while committing the murder, is replaced by the cold, calculated look of someone "doing a job" when he dismembers and skins the victim. Both expressions convey the severity of his character and indicate the complexity of his derangement. Plus, they disclose the quality of Anthony Wong's edgy performance, as does the earlier incident with the attorney. Rebuffed in his attempt to gain legal possession of the restaurant, the character's anger erupts as he screams, "Fuck! Fuck! Fuck! You are so fucking stupid!" Seemingly too furtive to step over the line in this "public" setting, however, his only action is to ruffle some documents. Wong Chi-hang's third killing exacts "revenge" from a woman he believes tipped off the police about his shocking activities while she was working as a waitress at "his" restaurant. Director Yau, extending the length of the savagery and upping the butchery with each gruesome act, shoots a scene too torturous for all but the most jaded of viewers to watch. Wong beats and rapes the woman before assaulting her a second time with chopsticks and mutilating her body. Then, as with his previous victim, he cooks her flesh into the pork buns responsible for the "rave reviews" and the increasing number of customers at the Eight Immortals Restaurant. Responding to criticism of the film's depiction of violence against women, actor Anthony Wong indicates, "I don't quite like the movie. I played a role; the character is an anti-hero. Once the job is given, I just have to make my best effort."

Yau asserts, "it was not my intention to perpetuate violence against women. I executed the rape and murder scenes the way I did because I thought the 'bunman' had a very high possibility to do it like that. It is not fair to generalize about the treatment in the movie as my attitude towards the issue. What people see is the behaviour of the 'bunman' according to my imagination based on the research I did. The torture that the 'bunman' put on the victims were ways to punish them since he thought they were bad to him or had cheated him. Of course, the ultimate punishment was the death penalty." The filmmaker doesn't eroticize the physical attacks of the woman, and the camerawork focuses upon close-ups of the assailant's twisted face rather than the frightful looks of his female victim. Still, Arjun Appaduri maintains that "fantasies of gendered violence [that] dominate the B-grade film...both reflect and refine gendered violence at home and in the streets."[18] If rape is a means by which men intimidate and keep women in fear, *The Untold Story* incident goes beyond male power and phallic domination to link cinematic voyeurism with sadism. As Laura Mulvey charges, "Sadism needs a story", a portion of which is punishing women for their alleged transgressions.[19] And the waitress's transgression is that she's smart enough to figure out that there's heat in Wong Chi-hang's kitchen. Unfortunately for her, however, she can't escape.

The film departs from the convention of having the cops pursue the perpetrator in a game of "catch me if you can" when Wong Chi-hang is arrested about halfway through the film. One of the world's largest operations, in per capita terms, the Hong Kong police force numbers approximately 30,000 officers in a city of 6.5 million people, a ratio of about one officer to 200 citizens. Moreover, the Hong Kong police have considerable discretion in regard to the use of force in the exercise of their duties. According to Criminal Ordinance Cap 221, S1101A, police may use "such force as is reasonable in the circumstances."[20] Allegations of police brutality by the Hong Kong police are legend. While reported complaints number about 3000 per year, the number of unreported cases is believed to be three to four times higher than that figure. Most victims of abuse and torture are low-income and working class people who may be further intimidated and threatened by the police if they file a formal protest.

The inept and ostensibly humorous investigative unit in the film turns macabre when Wong is apprehended trying to flee to China. Danny Lee's character appears willing to use any means necessary to extract a confession from the suspect against whom he has limited evidence. The interrogation of the barbarous Wong is itself barbaric; he is alternately subjected to physical abuse from the police and fellow cellmates in jail. Doctors tie the man to a hospital bed and inject him with drugs following an attempted suicide, as well as a failed escape try. As the police beatings continue, Yau accomplishes the unthinkable - he elicits momentary sympathy for a psychopathic killer who may be the most appalling character to ever appear on the screen of a "mainstream" film anywhere in the world. Accordingly, the filmmaker confirms that *The Untold Story's* portrayal of the cops is, "in a sense, an anti-police, anti-authority statement."

Eventually a nurse shoots Wong up with water causing painful boils to arise on his back, and he cracks under the collective weight of the authorities' treatment. As if the film has not already pushed the boundaries of cinematic cruelty, the "bunman's" confession consists of a visual flashback in which we learn that he not only murdered his boss Cheng Lam at the beginning of the movie, he slaughtered the entire family. As with the earlier rape scene, Yau agonizingly draws out the attack, shooting the slaughter in excruciatingly vivid detail. After tying up the wife and children, Wong inadvertently chokes one son to death with wire wrapped around the boy's neck. Whereupon he stabs the wife in the stomach snarling, "I'm going to kill your whole fucking family." Then, amidst stomach-curdling children's screams; he chops several daughters to death with a meat cleaver, decapitating one young girl as she crawls around helplessly on the floor. The death toll stands at ten when the

above:
Anthony Wong in
The Untold Story.

[18] Appaduri, A. (1994) "Disjuncture and Difference in the Global Cultural Economy." In Williams, P. and L. Chrisman (eds.), *Colonial Discourse and Postcolonial Theory: A Reader.* New York: Columbia University Press, 336.

[19] Mulvey, L. (1989) *Visual and Other Pleasures.* London: Macmillan, 22.

[20] UN Profile - Hong Kong, "World Fact Book of Criminal Justice." www.ojp.usdoj.gov (4 August 1998).

massacre is over, eight of which are innocent children, and the room is drenched in blood.

As in the earlier tortured waitress scene, Yau was adamant about not wanting low-key lighting for the killing of the entire family. He avows that "most directors would have it [low-key lighting] for such scenes." Instead, he made the lighting harsh, and the killer, meticulous and methodical once he has determined his actions. Delivering an almost clinical expose of relentless brutality, Wong and Yau out-Hannibal Hannibal Lecter by not having Wong's madman merely consume his victims, but by showing the labour-intensive process of Wong carefully preparing and disposing of the bodies and cleaning up the mess. The irrational pleasure the killer receives by watching the results eaten by others makes the effect even more gruesome.

Carol Clover has written that slasher films frequently trade in male killers whose sexual fury is vented against attractive, sexually liberated young women. She has also noted that the assailant often fails to survive the end of the movie. *The Untold Story* is one exception to Clover's first point, in that Wong's rage is not rooted in his sexuality but rather in his reaction to the powerlessness he experiences as a "member" of the working poor. The work does conform to Clover's second notion, albeit with a twist. Typically a "final girl" triumphs over monstrous evil by killing the perpetrator, but in this instance, the mass murderer commits suicide in jail.**21** Generalizing the cinematic mayhem, however, provides clues to the psychosis of Anthony's Wong's character. He is frenzied Hong Kong, caught in a web of magnified fears wrought by the Tiananmen tragedy, widening income polarization, and increasing pessimism associated with 1997.

Human interest stories: collecting debts in *The Underground Banker*

Wong says that most of what came his way following the Hong Kong best actor award win (for which he admits surprise) were "maniac roles."**22** Representative of this situation were the deranged intruder who torments a temporarily blind, self-centred wife of an out-of-town wealthy physician that he played in *Retribution Sight Unseen* (1993), and his depiction of a wealthy businessman whose tastes run towards torture, murder, and cannibalism in *The Day That Doesn't Exist* (1995). Regarding his typecasting as a villain, the actor says,

"From the creative point of view, of course I'm not satisfied, but from the money making standpoint, it doesn't really matter and I don't really care."**23**

Having established himself as the most ghastly screen presence in Hong Kong cinema as the "bunman", Anthony Wong plays against type for much of Bosco Lam's *The Underground Banker*. The actor's trucker character Tong Chi-ming is a "regular fella" with a wife and son. Tong owns his eighteen-wheeler but, as is the case with many sole proprietors, he is hardly his own boss. Thus, there is little to distinguish him from those who are working class. As a sub-contractor, he works long and hard to make ends meet, frequently on the road for a week at a time. He covers the costs of upkeep on the truck as well as family expenses, but has little time or money for leisure activities or material indulgences. Nicknamed "Marshmallow" because he's easily intimidated, Tong appears to "go along to get along" as when he says he just wants to "earn a living" while handing money over to some petty-thugs who claim that they control the lot in which he parks his rig.

Early in the film, Wong's character notices flickering hallway lights outside the apartment to which he and his family have just relocated and asks: "Is it a horror film?" Only partly so, as director Bosco Lam weaves elements of Hong Kong "horror/crime" flicks into a devilish lampoon of them (complete with lame comedy and obligatory Cat III misogyny and sexploitation). For example, there is the notorious serial killer Lam Kuo-jen of the earlier *Dr. Lamb* movie, played by Lawrence Ng this time rather than Simon Yam. "Rehabilitated" and released into the general population, Ng's Lam displays a sardonic wit; his character is cryptic, not evil. On the one hand, he saves Tong's son from a raging fire; on the other, he enthuses that "I'm really happy" to be killing again when he takes action against a group of thugs. In addition, an agitated Tong screams near the end of the film that "I'll chop you and make BBQ pork buns" making an all too obvious reference to Wong's own "bunman" character in *The Untold Story*.

The story line revolves around the apartment that the mild-mannered trucker and his family have secured in one of the "new town" high-rise complexes that now dot Hong Kong's New Territories. Housing has been at a premium since the trebling of the population in the years following World War Two and the Chinese Revolution half a

21 See Clover's (1992) *Men, Women, and Chain Saws: Gender in the Modern Horror Film*. Princeton: Princeton University Press.

22 Wood, M. (1998) *Cine East: Hong Kong Cinema Through the Looking Glass*. Surrey: FAB Press, 134.

23 Anthony Wong states that "I make only one real film a year - at least what I consider to be a real film." Such a movie was *Ordinary Heroes* (director Ann Hui's 1998 consideration of left-wing political groups in the "go-go" days of 1980s Hong Kong). Wong's character was based on a real-life Catholic priest with Maoist tendencies.

century ago. The government began public housing construction following a 1953 Christmas Day fire that left 50,000 people homeless. 1950s and 1960s housing estates, generally low quality urban structures, failed to keep up with demand driven by a further doubling of the population during those decades. In response, Hong Kong's government initiated residential development of the New Territories in the 1970s; today, about one-third of Hong Kongers live on former farm and swamplands.

The family's name finally reaches the top of the public housing waiting list following someone's mysterious plunge from an upper-story apartment floor to their death (as a sign of things to come, the individual is suspected of owing money to a 'usurer'). But he and his wife quickly turn apprehensive about their new residence upon learning that they live next door to Lam Kuo-jen. From his eerie yellow-tinted sunglasses, hooded jacket, and ever-present chainsaw, to his dimly lit flat, surgical knives, and foreboding kitchen, Lam exudes a disconcerting aura. Misgivings begin when the couple discovers their son playing video games at Lam's apartment. Subsequently, Lam serves Tong a large plate of spaghetti (reminiscent of intestines) topped with blood red sauce and says, "even you're biased against me, but you're better than the rest as we can be friends. I can't imagine they'd release me so soon. For me, I don't know if it's good or bad. It's very difficult to control myself. I think I will not kill anymore."

During the move into the new flat, Tong's wife Chun (Ching Mai) bumps into an old boyfriend named Canner (Wong Chi-yeung). Here the film begins a dark turn as Canner exploits the woman's desire for economic freedom by convincing her to invest with a stockbroker who buys and sells on the margin (symbolic of her lot in life). Initial success is followed by loss of the family's meagre savings whereupon Canner introduces her to his loan-sharking triad boss Chao (Ho Ka-kui), the "underground banker" of the film's title. No longer able to meet the family's basic fiscal obligations, much less pay the debt accumulated from failed market transactions, Chun (also called Kitty) borrows money at an exorbitant interest rate.

The woman's financial plight becomes the basis for *The Underground Banker's* Cat III rating; after all, the film's producer was Hong Kong cinema's "sleaze king" Wong Jing and its director (Bosco Lam) has helmed a number of "adult" movies, including *Chinese Torture Chamber Story* (1994). In this instance, "old flame" Canner slips an aphrodisiac into Chun's drink and rapes her. Then, ignoring her tears, he beats her into agreeing to become a prostitute in order to protect her family from harm. A second aphrodisiac and rape scene later in the film involves a gang-attack and the presence of video cameras. Shortly thereafter, the salacious Boss Chao is aroused by the youthful spunk of Tong's sister Chi-kwan (Hui Pui), who stands up to Canner's voyeuristic violation of her friends (he and his cronies surreptitiously film them in various states of undress at a "modelling school"). As a prelude of events to come, Chao's underlings terrorize Chun and her son; the former is coerced into arranging her sister-in-law's kidnapping for the purpose of sexual assault. By perpetually upping the ante, the "underground banker" ensures that the liability will never be settled.

Tong, obsessed with his sexual inadequacy and anxious over his psychopathic neighbour, appears oblivious to what is happening around him for much of the film. In quick succession, however, he learns that his wife has lost all their money, been forced into prostitution, and betrayed his sister. Tong, seeing no other solution than to sell his truck to pay the debt, raises most but not all of the needed cash. He begs Chao to accept the amount he has as payment in full but the latter informs the humiliated trucker that he must pay an additional $100,000 to keep sex tapes of his wife off the streets. Refusing to cower further, Tong leaves the usurer's office without paying anything at all. Triad members attack him in the street, break his glasses, and steal his money. While at the police station reporting the crime, Chao's henchmen barricade Tong's wife and son into their home, pour gasoline under the door, and set fire to the apartment. Chun dies in the flames and the boy, saved by Lam who cuts the chain blocking entry into the flat, is badly burned over his entire body.

Doctors remove the boy's bandages three months later to find him badly scarred and in need of extensive skin grafting. Chi-kwan assumes the role of the deceased Chun in asking her pusillanimous brother whether or not he is a "man." Dabbing tears from his eyes when the young boy says he'll never be able to play video games again, Lam tells his neighbour that the time for action has come and to "call me if you need help." Upon hearing his son counsel him to "kill those bastards", Tong finally acts and actor Wong's crazed screen presence that viewers have been awaiting during the film's entirety comes to the fore. The remaining footage is violent and bloody. Tong, dressed in camouflage, shoots off one man's penis, Lam slices and dices through several villains with piano wire, gutting Canner along the way, and Tong and Chao battle with meat cleavers, each hacking the other's arms and chest. In the final scene, Tong - with Lam's assistance - castrates Chao.

At movie's end the last camera shot is a pan of the Hong Kong that doesn't show up on Chamber of Commerce brochures - hillside hovel dwellings symbolizing the 450,000 households and almost 1.2 million people who reside in inadequate housing. Poor and lacking what conventional banks call "credit worthiness", this segment of the population is vulnerable to lending scams. Tong's voice-over is reciting the terms upon which he will loan money; driven over the edge, the one-time hard working family man has become an "underground banker", a blood-sucking parasite feeding upon the most disadvantaged. Thus the horror of the capitalist city about which Friedrich Engels notes: "Every great city has...slums, where the working class is crowded together...where removed from the sight of the happier classes, it may struggle along as it can."[24]

Working class rage: spreading the virus in *Ebola Syndrome*

Herman Yau and Anthony Wong capitalized on the success and sensationalism of *The Untold Story* with *Ebola Syndrome* three years later. Produced by Wong Jing, the latter film's shoot took seventeen 12-hour working days but its postproduction was only a week. "In a hurry", explains Yau, "because we had to catch up with the screening schedule in Hong Kong." A comparison of the two flicks reveals similar strains, most prominently, of course, Anthony Wong and his characterizations. Both begin with an establishing exterior

above:
Wong's character during the violent opening to **Ebola Syndrome**.

right:
Hong Kong VCD cover art for **Ebola Syndrome**.

[24] Engels, F. (1984) *The Condition of the Working Class in England*. Chicago: Academy, 60.

shot and crime appearing before the opening credits, and a restaurant serves as the main scene of the wrongdoing and objective for the main character's economic climb. Likewise, he takes on a new identity, food plays a major part in the horror, and there's a close look at the work process, whether preparing food or disposing of corpses (sometimes one and the same). Anthony Wong's role again involves the murder of his boss' family save for one young daughter (who, as a grownup years later, becomes nauseated when she recognizes his smell). Moreover, time and setting change when *Ebola* jumps ahead a decade and shifts it locale from Hong Kong to South Africa.

Regarding *Ebola*, Yau says his interest was "to create a world losing control... an attempt to create an anarchical situation. *Ebola Syndrome* is not a sequel to *The Untold Story*. But we secured an investor because of the box office success of *The Untold Story*, and the investor found some similarities in both during the scripting stage. You know, I don't like the part of making 'human meat hamburger' in the movie, but it was nearly a 'must' in order to secure an investor."**25** Audiences perhaps felt much the same, as *Ebola* proved to be a shadow of the box office draw of the earlier film; costing HK$5 million (almost US$600,000) to produce, it played only one week in Hong Kong theatres, grossing HK$1.6 million (approx. US$255,000).

In place of the brutal murders of the children witnessed in *The Untold Story's* flashback, *Ebola* focuses on perverse sexuality and extreme and detailed violence against women. Women serve as scapegoats for the working class (anti-)hero/horror to go on a virus-spreading rampage. Multiplying ironies, victimization at the hands of what actor Wong calls *Ebola's* "anti-society character" (variously called Kai, Sam, and Chicken in the film) serves as a simulacrum for his and other labourers' exploitation. First, as a Cat III movie, the film is by definition exploitative; second, the character's sublimated rage expresses itself as misogynistic physical abuse of women; and, third, Kai victimizes others just as he is being victimized by an entrepreneurial class. Both the boss he kills in the opening scene (after the man catches him in *flagrante delicto* with his wife) and the restaurateur couple who use him for the hard labour that food preparation requires - securing animals, slaughtering and preparing them, cleaning up - abuse and underpay him. Engels writes, "When one individual inflicts upon another such bodily injury that death results, we call the deed manslaughter; when the assailant knew in advance that the injury would be fatal, we call this deed murder. But when society places hundreds of proletarians in such a position that they inevitably meet a too early and an unnatural death, one which is quite as much a death by violence as that by sword or bullet... [I]ts deed is murder just as surely as the deed of the single individual..."**26**

Kai's violent actions result from his being excluded from Hong Kong's economic miracle. Director Yau suggests that "to a certain extent it was my intention to have class resentment in the movies [he is speaking of both *The Untold Story* and *Ebola Syndrome*]. I always think that the underdogs of society can be very powerful if they want to take revenge against the rich men and the people who control the rules."**27** What if such anger, however, is misplaced, as it is in Kai's circumstance?

That the first onscreen action is sexual ("suck it, lick it", Kai tells his boss's wife), and that their activity is interrupted and perverted - "pee on him", the husband directs his wife, and Kai barely avoids castration - introduces the twisted sexuality that follows. Kai masturbates into raw meat and later steams the pork to serve to a complaining diner. He gets off on overhearing the restaurant couple loudly engaged in acrobatic sex or by smelling the wife's bra. He rapes both a weakened African villager dying of Ebola and the restaurateur's wife. The former spews projective vomit in his face (as if other bodily fluids weren't enough to infect him); the latter struggles but is forced to perform oral sex and have anal sex, and after sloppy kisses Kai bites off her face and impales her. He is unusually literal when the assault is over, bellowing that "both of you bullied me long enough. I'll screw whoever bullies me."

The result is a horrifying and often nauseating series of violent acts that play upon sexist, racist, and homophobic attitudes. With an African setting for much of the story, featuring interludes during which the Ebola virus spreads, viewers can't help but think of anecdotal rumours of the spread of AIDS by a gay European flight attendant who ostensibly contracted the disease on the "dark continent." When a black man comes into the restaurant, the wife remarks in Chinese, "I daresay he has a soft dick" while Kai complains, "the Negroes are so dark, you never know if they

above: Anthony Wong during the climax of **Ebola Syndrome**.

25 Regarding Yau's comment that *Ebola Syndrome* is not a sequel to *The Untold Story*, the latter eventually spawned two films of the same name. Anthony Wong appeared in director Ng Yiu-kuen's *The Untold Story II* (1998), Herman Yau returned to direct *The Untold Story III* (1999) *sans* Wong but with Danny Lee (who also produced) in the role of police captain.

26 Engels, 126.

27 The filmmaker asserts, "I don't consider myself a political director. I don't like politics but there is no way to avoid it because we live in a world surrounded by politics."

Hong Kong

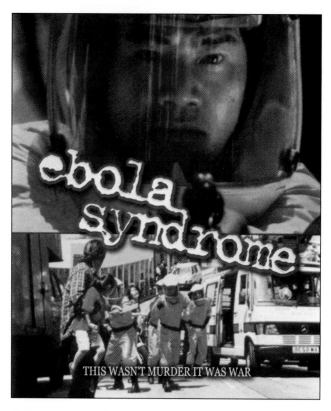

above:
Artwork from the Dutch DVD cover.

28 Dery, M. (1996) *Escape Velocity: Cyberculture at the End of the Century.* New York: Grove, 233-34.

29 Engels, 43.

30 Stringer, J. (1999) "Category 3: Sex and Violence in Postmodern Hong Kong." In Sharrett, C. (ed.), *Mythologies of Violence in Postmodern Media.* Detroit: Wayne State University Press, 362.

31 Among his wide-ranging projects, the actor did the voice-over for the comedic DreamWorks animation *Shrek* (2001), providing the dialogue for the title character (performed by Mike Myers in the U.S. release).

have expressions on their faces." He wonders whether tribesmen from whom they buy pigs are cannibals, to which his boss replies, "Asshole! No one will eat you. You're stinky and dirty", a judgment later confirmed by an English prostitute. She tells Kai, "Get out of here! I only do it with white people, not yellow crap. Fuck off! You're disgusting and smell like shit. Don't you people ever wash yourselves?"

Besides the murders and inadvertent cannibalism (restaurant-goers dining on "human meat hamburger" is a wry commentary on the devouring hungers of consumer materialism that runs rampant in Hong Kong), the depiction of the virus itself makes this a movie not for the squeamish. "The facial muscular tissue is badly composed", says one examiner of visible bodily remains. "I've never seen anything like it. It's as if the muscular tissues were trying to eat each other." Oozing mucus, projective vomiting, and blood from the hackings makes this a movie of bodily fluids. Cyber-theorist Mark Dery recounts that "horror has always taken the body as its central trope" while he declares that "the end of the twentieth century [was] a period of whose obsession with the body belies a widespread anxiety over the body's fate."

Accordingly, Dery asserts that "the *body horror* we see all around us is most obviously a waking dream about the AIDS pandemic, whose ravages have imprinted nightmare images on the mass imagination - bodies gnawed to skin and bones, flesh mottled by the purple lesions of Karposi's sarcoma."**28**

Kai, it seems, is a working class survivor of sorts, and after being infected, recovers from a high fever and body sweats to become a carrier physically unaffected by the virus, but mentally and metaphorically a spreader of destruction. Wong's characterization grows more and more frenzied as the film progresses, until he runs wild in the streets of Hong Kong, Milton Friedman's exemplar of successful laissez-faire economics. Engels, however, offers a different perspective: "Capitalist rule cannot allow itself the pleasure of creating epidemic diseases among the working class with impunity; the consequences fall back on it and the angel of death rages in its ranks as ruthlessly as in the ranks of the workers."**29**

Herman Yau states that *Ebola Syndrome* has a "kind of anarchy and chaos metaphor. One little man shocks society. In a way, revolutions in history share some similarities." At one level, then, the film's points to a scenario that had been laid out for Hong Kong's return to China. At another, it is an explosion before the expected (but by and large unrealized) "tighter and straighter" censorship following the hand-over. While he says that he still very much enjoys making movies, Yau notes that he has witnessed "the decline of the Hong Kong film industry from its climax. The budget for making a movie is getting tighter and tighter, the number of shooting days allowed is more limited, box office is important, critics' comments are always mean, and the audience is sometimes wonderful. People in the industry are not helping each other and there is keen competition." So in another sense, *Ebola's* bedlam and ferocity foreshadows current industry trends. Film scholar Julian Stringer maintains that "it is a truism of capitalist culture that film industries in decline often turn to sex and violence."**30** Anthony Wong disagrees. He reasons that since there are fewer movie productions, "only low budget movies will go for this type of strategy. These productions are fading away and won't last much longer." Hong Kong millennium horror flicks, he feels, "aren't horrifying at all. They're more like comedy, I think."**31**

fear without frontiers

Anthony Wong

**Interior decorating:
terrors of the mind in *New Tenant***

Like many actors, Wong looked forward to directing his own film and in 1995, he directed and starred in *New Tenant*, for which he also wrote the script, and for which he used his own music. The movie was made on a shoestring, approximately HK$3 million (about US$390,000), shot over ten days (14 hours a day average shooting), with a mini-crew, one camera, one track and seven days of editing and dubbing post-production. Of the experience, Wong says, "Acting is more comfortable, more fun, more income, and more relaxed. Working behind the scenes in Hong Kong is a dying job." Nonetheless, the film provides an interesting experiment in Wong's own appropriation of the horror genre and his onscreen image.

With a limited budget, Wong found inventive ways to get the most out of the money. Using lots of close ups and pull backs, voice over narration and eerie sound effects, two primary locations, a small, effective cast (plus a couple of cameos), he fashioned a dense plot relying on twists and turns foreshadowing a revelation from the beginning. Wong is Tam Ling-wun (whose name plays on that of pop singer Alan Tam), a newly-released mental patient who doesn't know whether he can adapt to the outside world. He has been reassured by his weird born-again Christian, Tai-chi-practicing, wormhole theorizing doctor that he recovered because he forgot everything. "Are you afraid of darkness?" asks a real estate agent who laughs maniacally as he rents Tam an apartment in an empty building slated for demolition in three month's time. At film's end, he will be asked the same question by his soon-to-be wife Shark, the identical twin to Dolphin (both played by Dolphin Chan), the woman he'll remember that he's murdered.

Wong exploits aslant camera angles that he saw work effectively in his work with Yau, but unlike the latter, he restricts what violence he actually shows making this movie much more an experience of tension and mood anxiety than in-your-face horror. Some strange shots, such as an inexplicable view of Wong and the agent from the roof of the building as they discuss rental arrangements, add to the creepiness and the unexplained atmosphere. Whereas Yau gives us body parts in his films, Wong provides pieces of evidence in the puzzle as the story progresses. Some fragments don't exactly fit, resulting not in a big picture whole, but instead contributing to a twilight zone world of the uncanny. Instrumental in creating the atmosphere of the unknown (and, possibly, the "we don't want to know, but can't help watching" result) is the disjunction between image and sound. Along with some voice distortion on the track, repeated musical cues, and a ticking clock, the voice-over or conversation among characters is intentionally slightly off from what the audience sees onscreen, making for an uneasy accommodation by the viewer kept on the edge.

The two main interior shot locations for the movie are the empty apartment building, mostly one room, and the hospital from which Tam has been released, with a few exteriors thrown in mostly for conversations between Tam and his physician. Both interiors share narrow hallways and small rooms, producing a psychically cramped and obscurely threatening space. The hospital is all light while the apartment building is mostly darkness and shadows. Shooting in the hospital, Wong says, was difficult because "there was another crew making a movie at the same time on the same spot, so basically, the progress was extremely slow. Weather was also a challenge with the actors' conflicting schedules, and the rainy season made it

left:
Promotional artwork for Anthony Wong's directorial debut **New Tenant**.

right:
Anthony Wong starring with Dolphin Chan in **New Tenant**, which he also directed.

difficult for us to complete the shots. But the greatest barrier was mainly from post-production, due to the lack of technical support in the Hong Kong industry." Generally, the apartment interiors serve as a visual metaphor for the claustrophobic clutter of a deranged mind, while the exteriors alongside water, with wind blowing, offer a breezy sweep through that mind and a respite from gloominess and confinement. The penultimate scene, set in a maze-like tunnel of darkness and dripping sewers, revels in the murky side and cancels out the tempered daylight and macabre humour of the film's end.

In tandem with the medium and medium-long shots of the corridors and rooms, along with pull back shots to reveal the character in his environs, there are numerous extreme and medium close-ups of Tam. Wong exploits his wonderful and extraordinary ability to believably run a gamut of emotions in facial expression alone. Indeed, the story opens with the character contemplating his face in the mirror, a bit bewildered, thoughtful about who he is, reluctant to re-enter the outside world. Soon, however, he's naïve and ordinary, and the strength of the performance encourages us to identify with him. When Tam becomes more pained and confused as memories begin to return to him, we share his predicament, still unclear ourselves as to the direction the events will take. Ultimately, though, a chilling insanity emerges.

Appropriating the clocks which run rampant in Wong Kar-wai films from *Days of Being Wild* (1991) to *Chungking Express* (1994), Anthony Wong uses a discarded clock Tam finds in the building to negotiate the time and space travel the character takes between 1984 and 1994. Running haphazardly, the ticking clock parallels the unstable character's returning memory. When the clock is running he can observe the life going on inside the building in the past, but the 'ghosts' can't see him and he cannot interact with them. But he makes contact with Dolphin because there is a relationship between them, and tellingly, he also is perceived by the anthropology professor (fiancé to Dolphin's sister Whale [Ng Kai-wah]) with whom he has a connection. At one point the "Doctor Lam"-like professor confides he's eaten Whale "out of love... The only way to possess his or her lover is to eat them so as to make them part of oneself." Shades of the "bunman"! In a flash, Wong incorporates his previous persona into this crazed former mental patient, Dolphin's "Angel."

Coupled with the clock is a masked and bloodied face most often seen in mirrors, as well as a slow moving turtle, a departing gift from a fellow mental patient; always appearing in relation to the ticking clock, the mask reveals Tam's true self. And always attempting to escape its shell across the pages upon which Tam writes his story, dream, novel, or movie, the turtle disappears when Tam finally discovers who he really is. "Usually, the couple in a romantic story will have a romantic ending. Dolphin and I, no, I mean Shark, we have a romantic ending too..." the voice over narrative concludes. *Bon appetit!*

"Like most Hong Kong citizens, you're slightly schizophrenic", a cop tells Tam, and of course the description is fitting. Examination of several aspects of Hong Kong identity discloses Hong Kong in relation to the British Empire and the PRC; a leviathan working class set against an elite rich; and Anthony Wong in relation to his on-screen characterizations, from crazed killers to likeable, ordinary schmucks. In the first regard, being Hong Kong Chinese means to be pulled both ways - between the conditions established in the colony under British rule as well as towards the homeland; and in 1995 when the film was made, the return ever-present in people's minds. Secondly, the former travel magazine writer Tam leads a Spartan existence in his past and present lives, and the dreariness of the apartment building in which he and the others reside points to all the luxuries of contemporary life they are missing and desire. Perhaps Wong best reconciles all perspectives in a judgment made on his characterizations: "I think nobody is normal. In my eyes everyone is crazy. I really want to explore the abnormal side of the human being."

Hyperbolic Hong Kong: the political-economic imaginary

Horror film specialist Tony Williams has noted that Category III Hong Kong films, despite their abusive nature, echo motifs found in dystopian literature. He remarks, "It is hard not to see a certain social relevance in these Hong Kong productions which are not as far removed from our world as we may think." Williams writes of a "cinematic future whereby capitalist exploitation and a supposedly primitive mode of cannibalism will logically co-exist in a brave new world."**32** Of course, capitalism is, by "nature", human-eating, its history strewn with the limbs and bodies of working people, its progress built upon the flesh and blood of the labouring classes. Unlike Western nations, however, Hong Kong's rapid development has included features of early and late capital accumulation simultaneously.

In the early period, force separates capital from labour, exchange-value in the market from immediate use-value, and owner from worker. Patterns of ruthless competition create unstable social relations; conquest, enslavement, robbery, murder, and gangsterism characterize this phase. Describing its violent genesis, Marx writes that "Capital comes [into the world] dripping from head to foot, from every pore, with blood and dirt."**33** Late capitalism, on the other hand, refers to the process of globalization and its accompanying commodification of almost everything. The accumulation process is increasingly based upon finance capital, global markets, and dual labour structures. As economist Robert Heilbroner notes, "'Made in Hong Kong' stamped on commodities that embody the most remarkable capabilities of scientific production becomes a symbol of the ability of capital to move wherever low labour costs or strategic sites for distribution offer competitive advantages."**34**

The territory's highly competitive industries - land speculation, real estate construction, electronics, apparel and textile manufacture, finance, and tourism - manoeuvre between two worlds, a local proprietary sector and a transnational corporate one. "Creative destruction" is on display everywhere in Hong Kong as industrial factories give way to opulent hotels, which in turn yield to office towers in only a few years. Perhaps it is such contradictory and turbulent circumstances that Anthony Wong speaks of when he says that Hong Kongers, "are a mad people. Everyone is mad." Novelist William Styron, himself hospitalized after being diagnosed with depression, writes that madness is a "simulacrum for all the evil of our world: of our everyday discord and chaos, our irrationality, warfare and crime, torture and violence, our impulse toward death and our flight from it held in the intolerable equipoise of history."**35** Wong's ability to turn that "madness" into creativity sheds light on the elaborate relationships of power, ideology, and representation that wonderfully play themselves out in the terrifying yet fascinating portrayals he has brought to movie and video screens. From *The Untold Story's* "bunman" to *Ebola Syndrome's* deadly virus carrier, Anthony Wong is hyperbolic Hong Kong, an expression of frantic paranoia in the pre-handover city-state; but he also reflects the insanity of the capitalist mode of production. As an actor and as a performer, Wong doesn't so much tease out the links between literal and metaphorical cannibalism as he rips them apart, revealing the fear and loathing that lies beneath his society's ideological structures along the way.

above:
A battered Wong in **Beast Cops**, one of the best millennium-era action/horror films to come from Hong Kong.

32 Williams, T. (2002) "Hong Kong Social Horror: Tragedy and Farce in Category 3", *Post Script: Essays in Film and the Humanities* 21.3, 61-71.

33 Marx, K. (1967) *Capital* Vol. 1. New York: International Publishers, 760.

34 Heilbroner, R. (1985) *The Nature and Logic of Capitalism.* New York: W. W. Norton, 171.

35 Styron, W. (1992) *Darkness Visible: A Memoir of Madness.* New York: Vintage, 83-84.

artists, actors, auteurs

The rain beneath the earth: an interview with Nonzee Nimibutr

Mitch Davis

The year 1897 marked the very first time a film was screened for public entertainment in Thailand. Three years later, Prince Sanpasartsupakij imported camera gear and became Thailand's first cinematographer. 1904 saw a new trend, with Japan exporting their films for Thai consumption. This proved so successful that the Japanese built Thailand's first dedicated movie theatre in 1905. In 1916, two years after the start of the First World War, the Pattanakorn Cinematograph Company was launched. It was Thailand's first foreign film distributor. 1922 saw the inaugural publication of *Parbpayon Siam*, Thailand's first movie magazine, but it wasn't until 1927 that the newly formed Bangkok Picture Company (alternately known as Bangkok Film) produced *Choke Song Chan* (*Double Luck*), the first *bona fide* Thai film. Audiences went wild. By 1931, Thailand had a full-fledged film industry, complete with government codes and regulations; and with the launching of the Srikrung Sound Film Studio in 1936, film production was executed under an enormous, Hollywood-like system.

From that point on, Thailand has enjoyed a rich and unusual cinematic heritage, one whose very mechanics were often shaped by crisis. One notable event saw almost every major filmmaker turning to 16mm when 35mm emulsions became scarce during World War II. This 16mm film wave officially came to an end in 1972. When the global oil crisis hit in 1974, the Thai government ordered cinemas to reduce screening times, which in turn impacted the running times of most productions during that period. When Thailand was ravaged by an economic crisis during the late 80s, the number of productions dropped dramatically, the country's film system slowing to a flickering crawl.

In 1997, times began changing back when *2499 antapan krong muang* (*Dang Bireley and the Young Gangsters*) took Thailand by storm, smashing box-office records and becoming the first large-scale event movie that Thai audiences had seen in ages. Its young director, Nonzee Nimibutr, hit the international festival circuit with the film and returned to Thailand with global cineaste recognition and the Grand Prize award at the 19th Festival International du Film Independent in Brussels. Nimibutr's 1999 follow-up was the haunting *Nang Nak*, a film that broke his own box-office records and, through its travels on the festival circuit, managed to put Thai cinema back on the international map - on a larger scale than ever before.

Nang Nak wasn't just a phenomenal success; it was a cultural phenomenon, comparable to what James Cameron's *Titanic* (1997) was to mainstream Western moviegoers. That Thailand's ultimate blockbuster production would be an eerie, tragic ghost story is indicative of the country's longstanding fascination with supernatural folklore. That the film also manages to be an effective love story is a testament to Nimibutr's uncanny ability to create works that are at once deeply personal and widely accessible. His films are atmospheric, calculated and captivating, the rare works of a genuine artist with an intuitive knack for commercial survival that allows his preoccupations to be explored freely.

The following interview was conducted in late January 2000 at the Rotterdam Film Festival, the day after I walked into a

opposite:
Artwork used to promote the Hong Kong release of **Nang Nak**.

screening of *Nang Nak* with no expectations and spent the rest of the afternoon in a daze, staring at cracks in the pavement. Since the time of this interview, Nimibutr has gone on to become one of the most important figures in the Thai film scene, producing gigantic titles like the Pang brothers' *Bangkok Dangerous* (2000), Wisit Sartsanatieng's *Fa talai jone* (*Tears Of The Black Tiger*, 2000), Tanit Jitnukul's *Bang Rajan* (2000) and Pen-Ek Ratanaruang's *Monrak Transistor* (*Transistor Love Story*, 2001), all of which played with exceptionally high profiles on the A-list international festival circuit. Further, the Pang Brothers' international success with *Bangkok Dangerous* afforded them the ability to make their unconventional horror film blockbuster *Jian gui* (*The Eye*, 2002), a picture that has been incredibly well-received across the world and was immediately licensed by Tom Cruise for a projected US remake following its first North American screening at the Toronto International Film Festival.

Nimibutr's directorial follow-up to *Nang Nak* was the controversially stark and equally beautiful *Jan Dara* (2001), a major co-production between Thailand and Hong Kong. Most recently, he produced, directed and co-wrote *The Wheel* - a chilling chapter of the omnibus horror film *San geng* (*Three*, 2002), a trail-blazing anthology co-production comprised of three segments, each hailing from a different Asian country. (The other segments in *Three* come from South Korea's Kim Ji Woon, best known for *Choyonghan kajok* [*The Quiet Family*, 1998] and *Banchikwang* [*The Foul King*, 2000], and Hong Kong director Peter Chan, who was actually born in Thailand, the maker of films like *Gum gee yuk yip* [*He's A Woman She's A Man*, 1994] and *Tian mi mi* [*Comrades: Almost A Love Story*, 1996]). While Thai productions have traditionally been exported almost exclusively to other Asian territories when they were exported at all, Nimibutr's films have, without exception, been screened in every part of the world. Perhaps more than any other contemporary Asian filmmaker, Nonzee Nimibutr is pulling his country's cinema culture into the consciousness of the global film community. And he is doing it without compromising a single frame of integrity.

Mitch Davis: Just to get a broad overview, approximately how many features would you say come out of Thailand per year?

Nonzee Nimibutr: Almost ten. Ten per year.

MD: What would their average budgets be?

NN: The average is middle. It's not huge, but not small. Often half a million US dollars.

MD: Is that what Nang nak *(1999) cost? $500,000 US?*

NN: Yes, a half-million dollars.

MD: Wow.

NN: But the half-million includes promotion.

MD: WOW. So then before you got to post-production, what was your shooting cost?

NN: About $200,000 US. In Thailand, post-production is really expensive. When you compare it to Hong Kong, it's the same price. Really expensive in Thailand.

MD: In general, how do you approach the financing?

NN: Fortunately, I was working in TV commercials before. Ten years of TV commercials. I had a show reel when I went to the company, and I had a script. Because I had a reel, everyone trusted that I could make a film. For me it wasn't difficult, but for other directors it's sometimes really hard because if he doesn't have a show reel, or wasn't already working before... Maybe someone will go to make a music video, or a TV program, and also make up a reel to show to potential investors. But now Thailand is in an economic crisis. Investors don't want to

below:
Nang Nak.

lose money! It's really hard to find investors, and really hard to make a film, because the film company, the distributor and the financiers will not invest in a Thai film now. It's really difficult these days. But my friends and I are trying to fight this problem. I have to build a film company myself, and try to find a financier from another country, or another company, like a TV channel or something, to make a film. In Thailand we have only six film companies.

MD: Which is a lot I'd imagine, if there are only about ten Thai films made per year.

NN: But five years ago, in Thailand, we made two hundred films per year.

MD: Two hundred locally-produced features?

NN: Yes, between six film companies! It's changed because of the economic crisis. And because of Hollywood...it's the same problem with most Asian countries. The good thing about Hollywood movies playing in Thailand is that when our production companies want to make a film, they screen like a filter - they screen the script, the director, everything. In Thailand, only good films are made!

MD: How would that fare for the more personal films?

NN: When I started making films, I made ones that I loved to do. I didn't care if the audience loved my movie or not, because I knew I would make the story the way I wanted to. But I always had the marketing in my mind, because I was involved in TV commercials for ten years. After I make a film, after it is finished, I realise how I can push it to the audience. This happens after I finish my films, but when I first started making movies I didn't care about anyone. But it's because my first film [*Dang Bireley and the Young Gangsters*] earned a lot of money in Thailand that, when I made the second one [*Nang nak*], it was really easy to find financiers. Really easy to get the budget. But I have a strong reason to talk with the film company - to tell them that I want to make my film the way I want. Don't get involved with my movie! There is actually another director, Pen-Ek Ratanaruang [*Ruang talok 69 (6ixtynin9*, 1999)]. Pen-Ek and I are in the same position and the same situation. Pen-Ek is also involved with TV commercials as a director.

above: Nonzee Nimibutr's **Nang Nak** is part of a select group of contemporary Thai movies to find acceptance in the West in recent years.

MD: Is it common for the directors of Thailand's larger-sized productions to emerge from advertising backgrounds?

NN: No, no, just three directors, not more. I wanted to make movies when I started in university but I couldn't because when you are a filmmaker in Thailand, you can't make enough money to live. That's the reason why I have to do jobs like make TV commercials. I can collect money from the commercials and that's enough for my family, for living. But to answer your question, I don't know if I would want to make something for my audience. I just cut it off. When I see my film, when the actors play their roles, and when I say "that is enough," I cut it. I know I should be playing for more time, but I don't want it to look like a Hollywood movie. That's the reason that I don't cater to the audience much. No more than I want to. The selling point of this film [*Nang Nak*] is atmosphere, and the period of the film, the period of the story.

MD: Also, the Nang Nak *folk tale looks like it will live forever in Thailand. I've been told that there were over twenty film productions made, but that in spite of the fable's foregrounded supernatural trappings, yours was the first film to play the horror elements straight.*

NN: Yes, well, you know, before my film, *Nang Nak* had been made in 21 versions in Thailand. In all of these versions, the directors never researched the tale as if it were a real story. Everyone made it like a fairy tale, as if it couldn't be a realistic story. When I saw these films, I didn't enjoy them, because it's like the ghost shows up and the people scream and run away or something, like a comedy. And the ghost

Thailand

above:
Hong Kong DVD cover for Nimibutr's **Jan Dara**.

opens its body and goes "bleeeeecchhhhh." One version ends with funny people like Ghostbusters sending Nang Nak away! I didn't think that had to be true. Why wouldn't anyone treat this story like it was real?! I spent two years researching everything I could about the legend of Nang Nak, because it's based on a true story.

MD: To what extent?

NN: There is the house of Nang Nak in Thailand, in a temple. There are sculptures of Nang Nak for people to pay their respect to her. When I did my research, I spoke with historical consultants and everyone that knows the story. I found it very interesting, because I love the old stories. I love the period films, and I would like to see Bangkok and Thailand one hundred years ago. Everyone in Thailand knows this tale, but they don't know when it happened. So, if there is any clear reason why the film has become so successful, it's this one: because it's a period film, and everyone will go to see something like this. And here's another reason: when the Hollywood movies came to Thailand, everyone loved to see them; but one day they became boring, you know? Because most Hollywood movies are like technical movies. They're not talking about real life. When the economic crisis occurred in Thailand, everyone saw that. When *Nang Nak* showed in Thailand, everyone realised that "Hey, this is Thai culture. This is Thai tradition." Everyone here likes to be reminded of Thai history.

MD: *And it's become the top-grossing film in Thai history.*

NN: Yes. More than *Titanic*! (laughs)

MD: *It feels so good to hear something like that. Would you say that there has always been a large audience for horror and fantasy films in Thailand?*

NN: I think that, on the inside, Thai audience love to see horror films. No one really knows what kind of movie audiences here want to see. The ten films released in Thailand last year, every one of them failed. They all flopped: the action movie, the love story, everything. Nobody knows what the audience wants to see; instead, people just say, "Well, well, well, this movie is not good. The love story is not good." No one knows, and I didn't know either. But like I've been telling you, I don't care because I like to make my movies the way I want.

Everyone in Thailand says the audience for movies here is young, like a teenager. Just that. But I don't believe it. That's the reason why, in Thailand, everyone makes films for the audience. For the teenage crowd. But it's not the whole. Like me, for example, now I'm 40. As an audience member in Thailand, when you are 30 and 40 years old, you don't have any films for you. Before *Nang Nak*, everyone was just making movies for the teenagers.

MD: *So then going to the cinema might be depressing for a lot of the audience. It could make them feel old or out of touch.*

NN: (laughs) Yes. I didn't have a movie for me in Thailand. "Ah, wow, what movie would I like to see...?" That's the reason why, when I made *Nang Nak*, I didn't make a movie for a teenage audience. I made a movie for everyone. I realise that teenagers like to see my films, but it's for the opposite reason. The teenagers *didn't* know this story. That's the reason why they wanted to

fear without frontiers

go see it. The teenagers would like to know, and so they went to see my movie. In the beginning, I didn't think the teenage audience would go to see it.

MD: *But they did.*

NN: A LOT! (laughs)

MD: *For many of the younger viewers,* Nang Nak *would be their first exposure to a Thai period film...*

NN: In Thailand, nobody makes period films anymore, not for many years. It takes a big budget. Like my film - it's *almost* a big budget (laughs). I had to use the techniques I learned from shooting TV commercials to make the film. I prepared everything in advance. I'm figuring out my film before shooting on the set. I know the problems. I know everything before I start shooting. That's the reason why I didn't need a big budget. I could control the budget because I was the producer also. Not everyone can control the budget. I wrote the storyboards too, and I knew that "in this scene, I would like to see all of this from here to here, so don't change *everything* from modern day." So, I could control the budget that way.

MD: *How much of the film was shot on studio sets as opposed to dressed or modified locations?*

NN: Everything was on a set... Set on location (laughs). I built some sets right on the locations. This is because I could find the locations that I knew from many years ago, but everything has changed since then.

MD: *You used many animals and insects in the film as supernatural symbols. Can you explain some of the beliefs behind this imagery?*

NN: In Thailand, everyone believes that when the lizards go *tsk-tsk-tsk-tsk*, you can't go out of your home. Everyone believes in the animal action. Just like, when you see the rat - a lot of rats in your house - you go "Why? Why?" It's like a hint of something.

MD: *I was particularly struck by the image of the spider acting almost as a door-knocker, slamming the mass of its body against the door. What do spiders signify to you?*

NN: If a spider goes *toc-toc-toc-toc* and falls to the floor dead, it means that someone in the house has died.

MD: *Did you encounter any particular problems shooting some of the more elaborate animal-driven sequences?*

NN: Nothing too bad because, fortunately, I had a very good team and a good crew. We rehearsed the animals beforehand. Like the owl: we practiced with the owl for six months before shooting.

MD: *And how do you rehearse an owl?*

NN: (laughs) We had something like a bird teacher. A trainer. He rehearsed the owl until it knew the sequences of movement, where to go. I feel sorry and awful because many animals died during the shooting.

MD: *Oh man, I'm sorry to hear that. What was it that killed them?*

NN: The shooting (laughs)! When I came back to Thailand on February...February 20...I made an ordain for the animals.

MD: *Sorry?*

NN: I made an ordain. To become a monk! (laughs)

MD: *What exactly was it that caused the animals to die during the shooting. Was it simply a question of the general conditions?*

NN: The reason was the whole nature of shooting. The lighting and the time and everything you keep captured for a long time...dies.

MD: *Would you consider* Nang Nak *to be a religious film? I understand that it's based on a fairy tale, and a historically-cherished one, but the film strikes me as something that came from a very spiritual state of mind. How do you see it?*

NN: I see it like a Buddhist lesson - like the Circle Of Life. When you die, your soul should die together with your body, you don't stick on someone like Nang Nak sticks on her husband. The Buddha teaches something in Thailand: when you live on the earth you don't stick to anything. Like the Circle Of Life, when you're born and when you're dead, you can't bring anything with you. I would like to say that this is also a story of love -

above:
Jan Dara.

because someone was telling me that in Thailand they don't believe in love. But I believe in love. When you love someone very much, you can do anything. In another version of the story, after Nang Nak goes away, they talk about Mak having a new wife, but then Nang Nak is jealous and tries to kill her! In my version, Mak becomes a monk in the end because that is like a promise. A promise to Nang Nak that she will always be the one woman for him.

MD: In the film, Mak has to bend down and look between his legs in order to see the truth through the mysticism. Does this come from the original fable or is it based on a wider superstition?

NN: It's a belief. When I was young, my grandmother told me about it. Upside-down, between your legs, you concentrate your mind until you are thinking with the Buddha. Everyone in Thailand knows that way you can see ghosts (laughs).

MD: In the climax of the film, there is great tension between the monks and the medicine man when he tries to dig up Nang Nak's grave. Since both sides were ultimately working towards the same goal, why were the monks so opposed to the medicine man's ritual?

NN: When someone tries to destroy a body and hits the skull with a rock, that means it destroys the soul also. The monks didn't want him to do it like that. When the soul is destroyed, it can't be controlled. In Thailand, everyone believes that when your skull is broken and your soul is released, this means you cannot control it. Maybe it means that the soul will become a ghost forever. But if the highest monk talks with her, that means she might be born again.

MD: What are some of the films that inspired you as a director?

NN: When I was young I loved to see Thai films very much - more than Hollywood films, because they were closer to me. But I like Martin Scorsese very much. I love *Goodfellas*.

MD: That's an almost perfect film.

NN: Yes. I love most of Scorsese's films. They are very intellectual and, I don't know, very good for me. My first film was a gangster movie, inspired by Scorsese's work. *Nang Nak* was the next step for me, but it was actually my first idea. I couldn't make it first though, because I thought that as a really dramatic film, it would be very difficult to make. So I decided to make the gangster film first because I thought it would be easier and I wanted to have that experience first. The gangster film is an action film - action/drama - so it wasn't too difficult to make.

MD: And also not as risky from a commercial perspective.

NN: Yes. After that, I felt like I could make a dramatic film and go to the next step. As for the next step after *Nang Nak*, I think I would like to talk about the philosophy of being human. What is inside of the human. *Everything* that is inside of the human.

MD: Where do you see the next few years of Thai film going in terms of their financing and international export?

NN: I think that now, fortunately, everyone would like to make a co-production in the Thai film industry. It is really interesting. For my latest project, I didn't work with the Thai companies, I worked with a foreign company.

MD: From which country?

NN: Hong Kong (laughs).

MD Good!

NN: Yes! And for the next one, I am trying to get funding from France, from Switzerland, from Sweden. It's possible now. It's possible. Now it's a great opportunity for the Thai filmmaker. We have companies that try to understand the filmmaker, more than in the past. Everyone would like to support the short film to encourage young blood. The new generation. Like me, when I have the money, I want to make a fund for the short film. I would like to support this form. I think Thailand should have more young blood filmmakers than it does right now. *Then* we can shoot. Because the old filmmakers...their old styles...they can't change! I almost want to say to them, "Please, please, don't make any more films!" I want to see the young blood. Something new. I would be really pleased to support them.

opposite:
Promotional artwork for **The Wheel**, Nimibutr's segment of the anthology feature **Three**.

artists, actors, auteurs

Cinema of the doomed: the tragic horror of Paul Naschy

Todd Tjersland

The Wolf Man cometh

Doomed love. Twisted desire. Ancient evil. These three themes dominate the cinematic landscape that is the career of Spanish horror legend Paul Naschy.

The Paul Naschy story begins 6 September 1934, in Madrid, Spain, when he was born Jacinto Alvarez Molina, the son of small-time industrialist Enrique Molina. He grew up under the censorious regime of General Francisco Franco, where horror films were rarely screened. Life under Franco was far more harsh than the absence of monster movies; indeed, it is rumoured that the young Naschy nearly lost his father to a firing squad when the elder Molina was betrayed by his own brother-in-law. Fortunately, fate intervened and his father was cleared of any charges.

From a very young age, Naschy's mother, Pilar, would take him on frequent trips to the cinema. There, in the hush and quiet of the darkened theatre, the boy delighted in the fantastic, flickering images on display. "I had entered the world of fantasy", Naschy would later recall. His cinematic interests at this point consisted primarily of serials, westerns and historical adventures. All of this would change, however, when, at the age of eleven, he saw a rare screening of Universal's *Frankenstein Meets the Wolf Man* (1943), a film which impacted him deeply. He became obsessed with the tragic character of the werewolf: a lost soul cursed to be half-man, half-beast; gifted with savage strength and cunning but doomed to destroy all those he loves. The dual nature of hero and villain in the same flesh, of rebel and outcast, held a powerful allure for the young boy. Many of history and literature's most memorable figures could be likened unto the werewolf: men fighting the enemy without and within and yet ultimately helpless in the face of their own dark destiny. This type of tragic anti-hero would prove central to Naschy's characterizations throughout a career encompassing over one hundred credits and spanning five decades. "I knew that I wanted to go into acting", Naschy mused, "especially the fantastic and horror cinema, and above all, as the character of the Wolf Man, by which I was completely fascinated."

But Naschy's parents had other ideas and determined that he should pursue a respectable career more fitting to his social status as the son of a successful industrialist. His early college studies were in agriculture, but he later switched to architecture, gaining a scholarship to the prestigious School of Architecture in Barcelona. He received high marks for his artistic talents and found work designing record sleeves for major record companies, including some for Elvis Presley. He drew comics, exhibited his paintings and wrote paperback westerns under the pseudonym Jack Mills. His energy never flagging, the ambitious Naschy exercised his body as well as his mind, excelling in soccer, javelin throwing and weight lifting. It was in the latter of these sports that he was destined to set new records, easily winning the Spanish National Championships in 1958 when he was unexpectedly called in to replace another competitor.

With such an impressive physique, it came as no surprise that he began to receive work as an extra in movies and television. His most prestigious roles as an extra were in the Biblical epic *King of Kings* (1961) and in a 1966 episode of the American television series, *I Spy*, entitled "Mainly On the Plains",

opposite:
Original Spanish poster artwork for **Dr. Jekyll versus the Werewolf**.

above:
Naschy drags away one of his murder victims in **Latidos de Pánico**, 1982.

which co-starred one of Naschy's childhood horror idols, Boris Karloff. It was shortly after this that Naschy decided to try his hand at screenwriting, and the sole inspiration for his first script was *Frankenstein Meets the Wolf-Man*. When he approached a director friend about the project, the friend told him he was insane! "The truth is", Naschy admits, "there was no tradition for this genre in Spanish cinema." Eventually, a German company expressed interest in developing the project, but no suitable actor to play the Wolf Man could be found. The original Wolf Man, Lon Chaney, Jr., was offered the part, but had to decline due to poor health. With no one to play the lead, Naschy was finally offered the role, and it was at this time that he took on his new name after he was asked by the German producers of the film to come up with a name that sounded less Spanish. He claims that he got Paul from a newspaper headline mentioning the then Pope (Paul VI). Naschy was a germanised version of the name of Imre Nagy, who had been a Hungarian weightlifter that Molina had got to know on the tournament circuit when he was in competition in the early 1960's.

Eagerly, Naschy threw himself (for what would be the first time of many times) into the part of his doomed protagonist, Count Waldemar Daninsky. The character's nationality was chosen to represent the suffering of the Polish people, who were being oppressed at the time under Communist rule. The fictional Count Daninsky was also bitter, persecuted and misunderstood - a perfect match in Naschy's mind. He would draw upon the pain those dark feelings engendered to create one of horror cinema's most long-lived characters: Waldemar Daninsky, El Hombre Lobo.

The film was completed and released in Europe as *La Marca del Hombre-lobo* (*The Mark of the Wolfman*, 1968), but it did not see U.S. release until 1972, where it was retitled as *Frankenstein's Bloody Terror* - despite the fact that there was no Frankenstein monster to be found in the film! The American distributor had promised theatres a Frankenstein movie, and justified the bizarre retitle by inserting a brain-dead new opening credit sequence informing the audience that, "The Frankenstein family had been cursed with lycanthropy and changed its name to Wolfenstein." The sequence showed a series of poorly drawn illustrations of the Frankenstein monster slowly turning into a werewolf, achieved through a process of dissolves. The film was also heavily edited and not presented in its original 70mm, 3-D format.

La Marca set the stage for establishing the conventions of the series: Daninsky is bitten while trying to kill his evil, lycanthropic ancestor, Count Imre Wolfstein, and therefore cursed to carry on the unholy taint of lycanthropy. He now bears the mark of the pentagon on his chest, and can never truly die except by an item forged of silver (a bullet in the early films, but later it is changed to a cross) thrust through his heart by a woman who loves him. The pentagonal "mark of the beast" and method of destruction requiring a woman's love were quite different from conventional werewolf films and folklore, having been wholly invented by Naschy. As *La Marca*'s story unfolds, the infected Count Daninsky seeks out a mysterious Hungarian professor to cure him, but the professor and his wife turn out to be evil vampires whom Daninsky is forced to destroy before they can do more harm. Naschy's love interest in the film, the stunning redheaded actress Dyanik Zurakowska, would team up with Naschy again as a scheming, sex-starved countess in *La Orgía de los muertos* (*The Hanging Woman*, 1973), but she is best known for her role as the bewitching vampire countess in León Klimovsky's disturbing *La Orgía nocturna de los vampiros* (*Vampire's Night Orgy*, 1972).

Naschy immediately followed up *La Marca* with *Las Noches del Hombre Lobo* (*Nights of the Werewolf*, 1968), but the picture was never released, having been impounded upon the death of director René Govar and never located. Undiscouraged, four more Daninsky werewolf pictures followed in quick succession: *Los Monstruos del terror* (*Assignment Terror*, 1969), shot in just six days, in which Naschy's werewolf

Paul Naschy

was just one of many classic monsters enslaved by a mad scientist; *La Furia del Hombre Lobo* (*The Fury of the Wolfman*, 1970), which recycles stock werewolf footage from *La Marca*; *La Noche de Walpurgis* (*Werewolf's Shadow*, 1970), the success of which would spark the Spanish horror boom of the 1970s; and *Dr. Jekyll y el Hombre Lobo* (*Dr. Jekyll versus the Werewolf*, 1972), featuring Daninsky turning into Mr. Hyde as well as a werewolf! The year 1971 also saw the first of Naschy's attempts to diversify his horror output with *Jack el destripador de Londres* (*Jack the Ripper of London*), a disappointing Jack the Ripper update, with Naschy playing the prime suspect.

Raining/Reigning Naschy

It was with the 1972-73 releases of a veritable flood of Paul Naschy movies that the Spanish actor finally hit his stride and started to achieve the international notoriety he deserved. While *Los Ojos azules de la muñeca rota* (*Blue Eyes of the Broken Doll*, 1973) was pure sadistic sexploitation, providing Naschy with one of his few non-monster roles of the period, *El Jorobado de la Morgue* (*Hunchback of the Morgue*, 1973) showed Naschy's attempt to create a sympathetic killer. As Gotho, the pathetic hunchbacked morgue assistant, Naschy truly shines, delivering one of his most sincere and emotionally riveting performances. Gotho is a good but simple-minded cripple driven to do terrible things for a love he can never hope to possess. When his childhood sweetheart dies of an illness, Gotho begs Dr. Orla (Alberto Dalbés) to "wake her up." The cruel doctor quickly agrees, but only if Gotho will procure fresh corpses to feed to his rapidly growing "primordial one." Dr. Orla believes that his artificial lifeform, begun as a single-celled protoplasm, will "grow" into the type of creatures it eats. The doctor's theory proves to be correct when the heretofore-unseen beast breaks out of its prison cell during the film's climax, resembling a slime-covered version of the Golem in *It!* (1966).

Cruelly used and abused by those around him, eventually Gotho realises he is being duped and so chooses to redeem himself. He joins his lover's corpse in the mad doctor's bubbling acid pit, taking the primordial one with him. *El Jorobado* is also notorious for its brutally gory violence and the infamous "rat scene", where Gotho discovers the body of his deceased love being feasted upon by dozens of rodents. The rats jump to attack the enraged hunchback (although astute viewers will note that the animals are merely being thrown at the actor by offstage handlers, providing some unintentional hilarity). Swarmed by the biting rats, Gotho sets those within reach alight and drives the rest off with his frantically waving torch. Flaming, shrieking balls of fire are thus sent scampering across the screen, which is all the more unbelievable when seen by the light of today's rather more humane view of animal rights. No special effects were used; the animals were "sacrificed" for the integrity of the scene. Naschy himself sustained many bites while filming, making the pain and panic of his performance all the more convincing. Because of the rat scene, he received the "Best Acting" award for *El Jorobado* at the 1973 Paris Convention of Fantastic Cinema.

El Gran amor del conde Drácula (*Count Dracula's Great Love*, 1972), directed by Javier Aguirre, miscasts the decidely robust and healthy ex-weightlifter as Count Dracula. It is nowhere near as elegantly filmed as his other Naschy collaboration that year, *El Jorobado de la Morgue*. The script of *El Gran amor* deals with a group of travellers trapped in a nursing home by the

below:
French poster for **La Noche de Walpurgis** (aka **Werewolf's Shadow**), 1970.

horror cinema across the globe

Count, who needs one of the young women to consent to becoming his undead lover so that he may reanimate his daughter. When the woman refuses, Dracula buries his daughter and thrusts a stake through his own heart! This is another example of Naschy's fascination with the doomed nature of his characters and his determination to see them come to a ghastly end, regardless of logic.

El Espanto surge de la tumba (*Horror Rises from the Tomb*, 1972), one of Naschy's many collaborations with director Carlos Aured, was the first film to star Naschy in a dual role as both hero and villain. This inspired bit of casting treats us to Naschy at his most humane and horrifying. As the devil-worshipping knight, Armand du Marnac, Naschy is suitably malevolent, and succeeds in projecting a powerful aura of supernatural menace by eye contact alone. In this respect, Naschy appears to be taking his cue directly from Christopher Lee's portrayal of Dracula in the various Hammer productions, where the sensuous, corrupting evil of the Count is conveyed more by mere presence than words. By contrast, Naschy's decidely more verbose performance as Hugo du Marnac, Armand's doomed descendant, shows him to be weak, vain and spoiled. Hugo would have to be able to overcome these flaws in order to have any chance against his demonic ancestor, whose list of crimes reads like a veritable grocery list of every conceivable blasphemy ever committed:

Armand du Marnac, you are about to hear all the evil crimes by which the just Tribunal of Carcasson has condemned you: You have drunk human blood. Of both the living and the dead you have eaten flesh; also, you have celebrated the Black Mass, with bloody sacrifice of the newborn and young girls. You are both the dog and servant of Satan! You are vampires and lycanthropes! For this, you will be beheaded, and your head and body buried in separate places, so that never again shall they be joined.

Upon hearing these charges, Armand places a curse on his accusers (including his own brother) and is summarily executed. Armand's wife is stripped completely naked, strung upside down from a tree, then cut in half.[1]

In modern day France, the cursed descendants, Hugo and Maurice (Víctor Alcázar), decide to return to Armand's old stomping grounds to look for his severed head. They are accompanied by their girlfriends, and after fending off some bandits intent on raping the women, arrive at Hugo's ancestral home. The knight's head, kept alive all these years by black magic, uses its fiendish power to enslave and murder, and eventually succeeds in reuniting his head and body. Armand's wife is reborn when a nude girl is sacrificed over her skeleton. Now mobile and hungry to devour human flesh, the unholy pair stalk the night, seducing and slaying the unwary. The film falters near the end, when a *deus ex machina* - a talisman called "The Hammers of Thor" - is suddenly dredged up out of a nearby well and proves effective in destroying the undead couple and their zombie army. The talisman is never so much as hinted at prior to its appearance, when the sole surviving female suddenly "remembers" that it exists. This comes off as both contrived and poorly thought out (what is a Norse talisman doing in France, and how does an obviously pagan symbol have power over the spawn of Satan?). This, combined with Hugo's demise and the less interesting Maurice unexpectedly taking over as the main hero, undermine the film's credibility and climax. Despite these problems, *El Espanto* remains an extremely entertaining exercise in Grand Guignol violence, with many memorably unsettling and gory scenes to its credit. A sadistic semi-sequel, *Latidos de pánico* (*Cries of Terror*, 1982), would resurrect the vengeful spirit of Armand du Marnac once more.

La Rebelión de las muertas (*Vengeance of the Zombies*, 1972), another Klimovsky collaboration, failed miserably, despite attempting to follow in the "colonial revenge horror" footsteps of Hammer's outstanding *The Plague of the Zombies* and *The Reptile* (both 1966). Not even a horde of zombies can save this film from Klimovsky's abysmal direction. Fortunately, Naschy would redeem himself and deliver one of the few truly great zombie films in history the following year with *La Orgía de los muertos*. In *La Orgía*, Naschy plays the role of insane necrophilic gravedigger Igor, supplying the severely misguided Dr. Bracula with bodies to reanimate as zombies.[2] Though the film is a superior chiller marred only by a muddled "surprise" ending, Naschy has very little to do except peep on naked girls and skulk through secret passages. Given his scant screen time, Naschy is regrettably unable to endow Igor with the same emotional depth as he did Gotho in *El Jorobado de la Morgue*. Still, we can glimpse Naschy's attempt to portray his character as more than just a one-dimensional maniac,

---

[1] In the American release, we only see the wife suddenly upside down, topless and screaming before freeze-framing and cutting to the opening credits. The full frontal nudity and bisection sequence are cut, though the rest of the film's gore and nudity seem to be intact.

[2] *La Orgía de los muertos* was also released as *Bracula - Terror of the Living Death*, which comes as no surprise since it came out the same year as American International Picture's more widely known *Blacula*. In fact, the name "Dr. Bracula" is mentioned only once in the entire English dubbed version's running time, leading one to suspect that this was not the character's name in the film's original Spanish version and was added purely for marketing purposes.

Paul Naschy

but as a frustrated man driven to madness by those who would treat him as nothing more than a mindless slave. Nowhere is this more evident than in the scene where he rejects the lust of the Countess and descends into the secret catacombs to kiss and fondle the decomposing collection of female corpses within, all the while apologizing to them for dallying with the living. "I'm sorry", Igor solemnly intones, "...I love only you." *La Orgía de los muertos* also features hallucinogenic lovemaking, an ever-deepening sense of mystery and eerily effective zombie make-ups, which appear to have had some influence on the design of those later seen in Jorge Grau's excellent *Non si deve profanare il sonno dei morti* (*Let Sleeping Corpses Lie*, 1974).

La Venganza de la momia (*The Vengeance of the Mummy*, 1973) reunited Naschy and director Carlos Aured in a misogynistic gorefest detailing the predictably gruesome exploits of a mummy who must drink the blood from the slashed throats of young women.[3] The film makes

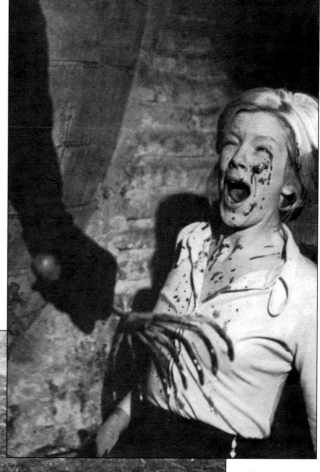

Women-in-peril; the motif most strongly associated with 70s and 80s European horror cinema.

above:
Los ojos azules de la muñeca rota (aka **The Blue Eyes of the Broken Doll** aka **House of Psychotic Women**), 1972.

left:
Latidos de Pánico, 1982.

[3] The gore scenes are drastically cut in most prints.

Spain

the most of its obviously shoestring budget, but still comes off as a crude imitation of the Universal and Hammer mummy films from which it is so obviously derived.

El Retorno de Walpurgis (*Curse of the Devil*, 1973) continued the Naschy-Aured collaboration with a seventh entry in the *Hombre Lobo* series. Aured's capable direction rewards us with the best film in the series up to that point. *El Retorno* wisely mixes in more nudity and gore than its predecessors, and includes the first time a dagger fashioned with a silver cross handle is used to destroy the werewolf, Waldemar Daninsky. This would quickly become a convention, replacing the traditional silver bullet as the preferred method of execution in all future *Hombre Lobo* pictures.

El Mariscal del infierno (*The Devil's Possessed*, 1974) starred Paul Naschy as Gilles de Rais, a French historical figure who was a great war hero but was later revealed to be a bloodthirsty sex maniac and cannibal, eventually documented as one of history's most prolific serial killers. Naschy has said that he based the character of Armand du Marnac from *El Espanto surge de la tumba* on Gilles de Rais.

Exorcismo (*Exorcism*, 1975) was one of many horror films from around the world to cash in on the success of William Friedkin's 1973 blockbuster, *The Exorcist*. Although allegedly written by Naschy before *The Exorcist*, he was unable to secure financing for the script until after Friedkin's film became an international hit. *Exorcismo* offers nothing new to the demonic possession subgenre. Instead, the picture merely reinforces the dangerous notion that any deviation from what is dictated as "normal" by societal or church standards is "the work of the devil." Strangely, this underlying message is in direct opposition to the compassion Naschy normally feels for all rebels and outcasts.

La Maldición de la bestia (*The Werewolf and the Yeti*, 1975) proved an odd but daring sequel in the *Hombre Lobo* saga. Waldemar Daninsky joins an expedition to the Himalayas, has a lusty ménage-á-trois with skin-ripping female cannibals in a cave and ultimately battles the Abominable Snowman! The fight between the werewolf and the yeti, sadly, is delayed until the film's finale. Although somewhat hampered by the lacklustre direction of Miguel

below:
Inquisición (aka **Inquisition**), 1976.

Iglesias Bonns, a haphazardly chosen stock music score and the inability of Naschy to convey the same sense of brooding, tragic intensity inherent in his prior performances as Daninsky, this film remains a fan favourite. Naschy was unhappy with the film, however, not only for the above reasons, but because Daninsky does not die at the end. Instead, contrary to all conventions of the series before and after, Daninsky is cured and walks off into the sunset with the girl he loves. Despite Naschy's disappointment, he received the "Best Acting" award for *La Maldición* at the 1975 Catalonian International Film Festival in Sitges, Spain.

The obscure *Último deseo* (*The People Who Own the Dark*, 1976), directed by the hit-or-miss Argentinian León Klimovsky, actually approaches near-classic status as a triumph of post-apocalyptic terror. Even though Naschy has only a supporting role as a self-serving and utterly unsympathetic adventurer (who gleefully sacrifices anyone if it will extend his life), his presence serves to further bolster an already excellent film. The story of *Último deseo* tells of a mysterious group gathering beneath a remote mansion. The group is dedicated to the perverse sexual philosophies of the Marquis De Sade, and a wild party ensues on the night of a nuclear attack. Miraculously, the group survives and leaves the ruins of their mansion. While exploring the surrounding countryside, they discover to their horror that whoever wasn't killed or sheltered underground from the blast has become a blind, zombie-like maniac, eager to rip out the eyes of anyone "normal." The film is tense and terrifying, echoing the themes of such horror/sci-fi classics as *Night of the Living Dead* (1968), *The Crazies* (1973) and *Soylent Green* (1973).

Branching out, all over

Inquisición (*Inquisition*, 1976), easily one of Naschy's best pictures - and the first to be directed by him - features the multi-talented actor in a surprising yet perfect dual role: that of the Inquisition-era witch hunting Judge de Fossey and Satan! Like fellow Spaniard Jesus Franco's *Les Démons* (*The Demons*, 1972), Naschy's film borrows heavily from the three landmark "witchcraft hysteria" pictures preceding it: Michael Reeves's *Witchfinder General* (1968), Michael Armstrong's *Hexen bis aufs Blut gequält* (*Mark of the Devil*, 1969) and Ken Russell's *The Devils* (1971). Naschy weaves a straightforward but titillating tale of love, lust and betrayal, filled with scenes of nudity and torture. Perhaps the most incredibly tasteless scene of his career comes when he orders an uncooperative young witch's nipple to be torn off with a pair of metal tongs. The satanic orgy scene in Hell (presided over by Naschy as the goat-headed Prince of Darkness) is also particularly hallucinogenic and thrilling. Even amidst all of this gratuitous nudity, gore and sadism, however, we feel for Naschy's character, seeing his tragic end well in advance and wishing he could escape his fate. Thus, Naschy succeeds once more in promoting his 'doomed antihero' concept, and injects his story with more emotion and humanity than one would expect from such a film.

Naschy played Satan once again in *El Caminante* (1979), an erotic black comedy about the devil in human guise leading people to ruin. For his "cultural contribution to film" with *El Caminante*, Paul Naschy received the Award of Honour at the 9th Annual Festival of Fantastic Cinema and Science Fiction in Paris. That same year, *El Caminante* received a special award from the International Festival of Imaginary Cinema and Science Fiction in Madrid for innovative work within fantastic cinema.

El Retorno del Hombre-Lobo (*Return of the Wolfman*, 1980) was the first Waldemar Daninsky outing to be directed by Naschy himself. His script for *El Retorno* is a throwback to the simpler Universal monster movies of the 1930s and 40s, albeit with nudity and graphic violence thrown in. The story remains completely faithful to the conventions of the *Hombre Lobo* series. Perhaps unsurprisingly, there are some striking similarities to *La Noche de Walpurgis*, *El Retorno de Walpurgis* and *El Espanto surge de la tumba*, all of which Naschy wrote. The devil-worshipping vampire Countess Báthory from *La Noche* returns, as does the *deus ex machina* "all-purpose talisman" of *El Espanto*, this time in the form of the silver cross/dagger needed to end Daninsky's lycanthropic curse (now effective in warding off vampires as well as werewolves).

The story concerns three German women searching for Countess Báthory's tomb, one of whom is a murdering witch who needs her unsuspecting companions as sacrifices for a satanic ritual which will reawaken the countess. In an unrelated

above:
Spanish admat for
Blue Eyes of the Broken Doll.

above:
Una libélula para cada muerto (aka **A Dragonfly for Each Corpse**), 1973

incident before the women arrive, some graverobbers foolishly remove the silver cross from Waldemar's heart, reviving him and ensuring their immediate and messy deaths. Since Waldemar was enslaved by Báthory's black magic before being killed, now that he is free he does not wish to come under her spell again. Thus, he fights to prevent the witch from restoring her back to (un)life. Naturally he fails in this attempt, and after a few skirmishes, the vampires and the werewolf fight to the death. Boasting the best make-up, soundtrack and sets of the entire series, *El Retorno* served as a breath of fresh air in the slasher-dominated horror market of the early 1980s, skillfully succeeding as a modern update to the classic horrors of the past. Perhaps because of a failure to cater to changing market tastes, however, *El Retorno* was a major international flop, nearly bankrupting Naschy's production company. *El Retorno* was released on video in America as *The Craving* in order to capitalise on the popularity of Joe Dante's *The Howling*, which came out the same year. Aside from being werewolf movies, though, the two pictures have little in common.

El Carnaval de las bestias (*Human Beasts*, 1980) was the first of Naschy's Spanish-Japanese co-productions, and turned out to be a routine gore movie. The plot concerns a jewel thief (Naschy) who double-crosses his Japanese partners and escapes to Spain, only to end up trapped in a house full of cannibals.

Naschy claims to have done the musical kiddie comedy, *Buenas noches, señor monstruo* (1982) strictly for the money, starring once again as his beloved Wolf Man. This time, he menaces four kids trapped in a castle by famous movie monsters. Picture *Home Alone* (1990) meets *Mad Monster Party?* (1967) and you get the idea.

Latidos de pánico, an erotic horror picture, was Naschy's attempt to recover from the financial disaster of *El Retorno del Hombre-Lobo*. It was made with the crew's agreement to defer payment unless and until the picture turned a profit. The story begins in the sixteenth century, with Armand du Marnac of *El Espanto surge de la tumba* murdering his unfaithful wife. His ghost then returns once every hundred years to visit painful death upon the immoral women of the du Marnac clan. The

above:
La bestia y la espada mágica (aka **The Beast and the Magic Sword**), 1983.

film is mean-spirited and pessimistic, though beautifully shot.

La bestia y la espada mágica (*The Beast and the Magic Sword*, 1983) was Naschy's tenth outing as the reluctant werewolf, Waldemar Daninsky, and his second Spanish-Japanese co-production. Daninsky is here transplanted to sixteenth-century Japan, where he is seeking a cure for his cursed condition. Unable to find this remedy, he returns to Europe with a beautiful Japanese lover who, after numerous lycanthropic transformations and attacks by Daninsky, ends up killing him with a silver sword. *La Bestia* benefited from a larger-than-usual budget for a Naschy production, and the film takes full advantage of it. Equally atmospheric and impressive, *La Bestia* could have served as a fitting end to the series. However, *La Aullido del diablo* (*Howl of the Devil*, 1987), co-starring Naschy's son Sergio, and *Licántropo: El asesino de la luna llena* (*Lycanthropus: The Moonlight Murders*, 1996), both followed. And in Fred Olen Ray's *The Unliving*, which filmed in March 2003, Naschy returns once again to play the part of the troubled wolf man.

As *The Unliving* indicates, the new millennium certainly hasn't slowed Naschy down any. In 2001 he had a lead role in the Spanish slasher flick, *School Killer*. Since then, he's appeared in no less than four features, two shorts and a TV series! Naschy has also written his autobiography, *Memoirs of a Wolf Man*, published in the United States by Midnight Marquee Press, with an extra chapter not included in the original Spanish edition. Earlier in 2001, Naschy was presented with Spain's highest honour, the Gold Medal Award, which carries with it the title of "Señor Excelentisimo" (similar to the title "Sir" acquired by being knighted in Britain). The award for his lifetime achievement as one of Spain's most important actors was presented by none other than King Juan Carlos I himself.

A dedicated and passionate horror fan, Paul Naschy deserves praise and recognition for pushing the envelope of sex and violence in horror, for defying the conventions of Spanish cinema and perhaps most importantly, for caring enough to endow his characters with a level of emotional depth and intensity unseen in most of the world's horror films.

Spain

Paul Naschy filmography

1960 KING OF KINGS Dir. Nicholas Ray. Extra (uncredited)
1960 EL PRÍNCIPE ENCADENADO ('The Chained Prince' / King of the Vikings) Dir. Luis Lucia. Extra (uncredited)
1963 55 DAYS AT PEKING Dir. Nicholas Ray, Guy Green (uncredited), Andrew Marton (uncredited). Extra (uncredited)
1966 MAINLY ON THE PLAINS (episode of US TV series I SPY) Dir. David Friedkin. Extra (uncredited)
1966 OPERACIÓN PLUS ULTRA ('Operation Plus Ultra') Dir. Pedro Lazaga. Extra (uncredited)
1966 LAS VIUDAS ('The Widows') Dir. Pedro Lazaga ("Luna de miel"); Julio Coll ("El Aniversario"); José María Forqué ("Retrato de regino"). Extra (uncredited) (segment "Luna de miel")
1967 AGONIZANDO EN EL CRIMEN ('Agonizing in Crime') Dir. Enrique López Eguiluz. Actor
1967 AVENTURA EN EL PALACIO VIEJO ('Adventure in the Old Palace') Dir. Manuel Torres. Assistant director
1967 CRÓNICA DE NUEVE MESES ('Chronicle of Nine Months') Dir. Mariano Ozores Jr. Assistant director
1967 DOVE SI SPARA DI PIÙ (La furia de Johnny Kid / The Fury of Johnny Kid / Ultimate Gunfighter) Dir. Gianni Puccini. Actor
1968 LA MARCA DEL HOMBRE LOBO ('The Mark of the Wolf Man' / Frankenstein's Bloody Terror / Hell's Creatures / The Wolfman of Count Dracula) Dir. Enrique Lopez Eguiluz. Actor, co-writer
1968 LA ESCLAVA DEL PARAÍSO (Sharaz / 'The Slave of Paradise' / 1001 Nights) Dir. Joe Lacy [José María Elorrieta]. Actor
1968 LAS NOCHES DEL HOMBRE LOBO (The Nights of the Wolf Man) Dir. René Govar. Actor, co-writer [note: Lost film; though on most Naschy filmographies, there is no concrete evidence for its existence.]
1968 PLAN JACK CERO TRES ('Plan Jack 03') Dir. Cecilia M. Bartolomé. Actor
1969 LOS MONSTRUOS DEL TERROR ('The Monsters of Terror' / Assignment Terror / Dracula Vs. Frankenstein) Dir. Tulio Demichelli, Hugo Fregonese. Actor, writer
1970 LA FURIA DEL HOMBRE LOBO (The Fury of the Wolf Man) Dir. Jose Maria Zabalza. Actor, writer
1970 LA NOCHE DE WALPURGIS ('Walpurgis Night' / The Werewolf Vs. The Vampire Woman / Werewolf's Shadow) Dir. León Klimovsky. Actor, co-writer
1970 EL VÉRTIGO DEL CRIMEN ('The Vertigo of Crime') Dir. Pascual Cervera. Actor
1971 DR. JEKYLL Y EL HOMBRE LOBO (Dr. Jekyll versus the Werewolf) Dir. León Klimovsky. Actor, writer
1971 JACK EL DESTRIPADOR DE LONDRES (Sette cadaveri per Scotland Yard / Jack the Ripper of London) Dir. José Luis Madrid. Actor, writer
1972 LOS CRÍMENES DE PETIOT ('The Crimes of Petiot') Dir. José Luis Madrid. Actor, co-writer
1972 DISCO ROJO ('Red Light') Dir. Rafael Romero Marchent. Actor, co-writer
1972 EL ESPANTO SURGE DE LA TUMBA (Horror Rises from the Tomb) Dir. Carlos Aured. Actor, writer
1972 EL GRAN AMOR DEL CONDE DRÁCULA (Count Dracula's Great Love / Dracula's Virgin Lovers) Dir.Javier Aguirre. Actor, co-writer
1972 EL JOROBADO DE LA MORGUE (The Hunchback of the Morgue / The Rue Morgue Massacres) Dir. Javier Aguirre. Actor, co-writer
1972 LOS OJOS AZULES DE LA MUÑECA ROTA (The Blue Eyes of the Broken Doll / House of Psychotic Women) Dir. Carlos Aured. Actor, co-writer
1972 LA REBELIÓN DE LAS MUERTAS (The Rebellion of the Dead Women / Vengeance of the Zombies) Dir. León Klimovsky. Actor, writer
1973 L'ORGIA DEI MORTI (La orgía de los muertos / Bracula - The Terror of the Living Death / The Hanging Woman / Return of the Zombies) Dir. José Luis Merino. Actor
1973 EL ASESINO ESTÁ ENTRA LOS TRECE ('The Murderer is One of the Thirteen') Dir. Javier Aguirre. Actor, co-writer
1973 LAS RATAS NO DUERMEN DE NOCHE ('Rats Don't Sleep at Night' / Crimson) Dir. Juan Fortuny. Actor
1973 EL RETORNO DE WALPURGIS (The Return of Walpurgis / Curse of the Devil) Dir. Carlos Aured. Actor, writer
1973 TARZÁN EN LAS MINAS DEL REY SALOMÓN (Tarzan in King Solomon's Mines) Dir. Jose Luis Merino Boves. Actor
1973 UNA LIBÉLULA PARA CADA MUERTO (A Dragonfly for Each Corpse) Dir. León Klimovsky. Actor, writer
1973 LA VENGANZA DE LA MOMIA (The Vengeance of the Mummy / The Mummy's Revenge) Dir. Carlos Aured. Actor, writer
1974 LA DIOSA SALVAJE ('The Savage Goddess' / Kilma Queen of the Jungle) Dir. Miguel Iglesias Bonns. Actor
1974 EL MARISCAL DEL INFIERNO (The Marshall of Hell / The Devil's Possessed) Dir. León Klimovsky. Actor, writer

Paul Naschy

1974 LOS PASAJEROS ('The Passengers') Dir. José Antonio Barrero. Actor
1974 TODOS LOS GRITOS DEL SILENCIO ('All the Cries of Silence') Dir. Ramón Barco. Actor, co-writer
1974 EXORCISMO (Exorcism) Dir. Juan Bosch. Actor, co-writer
1975 LA CRUZ DEL DIABLO (The Devil's Cross) Dir. John Gilling. Co-writer
1975 DOCTEUR JUSTICE (Ambicion fallida / Doctor Justice) Dir. Christian-Jaque. Actor.
1975 LA MALDICIÓN DE LA BESTIA (The Curse of the Beast / Night of the Howling Beast / The Werewolf and the Yeti) Dir. Miguel Iglesias Bonns. Actor, writer
1975 MUERTE DE UN QUINQUI ('Death of a Hoodlum') Dir. León Klimovsky. Actor
1976 INQUISICIÓN (Inquisition) Dir. Jacinto Molina. Director, actor, writer
1976 SECUESTRO ('Kidnapping') Dir. León Klimovsky. Actor, co-writer
1976 ÚLTIMO DESEO ('Last Desire' / The People Who Own the Dark) Dir. León Klimovsky. Actor
1977 COMANDO TXIKIA (Muerte de un presidente) Dir. José Luis Madrid. Actor
1977 EL FRANCOTIRADOR ('The Sniper') Dir. Carlos Puerto. Actor, co-writer
1977 EL HUERTO DEL FRANCÉS ('The Frenchman's Garden') Dir. Jacinto Molina. Director, actor, co-writer
1977 PECADO MORTAL ('Mortal Sin') Dir. Miguel Ángel Díez. Actor
1977 EL TRANSEXUAL ('The Transsexual') Dir. José Jara. Actor, co-writer
1978 MADRID AL DESNUDO ('Naked Madrid') Dir. Jacinto Molina. Director, actor, co-writer
1979 AMOR BLANCO ('White Love') Chief of production
1979 EL CAMINANTE ('The Traveller') Dir. Jacinto Molina. Actor, co-writer
1980 LOS CÁNTABROS ('The Cantabrians') Dir. Jacinto Molina. Director, actor, writer
1980 EL CARNAVAL DE LAS BESTIAS (The Carnival of the Beasts / Human Beasts / The Pig) Dir. Jacinto Molina. Director, actor, writer
1980 MISTERIO EN LA ISLA DE LOS MONSTRUOS (Mystery on Monster Island) Dir. Juan Piquer Simón. Actor
1980 EL MUSEO DEL PRADO (The Prado Museum) Dir. Jacinto Molina. Director, writer
1980 EL RETORNO DEL HOMBRE LOBO (The Return of the Wolf Man / The Craving) Dir. Jacinto Molina. Director, actor, writer
1981 LA MASCARA ('The Mask') [Spanish TV] Actor.
1981 EL PALACIO REAL DE MADRID ('The Royal Palace of Madrid') [Japanese TV documentary] Dir. Jacinto Molina. Director, writer.
1982 LATIDOS DE PÁNICO ('Panic Beats' / Cries of Terror / Heart Beat) Dir. Jacinto Molina. Director, actor, writer
1982 LA BATALLA DEL PORRO ('The Battle of the Dullard') Dir. Joan Minguell. Actor
1982 BUENAS NOCHES SEÑOR MONSTRUO ('Good Evening, Mr. Monster') Dir. Antonio Mercero. Actor

Spain

1982 LAS CUEVAS DE ALTAMIRA ('The Altamira Caves') [Japanese TV documentary] Dir. Jacinto Molina. Director, writer
1982 LA ESPADA DEL SAMURAI ('The Sword of the Samurai') [Japanese TV] Actor
1982 INFIERNO EN CAMBOYA ('Hell in Cambodia') [Japanese TV documentary] Dir. Jacinto Molina. Director
1982 LA MASCARA DEL JUYO ('The Mask of Juyo') [Japanese TV documentary] Dir. Jacinto Molina. Director, writer
1982 EL MONASTERIO DE EL ESCORIAL ('The Escorial Monastery') [Japanese TV documentary] Dir. Jacinto Molina. Director, writer
1983 LA BESTIA Y LA ESPADA MÁGICA (The Beast and the Magic Sword) Dir. Jacinto Molina. Director, actor, writer
1984 MI AMIGO EL VAGABUNDO ('My Friend the Vagabond') Dir. Jacinto Molina. Director, actor, writer
1984 LA TERCERA MUJER ('The Third Woman') [Japanese TV] Actor
1984 EL ÚLTIMO KAMIKAZE ('The Last Kamikaze') Dir. Jacinto Molina. Director, actor, writer
1984 OPERACIÓN MANTIS ('Operation Mantis') Dir. Jactino Molina. Director, actor, co-writer
1986 PEZ (Fish) [short] Dir. Santiago Aguilar, Raúl Barbe, Luis Guridi. Actor
1987 MORDIENDO LA VIDA ('Biting Life') Dir. Martin Garrido. Actor
1988 EL AULLIDO DEL DIABLO (The Howl of the Devil) Dir. Jacinto Molina. Director, actor, writer
1988 SHADOWS OF BLOOD Dir. Sydney Ling. Actor
1988 EL ÚLTIMO GUATEQUE II (The Last Party II) Dir. Juan José Porto. Actor
1988 SHH [short film] Dir. Escuadra Cobra [Santiago Aguilar, Luis Guridi, Raúl Barbe]. Actor
1990 AQUI HUELE A MUERTO . . .(¡PUES YO NO HE SIDO!) ('It Smells Like Someone Died Here . . . (But it Wasn't Me!)') Dir. Álvaro Sáenz de Heredia. Actor
1990 BRIGADA CENTRAL ('Central Brigade') [Spanish TV] Dir. Pedro Maso. Actor
1990 LA HIJA DE FU MANCHU ('The Daughter of Fu Manchu') [short] Dir. Santiago Aguilar, Luis Guridi. Actor
1990 HORROR EN EL MUSEO DE CERA (Horror in the Wax Museum) Dir. Jactino Molina. Director, actor, writer
1991 OLLA DE GRILLOS ('Bedlam') [Spanish TV] Actor
1992 LA NOCHE DEL EJECUTOR (The Night of the Executioner) Dir. Jactino Molina. Director, actor, writer
1992 STATE OF MIND Dir. Reginald Adamson [Reginald Van Severen]. Actor
1994 EL NECROFAGO [short] Dir. Gonzalo J. Fuentes Actor
1995 LOS RESUCITADOS ('The Resurrected') [unfinished] Actor
1996 EL ÁNGEL MÁS CAÍDO ('The Angel Has Fallen Very Far') [short] Actor
1996 CIENTIFICAMENT PERFECTES (Scientifically Perfect) Dir. Francesc Xavier Capell. Actor
1996 HAMBRE MORTAL ('Mortal Hunger') Actor
1996 MALA ESTRELLA ('Bad Star') [short] Actor
1996 LICÁNTROPO (Lycantropus) Dir. Francisco Rodríguez Gordillo. Actor, writer
1998 EL OJO DE LA MEDUSA ('The Eye of the Jellyfish') Dir. Jose M. Cabanach. Actor
1998 QUERIDO MAESTRO ('Dear Teacher') [Spanish TV] Actor
1998 CUANDO EL MUNDO SE ACABE TE SEGUIRE AMANDO ('I'll Still Love You When the World Ends') Dir. Pilar Sueiro. Actor
1999 RONDADORES NOCTURNO 2 (Night Prowlers 2) [short] Dir. Aure Roces. Actor, co-writer
2000 ANIMAS [short] Dir. Daniel Ortiz-Entrambasaguas. Actor
2000 ÉRASE UNA VEZ (Once Upon Another Time) Dir. Juan Pinzas. Actor
2000 LA GRAN VIDA ('The Great Life' / Living It Up) Dir. Antonio Cuardi. Actor
2000 ANTIVICIO [Spanish TV] Actor
2000 EL COMISARIO ('The Commissary') [Spanish TV] Actor
2000 EL LADO OSCURO ('The Dark Side') Dir. Luciano Berriatúa. Actor
2001 SCHOOL KILLER (El vigilante) Dir. Carlos Gil. Actor
2001 DESENLACE [Spanish TV] Actor
2001 EL CORAZON DELATOR ('The Tell-Tale Heart') [short] Dir. Alfonso S. Suarez. Actor
2001 EL QUINTO RINCON ('The Fifth Corner') [short] Dir. Mischa Müller Thyssen. Actor
2002 OCTAVIA Dir. Basilio Martín Patino. As himself
2002 MUCHA SANGRE ('Much Blood') Dir. Pepe de las Heras. Actor
2003 COUNTESS DRACULA'S ORGY OF BLOOD Dir. Donald F. Glut. Actor
2003 THE UNLIVING Dir. Fred Olen Ray. Actor

Filmography compiled by Francis Brewster, with reference to the excellent 'The Mark of Naschy' website (www.naschy.com)

artists, actors, auteurs

Sex and death, Cuban style: the dark vision of Jorge Molina

Ruth Goldberg (article), Steven Jay Schneider (interview)

How to describe Molina's films? Irreverent and very independent Caribbean style cult/horror. Think Jess Franco, an 80s dominatrix, Coffin Joe and Lydia Lunch all getting drunk together in Dario Argento's living room.
- Karyn Riegel[1]

We go to the Cinema to feel, not to understand.
- Tsui Hark[2]

An old dark house in Cuba

The small screening room upstairs at the Chaplin Cinema in Havana is packed to capacity. In the middle of the afternoon an audience of well-known filmmakers, critics, actors and students have turned out for the premiere of *Molina's Test* (2001); a short film which received no advance publicity and which was made, unusually enough, entirely independently of the state-run Cuban film industry. At the eleventh hour, it had been yanked from competition in the prestigious International Festival of New Latin American Cinema in Havana when a special committee deemed the film to be "not representative of Latin American Cinema."

The audience gets what they've come for. *Molina's Test*, the latest effort by maverick Cuban director Jorge Molina, is a bloody spectacle; full of all of the dark, transgressive elements that Molina fans look for, and laced with enough diverse cinematic references to keep "trash film" scholars busy for a long time to come.

One can trace the genealogy of *Molina's Test* back across film history, through a direct line of descent from James Whale's classic *The Old Dark House* (1932).

In scrutinising this legacy, however, it would seem that *Test* bears a much closer resemblance to later variations on the Old Dark House theme, including the camp reworking of that narrative in *The Rocky Horror Picture Show* (1975) and Paul Schrader's more recent *The Comfort of Strangers* (1990). The basic plot is familiar: disoriented, a young couple in transit take refuge in a strange house and are transformed by their experiences there. It is well worth noting that in virtually all reworkings of the Old Dark House narrative, the couple in question are either recently married or facing the prospect of marriage. They find themselves suddenly "not on any map," in a nightmare world where their bond is tested and in which past conflicts and sexual ambivalence are embodied, taking on the urgency of confrontation.

Molina's Test accesses the uncanny potential of this formulaic tale by a disarmingly circuitous route. It does not begin on a dark and stormy night, but rather in the broad Caribbean daylight of Central Havana. Luis (Leandro Espinoza) has arranged to borrow a motorcycle to take his fiancée Sara (Rachel Pastor) away for the weekend to an inn they visited five years earlier. He arrives to find that the motorcycle has instead been rented to an Italian tourist (Benny Casas) who has engaged the services of Leticia (Indira Valdez) the "jinetera" - or prostitute - for the day. The Italian paid for the rental in dollars. Under such lucrative circumstances, the owner of the bike could not have been expected to honour his promise to lend Luis the bike for free. We see the first of many brief, shimmering moments-out-of-time filmed in slow motion - an image of the

[1] Karyn Riegel, "Ocularis Newsletter" (29 April 2002): www.galapagosart-space.com.

[2] As quoted by Jorge Molina, personal interview with author. Havana, Cuba (10 December 2001).

horror cinema across the globe

81

right:
The character of Madame Tsu in **Molina's Test**.

jinetera laughing on the back of the motorcycle - a nod to Wong Kar Wai. Luis somehow manages to procure a car, and the couple sets off for the country, excitedly planning their upcoming marriage. Along the way, Rachel is seen reading *Tropical Animal*, one of Cuban author Pedro Juan Gutierrez's fictional works of "dirty realism,"[3] and she comments dryly that the book, a sordid exploration of life and sexual arrangements in greater Havana, is not published in Cuba.

Up until this moment, the film is indeed representative of Latin American cinema, and of Cuban cinema in particular, in the kinds of references it makes to the jaded realities and daily hardships of Cuban life - jineterism and the tourist trade, the two-money economy, a subtle reference to what the state-controlled press will or will not print, etc. - that might be found in virtually any Cuban film. This characteristic rootedness in the everyday, the natural, easy quality of the interaction between characters and the emphasis on social realism, all so typical of "Nuevo Cine Cubano," raise the troubling question of why Molina's work has been and continues to be so marginalised in his country of origin.[4]

"Why" soon becomes apparent. The couple lose their way in a forest and pause to, as Rachel puts it, "fuck like rats" in the car. The engine refuses to start up again, the map gives no indication of where they are and, compounding the sense of impending dread, they are soon passed on the road by the Italian tourist and jinetera heading back towards Havana on the coveted motorcycle. The jinetera is no longer laughing. Rather, she looks zombified, blood trickling from behind her ear. Without speaking, the equally zombified tourist points Rachel and Luis in the direction from which he has just come. Mystified, the couple set off on foot, and, as night falls, they arrive at a Chinese pagoda in the middle of the forest. ("Who lives here? Fu Manchu?!" Luis says, laughing.) What ensues is transgressive enough to ensure that Jorge Molina will never receive any money from the Cuban government to make a film.

The inhabitants of this bizarre domicile are the sinister "fake Chinese" couple Mister Wong and Madame Tsu, played by veteran Cuban actor Luis Alberto Garcia and newcomer Zulema Clares. The house and its inhabitants are a hallucinatory homage to tacky Hollywood stereotypes of Chinese villains throughout film history, with Madame Tsu revelling in her part as the insanely over-the-top dragon lady, and Mister Wong representing the unctuous Chinese torturer-cum-philosopher. Molina celebrates the trash/camp aesthetic while pushing deeper and deeper into uncharted transgressive territory as he probes various Asian stereotypes. This effect is heightened by an expansion of the film's narrative structure to include all possible actions, real or imagined. An intentional ambiguity is created as to whether Luis and Rachel are fantasising, hallucinating (possible victims of the so-called "Chinese Restaurant Syndrome") or actually witnessing what follows, as the "realistic" sequences are intercut with nightmare visions of sex and violence: M. Wong, practically in drag in heavy makeup, a kimono and four-inch press-on nails, clinks Qigong balls to announce that dinner is served, wields a giant cleaver with quiet menace and philosophises about love while first fondling and later having intercourse with a goat. M. Tsu, equally outrageously attired, alternately smokes an opium pipe, slurps at the carcass of a baby bird and sodomises a rapturous Mister Wong with an enormous cucumber.

In the midst of all of this, one fantasy sequence stands alone. Searching for Sara, Luis finds himself at a raucous party-turned-orgy somewhere in the house. Pedro Juan Gutierrez, the author of *Tropical Animal* is there, casually engaged in sex with Leticia the jinetera.

[3] A term which came into vogue in describing one tendency of Latin American literary fiction in the 1980s and 90s. The term indicates both the central focus on the everyday lives of individuals and the regionalist bent of this literature.

[4] The birth of the New Cuban Cinema dates back to the creation of the Cuban Art Institute and Cinematographic Industry, known internationally as ICAIC, in March of 1959. Although Cuban filmmaking has evolved in a number of different directions since 1959, and unarguably represents a range of practices including farce and fantasy, the national cinema of Cuba continues to be a contemplative cinema and to utilise the strategies of realism as a central tendency.

Jorge Molina

Pedro Juan tells Luis where to look for Sara, and we watch as Luis, in slow-motion, arrives to find his fiancée dressed in a bridal gown, being groped by Madame Tsu in a bathroom stall. The women laugh at him, taunt him. The worst is yet to come.

This small film, overtly violent and sexual and ultimately pessimistic about the bond of intimacy, achieves a profound subtlety through these slow-motion sequences. They are used to illuminate moments of the characters' transformation of vision. The narrative, rooted in stories of the body, slows down to betray Luis's inner vision moving at a different pace, a different level of paranoid detail than that of exterior reality. This is where the film most classically plays on themes of horror, as it reveals the idea that reality and inner vision can be inconsistent; that your inner eye might reveal that you are helpless and exposed, trapped in a nightmare of fulfilled suspicions, as each of Luis's fears are played out one by one. In each retelling of the Old Dark House narrative, it becomes clear in exactly this dreamlike way that the journey the characters *thought* they were on - the one which led them to these bizarre encounters in the first place - is only a pretext for their *actual* journey. As soon as the couple find themselves "not on any map" the viewer is signalled that they have entered the realm of the uncanny, and that this is, in fact, an interior journey which will reveal the full horror and ambivalence of intimacy, the fear of betrayal.

Pedro Juan Gutierrez's cameo appearance gives the sequence a further dreamlike integrity. His presence is not only a reference to an earlier waking idea, but also embodies this division of perception, between the calm one sees on the surface while underneath a storm rages. It is the revelation of this storm, the desperate acts people commit every day in Central Havana, the ubiquity of sex and squalor in Cuba that tourists rarely see but which is brought to light in Gutierrez's works, that puts him on equal footing with Molina, an artist who, in his own way, is committed to exposing an unseen interior world.

A reverence for reference

Molina's films, although rooted in his experience in Cuba, reflect a worldliness from other frames, a testament to his encyclopaedic knowledge of film history. (He has taught courses on subjects as diverse as Blaxploitation, Alejandro Jodorowsky, the *oeuvre* of Billy Wilder and the American Underground Tradition.) Perhaps more than any other, one sees the influence of Hong Kong cinema in Molina's work. *Test* is, in its own extremely low-budget way, as over-the-top as Ronny Yu's *The Bride with White Hair* (1993), at moments as intentionally silly as Ching Siu Tung's *A Chinese Ghost Story* (1987); given the budget, surely Molina's characters would be flying through the air. In speaking of this influence on his work, Molina has said that what attracts him to the cinema of Hong Kong is its quality of total creative liberation; the ethic it transmits that a filmmaker should be faithful to the integrity of their own imagination at all costs. In this particular case, Molina allows his imagination to run amok in *Test* in a kind of wild homage to world cinema. It is this vision which makes Molina's films most decidedly, proudly "*not* representative of Latin American Cinema."

By making horror movies, something which had not even been attempted in a mainstream Cuban production since before 1959, and moreover, by insisting on pushing his films well beyond the accepted Cuban film lexicon - beyond the official borders of realism, beyond the familiar territory of the absurd or the stylised tactics of magical realism or even the symbolic works of Fernando Perez - Molina adds a facet to Cuban cinema which Cuba may not be ready for. His films always begin realistically enough, but then immediately plunge the viewer into a world of cinematic cross-reference: the dark world of the *giallo*, the "trash" visions of Mojica Marins, Fulci and Franco, the cynical underworld of classic Hollywood *noir* - a sort of cinematic cyberspace contained within the skull of the director, ready to break out at any moment.

Perhaps the best evidence of this innate referential quality is that the few

left:
A quick taste before the real test:
Molina's Test.

writers to have tackled the task of describing Molina's work have been unable to do so except by comparing him to other directors. If screenwriter Ramiro Garcia Bogliano's words can serve as an example: "Maybe *Test* isn't Jorge Molina at his best, but it is, without a doubt, a highly disturbing movie that moves weirdly but successfully between the influences of Jess Franco, Jose Mojica Marins and the finest Ken Russell."[5]

(I am, obviously, equally guilty of taking this easy way out of describing Molina's difficult work. The first time I sit down to watch *Molina's Test* I scribble lamely, "Wong Kar Wai shooting with Jess Franco's lens. *Shanghai Gesture* and *The Old Dark House* remade by Fulci.") Most remarkable is the sheer range of conscious references and the strength of Molina's instincts as a filmmaker. This mix of talent and education combined with his natural inclination towards provocation is what makes the work at once engaging and unsettling. This is the art of a man who has lived and breathed cinema ever since he was very young.

Molina tells the story that his mother took him to see Kurasawa's *The Bad Sleep Well* (1960) in his hometown of Palma Soriano when he was ten years old, and that he emerged from that experience certain that he would dedicate his life to making movies. He went on to study filmmaking in Moscow before returning to Cuba and completing a degree in directing at the International School of Film and Television in San Antonio de los Baños. His appetite for film took on a life of its own early on, and he developed eclectic tastes: an absolute reverence for Billy Wilder, an unusual level of familiarity with the work of filmmakers as diverse as Seijun Suzuki, Carlos Sorin and Nick Zedd, and a not-so-secret penchant for police porn. Despite this range, the themes in his work remain constant: sex, death, desire, and monstrosity.

The recurrent themes of sex and the monstrous-feminine in Molina's work have been much discussed. What remains unexplored is his treatment of love, the overt theme of this most recent film. It is a dark vision of love, in which those who love are tested and ultimately punished for it. In Molina's other films[6] as well (*Molina's Culpa* [1993]; *Dolman 2000* [2000]), love always comes at a price - and often that price is humiliation. It is to this territory that Molina returns once again to play on classic themes of horror. In each remake of *The Old Dark House* the journeying couple encounters a "monstrous" counterpart in the strange house; a bizarre couple or family in whose company the travellers feel uncannily exposed, and in front of whom any ambivalence between them is made manifest and carried to its most twisted extreme. The lesson is simple: ambivalence is fatal. In horror cinema, at least, it results in the monstrous transformation of fear and desire, with unknowable consequences.

Whale ends his seminal *Old Dark House* on an "up" note. Roger Penderel (Melvyn Douglas) and Gladys DuCane (Lillian Bond), having weathered the storm and all manner of weirdness, and having survived attacks by brutes and madmen, profess their love for one another in "the cold light of day" and head towards matrimony as the credits roll, brought closer together by their ordeal. Molina leaves us with no such romantic vision of the enduring power of love. After glibly responding to Mister Wong's inquiry "What would you be capable of doing for one another? Would you give your lives for each other?" Luis and Sara are made to take a long hard look at the true nature of their bond. They emerge transformed, their future uncertain.

Most enigmatic of all is Molina's own stance on the subject. When asked about the cynical, tortured vision of love portrayed in *Test*, he responds with a wink, "I believe in love. With love *anything* is possible."

[5] Ramiro Garcia Bogliano, The Internet Movie Database (IMDB), 26 June 26 2001: http://us.imdb.com/Title?0280957#comment.

[6] I am referring here to Molina's fiction films only. His filmography also includes a number of documentaries, including *Machurrucutu II: Haz Lo Incorrecto* (1991) and *Sidoglio Smithee* (1998).

Jorge Molina

Testing Molina: a candid interview with Cuba's underground auteur

Steven Jay Schneider: What got you interested in becoming a filmmaker?

JM: It's all my mother's fault! My mother was a tremendous cinephile and she began bringing me to the cinema when I was a baby. She said that I never cried - I would just stare intently at the screen...

SJS: Where was this cinema?

JM: I grew up in Palma Soriano, a small town in the province of Santiago de Cuba. It's on the Eastern part of the island, more commonly known as Oriente de Cuba. There was a mobile cinema that would come and show movies against a sheet in front of a store.[7] When I was around eight or nine years old I began to see classic films by Kurosawa, by Fellini, Soviet cinema - all the classics. The one that struck me first was *The Bad Sleep Well* (1960) by Kurosawa. That was the one that really trapped me and made me say to myself, "I have to dedicate myself to this."

SJS: So how did you begin pursuing your dream?

JM: It was impossible to study film in Cuba - there was no film school at that point. You had to go to the University and study Humanities or Literature. I decided one day that I was going to make a film, though I didn't know how I was going to do it. A friend of mine sold me an 8mm camera for a ridiculously low price...and I began just filming everything. My friends used to escape to this nearby river, and I began shooting them. We were about 10 or 11 at the time. It's really prominent in that part of the country for one's first sexual experiences to be with animals - mares, goats, chickens. Adolescent adventures. I began filming this. The footage has been lost...my friends are very happy about that! Too bad, as it could have been a good document of what adolescent life is like in this place. It was filmed without any cinematographic knowledge, but it's fun to talk about.

At that age, I used to go alone to the movies because my friends weren't interested. For example, when I wanted to see *Jaws*, I said to a friend "Why don't we go see *Jaws*?" and he said "No, I'm going with my girlfriend to the park." I was the only one without a girlfriend so it left me more time for movies. Because none of the girls were interested in me at all, my partner was the cinema.

SJS: Didn't you get your training in Russia?

JM: I went to Havana to study education and fine arts: I had to be in Havana at that point because there was nothing happening in regards to cinema in Oriente. So I came to Havana to be closer to what was possible to do in cinema, but no opportunities presented themselves. Then I found out that there were special scholarships provided for children of Cuban military personnel to go and study film in Russia. (I'm the son of a captain in the army.) They finally sent me to the school in Moscow after taking the exam two times...there was a lot of bullshit before they let me go... I was 19 years old, and I was there for 15 months.

What I learned most of all in Russia is how to look at cinema, how to appreciate where the camera is positioned - all the technical elements. And I studied acting there as well. It was the happiest time in my life. The only time I felt completely free to do what I wanted to do, without anyone caring.

SJS: You didn't feel like a stranger in a strange land?

JM: No! They loved the Cubans there. It was such an exciting time. Capitalism was about to invade Russia, and there were all these things coming in that I had never been exposed to before. All these directors were making bizarre cinema than I had never experienced - Polish directors, Japanese directors...

SJS: When did you start getting interested in the horror genre?

JM: Ever since I was a kid horror films really scared me. I loved that. Classic horror films...even the bad ones! I still remember watching *Kronos* (1957). And *The War of the Worlds* (1953) was one of my favourites - the way the machines moved in that film scared the hell out of me.

SJS: Who are some of your favourite horror filmmakers?

JM: Robert Wise for *The Haunting* (1963). James Whale. Romero. Tobe Hooper. Cronenberg. I also love Jodorowsky - I'm something of an expert on him. I really love *El Topo* (1970)...

[7] As Ruth Goldberg explains, "The mobile cinema movement came out of Russia and came to Cuba right after the Revolution in 1959; the first cultural act of the Revolution was to create a film industry. Many parts of Cuba at that point didn't have electricity, didn't have any knowledge of cinema at all...so they mobilised cinema by strapping projectors on to the back of donkeys and they put them on trains, on boats and most often on trucks, and they took them out into all these parts of Cuba where people had never seen movies before. They installed electricity and they also brought these mobile generators and then they began to show movies up against the walls, against sheets, and it created this tremendous appetite for cinema. ...And along with that there's this television show called *24 Frames Per Second* which has been on the air continuously for more than thirty years to educate the Cuban public about how cinema works, so that they can more fully appreciate it and also so that they can't be taken in by the propaganda of Hollywood." Interview with the author (12 May 2002).

Cuba

above:
Molina's alter ego?
Mister Wong (Luis
Alberto Garcia)
preparing the tools
of his trade in
Molina's Test.

SJS: *What about European?*

JM: Jess Franco for one. And Bava, Franju, Argento, Fulci, among others.

SJS: *And at home? What has there been in terms of Cuban horror?*

JM: I think what's horrifying in Cuban cinema is how bad it is! [Laughs.] In the sense that it is too contemplative and superficial, for export more than anything else. There are some very old Cuban films that have maybe some elements of horror in them, like *The Red Serpent* [1939, dir. Ernesto Caparrós], Cuba's first feature film with sound. But since 1959 there has been nothing - no one has made a real horror film in Cuba. Unfortunately, the utopian idea of a New Cuban Cinema that began in 1959 was very idealistic - they worked to negate genre - and it did a lot of damage. There were a lot of directors who wanted to make genre pictures but because they knew they couldn't get support they ended up making films that were apologetic and didn't really come out of what they felt. Films about Cuban "reality," which wasn't what they really wanted to do. For that reason the films were bad, or just silly. In animation directors had better luck, because animation allowed them a little more creativity. The Cuban Film Institute didn't pay a lot of attention to what was happening in this area. People were able to do really fun things with genre and animation.

There are plenty of directors in Cuba who would like to do horror, but they're cowards. They go so long in between projects and are so desperate to work that they get involved in projects they don't really care about - that they don't really love - and it turns out badly. The resulting works are "safe." They won't provoke or bother anyone, but they are insignificant as a result.

SJS: *What about the horror elements in your own work?*

JM: I don't think I've made "pure" horror films. I've made films that have elements of horror in them. My real interest *is* in fact the horrific, but it's broader than horror: it's *all* of the dark elements of human nature.

SJS: *So it's not generic? There's no concern with making something conventional to fit within a particular category?*

JM: Not really. If there was a specific project that I fell in love with that really required that I stay within one genre, I would certainly do it. But my main emphasis is to enjoy the project and to make it have integrity. And to try to provoke sensation. If the sensation is of horror, then fantastic - I love to provoke fear in the audience! But the main idea is just to make the audience feel.

When I'm making a film I do what I feel is right. I'm not always consciously thinking, "I'm doing *this* to make the audience feel *this* at *this* moment." It's more organic than that. It comes out of what I think I should do at that particular moment as director.

I'm not the kind of artist who creates something to have an effect. I do it because it feels good when I'm doing it. And then once it's done it has it's own life, and often it does in fact have an effect on people.

SJS: *But you like the fact that it has an effect. Do you see that as posing any conflict?*

JM: I'm really thinking about myself when I make my films; I'm thinking about what *I'm* feeling, that *I'm* enjoying it. It's a problem: you do things because you feel them. You don't always know if they're going to work. You're really happy when they do. But really I'm thinking about whether it works for me. I love exploring themes of sex and death and bloody spectacle. These are themes that always interest the public, but they are themes that have interested me since I was a kid and so I keep exploring him for that reason, not because they're going to interest other people necessarily.

SJS: *In addition to the violence and the horror elements in your films, there is clearly an effort to turn people on. And there's also humour...so this is part of it as well?*

Jorge Molina

JM: Cubans have a very good sense of humour. They make comedic films about their own tragedies. All of these recurring themes...sex, death...in my work, I relate it to my childhood. I was a shy kid. *Very* shy. Even though my father was always really clear with me about sex, that it's a good thing and nothing to be ashamed of. I was always obsessed with women, naked women. As a kid I spent a lot of energy getting a hold of porn, pornographic magazines in particular - which are still illegal in Cuba, by the way. When I was sixteen I was arrested for having porno mags, for having prurient tastes.

SJS: I'm glad you feel comfortable talking about this! Based on your films, I would be surprised if you were embarrassed talking about anything. And we should get to that - the confessional nature of the material, and the non-exploitative presentation of sexuality, masturbation...it's all just kind of "there."

JM: At times I would really *like* my films to be more exploitative, to play around with that, to see what it's like, because I'm so influenced by Franco and all these kinds of directors. But my work doesn't really come out that way. I don't put sex scenes in so that people will say, "Wow. What a crazy, 'out there' guy for Cuba."

Everything that comes out in my films stems from an early feeling... one important early experience I had in an orange grove as a kid, when a girl went to kiss me and I fled from the scene. Women often turn up in my work as monstrous or menacing.

SJS: But in Culpa (aka Molina's Culpa, 1993) it's the man who kills the woman. Does that make it different to your other, later films?

JM: They're different stories, different contexts, but it's really the same woman. There is always a woman who shows up and changes the life of the man. There's always a sexual element. The man in *Culpa* has never had sex; he's devoted himself to prayer. Then this woman shows up...he would never have killed her had she not effected a change in his life.

In *Fría Jenny* [the segment in the three-part *Dolman 2000* (2000) directed by Molina], the guy's life is kind of fucked up. A woman shows up like this ray of light, but then she has this sort of decaying influence. She's not really there...she's not really alive.

above:
Molina at work behind the scenes.

SJS: Can you explain the end of *Fría Jenny*? What turns out to be the case? There's a woman who stops by again and again at this guy's apartment. It's kind of humorous, actually - she borrows all his stuff. Finally they have sex and then she leaves. At the end, he goes upstairs to find her but she seems to have been in a coma for a long time. It's ambiguous, though, because she is still holding on to a stuffed animal that he gave her...

JM: It's inspired by a story that shows up in a lot of different cultures. A woman appears - she shows up hitchhiking or something like that (it depends on the country) - and there's a romance. As soon as the man falls in love and goes to look for her, it turns out that she's been dead for twenty years. It's the ghostly maiden who turns out not to be alive.

This is the film of mine that the audience liked best when I recently showed my work in Miami... It was just three people having fun with a camera, not planning it at all. It demonstrates to me that seeing a lot of films really helps a lot as a director. My friends wanted to show that we could do something good, cheap and fast. As good as something planned out and made with a lot more money.

SJS: You yourself have a starring role in *Fría Jenny*. What's it like to direct yourself as an actor?

JM: It's strange. It's fun but it's very strange. Because I don't know until later if I'm doing a good job! So I become dependent on the photographer while shooting. I ask him all the time, "Did I really do it okay?" And he keeps telling me,

above:
The Last Supper: Molina directing his actors in **Molina's Test**.

"Yes, you did fine." But I feel bad about it and say, "Let's do it again" - and I do it worse every time!

SJS: *Let's go back to* Culpa *for a moment. What's the synopsis of this film?*

JM: The way I define it...it's about a young man completely - but in a disturbing way - involved in his faith. By accident he comes to know a prostitute, which results in an unexpected passionate encounter. It all takes place in a small town that's plagued by violence - there's a serial killer on the loose who kills young women. The idea was to bring together two people from totally different worlds into one room. The story really begins when they come to the guy's house, because then the two characters really start to reveal themselves. It was completely intentional to set it up as a tragedy. You can tell right from the beginning that someone is going to die as a result of this encounter. Actually, any audience member can tell from the start that he's going to kill her, because he's so repressed and she's so...overt.

SJS: *Except that earlier on, she looks like a temptress - she's mocking him, laughing at him - and seems just as capable as he is of doing something bad. Maybe even more so.*

JM: What she's capable of is making things up. You never know when she's telling the story of how she became a prostitute whether she's telling the truth, or making fun of him.

SJS: *What was the reception of* Culpa *in Cuba?*

JM: It appeared in various national festivals with a lot of success. People were surprised by it - they didn't think a Cuban would make something like this. In Camaguey, the Catholic Church wrote a letter of protest to Juan Antonio Garcia after he showed *Culpa* at the Annual Conference of Cuban Film Critics. But I said, "Look I don't believe in God. I can't be at fault!"

SJS: *At some points, the sex scenes look almost hardcore...*

JM: And so? What's your question?

SJS: *There's no question. I'm just mentioning it!*

JM: It's an homage to hardcore cinema. I know it's strong for anywhere, but it's time to change all that.

SJS: Molina's Test *(2001). This film seems much more advanced technically and stylistically than your previous works.*

JM: Yes, technically it's much better. But I feel like I'm missing the drive that I once had. It's not that it lacks the same passion, it's just that it took so long to finish. It took four years to make *Molina's Test*. By the time we got everything together to make it, I was less interested than I had been originally. To wake up your passion again is complicated. But I hope you can see from the film that it is passionate.

What I love most about *Test* is the scene in the bamboo forest when the sun is falling. It's just one little grove of bamboo. Behind it is a cafeteria! In general, filmmakers are absolutely too tied up with the idea of location. I learned that from Orson Welles...and from Jess Franco. You can shoot one thing in Switzerland, one thing in New York, cut them together and make it look like you did it all in one place. I've got that very clear: that you don't need to spend a lot of time and money searching for the perfect location.

SJS: *This film reminds me a lot of early David Cronenberg,* Shivers *(1975) and* Rabid *(1977) in particular. In the end, everybody ends up a zombie, but life just...goes on. It's very ambiguous in terms of what will happen once the story ends. What happens with the young couple after the film is over? It's interesting to think about: I guess life just keeps going for them.*

Jorge Molina

JM: But it's not the same - it's a different life that goes on. That's when their real life begins, at the end of the film. Until that moment they really didn't know each other. Everything had been very superficial...

SJS: Very romantic...

JM: But a modern romance. Not in the true spirit of romanticism. At one point, in the re-editing of the film, I began to talk with my editor and ask, "What story are we really telling here?" We reduced it down to this idea of a tragic love story: a couple that thinks life is one way, but it's really another way entirely... What interested me most was to leave the couple a pair of zombies - to zombify them. So that the audience would think, "Well, what's going to happen to them now?" And they would be clear that these people are not the same.

SJS: Do you think the film is pessimistic, or cynical? It begins with an attractive young couple both members of which claim they would die for each other. They go through an ordeal - maybe it's fantasy, maybe it's drug-induced, whatever it is - but at the end it turns out that they wouldn't die for each other. That might be taken to signify a loss of innocence - they no longer have any ideals about what love is - but also that this is the reality of relationships, that people are ultimately not willing to make the ultimate sacrifice. In that sense, the film seems de-romanticising.

JM: Yes, it is a de-romanticisation. But it doesn't necessarily reflect my own vision of love - I believe very much in love. But the film was intended to provoke these questions. If I make a totally romantic film, no one is going to care about it...nobody is going to want to see my version of Romeo and Juliet! It would be much more interesting if, at the end of the play, Juliet wakes up, sees Romeo dead and then says "Asshole! Why did you do such a stupid thing?" and then goes and has sex with the priest.

SJS: What was the thought behind the Chinese couple, which I'm sure people find very funny and unexpected in this context?

JM: I'm fascinated by China. I always have been. Hong Kong cinema is the best cinema in the world! So I was interested in the idea of making the villains Chinese: it's like an homage. I'm playing around with the classic stereotype of the Chinese villain, from Fu Manchu on. But to make that stereotype my own: to transform it through my own vision.

What bothers me now after making the film is that the two Chinese characters are too similar: I would have liked them to be more different. It would be much more interesting if they embodied a conflict between them. If, for example, when Mr. Wong says to the male protagonist, "I can prove to you that your love is not real," Madame Tsu had taken the opposite position. But you know, in hindsight... Maybe next time I'll have the foresight to make the two villains more complimentary, more interesting as a pair. That just shows me that I still have a lot to learn.

SJS: This couple, whom you refer to as villains, but who don't seem to me to be particularly villainous... they seem to offer the possibility of a kind of opening up of new realms of sexual experience. Both non-traditional sexualities and different partners. And that's very liberating. In this respect, Molina's Test is precisely the opposite of cynical.

JM: It's funny - in Cuba, when someone is opened up sexually, we call it being "de-avocadoed"! In that sense, yes, they aren't villains, because the young couple is fascinated by them and the possibilities they offer. They are opened up by all these new sensations. But that same source of knowledge brings suffering as well. They see that it's not all as romantic as they first thought.

SJS: But it might be more exciting... What was the budget for this film, by the way?

below:
An Escheresque view of Molina's already strange mise-en-scene.

right:
Jorge Molina.

JM: $3000 (US). I never saw a dime of it!

SJS: *Having discussed a few of your films in some depth, how would you characterise your directorial style?*

JM: I love that question! I don't really think that I have a style yet. I like certain shots in films. Often something will happen in a movie...I'll really love a certain image...and I'll say to myself, "I'm going to put this in mine. I'm going to transform it to make it my own, but it's going to be inspired by this shot." My films therefore are an accumulation of shots that I've liked in other films. Of course I take them beyond the original shot: I don't simply transpose the shot. That's how I would define my style if I had to: a love of reference. Cinema for me is totally referential. And certainly constantly watching films helps me make better ones. It's possible that I have a particular way of telling a story. But I think that's due to the sheer volume of images that I have stored away from other films, and that come out on their own, involuntarily. I have a storyboard that I almost never use. Whenever I'm on location I throw it away. I put the camera wherever my intuition tells me to put it. When the producer comes and says, "We have an hour to shoot twenty shots," I say, "Okay, I'm going to shoot it in five shots." And it comes out much more interesting in five shots than in twenty.

SJS: *So you prefer longer takes?*

JM: Long shots are fine as long as they don't get boring. What you have to know is where to cut...when to *stop* shooting. Films have to have a rhythm - the action can't ever stop.

SJS: *What is the next project that you have in mind, or that you are working on right now?*

Editor's Note:
This interview took place in New York City on 12 May 2002. I would like to extend my sincerest thanks to Ruth Goldberg for translating and assisting in all phases of the preparation of this joint chapter. My thanks as well - it goes without saying - to Jorge Molina, whose talent, spirit and love of cinema is immediately apparent to anyone who meets him.

JM: The next immediate project is a highly sexualised version of *Little Red Riding Hood*. With elements from *Lolita*. I'm going to shoot it on digital video. I don't want to do anything else on 35mm until I have the security that I can finish it correctly. I have on the shelf a project called "Panic in the Cathedral" that's sort of a variation on Jekyll and Hyde. That one I would really love to do. It is truly a horror film...sexual horror. The dark side of human nature - de-avocadoed! It would be a feature length film, a departure for me. I presented it to the Institute of Cinema in Cuba and they said it was very good but they're not interested in producing that "sort" of film. If I can get even minimal funds together, I'll do it. But I'll probably have to be the protagonist because I wouldn't be able to afford to pay the actors.

SJS: *You've done a lot of acting. How many films have you been in?*

JM: More than 90 shorts and 6 features. I'm the graduate of the International School of Film and Television that has been most filmed.

SJS: *What is your current position at the school?*

JM: I'm Head of the Department of the School called "Cultural Integration." I'm responsible for bringing in all the foreign professors, for creating a schedule of events so that we can be sure there is a rich life on campus. And to make sure that the students are exposed to what's happening culturally in Cuba. And I teach sometimes as well.

SJS: *Judging from the host of references and homages in your films, it would seem that your tastes are incredibly broad and varied, that you don't make firm distinctions between high and low cinema, between art and trash, etc. Is that accurate?*

JM: I agree with you totally. That comes through in my films. I learn more from bad films than from good films.

SJS: *Why is that?*

JM: The bad ones let you understand what you shouldn't do. But even in the bad films you sometimes see something involuntary on the part of the director that really amazes. And you think, "How can such a brilliant idea, such a brilliant shot, come out of this person with no talent." And that's when I ask myself, "What can I take from this?"

Part Two:
Films, Series, Cycles

Fantasmas del cine Mexicano: the 1930s horror film cycle of Mexico   93
- Gary D. Rhodes

The cosmic mill of Wolfgang Preiss: Giorgio Ferroni's *Mill of the Stone Women*   105
- David Del Valle

The "lost" horror film series: the Edgar Wallace *krimis*   111
- Ken Hanke

The exotic pontianaks   125
- Jan Uhde & Yvonne Uhde

Playing with genre: defining the Italian *giallo*   135
- Gary Needham

The Italian zombie film: from derivation to invention   161
- Donato Totaro

Austrian psycho killers & home invaders: the horror-thrillers *Angst* **&** *Funny Games*   175
- Jürgen Felix & Marcus Stiglegger

films, series, cycles

Fantasmas del cine Mexicano: the 1930s horror film cycle of Mexico

Gary D. Rhodes

Mexican cinema has long been famous for its horror films of the 1950s and 60s, particularly due to the familiar name of actor/director Abel Salazaar and the familiar masked face of horror film actor/wrestler of El Santo. Bizarre, atmospheric and sometimes silly, the films of that period possess a unique charm that continues to spawn books, articles, fan clubs, websites and even T-shirts. But the fandom which supports continued interest in those films, as well as the cinema scholars and academics that write about them, generally overlook the roots of horror in Mexican cinema: a cycle of some twelve movies produced in the 1930s, constituting probably the largest body of horror put out by any national cinema during this decade except for the United States. These films deserve an extended examination for many reasons beyond sheer numbers, however. They exhibit the work of some of the most gifted directors (e.g., Juan Bustillo Oro, Fernando de Fuentes) and onscreen talent (e.g., Cantinflas, Carlos Villarías) in Mexico at that time. They represent undeniable cinematic achievements in mood and *mise-en-scene*. And they also echo the sentiments and shifting attitudes of the Mexican people during a pivotal period in their country's history.

Beginnings

Horror films had actually been known in Mexico for many years before the country produced any of its own. For example, during the silent film era producer Germán Camus imported movies from various countries to screen in Mexican cities and towns. Among these were German Expressionist efforts like *The Cabinet of Dr. Caligari* (1919) and *The Golem* (1920). Mexican audiences of the 1920s also saw various US horror films, including *The Phantom of the Opera* (1925) with Lon Chaney. Indeed, most films of any genre that Mexicans viewed during this decade were Hollywood product. By 1928, ninety percent of all films screened in Mexico and Latin America as a whole were imported from the US.[1]

However, the sound film era created problems for a Hollywood used to exporting its product to Mexico. Subtitles were technically possible, but illiteracy rates in Mexico were very high and thus eliminated that option. And yet, the early years of talking pictures were among the least productive for the Mexican cinema. The first Mexican sound film was *Más Fuerte que el Deber* (*Stronger Than Duty*, 1930), but it was one of only eight films made in the country between 1930-32, presumably due to financial reasons as well as a lack of trained sound technicians.[2] Recognising the country's need for product, Hollywood studios began making Spanish-language films.

The most famous of these attempts is Universal Studios' *Dracula* (1931). After the crew for the English-language film directed by Tod Browning finished each day, another crew came onto the same sets at night to film an alternative version in Spanish. Carlos Villarías portrayed Count Dracula, and Lupita Tovar portrayed Mina Harker. Both actors would soon make their way from Hollywood to Mexican film studios, each garnering a degree of renown from the horror film in which they had starred.

While praised by many modern film critics for its visual style, fluid cinematography, and erotic imagery, the Spanish-language *Dracula* was not a major hit with

opposite: Pablo (Joaquín Busquets), his disfigured face hidden by a hideous mask, spies on her beloved Angélica in **El misterio del rostro pálido** (Juan Bustillo Oro, 1935).

[1] Hershfield, J. and D. Maciel (eds) (1999) *Mexico's Cinema: A Century of Film and Filmmakers*. Wilmington, Delaware: Scholarly Resources, 2.

[2] Riera, E.G. (1998) *Breve Historia del Cine Mexicano: Primer Siglo, 1897-1997*. Zapopan, Mexico: Instituto Mexicano de Cinematografía, 78.

Mexican audiences in 1931. Villarias had overacted in the lead role, but even more problematic was a pervading air of unreality, caused not by the supernatural storyline but by the conflicting regional accents of the Spanish-language actors. The novelty of sound film and the geographical immobility of many Mexican viewers meant that many had never even heard some of the dialects used in the film. Director George Melford, who was not Spanish and used an interpreter on the Hollywood set, could scarcely have realized this difficulty. And the problem that plagued Dracula was one repeated in other Spanish-language films of the period.[3]

During the silent era, competition from imported product and the difficulties of indigenous movie production had kept the Mexican film industry from emerging as a major force. But Hollywood's Spanish-language movies helped to spur the talking era of Mexican film production into motion. Though the problem of mixed dialects in the US-made films existed, some Spanish-speaking cast and crew members learned a great deal from their experiences in Hollywood, enabling them to contribute their experience and knowledge to Mexican-made films. For example, Lupita Tovar went to Mexico to star in the sound film *Santa* (1932). Though by no means a perfect movie when compared to the technological standards of Hollywood in 1932, *Santa* proved very successful at the Mexican box-office. More talkies went into production, with the Mexican film industry quickly growing during the 1930s. For example, though only seven sound movies were produced in Mexico in 1932, the number increased to 21 in 1933, 23 in 1934, 22 in 1935, 24 in 1936, 38 in 1937, 55 in 1938, and 36 in 1939.[4]

It was during this period of growth that the Mexican horror film cycle began. However, to speak of these films collectively risks overlooking the stylistic gulf between the earliest horror films and those that followed. The first three - *La Llorona* (*The Crying Woman*, 1933), *El Fantasma del Convento* (*Phantom of the Convent*, 1934), and *Dos Monjes* (*Two Monks*, 1934) - represent very different filmmaking styles and narrative forms than the subsequent movies in the cycle. Given that they *were* the first ones, and also that they appear at an early stage of major sound film production in Mexico, this fact is hardly surprising. The early efforts within a given narrative film form often illustrate a kind of generic indeterminacy; until the visual and storytelling codes in a genre crystallize, filmmakers must experiment with both form and content. The classical Hollywood style - meaning the narrative, visual, and editing conventions of Hollywood studios - clearly influenced this trio of films, almost certainly a result of the dominance of US silent films in Mexico. At the same time, however, these three films seem essentially untouched by the influence of 1930s Hollywood *horror* films.

Instead, *La Llorona*, *El Fantasma del Convento*, and *Dos Monjes* act as an important and fascinating barometer of the Mexican cultural experience of the early 1930s. However different in some respects the films are from one another, they each share a debt to the reality of Mexico and Mexican life as it existed at the time. For example, during the 1933 production of *La Llorona*, the revolutionary spirit in Mexico - which had burst forth in a major way during 1910 - was weak and dying. The Mexican Constitution of 1917 had created a kind of peace in the country, but also spawned a series of political leaders more interested in personal gain than in effecting improvements in their country.[5] Those politicians caused years of discontent among the Mexican people.

Pivotal to the Mexican political landscape of the 1920s and early 1930s was Plutarco Elías Calles. Performing a variety of governmental tasks during the twenties, his power grew at the time of the assassination of Alvaro Obregón, the unopposed presidential candidate of 1928. Rather than attempt to become president himself, Calles preferred to maintain his position as principal leader of the official state party, the Partido Nacional Revolucionario. As head of the PNR, he effectively controlled Mexico from 1928 to 1934, pulling the strings of a series of puppet presidents. Historian Robert E. Quirk claims that, "...by the early 1930s, the revolutionary spirit seemed to have fallen prey to the corruption and cynicism of Calles's strong-arm rule."[6]

Life for the everyday Mexican in the early 1930s was harmed not only by the political grip of the PNR, but also by wretched economic conditions. The Great Depression devastated Mexico, particularly in the years 1931-32. Important exports like oil and food diminished, and economic problems were exacerbated by the US deportation of over 400,000 Mexicans and Mexican-Americans back to Mexico.[7] These financial woes, together with anxieties over the political situation,

---

[3] Mora, C. (1982) *Mexican Cinema: Reflections of a Society, 1896-1980.* Berkeley: University of California Press, 32. See Chapter 6 of Skal, D. (1990) *Hollywood Gothic: The Tangled Web of Dracula From Novel to Stage to Screen* (New York: W.W. Norton) for an in-depth examination of the 1931 Spanish-language *Dracula*.

[4] *Ibid*, 146-52.

[5] Kirkwood, B. (2000) *The History of Mexico.* Westport, CT: Greenwood, 155.

[6] Quirk, R. (1971) *Mexico.* Englewood Cliffs, NJ: Prentice-Hall, 102.

[7] Hamnett, B. (1999) *A Concise History of Mexico.* Cambridge: Cambridge University Press, 237-38.

caused disappointment, malaise, and confusion among the Mexican people.

But these feelings also provided a rich cauldron of emotions for the filmmakers of *La Llorona*, *El Fantasma del Convento*, and *Dos Monjes*. All three films feature breakdowns or potential breakdowns of trust between family members and/or friends. Deceit and distrust run rampant, creating situations where characters must (or should) call into question their best friend, their wife, and their own grandmother (literally). Loyalties are displaced, and the one who implicitly says, "trust me" simply cannot be trusted. These themes mirror Mexicans' frustrations with their economy and their government.

Directed by Ramón Peón, *La Llorona* tells the story of the "Crying Woman", a character from Hispanic folklore who mourns her dead child. At least one critic has noted the similarity to D.W. Griffith's *Intolerance* (1916) in *La Llorona*'s narrative framework, though Peón's film is certainly less epic in scale and less complex in structure.[8] A modern framing story shows the kidnapping of a young boy, the son of the respected Dr. Cortés (Ramón Pereda); the cloaked villain turns out to be the boy's own grandmother on his father's side. A flashback to an earlier *La Llorona* encounter comes when Cortés's father-in-law reads him a tale from an old book. In it, a woman kills her bastard child and then commits suicide while her lover and suitor fight a duel; their costumes suggest an Elizabethan-era setting. The second flashback comes when Dr. Cortés finds a book belonging to the villainous grandmother. In what appears to be more traditional Mexican costumes, a woman commits suicide after her baby is stolen from her. The commonality between all these women is an Aztec-style ring they all wear, as well as the fact that their damned spirits visibly rise from their dead bodies.

In its themes and depictions of gender, *La Llorona* is a fascinating film. It begins ominously with the sound of a woman wailing as a man collapses and dies, an act that leads Dr. Cortés (who examines the body) into the world of the "crying woman." Close-ups of the man's hand, with his fingers slowly clutching inward, set up the recurring image of the hand as a symbol of death; later in the film, the hand of the crying woman is shown in close-up on several occasions. And in her various incarnations, she causes (or at least attempts to cause) death and mourning. Rather than the typical 1930s Hollywood horror film depiction, the females of *La Llorona* (with the exception of Dr. Cortés's wife) are portrayed as dangerous, even evil.

Visually, *La Llorona* features both clichéd and unique imagery. Able cinematography and mobile camerawork is complimented by the frequent use of music on the soundtrack. Though seemingly untouched by the influence of 1930s Hollywood horrors, the film does show the influence of silent works such as *The Bat* (1926) and *The Cat and The Canary* (1927). For example, the villain (dressed very similarly to the Bat) uses hidden passageways to reach Cortés's father-in-law, whom she murders. But such influences hardly detract from *La Llorona*'s more unusual imagery. For example, a sense of irony pervades the birthday celebration from which Cortés's child is kidnapped, its table, chairs, and cake all designed as four-leaf clovers - generally signifiers of good luck. And the three times the "Crying Woman" dies in the three stories, a superimposed ghost rises up from the corpse and walks away. In each case, the ghost walks with somewhat jerky movements, creating a particularly eerie effect. The first occasion

above:
The Indian Princess Ana Xicoténcatl (Adriana Lamar) in **La Llorona**, holding the stone knife with which she kills his son and herself, after learning that her Spanish lover - and father of the child - has married another woman (Ramón Peón, 1933).

[8] Hardy, P. (ed.) (1995), *The Overlook Film Encyclopedia: Horror*. Woodstock: Overlook Press, 56.

Mexico

even features the ghost taking to flight across the night sky, causing the duelling lovers to cease their fight. This ethereal image is one of the most memorable in Mexican horror film history.

Fernando de Fuentes, one of the three screenwriters of *La Llorona*, followed his work on the film by directing *El Fantasma del Convento* on location at a Teotzotlan monastery. The narrative begins in the dark of night; a shadowy figure directs a trio of wandering young friends to an old monastery for their evening's shelter. As an old monk escorts them to their rooms, tension between the three becomes obvious. Cristina (Marta Ruel) has plans to seduce Alfonso (Enrique del Campo), the close friend of her naive husband Eduardo (Carlos Villatoro). At dinner, Cristina slyly makes clear her intentions to Alfonso; medium shots of her and Alfonso (on screen right) are juxtaposed with shots of her and Eduardo (on screen left), visually and geographically reinforcing her narrative placement between the two friends. The three have little chance for conversation at dinner, as a number of silent monks are eating at the same table. The skeletal hand of one of them can be seen extending from his sleeve. At the head of the table is the monk who escorted the three inside; he tells a story about one of the prior monks who seduced the wife of another man. At death, the wicked monk's spirit returned to his room at the monastery, unable to move peaceably into the next world.

Despite the tale he hears, Alfonso seems to fall under Cristina's spell later that evening. While wandering around the monastery, he pauses when he hears groans coming from behind a barricaded cell. After entering, he sees a corpse whose hand drips blood and moves slowly, pointing to a diary. It is the deceitful and disloyal monk discussed at dinner. Alfonso then sees his own face on the monk's body, a doubling that frightens him into unconsciousness. When he awakes the next morning, he no longer considers having a sexual tryst with Cristina. Reunited with the married couple, Alfonso discovers that the monastery has become a tourist attraction. The three learn that no monks have lived in the building for years, and that their bodies exist only as mummies; the monks of the prior evening had evidently been spectres.

From the standpoint of a horror narrative, the film offers a fascinating group of characters. For example, the monks are not counterparts to the supernatural figures in US horror films of the 1930s. While ominous in appearance, they are actually present not for the sake of causing conflict and fright (as in the case of Hollywood's supernatural characters, e.g., Dracula of 1931, the Mummy of 1932, and Dracula's Daughter of 1936), but to prevent the potential horror and conflict stemming from Cristina. Similar to *La Llorona*, it is the female who is the villain here. As much as anything else, Cristina signifies the greed and wanton behaviour that consumed many of the by-then institutionalized Mexican revolutionaries, aparticularly Calles.

El Fantasma del Convento exudes an atmosphere of dread, decay, and death. Rather than being punctuated with moments of high and low intensity, an uneasy mood is effectively created and sustained throughout. The constancy of mood is coupled with a very slow tempo. But rather than becoming listless, the pacing creates a deliberate and brooding quality rarely matched by 1930s horror films of any national cinema. Actor's movements and expressions, editing style, and camera motion together function to achieve this effect. The unmoving shadow of a bat on the monastery wall, the deliberate movements of the dead monk's hand dripping blood as it slowly reaches for its diary, and the methodical camera pan of the mummies at the film's conclusion are all fascinating examples of this pacing.

Throughout the film, *mise-en-scene* reinforces the feelings of dread engendered by the slow pace. While string music plays early in the narrative, the age and decay of

below:
The supernatural atmosphere of the monastery in **El fantasma del convento** (Fernando de Fuentes, 1934) terrifies Alfonso (Enrique del Campo), Cristina (Martha Ruel) and Eduardo (Carlos Villatoro).

above:
Javier (Carlos Villatoro) is tortured by delusion in the climactic scene of **Dos monjes** (Juan Bustillo Oro, 1934).

the monastery becomes more and more obvious. Moving camerawork reveals ancient hallways and we soon see the minimal amounts of furniture in the trio's bedrooms. Costumes create additional anonymity for the monks, as they are all dressed in the same robes and all are silent at dinner save one. The look of the film thus shares the brooding and direful quality of its mood.

Juan Bustillo Oro's film *Dos Monjes* also represents a fascinating use of *mise-en-scene*, but one more directly inspired by the works of another national cinema. The film borrows heavily from German Expressionism, at least in its visual sensibilities. Exaggerated makeup, deep shadows, abrupt camera movements, and distorted angles mark the film. Whether Oro and cinematographer Agustín Jiménez were referring directly to the silent German films that they had seen years before in Mexico (e.g., *The Cabinet of Dr. Caligari* or *Schatten* [*Warning Shadows*, 1923]), or were in part inspired by the *mise-en-scene* of the Spanish-language *Dracula* is unknown, but the result was definitely a clear adoption of the Expressionist vision.

The narrative of *Dos Monjes* concerns a love triangle in which two friends, Juan (Víctor Urruchúa) and Javier (Carlos Villatoro), both seek the affections of Ana (Magda Haller). After she is shot and killed, they become monks. An unusual perceptual effect is created by the two different versions the audience sees of Ana's demise. First the audience witnesses the story from Javier's point of view, in which Juan accidentally shoots Ana after trying to charm her away from Javier. In his version of the story, he is costumed in white and Juan in black. Then the same story is repeated through Juan's eyes; in it, he and Ana were estranged lovers, reunited by fate at Javier's house. They decide not to re-ignite their affections, but unfortunately Javier believes otherwise and accidentally shoots Ana. In Juan's story, he is the character dressed in white and Javier is dressed in black. The film ends with Javier suffering from ominous visions while getting closer and closer to death.

Dos Monjes was innovative in its storyline, with its complex use of narrative point of view anticipating films like Welles's

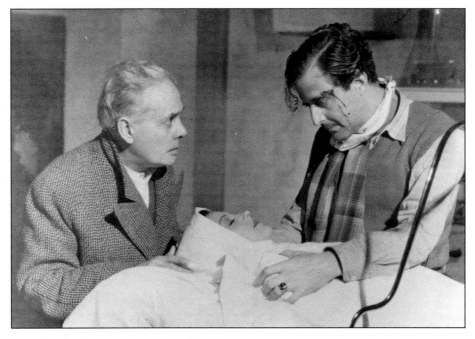

right:
Dr. Monroy (Manuel Noriega) and Dr. del Valle (René Cardona) look for signs of life in Alicia (Esther Fernández) after defeating the mad Dr. Renán in **El baúl macabro** (Miguel Zacarías, 1936).

Citizen Kane (1941) and Kurosawa's *Rashomon* (1950). Thematically, the story conveys ideas like distrust and deceit, which would have resonated strongly with Mexican audiences. At the same time, the film features a ponderous pace and sometimes juvenile dialogue that keep it from reaching the aesthetic heights of *El Fantasma del Convento*; as Mexican film historian Federico Dávalos Orozco has said of the film's experimental style, "...the public's disapproval was evident."[9]

Despite the unenthusiastic reception of *Dos Monjes*, the Mexican public of the period apparently had an interest in horror films, as many more were made between 1935 and 1939. But these films were very different than their three predecessors; though morbid and at times grisly, they do not reflect the same kind of cultural malaise and uneasiness as films like *La Llorona* and *El Fantasma del Convento*. The narrative differences are due in part to the changing political and economic landscape of Mexico, in which a degree of trust was restored between the people and the politicians.

Explorations

The election of PNR candidate Lázaro Cárdenas during the presidential campaign of 1934 brought major changes to the country. Rather than becoming yet another puppet, Cárdenas gained the loyalty of the army and moved to exile Calles. As historian Robert E. Quirk has noted, "...for the first time in Mexican history a strong populist executive committed his administration to effective social reform."[10] Great enthusiasm surrounded Cárdenas's various achievements, which included the restoration of religious peace, the remodelling of the PNR into a more populist party, the creation of a new labour federation, and the engineering of various industrial transformations.[11] As a result of these and other reforms, the people of Mexico did not generally feel the same kind of despondency as they had before Cárdenas's rise to power.

While reflecting these changing attitudes, from 1935-39 Mexican horror films also feature a far stronger influence from Hollywood horror films. The impetus for this might have been due to Mexican filmmakers viewing US product rather more than the everyday Mexican audience member, who likely had not seen the sound horror films of Hollywood. But more importantly, the narrative modes that dominated US horror at the time were readily adaptable to Mexican films made after Calles's control had ended. Generally positive and clear-cut story resolutions, frequent comic relief, and a greater emphasis on science gone wrong than on the supernatural - these aspects of the US horror film provided narrative prisms through which Mexican filmmakers could examine the changing sensibilities of their own country.

[9] Hershfield, 27.

[10] Quirk, 103.

[11] Suchlicki, J. (1996) *Mexico: From Montezuma to NAFTA, Chiapas, and Beyond.* Washington: Brassey's, 126; 128-30.

fantasmas del cine Mexicano

above:
The monster (Raúl Urquijo) attacks Sóstenes (Leopoldo Chato Ortín); on the left, Margarita (Consuelo Frank) takes care of Dr. Mont (Ramón Armengod) who has been knocked out by the creature in **El superloco** (Juan José Segura, 1936).

For example, the use of science and an emphasis on man rather than supernatural forces were major narrative components that Mexican horror films borrowed from their Hollywood counterparts. Though standout exceptions like Browning's *Dracula* and Freund's *The Mummy* (1932) exist, US horror cinema of the 1930s was mainly obsessed with science, whether in conflict with God (e.g., 1931's *Frankenstein*, 1933's *The Invisible Man*, 1935's *Bride of Frankenstein*), or as a tool for personal gain (e.g., 1935's *Mad Love* and *The Raven*), or as part of the evolutionary process (e.g., 1932's *Island of Lost Souls* and *Murders in the Rue Morgue*). In all of these examples, and in many others that could be given, the driving force is the use of scientists in the horror film narrative.

Much like their US inspirations, the scientists in Mexican horror films generally meet their doom after pursuing some life-long obsession. *El Misterio del Rostro Pálido* (*The Mystery of the Ghastly Face*, 1935) features a scientist (Carlos Villarías) who disfigures his own son due to an ill-fated experiment, and then kills those who discover his secret. Dr. del Vialle (Ramón Pereda) in *El Baúl Macabro* (*The Macabre Trunk*, 1936) dies alongside his wife after spending the entire film killing a series of young women. Dr. Dyenis (Carlos Villarías) in *El Superloco* (*The Crazy Nut*, 1936) dies when his own ape throws him out of a window after seeing the doctor menace the heroine. The insane Dr. Duarte (Miguel Arenas) in *La Herencia Macabra* (*The Macabre Legacy*, 1939) injects his wife's lover with a disfiguring virus. The use of science in *Los Muertos Hablan* (*The Dead Speak*, 1935) - which features a scientist who believes that the last image a person sees is frozen on their eye like a photograph - also becomes subjugated for personal gain.

These Mexican efforts also share another similarity with Hollywood horror: *thematic uncertainty*. The mad scientist films of both countries feature chaos created by a particular individual. Life is disrupted for those around him, as well as (potentially, at least) for society itself. Upheavals occur as the traditional parameters of acceptability are violated. Religion and the law are ignored or else challenged outright. And at the film's conclusion, normalcy is restored. But it is

Mexico

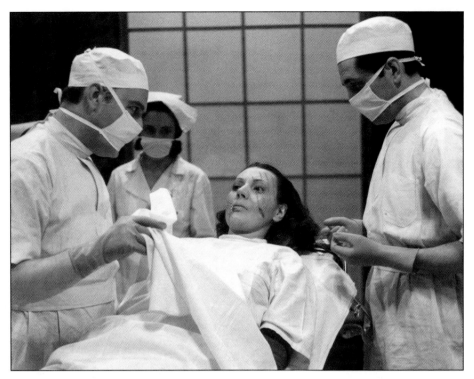

right:
Dr. Duarte (Miguel Arenas, left), and his assistant, Luis (Luis Aldás, right), look at a disfigured Rosa - Duarte's treacherous wife (Consuelo Frank) - in **Herencia macabra** (José Bohr, 1939).

restored at the heavy cost of all that has occurred narratively, and this restoration is not always a clear and unequivocal endorsement of the status quo. The deaths of the Frankenstein monster in *Frankenstein* (1931) and the giant ape in *King Kong* (1933), for example, hardly suggest that the rule of man is perfect. Goodness prevails, but what that means is typically not explored. Instead, after the villain is vanquished the credits quickly appear and the film is over. Films in the US such as *Dracula*, *Murders in the Rue Morgue*, and *The Raven* end very quickly after the foe is destroyed, with the greatest majority of these films' running time devoted to a detailing of his power and control. The same could be said of a film like *El Baúl Macabro* or *El Superloco*.

Other characters in these mad scientist efforts also echo Hollywood. The depictions of women in *La Llorona* and *El Fantasma del Convento* illustrate wicked traits, but by *El Misterio del Rostro Pálido* a different kind of major female role emerges. The female characters in this film and in subsequent mad scientist movies are stereotypically good in intention but weak in stamina. They are the quarry of the villain, and must be valiantly rescued by a hero. The heroines fit very much the narrative conventions of their US compeers.

The Mexican horror film also adopts the sympathetic but horrifying creature of the US horror film, the "freak" of society. Dr. Frankenstein's eponymous monster and the title characters in Tod Browning's *Freaks* (1932) are examples from the 1930s, possessing some of the qualities of Lon Chaney, Sr. in his silent era films *The Hunchback of Notre Dame* (1923), *The Phantom of the Opera* (1925), and *The Unknown* (1927). The horror stems from his appearance, but in turn this horror spawns sympathy. Such an uneasy combination of emotions proved important in the US horror film, just as it would in Mexican horrors like *El Misterio del Rostro Pálido*, where the scientist's disfigured son hides his face behind a waxen mask and strolls through the family estate wearing a cape and playing sad music on his violin. His ghostly mask peers in through the window of the home, anticipating a similar image in the US film *Scared to Death* (1946). And in a clear and poignant reference to *The Phantom of the Opera*, the son's mask is removed by the film's heroine. His ugly face is exposed to her, and then to himself when he stares at length into a mirror. After the heroine faints, he carries her limp body through the estate. He finally falls to his death after running along the top of a mountainous cliff, his accursed mask lying beside his lifeless body.

fantasmas del cine Mexicano

Flourishes

On a lighter note, Mexican horror films of this era also feature a good deal of comedy. Much to the chagrin of many modern viewers, US horror movies of the 1920s and 30s regularly employed comic relief. Charles Gerrard in *Dracula*, Robert Armstrong in the *The Most Dangerous Game* (1932), Maude Eburne in *The Vampire Bat* (1933), Charlie Ruggles in *Murders in the Zoo* (1933), Ted Healy in *Mad Love* - all of these actors provide that element of humour, just as, e.g., Creighton Hale had in *The Cat and the Canary* the prior decade. If we can believe the reviews printed in industry trades, fan magazines, and newspapers of the period, the original audiences of these films much appreciated the comedy as a counterpoint to the horror scenes, gaining a modicum of relief from the tension they felt.

If anything, the sheer amount of comic relief in several Mexican horror films exceeds that present in Hollywood product. Despite the horror framework of *El Superloco*, for example, much of the film's running time is spent following a comical drunk (Leopoldo Ortín) who is friends with one of the scientists investigating the mad Dr. Dyenis. More notably, *El Signo de la Muerte* (*The Sign of Death*, 1939) features a comical Aztec detective story with a heavy use of low-key lighting. Chano Urueta directs Cantinflas, the master of Mexican comedy, in the wild and humorous story by Salvador Novo. From offering crazy expressions to dressing in drag, Cantinflas delivers a wonderful performance. Much as horror in the US by 1939 was sometimes dominated by comedy (e.g., *The Cat and The Canary*, *The Gorilla*), the same had happened with *El Signo de la Muerte* in Mexico.

Though the comic relief is sometimes visual, these mad scientist films are heavily laden with dialogue. To be sure, the advent of the talkie required films to talk, and to talk extensively. At the same time, a sharp contrast can be seen from an early film in the cycle like *El Fantasma del Convento*, which features a relatively limited use of dialogue, and in the series of mad scientist films that follow it, which often feature an overabundance of dialogue. *Los Muertos Hablan*, *El Superloco*, and particularly *Herencia Macabro* are built far more on dialogue than mood, for example.

In tandem with the overuse of dialogue is the lack of special effects in these Mexican films. The US horror film of the 1930s was heavily dependent on these two factors. Some movies would hardly have been possible without a major use of special effects, such as *The Invisible Man* and *King Kong* (1933), but others more narratively aligned with the Mexican horror films were also dependent on such effects. The electrical devices of Kenneth Strickfaden in films like *Frankenstein* and *Bride of Frankenstein* are among the most prevalent images of the US horror film, influencing the *mise-en-scene* of most other Hollywood mad scientist films of the period. The mad scientists of Mexican cinema, however, make little use of elaborate laboratory sets. Labs they do work in, but ones more comparable to the lowest budget Hollywood horrors: little in the way of equipment, sparking or otherwise. For example, the labs in films like *El Misterio del Rostro Pálido*, *Los Muertos Hablan*, *El Baúl Macabro*, and *El Superloco* are drab and appear almost empty. And the laboratories, as well as the sets of most other locations in these films, feature a generally high key lighting style that is completely removed from the German Expressionist-inspired lighting of most Hollywood horror, or even of an earlier Mexican film like *Dos Monjes*. Perhaps the only standout moment for sets in the films after *Dos Monjes* comes in *El Misterio del Rostro Pálido*. Though not expressionistic by any means, the scientist's home features a fascinating art-deco design, but one that is limited by a cinematography that rarely highlights its uniqueness.

Special makeup effects and costumes are also at a minimum in the Mexican

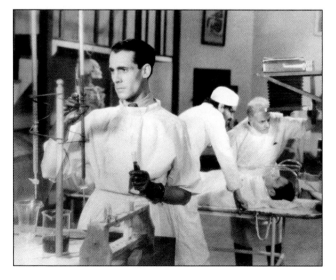

below:
Eduardo Molina (Julián Soler) prepares some formula, while Simón (Isidro D'Olace) and Dr. Jiménez (Manuel Noriega) take a picture of the pupils of a corpse's eyes in **Los muertos hablan** (Gabriel Soria, 1935).

horror cycle. However much a film like *El Misterio del Rostro Pálido* draws on *The Phantom of the Opera*, the character Pablo's makeup is not only far less effective than Lon Chaney's, it is also far less adventurous. He certainly appears different than before his face is harmed, but only to a minor degree. And yet this is the major example of makeup usage in these films to create a "monster." There are no Frankensteinian monster makeups, and even the mad scientist costumes are just standard laboratory coats; the more unusual appearances of, say, a Dr. Mirakle (Bela Lugosi) in *Murders in the Rue Morgue* are nowhere to be found. As with the near-total absence of special effects in general, the lack of makeup effects and more outlandish costumes was likely a result of the extremely low budgets of the Mexican horror films.

Nevertheless, isolated scenes in these films feature a grisly quality unmatched by their US counterparts. For example, the standout horror image of *El Misterio del Rostro Pálido* is certainly not Pablo's disfigured face, but a bizarre native ceremony which he witnesses with his father. Dancers circle a fire as the camera pans down from the drummers' faces to reveal that they are beating on human skulls to keep rhythm. In *El Baúl Macabro*, the police find the "macabre trunk" and have to place scarves over their noses and mouths as soon as it is opened; the decaying flesh inside is not shown, but its putridity is made clear from the character reactions. The most disturbing image in the film, however, is perhaps the goriest one in the entire era of the Mexican horror film. When a bum opens a sack discarded by Dr. del Vialle, he unknowingly pulls out the severed arm of one of the scientist's young female victims.

In addition to their more gruesome segments, the Mexican mad scientist films offer other memorable moments that break from the otherwise dialogue-laden visual plainness. Pablo in cape and mask playing his violin at night in *El Misterio del Rostro Pálido*. Photographic close-ups of a single eye in *Los Muertos Hablan*. Mourning of the dead viewed through a funeral wreath in *La Herencia Macabra*. A wizard-like figure at an altar in the moonlight of *El Signo de la Muerte*. Beautifully haunting images amidst numerous forgettable scenes.

However forgettable or unforgettable, the images in these Mexican films generally ignored one constant of Hollywood horror: stars. The importance of star personalities to the US horror film of the 1930s was pivotal, to the degree that audiences of the time and historians in the present sometimes use them to establish generic identity. Films like *The Black Room* (1935) become identified as *horror* films at least in part because of their association with Boris Karloff. The same could be said of *Murder By Television* (1935) with Bela Lugosi, or *The Sphinx* (1933) with Lionel Atwill. The reverse case is a film like *The Most Dangerous Game* (1932), one that bears many narrative commonalities to the horror film but is not always recognized as such, due mainly to its lack of a horror personality. The coterie of US horror actors in the early to mid-1930s (Karloff, Lugosi, and Atwill chief among them) proved important to genre identification and thus to marketing.

But the construction and repetitive use of horror personalities in Mexico never really occurred in the 1930s. We might mention Ramón Pereda, who appeared in both *La Llorona* and *El Baúl Macabro*, but in the former film he stars as not the villain but the hero. Carlos Villarías of Hollywood's Spanish-language *Dracula* represents the closest the Mexican cinema had to a Karloff or Lugosi. He appeared as the villain in *El Misterio del Rostro Pálido*, in *El Superloco*, and in Juan Bustillo Oro's *Nostradamus* (1936). Perhaps he was chosen for these films because of his work in *Dracula*; regardless, no evidence has as yet been unearthed to suggest he was a box-office draw for audiences in anything like the way Karloff or Lugosi was, or that his appearance in a film helped mark its genre identity as horror. But in a sense the lack of the Mexican cinema's creation of horror stars works to its advantage. *El Fantasma del Convento* plays with a particularly eerie and elegiac quality that would be minimized or absent had it been the vehicle for a star carrying the intertextual remains of prior films and the extratextual baggage of fan magazine articles and the like.

Horror stars or not, the first Mexican horror film cycle ended in 1939. But as the decade itself ended, Mexican cinema blazed a more exciting trail than ever before. The forties brought on what is often referred to as a "Golden Age" of cinema.[12] The rise of the *ranchera* and *rumbera* genres in Mexican film (genres which were never explored by the Hollywood studio system) coincided with the rise of actors like Joaquín Pardavé, Pedro Armendáriz,

---

[12] Hershfield, 33.

above:
Dr. Gallardo (Carlos Orellana) is also the sinister hooded priest, descendent of Quetzalcóatl, that intends to revive human sacrifice rituals in **El signo de la muerte** (Chano Urueta, 1939).

and many others. At the forefront of this new talent was Cantinflas; though hardly known at the time of *El Signo de la muerte*, his film *Ahí está el detalle* (*That is the Point*) scored internationally in 1940 and propelled him to a career of major importance. With popular onscreen talent like Cantinflas came a flurry of new producers and directors. All of these various elements - as well as historical factors such as World War II - combined to create an enormous flowering of fascinating Mexican movies in the 40s and beyond.

The Mexican horror film did not disappear after *El Signo de la muerte*, as several were certainly produced during the 1940s. But it would not be until the late 1950s that horror returned as a major force. These came in the form of US and British-inspired efforts; vampires (notably Fernando Méndez's 1957 *El Vampiro*), monsters, werewolves, and even a remake of *La Llorona* (directed by René Cardona in 1959) filled the screens. Horror also came in the guise of El Santo and unlikely cross-genre efforts that combined monsters and wrestling. The horror film had clearly returned, but in a vastly different manner than existed in the 1930s cycle.

And so what can we make of the Mexican horror films of the 30s? Rather than what would at first appear to be merely a body of works inspired by Hollywood horror, the films in question provide many fascinating moments, and at times classic stories (like *El Fantasma del Convento*) that are essentially untouched by external influence. Even when checkered with the stamp of Hollywood by the mid-to-late thirties, the Mexican horrors still emerge sporting unique enunciative techniques and visual motifs. They are often more subtle in *mise-en-scene* than their US counterparts, and occasionally more grisly in narrative execution. For modern viewers, they represent an untapped reserve of classic horror. For scholars, they are basically uncharted territory to explore; their landscape at present yields important insight into the Mexican experience of the time. But maps still need to be sketched in this important and overlooked cycle of 1930s horror to understand more fully what they have to offer.

The cosmic mill of Wolfgang Preiss: Giorgio Ferroni's *Mill of the Stone Women*

David Del Valle

Immortality is a clock that never runs down, a mandala that revolves eternally like the heavens. Thus the cosmic aspect returns with interest and compound interest.
- CG Jung, *Psychology and Alchemy* (1944)

Welcome to the Mill

In 1956, Riccardo Freda's groundbreaking *I Vampiri* gave rise to the Golden Age of Italian *fantascienza*, with masterworks like Mario Bava's *La Maschera del demonio* (aka *Black Sunday*, 1960) and Antonio Margheriti's *Danza macabra* (aka *Castle of Blood*, 1963), not to mention Freda's own magnum opus, *L'Orribile segreto del dottor Hichcock* (*The Terror of Dr Hichcock*, 1962) to follow. Among the more intriguing results of this influence would be Giorgio Ferroni's *Il mulino delle donne di pietra* (*Mill of the Stone Women*, 1960). An obsessively romantic homage to the expressionistic horror films of the silent era, its bravura set-piece - a life-size musical clock of historic statues in strange poses - creates a compelling dialectic of the animate/inanimate.

Derived from Pieter Van Weigen's short story of the same title from his collection "Flemish Tales," the image of the water mill recurs in Scandinavian and Finnish mythology as a cosmological symbol of the three realms of heaven, earth and hell. One may postulate that Van Weigen was influenced by a poem based on the legend of two giant women and the mill of Grottasongr - the mill being a convenient trope figuring prominently in the creation myths of the author's native land.

Mill of the Stone Women evolved from a tradition in cinema that captured our imagination as early as 1923 with Paul Leni's *Das Wachsfigurenkabinett* (*Waxworks*), in which a wax effigy of Jack the Ripper magically comes to life in order to kill. Maurice Tourneur's *While Paris Sleeps* (1923) has a sculptor (played by Lon Chaney) who is also a madman and a would-be killer. The advent of the 1930s with its own Golden Age of horror brought us *Mystery of the Wax Museum* (1933), *Mad Love* (1935) and *Midnight at Madame Tussaud's* (1936). Each of these films focuses on the theme of corpses being displayed as works of art; *Mad Love* is the most delirious of the trio, with a pale and bald Peter Lorre longing for his Galatea.

This tradition would reach an epiphany in 1953 with the introduction of the 3-D process in Warner Bros.' *House of Wax*, starring Vincent Price. One of the film's most macabre moments is repeated shot for shot in *Mill of the Stone Women* as we witness the figures of wax weep tears of their own substance while they perish in the flames. This image of the corpse viewed as a work of art would also play in a black comedy from Roger Corman entitled *A Bucket of Blood* (1959), culminating with the sado-masochistic *Crucible of Terror* (1971) and most recently *M.D.C. - Maschera di cera* (*The Wax Mask*, 1997), the latter of which comes full circle in paying a most obvious homage to both *Mystery of the Wax Museum* and *House of Wax* from the viewpoint of the generation obliged to Dario Argento.[1] Films such as these, which are invested with replicas of the human face in all of its incarnations and fallacies, drives us deep into a mythic nerve of fear that binds us together as human beings fearful of what lurks beneath the myriad of masks we wear in everyday life.

opposite: Lionel Atwill menaces Fay Wray in a gag shot offset in **Mystery of the Wax Museum** (Warner Bros 1933).

[1] Cf. Steven Jay Schneider, "Murder as Art/The Art of Murder: Aestheticizing Violence in Modern Cinematic Horror." In *Dark Thoughts: Philosophic Reflections on Cinematic Horror*, ed. Steven Jay Schneider and Daniel Shaw (Lanham, MD: Scarecrow Press, 2003), 173-96.

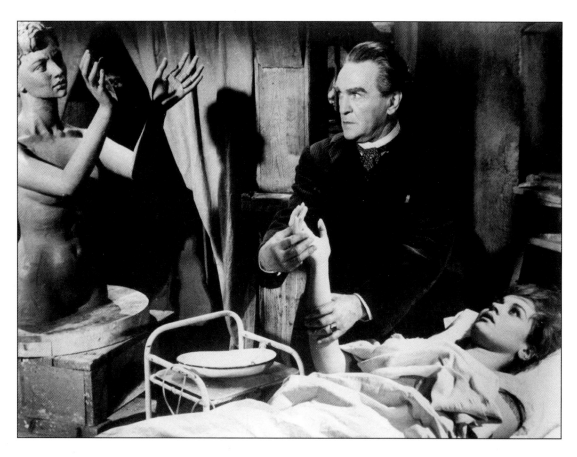

above:
Wolfgang Preiss with Scilla Gabel in **Mill of the Stone Women**.

opposite top:
Orfei Liana is about to have her worst fears realized within the cobwebs and shadows of the haunted Mill.

opposite bottom:
Pierre Brice is about to discover the deadly secret of the clock tower.

The medico-Gothic

Ferroni's film is an atmospheric fusion of medical and Gothic motifs, the guilt/obsession of the father towards a long-suffering and tragically ill daughter a literary conceit found in Nathaniel Hawthorne's "Rappaccini's Daughter" and Hanns Heinz Ewers's "Alraune." The film versions of these popular tales inevitably invest the father's motives with a perverse sexual ambivalence. In all five film adaptations of "Alraune," for example, a mad scientist artificially inseminates a streetwalker with the sperm of a murderer, adds a dash of mandrake root and - voila! - an emotionless siren of evil! Both the "father" and numerous suitors are eventually destroyed by her sensuous charm. The definitive 1928 version directed by Germany's Henrik Galeen contains an amazingly incestuous seduction scene between Brigitte Helm and Paul Wegener still shocking today. In "Rappaccini's Daughter," the child created from poisonous plants is "given" a mate by her demented father, who poisons his system to match hers - a horticultural version of *Romeo and Juliet*. Clearly, the father figures in all of these films are simultaneously fascinated and appalled by their daughters' sensuality.

Though shot in colour, *Mill of the Stone Women* remains steeped in the mythology of the 1960s black-and-white horror film. Jess Franco's masterful *Gritos en la noche* (*Screams in the Night*, aka *The Awful Dr. Orloff*, France/Spain, 1961) carries the same subtext of sex and death. Ferroni uses a rich and colourful palette, yet his frisson with Franco is unmistakable in that the visual motif carries the narrative in both films. In *Screams in the Night*, the chiaroscuro lighting combined with an oppressive atmosphere reinforces the German expressionistic look more than the film's pulp narrative. Ferroni, while working in colour, does much the same thing, utilising a macabre and dreamlike atmosphere that allows the delicate hues to project a Gothic feel no script ever could. A similar eroticism can be found in the silent cinema, and was revived in the 1960s - an era filled with emotional dislocation and erotic acts performed in the presence of the spectre of death.

Mill of the Stone Women

Mill of the Stone Women begins in the Holland of 1912. The flat countryside dotted with canals and windmills provides a Grimm's fairytale delicacy to an obsessive-romantic narrative. The protagonist, Hans von Arnam (Pierre Brice), while physically heroic, is decidedly lacklustre. Fortunately for viewers, the daughter, Elfi Wahl, is played with a perverse sensuality by Scilla Gabel. If denied, her sexual appetites can bring about a cataleptic semblance of death, a unique situation in films of this period.

The gothic flame is ignited by the presence of Wolfgang Preiss, a splendid actor who resembles Rudolf Klein-Rogge and who achieved some notoriety in the mid-1960s as Dr. Mabuse in Fritz Lang's *Mabuse* sequels. His turn here as a mad scientist and father who exsanguinates young women in order to give his daughter life is essential gothic. Equally obsessed is Herbert Böhme's Dr Loren Bolem, who assists Preiss (as Professor Gregorious Wahl) in his endeavours. As with Pierre Brasseur and Alida Valli in Georges Franju's like-minded medico-Gothic classic, *Les yeux sans visage* (*Eyes without a Face*, 1959), the pair are accomplices in murder and both are blinded by love for the sensuous Elfi.

Italy

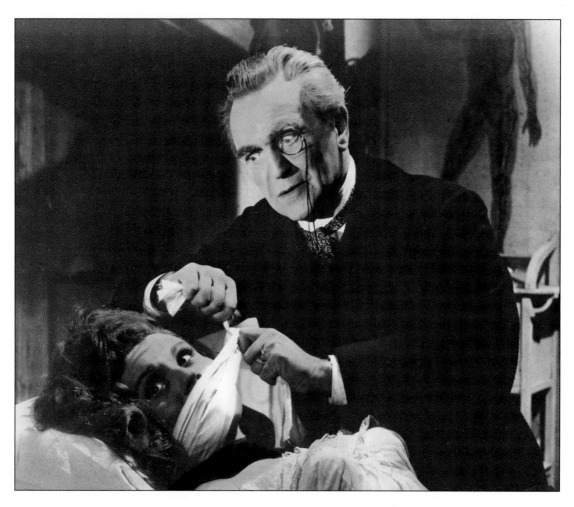

above:
Wolfgang Preiss prepares another sacrifice in the name of Science!

author's note:
I would like to dedicate this article to my late friend Alan Upchurch, who was so fond of **Mill of the Stone Women**. And I would like to thank Sergei Hasenecz for research.

From Expressionism to Surrealism

Although *Mill of the Stone Women* resonates with Expressionism, there is a nod to the golden age of Universal horrors with the rivalry between Dr. Bolem and Elfi's father. During a key exchange towards the film's end, Bolem advises Professor Wahl that he plans to marry Elfi, as he has perfected a formula to correct her diseased blood. This causes Wahl to lose control and kill the doctor, and in doing so he destroys the very antidote needed to save his daughter. The sequence recalls Lambert Hillyer's *The Invisible Ray* (1936), in which Dr. Janos Rukh's (Boris Karloff) own mother smashes the lifesaving antidote with her cane rather than let him live the life of a monster. As Oscar Wilde was fond of saying, "each man kills the thing he loves."

Ferroni also invokes Buñuel by utilising the Surrealist writer-director's theme of entrapment. In such Buñuel films as *Belle de jour* (1967) and *Tristana* (1970), the characters played by Catherine Deneuve are trapped inside a world of sexual longing and emptiness not unlike that of Elfi - a fairytale princess forbidden to leave her tower.

Drawn to Elfi's beauty and mystery, Hans ultimately succumbs to her advances. Soon after a night of passion he rejects her declarations of love, thereby inducing a seizure. However, after witnessing Elfi in her death throes, the young man flees the mill only to find her alive and well upon his return. Professor Wahl convinces Hans that he could be losing his mind and advises him to leave. But the disappearance of several young girls in the vicinity of the mill eventually jars our hero back to reality. Aided by a fellow student, the pair investigates the sudden disappearance of a music-hall singer, tracing her to the mill and ultimately thwarting the mad scientists at their own game. Ferroni imbues these proceedings with a weirdly poetic delirium.

Mill of the Stone Women

The poetry of horror

Ferroni has granted equal parts beauty, terror and madness to his film. Its magic lies within its imagery creating genuinely nightmarish set-pieces lit with brooding colours and Rembrandtesque shadows: the poetic language of horror typified by the lyrical image of Elfi standing in an alcove of the mill holding a single red rose longing for her lover, while Professor Wahl works nearby in a makeshift laboratory littered with severed limbs and mutilated corpses, an unholy mixture of eroticism and sadistic surgery. The windmill itself stands as a hideously beautiful music box filled with the corpses of beautiful women - a shrine to the altar of death and decay.

Elfi's denied sexual appetites, resulting in her catalepsy, brings to mind Edgar Allan Poe's "The Fall of the House of Usher," wherein the implied incest between Roderick Usher and his sister Madeline leads to the latter's catatonic state and subsequent premature entombment by her guilt-ridden brother. Roger Corman's adaptation of this novella was released the same year as *Mill of the Stone Women*. Interestingly, in Poe's original story, the outsider does not cause Madeline's catatonic state, nor does his presence trigger the House's fall. In the movie version, however, the outsider is a suitor of Madeline's, and while he does not seem to bring about her catalepsy (as Hans does to Elfi), he is in part the catalyst to the fall of the house, already teetering under the weight of the Ushers' transgressions.

Likewise in *Mill of the Stone Women*, where Hans is the final strain on a mill groaning under the pressure of Professor Wahl's sins.

Mill of the Stone Women's finale is a visually surrealistic mix of fire and brimstone enacted by Preiss's Professor Wahl in full flood - a King Lear minus the howls! With the mill in flames, he takes his Cordelia to the roof to die for the last time, and as the flames eat away at the musical clock of stone women a *danse macabre* is set in motion. The figures twist and writhe to a discordant melody as skulls and bones are liberated from their masks and costumes. With the flames consuming the Professor and his daughter, uniting them forever in blood and death, the cosmic mill of Wolfgang Preiss has at last come full circle.

above:
Wolfgang Preiss cradles the lifeless body of his daughter at the climax of **Mill of the Stone women**.

top left:
Pierre Brice rescues his true love from Preiss's clock tower.

below:
Scilla Gabel appears to have expired from lack of blood.

horror cinema across the globe

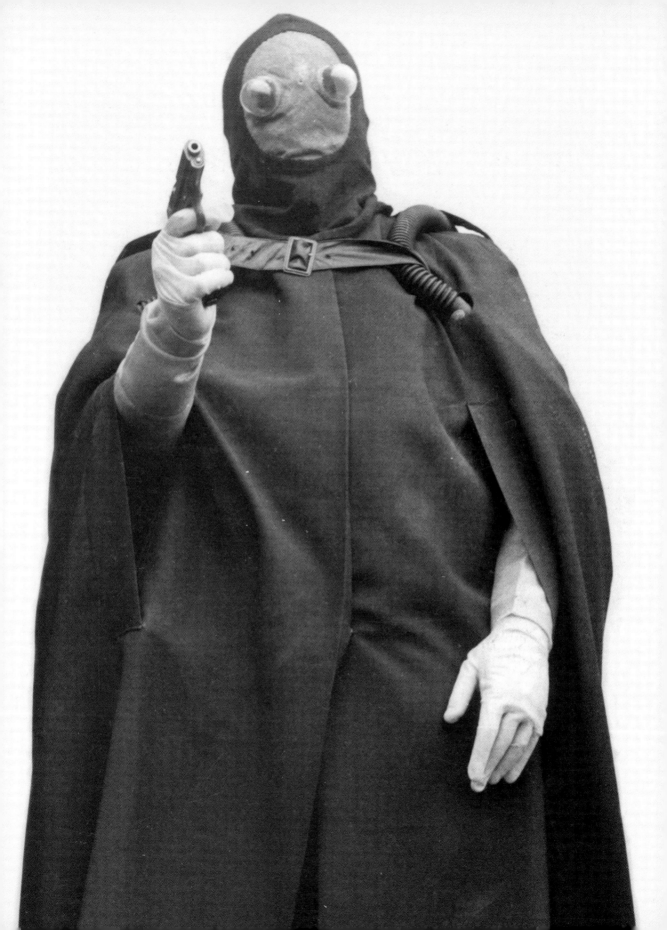

The "lost" horror film series: the Edgar Wallace *krimis*

Ken Hanke

The body of movies that make up the German adaptations of the crime thrillers written by Edgar Wallace (1875-1932), once an immensely popular and prolific novelist (there are some 180 books to his credit), is one of the most under-explored areas of the horror genre, and quite possibly the ultimate in the realm of "international horror cinema." After all, these films - called "*krimis*," a term derived from the word "*taschenkrimi*" (pocket crime novel) - are about as international as you can get. Produced in West Germany between the years 1959 and 1972, they were set in a studio-created England (beefed up with rear-screen stock shots and Hamburg streets passing for London's Soho), based on the works of an English writer, utilised actors from several different countries, and incorporated a strong American influence.

If you were a horror fan growing up in the 1960s, it was almost inevitable that sooner or later - once the *Shock Theatre* package and its minor offshoots were exhausted - you'd come across at least some of the odd West German film adaptations of Edgar Wallace's novels. The dedicated horror movie enthusiast of that era knew the name Edgar Wallace for his story credit on *King Kong* (1933) and as author of the source novel for the British Bela Lugosi vehicle, *The Dark Eyes of London* (aka *The Human Monster*, 1939, dir. Walter Summers). As a result, Wallace's name on these dubbed imports imbued them with an immediate curiosity value. They weren't horror pictures in the more literal sense associated with the films from American studios like Universal, but they were instead what might be called horrific. And they were sufficiently bizarre to capture a horror fan's attention, even if few people took them with any degree of seriousness for many years.

What none of us knew - or even began to guess - at the time were the peculiar origins of these films or how they were viewed in their source country. First of all, the question arises as to just *why* a German movie studio should have been mining the works of a once wildly popular English writer of thrillers. Certainly, it would have been far easier - and a great deal cheaper - to make movies that were not populated with British characters and were not set in London and other English locations. In order to begin to understand this, it's necessary to realise that Wallace's writings, while popular in Great Britain and America, had always enjoyed an unusual popularity in Germany.

Krimi conventions

In his landmark article on the German Edgar Wallace films, Tim Lucas cites a 1927 letter from Wallace to a friend: "For some extraordinary reason, there is a Wallace vogue in Germany."[1] Lucas goes on to suggest that this was not as extraordinary as Wallace made it sound, since the writer was no stranger to self-promotion in Germany. "Wallace's fictional universe of colourful crooks, dapper detectives, and lurking ladies coincided well with the increasingly corrupt atmosphere of pre-Nazi Germany," notes Lucas, going on to compare Wallace's work with such German films of the era as Fritz Lang's *Dr. Mabuse - The Gambler* (1922) and *Spies* (1928). (One might broaden this to include the depiction of the underworld in Lang's *M* [1931], too, and it's no stretch to add G. W. Pabst's *The*

opposite:
Harald Reinl's **Der Frosche mit der Maske** (aka **The Fellowship of the Frog**), 1959.

[1] Tim Lucas, "Dial 'W' for Wallace: The West German *Krimis*," *Gorezone*, November-December 1989.

Germany

above:
Alfred Vohrer's
Die Tur Mit Den 7 Schlössern (aka **The Door with Seven Locks**), 1962, starring Heinz Drache (left) and Sabine Sesselman (centre).

opposite:
Harald Reinl's **Der Frosche mit der Maske** (aka **The Fellowship of the Frog**), 1959.

2 Margaret Lane, *Edgar Wallace: The Biography of a Phenomenon.* London: Hamilton, 1964.

Threepenny Opera [1931] to this list.) In a peculiar way, the very British Wallace tapped into something that had a great appeal for the German people - and perhaps informed certain aspects of German pop culture of that era. (The situation is not wholly dissimilar to the German response to the work of British composer Edward Elgar, whose music was embraced in Germany before it was wholly appreciated in his own country.) A footnote in Margaret Lane's *Edgar Wallace: The Biography of a Phenomenon* stresses Wallace's popularity in Germany: "Miss Cicely Hamilton in her book *Modern Germanies* (1931) describes Edgar Wallace as the 'dominant English writer in Germany' and more popular than Shaw or Galsworthy."**2**

Just how far the impact of Wallace's fiction might have gone is impossible to say. After two German adaptations of his novels were made in the early 1930s, Hitler's rise to power and nationalisation of German cinema ended the possibility of further film adaptations of an English novelist. At this point, the translation of Wallace to the screen fell to British and, to a lesser extent, Hollywood studios, with varying results. There was, however, one fairly constant factor in these adaptations - a stress on the mystery element rather than the horrific, which perhaps goes a long way toward explaining why so few of these films have proved to have any lasting interest. This is borne out by the fact that the two best-remembered Wallace adaptations of the era - *The Dark Eyes of London* and *The Door with Seven Locks* (aka *Chamber of Horrors*, 1940, dir. Norman Lee) - are the two that can most accurately be called horror films, though in all fairness it must be noted that the mere presence of stars Bela Lugosi and Leslie Banks has more than a little bearing on these films' longevity.

The German explosion in Wallace adaptations didn't occur until 1959, when the Rialto Film Company made *Der Frosche mit der Maske* (*The Fellowship of the Frog*), directed by Harald Reinl. Viewed today, the film is not especially horrific, but it remains a marvellously entertaining crime thriller and establishes much of the basic format for the series that followed, including many of the actors. The standard premise is certainly there: a dashing hero (Joachim Fuchsberger), a heroine in distress (Eva Anthes), a dryly humorous Scotland Yard inspector (Siegfried Lowitz), a comic relief

112   fear without frontiers

sidekick for the hero (Eddi Arent) and a mysterious super criminal. Those are the basics and nearly every *krimi* that followed adhered to them, since it proved a successful formula. That formula needs to be clearly explained in order to understand aspects of the series' popularity in Germany, since many of the elements - not the least of which was the comedy of Eddi Arent - are difficult to judge in the dubbed versions of the films.

The elements that made up the basic *krimi*, however, do not in the least tell the whole story, since they do not account for what makes these pictures unique, and reveal little or nothing about how they paved the way for much of what we now accept as the modern horror film. The *krimis*' hybrid nature actually gave them a great deal of their tone. The romanticised German notion of England never successfully conveyed an accurate depiction of the country in which the films were supposedly taking place. Stock shots of London, oceans of fog, and the importation of British cars are hardly enough to make the films' Britishness convincing; indeed, these things often undercut the sense of reality. For example, the hero of *Fellowship of the Frog* tools around the countryside in an MG-A, a then fairly common and inexpensive car, making the fact that characters act like it's the *ne plus ultra* of pricey sports vehicles more quaint than convincing. The results, instead of evoking a real England, create a delightful fantasy world that affords the films a wholly unique quality. If anything, this works in their favour, since the unrealistic events seem far more plausible in this world than they would in a more believable one.

Despite the more "legitimate" pedigree of linking the *krimi* with the work of Fritz Lang, it would be ingenuous to suggest that the antics and style of the master criminals in these films are exactly in that league, having just as much in common with the colourful "hooded killer" of the more comic-strip diegesis of the serial film. (At the same time, it can be persuasively argued that Lang's own *The Testament of Dr. Mabuse* [1932] is not that far removed from the serial film's narrative universe.) It is hard to believe that Lang would have *ever* settled for a master criminal as lovably cheesy as "The Frog" (bearing the decidedly improbable real name of Harry Lime, no less). Decked out in something resembling a scuba diving outfit with a cape, sporting a black face covering and ping-pong ball-looking goggles over his eyes - not to mention very stylish elbow-length rubber gloves - the arch-villain of *Fellowship of the Frog* is a few light years away from Dr. Mabuse or Haghi (the master criminal in *Spies*; both characters played by Rudolf Klein-Rogge) in terms of seriousness of appearance. Visually, the Lang villains are considerably more intimidating, but the *krimi* villain makes a major - and startling - departure in terms of personal, extravagant, over-the-top violence. And this is where a good deal of the *krimis*' relation to the realm of modern horror cinema lies.

While relatively tame by later standards (indeed, *all* the *krimis* pale in this regard when compared to the modern horror film), it is nonetheless shocking to see The Frog at his most maniacally unhinged late in *Fellowship of the Frog*. Threatening to brand a voluptuous female victim (Eva Pflug) he has tied to a chair, he quickly changes his mind when her annoyance factor exceeds his patience. Rather than merely torture the victim, he opts to dispatch her altogether with frankly alarming overkill, pulling out a machine gun and blasting away until the

below:
Jurgen Roland's **Der Rote Kreis** (aka **The Crimson Circle**), 1959.

the Edgar Wallace krimis

chair she's tied to falls over. Not content with this, he merrily fires away, continuing to splinter the chair long after she is most surely very dead. It's so over-the-top - and the dubbed performance of The Frog so clichéd ("And you'll get the same treatment if you don't behave. You're coming with me. No one can stop me. I'm stronger than anyone!" he tells the hapless heroine) - that it's almost comic. But it remains unsettling all the same, and marks a clear path to the horror films of Italian auteur Dario Argento in particular, and to the modern horror film in general.

The fantastic horror of the old Universal films and even the contemporary Hammer movies is replaced in the *krimis* with what, as I indicated earlier, might better be termed the "horrific," with its greater emphasis on human horror and the sadistic. Despite the admittedly fanciful world of the films, and the retention of certain horror staples that were inherent in Wallace's work (such as the obligatory old dark house and certain gothic trappings), this emphasis constituted a significant break with the horror genre as it was typically perceived. And *Fellowship of the Frog* was merely the tip of the iceberg.

Fellowship of the Frog was successful enough to spawn two more films almost immediately - *Der Rote Kreis* (*The Crimson Circle*, 1959, dir. Jurgen Roland) and *Die Bande Des Schreckens* (*The Terrible People*, 1960, dir. Harald Reinl). Very much in the same mould as the first film, the stress was again on the horrific. *The Crimson Circle*, in fact, offers a "body count" of some 25 persons, though of course not all the murders are depicted on screen. The only comparable films in classic American horror are isolated instances like Columbia's *Night of Terror* (dir. Benjamin Stoloff) and Paramount's *Terror Aboard* (dir. Paul Sloane), both significantly from 1933, the year prior to the inception of the Production Code that brought sweeping censorship restrictions to the industry. The *krimis* were very much a different type of horror with a markedly different approach - one that was not lost on others in the movie business.

Independent producer Kurt Ulrich was the first to attempt to cash in on Rialto's success with the Wallace adaptations, coming out with *Der Rächer* (*The Avenger*), based on Wallace's novel *The Hairy Arm*, in 1960. Director Karl Anton's approach (whose last film this would be) was, if anything, more over the top than that of his Rialto predecessors. Any film that starts off with two old ladies finding a severed head in a box on the roadside is most certainly not interested in restraint! And it didn't end there, with its in-your-face horrors of a guillotine (referred to by the French slang name of "The Widow") and the inclusion of a hulking African "monster" called Bhag (Al Hoosmann), the "Hairy Arm" of Wallace's original title (though in the novel, the arm belongs to an actual orang-utan). Certain aspects of the Rialto series were directly copied, for example the hero is again given an MG sports car to reinforce his Britishness. All in all, the film did a good job of replicating the Rialto product.

In fact, it might be said that Ulrich did *too* good a job - at least so far as Rialto was concerned. They were sufficiently impressed by *The Avenger* that they threatened to sue Ulrich if he attempted to make any further films in

above:
Harald Reinl's
Die Bande Des Schreckens
(aka **The Terrible People**), 1960.

Germany

above:
Karl Anton's **Der Rächer** (aka **The Avenger**), 1960.

the series. Just exactly *how* Rialto viewed Wallace's entire body of work as their exclusive property is a little vague, but their threats successfully caused Ulrich to back down. In the process, Rialto opted to hire some of Ulrich's actors - notably Heinz Drache (who tended to alternate leading man status with Joachim Fuchsberger in numerous subsequent *krimis*) and Klaus Kinski (a valuable addition usually as a stock minor villain in the Dwight Frye mould) - thereby expanding on their original roster of *krimi* players.

With everything in place, the *krimis* fully came into their own with Alfred Vohrer's *Die Toten Augen Von London* (*The Dead Eyes of London*, 1961), arguably the best film in the series and the one most people immediately think of when they think of *krimis*. Some of the film's fame may stem from the fact that it's a remake of the most famous of all pre-*krimi* Wallace adaptations, *Dark Eyes of London* - not to mention that it's one of Wallace's strongest stories. Considering the sheer scope of the body of films that make up the *krimis*, I've opted to devote the largest section of this essay to an examination of *Dead Eyes of London*, since it is quite probably the *essential* film in the series, and a thorough understanding of it and the manner in which it is designed and executed provides a solid base for assessing the series on the whole and how it departed from horror as it was generally considered at the time. This is very evident if we compare *Dead Eyes of London* with the story's original cinematic incarnation. The two versions of the story are interesting both for their similarities and their differences.

The *Dark* and the *Dead*

The 1939 UK version, while first and foremost designed as a Lugosi vehicle, is remarkable for the way it pushed the envelope of what was and was not acceptable in a horror film. The picture is almost unbelievably sadistic for its time, with Bela's Dr. Orloff gleefully drowning his victims, mercilessly deafening a blind man so the police can't question him, etc. - and laughing all the while. *Dark Eyes of London* even ignored the then-censorable taboo of having a woman in bondage and took it a step further by allowing her to be touched (censors at the time seemed to think this

above:
Walter Summers's **The Dark Eyes of London** (aka **The Human Monster**), 1939.

made a significant difference). In terms of plot, the two films are virtually identical. For that matter, in terms of stretching the permissible, they are certainly soulmates, though occasionally it is the older film that packs more of a punch. But in other ways, there's a huge difference.

Of course, *Dark Eyes of London*'s status as a Lugosi vehicle is the most notable difference, since that fact meant a different focus to the film. Lugosi is at the centre of the proceedings and in a dual role (more accurately, he spends a good bit of the film in disguise with a dubbed voice). *Dead Eyes of London*, on the other hand, spends far more time concentrating on Inspector Larry Holt (Fuchsberger) and the investigation of the case, as well as splitting the Lugosi role into two different characters. As a result, the later film is considerably more complex in terms of events and characterisation - and much nearer Wallace in the bargain. That's not surprising, since in the world of the *krimi* Wallace is the star, more so than any individual actor.

Alfred Vohrer brought a slightly different look and approach to the series. While still revelling in the more overt style of horror pioneered in the earlier entries, Vohrer showcases a stronger, more creative visual style that is strikingly reminiscent of Hitchcock's early British films. This is particularly notable in the manner in which Vohrer cuts from scene to scene. A "shock cut" from a whistle to a doorbell ringing insistently is very like Hitchcock's cut from the screaming woman's face to the train whistle in *The 39 Steps* (1935). *Dead Eyes of London* is full of such touches, giving the movie a strangely antiquated feeling that is both atmospheric and pleasing. It is also a very conscious style, and one that Vohrer - unlike Hitchcock - can't always pull off without seeming forced. It doesn't help matters that he has a tendency to embellish only the beginnings and endings of his scenes, allowing the bulk of a sequence to play rather indifferently. (In this respect, Vohrer is more reminiscent of some of Lewis Milestone's lesser efforts at grafting style onto a film. And that's part of the problem - the style sometimes seems more of an add-on to the picture than something that naturally grows out of it.) Moreover, some of these embellishments are awkwardly achieved, for

Germany

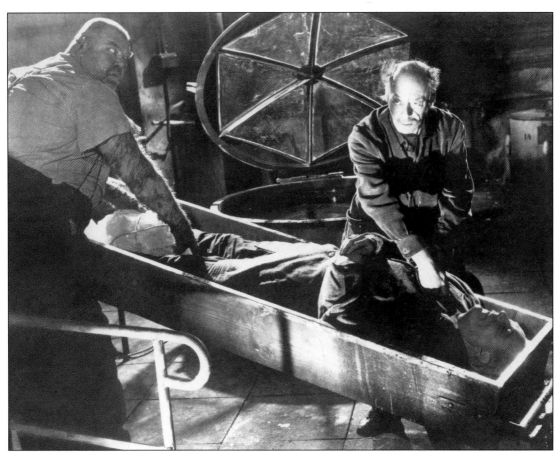

above:
Alfred Vohrer's **Die Toten Augen Von London** (aka **The Dead Eyes of London**), 1961.

example requiring actors to move objects - a hat, a glass, etc. - in unnatural ways toward the camera. At other times, Vohrer is just too tricky for his own good (the famous POV shot from inside a man's mouth as he uses a WaterPik, for example). But on many occasions, Vohrer's efforts pay off nicely, and the very fact that he went the distance to make *Dead Eyes of London* something special is in itself noteworthy.

Dead Eyes of London opens on a strong note, with a murderous attack on an unknown man by "Blind Jack" (Adi Berber) in an almost impossibly foggy London (so foggy, in fact, that some of the players' credits that follow are difficult to read!). Compared to the macabre, but relatively tame, opening of *Dark Eyes of London* with a corpse floating in the Thames (in essence, *Dead Eyes* backs up the action to the point of the attack that's already happened in *Dark Eyes*), this is much more compelling. Our early introduction to Blind Jack (it is many minutes into *Dark Eyes* before the viewer is introduced to Blind Jake [Wilfrid Walter], and there his villainy is not immediately apparent) sets the tone for the movie's horrors, and the addition of an obvious conspiracy afoot via Jack's accomplice in the matter puts the later film far more solidly into the *krimi* realm of master criminals and criminal gangs.

As with *Dark Eyes*, it is the finding of the body that sets the plot in motion, especially the discovery of a bit of Braille writing on the corpse. Since this is not the first such "accidental" drowning, Inspector Holt becomes convinced that this is murder and part of a pattern - "Always a foggy night, always men who wear glasses and can be easily attacked, and always rich men from abroad without a family in England." While not entirely buying into his theories (one wonders why, since the circumstances are suspicious to say the least), Holt's superior has at least gone so far as to recruit someone to read the Braille. This turns out to be Nora Ward (Karin Baal), who becomes an almost immediate romantic interest for Holt and figures rather more prominently and with greater

- and less believable - complexity than her counterpart in the earlier film. The Braille writing is in such bad shape, unfortunately, that Nora can only make out bits of it - "Crime...murder...the blind monster and his master..." That much, however, is enough to make Holt conclude: "It certainly looks as if the blind killers of London are at work again." He further explains, "They're a band of thieves and killers, blind peddlers who commit crimes in the dead of night." With typical *krimi* logic, this concept is accepted without question or even notable shock.

At this point, *Dead Eyes of London* introduces Eddi Arent's Sgt. "Sunny" Harvey, who wanders onto the scene greeting Nora with, "Not since the hatchet murderess, Lady Mixedpickles, was here for questioning have we been honoured by such beauty." Since Arent fulfils the function of comic relief in these films (and was a significant factor in their success in Germany), his contribution to the series is easy to overlook. In part this stems from the fact that it is difficult to judge a great deal of his comedy in the dubbed versions of the films. Not only are we deprived of his actual dialogue delivery, but there's no guarantee that we are even hearing the jokes as they were originally written. As a result, the English-speaking viewer is left with variable comedy dubiously delivered and a handful of Arent's physical schtick by way of *outré* costuming (here he removes his trench coat to reveal a garish plaid suit that makes one glad the film is in black and white) and whinnying effect he seems to have appropriated from Huntz Hall. However, Arent's characters are quite unusual in that they are usually there to provide more than just comic relief. In *Dead Eyes*, his absurdity is undercut by the fact that he's presented as a very capable buffoon, one who is constantly offering useful information about the case - and not, as might be expected, accidentally or unconsciously. In this sense, Arent's characters are perhaps unique in genre film. Indeed, it is Arent's legwork that leads Holt onto the path that ultimately solves the mystery by revealing that the drowned man had a life insurance policy with the Greenwich Assurance Company.

There is an intriguing parallel between Arent's "Sunny" and Edmon Ryan's Lieutenant O'Reilly in the original film. Both characters serve roughly the same function, though O'Reilly is a Chicago policeman in London studying Scotland Yard's methods. In both cases, the men are the creations of filmmakers putting forth their *own* ideas of a character who is foreign to them. O'Reilly is quite obviously a British screenwriter-director's idea of an American policeman grounded entirely in ideas cobbled from Hollywood movies. Sunny, on the other hand, is just as obviously a wholly German notion of a very proper English policeman, and one who is grounded far more in the movies than in reality.

The plot having been set up, *Dead Eyes of London* proceeds along its remarkably convoluted path with speed and assurance - not to mention an abundance of nice, often bizarre, touches. One wonders, for example, just what prospective clients make of the fact that insurance broker Stephen Judd (Wolfgang Lukschy) keeps a human skull that dispenses cigarettes! Even in its dubbed version, the official police description of Blind Jack (delivered by Arent, of course) is extremely thorough - "Age about 50, height six foot four inches, occupation peddler, has unusually great strength, tends toward acts of violence, mentally retarded, easily subject to bad influences" - and is beautifully economical in ending with, "Last known address: 25 Blossom Lane," followed by a jump cut to the Blossom Lane street sign with the camera panning down to Holt, Sunny and Nora arriving on the scene.

Unlike the straightforward narrative of *Dark Eyes of London*, *Dead Eyes* is simply filled with various plot tangents and a wide array of shady underworld characters. Most of it works, though some of it strains viewer credulity, especially in terms of characterisation. It's one thing in *Dark Eyes* to buy the idea that Diana Stuart (Greta Gynt) would agree to spy on the comings and goings at Dr. Feodor Dearborn's (Lugosi) home for blind vagrants, since she knows there is a connection between the place and the murder of her father. In *Dead Eyes*, it's more of a stretch to accept Nora taking on this task, since she agrees *before* her father is murdered and, for that matter, doesn't even know who her father is or if he's still alive. (This aspect of the plot is very telling, since Wallace was himself an illegitimate child.) She agrees to worm her way into Paul Dearborn's (Dieter Borsche) confidence *solely* as a favour to Holt, whom she has known a scant few hours! Presumably, her devotion is very easily aroused.

The collection of colourful underworld characters, on the other hand, is quite a nice addition to the later version, especially the dapper blackmailer, Fleabite (as the dubbed dialogue has it) or Flicker (as the cast list has it) Fred (Harry Wüstenhagen), and the immediately indispensable Klaus Kinski (given special "and KLAUS KINSKI" billing) - looking for all the world like the bastard child of Dwight Frye and Jean-Paul Belmondo - as yet another blackmailer. Blackmail figures quite prominently in the plot, and the blackmailers invariably come to a bad and generally grisly end; Fleabite Fred, for example, is dropped down an elevator shaft, but suffers the indignity of first catching himself, only to have one hand burned with a cigarette and the other stepped on to ensure his speedy descent.

Of course, the most spectacular of the villains is Adi Berber's Blind Jack. Without a doubt, this is one of the series' most memorably grotesque characters. A Tor Johnson-like figure (both men had been professional wrestlers) minus an ear, boasting an improbably hairy body, and "dead" eyes, Blind Jack is certainly unsettling and more than a little daunting (anyone who gets the upper-hand on his sighted victims by crushing light bulbs with his bare hand is not to be trifled with). Interestingly, his relationship with Lew Norris (Bobby Todd) is quite different from that between Jake and "Blind Lou" (Arthur E. Owen) in the original film. In *Dark Eyes*, the arrangement is a fairly traditional one (in horror film terms) of a "monster" and his simple-minded devotion to one other person. In *Dead Eyes*, however, there is evidently no love lost between the two. Here - and this is very much in keeping with the tone of the *krimis* - Blind Jack is completely unsympathetic and sadistically forces Lew into assisting him in his crimes (indeed, it is Lew who is slipping the Braille notes to the police via the corpses). Blind Jack is also a much more active and reasoning participant in the crimes than was Jake; this latter is a strange point considering the fact that the description drags in the idea that he is mentally retarded. While Lugosi's Orloff merely uses Jake as a strong-arm henchman, the villains here allow him to undertake the elaborate murders himself - strapping a large block of salt to the victim and dumping him into the Thames, assuring drowning in such a way that the body will float to the surface when the salt dissolves in order to collect on the insurance.

In the end, however, the original film's Jake is both more memorable and more menacing. Not only is the execution of Blind Jack long before *Dead Eyes*' conclusion something of a mistake, since it robs the climax of a level of peril that it badly needs, but Blind Jack (at least as far as the dubbed version is concerned) is far too articulate and cagey, pleading too coolly and even off-handedly for his life in the execution scene. This is a case where *Dead Eyes of London* settles for a bit of overt gruesomeness - Jack shot point blank in the head several times and left in a garbage dump for a grisly close-up - and undermines itself in the process.

The usual *krimi* procession of serial-like events - the attempted murder of the one person who knows the truth about Nora's ancestry (complete with last-minute rescue), a trick gun hidden in a TV set to dispose of intruders, the bound hero tortured with impending drowning in a laundry vat - make up the film's last section and provide some compensation for the ill-advised disposal of Blind Jack. The climax, however, for all of its sadistic thrills (Dearborn tormenting Nora with an acetylene torch and the delightful warning, "A corpse is ugly when it's been burned") feels slightly empty. The story leading up to it is just deserving of a much more spectacular finale than it is afforded here.

Another *Door* opens

One has to wonder if the success of *Dead Eyes of London* had a bearing on the choice to follow it up with a new version of *The Door with Seven Locks* (German title: *Die Tur Mit Den 7 Schlössern*), also directed by Vohrer, as this was the less-successful follow-up to *Dark Eyes of London* as well. (Leslie Banks made an effective villain in the 1940 UK version, but he lacked the drawing power of Bela Lugosi, and the resultant tepid response killed off what might easily have developed into a home-grown Wallace series at the time.) Whether or not this was the case, the resulting film in the *krimi* series turned out to be one of the best - and quite possibly the strangest.

The original *Door with Seven Locks* had been a fanciful, if rather simple, story about defrauding an heiress - hardly the most original concept ever to come down the pike. Vohrer's film is an altogether different matter, though a scheme to defraud is still the basic plot. However, the new *Door with Seven Locks* manages to bring in a Langian master criminal (not hard to spot), a mad scientist with a desire to graft a man's head onto a gorilla, a hulking brute and more. Vohrer's direction is as creative as in *Dead Eyes of London*, but minus most of the more awkward effects. It's just as well, since the storyline is so wild and woolly on its own merit that all it needed was the right atmosphere.

The entry replaces Joachim Fuchsberger with Heinz Drache and Karin Baal with Sabine Sesselman, but otherwise it draws heavily on the elements that made *Dead Eyes of London* a success: Eddi Arent's comedy, a great (albeit brief) bit for Kinski at his twitchy best, Adi Berber (now billed as Ady) as a murderous simpleton - minus the extra hair, and with both ears, but sporting scars instead - etc. The idea quite obviously was to take the best features of *Dead Eyes of London* and expand upon them. To a great extent, the effort is successful. Berber's character, for example, works better this time round, since he's given no dialogue to speak of, and while it may be a cliché, making him a sympathetic monster is strangely more satisfying. Moreover, the script shrewdly allows him to interact with the leads, keeping him less on the fringe of the proceedings. If nothing else, this results in a wonderfully bizarre moment where he attacks Eddi Arent (here playing a secondary cop with the name of Holmes!) and very matter-of-factly tries to bury him alive.

The most intriguing aspect of *The Door with Seven Locks*, though, is almost certainly the addition of Pinkas Braun's Dr. Staletti, the aforementioned mad scientist. This brings the series a bit closer to something like traditional horror. Staletti - who turns out to be more mad charlatan than mad scientist - is given a great secret laboratory (some of the props are recycled from *Dead Eyes of London*'s secret drowning room), wonderfully improbable dialogue (at least in the dubbed version) and the most lovably hokey man-in-a-gorilla-suit ever to grace the screen. What is especially interesting about all this, though, is the nature of Staletti's proposed experiment. Whether by accident or design, the idea of grafting a human head onto a gorilla was the dream of the father of the American horror film, Tod Browning, though Browning's concept was somewhat kinkier in that he was specifically interested in grafting a woman's head onto the animal. Nonetheless, it's of some note that this idea - one that Browning never managed to bring to fruition - should here see the light of day.

above:
Poster for Alfred Vohrer's **Die Tur Mit Den 7 Schlössern** (aka **The Door with Seven Locks**), 1962.

Even when it isn't successful as horror, the film is so much fun that no one is likely to complain; where *Dead Eyes of London* had been frequently chilling, *The Door with Seven Locks* is just too fanciful not to be amusing. And in many ways, that is the story of the *krimis* to come. *Dead Eyes of London* may be the closest the series ever came to making a horror film in the classic sense, but taken as a body, the films have a place in the history of horror that has never been adequately explored.

The growing success of the series on a purely popular level led Rialto's rival studio, CCC (Central Cinema Company) to try their hand at a blatantly imitative series. However, CCC had learned a lesson from independent producer Kurt Ulrich's

above:
Edwin Zbonek's **Das Ungeheuer Von London City** (aka **The Monster of London City**), 1964.

opposite top:
Franz Josef Gottlieb's **Das Phantom Von Soho** (aka **Murder By Proxy**), 1963.

opposite bottom:
Franz Josef Gottlieb's **Der Fluch Der Gelben Schlange** (aka **The Curse of the Yellow Snake**), 1963

run-in with Rialto, and, after risking one bona fide Wallace adaptation, *Der Fluch Der Gelben Schlange* (*The Curse of the Yellow Snake*, 1963, dir. Franz Josef Gottlieb), they opted to buy the rights to the works of Wallace's son, Bryan Edgar Wallace, for their source material. The younger Wallace, who had adapted his father's work for the screen back in 1937 with William K. Howard's *The Squeaker* (aka *Murder on Diamond Row*, UK), had then taken it on himself to write mystery novels in his father's style. CCC's offerings were very nearly as successful with audiences as the Rialto films, and soon the studio imported Wallace himself to craft original screenplays for them. Some of the films from CCC, such as 1963's *Das Phantom Von Soho* (*The Phantom of Soho*, aka *Murder By Proxy*, dir. Franz Josef Gottlieb) and the following year's *Das Ungeheuer Von London City* (*The Monster of London City*, dir. Edwin Zbonek), are considered to be on a par with the genuine Rialto article.

The series continued in various forms - often unsuccessfully attempting to change with the times - through 1972, by which time it had been overtaken by the works of Italian director Dario Argento, the most famous horror filmmaker to be directly influenced by the *krimis*. While Argento's early pictures, *L'uccello dalle piume di cristallo* (*The Bird with the Crystal Plumage*, 1970) and *Il gatto a nove code* (*The Cat o' Nine Tails*, 1971), are perhaps only *krimis* in a purely nor' by nor'west sense, they were certainly influenced by them and were co-produced by CCC, who marketed the films in Germany with the use of the Bryan Edgar Wallace name. These films mark the direction the actual series itself would have needed to move toward in order to survive any longer than they did. Much like the Universal horrors of the 1930s and 40s, and even like the Hammer horrors of the 1950s and 60s, it was a case of that which once seemed fresh and daring starting to pale as newer, bolder, though not necessarily better approaches to the genre came into being. The German film industry was giving way to the Italian one for the continuance of this particular

the Edgar Wallace krimis

brand of realistic horror film. The final film from Rialto, Massimo Dallamano's *Cosa avete fatto a Solange?* (*What Have You Done to Solange?*, 1972), was ultimately less a *krimi* than it was an early *giallo*, the form that took over from the *krimi* in many ways. Old Rialto favourites Joachim Fuchsberger and Karin Baal were in the cast and the film claimed to have been "suggested" by Wallace's *The Clue of the New Pin*, but it was a different sort of film for a different audience and a different time, and might best be viewed as an homage to the *krimis* rather than a true member of the series.

The unfortunate thing about the *krimis* is that they are insufficiently known and appreciated, even by fans of the stronger *gialli*, and, as a result, have never really gained a foothold in the history of the development of the horror film. This essay, which is really little more than a primer, is an attempt to at least suggest that the films in question are deserving of a closer look than they have generally been afforded. The films are so numerous and their history so rich that a book-length survey is really the only way to do them justice. Hopefully, the misbegotten *krimis* will one day attain sufficient interest to be afforded such a study.

The exotic pontianaks

Jan Uhde & Yvonne Ng Uhde

The horror film, rooted in the dark vision of German Expressionist cinema of the post-WWI era, is unquestionably one of the most extensive and influential genres of film history today. Thanks in particular to Hollywood's shrewd interest, it spread and crossbred, blending with other genres such as the thriller, science fiction, action-adventure, *film noir* and even comedy. One of its more salient subgenres, the vampire film, ushered in eight decades ago by Friedrich W. Murnau's unforgettable *Nosferatu* (1922), has also swollen enormously. Yet the image of the vampire as perceived by most Western audiences hardly extends much beyond that tall, fanged creature from the deep woods of the Transylvanian Alps.

In fact, other less well-known manifestations of the vampire exist in the tropics on the other side of the globe. The name *Pontianak* might ring a bell for readers of *National Geographic* magazine who would recall the capital city of West Kalimantan, lying exactly on the equator, in the Indonesian part of the island of Borneo. How the city got its name is unclear but for many in the region, the word "pontianak" denotes something much more sinister than just a geographical location; it is inextricably bound to the image of a female vampire. Pontianaks were - indeed for many still are - feared revenants of South-East Asia, particularly in Malaysia, Singapore and Indonesia.

In the same way that Hollywood's Universal Studios and later Hammer Films in England struck box-office gold with their Dracula and monster films of the 1930s, 40s and 50s, Singapore's filmmakers, on a much more modest scale, kept the till ringing with their own versions of the vampire film. Like their Western counterparts, the success of the early pontianak movies spurred spin-offs which brought to the screen other monsters, including the formidable "oily man" (*orang minyak* in Malay). In all, seven pontianak movies were produced in Singapore[1] between 1956 and 1965, during the "golden age" of Singapore cinema, in the two leading studios of the region, Shaw Brothers' Malay Film Productions (MFP) and Cathay-Keris (Cathay Organisation's Malay filmmaking arm). The immense popularity of these pictures was virtually a phenomenon in Singapore's Malay film production of the time. Many people in the region, especially in Singapore and Malaysia, still retain fond memories of the excitement and terror they felt upon viewing the pontianak films decades ago.

Vampires of the East and West

Like the mythologies of most cultures, old Malay and Indonesian legends are populated with a variety of supernatural creatures, not least bloodthirsty vampires. The latter include the *penanggalan* (aka *penanggal* or *penaggalan*), the *langsuyar* (also spelled *langsuir*) and the pontianak; the equally nocturnal and violent oily man is not a bloodsucker but a violator of women. Of these four spirits, the pontianak became the most prominent, thanks to its temporary movie stardom. In contrast to their Western counterparts such as Dracula (Nosferatu), the Malay/Indonesian vampires - the penanggalan, the langsuyar and the pontianak - are female.[2]

Other Eastern cultures such as the Chinese, Japanese and Korean are also familiar with female spirits. These ghosts too have found their way from legends into films, including works by well-known directors such as Kenji Mizoguchi's *Ugetsu monogatari* (1953) and Akira Kurosawa's *Dreams* (1990). Female phantoms in China

[1] In 1946, Singapore became a British Crown colony; the former Malayan Union became Federation of Malaya in 1948. Singapore obtained self-rule in 1959, and in 1963 it joined the new Federation of Malaysia. In 1965, it left the Federation and became an independent Republic.

[2] Judaeo-Christian cultural tradition offers legends comparable to those of the East-Asian langsuyar. Putting aside the relatively recent, reality-rooted story of the bloodthirsty Hungarian Countess Báthory, those about Lilith, Adam's first wife according to some Jewish legends, appear to be especially relevant. The American art historian L.C.E. Witcombe (2002) characterises Lilith "as a winged female demon who kills infants and endangers women in childbirth. ...As a female demon, she is closely related to Lamashtu whose evilness included killing children, drinking the blood of men, and eating their flesh. Lamashtu also caused pregnant women to miscarry, disturbed sleep and brought nightmares."

opposite:
Fadzlina Mohamad Shafie, star of **Return to Pontianak** (2000).

and Japan are often associated with foxes and may appear in their likeness. In a typical set-up, a beautiful woman would lure a young man into her lavishly appointed house; after spending the night with her, the man wakes up in a dilapidated, abandoned dwelling and eventually discovers that his lover was a phantom or fox spirit. Such "one-night stands" can in fact last quite long, sometimes a year or more. In South-East Asia, however, the most notorious female spirits are the pontianaks. Featured in countless ghost stories, it was just a matter of time before they appeared on the movie screen.

The pontianak and the langsuyar are closely related. The langsuyar is supposed to be the ghost of a woman who died in childbirth or from shock upon discovery that her child was stillborn. She may assume different physical forms (especially a night owl with long claws). However, she usually appears as a beautiful woman with long fingernails and long hair; the hair conceals a hole behind her neck through which she sucks the blood of infants. She can be tamed, though, when her hair and fingernails are cut and stuffed into the hole behind her neck; the man who manages this feat can become her husband and they can have children - as long as she is kept away from dancing and similar social activities. Otherwise, she will become what she was before and fly away.

According to the legends, the pontianak is the stillborn child of a langsuyar. Although its gender is not quite clear in traditional folklore, it is always depicted in female form on the silver screen, most probably because it is often confused with its mother. Like the langsuyar, it drinks infants' blood and can also appear in the form of a night owl; it is believed to live in kapok trees (white silk-cotton trees) during the day and attack at night. There are several etymological explanations of the word pontianak, none of which appears to be conclusive: "anak" means "child" in Malay (and in the Malay-derived Bahasa Indonesia). The word "ponti" is sometimes explained as "unknown"; according to this, "pontianak" would mean "unknown child"[3]; in Malaysia, the pontianak is also called "mati-anak"; "mati" means "death," therefore "dead child."

To prevent a woman who dies from childbirth from becoming a langsuyar, her body must be laid to rest by putting glass beads in her mouth, needles in the palms of her hands and an egg under each armpit. Her stillborn child would also be treated in the same way to prevent it from turning into a pontianak. Some believe that the effect of these rites is temporary as they only ensure that the dead woman or child will not transform into a langsuyar or pontianak until forty days after burial.

The penanggalan, one of the most famed and feared Malaysian and Indonesian ghosts, is a woman who was interrupted during prayer, causing her head to separate from her body, along with all the innards. The head with the entrails in tow then flies through the air, looking for the blood of newborn babies or pregnant women. The entrails' pestilential fluids spread disease. Pregnant women and small children were kept inside at night to protect them from the penanggalan. Unlike the pontianaks, the penanggalan never appeared in Singapore Malay movies, although its bloodcurdling potential has been tapped by other Asian filmmakers.[4]

Movies also extended the popularity of another Malay legend, that of the oily man. As his name implies the oily man is male. During the day, he behaves like an ordinary person but at night, he rapes young women whom he first hypnotises into submission with his bewitching stare; often, he kills his victims. Before setting out on his nocturnal adventures, this sub-human covers his half-naked body with oil to make it slippery so that he cannot be caught easily. He is very strong and makes frequent use of his supernatural powers to leap through air or to vanish from sight when pursued by the villagers or the law. In a modern twist on the old legend, ordinary rapists have been reported to exploit these old beliefs and fears by behaving like the "oily man."[5]

Indeed, many of the Malay and Indonesian vampire legends and black magic practices are still very much alive. The traditional help against all evil spirits comes from the *bomoh*, essentially a witch doctor called in to suggest the best way of getting rid of the plague. Some of their tools are similar to those of their Western counterparts (stakes for example), minus the Christian religious symbolism, while the proverbial garlic is replaced by local plants and fruits.

First Pontianak films

The first pontianak film appeared in 1957, and in many ways it set the stage for most of those to follow. Entitled *Pontianak*, (*The Vampire*), it was produced by the Cathay-Keris Studios in Singapore and directed by

---

[3] Francis 2002.

[4] In 1977, the Hong Kong director Lian Sing Woo made *The Witch with Flying Head*; *Léak* (aka *Mystics in Bali*) was directed by Indonesian filmmaker H. Tjut Djalil in 1981.

[5] One such incident was published by a Malaysian newspaper in 2001, under the heading "Man attacked in 'oily man' case." It was reported from Kuala Kedah in Northwestern Malaysia that a man was seized and beaten after trying to steal a talisman from a female *bomoh* who had apparently caught an oily man. (*The Star*, Kuala Lumpur, Malaysia, 23 September 2001). According to the report, four "orang minyaks" were eventually caught.

the exotic pontianaks

Balakrishna Narayan Rao (b.1908 in Tellicherry, Kerala, India). Rao was an experienced filmmaker with over thirty films to his credit. He had been working in the film business for more than twenty years when he made his first pontianak movie. In all, he directed four of the seven pontianak movies, and these were also the most successful ones.[6]

Pontianak was, like most of the Singapore-based productions of the 1950s and 60s, a Malay-language film shot in black and white. Against the rural setting of a traditional Malay *kampong* (village), a young female hunchback (Maria Menado) is transformed into a beautiful woman by magic forces. She marries but enduring happiness eludes her: when her husband is bitten by a snake, the venom she sucks out causes her to become a pontianak. She then tries to turn her daughter into a vampire but is destroyed after a nail is driven into her skull.

It is quite evident from the old Malay legends that the "pontianak" in this film is in fact a langsuyar. The true pontianak - the vampiric baby of the langsuyar - is not part of the movie at all. Whether due to a confusion among the filmmakers over these two closely related phantoms, or what is more likely, to a common semantic inconsistency, this factual error did not discourage the film-going public in the least. In all probability, most never even realised there *was* a mix-up. The power of popular misconception gave the old folklore another twist and so the term "pontianak" stuck.

The release of the first pontianak film must have been a pleasant surprise for Cathay-Keris, which had seldom seen its Malay feature productions turn a profit. As the Malaysian scriptwriter and historian Hamzah Hussin recalls, the movie was originally scheduled to open at Singapore's prestigious Cathay Cinema at Dhoby Ghaut for the Muslim holidays Hari Raya Puasa; after two days, it was to be moved to the Taj, in the city's predominantly Malay area of Geylang Serai. However, the long line-ups caused it to remain at the Cathay flagship theatre for two months, after which it played for another three months at the Taj. Similar success was recorded throughout Malaya, Sarawak and Brunei.[7] International distribution followed. In 1958, *Pontianak* was dubbed into Cantonese and released in Hong Kong, the first Malay feature to do so. Two years later, it was subtitled in English to be shown on television in the United States as part of an Asian film showcase, representing Malaya and Singapore.[8]

This success prompted Cathay-Keris to make a quick follow-up, *Dendam Pontianak* (*Revenge of the Vampire*, 1957). Here, the female vampire returns from the grave seeking vengeance. The circumstances of her death at the end of the picture were left unclear by the filmmakers, which offered them the possibility of another sequel, *Sumpah Pontianak* (*The Curse of the Vampire*, aka *Blood of Pontianak*) in 1958. That year, Cathay-Keris's feature production output almost tripled, compared to three in 1957 and four in 1956; this significant achievement helped the company to compete with its rival and the dominant producer of Malay features, Shaw Brothers' Malay Film Productions, on equal footing.

No less important was the pontianak films' multi-cultural appeal. The Singapore-based Australian lecturer and historian Kevin P. Blackburn quotes Cathay-Keris director and a pioneer of the Malay film industry Laksamanan Krishnan, who claimed that the *Pontianak* series made even more money than the films of the multi-talented director and Malay cinema's greatest star P. Ramlee because it attracted not only the Malays but the Chinese as well. As a result, "because the Chinese came everybody walked into the cinema."[9]

New Pontianaks and other monsters

Most of the pontianak movies were made in 1957 and 1958, all of them out of Cathay or Shaw studios in Singapore. Noting the overwhelming success of Cathay's pontianak films, Shaw persuaded *Pontianak* scriptwriter Abdul Razak to pen a vampire screenplay for its organisation as well; and so, in addition to the three Cathay-Keris titles already mentioned, Malay Film Productions released *Anak Pontianak* (1958), directed by Filipino filmmaker Ramón A. Estella. Unlike the original pontianak movie, this version featured the vampire's son - a bodiless monster called Polong - as the film's demon, together with Hnatu, the snake devil. It seems quite likely that the penanggalan legend played a part in contributing to *Anak Pontianak*'s narrative. Without the attraction of Menado's pontianak, however, this vampiric tale failed to catch on at the box office.

1958 was also the year that saw the arrival of three oily man films, starting with Cathay's *Orang Minyak* (*Oily Man*), directed by L. Krishnan. While Cathay exulted over

[6] B.N. Rao worked in India in Tamil, Hindi, and Telugu language movies. He started his career as an actor in 1926; later he became assistant director and assistant cameraman. His first feature as director was the Hindi *Veer Kumari* (1935). Rao moved to Singapore to work for Shaw Brothers' Malay Film Productions (1953-56); in 1957, he joined the Shaws' chief rival, the Cathay-Keris Studios. He stayed there until 1964 after which he returned to India. He directed his last film in 1974, the Telugu movie *Nitya Sumangali*. His Singapore career includes the remake of the first Singapore-made movie, *Laila Majnun*, released in 1962.

[7] Hussin, 41.

[8] Ibid.

[9] Blackburn 2002 [A].

Singapore

above:
Maria Menado, the Indonesian-born star and the most famous "Pontianak" of them all.
(courtesy of Cathay-Keris Film Pte Ltd)

its *Pontianak* profits, Shaw found its own horror goldmine in the sexually rapacious, greasy human monster. The Shaw Brothers' release, *Sumpah Orang Minyak* (*The Curse of the Oily Man*), was directed by P. Ramlee, who also played the main character. The film introduced the young actress Sri Dewi and featured Salleh Kamil as Buyong and Shariff Dol as Satan. The well-written tragic story of a hunchback cast out by the community had a philosophical depth which went far beyond most of the other Malay-language vampire films of the period. Not without flaws, this was nevertheless a remarkable film, beautifully photographed by A. Bakar Ali; it won the "Best Black and White Photography" award at the 5th Asian Film Festival in Manila in 1958.

Eager to cash in on Shaw Brothers' success, Cathay lost no time in producing their own oily man sequel. Entitled *Serangan Orang Minyak* (*The Oilyman Strikes Again*, 1958), the film was directed by L. Krishnan and starred M. Amin and Latifah Omar. This "modernised" version of the mythical subject, however, was stylistically quite incoherent, lacking in creativity and imagination.

The Pontianak in person: Maria Menado

The big crowd-puller, the real star of the pontianak films, and the secret of their record-breaking success was the pontianak herself, portrayed by the attractive Menado. Born Libeth Dotulong in Menado (Sulawesi, Indonesia) in 1931, she came to Singapore as a teenager looking for a job. She won a "Kebaya Queen" beauty contest (the kebaya is a figure-hugging tunic worn with a long sarong), which helped her land her first film role with Shaw Brothers, *Penghidupan* (*Livelihood*, starring P. Ramlee, 1951). Later, she switched to Cathay-Keris studios where her role in Cathay's pontianak films, scripted by her first husband, Abdul Razak, catapulted her to fame. The most eagerly awaited moment came when the audience saw her screen character - an ugly hag - magically transformed into a beautiful woman. Indeed, for Menado, who had received little attention from previous films, her first pontianak role was the breakthrough in her acting career. After *Pontianak*, her name became synonymous with the vampire and she became a star overnight.

Menado appeared in four pontianak films, all of them produced by Cathay-Keris. The first three, *Pontianak*, *Dendam Pontianak* and *Sumpah Pontianak* were directed by B.N. Rao; the fourth, *Pontianak Kembali*, was made by the Filipino director Ramón A. Estella. Menado often played powerful female characters; in addition to the pontianaks, she portrayed characters from Malay literature such as *Siti Zubaidah* (1958) and *Tun Fatimah* (1961). She also set up her own production company, Maria Menado Productions. This unusual career for a woman in South-East Asia in the 1950s has been noted by Blackburn, who commented on this aspect in his article "Maria Menado: Feminist Film Maker?"[10] Menado's film career ended abruptly when she married the Sultan of Pahang in 1963.

The departure of the one and only pontianak star had a significant impact on the future and profits of the Malay vampire film in Malaysia and Singapore. Moreover, the Sultan's palace had prohibited the screenings of those films featuring the star-turned-Queen. As a result, Malaysian television (RTM) programmes were also affected. This must have been of great concern to Ho Ah Loke, one of the two key Cathay-Keris producers who, upon leaving the company in 1960, had the first two pontianak films in his custody. The hot-tempered Ho, in a moment of despair or, as

[10] Blackburn 2002 [B].

the exotic pontianaks

Hamzah Hussin suggests, "out of disappointment and defiance,"[11] disposed of these two films among others, both negatives and positives; rumour has it that they were thrown into Kuala Lumpur's Gombak river. It hardly needs to be stressed that these events have contributed to the serious information shortage and frustrating factual confusion regarding the early pontianak films, a situation made more difficult with the passing of the years.

Unique stylistic blend

The second film in the Cathay-Keris series, *Dendam Pontianak*, also made in 1957, was even more successful at the box office than the first. The critical reaction too was more favourable, with the filmmakers' successful effort at blending traditional horror with elements of comedy and song especially pointed out. According to Hussin, this was also the first time that a Malay-language film included comical characters from the Bangsawan Malay opera.[12]

The third pontianak film - and the first Singapore Cinemascope movie - was made by Cathay-Keris shortly after the first two successes. The director, the story, the setting and the cast of *Sumpah Pontianak* were largely the same as in the earlier films, as was the presence of the comical and lyrical scenes. The latter were characterised by the daughter Maria (Salmah Ahmad) calling for her vampiric mother Chomel (Menado) through her songs. This film actually has a happy ending, as the mother saves both her daughter and herself: she overpowers the truly evil spirit, the "wild man" Hantu Raya, in mortal combat, saves Maria and regains beauty for herself.

The integration of antithetical generic components - violence, suspense and horror on one hand, comedy, song and dance on the other - is not a common feature of the Western vampire film, but it became one of the typical features of the Singapore-produced Malay pontianak pictures. Here, the comical and lyrical elements are inserted as semi-autonomous parts which constitute digressions from the main action. The humorous scenes usually assume the form of colourful village conflicts of minor importance, such as quarrels between competing satay and noodle sellers. The comical characters also blunder at night into the jungle and experience "pontianak" attacks, which are usually revealed as cases of mistaken identity, practical jokes, or the result of general confusion. These scenes are longer than the customary comic diversions filmmakers use to relieve accumulated suspense and dramatic tension. Nevertheless, they do not serve to change the film into a full-fledged vampire comedy such as Roman Polanski's *The Fearless Vampire Killers* (aka *Dance of the Vampires*, 1966).

The humorous sketches became the road to fame for a remarkably gifted comedian, Wahid Satay, who had originally worked as a set designer. In *Pontianak*, he was given the supporting role of a satay seller where the expressiveness of his pantomimic facial gestures, his nimble body movement and his amusing singing style quickly endeared him to the audience. This success secured him similar roles in *Dendam Pontianak* and *Sumpah Pontianak*. According to Hussin, Wahid was a "most unique star" of these films.[13]

In the pontianak films the lyrical intermezzos are usually reserved for the young heroine or other main characters. The camera would follow the characters during their leisurely walks through beautiful natural scenery. These moments, which virtually cause the action to stop, may remind the viewer of the familiar techniques of the film musical. A closer look at these musical numbers will show that they are rooted in the unflagging potency of popular Indian cinema.

This is not surprising, as it was mainly Indian directors, cinematographers, editors and other experienced film craftsmen - including B.N. Rao and B.S. Rajhans - who were invited to Singapore to help set up the local film production. These filmmakers brought with them the stylistic attributes of Indian cinema, including the musical component. They fused these with Malay, Indonesian, Chinese and Hollywood artistic traditions, eventually developing the style characteristic of the Singapore Malay cinema of the 1950s and 60s, reflected in the pontianak films and which no doubt contributed to their success.

These structural characteristics were quite different from the techniques used in the classical Hollywood paradigm. According to the National University of Singapore film historian Timothy White, what could be seen as stylistic inconsistency in Western eyes, "...is not unusual in Malaysian films; obviously, one reason for this is economic, but its acceptance is indicative of a culture that, unlike most Western cultures, does not seek absolute verisimilitude in the consistency of *mise-en-scène*. Such cultures tend to value performance, or presentation, over 'realistic' representation..."[14]

---

[11] Hamzah, 97.

[12] Bangsawan is a form of Malay opera developed through various stages from the Indian Parsi Theatre, which was brought to Penang, Malaysia by visiting troupes from India during the last quarter of the 19th century. From Penang the genre spread to the rest of the Malay Peninsula as well as to Singapore and Indonesia. Bangsawan is improvisational in character, with stereotyped roles and acting, and an extensive repertoire of stories derived from several sources, including Indian, Western, Chinese, Indonesian, and Malay. Music and incidental dance are optional. See Tan Sooi Beng 1993/1997.

[13] Hamzah, 43.

[14] White: 14-15.

A dialectical vampire

An interesting element of the pontianak subgenre, and one which can also be detected in some of the related oily man films, is the fact that these phantoms - the pontianak and the oily man - are not completely evil; often they are persons wronged or rejected by the community, or else they are victims of its customs. For example, a woman's death in childbirth and the death of her baby may be directly or indirectly caused by others; or the unfortunate individual may be ostracised because of his unappealing looks or physical impairment. The pontianak or the oily man then comes back to haunt the community.

One of the most appropriate examples illustrating the phantom's dialectical nature can be seen in *Sumpah Orang Minyak*. Although the film does not bring up the pontianak legend, and features instead a male protagonist, its narrative structure is similar to those of the early pontianaks. The film's main character, Si Bongkok (P. Ramlee), was born a gifted artist but an ugly hunchback. Because of this, he is frequently taunted by the villagers. When he reveals his love for a beautiful maiden, he is chased out of the village. Upon his appeal to God about this injustice he is taken to a magic kingdom where he is made beautiful after taking a bath in a magic pool. He will remain so upon one condition: he must never kill anyone. Si Bongkok's return to his village provokes a confrontation and his rival cowardly kills the girl he had loved. Enraged, Si Bongkok challenges his rival to a duel and kills him. Made invisible as a punishment, Si Bongkok is approached by Satan who promises him physical beauty again if he rapes twenty-one girls within seven days. Thus the protagonist begins his hideous career as the oily man, with no way out.

Not only is *Sumpah Orang Minyak* a beautiful and poignant tale, with resonances of the *Thousand and One Nights* and the great tragedies of antiquity, but it also points out the community's complicity in the fate of the doomed protagonist. Such stories, minus the supernatural elements, tend to be fairly accurate reflections of everyday life and its problems, and therefore have an undeniable moral purpose. This may be one of the less obvious reasons for these films' unusual popularity, in addition to the fact that many of the old superstitions have survived until today, despite the high-tech veneer of the region's metropolises like Singapore and Kuala Lumpur.

The decline

In 1963, Ramón Estella directed the last pontianak movie with Maria Menado, *Pontianak Kembali* (*The Vampire Returns*), produced by Cathay-Keris and Maria Menado Productions. The following year, Cathay-Keris once again engaged the experienced B.N. Rao to make *Pontianak Gua Musang* (*The Vampire of the Cave*, 1964). Set in a *kampong*, this was virtually a comedy version of the vampire film and one of the more interesting pontianak movies of the 1960s.

In general, however, the quality of the pontianak productions declined in this decade. Perhaps the most conspicuous change was the "modernisation" of the genre formula. The traditional - and in a way timeless - *kampong* setting was replaced by an urban one; the main characters shed their colourful sarongs for western-style attire; Malay tunes gave way to jazz and pop music. More importantly, the supernatural activities of the monsters were replaced by events that could be explained rationally.

A typical case illustrating these structural changes was Estella's *Pusaka Pontianak* (*The Accursed Heritage*, 1965), which was also the last of the pontianak series. The film tells the story of a group of urban, money-hungry contenders for a dead magnate's fortune. To make themselves eligible, they must follow the rich man's will and spend a couple of weeks in his mansion on a secluded rubber plantation. There, they are subjected to nocturnal attacks by a deadly "pontianak." However, it is revealed at the end that the whole thing was only a diabolical plot hatched by a pair of criminals trying - Agatha Christie-style - to eliminate the lawful heirs and secure the magnate's millions for themselves. To emphasise the atmosphere of contemporary sophistication, the characters drive swanky sports cars and dress-up in sexy clothes, while the musical numbers are provided by The Swallows, a pop group striving to emulate the Beatles.

The orang minyak movies, like those of the pontianak, reflect similarly unsuccessful attempts at modernisation. The second entry in the Cathay-Keris series, L. Krishnan's *Serangan Orang Minyak*, focuses on a young Singapore police inspector whose life, and that of his family, is threatened by a vengeful oily man. One of the few original generic elements in this film appears in the prologue, in which the oily man asks his mysterious "master" - an invisible character living inside a banana tree - to grant him supernatural powers to accomplish his revenge. After that, the film's plot switches gears and seems closer to a watered-down cops-and-robbers movie than to its vampiric cousins. In one scene, which was presumably not meant to be comical, the inspector dresses like Marlon Brando in *The Wild One* (1954) - complete with leather jacket and beret. *Serangan Orang Minyak* is less than a pale reflection of P. Ramlee's *Sumpah Orang Minyak*, which uses traditional plot and settings.

It would seem that the main problem and the eventual demise of the Singapore Malay vampire film was the precipitated disappearance of the traditional *kampong* community in which it was rooted and which had provided it with both subject matter and setting. The second half of the 1950s ushered in a period of political turmoil: the pullout of the British from its colonies in the region; the short-lived period of Singapore as a member of the Malaysian Federation (1963-65); and the establishment of the independent Republic of Singapore (1965). This was followed by a period of intense urbanisation and economic growth. In Singapore, there were no longer enough kapok trees where the pontianaks could hide. The attempts at modernisation of the pontianak genre, mostly synonymous with the grafting of Western models onto local cultural foundations, could not be successful and the pontianaks and oily men disappeared from the film screen, along with Singapore film production, to be resuscitated only in the 1990s, after two decades of production standstill.

Return of the Pontianaks?

In the mid-seventies, director/producer Roger Sutton made a valiant attempt to pull the pontianak film out of its grave by releasing his version of *Pontianak*, a modernised and bloodier variation of the familiar 1950s theme, including the humorous and musical breaks. Shot in full widescreen, this was the first colour feature in the Malay-language subgenre, which did little to salvage a movie plagued by weaknesses such as rough editing and bad post-synchronisation. Not surprisingly, the film fell quickly into obscurity.

More recently, interest in the pontianak horror film was rekindled by the emergence of a Singapore production with the tantalising title *Return to Pontianak* (2000). Written and directed by Djinn (Ong Lay Jinn), the 81-minute feature was shot on digital video on a shoestring budget of US $20,000 and transferred onto 35mm for the silver screen. Like the pontianak movies of the 1960s, the film attempts to breathe new life into the ancient legend by giving it a contemporary setting. As a sign of how modern things have become, the Malay language is now replaced by English.

In this tale, an Asian American girl, Charity (played by Vietnamese actress Hiep Thi Le, the lead actress in Oliver Stone's 1993 *Heaven and Earth*), together with four other young city dwellers, venture into a Malaysian jungle in search of a lost village, the place where her biological parents were said to have died. Instead of the village, they come across a dilapidated hut inhabited by an old Malay man and make the startling find of a beautiful if dishevelled young woman, living under the hut. Disturbed by this, the urbanites decide to find their way out of the jungle but not before the grisly discovery of the decapitated body of one of their friends. While the group had previously thought they were being followed by the mysterious white-robed girl, they now realise they are being slowly hunted down.

Thanks to the nostalgic longing for the old pontianak movies, and to a deeply ingrained cultural regard for the supernatural, there was no lack of interest in the new pontianak feature. *Return to Pontianak* premiered at the 2001 Singapore International Film Festival (appropriately on Friday the 13th of April) to a full house eagerly waiting to be terrified. What the audience saw instead was a less-than-impressive imitation of

above:
A publicity float for **Pontianak Gua Musang** (aka **The Vampire of the Cave**), 1964.
(courtesy of Cathay-Keris Film Pte Ltd)

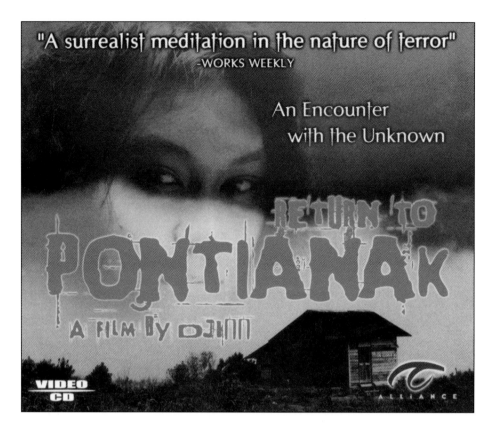

right:
VCD cover artwork for **Return to Pontianak** (2000).

the hugely successful American independent horror film, *The Blair Witch Project* (1999). Djinn's pontianak, played by 17-year-old Fadzlina Mohamad Shafie, is beautiful, subtle and mute, with a menacing stare. Atmospheric though the film may be, it never quite manages to hold the audience in a grip of terror. On the positive side, *Return to Pontianak* was among the first film experiments in the city state shot on digital video. Despite general disappointment with the new pontianak film at home, the movie has been making its share of rounds at international film festivals, particularly in Asia and North America.

With the advantage of half-a-century's distance, one can view the transparent horror special effects of the faded pontianak and oily man pictures with the benevolent smile of one who knows better. However, there is more to these old B-movies than first meets the eye: they are in fact unintentional witnesses of a vanished world of lost customs and lifestyles of a recent past. The best of these movies exemplify the inventive craftsmanship, imagination and artistic honesty so difficult to find in much of today's commercial film production.

Appendix 1: Pontianak films

1. *Pontianak* (*The Vampire*, 1957). Director: Balkrishna Narayan Rao. Producer: Cathay-Keris (Ho Ah Loke). Cast: Maria Menado, M. Amin, Salmah Ahmed, Dollah Serawak, Aminah Yena, N. Kassim. Malay language, b/w. Prints presumed lost.

2. *Dendam Pontianak* (*Revenge of the Vampire*, 1957). Director: Balkrishna Narayan Rao. Producer: Cathay-Keris. Cast: Maria Menado, Puteh Lawak, S. M. Wahid, Mustapha Maarof, Salmah Ahmad, Rahimah Alias. Malay language, b/w. Prints presumed lost.

3. *Sumpah Pontianak* (*The Vampire's Curse / Blood of Pontianak*, 1958). Director: Balkrishna Narayan Rao. Script: Abdul Razak. Producer: Cathay-Keris. Cast: Salmah Ahmad, Mustaffa Maarof, Maria Menado. Malay language, b/w Cinemascope, ca 90min.

4. *Anak Pontianak* (*Son of the Vampire*, 1958.) Director: Ramón A. Estella. Script: Abdul Razak. Producer: Shaw MFP. Cast: Kemat Bin Hassan, Sofia Dyang, Hasimah, Jins Samsuddin, Haj Sattar. Malay language, b/w.

5. *Pontianak Kembali* (*The Vampire Returns*, 1963). Director: Ramón A. Estella. Producer: Cathay-Keris

and Maria Menado Production. Cast: Maria Menado, Malik Selamat. Malay language, b/w.

6. *Pontianak Gua Musang* (*The Vampire of the Cave*, 1964). Director: Balkrishna Narayan Rao. Producer: Cathay-Keris. Cast: Suraya Haron, Ghazali Sumantri, Malek Siamat, Ummi Kalthoum. Malay language, b/w 121min.

7. *Pusaka Pontianak* (*The Accursed Heritage*, 1965). Script and Director: Ramón A. Estella. Producer: Shaw MFP. Cast: Sa'adiah, Ahmad Mahmud, Dayang Sofia, Salleh Kamil, Normadiah, Aziz Sattar, Ahmad Daud, Ibrahim Pendek. Malay language, b/w, 100 min.

8. *Pontianak* (ca 1975). Director and Executive producer: Roger Sutton. Producer: Hamid Bond Organisation and Kobe Trading Company. Cast: Hamid Bond, Ah Leng, Herdawati (Indonesia), Piya Johnny (Thailand), Sharif Medau (Singapore). VCD release Lokasari (Malaysia). Malay language. Colour, cinemascope, 89 min.

9. *Return to Pontianak* (aka *Voodoo Nightmare*, 2000). Script and Director: Djinn (Ong Lay Jinn). Cast: Hiep Thi Le, Fadali, Eleanor Lee, Fadzlina Mohamad Shafie, Steven Banks, Victor Khong. English language, colour, digital, 81min.

Appendix 2: Orang Minyak films

1. *Orang Minyak* (*Oily Man*, 1958). Director: L. Krishnan. Producer: Cathay-Keris. Cast: Salmah Ahmad, Noordin Ahmad, Roomai Noor, Latifah Omar, M. Amin. Malay language, b/w. Prints presumed lost.

2. *Sumpah Orang Minyak* (*The Curse of Oily Man*, 1958). Script, Director: P. Ramlee. Producer: Shaw Brothers MFP. Cast: P. Ramlee, Sri Dewi, Salleh Kamil, Marion Willis, Daeng Idris. Award: Best Black and White Photography (Abu Bakar Ali). Malay language, b/w, ??min.

3. *Serangan Orang Minyak* (*The Oilyman Strikes Again*, 1958). Script, Director: L. Krishnan. Producer: Cathay-Keris. Cast: M. Amin, Latifah Omar, Noordin Ahmar, S. M. Wahir. Editor and Music supervision: Hussain Haniff. Chinese number: S. K. Law Wah. Malay language, b/w, ca 112 min.

Appendix 3: Literature on Singapore cinema (including works cited)

Blackburn, Kevin P. [A]. "The Golden Days of Cinema in Singapore." www.arts.nie.edu.sg/his/blackburn/Singapore.htm (National Institute of Education at Nanyang Technological University.) 23 March 2002.

Blackburn, Kevin P. [B]. "Maria Menado: Feminist Film Maker?" www.arts.nie.edu.sg/his/blackburn/Menado.htm. (National Institute of Education at Nanyang Technological University.) 29 March 2002.

Francis, Sean D. "Malayan Vampires," www.stygian-labyrinth.net/forvampires/lifestyleculture/malayan.html, 17 March 2002.

Gladwin, Stephen. "Witches, spells and politics: the horror films of Indonesia." In *Fear Without Frontiers: Horror Cinema Across the Globe*, ed. Steven Jay Schneider. Surrey: FAB Press, 2003, 219-29.

Hussin, Hamzah. *Memoir Hamzah Hussin. Dari Keris Film ke Studio Merdeka*. Kuala Lumpur: Penerbit Universiti Kebangsaan, Malaysia.

Lim, Kay Tong. *Cathay: 55 Years of Cinema*. Singapore: Landmark Books, 1991.

Mohamed Anis Md Nor. *Zapin: Folk Dance of the Malay World*. Singapore: Oxford Uni. Press, 1993.

Skeat, Walter W. *Malay Magic: Being an Introduction to the Folklore and Popular Religion of the Malay Peninsula*. 1900. Reprint, New York: Benjamin Blom, 1972.

Tan Sooi Beng. *Bangsawan: A Social and Stylistic History of Popular Malay Opera*. Kuala Lumpur: Oxford University Press, 1993; and Penang: The Asian Centre, 1997.

Uhde, Jan and Yvonne Ng Uhde. *Latent Images: Film in Singapore*. Singapore: Oxford University Press, 2000.

Wazir Jahan Karim (ed.) *Emotions of Culture: A Malay Perspective*. Singapore: Oxford University Press, 1990.

White, Timothy: "Historical Poetics, Malaysian Cinema, and the Japanese Occupation." *Kinema: A Journal for Film and Audiovisual Media* 6, Fall 1996, 5-23.

White, Timothy. "Pontianaks, P. Ramlee and Islam: The Cinema of Malaysia." *The Arts* (Centre for the Arts, NUS) June 1997, No 4, 18-21.

Witcombe, L.C.E. "Eve and the Identity of Women" http://witcombe.sbc.edu/eve-women/7evelilith.html, 24 March 2002.

Zinjuaher H.M. Ariffin, Sharifah. *Serajan Filem Melayu/The History of Malay Motion Pictures*. Kuala Lumpur: Sri Sharifah, 1980.

Playing with genre: defining the Italian *giallo*

Gary Needham

In 1929, the Milanese publishing giant Mondadori launched a line of books in yellow cover, hence "giallo" - the Italian word for yellow - as part of a large campaign to promote, specifically, tales of mystery and detection. These works consisted primarily of imported translations of British "rational-deduction" fictions of the Sherlock Holmes variety and the early twentieth century American quasi-fantastic murder mysteries built on the Edgar Allan Poe model.

Before 1929, the notion of the detective was something unknown to the Italians, but that isn't to say that works of detection, mystery and investigation were not in circulation; rather those sorts of fictions were to be found under the banner of adventure. The publication of *gialli* increased throughout the 1930s and 40s, however the importation and translation of the 1940s "hard-boiled" detective fictions from the U.S. were prohibited from publication outright by Mussolini on the grounds that their corrupting influence and glamorisation of crime would negatively influence "weak-minded" Italians.

It wasn't long before Italian authors began writing under anglicised pseudonyms their own *gialli* based on the early British and American models of rational thought and logical deduction. Only after the war did a truly Italian form of the fiction began to emerge, principally in the work of Leonardo Sciascia. Not only did Sciascia write his own important *gialli* (including *Il giorno della civetta* [*The Day of the Crow*] and *A ciascuno il suo* [*To Each His Own*]); he also published two polemical articles in the 1950s on the specificity of the Italian *giallo* and its need to be taken seriously by Italian intellectuals, particularly those on the left influenced by Gramsci. Today, *gialli* continue to be written by Italians, Umberto Eco's *Il nome della rosa* (*The Name of the Rose*) in 1984 being the most famous and prestigious outside of Italy. There are also numerous translations into Italian of novelists such as Thomas Harris, Patricia Cornwell, et al.

It is the *giallo* on film that concerns us here, however, and it emerges during the "Golden Age" of Italian cinema in the early 1960s. One interesting point about the *giallo* in its cinematic form is that it appears to be less fixed as a genre than its written counterpart. The term itself doesn't indicate, as genres often do, an essence, a description or a feeling. It functions in a more peculiar and flexible manner as a conceptual category with highly moveable and permeable boundaries that shift around from year to year to include outright gothic horror (*La lama nel corpo* [*The Murder Clinic*, Emilio Scardimaglia, 1966]), police procedurals (*Milano, morte sospetta di una minorenne* [Sergio Martino, 1975]), crime melodrama (*Così dolce, così perversa* [*So Sweet So Perverse*, Umberto Lenzi, 1969]) and conspiracy films (*Terza ipotesi su un casa di perfetta strategia criminale* [*Who Killed the Prosecutor and Why?*, Giuseppe Vari, 1972]).

It should be understood then that the *giallo* is something different to that which is conventionally analysed as a genre. The Italians have the word *filone*, which is often used to refer to both genres and cycles as well as to currents and trends. This points to the limitations of genre theory built primarily on American film genres but also to the need for redefinition

opposite:
L'uccello dalle piume di cristallo (aka **The Bird with the Crystal Plumage**), 1970.

right:
L'occhio nel labirinto
(aka **The Eye in the Labyrinth**), 1972

opposite:
Lo strano vizio della Signora Wardh (aka **Next!**), 1970

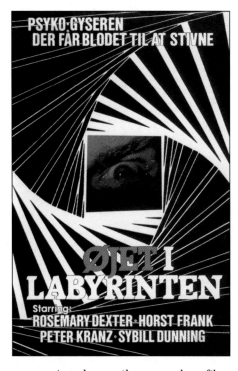

1 Though in George Pollock's *Murder She Said* (UK, 1961), which predates the Bava by two years, we see Miss Marple (Margaret Rutherford) get on the 4:50 from Paddington (the original title of Agatha Christie's source novel); as she settles down to read her murder-mystery novel, she glances out the window at a passing train to see a black-gloved and black raincoat-wearing killer strangling a beautiful blonde woman in a passing train. (In the novel, it is a friend of Miss Marple who sees this.) Thanks to Mikel Koven for this example.

2 Cf. Humphries, R. (2001) "Just another fashion victim: Mario Bava's *Sei donne per l'assassino* (*Blood and Black Lace*, 1964)", *Kinoeye: A Fortnightly Journal of Film in the New Europe* 1.7, 26 November, www.kinoeye.org/01/07/humphries07.html.

can be argued that the Italian *giallo* predates Bava's film, as the term has frequently been used to associate Luchino Visconti's *Ossessione* (1943) with the tradition. However, the reason why Bava's film is the "true" starting point of the *giallo* is its explicit and successful attempt to say to the spectator, in effect, "The Italian *giallo* has arrived."

The opening sequence has Nora Davis (Letícia Roman) reading a *giallo* novel on an airplane. The entire scene is essentially a foundational gesture that brings together several elements all at once: the staging of the *giallo*'s literary origins through *mise-en-abime*[1] (also central to Dario Argento's *Tenebre* [*Tenebrae/Unsane*, 1982]); the foreigner coming to/being in Italy; the obsession with travel and tourism not only as a mark of the newly emerging European jet-set (consider how many *gialli* begin or end in airports), but representative of Italian cinema's selling of its own "Italian-ness" through tourist hotspots (initiated by the murder on the Spanish Steps in Bava's film as well as countless deaths in or around famous squares, fountains and monuments throughout the *giallo*); and of course fashion and style.

I am confident in suggesting that the familiar black raincoat associated with the *giallo* killer stems from continental fashion trends in the 1960s and has since shifted its meaning over the decades to become the *couture* choice of the assassin by default in addition to serving as one of the *giallo*'s most identifiable visual tropes. Bava's *Sei donne per l'assassino* (*Blood and Black Lace*, 1964), set in a fashion house, confirms this observation as the use of a black Macintosh for disguise purposes potentially means it could be any number of the models and, at the same time, situate itself on the pulse of fashion.[2]

Returning to *La ragazza che sapeva troppo*, the American title of the film is *The Evil Eye*, illustrating the *giallo*'s obsession with vision and the *testimone oculare*, or eye-witness. *La ragazza che sapeva troppo* (*The Girl Who Knew Too Much*) might have been called *The Girl Who Saw Too Much*, but that would have betrayed the allusion to Hitchcock in the title. Nora questions the authority of her own witnessing of a murder on the Spanish Steps in Rome. She ends up unconscious and delirious in a hospital, and is subjected to scrutiny by both the police inspector and her doctor - the twin

concerning how other popular film-producing nations understand and relate to their products. This introduction to the *giallo*, therefore, begins from the assumption that the *giallo* is not so much a genre, as its literary history might indicate, but a body of films that resists generic definition. In this respect it is unlike the Italian horror and *poliziotto* (police) genres yet, at the same time, the *giallo* can be understood as an object to be promoted, criticised, studied, etc.

By its very nature the *giallo* challenges our assumptions about how non-Hollywood films should be classified, going beyond the sort of Anglo-American taxonomic imaginary that "fixes" genre both in film criticism and the film industry in order to designate something specific. As alluded to above, however, despite the *giallo*'s resistance to clear definition there are nevertheless identifiable thematic and stylistic tropes. There is a stereotypical *giallo* and the *giallo*-fan has his or her idea of what constitutes the *giallo* canon. The following points therefore, are an attempt to clarify and define familiar aspects of this "canon."

Early efforts

In 1963, Mario Bava directed the first true Italian *giallo*: *La ragazza che sapeva troppo* (*The Girl Who Knew Too Much*). It

agents of naming sickness and of doubting female testimony.

The hybrid medico-detective discourse is a popular one in the *giallo*. Hallucinations and subjective "visions" are central both to the protagonists and the narrative enigma in *Una lucertola con la pelle di donne* (*Lizard in a Woman's Skin*, Lucio Fulci, 1971) and *Lo strano vizio della signora Wardh* (aka *Next!*, Sergio Martino, 1971) and are part of the *giallo*'s inherent pathologising of femininity and fascination with "sick" women. Hysterics are in abundance here: films such as *Il coltello di ghiaccio* (*Knife of Ice*, Umberto Lenzi, 1972) and *Tutti i colori del buio* (*They're Coming to Get You*, Sergio Martino, 1972) anchor their narratives around the collapse of the "sickness" and mystery, albeit through the conduit of femininity.

The 1960s made a slow but sure inroad for the *giallo* in Italian cinema. The period following 1963's *The Evil Eye* was clearly a mapping out of new territory for Italian directors, not only for the *giallo* but also for the Italian horror film. The early- to mid-60s *giallo* didn't exhibit the strength of other genres of the period such as the western, the horror and the *peplum* ("sword-and-sandal" movie). However, one remarkable thing about the *giallo* is its longevity; even if its presence has been slight at times, it has still spanned over four decades of Italian cinema with the latest Dario Argento film, *Nonhosonno* (*Sleepless*, 2001). Not only does *Sleepless* constitute a return to form for the director, but it signals a revisting of his own debut, *L'uccello dalle piume di cristallo* (*The Bird with the Crystal Plumage*, 1970). Perhaps again the *giallo*'s staying power can be reduced to a resistance of the homogenising constraints that traditional genre membership often imposes on bodies of films by making them fit particular historical and critical categories.

Instead of defining the *giallo* in generic and historical terms, I would like to suggest that we understand it in a more "discursive" fashion, as something constructed out of the various associations, networks, tensions and articulations of Italian cinema's textual and industrial specificity in the post-war period. It happens that the *giallo* revolves around murder, mystery, detection, psychoanalysis, tourism, alienation and investigation. Therefore, I would like to tentatively flag the following issues as a starting point for future study.

Psychoanalysis

The *giallo* literally begs for psychoanalytic inquiry and at the same time stages both the "analytical scene" and the "classic symptoms." As usual, this staging occurs through the conduit of femininity but in some cases - as in (almost) every Dario Argento film - masculinity becomes the focal point. The typical Argento protagonist is the victim/witness of trauma who must keep returning to the scene of the crime (the Freudian "*nachtraglichkeit*" or retranscription of memory; popularly represented via flashback sequences), often committed by a killer who just can't resist serial murder (the psychoanalytic "compulsion to repeat").

L'occhio nel labirinto (*The Eye in the Labyrinth*, Mario Caiano, 1972) is about the murder of a male psychoanalyst by his female patient who confuses him as lover, doctor and father. *L'occhio nel*

below:
Il gatto a nove code (aka **The Cat O'Nine Tails**), 1970

defining the Italian giallo

above:
Gatti rossi in un labirinto di vetro (aka **Eyeball**), 1974

labirinto also goes so far as to open with a cryptic quote from Borges, from which the film constructs the triple analogy of labyrinth:mind:narrative before structuring the old Freudian war-horse of "woman as mystery." Many of the *giallo*'s female protagonists are either in therapy, have had therapy or are told that they *need* therapy. (The *giallo* queen of psychic discontent has to be Edwige Fenech, whose performances confirm that hysteria is always histrionic when it comes to Italian cinema.)

The *giallo* is a paradigm case in defence of psychoanalysis. It solicits psychoanalytic interpretation and stages every oedipal scenario literally and spectacularly.

Italy

above:
La dama rossa uccide sette volte (aka **The Lady in Red Kills Seven Times**), 1972

opposite:
Giornata nera per l'ariete (aka **The Fifth Cord**), 1971

[3] See Clover, C. (1994) "The Eye of Horror." In *Viewing Positions: Ways of Seeing Film*, ed Linda Williams (1994). New Brunswick: Rutgers University Press.

Testimone oculare

The Italian term for the eye-witness of a crime. Those who watch their *gialli* in Italian will hear these two words frequently. The *giallo* makes a point about the failings of vision as a source of authority and knowledge. *Il gatto a nove code* (*The Cat O' Nine Tails*, Dario Argento, 1971) goes as far as to create an "aural mystery", a restaging of Alfred Hitchcock's *Rear Window* (1954), including a blind crossword-puzzle maker as one of its detectives.

All sorts of vision/knowledge dynamics are explored in the *giallo*, but never to such great effect as in *L'uccello dalle piume di cristallo*, whose foreigner abroad, *flaneur* Sam Dalmas (Tony Musante), is eye-witness to a knife assault in a chic Roman art gallery. The gallery is explicitly concerned with maximising clarity and vision: the space is minimal so there are no distractions for the gaze other than that of the crime; the doors/façade are enormous glass panels; nothing is obscured; the entire area is brightly lit. However, despite all of these supports aiding Dalmas's vision, he fails to see (or in psychoanalytic terms, he *misrecognises*) the truth of his gaze. Other *gialli* which foreground the eye-witness narrative strand are *Passi di danza su una lama di rasoio* (*Death Carries a Cane*, Maurizio Pradeaux, 1972) and, of course, *La ragazza che sapeva troppo*.

Quite related to the theme of eye-witnesses and unreliable sight - and in the spirit of Carol Clover[3] - are the numerous incidents of violence done to the eyes (including those in *Gatti rossi in un labirinto di vetro* [*Eyeball*, Umberto Lenzi 1974] and *Opera* [Dario Argento, 1987]) and the generous amount of titles with "*gli occhi*" in them, whether this refers to the eyes of detectives, victims, killers or cats (e.g., *I gatto dagli occhi di giada* [*The Cat's Victims*, Antonio Bido, 1976] and *Gli occhi freddi della paura* [*Cold Eyes of Fear*, Enzo Girolami Castellari 1971]). The *giallo* eye is both penetrating and penetrated.

Detection

As a work of detection, the *giallo* is less a set of conventions than a playful resource about them. Detection is often the point of entry for an exploration of how to sort out the normal from the pathological through identity and representation. Along with psychoanalysis, detection was one of the great ends of nineteenth-century epistemology and it is by now a cliché to make the analogy between detective and analyst.

Many *gialli* clearly define the pathological other, including *Sette scialli di seta gialla* (aka *Crimes of the Black Cat*, Sergio Pastore, 1972) and *La bestia uccide a sangue freddo* (aka *Slaughter Hotel*, Fernando Di Leo, 1971), and it is the sole purpose of these particular films to exploit this characterisation. The detective's job thus becomes one of uncovering, naming and containing otherness as something socially and morally threatening. However, several progressive *gialli* (again mostly those of Argento, but also *Giornata nera per l'ariete* [aka *The Fifth Cord*, Luigi Bazzoni, 1971]) play with the conventions of detection and investigation procedures in order to explore issues of masculinity and identity. Key themes in such *gialli* include alienation, failed detection, otherness and the well-worn European concept of the "subject in process/on trial."

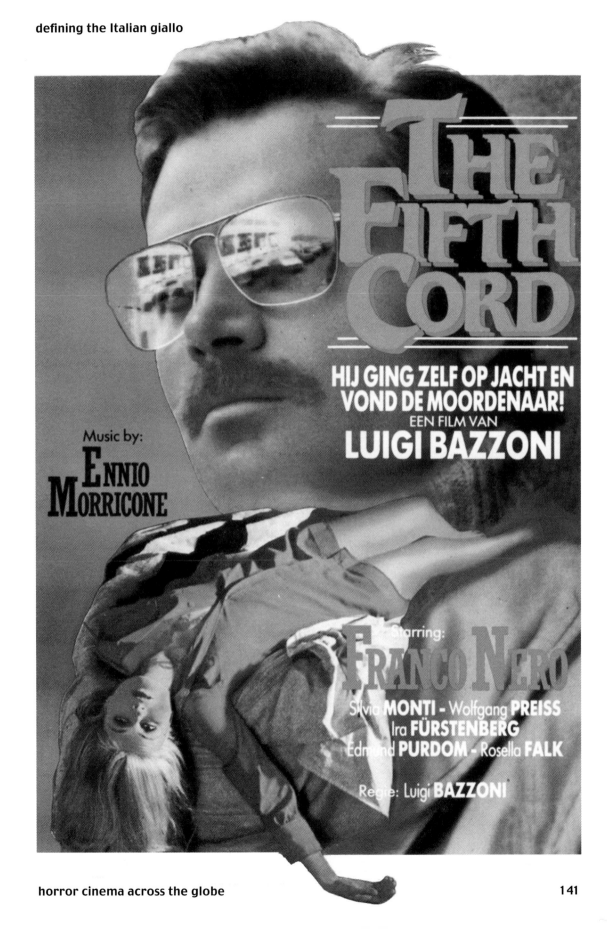

right:
La bestia uccide a sangue freddo (aka **Slaughter Hotel**), 1971.

[4] See, e.g., Doty, A. (1993) *Making Things Perfectly Queer: Interpreting Mass Culture.* Minneapolis: University of Minnesota Press.

Camp

While many *giallo* viewers await the ubiquitous Susan Scott's next undressing scene, many many others are waiting to see her next fabulous outfit. Such is the *giallo* that it panders to both readings: erotic anticipation and camp sensibility. The *giallo* is a document of 60s and 70s style that years later can be seen as utterly camp. Even the most tired of *gialli* is capable of being resurrected as a "masterpiece", thanks to Alexander Doty's example of making things queer[4] and wardrobe departments whose creativity and expression at times exceeds that of the director.

How many *gialli* are set in and around fashion houses and photographers' studios? *Sei donne per l'assassino*, *Nude per l'assassino* (*Strip Nude for Your Killer*, Andrea Bianchi, 1975) and *La dama rosa uccide a sette volte* (*The Lady in Red Kills Seven Times*, Emilio P

defining the Italian giallo

Miraglia, 1972), just to name a few. How many of the *gialli*'s victims are fashion models?**5**

The literary

Referring back to the *giallo*'s origins in the 1930s with the translations of British and early American murder mysteries, it appears that the cinematic *giallo* has never quite forgotten its debt to the literary. The most explicit examples include the staging of the *giallo* book as an object in *La ragazza che sapeva troppo* and the author/reader of the *giallo* as central to the narrative in *Tenebre*. In the latter film, Peter Neal (Anthony Franciosa) is an American *gialli* author, and Giuliano Gemma's detective is an avid reader of Sherlock Holmes stories who even quotes what is perhaps the mantra of the *giallo*'s dénouement: "whatever remains, however improbable, must be truth" (from Arthur Conan Doyle's *The Sign of the Four*).

Although uncredited, Agatha Christie is the main source of inspiration and imitation for *Concerto per pistola solista* (*The Weekend Murders*, Michele Lupo, 1970) and *5 bambole per la luna d'agostso* (*Five Dolls for an August Moon*, Mario Bava, 1969). Edgar Allan Poe is also represented in *gialli* such as *Sette note in nero* (aka *The Psychic*, Lucio Fulci, 1977), not to mention Argento's ineffectual cut-and-paste of Poe's world in the "black cat" episode of *Due occhi diabolici* (*Two Evil Eyes*, Dario Argento and George Romero, 1990).

The postcolonial question

Travel, tourism, exoticism, hybridity and foreignness are all familiar features of the *giallo*. The textuality of Italian cinema after the 1950s has many features that seem to open up queries problematising the concept of a national film movement and a national identity. The main protagonist of the *giallo* is often the foreigner in Italy or the Italian on holiday. "Exotic locations" include Dublin (*L'iguana dalla lingue di fuoco* [*The Iguana with a Tongue of Fire*, Riccardo Freda, 1971]), Haiti (*Al tropico del cancro* [aka *Death in Haiti*, Edoardo Mulargia and Giampaolo Lomi, 1972]) and Africa (*L'uomo più velonoso del cobra* [*Human Cobras*, Bitto Albertini, 1971]). Characters don't seem fixed to a home or location; they are always (in) between different places. This justifies the advertisements for various transatlantic airlines that bookend the *giallo*, not to mention the promos for every traveller's favourite drink - a J&B whisky. This must be the most plugged product in the history of European Cinema. Look out for it.

When the *giallo* is set in Italy it typically takes one of three different routes. Sometimes it promotes "Italian-ness" through a foregrounding of identifiable tourist spots that often halt the narrative and serve as sheer spectacle. Other times it strives to erase Italian-ness by establishing the setting as an(other) anonymous European city, avoiding distinctive signifiers of Italy altogether. And still other times it constructs a "rural-historical" locale as a place of the uncanny, as in *La casa dalle finestre che ridono* (*The House with the Windows that Laugh*, Pupi Avati, 1976).

Italian popular cinema tends to promote the non-national, and this variably results in a tendency to exaggerate and exploit the "foreign" through the tropes of travel and the tourist's gaze. Ugo Liberatore's *Incontro d'amore a Bali* (1970) and the *Black Emanuelle* series (1975-83) instigated a whole *filone* of soft-porn desert island and globe-trotting adventure films, fueling what Anne McClintock calls the "porno-tropics",**6** and which in turn influenced the direction of the *giallo* towards a more pan-exotic exploration of mystery, detection and murder to sustain the public's interest and changing tastes.**7**

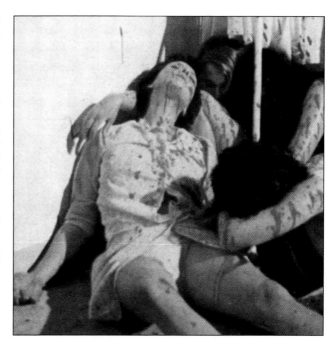

above:
A pile of corpses; archetypal giallo imagery from **Slaughter Hotel**.

5 See Humphries, *op cit*.

6 See McClintock, A. (1995) *Imperial Leather: Race, Gender, and Sexuality in the Colonial Contest*. New York: Routledge.

7 For more on colonisation and (post-)colonial issues in the *giallo*, see Burke, F. (2002) "Intimations (and more) of colonialism: *L'uccello dalle piume di cristallo* (*The Bird With the Crystal Plumage*, 1970)", *Kinoeye: A Fortnightly Journal of Film in the New Europe* 2.11, 10 June, www.kinoeye.org/02 /11/burke11.html.

right:
L'iguana dalla lingua di fuoco (aka **The Iguana with a Tongue of Fire**), 1971.

below:
Passi di danza su una lama di rasoio (aka **Death Carries a Cane**), 1972

opposite:
La dama rossa uccide sette volte (aka **The Lady in Red Kills Seven Times**), 1972

author's note:
This essay originally appeared in *Kinoeye: A Fortnightly Journal of Film in the New Europe* 1.6, 12 November 2001, www.kinoeye.org/02/11/needham11.html. Reprinted here by kind permission of the publisher.

Conclusion

The *giallo* is quite difficult to pin down as a body of films. Criticism tends to gather around auteur directors or singular examples. However, if we can understand the *giallo* discursively, we may begin to make interesting connections between its textual, industrial and cultural features. Such a strategy would allow us to open the *giallo* up rather than close it down. One final note specifies the *giallo*'s discursive potential in everyday criticism. A recent Japanese animated feature, *Perfect Blue* (Satoshi Kon, 1997) was referred to as an animated Japanese *giallo*. There is also a frequent and longstanding tradition of appropriating Spanish (*Una libélula para cada muerto* [*A Dragonfly for Each Corpse*, Léon Klimovsky, 1973]), Belgian (*Die Potloodmoorden* [*The Pencil Murders*, Guy Lee Thys, 1982]), Japanese, French and Dutch films for inclusion in the *gialli* tradition.

this page top, and opposite page:
Scenes from Alejandro Jodorowsky's **Santa Sangre** (Chile/Mexico).

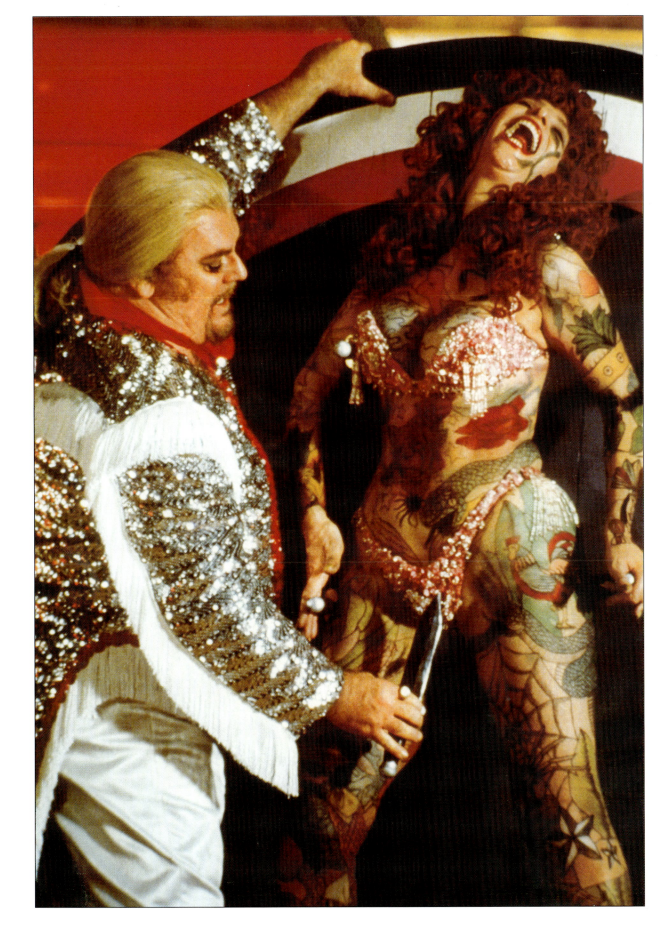

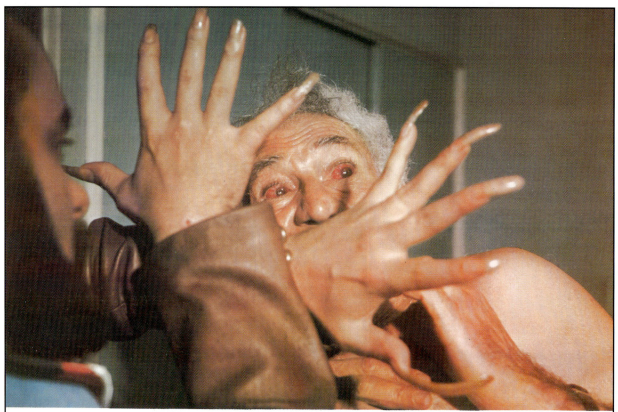

 JOFRE SOARES
WALTER STUART
GEORGIA GOMIDE
ADRIANO STUART

EXORCISMO NEGRO
JOSÉ MOJICA MARINS / ZÉ DO CAIXÃO
Colorido

ALCIONE MAZZEO
ARIANE ARANTES
WANDA KOSMO
MARCELO PICCHI
e a menina MERISOL

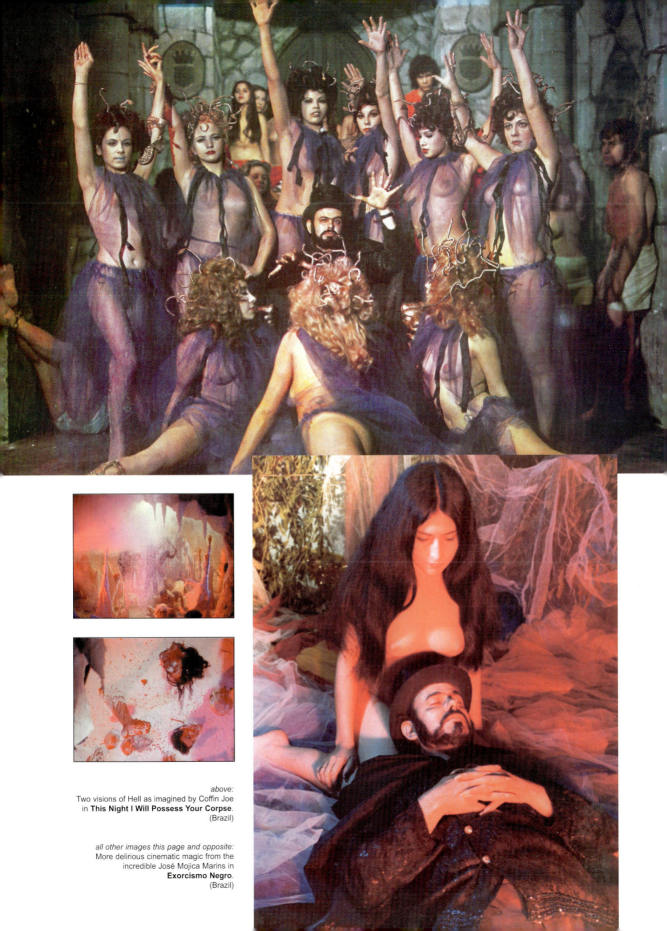

above:
Two visions of Hell as imagined by Coffin Joe in **This Night I Will Possess Your Corpse**. (Brazil)

all other images this page and opposite:
More delirious cinematic magic from the incredible José Mojica Marins in **Exorcismo Negro**. (Brazil)

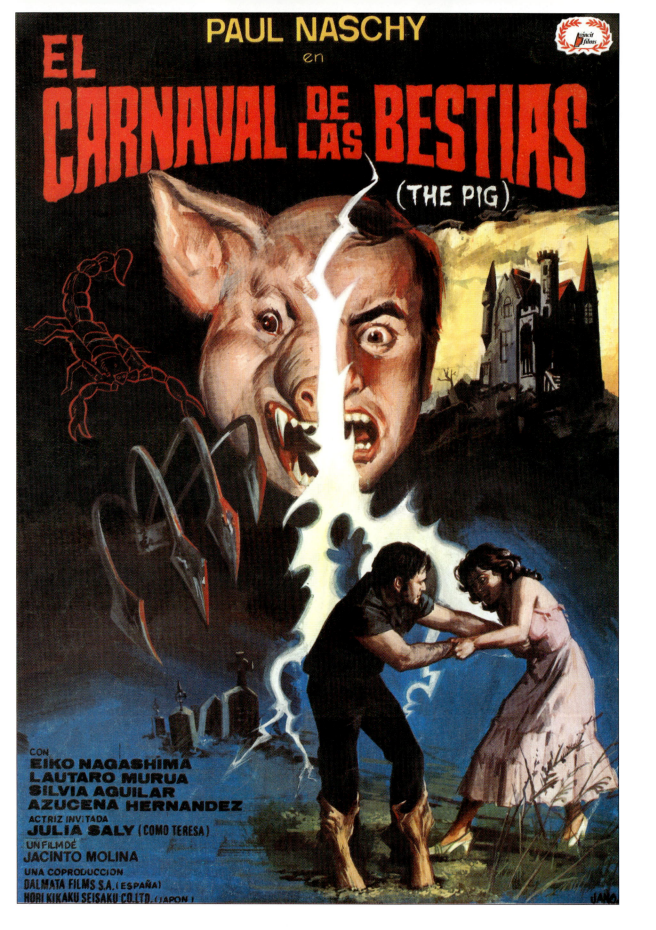

Promotional artwork for Paul Naschy movies (Spain).
opposite: **Human Beasts** (1980), *top:* **Howl of the Devil** (1987),
above: **El vertigo del crimen** (1987), *right:* **Latidos de pánico** (1983).

top: **Angst** (Austria); *above:* **The Saragossa Manuscript** (Poland); *opposite:* **Seytan** (Turkey)

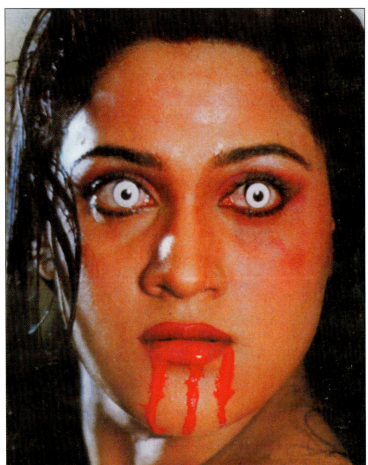

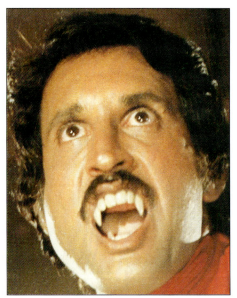

top:
Anthony Wong with director Herman Yau during the making of **Ebola Syndrome** (Hong Kong). *(courtesy of Herman Yau)*

above:
Kiran Kumar, superstar of Bollywood horror films (India).

left:
A vampire strikes in Vinod Talwar's **Khooni Panja** (India).

opposite top:
Wohi Bhayaanak Raat. (India)

opposite bottom:
Khooni Panja. (India)

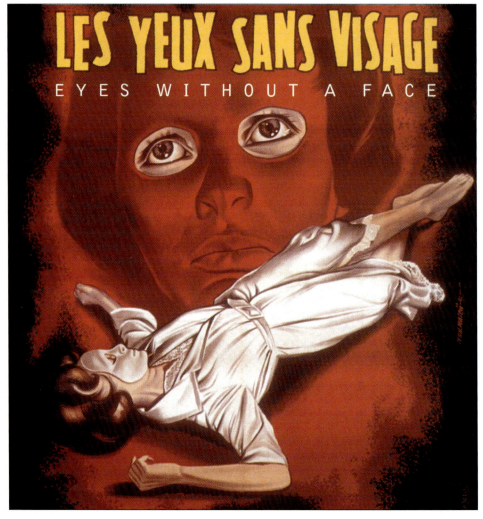

above:
Nyi Blorong (aka **Hungry Snake Woman** aka **The Snake Queen**) (Indonesia).

right:
Les yeux sans visage (aka **Eyes Without a Face**) (France).

opposite:
Die Blaue Hand (aka **The Creature with the Blue Hand**), a 1967 entry into the Edgar Wallace *krimis* cycle (Germany).

above: **Shiri** (South Korea); *below:* **Memento Mori** (South Korea)

this page: **Ichi the Killer** (Japan)

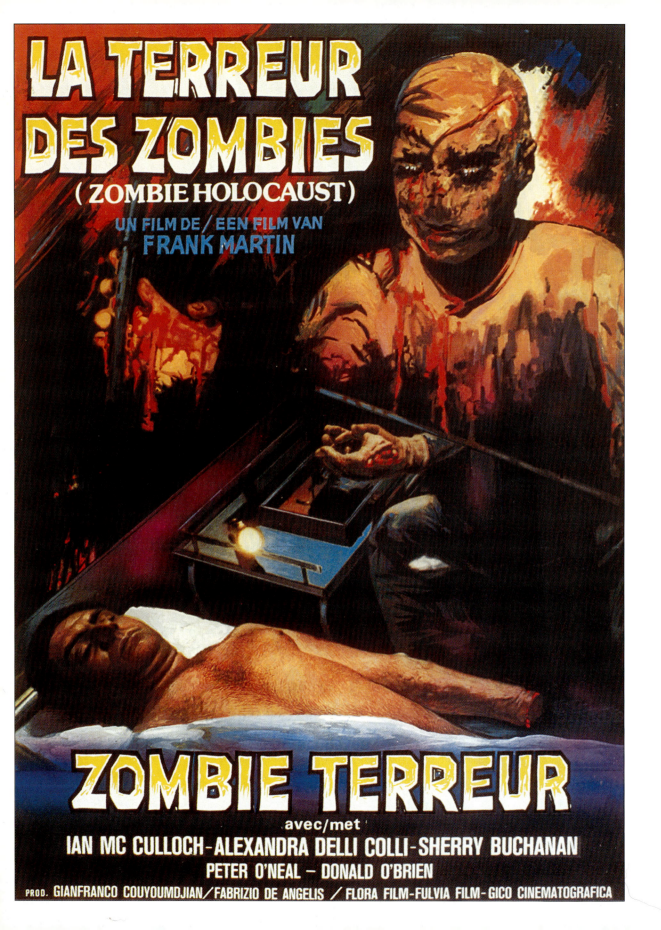

films, series, cycles

The Italian zombie film: from derivation to reinvention

Donato Totaro

Setting the table

Since the late 1950s, with Riccardo Freda and Mario Bava leading the way, Italy has produced some of cinema's most excessively stylised and passionate horror films and cycles: from the *giallo* thriller to the mondo film, the Third World cannibal epic, the Devil possession film and the gut-wrenching zombie movie. Even with this impressive genre pedigree, however, the Italian horror industry has continually struggled against cultural stigmatisation,[1] financial constraints, industry apathy and the overbearing presence of American cinema. Because of this latter fact, the industry developed a parasitic relationship with American cinema. Sometimes out of financial necessity, sometimes out of creative laziness, Italian cinema became (especially in the 1980s) extremely derivative of popular American cinema. But the Italians, with their spirit of reconciliation and ability to make the best of a situation ("*arte di arrangiarsi*"), managed to turn a negative into a positive by adapting their own cultural and artistic temperament to an American model.

A case in point is the Italian zombie film. It would be ludicrous to deny the influence of American cinema, especially George Romero's, on this cycle. Romero - whose key films in this context are *Night of the Living Dead* (1968), *The Crazies* (1973) and *Dawn of the Dead* (1978; an Italian co-production with Dario Argento) - clearly moulded the template for the modern zombie film. As I hope to show in what follows, however, the more talented of the Italian directors learned to recast the mould.

Although one rightly thinks of the late 1970s and early 1980s as the prime period for the classic Italian zombie film, the *idea* of the walking or reanimated dead has been a mainstay of Italian horror cinema since its first modern incarnation, Riccardo Freda's *I vampiri* (Mario Bava uncredited, 1956). In this film an 'overachiever' doctor named Julien Du Grand (Antoine Balpêtré) feigns his own death by filling his coffin with the murdered body of his "Renfield", Joseph Seignoret (Paul Müller). After the funeral, the doctor smuggles Seignoret's corpse into his laboratory to continue his research in human reanimation. While attending to some laboratory machines he relates his medical philosophy to his assistant: "I'll use this device to artificially oxygenate the blood, with no need to rely on the body itself, which now lies dead and inert. I'll discover the very energy that creates life and make it flow forever through my subjects." Then in a subsequent scene, which foreshadows Asa's (Barbara Steele) reanimation in Bava's *La maschera del demonio* (*Mask of Satan*, 1960), Seignoret, lying motionless on a table, opens his eyes and slowly rises to a seated position.

In the next scene, Seignoret is seen groping his way along the mansion's grounds, where he meets a reporter, Pierre Valentin (Dario Michaëlis). The frightened Seignoret pleads with the reporter to take him away from the doctor's estate. The reporter brings him to the police station, where he is queried by a detective about the doctor's activities. Seignoret replies, "They forced me to help them, and then they killed me!" Understandably, the perplexed detective replies, "What! You're crazy!" Although a distant cry from his

[1] For example, Italian audiences never could accept Italian filmmakers as being able to make fantastic films. Riccardo Freda once claimed that he saw a group of Italians outside the theatre marquee of *I vampiri* (1956), but they walked away when they saw that it was made by an Italian, believing that an Italian could not make such a film. Hence his adopted pseudonym of Richard Hampton, and the subsequent tradition of Americanised pseudonyms for Italian actors and directors.

opposite: Poster from Belgium advertising **La Regina dei Cannibali** (aka **Zombi Holocaust** aka **Dr. Butcher M.D.**), 1980

2 Keeping track of the alternate release titles of most Italian zombie films is a laborious task in itself. For example, Jorge Grau's Italian-Spanish co-production *Non si deve profanare il sonno dei morti* (aka *No profanar el sueño de los muertos*, 1974) has been retitled as *The Living Dead at Manchester Morgue*, *Breakfast at Manchester Morgue*, *Don't Open the Window* and *Let Sleeping Corpses Lie*.

3 De Rossi set the standard for zombie make-up effects in Italy with his work on the first outstanding Italian zombie film, *The Living Dead at Manchester Morgue*, and the four Fulci zombie films, *Zombie Flesh Eaters*, *Paura nella città dei morti viventi* (*The City of the Living Dead*, 1980), *L'aldilà* (*The Beyond*, 1981) and *Quella villa accanto al cimitero* (*The House by the Cemetery*, 1981). The latter four films were also all photographed by Sergio Salvati.

4 De Rossi made a conscious effort to distinguish his make-up from that of *Dawn of the Dead*. He explains, "...[Fabrizio] De Angelis and Fulci...wanted to make a remake of Romero's *Dawn of the Dead* and asked me to copy Tom Savini's zombie make-up, which I hadn't particularly liked, because the extreme pallor of the zombies' faces on film gave them a bluish tinge. And so, realizing that our film was going to be a low-cost imitation, I decided to at least try and give the special effects a touch of originality and if the box-office takings are anything to go by, I think I did the right thing." In Palmerini, L. and G. Mistretta (1996) *Spaghetti Nightmares*. Key West, Florida: Fantasma Books, 119.

later flesh-eating and blood-drinking brethren, Seignoret represents Italian cinema's first reanimated corpse. Bava's own revenge-seeking demon couple Asa and Yavutich (Arturo Dominici) in *Mask of Satan* can be seen as transitional figures between Seignoret's victimised, human zombie figure - representative of the pre-1950s American voodoo zombie-as-slave film - and the aggressive predatory zombies of the late 70s and early 80s: the slumbering, decaying, flesh- (and brain-) eating 'undead'.

Seminal works: establishing an Italian zombie film lexicon

The seminal modern Italian zombie film of the latter variety is Lucio Fulci's *Zombie Flesh-Eaters* (1979). Although it was released as *Zombi 2* in Italy to capitalise on the popularity of *Dawn of the Dead*, which was known there as *Zombi*,[2] *Zombie Flesh-Eaters* has less in common with Romero's classic than one would assume. To begin with, it is far more relentless in its nihilism, lacking any of the former's comic tone or black humour. This is partly due to the zombie make-up effects by Giannetto De Rossi who, along with the film's cinematographer Sergio Salvati, is one of the seminal creative figures of the Italian zombie movie.[3] In contrast to make-up artist Tom Savini's garish, blue-tinged zombie pallor (and more identifiable clothing) for *Dawn of the Dead*, De Rossi's muddier earth tones and ashen frocks render the zombies a homogeneous mass of undead beings who have, in some cases, just risen from the bowels of the earth - a more direct and Catholic localisation of Hell and the apocalypse.[4]

Zombie Flesh-Eaters established and/or perfected much of the Italian zombie lexicon, some of which was taken from Romero, some not. Included among these filmic elements, thematic-narrative conventions and visual iconography are the following: a pulsating soundtrack that establishes dread and drives the film's rhythm; extreme levels of viscerality (through both violence and grotesque imagery); the mixture of zombies in a Third World setting (which stems from the mondo genre[5]); an unresolved or open-ended conclusion; and a philosophical bleakness which can be best described by the motto, "Nobody gets out of here alive."

Aligned with the element of extreme viscerality is the penchant for inflicting violence on particularly vulnerable body

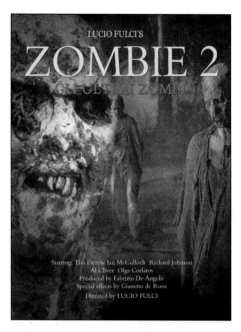

parts, the eyes being the most common. *Zombie Flesh-Eaters* signals this in a scene where Dr. Menard's (Richard Johnson) wife has her right eye pierced by a jagged piece of shattered wood lattice in a series of unflinching close-ups. This single moment has achieved cult status in the annals of Italian horror cinema. Moreover, it derives from a larger scene whose structure forms part of another unmistakable element of the Italian zombie film: the protracted or elaborate set-piece. In fact, Fulci's four zombie entries - *Zombie Flesh-Eaters*, plus his zombie trilogy *Paura nella città dei morti viventi* (*City of the Living Dead* aka *Gates of Hell*, 1980), *E tu vivrai nel terrore... l'aldilà* (aka *The Beyond*, 1981) and *Quella villa accanto al cimitero* (*The House by the Cemetery*, 1981) - have been pillaged for gore sequences and set-pieces by a veritable legion of lesser-skilled craftsman, from Andrea Bianchi to Aristide Massaccesi.

A set-piece is a choreographed scene that usually, though not exclusively, takes place in one location. By an "elaborate" set-piece, I mean a situation or set of actions where narrative function (character development, plot exposition or key story point) gives way to 'spectacle'. In other words, the scene plays on far longer than what is strictly necessary for the narrative purpose. The Italian zombie film set-piece typically involves one to three characters, builds toward an anticipated danger, takes particular relish in the

the Italian zombie film

left:
Non si deve profanare il sonno dei morti (aka **The Living Dead at Manchester Morgue**, aka **Let Sleeping Corpses Lie**), 1974.

depiction of pain and anguish and climaxes with a violent death. For example, the 'mutilated eye' scene mentioned above consumes approximately six minutes of narrative/screen time just to kill off a minor character. The scene begins with voyeuristic subjective camera shots outside a house, first from afar through foliage, and then through the bathroom windowpane as Mrs. Menard (Olga Karlatos) takes a shower. The camera then tracks her nervous pacing across the adjoining central room as she hears loud shuffling and breathing noises outside her window. The atmospheric build-up ends with a zombie arm smashing through a boarded window to grab her by the hair and slowly draw her eye into the splintered wood fragment. Consequently, every well-meaning Italian zombie film would include at least one such 'Buñuelian' attack on the eye.

This manner of set-piece typifies an aspect of the transformation that perhaps best differentiates the Italian horror film from its American counterpart, which is more character-based, plot-driven and attentive to verisimilitude. The focus on spectacle as a mode of entertainment often comes at the expense of narrative coherency and characterisation, but is a conscious decision based on many varied factors (economic, aesthetic and stylistic). Therefore, when mainstream critics complain about the 'weak' narratives in Italian horror films, they are missing the point. In most cases, narrative is merely a pretext for spectacle. The Italian zombie film set-piece serves the same function as the showdown in a Sergio Leone spaghetti western, the dance number in a musical, the car chase in an action film or the fight sequence in a martial arts movie: entertainment as pure spectacle.

Although Fulci's *Zombie Flesh-Eaters* is often associated with Romero's *Dawn of the Dead*, a more accurate and thorough assessment would also consider the influences of Erle C. Kenton's *Island of Lost Souls* (1932) and Jacques Tourneur's *I Walked With a Zombie* (1943). *Zombie Flesh-Eaters*, in fact, positions itself between two discourses represented by each of these films: scientific experiments (*Island of Lost Souls*) and voodoo witchcraft (*I Walked With a Zombie*). A film which is more indebted to George Romero (especially his *Night of the Living Dead*), but which distinguishes itself nonetheless, is the Italian-Spanish co-production by Catalonian director Jorge Grau, *Non si deve profanare il sonno dei morti* (*The Living Dead at Manchester Morgue*, aka *Let Sleeping Corpses Lie*, 1974). Although there are many similarities between the films, such as the first zombie attack in an open field and the senseless death of the hero at the end, *Morgue* represents a clever colour re-working of *Night of the Living Dead*.

Grau transplants the mainly rural American location to a mainly rural English setting, and brings to surface the anti-establishment sensibility lurking

[5] As Neil Jackson explains, "the 'mondo' documentary (or 'shockumentary') ...mixed documentary and staged footage, presented as travelogues which purported to demonstrate the lifestyle conditions and peculiarities of cultures in underdeveloped nations. Initiated in 1962 by Gualtiero Jacopetti's *Mondo Cane*, and characterized by titles such as *Africa Addio* (1966), *Ultime Grida Dalla Savana: La Grande Caccia* (aka *Savage Man, Savage Beast*, 1974), the mondo film is not strictly Italian in origin but developed there as a distinct sub-form, showcasing footage of tribal initiation ceremonies, animal deaths, and human executions." In Jackson, N. (2002) "*Cannibal Holocaust*, Realist Horror, and Reflexivity." *Post Script: Essays in Film and the Humanities* 21.3 (Summer 2002): 320-45.

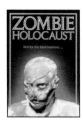

above:
Zombie Holocaust is the English language re-titling of Marino Girolami's **La regina dei cannibali** (1980).

[6] The American version of this picture, *Dr. Butcher M.D.*, includes a pre-credit sequence filmed in the US by Roy Frumkes.

below:
Zombie Flesh-Eaters (1979).

within Romero's b&w classic. Whereas Romero's film merely hints at nuclear radiation as a possible cause of the zombie outbreak, Grau places the cause squarely on the government's agricultural program of "ultrasonic radiation pesticide", reflecting a distrust of the political establishment which is much more endemic to Italian (and European) culture than American. Grau also brings to the forefront the generational conflict between the young, long-haired hero (Ray Lovelock) and the ageist, redneck detective (Arthur Kennedy).

In terms of the evolution of the Italian zombie subgenre, *The Living Dead at Manchester Morgue* is important for its foregrounding of the ecological and environmental aspect of the zombie mythology. Subsequent to the post-*Night of the Living Dead*, *Manchester Morgue* and *Zombie Flesh-Eaters* period, the majority of Italian zombie films explain the cause of the zombie contagion in one of two ways: (1) science (ecological, environmental, geological or biochemical) or (2) supra-nature (voodoo, witchcraft, alchemy or religion). Examples of the former include *Incubo sulla città contaminata* (*Nightmare City*, aka *City of the Walking Dead*, 1980), *Virus* (*Night of the Zombies* aka *Inferno dei morti-viventi* aka *Apocalipsis caníbal* aka *Zombie Creeping Flesh*, 1980) and *Zombi 3* (1988). Examples of the latter include *The Beyond*, *Le notte del terrore* (*Nights of Terror*, aka *Burial Ground*, 1980) and *Dawn of the Mummy* (1981). In some instances, the two causes - science and supra-nature - are combined, as in *The House by the Cemetery* and *Zeder: Voices From the Beyond* (aka *Revenge of the Dead*, 1983).

One of the oddest concoctions is *La regina dei cannibali* (aka *Zombi Holocaust / Dr Butcher M.D.*, 1980), where director Marino Girolami (aka Frank Martin) blends as many scenarios as possible by featuring both science-made zombies and 'real' mondo-style native cannibals.[6]

A common formal method for ending the Italian zombie film is the freeze-frame, which helps to underscore the often ambiguous or open-ended conclusion. The following films, for example, all conclude with a freeze-frame: *The Living Dead at Manchester Morgue*, *Nightmare City*, *Burial Ground*, *The City of the Living Dead*, *Zombie Creeping Flesh*, *Dawn of the Mummy* and *Zeder*. An obvious explanation is the continuing influence of *Night of the Living Dead*'s bleak photographic freeze-frame ending. But the freeze-frame also provides a suggestive form/content fusion, since the effect of ending with paralysed time and narrative indeterminacy is a perfect match to one of the central thematic drives of the Italian zombie film: the fear of death in its most brutal and primal bodily sense. Since we can only put an end to this fear at the moment of our *own* death, the freeze-frame is a natural formal means of keeping this primal fear alive (in suspended animation, like our own death). In addition, the sense of prolonged fatality afforded by the freeze-frame is especially fitting for the bleak philosophical outlook on life offered in the Italian zombie film.

Given the nature of the beast (death and the undead), a handful of locations consistently reappear in this subgenre. The western has Death Valley, the saloon, the church, the ranch and the campfire; the Italian zombie film has crypts, catacombs, cemeteries, necropolises, ossuaries, mortuaries and hospitals. The latter may appear an odd inclusion, but not if one considers the hospital as a place where people are most vulnerable, and as a place which represents a type of terrestrial purgatory between life and death. The list of zombie films which feature hospital scenes is surprisingly long, and includes *The Living Dead at Manchester Morgue*, *Zombi Holocaust*, *Nightmare City*, *Zombi 3*, *The Beyond* and *Dellamorte Dellamore* (1994).

the Italian zombie film

The summit:
Lucio Fulci's zombie trilogy

Fulci exploits the hospital setting to interesting effect in *The Beyond*, the middle instalment of a gothic trilogy that represents the pinnacle of the Italian zombie film. From the moment in *The Beyond* when a plumber unwittingly opens a gateway to hell in the basement of a Louisiana hotel, spatiotemporal narrative order begins to go out of whack. This spilling over of the irrational into the rational world is represented through several hospital scenes. At one point, the dead plumber is brought to the town hospital, but we next see him as a zombie emerging from a bathtub in Liza's (Catriona MacColl) home. The most striking subversion of spatiotemporal order occurs in the film's final scene, as the protagonists Liza and John (David Warbeck) seek safety from the marauding zombies through an exit door along the hospital corridor, only to find themselves immersed within the hotel's surreal basement landscape.

Fulci's treatment of temporal and spatial disorientation is part of a larger metaphysical subtext that makes his zombie trilogy a landmark achievement. While in *Zombie Flesh-Eaters* he introduced the physical destruction of an eye which would be copied *ad infinitum* in subsequent Italian zombie films, in *The Beyond* eye fetishism goes beyond mere graphic sensationalism to achieve thematic and philosophical relevance. The blindness of one of the central characters, Emily (Sarah Keller), is accorded powerful visual significance through her blank, blue-grey, eggshell eyes. Devoid of any identity, her eyes become a central metaphorical image in *The Beyond*: an act of 'looking' that goes 'beyond' the physical to the metaphysical. When at the end of the film Liza and John find themselves trapped in the apocalyptic Hellscape, they turn to the camera and reveal (for the first time) the same blank, lifeless eyes as Emily. These de/void eyes mirror the surreal, ashen landscape that expresses Death and/or Hell as eternal nothingness. As the concluding voice-over confirms: "And you will face the sea of darkness and all therein that may be explored."[7]

Another distinguishing feature of Fulci's zombie trilogy is its impressive depiction of a form of evil associated with the fiction tradition of H.P. Lovecraft (1890-1937). According to Lovecraft's "Cthulhu" myth, the Earth was once inhabited by a previous race, the "Ancient" or "Old Ones", who turned to evil and were kept at bay by the goodly "Elders." A forbidden book, the *Necronomicon*, holds the key to the tenuous portal separating our world from the world of the Ancients. An important character in this myth is the "researcher-seeker" who dabbles in the unknown and unleashes the primordial, amphibian-like "Ancient Ones" on earth. These Lovecraftian elements appear throughout Fulci's zombie trilogy. For example, there is Dr. Freudstein's (Giovanni De Nava) "chemical reanimation and cannibalism", his amphibian-like appearance and the "researcher-seeker" Dr. Peterson (Ranieri Ferrara) in *The House by the Cemetery*; the forbidden book of Eibon in *The Beyond*; the portals that open up between life and death, past and present in all three films; and the zombies themselves as earthly representations of the "Ancient Ones." At the base of Fulci's zombie trilogy, as in Lovecraft's Cthulhu myth, is a metaphysical horror that comes from the haunting revelation that there is another, 'unspeakable' world living parallel to our own.

In Fulci's trilogy, evil is given its richest and most sustained treatment in *The*

[7] Not only Fulci, but Italian horror films in general have a fondness for ending with voice-overs and textual citations.

below:
Classic comic-book style promotional artwork for **Paura nella città dei morti viventi** (aka **City of the Living Dead**), 1980

Beyond. The film's opening and closing scenes serve as paradigmatic examples here. In the pre-credit sequence, we are led to assume that the man named Schweik (Antoine Saint John) is an innocent painter hunted down by superstitious, torch-bearing townsfolk. Our understanding of good and evil is thwarted, however, when we realise that the Hellish "Sea of Darkness" in the final scene bears a striking similarity to the crucified Schweik's canvas. The artist whom we initially thought was the innocent victim of mob mentality has apparently played a key role in opening one of the gates to Hell. Hence, in retrospect, the townsfolk were playing the role of Benign Elders in attempting to stop the painter's Hell-invoking brushstrokes. The opening and closing scenes suggest two forms of evil: physical and metaphysical. While the chain whipping, crucifixion and eventual zombies represent physical horror and evil, the ending depicts evil as a boundless sea of quiet emptiness. The blank eyes and expressions on the faces of Liza and John do not express physical horror, but rather existential terror at the prospect of infinite nothingness. A passage on the nature of evil from Paul Oppenheimer's 1996 book *Evil and the Demonic* captures quite well the sense of metaphysical evil in the closing scene of *The Beyond*: "The final effect of evil is not one of horror. It is of a pathetic helplessness... The very physics of the universe, their natural laws, have devoured themselves, to leave a silent state of nil."[8]

The good, the bad and the terrible

In this section, I will discuss some representative works that are perhaps of lesser quality, but certainly not without interest; films that are good, bad and terrible, sometimes all at once. I will begin with two films which borrow heavily from George Romero's zombie iconography, *Nightmare City* and *Zombie Creeping Flesh*. The latter, directed by Bruno Mattei, opens with a leak at a nuclear power plant in Papua New Guinea, whose undisclosed mission is an experimental project called "Operation Sweet Death." The leak causes the plant workers to attack and cannibalize each other, and ends with the plant manager leaving behind a cautionary tape message: "May God forgive us for what we have produced here...." Throughout this opening scene, we hear a soundtrack from the musical group Goblin, which is a direct lift from their own *Dawn of the Dead* score.

The next scene continues the *Dawn of the Dead* connection by introducing a trigger-happy SWAT team gleefully killing a terrorist gang at a hostage-taking. The film then shifts gears as the SWAT team join up with a couple of television reporters in search of the nuclear plant. Once at the nuclear site we discover that the plant's operative mission "Sweet Death" was a response to the problem of Third World overpopulation: turn the natives into zombie-cannibals and let

right:
Incubo sulla città contaminata (aka **Nightmare City**, aka **City of the Walking Dead**), 1980.

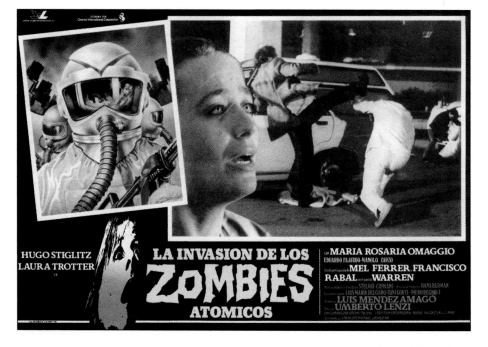

[8] Oppenheimer, P. (1996) *Evil and the Demonic: A New Theory of Monstrous Behavior.* New York: New York University Press, 7.

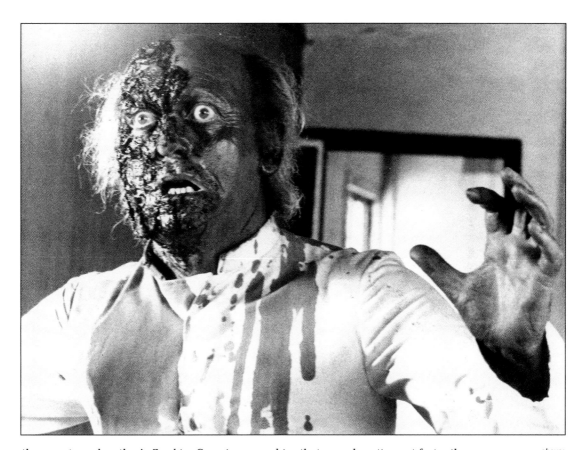

above:
Inferno dei morti-viventi (aka **Night of the Zombies**, aka **Zombie Creeping Flesh**), 1980.

them eat each other! *Zombie Creeping Flesh* belongs at the bottom of the Italian zombie heap. The film makes a token anti-colonial statement ('white man meddling with native culture') and a thinly-veiled political point concerning the practice of First World nations setting up military training camps, air strips or nuclear testing sites in Third World countries. But this message is hard to swallow given the unconvincing representation of Papua New Guinea: terrible canned sound effects, ill-matched animal stock footage, etc. Or the scene where the white, blond, female reporter strips nude and applies colourful face paint so she can move about among the natives 'unnoticed'.

A notch above *Zombie Creeping Flesh* is *Nightmare City*, if only for its jaw-dropping opening airport sequence where director Umberto Lenzi turns the convention of the zombie as lumbering and slow-thinking on its head. Reporter Dean Miller (Hugo Stiglitz) is sent to the airport to interview a nuclear physicist. Tension reigns when an unauthorised plane lands and is quickly surrounded by airport security. The plane's door slowly draws open and lets out a gang of armed 'terrorist' zombies that come bursting out faster than a team of Olympic sprinters.[9] A radiation leak appears to be the cause of the contagion, but these undead - sporting perhaps the shoddiest zombie make-up of any film in the cycle - seem driven by a plan to overthrow the government, as they attack high-ranking military officials and strategic locations (TV station, military airbase). This is brought out in one of several clunky dialogue exposition scenes between Miller and his wife Ann (Laura Trotter), where Ann likens the military's 'create and obliterate' mentality to the actions of the zombies. Ann sees in the actions of both groups a search for power ('will to power'). As one military official puts it, "We've got to get control back!"

This subtext on military-patriarchal power[10] is reaffirmed by the film's subtle homage/reference to Stanley Kubrick's *Dr. Strangelove* (1963), a classic satire on the phallocentric nature of military might. In the scene in question, a romantic liaison between Major Warren Holmes (Francisco Rabal) and his wife is rudely interrupted when he receives an emergency phone call ordering him to report to work. This recalls a similar scene in *Dr. Strangelove* where

[9] The undead are also fast moving in Fulci's *City of the Living Dead*.

[10] All of the zombies that come bursting out of the plane in the opening scene are male, as are all of the military officials.

above:
Le notte del terrore (aka **Burial Ground**), 1980.

Major Turgidson (George C. Scott) is interrupted by an emergency phone call during a romantic hotel liaison with his secretary. To push the link even further, the person placing the order to Major Holmes in *Nightmare City* is named Major 'Murchison' (Mel Ferrer)!

The film climaxes at an amusement park, with Miller and his wife taking refuge from the zombies on top of a rollercoaster. A failed helicopter rescue mission sees Ann fall to a gruesome death. However, after her fall the shot cuts quickly to Miller waking up from a bad nightmare, his wife sleeping safely next to him. Borrowing a page from William Cameron Menzies's *Invaders from Mars* (1953), Miller leaves for the airport in a déjà vu scene following which his nightmare will become reality. *Nightmare City* may lack the subtle touches necessary for the build-up of proper horror film atmosphere, but it is well-paced and earns points for being the only true Italian 'zombie-action' film.

In contrast to Lenzi's fast-moving zombies, the undead in Andrea Bianchi's *Burial Ground* are appropriately slumbering and ceremonial, owing more to Spanish director Amando de Ossorio's *Blind Dead* films than previous Italian zombie pictures.[11] In this film, the zombies have a taste for blue blood, munching on a group of Italian bourgeois who have been invited by a professor/scientist to stay at a villa. In the opening Etruscan catacomb scene, the professor's research into necronomics reanimates the dead. He quickly becomes their first victim, after which the undead turn to the guests. *Burial Ground* is a *Night of the Living Dead* clone, minus the character development and social import. Characters simply arrive at the villa to serve as zombie fodder. Under proper conditions, this is more than enough to constitute a decent zombie film, but where it fails here is in the uninspired set-pieces. In a good set-piece, the moment of death is only icing on the cake. The build-up is equally important. But Bianchi's direction is lazy, as he relies exclusively on the depiction of blood and entrails to achieve a sense of climax.

The one exception - and the film's best scene - comes with the killing of the maid. For once, Bianchi stretches out the scene with moments anticipating the violence to follow. A group of zombies roost beneath a bedroom window, and the maid opens the shutters to investigate the noise. A zombie throws a stake that pins the maid's hand up against the wooden shutter, with her torso caught in a bent position over the

[11] De Ossorio's cycle of Spanish zombie films include all of the following: *La noche del terror ciego* (*Tombs of the Blind Dead*, 1971), *El ataque de los muertos sin ojos* (*The Return of the Blind Dead*, 1973), *El buque maldito* (*Horror of the Zombies*, 1973) and *La noche de los gaviotas* (*The Night of the Seagulls*, 1975).

window sill. The zombies slowly make their way to her hanging torso and proceed to decapitate her with a scythe. The shot cuts to an overhead angle looking down at the headless, blood-splattering maid, with the zombies perched below using her head as a blood cauldron. The only thing that comes close to passing for characterisation in *Burial Ground* is the Oedipal relationship between a young boy, Michael (Peter Bark), and his "Mamma", Evelyn (Mariangela Giordano). In a twist on *Night of the Living Dead*, Michael returns as a zombie and is encouraged by his mother to suckle her breasts; suffice to note that junior does not keep his teeth in his mouth for long.

Keeping *Zombie Creeping Flesh* company at the bottom of the Italian zombie heap is Aristide Massaccesi's sequel to his cannibal atrocity *Anthropophagus the Beast* (1980), *Rosso sangue* (*Absurd*, aka *Zombie 6: Monster Hunter*, 1981). Mikos Stenopolis (Luigi Montefiori, billed as George Eastman) returns as a bland killing machine stalking a quiet community. Hot on his trail is the Greek scientist-priest (Edmund Purdom) responsible for his present physical state. Recalling the words of Dr. Julien Du Grand from *I vampiri*, the priest tells the local authorities that Mikos's dead body became contaminated in his laboratory and attained the ability to regenerate dead cells. *Absurd* has a certain morbid realism due to its budgetary-enforced static long takes and gruesome, over-the-top moments of gore: a medical drill is worked through a nurse's head from temple to temple; a butcher's head is sliced through a band-saw (both of these death scenes are derived from Fulci's *City of the Living Dead*); and a woman's face is burned in an oven (lifted from Hitchcock's *Torn Curtain*, 1966). But the dull narrative padding overwhelms the shock effects.

However, in a subgenre where women are either victims or utterly useless in combating the source of terror, it is refreshing to see this films' bizarre narrative twist, in which a crippled teenage girl, bedridden for most of the film, becomes the heroine. Mikos has entered the house and murdered the nanny, leaving the invalid Katya (Katya Berger) and her younger brother Willy (Kasimir Berger) to fend for themselves. As Willy bangs on her door for help, Katya finds the strength to untie her bed straps and walk. When confronted by the zombie she gouges him in both eyes with a compass instrument. This leads to one of the most absurd (in the good sense) chase scenes in all of Italian zombie cinema. With the camera positioned at the end of a dimly-lit hallway, we see a weak-legged Katya, supported by the wall, inching along slowly, and a few paces behind her the blind zombie, arms flailing as he cautiously moves forward. The image is ludicrous and sublime at the same moment, made all the more bizarre within the context of an otherwise mainly terrible movie.

The climax of *Absurd* sees the priest reappear to confront his monster. While Mikos strangles the priest, Katya picks up a fallen axe and, framed from below, strikes repeatedly at the zombie's neck. The touchstone for this odd film is not Romero, but John Carpenter's *Halloween* (1978): from the priest who is clearly modelled on Donald Pleasence's Sam Loomis, to the little boy who refers to the zombie as "the boogeyman", to the final shot which follows the scene described above, where a blood-drenched Katya stands on the porch in front of her homecoming parents, holding the zombie's head in one hand like a modern-day Judith of Bethulia holding the severed head of Holofernes.

In just a few short years (1979-81), the Italians had so exhausted the zombie formula that they attempted to 'redress' it with films such as *Dawn of the Mummy* (Frank Agrama with Armand Weston uncredited, 1981), an Italian, US and Egyptian co-production which is nothing but a zombie film in mummies' clothing. The crypt of a 3000 BC Egyptian Prince named Zevraman is desecrated by treasure seekers and an American fashion photo crew. The film groans along with insipid characterisation and bland plot development until the Prince and his army of slaves come to life for payback. The first

left:
Le notte del terrore (aka **Burial Ground**), 1980.

right:
Dawn of the Mummy, 1981.

desert resurrection scene is the film's most impressive moment. The lumbering, bandaged mummies rise up from the ground in the foreground in soft silhouette, while an orange sunrise burns behind them. Once resurrected, the mummies move and behave like zombies, attacking the jugular and devouring human entrails. From this point on, the film becomes a gorefest of mummy mayhem, up until the proverbial open ending. The final few survivors think they have trapped and burned the mummies. The camera films the burning houses from a distance, lingering just long enough for the inevitable mummy hand to burst into the bottom foreground of the frame. The film ends on a freeze-frame of this 'pregnant' image.

Although even the lesser-quality works discussed in this section have their moments of interest, by 1982 the Italian zombie film had run its course. It would be a few years before the dormant subgenre would itself be resurrected by one of the most compelling and unusual of all Italian zombie films, *Zeder: Voices From the Beyond* (1983).

**Invention and innovation:
two late-period zombie classics**

Zeder, directed by Italy's reluctant horror auteur, Pupi Avati,[12] is in effect an *anti-*zombie film, relying not on traditional zombie imagery but on deliberate plotting and an escalating sense of paranoiac dread driven by a relentless minimal score by Riz Ortolani. It is also the most despairing and bleakest of films in a subgenre known for its distinct fatalism, largely because its horror obliquely recalls one of human history's darkest moments, the Holocaust. A writer named Stefano (Gabriele Lavia) receives an old typewriter as a gift from his wife Alessandra (Anne Canovas). He becomes obsessed with the words he finds imprinted on the old ribbon, which lead him to a bizarre, quasi-scientific/religious cult attempting to incarnate the writings of a 19th-century author named Paolo Zeder. According to Zeder, there are geological spots on earth ("K-zones") where time, space and death are suspended. A person buried in a K-zone could, theoretically, attain immortality.

The film's deliberate yet engrossing pace, detailed plotting and concern with questions of textuality (the arcane sentences inscribed on the typewriter ribbon) recall Avati's earlier *giallo* classic *La casa dalle finestre che ridono* (*The House*

[12] Unlike other Italian horror auteurs (Fulci, Bava, Argento, etc.), Avati has never embraced the horror film and feels his best work is outside the genre. When asked in a published interview if he agrees that his 1976 *giallo*, *La Casa dalle Finestre che Ridono* (*The House with the Windows that Laugh*) is his masterpiece, he replies, "Please! ...As a horror film it did its work, but I would not count it among my favourite films." Avati sees himself much more as a director who does his best work when not constrained by genre. In the same interview he states, "I experimented with almost every film genre without ever fossilizing myself in any one." So even though most critical writing on Avati's films concentrate on his horror work, he does not see them as being any more important than his non-horror work. It is the fans and genre critics who refer to him as a horror auteur. (Quotes from Palmerini, L. and G. Mistretta, *Spaghetti Nightmares* (M&P edition, 1994 & 1996; reprint Pubbliprint Service s.n.c., Roma, 1997), 32 (page citation is to the reprint edition), my translation from Italian.)

with the Windows that Laugh, 1976) and foreshadow his later horror film *L'arcano incantatore* (*Arcane Enchanter*, 1996). Stefano's trail leads him to a necropolis in the Northern Italy town of Spina, and a derelict building with an unusual history. In the narrative present, the building is site of a byzantine research project run by an elite French consortium, who claim the area as one of the most fertile K-zones they have yet come across. We learn from a priest that sometime after World War II until 1956 the place was run by the Catholic Church as a "kid's holiday camp." Before then, we hear from a local that the building was used by the Germans during World War II to house prisoners: "There were Germans here during the war, rounding people up, but some found a way to save themselves." When Stefano asks about investigating the building, the local warns him: "They [the French researcher consortium] put up a kind of electrified fence, like Auschwitz." Through another local, we learn that the building contained an "incinerator." Collectively, these snippets of information recall the Nazi concentration camps.

Zeder's frightening climax includes a scene where Stefano enters the K-zone and comes across a room with a television set tuned into a video camera placed within the lit coffin of a dead defrocked priest. As Stefano watches transfixed, the priest opens his eyes and begins to laugh maniacally, then comes crashing up through the floorboards. Stefano escapes and entrusts the videotape to his wife, but the consortium murders her before she is able to pass on the incriminating evidence. In the final scene, Stefano buries his wife in the K-zone and waits for her return. She does not disappoint, in a moment whose setting and action recalls Jean Cocteau's classic 1950 film version of the Orpheus myth, *Orphée* (in which a man enters a limbo realm between life and death called the "zone" to retrieve his wife). The still-beautiful Alessandra embraces Stefano. As they turn, Stefano faces the camera and we only see Alessandra's back. Stefano's face slowly forms a look of horror and he lets out a primal scream as, we must assume, Alessandra bites into his neck. The disquieting ending dissolves to the closing credits scrolling over a distant freeze-frame view of the concrete building façade housing the K-zone.

The Italian zombie film rarely inscribes profound social and/or political

right:
Zeder: Voices From the Beyond, 1983.

messages (nor am I implying that they should). When they do, it is of a general nature, such as the superficial (and usually compromised) references to Third World policy or Western attitudes to native cultures noted in some of the films above. In *Zeder*, however, there is a veiled reference to Italy's historical past in the scattered bits of plot information that allude to World War II and the Nazi concentration camps (Germans housing prisoners there, incinerator, electrified fences, analogy to Auschwitz, the physical appearance of the building itself, the setting in Northern Italy, etc.). The clandestine nature of the K-zone operation, coupled with the secretive experiments being conducted there, is yet another echo of the concentration camps. Given the implied textual parallels to Italy's history, one wonders how it is that the Church assumed ownership of the building after the Nazis. And might they still have a connection to the current owners of the building, or be aware of the experiments being run there? With a bit of interpretive muscle one can read into this and other plot fragments a possible political subtext relating to the Roman Catholic Church's place in World War II vis-à-vis Nazis, anti-Semitism and the Holocaust itself.

After an even longer hiatus of approximately ten years, the Italian zombie film returned once again with a creative vengeance. Michele Soavi's *Dellamorte Dellamore* (1994, US re-release title *Cemetery Man*, 1996) is clearly a zombie film of a different ilk, introducing a dark humour previously absent in the subgenre, and for the first time featuring strong characterisation (Rupert Everett as the titular Francesco Dellamorte and French pop star Francois Hadji-Lazaro as his Curly Howard-like sidekick Gnaghi). *Dellamorte Dellamore* - literally "of death, of love" - deals ostensibly about death, necrophilia and impossible love, but from a decidedly lyrical and metaphorical perspective.

The narrative concerns a young, handsome introvert, Francesco Dellamorte, who works as a cemetery custodian with his dim-wit sidekick Gnaghi in the fictional Italian community of Buffalora. But this is not your average cemetery, as certain of Buffalora's dearly departed have a bothersome habit of returning to life as flesh- and blood-seeking zombies on the seventh night after burial. The laconic Francesco and the indifferent Gnaghi re-kill the "returners" in time-honoured zombie-film fashion: via a blow or shot to the head. They act not out of a sense of survival, however, but as guardians of the outside world. In keeping with the film's tragic romanticism, both Francesco and Gnaghi suffer fatal love affairs with "returners." While bound to their role of earthly guardians, both characters dream of escaping their dreary cemetery existence to discover (or re-discover) "the rest of the world." But the world is of their own making and they stand no better chance of escaping it (or society), as do the two lifeless figures standing side-by-side in the glass snowball seen at the beginning and end of the film.

Although perfectly enjoyable as a zombie picture, *Dellamorte Dellamore* becomes infinitely richer when also seen as a tragedy and a parable. The film's use of nearly every imaginable authority figure - mayor, bureaucrat, policeman, doctor and nun - gives credence to a reading of the cemetery as a microcosm for social decay in the outside world, and one person's inability to adjust to it. Soavi plays this metaphor as a subjective world-within-a-world, a world contained in a dark, circular void. The circular motif is underscored in many ways: the glass ball seen at the beginning and end; the earth-shaped form at the top of the cemetery gates; the glowing moon; the 360-degree camera movements; the many repeated lines of dialogue; and the three returning "she" figures (all played by Anna Falchi). The over-the-top hospital sequence includes a scene in which Francesco, visiting his comatose namesake/alter-ego Franco, nonchalantly shoots, in succession, a nun, doctor and nurse. Francesco's social isolation and invisibility is reflected in the next shot, an overhead angle that zooms out until the room is a tiny enclosed circular speck within a black hole - a pointed world-within-a-world metaphor which makes it clear that we have fully entered into Francesco Dellamorte's fantasy state.

Many of the film's apparent narrative inconsistencies make sense when viewed as part of Francesco's subjective dreamscape. The film opens as if in mid-dream, with the camera pulling back out of a dark void (a skull's eye) and dollying backward through the physically impossible space of a coiled telephone cord. This receding motion from within the literal space of a skull can be read as a symbolic descent into/out of the unconscious. By film's end, we can assume (though not with certainty) that Buffalora is but a figment of Francesco's existentially-challenged imagination, a 'dream-fantasy' reality that makes *Dellamorte Dellamore* the *8 1/2* (1963) of Italian zombie films.**13**

Fellini's masterpiece may seem an esoteric reference for a zombie movie, but *Dellamorte Dellamore* is proud of its rich Italian heritage. A film not ashamed of its horror pedigree, neither is it confined by its generic boundaries. Though many critics and fans reacted positively to *Dellamorte Dellamore*, the fact that it veers into rather alien terrain for a zombie film also left many viewers befuddled or indifferent. The indifference stems largely from not wanting to accept, emotionally or intellectually, the generic rejuvenation accomplished by Soavi.

In the decades following World War II - and to some extent even today - every Italian director felt the need to exorcise the rich legacy of Italian neo-realism. Some directors left the neo-realist legacy by exploring the inner realities of their characters (Michelangelo Antonioni, Roberto Rossellini) or themselves (Federico Fellini). But many clung to neo-realism's allegiance to external social realism, only moving away from neo-realist aesthetics ("realism") by employing a more expressive visual style (Mario Monicelli, Alberto Lattuada, Pier Paolo Pasolini, Luchino Visconti, Pietro Germi, Nanni Moretti). Soavi is going through a similar process with the zombie film, attempting to exorcise the spirits of Riccardo Freda, Mario Bava and his son Lamberto, Lucio Fulci, Aristide Massaccesi, Umberto Lenzi, et al., by employing an 'external' surface resemblance to the zombie film - traditional zombie makeup, behaviour, killing method, etc. - to explore an inner, lyrical-subjective reality. In so doing, Soavi takes the risk that all directors take when deciding to challenge or subvert genre expectations, namely fan alienation. This chapter accounts for a nearly forty year history spanning from 1956 to 1994, a legacy Soavi both invokes and manipulates. A decade later, the Italian zombie film still awaits its next reincarnation.

13 The analogy to *8 1/2* is apt when one also considers the breadth of *Dellamorte Dellamore*'s intertextuality, drawing from a broad range of horror and non-horror films alike. One key film from which Soavi draws creative inspiration is Orson Welles's *Citizen Kane* (1941). Some brief textual examples: in both films we have two men who isolate themselves from the 'outside' world; Kane isolates himself in a cemetery-like compound, Xanadu; and both films have an early scene with a glass snowball whose meaning will only be dispelled at the end. Though it would take far too much space to fully explicate, the other key influence on *Dellamorte Dellamore* is Alfred Hitchcock's classic study on male psychic breakdown, *Vertigo* (1958).

Austrian psycho killers and home invaders: the horror-thrillers *Angst* & *Funny Games*

Jürgen Felix & Marcus Stiglegger

The horror genre is virtually non-existent in Austrian cinema. Well-known especially for their avant-garde and experimental productions, everyday topics and problematic dramas, Austrian films are comparable to the art films of New German Cinema or to the kind of German TV movies that share a similar "anti-cinematic" take on the medium. Therefore, it should come as no surprise that at the time of writing Gerald Kargl's serial-killer film *Angst* (*Fear*, 1983) has never been distributed commercially outside of selected North European territories, not even on videotape or DVD. Even today this disturbing horror-thriller - which follows the bloody course of a twice convicted serial-killer through the Austrian countryside - is hard to watch because of its disgusting crime scenes. In contrast to Kargl's only film to date, Michael Haneke's *Funny Games* (1997) was shown at film festivals all over the world (from Cannes and Munich in 1997, to Rotterdam and Miami in 1998), and could be considered something of a box-office hit. But even if writer-director Haneke - born in Munich, Germany in 1942 - had already received several prizes for *Der Siebente Kontinent* (*The Seventh Continent*, 1989), *Nachruf für einen Mörder* (1991), *Benny's Video* (1992), *Die Rebellion* (1992) and *71 Fragmente einer Chronologie des Zufalls* (*71 Fragments of a Chronology of Chance*, 1994), his films have been heavily criticized, even by young Austrian film critics, for their didactic approach to the mass media and mainstream cinema. Nonetheless Haneke's "Kammerspiel"-like *Funny Games* is a rare and important example of the Austrian horror-thriller, as is Kargl's semi-documentary psychodrama *Angst*.

Deadly passions of a home invader

Angst is based on an actual case of triple-murder, the "Kniesek case", which is as famous in Austria as the Fritz Haarmann and Peter Kürten trials in Germany, or the Ed Gein case in America. Like these and other serial killers, Werner Kniesek from Salzburg - who killed three people out of pure lust in 1980 - stands as a threatening symbol of senseless death and destruction for its own sake. "I just love it when women shiver in deadly fear because of me. It is like an addiction, which will never stop", said Kniesek in front of the judge. His psychiatrist classified him as "extremely abnormal but not mentally ill" - an explosive mixture of lust for destruction and addiction to physical violence. He probably should never have been set free.

Kniesek was born in 1946, the spoiled son of an Austrian widow and an African-American soldier. His mother used to call him a "cute little black baby", and as a child he really was what his mother expected: a nice young boy. In his adolescent years, he developed a criminal instinct, which lead him to commit a number of burglaries in his hours off school. In 1962, Kniesek planned to leave the country. First he took a great amount of money from his mother, then he stabbed her several times with a bread knife. Kniesek was then sixteen years old. He left behind his critically wounded mother and took the train to Hamburg. Two days later he was caught by police, convicted, and sent to prison. Only two years later he managed to obtain his release. He married a prostitute, committed several house break-ins, and again tried to kill a woman, but his 73-year-old victim survived. For the second time in his short life, Kniesek was locked up in jail.

opposite:
Hunting for Humans in **Angst**.

Austria

above:
Angst.

In 1980, a few weeks before his sentence was up, Kniesek got the chance to go free to search for some work. Immediately he drove to Upper Austria, the town of St. Poelten, where he broke into the villa of a middle-aged widow named Gertrud Altreiter. There he found the son of the family, who was dependent on a wheelchair. In his confession, Kniesek explained that he knew he would kill the boy, but not at that moment. Later that day the mother and her daughter returned home from a shopping trip. Kniesek threatened the two women with a gas-pistol, bound and gagged them, and carried his helpless victims into two different rooms. In self-defence the daughter tried to seduce Kniesek, but the cold-blooded killer just stated that soon they would all be dead. His first victim was the disabled son whom Kniesek strangled to death, subsequently showing the corpse to the panicking mother before killing her as well. The horrifying chain of events climaxed in the violation and torturing of the 25-year-old daughter for several hours. Finally, Kniesek murdered her, along with the family cat, whose crying had bothered him. Afterwards, the killer spent the night side-by-side with his dead victims.

"I killed them simply out of the lust for murder", Kniesek later stated. "I even gave the elder woman some medicine so that she would live longer." His attempt to commit suicide in his single cell failed. During the trial, the killer expressed the wish to be jailed in a special institution for pathological criminals, because from childhood on he had felt the desire to kill people, and given the opportunity he would commit murder again and again. The case escalated again when Kniesek nearly managed to escape from prison three years later. During this period of public outrage, the possibility of reintroducing the death penalty in Austria was discussed more seriously than ever.

Inside the mind of serial killer

In *Angst*, Gerald Kargl's cinematic adaptation of the Kniesek case, some of the authentic facts are changed, the names of the people and cities altered, and certain of the events modified. The most obvious and significant change is the director's decision to add the killer's voice-over, as he quotes passages from other serial killers' confessions, especially those of Peter Kürten, the so-called "Vampire of Düsseldorf." This strictly subjective one-person drama is shot with a strong use of high-angle shots and handheld camerawork, and the minimal narration shows similarities to Aristide Massaccesi's Italian stalk'n'slash-epic *Rosso sangue* (*Absurd*, 1981). But in fact, Kargl manages to direct a European counterpart to John McNaughton's *Henry: Portrait of a Serial Killer* (USA, made 1986): irritating, gory, and absolutely hopeless.

Angst is exceptional in Austrian cinema for at least two reasons: it is both a "true crime" semi-documentary, and a horror-slasher film resembling those from the Italian tradition. Yet it is different as well. The film confronts the viewer with the most horrible details of the authentic case, and stands as the collaborative effort of first-time-director Kargl and his writer-cameraman Zbigniew Rybczynski; the third "author" is composer Klaus Schulze (from the "Krautrock"-group Tangerine Dream), whose cold yet haunting electronic rhythms add a great deal to the alienating atmosphere. The soundtrack mainly consists of pre-existing pieces, most notably the charming melody of "Freeze" - a track also used to great effect in the moonlight love scene of Michael Mann's serial killer drama *Manhunter* (USA, 1987).

Angst uses real-time narration nearly all way through; only a few ellipses appear in the second part, but most of the film is staged in detailed on-screen action, filmed with long handheld shots, sometimes even in planned sequences. Dialogue scenes are extremely rare, due to the concentration on a subjective, one-person drama. The film starts in a prison cell, establishing the killer (Erwin Leder) through an off-screen monologue in which he reflects about his past, his deeds, his needs, his sexual desires, and his supposedly lost childhood. The film's irritating atmosphere is established via clear, often high-key, but always greyish visuals - only broken by some stylish chiaroscuro in the cell. When released from prison ten years later, the off-screen narration leaves the viewer with no illusions: the killer will be stalking his next victim soon. When he enters a small diner we are forced to "scan" the guests through the killer's eyes. Every human being is a potential victim. First he enters a taxi, directs the female driver into a forest, and tries to strangle her. But he fails, as she has sensed something weird the whole time. His potential victim manages to kick him out of the car and escapes. The killer flees through the forest until he reaches a huge villa. He breaks into this supposedly empty house and meets - here the semi-documentary begins - a disabled and mentally retarded young man in a wheelchair (Rudolf Götz). Soon the other occupants of the house arrive: a middle-aged woman (Silvia Rabenreither), and her adolescent daughter (Edith Rosset).

Accompanied by his own quietly spoken voice-over, the killer starts his bloody "work": the son is drowned in the bathtub, and the mother gets strangled in her bedroom. The daughter tries to escape, but the killer hunts her down in the basement garage and viciously stabs her with a bread-knife. Here the most disturbing sequence of *Angst* runs its course: after massacring the young woman in a total frenzy, the killer rapes the corpse post-mortem. All of this is shot in real-time. After this disturbing climax, the film returns to its low-key narrative, and shows us the killer's actions after the murders: having slept at the crime scene, he washes himself, stuffs the corpses in the trunk of the family's car, and - once again - visits the diner from earlier in the picture. While there, he behaves so suspiciously that immediately the police are on to him. Finally they force him to open the trunk, a sequence filmed in the long, circling tracking shots Hollywood-cameraman Michael Ballhaus would later become popular for, symbolizing the circle of crime and punishment in which the killer is so consciously trapped.

What is so frightening about *Angst*, what makes the film a *horror* film in the true sense of the word, is that the killer is characterized as a threat to every human being crossing his path. To be seen by him is to be his potential victim. He easily invades the residence of a bourgeois household - a place that is normally synonymous with warmth and safety. And he brings murder to a dispassionate middle-class society in which

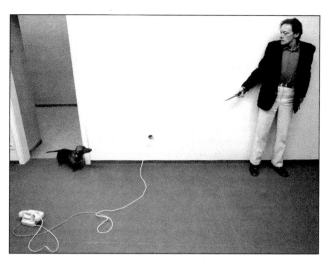

"death" would appear to be the only and last taboo. Interestingly, the disabled son seems to be "hidden" by his own family in this villa by the edge of the forest.

As noted earlier, *Angst*'s dramatic structure is reduced to only a very small amount of narration: we are simply shown the killer's murder spree on his one and only day of freedom. What might cause some empathy with this dangerous character - his own first-person-narration - in fact functions to alienate the viewer even more. This because the voice-overs simply double on the verbal level the monstrous incidents shown to us in all their graphic horror. Through the use of this technique, the film creates a distance between audience and protagonist that never really subsides. The murder sequences may be visually shocking, but they are also deeply reflective. Kargl avoids providing any type of entertainment, conventional thrill, or suspense. In fact, both Kargl and Haneke seem to believe that entertainment through stalk'n'slash splatter films is a sign of cynicism and should be avoided. As a result,

above and below:
Angst.

right and below:
Angst.

both have tried to develop directing methods marked by intellectual distance. Austria is a true middle-class society, and the greatest fear of the middle class is the invasion of the bourgeois home by unpredictable elements, be they of foreign origin - this is where racism comes into play - or be they mentally ill. To make his fable even more extreme, Kargl avoided the African-American origins of the real Werner Kniesek; in his film, the killer looks more like a "normal" guy no one would recognize or pay much attention to in the streets. *Angst*'s killer belongs to virtually the same bourgeois background as his choice of victims. This would seem to be the real Austrian nightmare, one which Michael Haneke has used as inspiration for several of his films.

Trapped in fear

The situation is quite simple, clearly structured, and well known from numerous thrillers and horror films: an upper-class family (father, mother, son) is trapped in an isolated house (their own luxurious holiday home nearby some Austrian lake), captured by two dangerous criminals who turn out to be serial killers. But unlike other home invaders - for example the psychopathic criminal in *Cape Fear*, played by Robert Mitchum in 1961 and by Robert De Niro in Martin Scorsese's 1991 remake - *Funny Games* confronts the viewer with a pair of seemingly harmless, almost innocent looking young men. They aren't much older than eighteen, and they look just like regular boys from a bourgeois neighbourhood. They are both wearing white sweaters and short trousers; only their white gloves, which may remind viewers of the "horror-shows" in Stanley Kubrick's *A Clockwork Orange* (1971), don't fit in with the fresh boyish look. Peter (Frank Giering) and Paul (Arno Frisch) - who refer to themselves with nicknames such as "Tom and Jerry" or "Beavis and Butthead" - seem well-educated, talk eloquently, and act politely. At least at the start. They are not the "usual" criminals who will break into a house to steal money, or to commit rape. They are just boys who want to play games. Only their kind of game is a very disgusting and ultimately deadly one.

First of all, Peter and Paul (two Christian names, as we know) have to choose their "teammates", and the newest member of the cast is the Schober family, who has just arrived at their holiday residence. Anna Schober (Susanne Lothar) is preparing supper in the kitchen, while husband Georg (Ulrich Mühe) and son Schorschi (pronounced "Georgi", Stefan Clapczynski) are busy fixing the sailboat for tomorrow's voyage. Meanwhile, Peter waits at the entrance, and when Anna finally notices the shy-looking, embarrassed boy at the front door, he introduces himself as a guest of the Berlingers, a neighboring family, and kindly asks if he might borrow some eggs. Unlike the family dog, a German shepherd named Rolfi who instinctively attacked him in the garden earlier, Anna doesn't recognize the danger posed by Peter. So she believes it is an accident, mere clumsiness - not bad will or a calculated act - when he drops the eggs in the hallway and a little later on the mobile phone in the sink.

Soon the awkward-looking boy is joined by a pert and insolent friend. First, Paul asks Anna if he may use one of her husband's golf clubs (with which he will kill the dog a little later), then he begins to patronize her harshly. At first the woman is irritated, and then she is frightened, but she is not willing to be in a "game" she does not know and the rules of which she cannot understand. In a first act of resistance, Anna bravely orders the home invaders to leave. But Peter and Paul won't go, leaving Anna

feeling upset, insulted, and humiliated. She attacks Paul. Just at that moment, father and son return from the lakeside. Georg doesn't understand what is going on, and is willing to believe in a kind of "unfortunate misunderstanding", as Paul puts it. Although Peter and Paul are back to behaving very politely, the situation is already strange, explosive, and threatening - getting out of control. So it comes as little surprise to the viewer when Paul threatens Georg with physical violence after being ordered to leave, and that Georg reacts by slapping Paul's face, like a father might do to punish his naughty child. But it comes as a total shock when Peter responds by striking Georg with the golf club, shattering his kneecap and sending the entire family into a state of utter panic. From that moment, right up to the end of the film, we are all involved in a "game" that we cannot accept or explain, one which isn't "funny" at all - not for the terrorized family, and not for the viewer who is terrorized as well because he or she can't help but identify with the victims.

All the way through the film - and increasingly as Georg, Anna, and their young son Schorschi are degraded, tortured, and eventually "dehumanized" by the cold-blooded home invaders - one thinks about how this innocent family might escape from their horrible, inhuman, and apparently fatal situation. Although there appear to be several chances for a happy ending (e.g., some friends come along with their boat, Schorschi escapes from the house, Peter is shot by Anna), in the end we come to realize that there is no way out, just as there is no real reason for the brutal and cynical actions of the assailants. For Schorschi, Georg, and Anna - and for the viewer as well - the "game" goes on and on, until the family finally loses the "bet" made on their behalf by the young men: that, as Paul says, "in twelve hours, you three will be kaput." It is a bet the family is forced to accept, and one it never had a chance to win.

First the family has to guess why Paul still has a golf ball in his pocket, even though he has already used the club (to kill the dog). Afterwards, Anna must search for Rolfi's corpse with Paul - who leads her around by saying "hot" or "cold" - acting as her guide. Later she has to take off her clothes in order to stop the torturing of her son. Her husband too must participate in this "game": "Take off your clothes, my sweetheart", he is forced to say. Up to and including the final "Good Wife" game, in which Anna is presented with two options - one, she must choose whether her husband dies by knife or by gunshot; or two, she can take his place and die first - all of the "games" are based upon physical torture and psychological humiliation, beginning with Paul's killing of the family dog with a golf club (off-screen), and reaching a dramatic climax in Peter's murder of Schorschi with a hunting rifle. We do not see the shooting of the little boy, because the camera stays with Paul calmly making some sandwiches in the kitchen. But we can hear the shot, despite the fact that the television set is roaring the whole time. And we can hardly ignore the screams of Georg and Anna, filled as they are with grief and despair.

above:
Funny Games.

Haneke and his cinematographer Jürgen Jürges - who worked with Rainer Werner Fassbinder several times in the 1970s, and with Helma Sanders-Brahms on *Deutschland Bleiche Mutter* (*Germany Pale Mother*, 1980) - withholds from the viewer all the familiar images of blood and gore. As opposed to Kargl or (to mention just one example of a prominent and ambitious Hollywood auteur) Oliver Stone, Haneke seems to have no confidence in the cathartic effect of violent images. Haneke's films instead force the viewer to listen to, and imagine, violent action, its effects discovered afterwards, reflected on the victims' faces. In *Funny Games*, it is Anna's ravaged face especially that we must stare at again and again: a face that gradually loses - torture by torture - all traces of human dignity, destroyed by escalating acts of humiliation forced upon her by her tormentors.

When Paul returns to the living room after Peter's killing of Schorschi, all we see at first is the blood-splattered screen of the blaring TV set. We can't see the perpetrators or the hostages; we just hear the broadcasting of an auto race, and Paul talking with Peter about the latter's "bad timing." With a simple cut, the entire perspective changes. From a distance, the camera now shows us the whole room,

opposite:
Funny Games.

revealing the immediate aftermath of a horrible act of senseless brutality. The boy's dead body lies on the floor; Anna, legs bound and hands tied behind her back, squats in a corner, staring motionless at the floor; and Georg lies between two sofas, tied up and semi-conscious. For almost ten minutes - what seems like an eternity - we are forced to stare at this scene, without any cuts to alleviate our discomfort. We watch Anna hop about helplessly, first to the television set in order to turn it off, then out of the room, into the kitchen. The killers have left (but only for a while); their victims are all alone. When Anna returns to her bound and injured husband, she puts her arms around his tortured body. Georg starts crying, filled with a despair so intense that he quickly reaches a point of near-total exhaustion. It is during the moment of silence that follows that we as viewers might begin to understand what Colonel Kurtz (Marlon Brando) could have meant by the phrase, "the horror", at the end of his journey through darkness in Francis Ford Coppola's *Apocalypse Now* (1979). In a situation that is both terrible and absurd, one that exists beyond the pale of all reasonable behaviour, psychological motivation, or logical explanation, monsters rule the imagination - monsters of a deranged mind which can be evoked but not exorcised by violent pictures. Imagination is thus the true home of horror.

Welcome to the circle

Haneke's *The Seventh Continent* confronts us with the suicide of a family. *Benny's Video* presents a young video freak, played by Arno Frisch ("Paul" in *Funny Games*), who first watches the killing of a pig several times, then murders a young girl just "to see what killing is like." In *71 Fragments of a Chronology of Chance*, a confused boy runs amuck in a bank. In *Funny Games*, Georg asks his torturers at least two times, "Why are you doing this?", but Paul's replies can't be taken seriously. He is just playing "answer the question", and repeating the kind of psychological verbiage offered in numerous crime stories again and again: his parents got divorced, and therefore the boy became homosexual, or had an incestuous relationship with his mother, or became a drug addict because of the brutalizing milieu in which he lived, etc. But none of these more or less "politically correct" explanations fits the "game" being played here. The only aim and motivation of these killers is fun, pleasure, amusement, or - as Haneke himself believes - the satisfaction of that pure, sadistic lust typically evoked and fulfilled by mainstream sex-and-crime cinema, and especially by horror movies.

Paul is upset about the premature killing of the boy, but only because Peter's rash action reduces the perverse possibilities of their sport. When Georg begs him to finish the deadly game because "it's enough", Paul replies that "We are still under feature length." Directing himself to the viewer, he continues: "Is it already enough? You want a proper ending with a plausible development, don't you?." The rules of the game determine the action, and the supreme rule is to obtain pleasure from humiliating one's captives. As soon as the victims can no longer stand the torture, and so submit to their predicted fate - as soon as they surrender unconditionally - the lustful possibilities of the game are exhausted, and these "teammates" aren't of interest anymore. Only now can the dehumanizing play be finished. Georg, lying tied up and practically unconscious on the sofa, is shot with the hunting rifle, just like his son before him. Anna is thrown overboard off the boat in the morning, her legs bound together and her hands tied behind her back; "Ciao, bella", is Paul's cynical farewell. All dead, game over, time to start a new game, maybe a variation of the last game or perhaps just the same old game once again. It is 8 a.m. when Peter and Paul arrive at another luxurious holiday home on the same Austrian lake. This time it is Paul who gently asks for some eggs, and as the young man enters this next victim's house the frame freezes, with the home invader's diabolic look staring directly into the camera, right into the viewer's eyes.

"I try to find ways of representing violence as that which it always is: as unconsumable", Haneke says. "I give back to violence that which it is: pain, a violation of others."[1] Most of his films, not only the well-known *Benny's Video* and *Funny Games*, are reflections on violent life in a media saturated society, or, to be more precise: reflections on mediated life in a violent society. Haneke studied philosophy, psychology, and drama in Vienna, then became a playwright with the Südwestfunk Theatre Company from 1967-70 before writing scripts for German television. As a filmmaker, he uses generic topics as experiments in which the protagonists - the good ones as well as the bad ones - are forced to behave like laboratory rabbits. There is no such thing as free will allowed, and no "emotional development" either.

[1] Haneke, M. "Director's Statement": www.attitude.hostrack.net/AttitudeFilms/

Angst & Funny Games

The characters we watch in *Funny Games* are just figures ("experimental subjects", one might say) playing roles, testing the limits of the human subject. When Anna shoots Peter in an act of desperate resistance, Paul panics. Having lost control over the "game", he hysterically grabs the TV remote control and rewinds the scene - the same diegetic episode we have just witnessed. This sequence, criticized for its obvious didacticism, may remind us of Pirandello, or it may be understood as a kind of "class-action revenge" taken by the director against all those viewers who fast-forward through the "boring" parts of movies watched on video (as David Bartholomew puts it). Nevertheless, the sequence does make sense within Haneke's *vision du monde*. The issue is not whether the viewer mixes up fact and fiction. For the fact of the matter, according to Haneke, is that fiction is real and reality a fiction. During their sailboat ride on the way to their next victims, Peter tells a science-fiction story which deals with two "parallel" universes, one real, the other fictional. The hero of the story lives in cyberspace, in the "anti-material world", while his family remains in the "real" world. There is no communication between these two worlds, and if there is any difference between them, one has no way of telling what it is. The fiction you see in a movie is as "real as reality", Paul says, a reality you can observe "as well as a movie." In today's mass mediated society, the "ecstasy of communication" just doesn't make sense anymore.

Shock value

Kargl's almost unknown psycho-thriller *Angst* and Haneke's notorious "Kammerspiel"-like horror-drama *Funny Games* are separated by a gap of almost fifteen years. During this time, cinema itself underwent major changes. In the early 1980s, when postmodernism emerged as a dominant cultural form, the last lethal whimpers of the sexual revolution which took place in the late 60s-early 70s finally led to the success of the slasher genre. In *Halloween* (1978), *Friday the 13th* (1980) and the like, juvenile bodies, once engaged in "free love", were stalked and slashed by perverts who represented the restrictive morality of a "new conservatism." In effect, the psycho-killers of these films act as moral executors to punish the lustful behaviour of a sinful youth. At their hands, the "sexual body" experienced its total destruction. "Free love" was shown to be a risk -

horror cinema across the globe

corresponding to the era's new conservative politics, especially in the USA - in the age of an ever-growing HIV plague. Kargl's *Angst* appeared shortly after the slasher genre reached its height with Lucio Fulci's graphic and disturbing *Lo squartatore di New York* (*The New York Ripper*, 1982). But the Austrian director was not willing to join the ranks of his exploitation horror peers. His work is contrary to the likes of Fulci's misogynistic thriller or Ruggero Deodato's home invader-class drama *La casa sperduta nel parco* (*The House on the Edge of the Park*, 1980). *Angst* avoids any moralistic subtext in its pursuit of depicting the ultimate in alienating, antisocial behaviour. The killer embodies the precise opposite of the utopian sexual being the 60s so desperately attempted to invoke: his sexual pleasure is the termination of life.

Funny Games also employs the theme of bourgeois-home invasion, but in a very different way. Haneke's film was made around the same time that Wes Craven began his comeback with the semi-ironic high school slasher *Scream* (1996), in which two boys terrorize and finally kill their classmates just for the fun of it, and corresponding to genre rules.[2] *Scream* may be seen as the sensationalistic, mainstream companion to the Austrian film. When the "master narratives" of bourgeois morality have all but disappeared, the killing game becomes party event - nihilistic but entertaining. Like the Kniesek character in *Angst*, the killers in *Funny Games* enjoy the "angst" of their victims, so long as they show the will to resist. But unlike him, they are not driven by destructive instincts; in fact, they don't seem to have emotions at all, save perhaps a desire for amusement. Here, all efforts at psychological explanations fail, all negative emotions expressed are simulated, just strategies in a game. Haneke doesn't show the gruesome act of murder itself - the destruction of the body actually happens outside the frame. This makes a kind of sense, considering that the death of the victims marks the end of the "game."

The pleasure of these (not at all funny) games lies precisely in breaking the victim's will to resist. When that will is broken, the killers loose interest, get bored. Killing becomes a mere triviality. Thus, the end of the film marks the beginning of a new circle. Playing with the last taboo of Western civilization, the taking of life, the killers manage to rise up against the unwritten laws of materialistic society. Their "game" produces nothing but morbid entertainment. What makes no sense, what lacks any productive value, may not be, and probably never has been. The fatal system of the boys' game reflects the Sadean orgies of destruction: every living body is just another toy in the hands of the "master." What is truly shocking about this cold and cynical film is the fact that two well-educated, sometimes seductive young killers are shown to embody the apocalyptic, self-destructive side of a society that has already lost its ethical values: if "anything goes", nothing will preserve the utopian dreams of the reasonable, moral human being.

right:
Angst.

[2] For more on the slasher/stalker subgenre and its revival in the wake of *Scream*'s phenomenal success, see Dika, V. (1987) "The Stalker Cycle, 1978-81", in Waller, G. (ed.), *American Horrors: Essays on the Modern American Horror Film* (Chicago: University of Illinois Press), and Schneider, S.J. (2000) "Kevin Williamson and the Rise of the Neo-Stalker", *Post Script: Essays in Film and the Humanities* 19.2, 73-87.

Part Three:
Genre Histories and Studies

Coming of age: the South Korean horror film   185
- Art Black

Between appropriation and innovation: Turkish horror cinema   205
- Kaya Özkaracalar

Witches, spells and politics: the horror films of Indonesia   219
- Stephen Gladwin

The unreliable narrator: subversive storytelling in Polish horror cinema   231
- Nathaniel Thompson

The Beast from Bollywood: a history of the Indian horror film   243
- Pete Tombs

In a climate of terror: the Filipino monster movie   255
- Mauro Feria Tumbocon, Jr.

French revolution: the secret history of Gallic horror movies   265
- David Kalat

Coming of age: the South Korean horror film

Art Black

The essentials of film are to surprise people, to touch people and to give them pleasure. Those three essentials are all in horror films.
- Kang Je-gyu[1]

On 24 December 1999, one day before Christmas, one week before Y2K failed to wipe out civilisation as we know it, a film opened in Korea that set a new standard for the horror genre both locally and internationally. *Memento Mori* takes place in one of Korea's unimaginably oppressive girls' high schools, where the pressure to conform, to perform, to *succeed* drives teenagers to desperate acts. A pair of outsiders, Yoo Shi-eun (Lee Young-jin) and Min Hyo-shin (Park Yeh-jin), form a lesbian alliance and together create an intricate and elaborate piece of art that functions as diary, suicide note and portal into the metaphysical and hallucinatory.

Unfolding in layered, nonlinear fashion, the film interweaves the girls' tragic romance with the voyeuristic tale of a fellow student who discovers their dark secret. Intrinsically criticised in the narrative is the strict, cruel, sexist and debasing Korean scholastic system and, by implication, the misogynistic nature of Korean society as a whole. *Memento Mori* simultaneously utilises numerous horror conventions while slyly inventing a whole new mode of storytelling, becoming in the process a horror film with few outright frights and fewer deaths - a psychic, psychological dissection of youth struggling for identity against infinite odds.

Memento Mori is theoretically a sequel, albeit in the loosest sense of the term. Also known as *Whispering Corridors 2*, it was made by different filmmakers, featuring new characters and an entirely dissimilar plot, sharing only the setting of a girls' high school and a palpable concern for the social pressures haunting the protagonists, both living and dead. The original *Whispering Corridors* was structured far more conventionally along the lines of a traditional scare flick, however it struck a deep chord with young Korean audiences by virtue of its familiar academic setting and postmodern slang. Capitalising on its teenage viewers' cultural apprehension and anxiety, it became the second-highest grossing domestic release of 1998 (seventh overall, trailing American juggernauts like *Titanic* and *Armageddon*).

Together the two pictures helped fuel a renaissance of fright films in Korea, spawning everything from scholastic creepers (*School Legend*, *Harpy*) to teen slasher flicks (*Bloody Beach*, *Rec*) to supernatural romances (*Il Mare*, *Calla*, *Ditto*) to violent serial killer psychological mysteries (*Tell Me Something*, *Say Yes*) to sadomasochistic surrealism/hyperrealism (*The Isle*, *Sorum*) and various combinations thereof. *Whispering Corridors* and *Memento Mori* are also highly indicative of the recent wave of Korean films by innovative, young directors intent on pushing the envelope, powering their productions with inventive style and provocative content, challenging old conventions and positing Korean film as the highest profile "new Asian cinema" of the third millennium. Neither picture could have been made as recently as a few years ago, with censorship still pervasive in Korean cinema. *Memento Mori*, in fact, was scripted with considerably more focus on the lesbian relationship, but both the government censorship board and the

[1] Kang Je-gyu, interview with the author.

opposite:
The Ring Virus.

releasing company insisted on cuts. Many of the best Korean films of the past few years have fought similar battles; some have won, many have lost, but all have helped to change the topography of the battlefield.

Golden times, early horrors

Following the ceasefire between North and South Korea in 1953, the South Korean government reorganised the film industry with the aid of technology and assistance from the United States. Modern studios were established, new equipment brought in, and in 1955 a landmark was established when Ch'unhyang-jon was seen by 200,000 viewers in Seoul alone - one tenth of the city's population - sparking the first "golden age" of Korean cinema, lasting through the 1960s. One of the most enduring of Korean folk tales, the story is often referred to as the local version of *Romeo and Juliet*, albeit with torture and revenge. The focus of the narrative is in fact on the torment and abuse endured by young Ch'unhyang as she struggles to remain loyal to her absent man despite the evil intentions of a lustful local lord. The story, likened by some to a symbolic retelling of divided Korea and its rape by foreign powers, has formed the basis for about a dozen films, including Korea's first features with sound (1935), colour (1958) and cinemascope (1961), along with a black and white satire in which the characters, clad in period costume, cavort with booze, jukeboxes and convertibles. Following the hit 1955 version, female rape became an enduring genre unto itself in Korean film. "A Korean movie in which the heroine is not routinely stripped and ravished by the third reel can be quite refreshing," commented *The Economist*, years later.**2**

Shin Sang-ok was one of several notable directors to begin challenging convention with bolder and more artistic works during this period. His 1958 film *Flowers of Hell* was the first to show a kiss on-screen and his pictures frequently included erotic elements, influencing later generations of filmmakers. Shin has remarked that although the country was poor in the 1960s, there was considerable freedom of speech - a statement belied by the fact that he was one of three directors booked on charges of obscenity in 1969 (for *Eunuch*). Indeed, ideological filmmaking could be a dangerous venture in Korea. As early as 1956, director Han Hyong-mo's *Chayu Puin* ("Free Wife") raised the ire of college professors, who protested the film as an insult to their profession. Director Lee Man-hui (*Seven Woman Prisoners*) endured far greater adversity when he was prosecuted by the government in 1965 for violation of the Anti-Communist law.

That same year, Yu Hyon-mok, a highly-stylised director credited with creating Korea's first avant-garde film in 1956 and introducing the techniques of counterpoint and psychological interactions to local cinema, released his film *The Martyred*, only to have a group of Presbyterian clergymen sue to have one-third of the picture cut, claiming that it defamed the clergy and encouraged communists. The film, based on a best-selling novel, escaped censorship due in part to strong support from liberal factions, but Yu's follow-up, *Ch'unmong* ("Spring Dream") wasn't so lucky. A psychological fantasy with parallels to *The Cabinet of Dr. Caligari* (1919) and *Spellbound* (1945), consisting in part of expressionistic, surrealistic dream sequences, the picture ran afoul of the censors as a result of supposedly "sadistic" sequences and a simulated nude scene. Yu countered that certain foreign films had been distributed with equally strong sequences, but the government countered that while the foreign releases (Edward Dmytryk's *The Carpetbaggers*, the Italian nudie *Adam and Eve*) were works of art, Yu's was not. *Ch'unmong* was exhibited in a scissored version and Yu was indicted on charges of making an obscene movie. He has since demurred from making anything remotely contentious.

Of course, the bulk of Korean productions during this period were anything but controversial. Gangster and juvenile rebellion films and the ever-popular melodramas made up most of the country's releases during the golden age. Sadism may have been cause for indictment when presented in the form of an intellectual discourse, but usually it was "mere" entertainment - just like rape. In Yi Yong-min's *Gate of Hell* (1962), for instance, an evil tyrant is given to all manner of torture and cruelty, including drowning an enemy and his son in the palace cesspool. Naturally the tyrant gets his comeuppance when he and his minions die and wind up in Buddhist hell. High-quality special effects and colour filming ensured that audiences got their money's worth with the graphic torture scenes.

Supernatural elements suffused such golden age films as Shin Hyeon-ho's *A Man*

---

2 *The Economist* 1985: 82.

coming of age

Sells His Life (1966), as well as *A Flower of Evil* (1961), *A Devilish Homicide* (1965) and *A Bridegroom From a Grave* (1963), all three from Lee Yong-min. The latter film hinges on a honeymoon during which a bride digs up the corpse of a child to suck its blood. Monsters made appearances in Gweon Hyeok-jin's *Wang-Magui* ("King-size Monster") and Kim Ki-duk's *Grand Evil Monster Yonggary* (released in America by AIP as *Yongary, Monster From the Deep*), both from 1967. *Wang-Magui*, cited as Korea's first science-fiction film, stars a giant ape that is dropped from a flying saucer by belligerent aliens and proceeds to kick its way through a cardboard Seoul. At one point a youngster jumps onto the creature's head, crawls into its ear and watches through one nostril as the ape stomps the city. The sequence ends with the monster stopping to slap itself and bellow, and the scene cuts to the youngster urinating inside its head.

Whereas *Wang-Magui* proved a commercial flop, *Yonggary* went on to sell over 100,000 tickets in Seoul alone (one of only fourteen films to achieve those sales in 1967). Engineered to cash in on the Godzilla craze, *Yonggary* was made with the participation of Japan's Daiei company and is a camp gem featuring a flame-spitting rubbersuit giant with a rhino nose, a pre-pubescent hero with an "itch ray" and an unforgettable scene of the title creature doing the twist. Nine years later, the US/South Korean co-production *A*P*E* would similarly swipe from the 1976 *King Kong* remake, beginning with a scene of a silly-looking ape flopping around pretending to fight with an equally oversized rubber shark. An interminable mess, the 3-D film features characters tossing things at the lens (including rubber snakes that hit the camera and cause it to wobble), along with countless dull scenes of bad models crumbling to the ground, toy planes and tanks, and the title beast giving his attackers the finger.

Kim Ki-Young: Korea's horror auteur

By this time the South Korean film industry was in steep decline, due in part to the increasingly oppressive dictatorship and stricter censorship regulations. In 1972, President Park Chung-hee announced that due to the Communist threat from North Korea, he was declaring a state of emergency, suspending all civil rights. The Korean CIA established a network of spies and conducted surveillance of schools, churches and the media. Any hint of dissent was met with imprisonment, torture, forced confessions and/or executions. This naturally sparked a dramatic increase in student protests calling for democratic reform, paralleled by filmmakers petitioning for changes to the restrictive regulations strangling the industry. Government strictures continued to limit artists' ability to create original and challenging works, even as the lack of good equipment and shortage of skilled technicians and writers (along with the exploding popularity of TV) resulted in a marked decrease in the size of audiences.

Further amendments to the Motion Picture Law, intended to strengthen the industry, resulted in exactly the opposite effect. Recognising that larger-budgeted, more slickly crafted imports were vastly more popular than local films at the box office, the government modified the quota system so that in order to gain a license to import one foreign film, filmmakers were required to produce four local ones. Additional import incentives were given to producers who managed to export films to foreign countries. As a result, film

below:
Artwork for the US/South Korean co-production **A*P*E**.

production boomed as companies began cranking out "quota quickies" in the late 1960s and early 1970s; movies were made for pennies and sold for export without ever seeing a screen, in order that the producers could import profitable foreign films. Local productions were chintzy looking, poorly written and flatly directed, with out-of-focus scenes, excessive use of zooms and bad post-dubbing. Following the Bruce Lee hysteria, kung-fu pictures flooded the market in co-production with Hong Kong and Taiwan. Most were cheap throwaways, although there were more prestigious offerings from Hong Kong's Shaw Brothers studio.[3] In 1971, noted Chinese director King Hu travelled to South Korea to shoot his ghostly tale of an evil spirit seductress, *Legend of the Mountain*. For the most part, however, Korean horror fans had to settle for the usual tragic melodramas disguised as cheaply-made ghost stories.

Among the most notable local directors during this period was Kim Ki-young. Born in 1919, Kim went to medical school before becoming a writer-director of maverick genre pictures. Melding excessive B-movie sensibilities with deeply personal psychodramas, Kim created a highly influential body of work that both typifies and surmounts Korean film melodrama. In the typical Kim Ki-young scenario, a family's domestic bliss falls victim to uncontrollable sexual desire and a menacing, vengeful woman. A husband is likely to commit rape; the rape victim is likely to become obsessed with her attacker; the rapist's wife is likely to find herself battling fiercely to keep her family together while the "other woman" manipulates the weak husband and tears apart the matrimonial bond. In addition to his wild proto-gothic visuals, Kim made liberal use of rats, poison, shamans, necrophilia, bizarre dialogue, extraordinary characters and an idiosyncratic juxtaposition of styles and generic conventions to create a wholly unique cinematic universe.

Following his 1955 debut *The Box of Death*, Kim finally found success with his ninth film, *The Housemaid* (1960), a modernist film noir with naturalistic opening and closing scenes bookending the expressionistic main story, in which the manipulative title character seduces her boss and goes to work destroying his family. In 1971, Kim remade the story as *The Woman of Fire*; eleven years later he remade it again as *The Woman of Fire 82*. During the 1970s Kim triumphed with films such as *The Insect Woman* (1972, remade by Kim in 1984 as *Carnivore*), *Iodo* (1977) and *Killer Butterfly* (1978). An art-house curiosity, *Iodo* posited a murder suspect on an island populated by native women. *Killer Butterfly* (roughly translated from Korean as "A Woman Chasing Horrible Butterfly") is an episodic murder story mixing science fiction, horror, melodrama and various other genres as a man survives an attempted murder/suicide only to find himself engaged in a desperate bid to kill another man. Unfortunately the victim won't stay dead, even as a skeleton. Kim apparently didn't want to make the film (it was written by someone else) and in later years would dismiss it off-handedly. Although it doesn't quite fit with his other, more personal works, it is nonetheless an entertaining slice of pan-genre filmmaking. "Kim Ki-young wasn't really a horror director," says playwright and filmmaker Kim Ji-woon, "but he has a sense of horror that's pervasive in his films. [He was] Korea's only director of cult movies. I think his ideas and thoughts were a step ahead back then. Because his films were unique they were kind of commercially successful, but his real philosophy toward his work, because he was very advanced, wasn't really embraced by the society."[4] Sadly, Kim's work was essentially forgotten over the years, before a 1997 film festival retrospective in Korea reintroduced his shocking and singular visions to the world. As the accolades began to pour in and his star began to rise once again amidst screenings at various international festivals, Kim and his wife died tragically in a house fire on 4 February 1998.

Real-life horrors

In 1978, the same year that Kim Ki-young made *Killer Butterfly*, director Shin Sang-ok encountered a very different type of horror. Long regarded as one of Korean cinema's leading lights, Shin often cast his wife, popular actress Choi Eun-hee, in starring roles. After being offered a lucrative film contract, Choi visited Hong Kong and promptly disappeared. Shin went looking for her and soon he too vanished - kidnapped by agents of Kim Jong-il, son of North Korean leader Kim Il-sun. A notorious cinema aficionado (and future leader of his country), the younger Kim firmly believed in film's persuasive powers and authored the polemical book, "Cinema and the Art of Directing." He argued that the industry should be

---

[3] These including Yueh Feng's *The Last Woman of Shang* (1964) - a grand costume epic of warfare and vengeance starring screen goddess Lin Dai and Korean actor Shin Yungkyoon - and the spiritual fantasy *Goddess of Mercy* (1967), co-directed by Shin Sang-ok in two versions with the same locations and cast, starring Chinese superstar Li Li-hua for the Hong Kong release and Shin's wife Choi Eun-hee for the Korean one.

[4] Kim Ji-woon, interview with the author.

controlled by government and advocated heavy-handed propagandist filmmaking with politically correct, anti-Japanese, anti-classist messages. Spirited to North Korea, the idealistic Shin Sang-ok allegedly spent four years in prison before he and his wife agreed to help Kim improve his country's film output. The couple lived lavishly for the next three years, directing and acting in about half a dozen pictures on a stipend of US $3 million per year.

Meanwhile, South Korea underwent dramatic changes. In December 1979, military dictator Park Chung-hee was assassinated by his close ally, the Director of the Korean Central Intelligence Agency. The "Seoul Spring" began, as the succeeding president released many political prisoners and promised genuine political reforms. *P'Imak* (aka *House of Death/The Death Cottage*, 1980) brought Korean shamanism to the Venice Film Festival, in the story of a sorceress enlisted to exorcise the curse that is killing all the male children of a local aristocrat. In a convoluted tale of sexual frustration and ghostly vengeance, a woman becomes infected after repeatedly stabbing herself in the thigh to stem her carnal desires (a perversely common image in Korean lore and films, in keeping with the traditional focus on wounds and torture). Taken to the Death Cottage, she recovers unexpectedly and has a child with the keeper of the house. When the lovers are killed by the aristocrat's family, they find their revenge through supernatural means, leading to a violent climax involving the shaman sorceress and her hidden secret.

But cinematic horror paled before reality. In May 1980, Korea was devastated by the Kwangju Massacre. Students at Chonnam National University were demanding release of an opposition leader who had been imprisoned for political activities, when black-bereted paratroopers began to indiscriminately kill protesters. In a parallel to the Tiananmen Square incident, civilians joined the students and succeeded in driving the army out of the city, but on 27 May, the 20th Army Division returned in force. The official number of dead was declared to be about 200, although witnesses claimed the figure to be closer to 2000. General Chun Doo-kwan used the incident to cement his power base and seized control of the country for the next seven years, while anti-government demonstrations continued to grow more violent and political corruption more prevalent. An underground film movement ("open cinema") evolved out of university film clubs of the 1980s, as young directors began to make illegal movies on campuses. Many of them began by making shorts, creating a thriving short film industry that remains to this day a healthy training ground for new talent. A distinct counterculture evolved among artists as the new wave of dissident filmmakers began to produce works with deeper cultural and political consciousness, addressing current social issues with increased realism. As a result, the modern independent Korean cinema came into being; a rebellion modelled after France's Nouvelle Vague and eventually dubbed *minjung* ("the masses") films. Commercial filmmaking felt the impact as subject matter became more mature, with newcomers producing important social dramas that brought local cinema to the attention of the international festival circuit.

Genre films generally fell by the wayside during this period, although Shin Sang-ok managed to make a notable contribution from his new home of North Korea. In 1985, he directed the giant monster movie *Pulgasari*, a remake of Kim Myeong-jae's 1962 film, *Bulgasari*. In the remake, oppressed peasants find a new champion when the local blacksmith crafts a protective talisman named *Pulgasari*. It turns out that the golem-like creature has an appetite for metal, which causes it to grow, and before long it is knocking over cardboard temples and chasing enemy armies. Produced with the participation of Toho's original Godzilla team, the rubber monster suit gives a commendable performance and the film has a cheesy sense of spectacle that goes nicely with the storyline. It was nearing release when director Shin, in Vienna with his wife to promote North Korean filmmaking, managed to make his way to the US Embassy and eventually received political asylum in Hollywood, where he has since worked on the *Three Ninjas* movie series under the name Simon Sheen. *Pulgasari* went straight into obscurity following its initial North Korean release, only to be resurrected once again in 1998 to play Japan as old-school competition against Hollywood's shiny new-tech *Godzilla*. In 2000 it flopped miserably when released in South Korea to complement the establishment of tentative relations with the country's northern neighbours.

South Korea

New blood in the 90s

Although the quota system ensured that locally-produced films were given substantial screen time in South Korea, foreign releases still ruled the box office. Nonetheless, by the mid-1980s the tide was slowly beginning to turn. For decades, Korean filmmakers had been stifled by outdated equipment, lack of schooling and governmental policies restricting film imports to a precious few commercial releases, effectively limiting local exposure to innovative and challenging international works. The 1990s saw the rise of a new generation of filmmakers, schooled overseas and with a vast knowledge of cinema history. Director Kang Je-gyu found himself the poster-boy for this new breed of Korean talents. A former student at New York University, Kang was a photographer turned award-winning, pan-genre screen-writer (mystery, noir, political thriller) who found himself constantly disappointed with the films made from his scripts, eventually deciding to take the reins himself.

"When I established my film company in 1993," says Kang, "we made a film, an omnibus film, sort of like three short films, and I directed two of them. Those two were horror films. Recently, *Chosun Daily*, one of the biggest newspapers, did a feature on rare videos, and it was one of them. Really, really hard to find. It's called *Horror Express Train* but it was never translated in English."[5] Kang debuted as a full-length director in 1996 with the genre opus *The Gingko Bed*. This film - a supernatural romance about reincarnated love and pursuit from beyond the grave - began with a rewrite of *The Terminator*'s (1984) famous opening and went on to include numerous effects hitherto unseen in Korean cinema. It quickly became the highest-grossing South Korean film to date. That same year, the Pusan International Film Festival was inaugurated. In no time at all, it became one of the pre-eminent festivals in Asia, attended by masses of cinema-literate Koreans with a thirst for innovative work.

By this time the educational opportunities for filmmakers in Korea had increased exponentially as film schools proliferated and expanded, with even the government becoming interested in promoting this developing product. Along with the outstanding technical improvements in South Korean filmmaking, a constitutional court ruled that film censorship violated constitutional law, theoretically allowing for an increased freedom in subject matter and approach. The governmental screening authorities were replaced in 1996 by a civic body, the Korean Performing Arts Promotion Committee (KPAPC), which promptly clamped down on director Jang Sun-woo's *Bad Movie* (aka *Timeless, Bottomless, Bad Movie*, 1997). Jang, a former student activist who was jailed for six months in 1980 and allegedly tortured, had made a name for himself as the controversial creator of such films as *Seoul Jesus* (1985) and *A Petal* (1996), the latter centering on the psychological aftermath of the Kwangju Massacre. *Bad Movie* was conceived as a semi-documentary about troubled teens and was cast through open auditions with "real-life juvenile delinquents." Jang and his crew spent a year with a group of punks, and in addition to handing over the cameras and allowing them to create their own autobiographical vignettes, he shot footage of them stealing, breakdancing, having sex with strangers, getting molested and being beaten by their teachers.

1997 was perhaps the biggest turning point for South Korean cinema, what with the popularity of crime films like *Green Fish* and the viciously funny gangster satire *No. 3*, and particularly the surprisingly successful romantic drama *The Contact*. In November of that year, Kim Sung-hong's *The Hole* brought horror home with wit, polish and a uniquely Korean perspective on traditional family values. When a new bride moves into the house where her husband lives with his widowed mother, the newlywed must kowtow and serve mom as the lowest and most subservient member of the household.

[5] Kang Je-gyu, interview with the author.

below:
The Gingko Bed.

coming of age

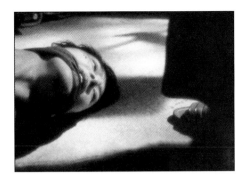

left:
The Hole.

Unfortunately, as hard as she tries to win mom over, she is rebuffed, reviled, despised, degraded and ultimately much worse for her efforts. The Hitchcockian twists mount as the bride discovers the secrets in her new family's closet, resulting in a taut and claustrophobic bloodbath. *The Hole* is a superbly mounted example of domestic horror, made all the more appealing by the distinctly Korean flavour of the relationships.

The following year, the Korean cinema industry underwent a seismic generational shift, as the box office was dominated by young, first-time directors, completely eschewing the traditional protégé approach to a career in filmmaking - i.e., starting off as a production assistant and slowly working one's way up the ranks. It has been noted that the country currently has the youngest filmmakers in the world and a cinematically astute audience comparable to Paris in the 1960s, fuelled by numerous film magazines and TV programs about movies. Advertising and distribution methods have developed in pace with production capabilities, and screening conditions have improved as multiplexes proliferated. Young audiences have increasingly flocked to theatres to catch the new wave of releases by brash, modern filmmakers, and in 1998 horror connected with Korean movie fans in a major way.

In April of that year, Kim Ji-woon debuted as director with the self-written black comedy *The Quiet Family*, about a peculiar clan whose guesthouse in the mountains is failing for lack of visitors. To make things worse, once guests do start to arrive, they mysteriously drop dead, and the family must cautiously dispose of the bodies in order to avoid arousing the curiosity of the police. Complications arise as the family, by now involved in murder and routinely engaging in ritual burials, discover that construction is about to begin on the land where the bodies are buried.[6] Kim would go on to direct an even more barbed satire, *The Foul King* (2000), about a downtrodden office worker who gets out his frustrations as a brutal, rule-breaking masked pro-wrestler. "Basically life is a horror," Kim says, "life is fear. Actually my movie *The Foul King* is also about the fear, you know, of facing...reality. I think that this horror element is going to be in my films all the time."[7]

In August 1998, *The Soul Guardians* provided a showcase for the newly opened Seoul Cinema Complex, a facility designed in part to provide state-of-the-art optical effects for local filmmakers. The story first saw light of day as a series of short, linked episodes by Lee Wu-hyeok on a Korean website. The hugely popular tales were then crafted into a blockbuster novel followed by a screenplay by the same author. Debut director Park Kwang-Chun skewed the original story slightly by focusing on the handsome twentysomething hero (Shin Hyun-jun, previously of *The Gingko Bed*) and relegating his battling cohorts - a young kid and an older, embittered priest - to lesser roles. The nominal plot concerns evil supernatural forces pursuing a girl, while the heroes put themselves in harm's way to protect her. It begins superbly with a SWAT team intruding on the eerie scene of a mass-suicide, and proceeds with excellent CGI effects and tremendous set-pieces, making for big local box-office. But the truly standout horror event of the year was the release of *Whispering Corridors* on 30 May.

[6] The film has been remade by maverick Japanese director Takashi Miike as the horror musical *Katakuri-ke no kôfuku* (*The Happiness of the Katakuris*, 2001), complete with dancing zombies, and in Hong Kong by Mok Kei Ying Hung as a direct-to-video film entitled *A Mysterious Murder* (2002).

[7] Kim Ji-woon, interview with the author.

above:
Kim Ji-woon, director of **The Quiet Family**.

left:
Promotional flyer for **The Quiet Family**.

South Korea

above:
Lobby card for **Whispering Corridors**.

Education over-kill:
Whispering Corridors

The Korean title *Yo-go-kuei-dam* translates as "Girls High School Ghost Story," with *kuei-dam* a traditional Korean genre of ghost stories in which the souls of those who have died nasty deaths are not permitted to proceed to the next world. *Whispering Corridors* is in many ways a traditional story, updated with a thoroughly contemporary setting and concerns. Schoolteacher Mrs. Park (Lee Yong-nyeo), known to her students as Old Fox, discovers something strange while reviewing school materials late at night. As she makes a frightened phone call, a shadowy figure in a school uniform unexpectedly confronts her and the next morning Old Fox is found dead.

New to the faculty is Miss Hur (Lee Mi-Youn), a former student of Old Fox. It was she that Old Fox was calling to warn that Jin-ju was back - Jin-ju who died nine years earlier. Old Fox's replacement as teacher is the abusive and sadistic Mr. Oh (Park Yong-su), known as Mad Dog. Among his current class are Lim Ji-oh (Kim Kyu-ri), a troubled student with average grades, and the wallflower she befriends, Yoon Jae-yi (Choi Se-yeon). Also in the class are Park So-young (Park Jin-hee), the number one student in the school - with an arrogant attitude to match - and Kim Jung-sook (Yoon Jy-hye), a strange, quiet girl who seems to spend her entire life studying. Mad Dog blatantly favours So-young, while constantly berating Jung-sook for not being good enough. He literally attacks Ji-oh, heaping verbal and physical abuse on her, insulting her as the child of a shaman mother.

Mad Dog, naturally, is next to die. After he vanishes from the campus, Miss Hur questions what part her former best friend Jin-ju may have played in Old Fox's death. Eventually the sad tale of Jin-ju is revealed in flashback; her untimely death and the reason for Miss Hur's guilt and shame. Back in the present, Ji-oh, with her shaman ancestry and ability to contact the dead, wonders if she is somehow responsible for the current unpleasantness, while Jung-sook lurks forever in the background like a vengeful wraith.

Debut director Park Ki-hyung presents the story as supernatural mystery, offering numerous suspects in the murder of the teachers. His delivery is dark and humourless, sober and conservative. Windows and doors slam shut on their own, a stalker is always directly in front no matter which way one runs, and the films of Dario Argento are recalled in details such as the location (a deserted girls' school at night) and the bleeding walls toward the end. What sets the film apart, then, is not so much the execution as the situation. The Korean school system is among the harshest and most punishing in the world. Students regularly sleep for less than half a dozen hours and spend every waking moment in class or studying. The pressure to achieve high scores is overwhelming, the competition for college admission positively excruciating. Upon taking over Old Fox's class, Mad Dog threatens that his students will have "no personal life for a year." He goes on to warn that, "you're each others' rival...you're each others' enemy."

This is made explicit via the creepy and mysterious student Jung-sook. Ultimately, she is revealed to be not so much creepy as sad; not mysterious but lonely, unhappy, anxious. It turns out that she and top student So-young were formerly best friends. "We used to be close during our freshman year," explains So-young. "We would share our most private secrets. The teachers started comparing us and we drifted apart. She became distant. I never reached out to her. But I never thought it would come to this..."

Ultimately we discover that the dead girl, Jin-ju, and Miss Hur were driven apart by similar academic pressures in the past. The film is in fact a curious study in parallels, both in character and incident. Old Fox is found hanged; so is another character later in the film. Jin-ju once gave Miss Hur a gift of tiny bells; Miss Hur's curiosity is aroused when she discovers that Ji-oh has an identical set of bells. Jin-ju's mom was a shaman, just like Ji-oh's. Toward the end, Miss Hur, resurrecting her own past in search of an answer to the present horrors, revisits the art room where Jin-ju painted her portrait, only to see Ji-oh sitting in the abandoned building sketching on a canvas.

Interestingly, the true outsiders in Park's film - the individualists, the shamans and the ghosts - are all artists. Art increasingly dominates the second half of the film, after Ji-oh creates a morbid portrait that Mad Dog rips to pieces and uses as an excuse to beat her mercilessly. Jae-yi encourages her to continue painting and Ji-oh retreats to the outer buildings of the school, the former art room where, it turns out, Jin-ju died violently. The definitive weapon in the film is in fact a palette knife given to Ji-oh as a parting gift, while Mad Dog is supernaturally assassinated and left dead amidst the dual symbolism of a severed ear, obviously recalling Van Gogh while metaphorically illustrating the teacher's disregard for his students' needs and feelings.

Although Ji-oh is the film's anchor, the character of Miss Hur provides the necessary link between present and past. The quintessential parallel, she is not only a former student and artist but the best friend who betrayed Jin-ju in the past at the behest of Old Fox; in the present Miss Hur is now a teacher herself, observing Ji-oh as she suffers abuse for being born of shaman lineage.

As a literal victim of the scholastic system, Jin-ju haunts the classrooms, unable or unwilling to move on. But the film makes it clear that she is only one victim among many. "I prefer ghosts," one character asserts. "Besides, didn't you know? I'm one myself." Ghosts, in this case, are lost creatures, sad, invisible, overlooked, in search of friendship, companionship, love. All the things denied by the dehumanising Korean scholastic system.

"School can be a horrific experience for both students and teachers," explains Ji-oh, summing up the film's theme. The mainstream media has made no secret of the problems with Korea's educational system, including the extreme pressure on students, the favouritism among teachers and class bullying. Director Park's innovation was to incorporate these issues clandestinely into an ostensibly straightforward horror movie. The national teachers' association was not amused, claiming *Whispering Corridors* "disgraced teachers and distorted the reality of education." They unsuccessfully attempted to have the film banned. Instead, their efforts fuelled a national furore among students to see the controversial movie, and it flew to the top of the charts, reinventing the South Korean horror film.

99 horror shows

Although 1999 was marked by increased pressure from US studios to strike down the quota system and local protests to keep it in place, the South Korean film industry continued to rally, in part due to an increased focus on marketing. The year's biggest success story was Kang Je-gyu's much-anticipated follow-up to *The Gingko Bed*, the phenomenon *Shiri*, an action flick

above:
Atmospheric horror in **The Ring Virus**.

[8] Kang Je-gyu, interview with the author.

below:
The clinical body-horror of **Tell Me Something**.

with a terrorist theme that curiously echoes the post-Korean War thriller *The Manchurian Candidate* (1962). *Shiri* outgrossed *Titanic* to become the most popular movie of 1999 in Korea and the highest grossing Korean production in history - at least for the moment. "Until *Shiri* came out, people in the Korean film industry didn't realise the importance of the international market," Kang says. "It gave a lot of confidence to people in the Korean film industry. It had a lot of influence."[8]

The year also saw a decided upsurge in horror and supernatural tales, beginning with *Doctor K*, the story of a loner surgeon and his miraculous, otherwordly healing powers. In addition to the mystery and romance elements, the film refers explicitly once again to Korean shamanism. In June, the monstrously influential Japanese film *Ring* (1998) was remade for Korean audiences by director Kim Dong-bin as *The Ring Virus*, starring popular TV actress Shin Eun-Kyung. Based on the novel by author Suzuki Koji and co-produced by the Japanese company that released Hideo Nakata's original film, the Korean version is more coldly clinical and stylised than its predecessor, with a few cosmetic changes to the plot that recall Nakata's sequel, *Ring 2* (1998). A videotape and a ringing phone still signal impending doom in *Ring Virus*, but here the story emerges in a more linear fashion, resulting in a hint more mystery in the early reels - although Kim's direction is more detached and less atmospheric.

Yonggary rose from the grave once more in 1999 in the form of a hugely expensive spectacle aimed for international release. Popular comedian Shim Hyung-rae conceived and directed the remake, utilising a cast of lousy Western actors and a monumentally stupid script in what amounts to a laughably bad 1950s monster movie with state-of-the-art visual imagery. Reportedly the most expensive Korean film ever made, it was bankrolled in part by Hyundai and did well enough at the box office that it was re-released in 2001 with augmented effects. Pre-sold internationally for US$2.7 million, it was dumped direct-to-video in the US under the title *Reptilian*. Shim promptly announced his intention to film *Imoogi*, the story of a 1000-year old snake.

Ghost in Love, released in August, was a lightweight but entertaining effects-laden tale of a disconsolate girl who contemplates suicide, only to be pre-emptively killed by two ghostly recruiters from a "suicide club" in their somewhat overzealous attempt to enlist new members. Her spirit joins their society, encountering demonic rapists, a brutally vengeful ghost, cruel emissaries from heaven with a vendetta against suicides and a renegade from heaven with his own agenda. With comic relief from a fat comedienne, the film casually lifts from sources as disparate as *Ghost* (1990) and *Hellraiser* (1987). November saw the release of *Tell Me Something*, a bleak and oppressive serial killer thriller in the *Se7en* (1995) mould, with smarts to spare and gruesome, casual violence. A murderer is dismembering his victims and playing jigsaw puzzle with the pieces, putting them back together in various combinations. A grizzled cop is obsessed with finding the killer, and one woman knew all the victims. Director Chang Yoon-hyun cut his teeth working on minjung films before debuting as director with the smash hit melodrama *The Contact* in 1997. *Tell Me Something*, his sophomore film, was Korea's third-biggest local hit of the year (aided by a stellar ad campaign). Gritty, grimy and suspenseful, it is quite striking and memorable, despite the obscure resolution.

coming of age

Lesbian dreams and nightmares:
Memento Mori

Millennium 2000 was introduced one week early by *Memento Mori*. High school student So Min-ah (Kim Min-sun) finds an elaborate diary created in tandem by her unpopular classmates Yoo Shi-eun and Min Hyo-shin. Intrigued by the book, So begins to shadow the pair, discovering their apparent lesbian relationship. But that relationship is clearly crumbling, in part due to pressure from their classmates, and when Min commits suicide by jumping from the school's rooftop, the entire campus is haunted by her lingering presence. Death, it turns out, is no end to unhappiness. Deserted, abandoned, spurned, Min literally cloaks her spirit around the school, trapping her classmates inside, terrorising them over the course of one stormy night. Among other things, she wants her diary back.

There is very little story here in the conventional sense. Scenes follow one another in non-chronological sequence, puzzle pieces awaiting reconstruction. The tale is told from multiple points of view, with Yoo and Min the focus and So the nominal audience surrogate, assembling the story bit by bit. Since nothing is sequential, context is supplied by accretion, with no distinction between present time and flashbacks. The diary turns Min and Yoo's life together into a literal open book, as So immerses herself in its Wonderland mysteries, swallowing a piece of candy hidden in the binding only to discover immediately thereafter that it is poison. Literally infected by the lesbian relationship, she becomes fascinated by the ill-fated lovers; ultimately she begins to fill Min's shoes, perhaps inciting the dead girl's troubled spirit. Following the suicide, when talk begins to circulate that Yoo may have been involved with Min's death, So not only defends Yoo but also provides her with a false alibi.

The story is replete with parallels and reflections, both visual and metaphorical. At one point, Min is called upon in class to recite a poem and relates a strange Dadaist chant at increasing speed; her classmates immediately label her a freak. Later, enchanted by the diary, So whispers aloud the words "Memento Mori" (Latin for "remember the dead"), repeating them at increasing speed. The incantation seems to call forth Min's spirit, and So finds herself caressed by phantom hands. She immediately freaks out and collapses from her desk. The incident can be read as an indication of So's vicarious infatuation with the lesbian relationship and her incipient fear of engaging in one herself.

above:
DVD cover for **Memento Mori**.

At one point, during a physical exam at school, So provides quiet assistance when Yoo encounters trouble during the hearing test. Yoo suffers from hearing loss, we discover early in the story, and sound is a crucial element of the film. The lesbian couple communicate in part by telepathy, hearing each other without words, without conventional language, without sound at all. Yoo's partial deafness causes her to remain silent during choir practice, an outsider, unable to fit in with her classmates. The teacher notices, singles her out and embarrasses her. Min, meanwhile, is musically gifted, leading the choir on piano. Following the incident with the choir, Min cuts the piano's strings, leaving the keys silent and thereby reassuring Yoo that it is okay to accept imperfection.

The purposeful use of sound extends from the literal (the genuinely chilling sound of an empty can hitting the pavement) to the metaphorical. Min hides her belongings, her feelings, inside the piano, turning it into a shrine. It is there that So finds the antidote to the poison she ingested from the diary. Following the climactic mayhem, Yoo, having betrayed her lover, lies on the ground amidst scattered sheet music. Similar symbolism is rampant throughout the film, usually astute but occasionally heavy-handed. Animals appear as frequent metaphors: deer in cages, a red bird trapped in the classroom and flying desperately from window to window, a caged turtle freed when his tank is smashed in the final melee, crawling deliberately among the panicked rush of fleeing students.

As we eventually learn, the love between the two girls has been corrupted by various pressures. Peer pressure from classmates has caused Yoo to back away, while Min has no reservations about making their relationship public. When a teacher snatches the diary and reads aloud from it, Min is proud. Yoo, on the other hand, is ashamed, and when Min attempts to kiss her in front of the class, Yoo violently shoves her away. A victim of rumours while alive, Min cannot escape even in death. Her suicide occurred on the day of the physical exams, something her classmates are certain is more than coincidence. She was pregnant, they whisper, and afraid that it would be revealed. Min is not only a lesbian schoolgirl, but also a pregnant one - the definitive freak. In fact, Min did engage in a one-night stand with one of her teachers, Mr. Goh (Baek Jong-hak). It is one of the film's strengths that he is depicted as thoughtful and concerned, and yet is the monster responsible for death, despondency and unhappiness. It is when Yoo discovers Min's dalliance that their relationship effectively ends. Heterosexuality, in the context of the film, is corrupting and evil.

Memento Mori begins with a visual metaphor: Min and Yoo with their ankles tied together, sinking into still blue waters. (It is worth noting that suicide in Korea is frequently accomplished by drowning, and always with one's shoes removed. This allows for freer, easier reincarnation.) Yoo frantically unties the knot binding their shoeless feet together, scurrying to the surface while Min sinks alone. Later, the girls are punished by having to clean the empty swimming pool, a waterless hole. In addition to the blatant sexual metaphor, the pool walls are painted with crosses, likening it to a cemetery, with the lovers six feet underground. The lovers themselves are first seen together hiding in a bathroom stall; later the bathroom appears to be haunted (a recurring theme in Asian films), with water retreating from the pipes.

Memento Mori offers little in the way of conventional suspense, instead opting for sophisticated, intellectual horror. The few minor jolts are mostly glimpses, reflections of *Repulsion* (1965): a face seen in a mirror or scurrying past a half-opened door. At one point a severed head is seen, the film's only outright shock; it is a hallucination. The entire ending is similarly hallucinatory, imagistic, as Min seals the school and drives her schoolmates into a frenzy. The students engage in a surreal, nonexistent birthday party that ends badly, recalling *Carrie* (1976). Argento's girls' school films are similarly evoked, although *Memento Mori* is considerably more thoughtful, less visceral. The parallels to *Whispering Corridors* are apparent in the setting, the pressures endured by the main characters, the abuse by teachers. The Korean title, in fact, refers to this as "the second story," and the narrative obliquely mentions that Min's is the sixth death out of seven. "The first day a girl dies," begins a voice over the opening credits, "with her head emptied out. Perhaps she had remembered the truth..." As of this writing, the third film in the series had just begun production, with a female director slated to helm the project.

(Sub)genre testing

Memento Mori wasn't the only film spawned by the box office success of *Whispering Corridors*. One week after *Memento Mori*'s release, the New Year was ushered in by the release of director Kim Hyun-myung's *School Legend* (aka *Spooky School*). This time it's elementary school students who encounter ghosts, initially in the girl's bathroom. Although the execution is rote at best, the film is notable as a specifically Korean horror story. Residents of Seoul traditionally think of country people as stupid, while country dwellers perceive Seoul residents as arrogant. The film concerns Seoul students sent in an exchange program to a summer school in the country, where their teacher recounts the "legend" of a *wangdda*, or outcast - a child ostracised and persecuted by his peers. The kids

coming of age

spend the rest of the film alternately pursuing the *wangdda* and running screaming from his shambling, cheaply made-up zombie minions, until one sensitive Seoul soul tries to connect with the poor, lonely phantom child. The ending steals blatantly from *Ring*, with a body in a well, and thematically from *Whispering Corridors*, with the counsellor talking the dead child into giving up the ghost.

March of 2000 saw the dual release of Kim Kuk-hyung's *Black Hole* and Na Hong-kyun's *Black Honeymoon*. The former centres on a surgeon who wakes up on the floor of a mansion the morning after a wild party, suffering from selective amnesia. Gradually he comes to discover that he has been privy to horrific acts, and encounters both suicide and murder in his attempt to unravel his own mysterious past. The ending drifts toward the hallucinatory as the final, existential truth is revealed. *Black Honeymoon* is a mystery/horror film set on Cheju Island, traditional destination for honeymooning couples. The picture begins on a comic note, depicting the different approaches to sex among half a dozen couples. One new husband gets drunk and climbs into the wrong bed. Next morning, he is dead and his eyes are missing. In July, Ra Ho-beom's *Harpy* offered the rote tale of high school students shooting a horror film in a remote location. Jealousy and resentment fragment the group and death, needless to say, quickly follows. For students shooting a post-*Scream* (1996) horror film, they certainly seem oblivious to the generic conventions that quickly envelop them.

In August, actress Kim Kyu-ri from *Whispering Corridors* returned in her second horror film, *The Horror Game Movie* (aka *Nightmare*, aka *Scissors*) from the producers of *Soul Guardians* and writer-director An Byung-ki. An elite club of schoolmates share a secret involving a classmate's death. Several years after graduation, the secret comes back to bite them. In yet another parallel to *Ring*, a videotape holds the clue to the various supernatural deaths, while other elements recall *Memento Mori* (the suggested lesbian pact, the girl held underwater by her ankles in a swimming pool). Despite the heavy-handed use of lightning accompanying virtually every action scene (including the ones indoors), the storytelling is structurally interesting and moderately engaging, beginning as a psychological suspense tale before veering into conventional *Nightmare on Elm Street* (1984) territory. The film has more than its share of phallic imagery and penetrations, including a scene of blatant castration anxiety as a former baseball star, now crippled and wearing a leg brace, accidentally kicks away the bat between his legs in his haste to escape the avenging female spirit.

Bloody Beach and *Rec* (aka *The Record*) were released two weeks later, on 12 August 2000. Both are technically proficient, modestly entertaining slasher flicks. Kim In-su's *Bloody Beach* concerns a group of internet-savvy students who retire to a remote cottage, only to be pursued by a sadistic psycho with the ID "Sandman." The requisite false scares are on offer, including handheld sequences from the killer's POV, teens cavorting in bathing suits, having sex and dying accordingly. Familiar tropes include the girl hiding from the killer in a closet with slatted doors and the intended victim who can't seem to get away from the slow-moving, limping killer no matter how fast

above:
Bloody Beach.

below:
The Horror Game Movie.

horror cinema across the globe

South Korea

above:
Hong Kong DVD cover for **Rec** (aka **The Record**).

[9] Kim Ji-woon, interview with the author.

[10] Kang Je-gyu, interview with the author.

[11] This is not the same Kim Ki-duk who directed *Grand Evil Monster Yonggary* (1967).

"We have a tendency of imitating success," offers Kang Je-gyu. "If an action film does well in Korea there are some people who imitate the trend but it's not like everybody does it. I think we're still in a testing period. We're trying these kinds of action and horror films, a lot of different things and different angles. But we're still testing out these genres. It's very hard to say what kind of horror films can be made in Korea. I think the ones that were made before, like in the 1970s, were more like situational horror. But the ones made recently are more psychological."[10] *The Isle* (2000) from director Kim Ki-duk[11] is genital horror - a brainy deadpan comedy about a mute prostitute at a lakeside resort, and her sadomasochistic-*cum*-homicidal interactions with the assorted criminals and reprobates who drift through her floating cottages. Depravity lurks just below the surface - of the lake, of the flesh - in a wholly unique and perversely metaphorical story punctuated by truly bizarre violence. Fishhooks through flesh form the central, unforgettable image of this sarcastic and surreal film, and Kim's quiet, matter of fact direction only makes the grue that much more gruesome.

Whispering Corridors director Park Ki-hyung returned in 2000 with *Secret Tears*, the tale of three friends who go out for a night of drinking and karaoke and accidentally hit a young girl with their car on the way home. The girl, seemingly unhurt but mute and without memory, is taken to the driver's home to recuperate. There he develops an unhealthy obsession with her, gradually discovering her paranormal powers, while his friends investigate her mysterious past. It's a slow, gentle and marvellously moody story, culminating in supernatural violence and tragedy. It's also an interesting dissection of social and sexual mores: the two friends who condemn the man's chaste love for a minor are themselves engaged in a carefree extramarital affair, while the girl's troubled past involves a middle-aged man having sex with schoolgirls - an all-too-prevalent scandal in Korean society. Yoon Mi-jo is superb in a slow-motion performance as the otherworldly child goddess, whose powers, interestingly, revolve around water. She manipulates it telekinetically, drawing moisture from the ground, moving droplets like magnetic beads, ultimately using it as a weapon. The film begins softly, with a very deliberate use of sound, little camera movement or music and at least one genuinely bizarre moment of absolute

she runs. Kim Ki-hoon's *Rec*, meanwhile, centres on (yet again) a group of internet-savvy students who retire to a remote cottage, where a prank involving a chainsaw goes awry and one of their members dies. The disposal of the body naturally doesn't go as planned, and before you know it they are being individually pursued and snuffed by a mysterious killer. The final set-piece is an enjoyable piece of over-the-top bloody nonsense. "I think there's a trend of general interest in horror films in the world these days," says Kim Ji-woon. "Especially after *Scream*. I think that Korean people are very perceptive to what people in other countries think and also due to the internet they get a lot of information on these films, so it sort of became a trend in Korea to make these films. I think a lot of people who were born in the 60s are making films, and a lot of them grew up watching B horror movies and think that it's a genre that they have to make in order to become a feature director. And so it's kind of like a trend among these young Korean filmmakers."[9]

coming of age

stillness, building a sombre ambiance and ending with a scene that alludes to the opening of *Memento Mori*, but played for very different effect.

Exactly opposite in tone and approach is the campy, tongue-in-cheek horror comedy *Ghost Taxi* (aka *Scary Taxi*, 2000), an episodic, techno-soundtracked B flick about the lovestruck driver of a supernatural, flying cab that runs on blood. Bong Joon-ho's *Barking Dogs Never Bite* (2000) isn't exactly horror - unless you're a dog. A brilliant black comedy about a henpecked husband driven to caninicide, it features several eye-popping scenes of animal cruelty that belie the opening credit claiming no living creatures were injured during the making of the film. When one man snaps and takes out his frustrations on a puppy, he has no idea how severely his life is going to spiral out of control. The film is a superb example of the new fatalism gripping alternative Korean cinema.

Just Do It (2000) from director Park Dae-young is vaguely reminiscent of *The Quiet Family* in its tale of a bitter and bizarre clan unexpectedly plunged into poverty when dad's business fails. Angry and despairing, they suddenly discover the joys of pain when dad is hit by a truck, only to find himself the recipient of a healthy insurance settlement. Before long, the family members are drawing straws to see who will be next to suffer in the name of cash. Soon they are contemplating the even greater payout of death benefits and begin to view each other differently. When an insurance investigator arrives to look into the series of "accidents," they add murder to the menu. Beginning with an inspired lampoon of *Forrest Gump*'s (1994) opening feather and ending with an underwater climax, it is a terrific skewering of modern Korean materialism, family dysfunction and greed.

The year 2001 saw only two pure horror films produced in Korea. *Sorum* (aka *Goosebumps*), produced by Baek Jong-hak from *Memento Mori*, is a strikingly composed and painfully gritty tale of a solitary taxi driver who moves into a filthy, rundown tenement, taking a room where the previous tenant died in a fire. He becomes intrigued by the battered woman down the hall and when she shows up one night covered in blood, he immediately steps in to help her cover up a crime. Meanwhile another neighbour is writing a book based on earlier deaths in the same ill-fated building, crimes involving an

above:
Secret Tears.

left:
Sorum.

abusive husband and baby hidden in a closet - crimes that turn out to have unpleasant repercussions in the present. The lead actors are both television veterans making their debuts in film, and director Yoon Jong-chan made several shorts at Syracuse University with similar themes before returning to Korea for this impressive first feature. Gloomy, detached and desperately downbeat, *Sorum* unfolds slowly and meticulously, holding back everything at first, revealing in layers the characters and parallel stories of very human horror. Initially presented as an emotionless cipher, the taxi driver first reveals his dark side while ferrying a nasty passenger; passing by the scene of a fatal accident, both men share a laugh at the victim's misfortune.

Say Yes, from Kim Sung-hong (director of *The Hole*), is the thoroughly conventional tale of a young couple on vacation who find themselves stalked by a mysterious, manipulative stranger. The violence begins small but quickly escalates to epic vehicular proportions as the husband becomes determined to fight back. It's a well-made and effectively brutal little thriller with not an original idea in its head, borrowing liberally from numerous familiar sources, including *Duel* (1971), *The Vanishing* (1988), *Se7en* (1995) and the near-drowning scene in *The Hole*.

Video voyeurs

In a country that has survived decades of dictatorship, a country with a reputation for ideological repression and governmental invasion of privacy, a country officially still engaged in a cold war with terrorists a stone's throw away, a country with a mandated curfew, where every male is required to serve in the army and everyone male or female is required to carry proof of their identity at all times, it is little surprise that the popular cinema is pervaded by a vague Big Brother paranoia. Add to this the cinematic savvy evidenced among young Koreans at the Pusan International Film Festival and elsewhere, and the pervasive voyeuristic element of modern Korean horror films becomes more understandable. *Memento Mori*, for instance, introduces several key characters via a student video camera early in its narrative. The voyeurism quickly escalates by way of numerous shots from above, showing the action from an omniscient point of view, one we ultimately come to recognise as that of the dead girl Min. Characters in the film are constantly being watched - being judged - without their knowledge. In the end, Min's face appears enormous above the school, looking down on the scene of panic through the glass ceiling.

The derivative *School Legend* cluelessly introduces a video camera as a simple prop, while *Harpy* offers a group of film students actually making their own horror movie, one which not surprisingly turns around and becomes real. *Rec* presents another group of students who decide to create a faux snuff film - and succeed all too well. The videotape wherein they "pretend" to kill a classmate ultimately returns to haunt them via the internet. *Black Honeymoon*, during its comic intro, includes a scene of a husband surprising his wife in the shower with a video camera. He jokingly tapes her as she protests and struggles to hide herself, a blatant visual rape. The voyeurism continues with scenes shot through blinds and two-way glass, or over people's shoulders. Early on, one character sees something forbidden, something off-limits, and is soon found dead - with his eyes torn out. *The Horror Game Movie* also features a character who loses an eye to a vengeful ghost. In this case, one girl's ignoble death was not only witnessed by her ostensible friends - it was videotaped, and everyone who observed the incident must die.

Director Kim Ki-duk's *Real Fiction* (2000) is not only the last word in voyeuristic cinema, but a fascinating (if not entirely successful) experiment in guerrilla filmmaking. A local portrait artist is shaken down by thugs and insulted by clients as he plies his trade in a park, while a woman videotapes his every humiliation. When she too insults him and walks off, he follows, entering a theatre advertising something called "Another Me." There he is confronted on stage by a performer who beats him, berates him and recounts demeaning episodes from the artist's life. Ultimately the artist kills the performer, and then heads out to begin murdering the people who made his life miserable. A woman who insulted his artwork dies at the point of his drawing pencil. The former best friend who stole his one true love and is now a serpent salesman dies by snake. His most recent girlfriend, who cheated on him while working in her flower shop, is...well...flowered to death. The cop who tortured him, the bully who beat him in the army and now owns a butcher shop,

opposite:
Promotional artwork for **Say Yes**.

right:
Whispering Corridors.

the thugs who constantly harass the park vendors - all meet untimely deaths, while the woman with the camera reappears periodically to hover around the perimeter and capture him on tape.

Shot in a cold, minimalist, almost documentary style, *Real Fiction* was made as an experiment in real time, with a dozen sequence directors, eight 35mm cameras, two steadicams and ten digital cameras. After documenting the artist's initial breakdown, the ensuing sequences begin by introducing the additional characters, followed by the artist entering the scene to exact his revenge. Altogether it was filmed in three and a half hours without retakes. The story ends with *Twilight Zone* irony, culminating in a long-shot of violence in the park. After the fade out, the same scene fades back in, the director calls "cut," and the crew scurries into view as the credits roll.[12]

Latest but not least

Korean cinema continues to expand in popularity both locally and abroad, with 2001 another banner year. The box-office record set by *Shiri* in 1999 was broken in late 2000 by *Joint Security Area* (aka *JSA*), which was quickly surpassed by *Friend* in 2001. At the end of 2001, the country's five highest grossing pictures were all local productions and Korean film as a whole had captured almost 50% of the national box office - an unprecedented figure. More companies entered the production arena, and budgets rose steadily as filmmakers vied for the next blockbuster hit. Genre films were prominent as early 2002 saw release of the hugely hyped science-fiction actioner *2009 Lost Memories*, a mystery set in an alternative Seoul wherein Japan won World War II, and the greatly anticipated *Sympathy for Mr. Vengeance*, described as a "very dark-themed, *noir*ish thriller" from Park Chan-wook, director of *JSA*.

With all this activity, distributors began looking at overseas markets as viable sources of income, and not only have recent Korean films such as *Tell Me Something* started to see release in America, but DVD has opened up a whole new avenue, with companies releasing English-subtitled versions of Korean films for the first time. International co-productions have also become increasingly common, with prominent Chinese actresses Cecilia Cheung and Zhang Ziyi appearing in high-profile Korean releases (*Failan* and *Musa: The Warrior*, both 2001) and Jackie Chan employing Korean locations and actress Kim Min in *The Accidental Spy* (2001). Prolific Japanese director Takashi Miike utilised funding from Korea, Hong Kong and Japan to make his explosive splatterfest *Ichi the Killer* (2001), and Chinese auteur Wong Kar-wai cast Korean actress Shim Hye-jin (*The Gingko Bed*) in his science-fiction film *2046*. Meanwhile, Park Joong-hoon, so memorable as the nasty cop in *Nowhere to Hide* (2001) and the even nastier psycho in *Say Yes*, traveled to Hollywood to act in Jonathan Demme's *The Truth About Charlie*.

Yet the most intriguing films coming from South Korean film remain not the mega-budgeted blockbusters, with their increasingly international veneer, but the smaller, more individualistic and iconoclastic rule-breakers. Released in October 2001, *Nabi* (aka *The Butterfly*) is a low-budget film with a marvellous premise: in a future Korea plagued by environmental breakdown, a new "Oblivion Virus" is erasing people's memories in a certain district. People with unhappy pasts begin to take advantage by scheduling tours through the area to have their memories cleansed. Director Moon Seung-wook shot the film on handheld digital video with creative editing and lighting, and it has become a festival favourite, winning Kim Ho-jung several Best Actress prizes for her performance.

[12] Following the impressionistic *The Isle* and the expressionistic *Real Fiction*, Kim Ki-duk, arguably the most ambitious provocateur working in the mainstream Korean film industry today, went on to direct *Address Unknown* (2001), a monumentally grim comedy - or hilarious tragedy - with a recurring motif of eye-injury, set among the miserable misfits scrounging a living alongside an American military base (paralleling Shin Sang-ok's classic *Flowers of Hell*); and *Bad Guy* (2001), the controversial and misogynistic tale of a lowlife creep who fixates on a total stranger, driving her to prostitution and degradation. With a budget of nearly three-quarters of a million US dollars, it is Kim's most expensive film to date.

coming of age

A drastically different festival fave is the anarchic, tongue-in-cheek tale of death, resurrection and vengeance, *Teenage Hooker Becomes Killing Machine* (2000). The Korean title is even more revealing: "The High School student who got chopped up while selling herself in Daehakroh is still in Daehakroh." The title character is plying her trade, providing a client with "voluntary date rape," when one of her teachers happens by. A human monster who looks like the entire Munster family combined into one, he coerces her into providing sex, then kills her when she becomes pregnant. After he enlists three gibbering psychos to dismember the body, a crazed scientist stitches her back together with an old-fashioned sewing machine and sends her out as an unstoppable killer. Although the film borrows shamelessly at one point from *La Femme Nikita* (1990) and at barely an hour it suffers from lackadaisical pacing, it is a unique and singular vision of high-voltage genre weirdness.

Teenage Hooker director-screenwriter-cinematographer-editor Nam Ki-woong refuses to provide a straightforward image when he can offer a manipulated one, and the audacious use of distorted colours and wide-angle lenses wandering deserted streets and alleys, lofts and bars produces a grainy psychedelic dreamscape two steps removed from Wong Kar-wai's *Fallen Angels* (1998). Nam's inspired lighting is particularly notable, along with his bizarrely eclectic soundtrack, mixing Latin rhythms with droney trance music, opera with punk, even allowing for an impromptu dance number between the schoolgirl and her teacher. Ultimately Nam reveals himself to be commenting on the same themes as the *Whispering Corridors* films and *Secret Tears*: societal pressures on young girls, the need to be needed and sexual misconduct with minors. The schoolgirl falls in love with her teacher-rapist and allows him to have sex with her for free - unlike her other teachers, who have to pay. She reveals that she will soon be displaced from home, once her mother remarries a man she has serviced sexually. Betrayed and discarded, the girl returns to exact her vengeance in a brutally sexual manner. Similar in stylistic approach to the radical splatterpunk films of Japan's cyber generation, Nam's film signals a bold new direction for Korean cinema, a milestone for local independent filmmakers and an intriguing alternative to the big-budget blockbusters that are increasingly dominating the Korean film market.

below:
Tell Me Something.

genre histories and studies

Between appropriation & innovation: Turkish horror cinema

Kaya Özkaracalar

The first Turkish-made feature film to be released in Turkey appeared in 1917. Annual film production, however, totalled nowhere near a dozen titles until the late 1940s. Properly speaking, the Turkish film industry emerged only in the 50s, when competing studios were formed one after the other and a Hollywood-style star system developed. It was also during this period that filmmakers tentatively began experimenting with various genres from all ends of the spectrum, experiments which included a few attempts at fantastic cinema. It is widely accepted that the Golden Age of Turkish popular cinema dates from the early 1960s to the mid-1970s, with annual film production hitting the 300 mark in 1972. While melodramas dominated the mainstream cinema aimed at family audiences, a number of other genres also flourished. As Italian and later also Hong Kong influences rivalled that of Hollywood, mildly erotic and highly violent costumed historical epics, crime and action movies, masked/costumed superhero movies, westerns and eventually martial arts movies, soft-core sex farces and even hardcore pornography found eager audiences in Turkey. Besides a few isolated exceptions, it seems that only the horror genre was largely missing from the scene.

The reason (or reasons) for the failure of horror to ever become a fad in Turkish cinema is open to question. It might be tempting to jump to quick conclusions from the perceived absence of "traditional" (read "Western") horror motifs in Turkish culture, such as vampires, werewolves, gothic castles, or serial killers in contemporary Turkey. A counter-argument would point out that Turkish culture does in fact make room for plain and simple ghosts, as well as for indigenous motifs with horrific overtones (such as *cin*, *umacı* and *karakoncolos*) in its own folklore. It should also be noted that, for example, while cowboys are obviously absent from Turkish history, enterprising Turkish filmmakers clearly did not care at all and, in the wake of the "spaghetti western" boom abroad, turned out dozens of homemade westerns set in the American Wild West.

One noteworthy explanation for the failure of horror to take root in Turkish cinema has been offered by Bülent Oran, a prolific scriptwriter of Turkish popular film who in his youth also happened to act in the first known Turkish horror movie, *Drakula Istanbul'da* (*Dracula in Istanbul*, 1953). Oran stresses the fact that Turkish audiences like to identify strongly with the characters on the screen. According to Oran, the horror genre does not offer sufficient avenues for such a strong level of identification.[1] Of course, horror movies like all films work with complex identification processes, but often in the case of this genre such identification is at a more subconscious level, and is even directed towards the monster. Oran's claim should be understood as stressing that Turkish audiences are inclined to identify themselves unambiguously with the hero (or heroine) of the narrative, that is the protagonist, rather than with the monster, the "other." Although such an explanation begs further questions, such as why foreign horror films persist in the Turkish market, Oran's answer does seem to lie in the right direction.

While horror films are not very numerous in Turkish popular cinema, the few that are available are quite interesting,

[1] Group interview with Bülent Oran, 4 July 2001, in Istanbul.

opposite: Metin Erksan's **Seytan** (1974) was an **Exorcist** rip-off. **The Exorcist** itself was not released in Turkey until 1982!

horror cinema across the globe 205

Turkey

2 From a reference guide of credits and plot synopses of Turkish films: *Türk Filmleri Sözlüğü* v.1: 1914-1973, compiled by Agah Özgüç, published by SESAM (Union of Owners of Cinematographic Works), Istanbul, 1998.

3 Information on the initial publication date of this novel is unconfirmed. It was reprinted in 1997, retitled as *Drakula Istanbul'da*.

4 Actually, actor Bülent Oran has told this author in an interview that the actress playing the vampire literally bit his lip during this scene.

below:
Drakula Istanbul'da.

and for a multitude of reasons. At first glance, one common feature of Turkish horror is the extent to which it draws upon foreign (Western) sources for inspiration instead of sources more firmly based in local culture and mythology.

Dracula in Istanbul

The first Turkish horror film or thriller is most likely *Çığlık* (*Scream*, 1949). However, little is known about this obscure movie, an Atlas Film production directed and written by Aydın Arakon and starring Muzaffer Tema, other than that the story takes place in a "mysterious mansion."**2**

The oldest Turkish horror film currently available for viewing is Mehmet Muhtar's *Drakula Istanbul'da*. This picture is particularly useful for observing and comparing the transformations a text undergoes when subjected to two different series of adaptations. Universal Pictures' *Dracula* (1931), directed by Tod Browning, was based on a stage adaptation of the Bram Stoker novel. The Turkish version, however, was based on an abridged and altered translation of the novel *Kazıklı Voyvoda* (*The Voivode with the Stakes*) by Ali Rıza Seyfi.**3** A comparison of the American and Turkish Dracula films yields the surprising result that, in many ways, the latter is more faithful to Stoker's original novel even though characters and setting have been altered.

Drakula Istanbul'da begins with a Turkish national named Azmi (Bülent Oran) arriving in Romania to visit Dracula at his castle. After the now-familiar scene of frightened locals warning him not to go the cursed castle, he is taken to his destination by a mysterious and spooky driver. The scenes at the castle follow the book fairly closely, complete with Dracula's famous "Listen to the children of the night - what music they make!" remark concerning the howling of the wolves.

The only major novelty the Turkish film version brings to bear is the presence of a hunchbacked servant who is sympathetic towards the guest. It should also be noted that only a single female vampire, and not three as in Stoker's novel (and most other cinematic adaptations), haunts Azmi as he falls asleep. Interestingly, the advance publicity booklet for the film also mentions three female vampires; the reduction in number must have been a last-minute change made during the course of production.

Beyond these digressions, *Drakula Istanbul'da* sticks considerably closer to the original novel at numerous points than does Universal's adaptation. First of all, Dracula in the Turkish movie, played by Atif Kaptan, sports fangs at his canines, whereas Bela Lugosi's Dracula was virtually fangless (Max Schreck's vampire in the earlier, German-made *Nosferatu* [1922] had fangs at his central teeth). It is often claimed by experts on the vampire film that the 1970 Hammer production *Scars of Dracula* was the first to depict the Count scaling down the castle walls, but *Drakula Istanbul'da* had already reproduced that scene almost two decades earlier. Azmi's encounter with the female vampire at the castle is also more explicit (relatively speaking) than the corresponding scene in the censor-sensitive Universal production, where the female vampires cannot even touch Jonathan Harker (David Manners); in the Turkish movie, she first seems to kiss him on the mouth and then moves her lips to his neck before Dracula appears.**4** *Drakula Istanbul'da* even has the

between appropriation & innovation

Count almost feeding the baby to the female vampire - a scene completely absent in the Universal film - albeit in an implied manner: the female vampire asks Dracula if he has brought anything for her and the Count points to something barely visible to the audience, then we hear a voice from outside calling on "the monster to give back her child."

It is significant that in *Drakula Istanbul'da* the tenuous link between the fictional Count Dracula and the historical Dracula, Vlad Tepes, is firmly expressed. In Stoker's novel, Count Dracula is said in passing to be a "voivode" who had fought the Turks in the past. It would take several decades for Western literary scholars to realise that this was a reference to Vlad Tepes, and therefore that a real historical figure provided one of the inspirations for Stoker. Tepes was a Walachian ruler (*voivode*) nicknamed "Dracula", which means "Son of the Dragon" (or "Son of Satan", according to an alternative translation), who was notorious for impaling his enemies - including the Turks. Since "the Voivode with the Stakes" was an integral part of Turkish history as taught in every high school-level Introduction to History course in Turkey, Stoker's brief reference to a *voivode* fighting the Turks must have immediately rang a bell to Ali Rıza Seyfi as he was translating and abridging the novel. In his own "nationalised" version of the text, he naturally expanded upon this connection.

Muhtar and his crew naturally preserved this feature as well, if not to the same extent as in *Kazikli Voyvoda*. When Azmi asks Count Dracula why the locals fear him, he replies by saying that he is a descendent of "the Voivode with the Stakes." Such references to the historical figure of Vlad Tepes are completely omitted in the Universal version, as well as in Britain's 1958 Hammer remake starring Christopher Lee. Only after Raymond McNally and Radu Florescu popularised the connection between Dracula and Tepes in their best-selling study *In Search of Dracula* (1972) and the more academic *Dracula: A Biography of Vlad the Impaler, 1431-1476* (1973) did Western filmmakers become aware of it. The first Western film to capitalise on the Tepes connection was Dan Curtis's television adaptation *Dracula* (1973; also released theatrically in an abridged version) starring Jack Palance in the title role. A better-known example is Francis Ford Coppola's box-office hit, *Bram Stoker's Dracula* (1992).

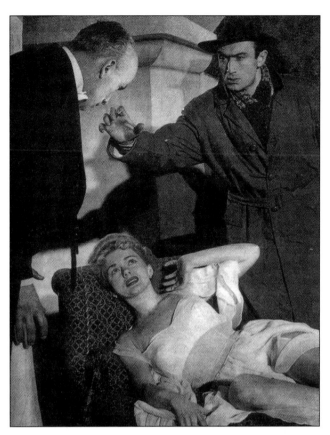

above:
Drakula Istanbul'da.

The second half of *Drakula Istanbul'da* is set in Istanbul. The Count moves there after purchasing a mansion in this city through the services of Azmi, who follows after escaping from the castle where he was imprisoned. Azmi's fiancée, Güzin, is a dancer, and stands as a marked contrast to both the original novel and other film adaptations. There is even an odd scene in which the Count makes her dance for his pleasure as a piano plays without a player. Güzin is played by Annie Ball, an Austrian dancer-turned-actress "discovered" by Turkish filmmakers while she was working in an Istanbul nightclub. Nevertheless, *Drakula Istanbul'da* continues to be more faithful to Stoker's novel than its Universal Pictures counterpart. Although the Lucy subplot is incomplete in Browning's film as the fate of the vampirised British girl is left unresolved (apparently due to self-censorship[5]), the graveyard encounter with the walking-dead Sadan (Ayfer Feray, one of Turkish cinema's rising stars at the time) and her staking in the coffin are all present in *Drakula Istanbul'da*. First we see a stake being placed on Sadan's body, then the camera zooms in to her face, which becomes distorted in pain.

[5] Though Turkish cinema was also far from being free of censorship, it seems that horror did not cause much concern.

Turkey

above and below:
More scenes from
Drakula Istanbul'da.

Another interesting feature of Muhtar's film is that the way Dracula is destroyed is in conformity with folkloric practice: cutting off his head and stuffing it with garlic after staking him (all off-screen), rather than simply driving a stake through his heart as is in the Browning version and others. Since Turks are a predominantly Moslem people, no rosaries or holy wafers are to be found in *Drakula Istanbul'da* - it is only garlic that repels the vampires. The movie ends with Azmi telling Güzin that he cannot stand the smell of garlic anymore, and that from now on she should never even use it while cooking.

Besides comparing the Turkish film with the earlier American one in order to determine their relative loyalty to Stoker's novel, another sort of comparison can be made between the novel, the intermediary Turkish novelisation and *Drakula Istanbul'da*. This latter comparison reveals that the Turkish novel on which the film was based had a strongly nationalistic - even chauvinistic - theme at the centre of the narrative, but that this theme was all but eliminated in the Turkish film adaptation. *Kazikli Voyvoda* was written during a time when the young Turkish Republic, formed in 1923 out of the ashes of the collapsed Ottoman Empire, was in the process of fervent nation-building. Nationalist feelings were being highly cultivated. As noted above, Ali Riza Seyfi placed the "Vlad connection" at the centre of his version of the Dracula story, and while *Drakula Istanbul'da* included one reference to this connection (in contrast to the other film adaptations of this period), it was not nearly as emphasised as in *Kazikli Voyvoda*. In Seyfi's novel the reader is made aware of this connection in the very first entry of Azmi's diary, where he notes that Güzin had reminded him that his destination was the land of the "monstrous" *voivode*.

between appropriation & innovation

Thus, the Turkish vampire hunters' crusade against Dracula in Istanbul is invested with a pronounced nationalist dimension. On the book's final page, Dracula's antagonists cry, "For the revenge of our compatriots who were impaled along the banks of Tuna [a river in the Balkans]!"

All in all, *Drakula Istanbul'da* is not a great film and would not rank with the best of Turkish cinema, but it is certainly above average for its time. One of its handicaps, besides the low-budget limitations of the Turkish studios, is that the score in some scenes - stock library music - does not really suit a horror movie, and indicates a lack of understanding of the genre on the part of the filmmakers. Yet the photography in some scenes is quite sophisticated. Most memorable is the beautiful scene in which Dracula victimises Sadan for the first time: we see them silhouetted on the rocks against a sea shining with reflections from the moonlight. The film's cinematographer was Özen Sermet, one of the most talented at his craft in Turkey. Sermet would later settle in America, where his subsequent credits included the cinematography for Paramount's *Tarzan and the Jungle Boy* (1968).

Horror motifs in miscellaneous genres

Not surprisingly, Vlad Tepes was a historical villain in numerous Turkish costumed epics. One of them, *Kara Boğa* (1974), is especially notable for being the first film ever to portray the historical *voivode* as a vampire himself in his own time, and not simply as an ancestor of the fictional Count Dracula. *Kara Boğa*'s scenario was written by none other than Bülent Oran, who had played the main protagonist in *Drakula Istanbul'da* almost two decades earlier; over the years, Oran gradually moved away from acting and had taken up a career as a screenwriter. The film was directed by Yavuz Figenli, a prolific exploitation filmmaker.

Kara Boğa begins with a prolonged flashback which borders at times on the horrific. At a castle guarded by warriors in skeleton masks, the *voivode* (Altan Günbay, a bald actor who was a favourite in villainous roles) is seen fervently kissing almost-nude girls, biting one of them on the neck to drink her blood and enjoying the spectacle of impaled men. Turkish warrior Kara Bey (Behçet Nacar, a well-known star of low-budget sex and violence movies), at the request of foreign emissaries pleading to

above:
Written by Bülent Oran and directed by Yavuz Figenli, **Kara Boga** (1974) is notable as the first ever historical *voivode* film.

Turkey

be saved from the *voivode*'s tyranny, defeats him on the battlefield and stakes him. He refrains from beheading the monster, however, on the grounds that it would not be manly to desecrate a corpse - a grave mistake, of course.

The *voivode* is revived as his hunchbacked servant kidnaps and sacrifices a "virgin girl", wetting his master's lips with her blood. The tyrant and his henchmen then proceed to raid Kara Bey's village, brutally massacring the women and children and capturing the Turkish warrior. Only his small son is rescued and brought to safety. Henceforth, the film tells the exploits of the grown-up son, Kara Boğa (again Behçet Nacar), as he seeks revenge and looks to save his father if he is still alive. After the flashback prologue, most of the picture follows the routines of a standard low-budget costumed epic. However, the gory finale again enters vampire territory, as blood spurts from the *voivode*'s mouth while Kara Boğa slowly drives a wooden stake through his heart using only his bare hands. The blunder of his father is not repeated this time, as the monster is also beheaded (off-screen).

between appropriation & innovation

Female vampires also made an appearance in a few other Turkish historical epics. One quite atmospheric scene in *Malkoçoğlu* (1966; the first entry in a series based on a comic strip of the same name) has the title hero descending several stories down a pit towards the centre of the earth, to fetch a crown hidden in the crypt of a lady vampire. On the way, he gets covered in cobwebs and encounters owls and skeletons. Dizziness overcomes him as he looks upon the vampire's corpse, but he manages to accomplish his mission without any reanimation of the vampire - a relief to himself, but a disappointment to those anticipating the springing forth of full-fledged horror elements.

Comic strip adaptations such as *Malkoçoğlu* were popular in Turkish cinema in the second half of the 1960s and the first half of the 1970s. A vampire-witch plays a far more central role in two films from a different series based on another popular comic. *Tarkan*, created by Sezgin Burak (who also scripted many of the movie adaptations), is regarded as one of the very best Turkish comic series. The stories take place in the 5th century, at a time when the hordes of Attila the Hun ravaged Europe (the hero of the title is a fictional warrior of this historical figure). This setting in the distant past, close to the so-called "Dark Ages", distinguishes *Tarkan* from most other Turkish comics (and other comics-based films) which are set in the Middle Ages, and brings Burak's strip closer to the Italian sword-&-sandal epics (*peplum*) or to the later Conan comic books and movies.

In *Tarkan: Gümüs Eğer* (*Tarkan: The Silver Saddle*, 1970), the main attraction is a blonde witch named Gosa, played by Swedish national Eva [Ewa] Bender - another "discovery" made by Turkish filmmakers from the Istanbul nightclub scene. Gosa, living in a mountaintop castle amidst whirling mists, has the power to mesmerise her male victims. Before stabbing them to death, she dances around them naked while they are tied to a stake. Although she is eventually killed, Gosa is revived in the truly delirious sequel, *Tarkan: Altın Madalyon* (*Tarkan: The Golden Medallion*, 1972), in an amazing scene rivalling anything in Western sado-erotic horror cinema.[6] A nun and a brothel dancer are kidnapped and tied up naked to crosses. Stabbed by a monk, flowing rivers of their blood fill channels at the base of the crosses, leading to a pit where the nearly decomposed corpse of Gosa now lies. The blood revives her naked body. Gosa's vampire nature is revealed in this sequel during a hallucinating scene in which she (naked, as always) sucks the blood spurting from the neck of a female victim caught in a giant spider's web that had materialized out of nowhere. Later, Gosa even manages to capture Tarkan himself, but is nevertheless destroyed at film's end.

Besides those turning up in costumed historical epics, horror motifs also appeared in various other genre efforts of Turkish cinema. *Kilink Istanbul'da* (*Killing in Istanbul*, 1967), features the fictional Italian anti-hero, "Killing."[7] The macabre imagery of the villain's skeleton costume is supplemented by several atmospheric scenes shot in dark alleys and basements, as well as by adult-comics-styled sado-erotic torture chamber sequences. *Kilink Istanbul'da* was a huge hit at the Turkish box office and spawned more than half a dozen other Killing films within the same year. In one of the more obscure offerings, the eponymous anti-hero confronts none other than Frankenstein's monster; despite the best efforts of Turkish movie hounds,

opposite top: A scene from **Tarkan: Altın Madalyon** (aka **Tarkan: The Golden Medallion**), 1972.

opposite bottom: A page from one of Sezgin Burak's *Tarkan* comics, upon which the films were based.

[6] Not surprisingly, this scene is always cut when the film is aired on television.

[7] The on-screen title (as well as the title featured on the posters, lobby cards, etc.) is *Kilink Istanbul'da* rather than the original word "Killing", which was not used for fear of copyright infringement.

below: Poster for **Kilink Istanbul'da** (aka **Killing in Istanbul**).

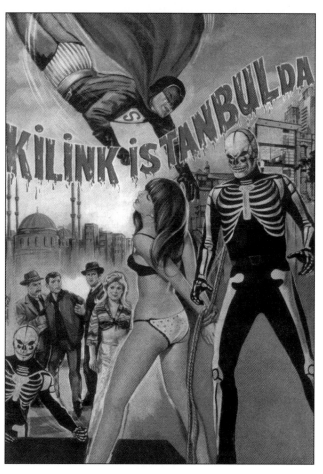

horror cinema across the globe

Killink Frankeştayn ve Dr. No'ya Karşı (*Killing versus Frankenstein*) remains a lost film, and no information on it is available besides credits and release data.

Frankenstein's monster would make a second appearance in Turkish cinema in the 1975 comedy *Sevimli Frankestayn* (*Cute Frankenstein*), which was obviously inspired by Mel Brooks's *Young Frankenstein* the same year. *Maskeli Seytan* (*Masked Devil*, 1970), another caped/costumed hero movie from the makers of the first Killing title, features a walking mummy who is revealed to be a criminal masquerading as part of a conspiracy. In the next decade, the Z-grade patch-up karate movie *Ölüm Savasçisi* (*Death Warrior*, 1984) included ninjas-turned-zombies, killer plants, ground-level prowling camerawork in the woods (*à la* Sam Raimi's 1982 cult classic, *The Evil Dead*), not to mention sundry other elements in footage some of which was directly cut-and-pasted from foreign pictures.

The Dead Don't Talk

In addition to the appearance of vampires in films outside the horror genre *per se* in the first half of the 1970s, Turkish cinema also produced two straight horror movies during this period. The first, *Ölüler Konusmazki* (*The Dead Don't Talk*, 1970), is a largely forgotten low-budget effort that deserves a second look. This black-and-white film was produced and directed by Yavuz Yalinkiliç, who would go on to make the ultra-trashy *Süper Adam Istanbul'da* (*Superman in Istanbul*, 1972). It features a largely unknown cast, the only familiar face being that of Aytekin Akkaya, best remembered for his supporting role in *Dünyayi Kurtaran Adam* (*The Man Who Saves the World*, 1983), the Turkish rip-off of *Star Wars* (1977).**8**

The film opens with a couple (the groom played by Akkaya) arriving at a spooky mansion. The place is abandoned but for a mysterious man in black who tells them it is a hotel where the customers don't pay any fees. The couple eventually pays the price for staying overnight with their lives. It is difficult to make much sense of the picture's rather incoherent plot. The man in black is apparently still lamenting the loss of a loved one from the past whose framed painting he almost worships. There is also an undead man who has risen from the grave to haunt the mansion. After the demise of the unfortunate couple, a newly-appointed female teacher to the town school is hosted at the mansion and subjected to more of the same perils. She volunteers to lure the undead man to a trap, where he is destroyed by a *hoja* (Islamic priest) reciting from the Quran while his accomplices hold up copies of the holy book.

If any film can be legitimately called "uneven", *Ölüler Konusmazki* is that film. At times, Yalinkiliç and his crew exhibit signs of expertise not evident in the director's other work. The cinematography makes good use of full-length wall mirrors at several points when characters suddenly appear in the frame. The film has some genuinely eerie moments, such as when the undead man appears outside the mansion's windowpanes in the dark of night, recalling a similar scene in Werner Herzog's *Nosferatu the Vampyre* (1979). Even the incoherence of the plot (and some apparently random continuity errors) might be seen as involuntarily adding to the force of the movie, puzzling the audience to such a degree that logic and rationality are abandoned. The result is to put the audience more in tune with the film's supernatural narrative, similar to Renato Polselli's *Riti, magie nere e segrete orge nel trecento* (*Reincarnation of Isabel*, 1972) and Luigi Batzella's *Nuda per Satana* (*Nude for Satan*, 1974). On the negative side, one must cite the introduction of a character who is there only to provide unnecessary comedy relief - a major defect which spoils the film's rhythm and atmosphere - and the overuse of the undead man's supposedly "uncanny" laughter, which is rather ineptly produced and more ludicrous than uncanny.

Ölüler Konusmazki has sank into obscurity after its brief and largely unnoticed theatrical release. It has never been released on video or aired on television, and is currently gathering dust on the shelves of a small backstreet studio in Turkey.

Turkish *Exorcist*

The second straight Turkish horror film from the decade is rather more famous: *Seytan* (*Satan*, 1974), the Turkish version of William Friedkin's phenomenally successful American film, *The Exorcist* (1973). Unlike the Dracula films, where both the Turkish and U.S. versions were based on different intermediary sources (which in turn were based upon the same

8 Akkaya also had roles in two Italian movies shot in Turkey: *Il Mondo di Yor* (*Yor, the Hunter from the Future*, 1983) and *I sopravvissuti della città morta* (*Ark of the Sun God*, 1984).

between appropriation & innovation

above:
Metin Erksan's
Seytan (1974).

source), *Seytan* is almost a direct remake of *The Exorcist*, albeit one that takes place entirely in an Islamic setting.

The Exorcist was not to be released in Turkey until 1982, and so entrepreneurial producer Hulki Saner hired well-known director Metin Erksan - one of the acclaimed auteurs of Turkish cinema, who had shifted to mainstream fare later in his career[9] - to make a Turkish version, obviously to cash in on the public interest aroused by widespread media coverage of Friedkin's film. Saner also produced a Turkish parody of *Star Trek*, titled *Turist Ömer Uzay Yolunda* (*Ömer the Tourist in Star Trek*, 1974), but the Turkish version of *The Exorcist* was intended to be a pure horror effort with no tongue-in-cheek. Erksan for his part, while acknowledging that he had watched *The Exorcist* abroad, claims in interviews that he made *Seytan* by following William Peter Blatty's original novel (from which *The Exorcist* was adapted) rather than by copying the American movie. However, the fact that *Seytan* even utilises the music score of *The Exorcist* does not grant much credibility to this claim.

Seytan opens with a prologue set in the Middle East, where an archaeologist (Agah Hün) discovers a medallion in the sands of the deserts where a giant statue of the Devil hovers nearby. In Istanbul, we are introduced to Ayten (Meral Taygun) and her daughter Gül (Canan Perver). Noises attributed to rats are coming from the attic of their house. In *Seytan*, the role of *The Exorcist*'s troubled priest is played by Tuğrul (Cihan Ünal), a medical doctor by training who chose to pursue an eccentric interest in researching the "belief and practice" of exorcism rather than take up a more lucrative career. His mother, living in dire poverty, has to be locked up in an insane asylum where she eventually dies, haunting Tuğrul in his nightmares. Meanwhile, all of *The Exorcist*'s possession scenes are reproduced here, though with less spectacular special effects - not surprising, given the incomparable budgets available to commercial American versus Turkish filmmakers. It should also be noted that the most notorious scene in *The Exorcist* is remade with a paper-cutting knife standing in for a cross, naturally because of the religious difference. When all attempts at medical treatment for Gül fail, Ayten calls on Tuğrul for help. Tuğrul in turn contacts the archaeologist, setting the stage for the exorcism scenes replicated from the American version. At the end of the film, Ayten and her de-possessed daughter

[9] Erksan's *Susuz Yaz* (*Dry Summer*, aka *I Had My Brother's Wife*, 1963) had won top prize at the Berlin Film Festival.

Turkey

above:
Karanlik Sular (aka **Serpent's Tale**, 1993), produced and directed by Kutlug Ataman.

[10] Arslan, S. (Autumn 1999) 'Yesilçam'ın *Seytan*'ı Holywood'un *The Exorcist*'ini Döver!', *Geceyarısı Sineması* 5, 50-61 [revised and expanded version of an unpublished English-language paper].

piously visit a mosque. Gül feels an impulse to kiss the hand of a *hoja*, the same person who put Tuğrul in contact with the archaeologist (inexplicably, this hand-kissing scene is missing from video prints of the film released by Alparslan Video). *Seytan* ends with the camera panning the interiors of the mosque as religious (Islamic) music plays on the soundtrack.

A key point, which is either missed or ignored in previous discussions of Seytan, is that the plot of *The Exorcist* actually fits very well and makes perfect sense in a Turkish setting. Even Savas Arslan's comprehensive study of the film, boasting a detailed, scene-by-scene (sometimes even replica-by-replica) comparison of the Turkish and American versions, and supplemented with intelligently written analysis, is not exempt from this criticism.[10] To be fair, Arslan does acknowledge in a footnote that *Seytan* might be read as a story of the failure of "Westernism" and the triumph of the Orient, but he claims that such a reading would be "complicated" in the face of what he sees as the "Christian codes" present in the film. Arslan's meticulous essay, the main strain of which is to prove that *Seytan* is "identity-less" due to the "transformation of Christian codes into Islamic ones", is nevertheless marked by cultural essentialism. Had he not regarded Christian and Islamic cultural codes as mutually exclusive ones which cannot be transformed into each other without a resulting loss of identity, but instead as already overlapping systems of thought which can be flexibly played with and manipulated, Arslan would have been able to go beyond "Westernism versus the Orient" and see the conflict between modernisation/ materialism and religion/ tradition which is present in *both* Western and Turkish (or, Oriental, for that matter) culture.

The main theme of *Seytan* is clearly the reconfirmation of Islam's power and validity. This is by no means a cosmetic issue for Turkey, but on the contrary, one of the major causes of social unrest in this country (even more so than in the U.S.). In Turkey, the roots of the modernisation/ materialism versus religion/tradition conflict can be traced back to the 19th century, when the ailing Ottoman state began taking some tentative steps towards modernisation - steps which were opposed by the religious elite and the masses under their influence. Turkey's modernisation drive became radicalised under the subsequent Republican regime, which initiated secularisation programs in all areas of life. Today this tension remains not only at the forefront of the Turkish political scene, but deeply embedded within the Turkish socio-cultural psyche as well.

Turkish *Psycho*

Another Turkish remake of a world-famous American horror film is the unreleased *Kader Diyelim* (*Let's Say It's Fate*, 1995). This ultra-low budget, 16 mm movie is a Turkish version of none other than Alfred Hitchcock's *Psycho* (1960). The most interesting and scarcely believable aspect of this oddity is that it is a film whose narrative is punctuated/punctured by singing, as in many Indian productions.

Kader Diyelim was produced and directed by Mehmet Alemdar, who also appears in a small role in the picture. Years ago, Alemdar had lent some money to Turkish singer Vahdet Vural, who had failed to pay him back. Alemdar eventually reminded Vural of his debt, and asked Vural to star in a movie of his for free in return for forgetting about the money forever. Alemdar, whose sparse credits as director are mainly of melodramatic films featuring popular singers, was privately a fan of horror movies. He resolved to use this cheaper-than-ever opportunity to blend the two genres. Thus, *Kader Diyelim* was shot in a few days.

The first part of the film follows its source of inspiration fairly closely: a girl steals some money from her workplace (Alemdar plays the customer whose money is taken) and arrives at a desolate motel, where she is killed by the clerk while taking a shower. Then her lover (Vural) investigates her disappearance, accompanied by a number of extra-diegetic singing scenes. No "mother" turns up in the end.

Not surprisingly, especially during a time like the post-1980s when distribution has been taken over by American oligopolies, *Kader Diyelim* did not receive any theatrical release. Actually, it is doubtful whether the film could have made it to theatres even in a less demanding distribution environment, since its production values are below the average of those low-budget exploitation movies which proliferated from the late 60s to the early 80s. However, Alemdar feels frustrated that he was not even able to sell his picture to television networks and is holding on to it at present.

Also in 1995, Alemdar went ahead and made another 16 mm go at the horror genre, this time without any singing numbers. The unreleased *Süphenin Bedeli* (*The Price of Doubt*) is about a serial killer who drugs his wife into confusing reality and hallucinations. The final scene is a setpiece rarely if ever to be found in Turkish cinema: a cellar full of the victims' bloody corpses. The only other Turkish serial killer film is the 1983 video production *Lanetli Kadınlar*; this sexploitation effort was made by Kadir Akgün, a director mainly specialising in direct-to-video pornography.

Dark Waters

The most "well-made" Turkish horror film is undoubtedly *Karanlik Sular* (*Serpent's Tale*, 1993), produced and directed by Kutluğ Ataman as his debut feature. This art-house horror movie has a deliberately multi-layered narrative rich in metaphors concerning, among other things, the identity crisis of the Turkish nation.

Lamia (Gönen Bozbey), who comes from an aristocratic background and lives in a seaside mansion in Istanbul, is told by an American named Richie Hunter (Daniel Chace) that her son Haldun (Metin Uygun), who was believed to have died in a drowning accident, is actually still alive. Hunter's intention is to get hold of an archaic manuscript that was discovered by Haldun. Various other people and groups - including a false prophet planning to declare a new religion, and a little girl called "Theodora, the Byzantium Queen" who works in nightclubs performing "vampire" shows - are also after this manuscript. Meanwhile, a series of grotesque murders begin to unfold in the dark alleys and ruined chapels of Istanbul. A subplot involves the pressures put on Lamia by Hasmet (Haluk Kurtoğlu) to dispose of her mansion for insurance money. Both stories end in fire, as the mansion is arsoned and Lamia burns the cursed manuscript. Haldun, who is implied to have a vampiric existence, intentionally goes out in broad daylight for the purpose of self-destruction.

Although the Ottoman Turks conquered Byzantium (remnant of the Eastern Roman Empire and site of today's Istanbul) centuries ago, a certain degree of Byzantine heritage has survived through the centuries. This heritage can be located in the presence of a small Greek community in cosmopolitan Istanbul, in the countless historical monuments dating from the Byzantine period which form an integral part of the urban landscape and in the traces of Greek culture reflected in the city's cuisine and other cultural features. In *Karanlik Sular*, the figure of the little girl Theodora, introduced as "the Byzantian Queen" during her nightclub shows, is clearly a symbol of this Byzantian/Greek heritage. Lamia, hopelessly attempting to hold on to her luxurious mansion and living with memories of a long-gone grandiose past, is apparently a symbol of Turkey's Ottoman heritage, and Hasmet, of the modern Turkish Republic. By and large, the Republic's founding fathers opted for a radical repudiation of Ottoman heritage, burning bridges with the past to gain a stronghold in the modern world - just as Hasmet wants Lamia's old mansion burned down for financial profit. Needless to say, Richie Hunter symbolises modern American imperialism, which puts up a cordial face to hide its self-serving motives.

On the other hand, it is difficult to pinpoint the metaphoric meaning behind the figure of Haldun, living a ghostly existence and eventually seeking self-annihilation. Perhaps it is the Turkish psyche, tortured by an identity crisis and torn apart by all the conflicting forces pulling it in different directions. Perhaps it is Kutluğ Ataman himself, an American-educated artist of Turkish origin, who feels this identity crisis even more acutely due to his own personal history. It can be added that Ataman also happens to be a gay filmmaker, which may have contributed to his feelings of alienation; his next feature was *Lola+Bilidikid* (*Lola + Billy the Kid*, 1999), a biting drama about the gay subculture within the Turkish community in Germany, a special case of multiple alienations.

Karanlik Sular was screened in several festivals abroad under the title *Serpent's Tale*. When it finally received a very limited theatrical release in Turkey, it flopped at the box office, selling a dismal figure of only 1,738 tickets. However, it should be noted that 1995 was one of the low points for Turkish cinema in general, with just ten Turkish films reaching the big screen, half of them selling fewer than 10,000 tickets and only two more than 100,000 (in subsequent years, several Turkish films have passed the 1 million tickets benchmark).

Although *Karanlik Sular* failed at the box office, it did receive near-unanimous positive critical reception, with more than one reviewer comparing it favourably to Alain Robbe-Grillet's directorial debut, *L'immortelle* (1963), also shot in Istanbul. While both films have enigmatic plots, Ataman's is actually far more socially and politically conscious than Robbe-Grillet's, for the reasons discussed above. Where *Karanlik Sular* is most reminiscent of *L'immortelle* is in its perfect use of Istanbul locales (credit must be given here to cinematographer Chris Squires). It fully succeeds in giving this ancient and cosmopolitan (but also quite modern) city at the cultural and geographic crossroads of two continents a mysterious atmosphere, one that is both menacing *and* alluring - wholly in tune with the film's Turkish-language title, which translated means "Dark Waters."

Conclusion

Whatever the future may hold, the fact remains that, to date, Turkish cinema has produced only three features unambiguously falling within a strict definition of the horror genre, plus one art-house horror movie and a few additional pictures located within other genres but featuring horror motifs.[11] None of these films build on the horrific elements present in Turkish folklore and mythology. Instead, they are either directly inspired by internationally-renowned American horror movies (as in the cases of *Seytan* and *Kader Diyelim*) or they feature vampires who should be regarded more as imports from Western popular culture to Turkish popular culture than as an indigenous Turkish folkloric element. This despite the fact that Turkey geographically neighbours Eastern Europe, the birth of the vampire myth.

The case was emphasized above as not to dismiss *Seytan* as a senseless attempt to copy a foreign text into an alien cultural background. Whereas the source material was of foreign origin (an American movie based on an American best-seller novel), it nevertheless had connotations which could make sense in a Turkish setting once some modifications were made. On the other hand, *Kader Diyelim* as a semi-musical pseudo-remake of *Psycho*, is a telling example to what degrees national filmmakers could go in bending and perhaps breaking with generic conventions if they want to blend foreign sources with local conventions.

The case of vampirism also provide examples as to the degree popular culture

---

[11] Horror does seem to be enjoying a growing popularity amongst young, prospective filmmakers in Turkey today, a trend witnessed in the recent proliferation of horror shorts entered into national film festivals. Examples include Baris Yös's black-and-white surreal Freudian drama, *Dr. Caligari'nin Karisi ve Oglu* (*The Wife and Son of Dr. Caligari*, 2000), Biray Dalkiran's slickly made *Sis* (*The Fog*, 2001) about a haunted apartment and Ahmet Uluçay's prize-winning *Seytan Kovma* (*Exorcist*, 2000), which depicts an Islamic exorcism séance.

author's note: Sincere thanks to Bülent Oran, Sadi Konuralp (to whom credit is due for coming across the only surviving print of *Ölüler Konuşmazki*), Mehmet Alemdar and Özlem Öz.

between appropriation & innovation

elements are flexible rather than being tied with fixed functions with respect to their original breeding grounds. The seductive vampire-witch of the popular *Tarkan* movies (and comics) fits perfectly into the pattern of vampires as metaphors for aggressive and threatening sexuality as observed in most Western vampire fiction and cinema. On the other hand, the utilisation of the vampire is not exclusively confined to such sexuality-oriented imagery neither in the west nor in Turkey, as in the cases of the anti-fascist themed *Jonathan* (1969) from West Germany and Kutluğ Ataman's *Karanlık Sular* where vampiric characters are employed in perhaps less explicitly political but nevertheless clearly socially-relevant plots.

Within the vampire subgenre, the specific case of the adoption of the Dracula theme is particularly interesting in Turkey since the source novel was partly inspired from a historical figure definitely part of Turkish history whereas being completely unknown to Western readers and spectators until a few decades ago. In other words, whereas in the west, the vampiric side of Dracula was more familiar and the historical connection completely alien, it was the reverse in Turkey. Thus, Turkish filmmakers could exploit this connection far more early than their Western counterparts. Neither Dracula nor any other popular culture element can be 'staked' so to speak with fixed origins to any ground.

above:
Drakula Istanbul'da.

below:
Tarkan: Gümüş Eger (aka **Tarkan: The Silver Saddle**), 1970.

SUZZANNA

THE HUNGRY SNAKE WOMAN

Witches, spells and politics: the horror films of Indonesia

Stephen Gladwin

Appreciating Indonesian cinema's horror output is not an easy task for the Western psyche. First impressions typically range from outright bewilderment to sarcastic humour accompanied by nervous laughter. Western viewers often find amusement in the impoverished budgets, cut-rate special effects and clumsy dialogue of Indonesian horror films. But to pass off this entire country's *cinefantastique* is a loss not only for fright fans. Unbeknownst to most adventurous Western viewers, Indonesian horror and fantastic cinema is one of the least adulterated conductors of the traditional customs, history and fears indigenous to the Indonesian people. We begin with an overview of the history of Indonesia's film industry, which, rife with political strife and fluctuating national outlook, greatly shaped the format of the country's contemporary horror cinema.

A brief Indonesian (horror) film history

Indonesia's film history is comprised of three periods of occupation by three respective countries. The Dutch were the first to utilise the archipelago's rich resources, and soon began making mostly exotic documentaries to export back to the mainland during the early 1920s. In fact, a Dutch studio in Indonesia was constructed solely for the purposes of documentary/propaganda production: the "Algemeen Nederlandsch-Indisch Film" (ANIF) in the mid 30s. This was an important company primarily because in 1950 it would metamorphose into the "Perusahaan Film Negara" (PFN), Indonesia's first government-run film production company. The company would change hands twice before the government took control: first when the Japanese controlled the country in 1942, and later when the country was handed over to the Dutch after the war. Although exploitive, these documentaries share some traits with Indonesian horror films of the early 1980s in that both genres eagerly showcase Indonesia's complex culture. It must also be noted that the Chinese were present during this time and even had theatres established by 1910 in Chinese provinces in Jakarta such as Glodok and Senen.[1]

The first true Indonesian film was largely a Dutch production, 1926's *Loetoeng Kasoroeng* (*The Enchanted Monkey*). It was blandly received, due in no small part to the primarily foreign (Dutch) cast. The first Indonesian film that made an impact came from China's Wong Brothers. These two immigrants arrived in Bandung from Shanghai in 1928 and found their first success in *Si Conat* (1929), a story detailing the duel between an Indonesian nemesis and a Chinese hero.[2] It was set in Jakarta and, more importantly, was made there as well. Jakarta would later become the hub of Indonesian filmmaking and assorted televised media, as well as the city of choice for many modern Indonesian horror narratives. *Si Conat*'s success resulted in large part from its mixture of Western cinematic technique (with all of the elaborate action set-pieces and staging this implies) and indigenous ethnic folktales.

Although the Dutch were keen on exporting propaganda and exploitation films flashing Indonesia's exotic qualities, it wasn't until Japan's brief occupation of the country from 1942-45 that Indonesians truly learned the power of politics in cinema. The Japanese recognised the

[1] Sen, K. (1994) *Indonesian Cinema: Framing the New Order*. Atlantic Highlands, N.J.: Zed Books, 14.

[2] Ibid.

opposite: Poster artwork for **Nyi Blorong** (aka **Hungry Snake Woman** aka **The Snake Queen**), one of the many films starring Indonesia's first lady of horror, Suzzanna.

opposite:
British DVD cover for **Leák** (aka **Mystics in Bali**).

capacity of film to serve as propaganda and employed it liberally to fuel the war effort. Indonesians themselves would later employ this cinematic tactic in horror films to enforce their perspective on the country and its customs. Most importantly during this period, however, was the freedom, however restricted, that the Japanese granted burgeoning Indonesian filmmakers. While still under tight supervision, the Japanese allowed the Indonesians precious control over the industry, and the country's indigenous people could finally feel secure behind the camera. Indonesians also absorbed essential technical film-making knowledge from their regents.

Once the Dutch reclaimed their territory on 17 August 1945, new film and television corporations began to spring up. One of them, the South Pacific Film Company (SPFC), harboured Indonesian film's future superstar, Usmar Ismail. Ismail was the first to appreciate cinema as a true art form, and such films as his debut *Harta Karun* (*Hidden Treasure*, 1949) remain widely admired among his fans and Indonesian film-goers generally.

Indonesia's true independence came four years later on 27 December 1949, and proved to be a potent stimulus for Indonesian film. The threat of war was lifted and the people could finally concentrate on their film-making. Imports were also popular, and by 1955, 184 films were being imported from India. The surplus of indigenous filmmaking was partly the result of American intervention and aid by the AMPAI ("American Motion Pictures Association in Indonesia"). This firm further solidified Indonesian filmmakers' talents by instructing them in advanced film technique and contributing sizable sums of money toward the cause. Such a partnership paved the way for future American co-productions in more modern Indonesian horror films. It proved to be a trade-off, however, as an influx of American imports came to the country, often portraying Asians as savages and primitives. Finally, it must be noted that the Indonesian language truly began to mature into what is widely spoken today due in no small part to the rise of film in the country. The dialect that was spoken onscreen (almost always the same) soon reached more and more people and stimulated its increasingly widespread use.

However, the fruitful times of this era were shattered in the late hours of 30 September, 1965, when General Sukarno's old regime, featuring his "guided democracy", was crushed by a coup. Soon General Suharto stepped in and introduced many new policies for Indonesia, including his most famous and comprehensive one, the so-called "New Order." Suharto aimed at Westernising Indonesia to some extent by, among other means, increasing consumerism. This point carries significant weight because it stimulated the rise of the Indonesian middle class, images of which would prove to be both an accurate (and often inaccurate) mirror of Indonesian life on screen, especially in more contemporary horror movies. What follows is an in-depth chronological look at five Indonesian horror and fantasy films, what makes them work (and why they sometimes don't), and the culture hidden within.

The early years: 1980-1986

The general rule of thumb for Indonesian horror cinema is that films incorporating the country's rich, Indian-derived mythology constitute the sweet spot of the genre. The various creatures contained in this mythology are outlandish, gory and bizarre enough to hold their own with their Hong Kong, Filipino and Japanese counterparts. To name but a few, there is the South Seas Queen, the *Sundelbolong* (ghosts of women who died during childbirth, rendered cinematically with a gaping hole in their stomach and an eternal longing for a child) and the Snake Queen (daughter of the South Seas Queen and a popular figure in Indonesian horror cinema).

And then there is the *Leák*, a mystical process indigenous to Bali, which enables its practitioners to transmogrify into a variety of objects. Prolific Indonesian director H. Tjut Djalil employed this intriguing strand of local mythology in his 1981 film of the same name - most commonly known outside Indonesia as *Mystics in Bali*. He also uses a common creature of South East Asian folklore, the *Penanggalan*. This hideous creature is a detached woman's (usually) head with spine and organs still intact. The thing looks like a sort of fleshy jellyfish with its trailing baggage of viscera. It also appeared in a Hong Kong production: 1977's *Fei taugh Mo Neuih* (*The Witch with Flying Head*). But in *Leák*, Djalil incorporates a literary source as well: Putra Madra's *Leák Ngakak*.

Djalil's film begins with yet another Indonesian custom, as the two protagonists watch a *barong* dance taking place. It is of the *wali* (sacred) class of Indonesian

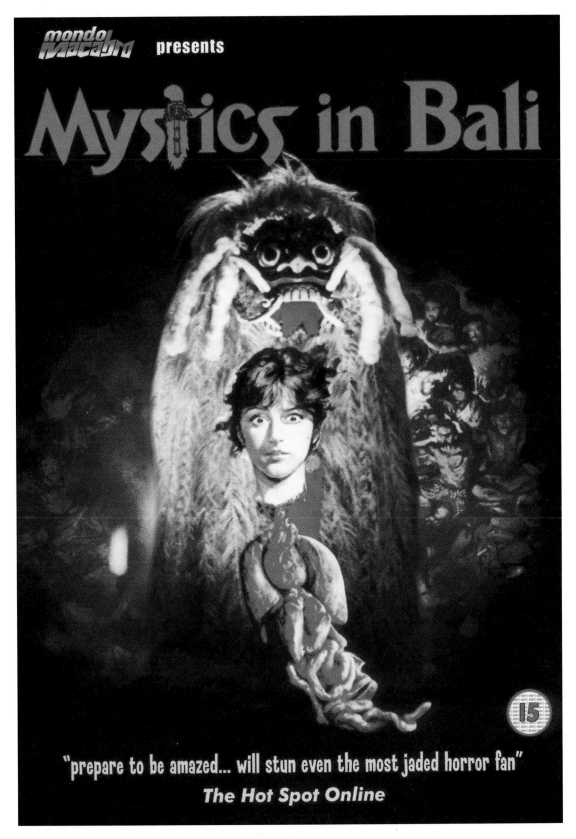

right:
Suzzanna stars in **Nyi Blorong**.

dance, and it tells the story of frightened villagers ridding their province of an evil presence. Djalil may well have been engaged in some foreshadowing here, since his Indonesian audience would obviously know such a dance and what it entailed (the haunting of a village by some mythological force) and would realise that the film could follow a similar storyline, which it does.

The basic premise of *Leák* concerns an American (in some prints, an Australian) woman named Cathy Kean (Ilona Agathe Bastian) who travels to Indonesia wishing to learn about the mysterious *leák* magic. She is befriended by a local, Mahendra (Yos Santo), and the two of them set out together to meet the *leák* priestess, whom Mahendra says possesses the power to transform her followers (in keeping with the legend).

Unsurprisingly, the confrontation with the priestess and Cathy's subsequent tutelage throw the town into turmoil. In exchange for lessons, Cathy is forced to offer herself (well, only her head) to the priestess, who will use it to scour the town in search of blood from the foetuses of pregnant women. The blood will then be used to rejuvenate the haggard priestess. Soon enough, the town is terrorised by the *Penanggalan* and the villagers fight back with traditional magic to end the terror.

Leák is an important film in the genre, not least because it showcases more than a few Indonesian horror customs and

[3] See, e.g., Heider, K.G. (1991) *Indonesian Cinema: National Culture on Screen.* Honolulu: University of Hawaii Press.

below:
Perkawinan Nyi Blorong, another of the many "Snake Woman" films starring Suzzanna.

provides insight into the Indonesian psyche. First, the notion of a grotesque, evil priestess utilising dastardly techniques in order to replenish her youth is a common stand-by in Indonesian horror, since beauty and complacency are essential components for a traditionally-accepted Indonesian woman. However, the most important cultural current running through the film concerns Cathy. Because of her ignorance, Cathy (a foreigner) interrupts the country's careful balance by ignoring warnings of the magic's powers, and the end result is disorder. Although previous scholars have looked at the presence of disorder in Indonesian cinema,[3] this theme has never truly been explored with respect to the horror genre. Disorder is signified in *Leák* by the collective hysteria of the villagers and the rampant deaths caused by Cathy when she is a possessed Penanggalan. The various sequences of angry villagers swinging flaming torches at the creature in the black night are a very common image of chaos in Indonesian horror.

In a rebellious move typical of Djalil, *Leák* does not end with the restoration of order, as many other contemporary horror films do. Undoubtedly, the Indonesian audience would expect a "cure" for Cathy and the demise of the priestess, but this proves only half correct. Mahendra's uncle, having successfully battled the priestess once before, has extensive knowledge of how to destroy her. He dispenses *ilmu* (knowledge) on how to destroy the Penanggalan menace: they must bury Cathy's decapitated body and ensure that the head does not re-attach itself to the corpse. Doing so will weaken the priestess, thereby making her demise that much easier to obtain. The priestess is destroyed in spectacular fashion (via dated albeit energetic optical effects), but unfortunately

witches, spells and politics

Cathy's fate is sealed, as her body must remain separate from her head. The film ends abruptly with an exhausted Mahendra and his uncle looking sorrowful and pensive. Hardly the "happy ending" usually brought about by restored order in Indonesian horror cinema! This untraditional, brooding ending is atypical of most films in the genre and helps to elevate *Leák* above lesser efforts.

Despite all the outlandish, gory special effects in *Leák*, including the Penanggalan and some rather clever transformation scenes, the film is surprisingly asexual. There is no sex whatsoever, not even a brief flash of nudity. This may seem strange to Western horror fans, suckled on the raunchy slasher films of the early 80's, the time of *Leák*'s production. However, one must consider the circumstances of the time. During this period, Indonesian cinema had a rigid "no sex" policy strictly enforced by the BSF (*Badan Sensor Film*), the country's censorship board. But over the next few years, the BSF would relax its censorship code somewhat, due in part to the increasing amount of foreign product that was exempt from censorship and thus was significantly more erotic. It was, as they say, the right time and right place for Indonesia's first horror bombshell, Suzzanna, to strut her stuff...

Among Suzzanna's earliest roles, one that she would grow into over the years was that of the Snake Queen, another standby of Indonesian legend transported to celluloid. The Snake Queen is the daughter of Nyi Roro Kidul, the "Queen of the South Seas", and resembles the Western Genie, with a few key exceptions. The Snake Queen is far more malicious than the Genie, and "deals in human lives" (to quote one Indonesian horror film) since she demands the blood of her customers' loved ones as payment for earthly riches. According to legend, the Snake Queen's sole gift is wealth. This fact has provided a useful springboard for Indonesian directors, such as Sisworo Gautama Putra, to balance the shocks with a tone of morality.

Such is the case in Putra's 1982 film, *Nyi Blorong Putri Nyi Loro Kidul* (*Snake Queen*), an exemplary entry in the Snake Queen cycle. The film begins with a well-worn Indonesian horror tradition: the graphic creation of a mythical monster (in this case, the eponymous Queen), accompanied by a narrator. We see Queen Kidul praying to the gods for a child, and soon an oversized snake egg appears. In typically spectacular fashion, a bloodied young woman (Suzzanna) hatches from the egg, while lightning pulses throughout the cave. Prolific Indonesian horror composer Gatot Sudarto's sonic cues are especially frenzied here, punctuating the activity. The narrator confirms the Snake Queen's appearance, and dictates to the audience that she is "a beautiful woman with the soul of a serpent." This declaration is significant because it carries with it an air of danger, suggesting that the Snake Queen is to be feared and dealt with quite cautiously. The Snake Queen is just one of many fearful women in Indonesian horror cinema. In general, women in the genre fall into one of two groups: those who possess fearful magic and exercise a reign of terror over the populace (especially men), or those "proper" women who are more traditionally restrained, pleasant and obedient. Often, the fearful women

above:
Nyi Blorong (aka **Hungry Snake Woman** aka **The Snake Queen**).

left:
More delirious horror imagery from **Nyi Blorong**.

represent the collective unconscious fear of female sexuality, as they almost always aggressively indulge in sex.

In the next scene we see a traditional Indonesian funeral, in which a husband, Kukro, mourns his wife's death. This is a social affair, as evidenced by the entire family's presence as well as countless other relatives and friends. Included in the familial procession is Delvi, Kukro's new wife. Delvi is in fact the Snake Queen, with whom Kukro is secretly conspiring to gain wealth. Upon closer inspection of the corpse, Andika (Barry Prima, sometimes billed as Berry) remarks that the fatal wounds on her neck appear to be snakebites. Director Putra has given the audience an obvious clue as to what is going on: Delvi (the Snake Woman) has taken the life of Kukro's former wife in return for the riches she has bestowed upon him.

The film's plot is a seemingly simple story of greed and its catastrophic results. But beneath this rudimentary premise again lies fascinating evidence of a particular culture. Kukro's greed clearly reflects Indonesian society's contrasting views on the individual and the group. While Westerners treat individual liberties not only as a blessing, but as a right, Indonesians consider too much individuality selfish. Perhaps Karl Heider put it best when he wrote: "For Indonesians, who place more value on the health of the group, this blatant individualism (of the west) seems peculiarly selfish."[4] If one is to strive for riches, why not include the family, or some other group for that matter? Kukro admits to his daughter Sasti later in the film that he always kept his family in mind during his monetary pursuits, but Sasti (and the audience) knows better, especially when she learns that Kukro also fed his son to the Snake Woman in return for riches. An individual's selfishness causes death and the break-up of the family unit, all of which results in chaos.

The scenes with the Snake Queen in her lair also provide valuable insights into the progressive loosening of censorship. In all the films of the Snake Queen omnibus, she possesses a cabal of eternally youthful female servants. In subsequent films, they are more and more scantily clad, eventually resembling strip-tease dancers. In this early entry, however, the servants are well covered except for their bare arms. The most blatantly sexual sequence comes from another generic Snake Queen standby - the seduction of a new "customer." These

[4] Heider, 30.

below:
Pengabdi Setan is a rare exception among Indonesian horror films, being based on a well-known Western model (**Phantasm**).

witches, spells and politics

seduction sequences are always garishly lit with trenchant costume and set design and provide some of Indonesian cinema's most spectacular set-pieces. The shocking sexuality is always on centre stage, however. Although tame by foreign film standards, these set-pieces are nonetheless important for their increasingly bold portrayals of sexuality. In Indonesian cinema, sex is often a means to an end. For example, many sex scenes are used to signify pregnancy, while others go for the exploitation approach by showing rape. *The Snake Queen*, however, uses its sex scene to create suspense, signalling as it does an imminent threat. Whenever a sex scene in Indonesian horror portrays the act as simply pleasurable, there is an inherent element of naughtiness...and danger. Not surprisingly, many of the Snake Queen's victims in subsequent films die a horrible post-coital death.

There are more profound instances of disorder in the family unit later in the film. Andika also falls under the Snake Queen's spell, and the result is disaster. As his lovesick obsession progresses, Andika's life falls apart. He misses his classes. He isolates himself from his friends and family. And the Snake Queen's world is equally warped, for she has found true love in Andika. She, too, abandons her lair and leaves her maidens behind. Soon the Queen is torn between her duties and her earthly love. She ultimately breaks off the relationship with help from her mother, Queen Kadul. Soon the Queen returns to her lair and resumes her duties. Order is restored for the Queen, but not for Andika and his family.

In another direct effect of the family's chaos, Sasti takes an angry drive after being told off by her husband Andika, and crashes in a near-fatal accident. While lying in her hospital bed, Sasti has a fevered dream. The dream sequence that follows is one of Indonesian horror cinema's most hallucinogenic and wildly imaginative: she views an all-female group of dancers who soon turn to snakes (a potent "women as monsters" image if ever there was one) and sees all of the Queen's victims in a hellish, bizarre sequence that would fit well in one of Brazil's "Coffin Joe" movies.[5] She soon views Andika passionately kissing the Snake Queen (who now resembles the Medusa) and learns of his terrible secret. She then bolts awake.

The remainder of the film concerns the resolution of the disorder and a possession sequence obviously lifted from William Friedkin's *The Exorcist* (1973). Part of what makes Indonesian horror cinema so unique is its refusal to localise recognisable horror sequences from successful foreign horror films. Exceptions do exist, such as the *Phantasm* (1979)-inspired *Pengabdi Setan* (made the same year and also lensed by Putra), but for the most part, foreign horror sequences remain untouched. Such is the case with the scene of Sasti's possession. All the stops are pulled out here: her bed levitates, her voice is a marvel of spooky post-synching and she is shown levitating above the bed. It is a surreal effect indeed to view such a familiar sequence amidst such an exotic film.

left:
Sundel Bolong, another horror role for Suzzanna.

While the climatic duel between The Queen and a local, competing mystic is visually compelling, the final Indonesian horror convention present in the film - the Queen's closing moral diatribe - provides the most impact. When Kukro has died a gruesome death after failing to provide another sacrifice, the Snake Queen warns Sasti: "Your father's death is his own fault. He tried to get rich the easy way. Work hard and struggle to make a good life." Whether intentional or not, such a statement is symptomatic of Suharto's "New Order" and emphasises hard, honest work for personal (and national) gain.

Although Prima occupied a substantial amount of screen time in *Snake Queen*, it wasn't until *Jaka Sembung* (aka *The Warrior)*, 1981, that he really came into his own. *The Warrior* and its two sequels remain the high point of Prima's career. It helps that the films themselves are greatly compelling and are dense with Indonesian culture and cinematic tradition. While the two subsequent instalments were winners in their own right, the original entry remains the crowning jewel of the series.

[5] See André Barcinski's chapter in this book, from p.27.

Prima plays the role of nationalist hero Jaka Sambung in the Dutch colonial period of Indonesia (the 1820's, approximately). Jaka's local anti-authoritarian antics bait the wrath of Dutch general Van Schramm, who soon takes action to claim Jaka's life. Van Schramm employs a local mystic who resurrects the body of Ki Item, a long-dead warlock. This resurrection sequence recalls Cathy's death in *Leák* in reverse: Ki Item's headless body is reunited with his head in lurid fashion. Lightning pierces the inky-black sky atop a mountain and pulsating, phosphorescent rocks levitate through the air. It is important to note the mountain location. Often in Indonesian horror and fantasy films, a mountainous region is used to symbolise isolation, a separation from the village, where devious black magic is performed. Upon his resurrection, Ki Item begins the hunt for Jaka, which culminates in an astonishing climax.

The Warrior is so memorable because it has such an eclectic foundation of three genres: horror, *silat* (Indonesia's own variant on Hong Kong chop-socky), and "compeni" (Dutch period drama). Such an ambitious construction yields a higher volume of Indonesian traditions and glimpses of life, and Putra's keen eye for striking visuals is in full force here as well.

Jaka and his fellow villagers practice Islam, one of Indonesia's main religions, and one that typifies the Indonesian belief in the virtues of selflessness. Jaka is fighting for the public cause of overthrowing the Dutch oppression. Even the enemy's daughter falls for him when she witnesses his courage and loyalty; she is amazed at how he is able to "put his people and his religion always ahead of himself." In perhaps the most extreme (certainly the most graphic) instance of self-sacrifice, Jaka's wife Sertei makes it her dying wish to donate her eyes to Jaka, who has been blinded by Van Schramm in a vicious confrontation. While Pete Tombs describes the gory transplantation scene that follows as an "excuse for some *Eyes Without a Face* surgery scenes and creaky special effects",[6] it behooves the viewer to grant the scene in question more than a passing glance because of its cultural significance. Finally, the villagers and the village itself act as a unit, further punctuating the importance of the group psyche in Indonesian life. Nowhere is this concept more apparent than during the climactic battle, where Ki Item is sorely outnumbered, taking on an entire village of opponents along with the powerful Jaka.

The other major source of insight is in the representation of the Dutch. In the film (and in most Indonesian films featuring the Dutch), the foreign oppressors dwell in an isolated, typically opulent Western mansion. Once again, the idea of isolation from a group suggests to the viewer the moral bankruptcy of the people depicted. Most curious, however, is the presence in *The Warrior* of a Westerner among the Dutch ranks. The bulk of the Dutch forces in the film are Indonesians, but one white general stands out. White actors in Indonesian cinema are typically relegated to historical roles such as these and are otherwise absent in the horror genre. The Dutch presence in the film also signifies the "bad" of the west, and as such the film stands as a sort of lesson on Western evils. This ties into Suharto's New Order ideology: he wanted to facilitate the best the west had to offer (technology, business) but to avoid the pitfalls (slavery, bigotry).

The later years: 1987-1993

As the decade came to a close, so did an era of vibrant Indonesian horror film-making, with originality progressively giving way to cheap exploitation. Indonesian filmmakers were showing more skin in their pictures than ever before. Overseas competition, both voluntary and involuntary, accounted for much of the change; try as it might, the Indonesian government was powerless to prevent the influx of black market pornographic videotapes seeping in from overseas. And then there was the pressure from mainstream foreign films, many of which sported heaping amounts of nudity and sex, resulting in the loss of Indonesian directors' core audience of adolescent boys. Indonesian horror filmmakers thus turned to the lurid marketing tactics of such exploitation directors as H.G. Lewis and Russ Meyer. Soon, wallpapering Jakarta were outrageous posters with busty Indonesian women in various compromising situations, and the gore-drenched victims of outlandish monsters. Another important component of the increasingly relaxed censorship code was Suharto's revision of his New Order. By the late 1980s, Suharto either realised the fruitlessness of his endeavours to mould Indonesian cinema so as to better portray his country or he simply stopped caring. As a result, films were no longer a priority for the New Order regime.

[6] Tombs, P. (1998) *Mondo Macabro: Weird and Wonderful Cinema around the World.* New York: St. Martin's Griffin, 71.

witches, spells and politics

Not surprisingly, Indonesian horror directors were quick to take advantage of this new freedom. One of the earliest was H. Tjut Djalil (director of *Leák*) in his 1987 film *Pembalasan Ratu Pantai Selatan* - also known under such titles as *Nasty Hunter* and *Lady Terminator* - an astonishing picture overflowing with pent-up frustrations brought on by censorship and a growing fear of modernism and its precarious benefits.

Nasty Hunter begins with a fairly traditional sequence recalling Suzzanna's best films. A narrator recounts the Indonesian fable of the South Seas Queen (the Snake Queen's Mother), a fearsome nymph with an insatiable sexual appetite. Her lair, populated with scantily clad handmaidens, recalls the Snake Queen's cave. At the conclusion of each sex session she dispatches her partners in particularly squirmy fashion, as a wriggly serpent extends from her vagina and bites the males' member off. However, one suitor tricks her and grabs the snake before it can strike. Powerless and enraged, the Queen vows to avenge this humiliation by possessing the man's great-granddaughter. She than retreats to the sea to discuss with "evil powers" how to handle "this insult."

Flash ahead to present-day Jakarta, where Tanya, an Indonesian anthropologist, is investigating the myth of the South Seas Queen. She soon arrives at the infamous ocean where the Queen is supposedly slumbering and happens upon her underwater lair. Tanya lies atop the Queen's bed and is suddenly spread-eagled by an invisible force, the Queen's snake slithering into her vagina. Tanya is now possessed and, after donning a bloodthirsty alter-ego, both seduces and castrates random men for much of the subsequent running time, until the police force confronts her in an excessively loud finale.

Above all, *Nasty Hunter* is a transitional picture. It forms a bridge between traditional Indonesian horror films and the slickly made, American co-produced horror films to follow (the soundtrack of *Nasty Hunter* was recorded in LA's "Intersound" studios). Indonesian horror filmmakers had been receiving financial assistance from the States since the 1950s, but only in the late 80s were their films largely (and explicitly) co-produced by the US. *Nasty Hunter* is especially interesting since it benefits from an old veteran of the genre (Djalil, working under

above: American video sleeve for H. Tjut Djalil's 1987 film **Pembalasan Ratu Pantai Selatan** (aka **Lady Terminator** aka **Nasty Hunter**).

the pseudonym "Jalil Jackson") seasoned enough to update old conventions with more modern visages. Tanya is really a sociological update of *Leák*'s Cathy; she too is an intellectual woman interested in local myth but is even more assertive and bold (while on a boat ride to the Queen's palace, the boater calls her "lady" and she promptly replies that she would rather be called an anthropologist). Another role in *Leák*, that of the local mystic who dispenses *ilmu*, becomes in *Nasty Hunter* a librarian who refers Tanya to a book on the same topic.

Of all the horror films lensed under Suharto's New Order, *Nasty Hunter* quite possibly possesses the most resonance and insight. The city of Jakarta is at the epicentre of Djalil's often-vitriolic critique. It is populated with sleazy, perpetually horny young men, dive bars and those proverbial shrines to consumerism, the shopping mall. The scenes in the malls echo George Romero's 1978 classic *Dawn of the Dead*, as Djalil's camera focuses on young Indonesian girls and their giddy excitement over flashy jewellery and other hollow, monetary trinkets. Djalil obviously has a bone to pick with Suharto's initiation of modernism, as one such girl (replete with 80s-style leg warmers) is messily gunned down by Tanya. On the other hand, Djalil's comments on economic change are less venomous than Romero's, as he is careful to include a high amount of product placement and sprawling skyscrapers in the *mise-en-scene*. Here the director appears to side with Suharto as he eagerly showcases Indonesia's prosperity.

Perhaps the ultimate criticism of modernism in the film is Djalil's implication that Western techniques and tools are useless for solving problems that are indigenous to Indonesia. Throughout the film, Jakarta's police force provides comic relief through their utter ineptitude. This wouldn't garner much attention if the officers investigating the case weren't almost all Westerners. The team on the case includes Snake, a burned-out stoner with a correspondingly stoned voice-over and Max McNeal, a sceptical Westerner who just happens to be the boyfriend of Erika, the great-granddaughter targeted by the scorned South Seas Queen. Max finds Erika's tales of Indonesian legend and the current situation unbelievable, and the result is near tragedy as Tanya escapes a hail of bullets in the police station. The fact that Tanya is invincible towards Western weapons stands as a strong criticism by Djalil. His film epitomises the concept of "reluctant modernism" because it suggests that the only way to deal with such a menace is to combat it with traditional, uniquely Indonesian mysticism. Erika's uncle is an Indonesian wise man (in one scene he even sits atop a mountain, recalling past films with mountainous imagery and its connotations) and he ultimately dispenses the skills necessary to destroy Tanya. Djalil hammers home the need to honour tradition by ending the film with a final cautionary strand of narration: "The stars will be here long after we are no more."

Such insights fare a great deal better than the film's visceral sequences, which border on numbing. The initial "You go girl!" sentiment is jarringly torn away once Tanya is possessed and begins shooting up Jakarta with her inexhaustible Uzi. The kill sequences, while bloody, are largely unimaginative and unspectacular. And while the nudity is the most graphic Indonesian film audiences had seen until that time, it is hardly put to more use than mere exploitation. Finally, and possibly because the film is an American co-production, the dubbing is particularly obnoxious, rife with snide quips and incongruous American idioms.

Although critic Tim Lucas calls it "...a sell-out of their [Indonesia's] national legends to Hollywood commercialism",[7] *Nasty Hunter* has a great deal to offer. In fact, it has the distinction of being the best of the "new wave" of Indonesian horrors since it bothers to examine the

7 *Video Watchdog* 50, 1999, 17.

below:
A painted billboard on an Indian city street (this shot was taken in Mumbai). The big 'A' is the Indian equivalent of an 'X' cert.

Indonesian people's largely unconscious fear of the modernist machine.

Dangerous Seductress (1993) lies on the *other* half of the spectrum of new wave Indonesian horror. It is a tedious, vacuous cash-in of a film. This is doubly sad considering the talent on board, as H. Tjut Djalil serves as the picture's associate director (as well as a co-director under the collective pseudonym "John Miller"). If nothing else, *Dangerous Seductress* sees the Indonesian horror film industry come full circle from localised shocks to sleekly-made, sell-out cinema.

The film opens with some attractive aerial photography of a clear Jakarta night. A gang of jewel thieves, including a Westerner, is engaged in a frenzied car chase with Jakarta's finest. Crashing in a nearby forest, one gang member's arm is severed and a shard of glass swiftly slices off his finger. In a sequence that owes much to horror films of the past, the finger crawls off into what appears to be a make-up compact (!) and burrows into the ground. Almost on cue, lightning strikes and, in a sequence obviously inspired by Clive Barker's *Hellraiser* (1987), a gloppy skeleton punches out from the ground and regenerates itself with the victim's blood. Soon the skeleton has transformed into a beautiful nude woman (Amy Weber), who promptly begins a hunt for human haemoglobin to replenish her body.

Then, in a sequence that plays like a live-action sentence fragment, the direction cuts to a seemingly unrelated vignette in sunny Los Angeles, where Susan (Tonya Offer) and boyfriend John (Joseph Cassano) are having a particularly nasty fight, which ends in an attempted rape. Fleeing her apartment in terror, Susan decides to visit her sister Linda (Kristin Anin), a bubbly blonde who just happens to live in (you guessed it) Indonesia. Before long, Susan becomes ensnared in Weber's grasp, luring men to their deaths to regenerate her master's body.

Like *Nasty Hunter*, the best asset of *Dangerous Seductress* is its new look at existing Indonesian traditions. It just doesn't do it nearly as well as the former film. For one thing, Weber's character is simply an update of the wicked priestess in *Leák*, but nowhere near as imaginative since she merely growls and looks increasingly silly in her body paint. Also, there is the familiar theme of foreigners inappropriately intervening in mystical affairs, as two men from New Guinea conduct research on primitive occultism in Indonesia and provide Susan with a forbidden book of Sumatran legend. This standby, however, is cheapened by a hackneyed *Evil Dead* (1982) rip-off: as Susan picks up the book of Sumatran legend and recites its incantations, the fog machine is turned up to full blast and there are more tacky visual effects. When combined with genuine Indonesian legends and intriguing cultural meditations such effects would be easier to forgive, but here they come off as cheap and obvious.

Perhaps the most easily recognisable trait possessed by the film is its updated image of women. Certainly, Susan and Linda are two of the most independent, modern women in Indonesian cinema (although they are both Westerners). They join other women at bars and enjoy drinking and smoking - strict cultural taboos for Indonesian females until quite recently. But have gender roles really changed that much? Both women are often portrayed in the tired role of sex object: Linda has a career in bikini modelling, and Susan uses her fetching looks to lure men into post-coital deaths. Hardly anything new for women in film.

There is one flash of worthy social commentary in the film, although this may have been a lucky coincidence. The scene in question begins with what appears to be a traditional Balinese dance in a temple. The viewer, understandably disoriented, soon realises the trick when the camera pans out and the shouts of a director can be heard: it turns out that the "dance" is really just a bikini photo shoot, and the scantily clad dancers are, in reality, mere models. The transition from tradition to modernism is perfectly encapsulated here. In fact, it is one of the best comments on Indonesia's movement towards modernism to appear in an Indonesian film.

It is all downhill from there, however. *Dangerous Seductress* concludes with a lame battle between Weber and a mystic, one that fails to distinguish itself from similar mystical *battle royale*s in previous films. This constitutes an especially disappointing ending not just to a particular film, but also to an era. Unlike European or even Hong Kong horror cinema, Indonesian horror never had an outside audience during its Golden Age. The result was a loss of opportunity for foreign enthusiasts to bring their own ideas and techniques to bear on future productions, and when they did it was only to dilute the core of the films, namely the history and culture of one of the world's most diverse countries.

The unreliable narrator: subversive storytelling in Polish horror cinema

Nathaniel Thompson

"Frasquita told her story to Busquenos. He told it to Lopez Soarez, who in turn told it to Senor Avadoro. It's enough to drive you crazy."

This bewildered observation from *Rekopis znaleziony w Saragossie* (*The Saragossa Manuscript*, 1965) could serve as the mantra of the colourful, crazy quilt state of European cinema in the two decades immediately following World War II, where formerly occupied territories found new voices after undergoing the harrowing ordeal of global combat. Multinational productions became the norm as countries like Italy, Germany and France forged cinematic alliances which allowed the cross-pollination of talent both in front of and behind the camera; though more restricted by the Iron Curtain, Poland and other Communist nations also joined in the new film renaissance led by such directors as Andrzej Wajda, who garnered international attention with such art house favourites as *Popiól i diament* (*Ashes and Diamonds*, 1958).

That film's celebrated lead actor, Zbigniew Cybulski, returned in *Saragossa* as Alphonse van Worden, a captain of the Wallonian Guards whose story is immortalized in the title scripture. The multi-layered, occult narrative follows his descent into the supernatural as he embarks on a trip through the mountains towards Madrid, only to encounter a demonically possessed beggar, two tempting incestuous sisters, a dark magician and even the forces of the Inquisition. Stories related by the various characters weave in and out of reality, with parallel histories in Spain directly impacting the present. The soldier realizes by the story's end that the events have formed an elaborate test of his worthiness to sire the heirs for a royal Moorish family with otherworldly connections.

The sprawling original text of *Saragossa* was written in segments somewhere between 1805 and 1815, the year in which the mysterious author, Count Jan Potocki, committed suicide. A sort of romantic, gothic alternative to such anthologies as *The Decameron* and *The Arabian Nights*, Potocki's inventive fantasia recounts van Worden's sixty-six days of interlocking stories in which characters constantly slip in and out from one narrative plane to the next, plot strands are continuously broken and juggled within each other, and no one can be truly be trusted, even the hero. The novel's conclusion finds him successfully embraced by his supernatural family, whose riches he spreads to his two children. As for the manuscript itself, he concludes, "I have copied it out in my own hand and put it in an iron casket, in which one day my heirs will find it."

The late director Wojciech Has opts for an even more difficult and challenging structure in his filmed adaptation. We begin with two soldiers retreating from warfare in the streets to read the Saragossa manuscript, which so entrances them that the violence outside becomes little more than an annoyance. This framing device is then abandoned for the rest of the film, in which a variety of storytellers leads the viewer downward through tale within tale until any sense of narrative security has been completely displaced. The ambiguous coda finds van Worden meeting his destiny by riding from the supernatural cabin which serves as the stories' axis and off

opposite:
Marina Pierro in Walerian Borowczyk's **Dr. Jekyll et les femmes**.

Poland

into the mountains, where he finally joins the two sisters for an unholy but triumphant final communion.

An ambitious and intellectually lively exploration of the occult, *Saragossa* is an epic in both length and scope. Its sense of the uncanny is balanced by a buoyant dark wit in keeping with the controversial notion of Satanism as a puckish, jovial practice which speaks to the natural inner beast in mankind. The moments of bona fide horror, as when van Worden and other characters repeatedly awaken to find themselves in a scorched landscape filled with hanging bodies and skeletons, attain a transcendent, nightmarish atmosphere both through the skilful scope photography and the experimental score by composer Krzysztof Penderecki, whose music later cropped up in *The Exorcist* (1973) and *The Shining* (1980). Though now commonly available in its complete 175-minute form, the film was often seen only in substandard or terribly abbreviated prints, which only hinted at its intellectual and visceral pleasures.[1] Best experienced on a big screen, fortunately this film can now be appreciated as one of the key foundation works in modern horror and art house cinema, two categories more inextricably linked than many critics cared to admit at the time of its release.[2]

The narrative experimentation of *Saragossa* earned the already seasoned Has a solid reputation as one of Poland's finest directors, but no other films came close to an international breakthrough. His next most widely seen film, *Sanatorium pod klepsydra* (*The Sandglass*, 1973), was not so coincidentally his second foray into the supernatural.[3] This eerie mood piece finds Josef (Jan Nowicki) arriving by train to a remote, snow-covered sanatorium to visit his ailing father (Tadeusz Kondrat). The doctor, Gotard (Gustow Holoubek), informs Josef that in terms understandable to the outside world, his father has passed away; however, the doctors have conquered time and slowed it down so that "dead" people now hover just over the abyss in a sort of dream state where events from the past can even be revisited. Josef encounters his father in younger guises amidst an assortment of colourful characters of variant nationalities, all bathed in eerie ambient light and framed once again in expert Cinemascope.

As visually ambitious as *Saragossa* if not quite as immediately satisfying, *The Sandglass* operates on a similar number of cultural and historical planes as it

fear without frontiers

explores the Jewish experience both past and present while depicting the uneasy transition from post-adolescence into full manhood, an experience similar to the acceptance of death. Once again Has draws upon a collection of related literary stories, this time by Jewish writer Bruno Schulz, to craft a nonlinear structure that bounces between scenes of warfare, otherworldly landscapes, and ambiguous interactions between the living and the dead. The playful satanic philosophy of the preceding film is taken over here by more of a pure cinematic anarchy, augmented by the blurry line between reality and illusion, life and death. "The whole thing is a question of relativity", explains Gotard early in the film. "Here, your father's death is yet to occur, though that death has already struck him." This explanation from a dubious source recalls *Saragossa*'s Pascheco (Franciszek Pieczka), a one-eyed priest's assistant suffering from violent bouts of demonic possession who is revealed to be another entity entirely later in the film. Pascheco's frenzied behaviour abruptly halts early on when he tells the story of how his possession and disfigurement came about, though even this proves to be a ruse functioning as part of a larger tapestry. In *The Sandglass*, facts related by Gotard and the father (in his various incarnations) prove to be even more of a dead end, pointing Josef instead to a fate ultimately as unknowable as life itself.

Burden of the beast

While Has expanded the boundaries of fantastic cinema by adopting a Chinese puzzle form of literary gamesmanship, his fellow Polish directors drew upon other influences for their own unique cinematic visions. The most volatile of these was Walerian Borowczyk, a skilled painter and visual designer who, like many of his peers, relocated to France for much of his career. His ventures into film began with a number of acclaimed animation projects geared towards adult audiences in which he ruminated upon the dreamy, antiquated erotica which would ultimately become his trademark. His first breakthrough, *The Theatre of Mr. and Mrs. Kabal* (1967), became a festival favourite throughout Europe and earned him the clout to film his first live action feature, *Goto, l'île d'amour* (*Goto, Island of Love*, 1968). This stylized exercise takes place on an island in which every inhabitant's name begins with the letter "G", and the characters' actions are controlled by love and betrayal.

The more ambitious *Blanche* (1971), the first specifically medieval venture for Borowczyk, explores that beloved male artistic construct: the beautiful, innocent girl (Ligia Branice) who sparks desire in everyone she encounters. Depicted with all the detail and loving care of an elaborate tapestry, this film promised great things from its creator and gave some hint of the more ornate explorations of sensuality through narrative construct which he would later establish in his most well known film, *Contes immoraux* (*Immoral Tales*, 1974). That quartet of stories explores eroticism through the ages: "The Tide" depicts a rakish youth (Lorenzo Bernini) sweet talking his cousin (Lise Danvers) into servicing him while surrounded by the rising tide; "Thèrese Philosophe" gives away its ending through a title card as it depicts a young girl (Charlotte Alexandra) discovering her sexuality with the aid of numerous antiquated objects before being ravaged by a madman;[4] "Erzsébet Báthory" features Paloma Picasso (daughter of Pablo) as the notorious countess who bathed in virgins' blood to say eternally young; and "Lucrezia Borgia" takes a brief look at one of history's most infamous families, here represented by Lucrezia (Florence Bellamy) enjoying the favours of her brother (Lorenzo Berinizi) and the Pope (Jacopo Berinzini) while a heretic is burned nearby.

Though three of the four stories are anchored in historical events, Borowczyk's film is anything but a literal depiction of the facts. Staid and dreamy even when actors are being tortured or slathered in blood, the film moves along at its own deliberate pace. Devoid of any traditional romantic entanglements or socially redeeming narratives, *Immoral Tales* instead aims to persuade the viewer that eroticism in its purest form, no matter how deviant it may seem to middle class sensibilities, can be appreciated as art.

Unfortunately audiences were not so willing to embrace his next film, *La bête* (*The Beast*, 1975), which began as a short intended for *Immoral Tales* in which noblewoman Romilda de l'Esparance (Sirpa Lane) is chased and ravaged by a wolf-like monster in the woods. Eventually she succumbs to the animal's lust until it dies from pleasure amidst hyperbolic displays of jetting fluid and hardcore

opposite:
Images from **The Saragossa Manuscript**.

[1] Many American and U.K. viewers initially encountered a brutalized two-hour version under the title *Adventures of the Nobleman*; much of the erotic content (which is still fairly potent by today's standards) was the main target of the distributor's scissors.

[2] See Bissette, S. (2002) "Curtis Harrington and the Underground Roots of the Modern Horror Film." In Mendik, X. and S.J. Schneider (eds), *Underground USA: Film-making Beyond the Hollywood Canon*. New York: Columbia University Press / London: Wallflower Press.

[3] The film won the 1973 Jury Prize at the Cannes Film Festival, but it failed to receive much theatrical play outside Europe and has only intermittently cropped up on television in squeezed 1.85:1 prints.

[4] A lengthy prologue, thematically similar to this story, contains footage of Borowczyk's own collection of nostalgic erotica. It was inexplicably removed from most prints and has yet to surface on any of the film's video editions.

above and opposite: Erotic horror imagery from Borowczyk's **Dr. Jekyll et les femmes**.

prosthetic manipulation. Though this sequence earned the film a place in the history books for offending and sickening critics throughout Europe, the rest of the film is in many ways more interesting and representative of Borowczyk as an artist. The bulk of the story concerns an English woman, Lucy Broadhurst (Lisbeth Hummel), who travels by car with her aunt to the l'Esperance estate, where she will marry the decidedly non-charismatic son, Mathurin (Pierre Benedetti). As the family prepares for her arrival, Mathurin undergoes an impromptu baptism while other household members fornicate and plot murders under the guise of social respectability. Lucy's arrival is greeted by the sight of horses breeding explicitly in the driveway, which she preserves through one of many Polaroids shot around the estate. After uncovering an illustrated album by the notorious lady of the estate, Romilda, Lucy experiences a feverish dream (the aforementioned short film) intercut with the nocturnal activities of the household. The next day, Mathurin's true bestial nature is exposed when he dies after Lucy's sexual awakening, an event which coincides with the arrival of the Cardinal who expounds his own philosophy about bestiality as Lucy and her aunt speed away in their chauffeured automobile.

The sense of the past impinging upon the present lingers throughout *The Beast* more potently than any other Borowczyk film. The image of Romilda's torn corset from her encounter with the beast remains frozen, an historical fetish object inside a glass case in the family sitting room, while the flashback lingers on the same discarded garment floating endlessly in a nearby pond as its owner's libido is awakened. The parallel narratives of Lucy and Romilda are never explicitly spelled out, leaving us instead to sift through the clues Borowczyk has provided. Why exactly does Mathurin die, and why does Lucy scream in his bedroom? When she speeds away at the end, how does one read the expression on her face, a sadder and more conflicted representation of the giddy smile she displayed during her earlier, photo snapping arrival? Borowczyk has gradually stripped away any semblance of polite convention; this goal may not seem too surprising for a film whose opening shot depicts horses coupling on camera, but the sensitivity and intelligence behind such a scenario can be genuinely startling.

Though *The Beast* can be categorized as a horror film, a work of erotica, or a dark fantasy influenced by classic fairy tales, its central thesis - the exploration of bestial behaviour in all its guises both

the unreliable narrator

natural and assumed - is most powerfully contained in its least recognized genre categorization, a witty comedy of manners laced with subversive, surreal touches worthy of Buñuel. The priest (Roland Armontel) who arrives to baptize Mathurin is the most obvious example, as he assumes pious positions while quietly enjoying the carnal company of his harpsichord-playing acolytes. In the spirit of *The Discreet Charm of the Bourgeoisie* (1972), much humour is derived from the insatiably lustful younger l'Esperance sister, Clarisse (Pascale Rivault), who amusingly sets aside her babysitting charges in favour of unlikely wardrobe dalliances with the studly houseboy.[5] In these quietly winning moments of frustration and transgression as much as the more legendary highlights, *The Beast* casts a firm, unforgiving eye on human nature in all its spiritual aspirations and physical temptations, a spectacle both pitiable and worthy of celebration. The final transition of Lucy's car tearing off in a swirling cascade of leaves, only to revert back to the body of the beast interred by Romilda as she walks off naked into the misty forest, offers no answer to the problem; instead, we must wonder how one can ever go home again after realizing that the aristocratic principles of Western society are nothing but a façade.

The same principle forms the basis of Robert Louis Stevenson's seminal Victorian short novel, *The Strange Case of Dr. Jekyll & Mr. Hyde*, which proved to be ideal source material for Borowczyk with *Dr. Jekyll et les femmes* (*Dr. Jekyll and His Women*, 1981). His first purely fantastic work after *The Beast*, *Jekyll* repeats many of its themes and echoes the setting with an isolated country estate housing a dark, sensual secret, in this case the formula which allows Dr. Jekyll (Udo Kier) to transform into an animalistic sadist who terrorizes his houseguests. The sexual and violent aggressiveness of Jekyll (complete with an outrageous, knife-like phallus)[6] eventually dissolves when his alter ego is finally externalized in the form of Fanny Osbourne (Borowczyk regular Marina Pierro), who enjoys a bloody communion in Jekyll's carriage after partaking of his bathtub formula. As they speed off into the morning light during the final scene, their departure (which likewise carries the viewer out of the dreamlike film) echoes the identical finale of *The Beast*, here rendered in more graphic terms as their intertwined, blood soaked flesh seems to blend into one entity. This resolution seems appropriate as the closing image of Borowczyk's excursions into cinematic fantasy; of his subsequent work, only the macabre S&M

[5] In the excellent book *Immoral Tales: European Sex and Horror Movies 1956-1984* (New York: St. Martins Griffin, 1995), whose title choice is extremely apt in this case, Cathal Tohill and Pete Tombs connect the scenario of Borowczyk's *Dr. Jekyll and His Women* to *The Exterminating Angel* (1962), though one could probably compile a small book's worth of similarities between the two directors.

[6] As with *The Beast*, this film suffered tremendous censorship around the world. The U.S. and U.K. video versions (entitled *Blood Lust* and *Bloodbath of Dr. Jekyll*, respectively) are hacked down to the point of incoherence.

right:
British video cover for Andrzej Zulawski's **Possession**.

7 The circumstances behind this production's abandonment are similar to those which befell Alejandro Jodorowsky's *Dune*, namely a projected budget that skyrocketed as shooting until financing was withdrawn completely. In Zulawski's case, the change of guard in the Polish government was dispiriting enough for him to leave not only his incomplete film but his homeland as well.

below:
Isabelle Adjani in award-winning form; **Possession**.

chamber piece *Cérémonie d'amour* (*Rites of Love*, 1988) evokes the same mixture of dread and arousal, with prostitute Pierro physically and emotionally tormenting client Mathieu Carrière. Given the degrading quality of both erotic and fantastic cinema in the overseas markets, perhaps Borowczyk's absence after this film could be considered a regrettable but inevitable example of quitting the game while one is still ahead.

Sex, monsters and mystics

Like Borowczyk, the younger Andrzej Zulawski revels in beautiful actresses who draw audiences in through physical appearances and then twists their emotions in storylines most accurately be described as abrasive. While Borowczyk remains grounded to the similar dichotomies of Polish/French culture (such as refined settings, formally composed camerawork, and escalating emotions kept barely in check by social conventions), Zulawski's films widen the net to encompass a dizzying amalgamation of various European influences, from the schizoid geography and emotional angst of Berlin to the passionate, visually aggressive excesses of Italy. His first international breakthrough, *L'important c'est d'aimer* (*The Most Important Thing Is to Love*, 1975), assembles an international cast in a more perverse, heterosexualized rendition of Fassbinder's *Beware of a Holy Whore* (1971), as photographer Fabio Testi

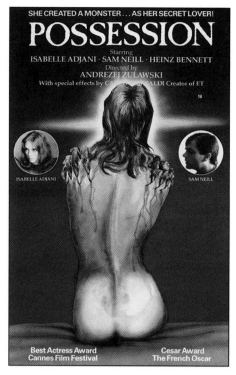

becomes torn between the worlds of art and pornography when he becomes the romantically inclined but reticent patron of sex actress Romy Schneider, who is surrounded by a colourful gallery of characters (including a memorable turn by Klaus Kinski). Offbeat, steamy, and stylish enough to grab critical attention, the film earned Zulawski positive notices but proved to be the harbinger of a lengthy hiatus caused by *Na srebrnym globie* (*The Silver Globe*), a fragmented science fiction project begun in 1977 (and more or less completed a decade later) that became derailed by the Polish government and led to Zulawski's self-imposed artistic exile.[7]

In 1981, Zulawski finally returned with a roar in the form of *Possession*, a divisive and uncompromising study of deteriorating human relationships cloaked in the guise of a bloody monster film. The marriage between Anna (Isabelle Adjani) and Mark (Sam Neill) disintegrates when he returns home to Berlin and finds that she has been unfaithful with Heinrich (Heinz Bennent), a boorish snob, as well as a third, unnamed lover she visits in a grungy flat. Mark begins an affair with Helen (also Adjani), his son's schoolteacher, who represents the most obvious example of repetitive doubling and echoing throughout the film. Driven insane by Anna's behaviour, Mark kills Heinrich by clubbing

the unreliable narrator

above: Isabelle Adjani and Sam Neill during the shattering climax of **Possession**.

and drowning him in a men's washroom, then discovers that the "other" lover is actually a mutating beast presumably borne from Anna's tortured psyche. Eventually the "flawed", human representations of Anna and Mark are gunned down on a vertiginous staircase while the monster, now transformed into Mark's indestructible and idealized double, ominously returns to the apartment to meet with Helen as the city collapses back into warfare outside and the son drowns himself in the bathtub.

As a surface text, *Possession* is deliberately confounding and repeatedly distances the audience with its violent, unrestrained performances and dizzying camerawork. Often the viewer must contemplate who is more insane, the actors or the director,[8] as numerous characters and plot points collide. Here narrative is turned inside out as the audience is dropped into the middle of a story and left to sort it all out; most of our information comes from what is told by Anna (not only an unreliable source but a self-mutilating and murderous psychopath) and what is uncovered by Mark, who proves to be equally dangerous halfway into the film. During one pivotal sequence, Mark sits and watches a homemade film (presumably shot by Heinrich) in which Anna sadistically pushes a ballet student past the point of endurance and then explains the circumstances behind her gruesome miscarriage in a metro station, the most audacious and physically repellent moment of the film. Here both Mark and the audience are granted a solid, cold look into Anna's mind, and what we see isn't pleasant. Earlier when Mark interrogates her about the reasons for her behaviour, she only nods positively when he asks whether she's upset "because I won't like you." Here the need for love versus sex and the inability to communicate this desire (a common thread in Zulawski's films[9]) is set in stark relief, and all of Anna and Mark's suffering for the ensuing running time brings them release only in the form of death after a final, bloody embrace.

The concept of a monstrous, semi-human entity intruding upon a bond between man and woman was revisited in Zulawski's long delayed return to Polish cinema, *Szamanka* (*The Shaman*, 1996). Rarely seen outside its native country, this erotic and unsettling essay on human desire is shot in the same austere, colour-coded style of *Possession*, but with a more suggestive and linear approach to its storyline. A young woman (Iwona Petry) commences a passionate, animalistic affair with an anthropology professor (Boguslaw

[8] In his invaluable commentary track on the U.S. DVD of the film, Zulawski explains that Adjani was emotionally shattered by the film and may have even attempted suicide after witnessing the final results. At least she received a Best Actress award at Cannes for both this and *Quartet* as compensation for undergoing a very stressful year.

[9] This theme erupts again full force in Zulawski's *La Fidélité* (2000), which stars Zulawski's long-term romantic partner, Sophie Marceau - who, perhaps not coincidentally, bears a striking resemblance to Ms. Adjani.

Poland

above:
French poster for Andrzej Zulawski's **Szamanka** (aka **The Shaman**).

Linda); in a parallel narrative, his discovery of the ancient body of a mystical shaman awakens latent facts of Petry's personality, triggering an inevitable descent into erotic mania. Though not overtly horrific, the film constantly flirts with the supernatural, teasing at the connections between sex, mysticism, and death, leaving most of its puzzles open to viewer interpretation.

The devil inside

Unquestionably the most commercially successful director to emerge from Poland, Roman Polanski shares with his fellow Polish directors a love for overturning genre conventions and disrupting traditional narrative patterns, though in a style distinctly his own. While directors like Zulawski and Borowczyk are known for keeping a safe aesthetic distance from their subjects, Polanski's most successful films instead offer easily accessible audience identification figures while allowing the uncanny incidents to escalate almost without notice.

In two of his earliest feature films, *Noz w wodzie* (*Knife in the Water*, 1962) and *Cul-de-sac* (1966), Polanski expertly depicts the dynamics of a married couple torn apart by infiltrating external male figures, but he achieved more shattering results with *Repulsion* (1965). His first foray into genuine horror stars Catherine Deneuve as a beauty salon employee whose sanity deteriorates over a period of days when she's left alone in the apartment she shares with her sister (Yvonne Furneaux). Her increasing dementia (symbolized by the decaying body of a rabbit intended for food) leads to a pair of murders and disturbing hallucinations involving intruders and groping hands thrusting from the walls. Though as beautiful as any of the women in the films discussed above, Deneuve is an entirely different presence here, a sympathetic but terrifying figure whose psychological destruction thoroughly undermines the viewer's sense of security. The final shot of her as a child, casting a terrified eye towards one of her older male relatives, offers only the flickering of a clue towards a mystery we know we will never be able to completely solve.

Critical and commercial indifference greeted Polanski's widely mistreated *The Fearless Vampire Killers* (1967), in which the established rules of vampire cinema are hurled aside, producing instead Jewish and homosexual bloodsuckers and a peculiar, chilling finale which finds the vampires (represented by Polanski's tragically murdered wife, Sharon Tate) victoriously overcoming the heroes (including Polanski himself as the neurotic Alfred) while they ride off into the snow. Polanski returned to *Repulsion* territory the next year with *Rosemary's Baby*, adapted from Ira Levin's best-selling novel, in which the desire to become pregnant proves to be a nightmarish experience for Rosemary Woodhouse (Mia Farrow), who grows to suspect that the eccentric neighbours in her brownstone apartment complex are actually devil worshippers with designs set on her expected child.

By confining his camera to Rosemary's point of view, Polanski never offers concrete reassurance that Rosemary is either right or wrong, at least until the nightmarish (but darkly comic) final minutes in which we learn that her suspicions have been correct all along. However, even here the supernatural is not rigidly reinforced; apart from a subliminal glimpse of the baby's sinister eyes and a druggy dream sequence, Polanski does not confirm the genuine existence of Satan via blatant special effects or gothic hocus pocus. In the grand tradition of producer Val Lewton, the entire experience could be the skewed perception caused by a troubled pregnancy or by the ruthless brainwashing engineered by the neighbours. Here, Satan is but an unseen supporting character in a drama whose implications are far more frightening for what it says about modern city dwelling, where one cannot trust the people next door and, even worse, perhaps not even one's own senses and consciousness.

These explorations of unstable protagonists reached their logical conclusion with Polanski's most neglected horror film, *The Tenant* (1976), the end product of a difficult decade which included Tate's murder by the Manson family, the chilly reception of the underrated *Macbeth* (1971) and *What?* (1973), and Polanski's comeback with his final American film, *Chinatown* (1974),[10] which was followed by his U.S. exile after charges of statutory rape. The film was shot in Paris, which has served as Polanski's home and favourite film locale after his voluntary flight from the American law, and in the tradition of 1970s European productions, the cast consists of an odd but striking array of international personalities for maximum box office potential. Polanski himself appears in the lead role of Trelkovsky, an even more jittery turn than Alfred in *The Fearless Vampire Killers* and a demanding performance, which would have intimidated most professional actors. Trelkovsky, an insecure Pole in Paris, rents an apartment despite the reservations of the concierge (Shelley Winters) and the building supervisor, Monsieur Zy (Melvyn Douglas). The sinister history of the apartment's previous resident, Simone Choule, involves a gruesome suicide attempt and the odd behaviour of the neighbours, who may have had a hand in her drastic road to self-destruction. Trelkovsky visits Simone (now lingering near death in a body cast) and meets the lovely, enigmatic Stella (Isabelle Adjani again), with whom he tremulously begins an unconsummated affair. Eventually Trelkovsky's insecurities devour him, possibly from the inside or due to his conspiratorial neighbours, and while decked out in drag, he hurls himself from his window - twice! - in a failed suicide attempt, only to relive the hospital visit from Simone's point of view during the horrific, time-bending final scene.

A more personal project than the similar *Rosemary's Baby*, *The Tenant* avoids the more literal resolution of Levin's narrative and instead becomes more mysterious and discomfiting as it progresses. The director's penchant for black humour and eccentric character roles proves to be a skilful match for the source novel, written by actor/writer Roland Topor.[11] The odd accumulation of details, such as the neighbours passively standing at bathroom windows all night long and the discovery of a dislodged human tooth imbedded into a wall, adds to the air of unease but only realizes its full horrific power after the film has concluded. Polanski also makes ingenious use of the Parisian locales, transforming the traditionally romantic city into a sinister, inhospitable den of schemers and lunatics.[12] As with *Repulsion* and *Rosemary's Baby*, the viewer remains trapped within the outsider protagonist's perspective even after any semblance of sanity has been lost for good; when the blood-smeared Polanski pathetically insists "I'm not Simone Choule!" as he clambers back up the stairs in high heels, the tragic horror of the situation overcomes the black comedy, becoming instead a chilling portrayal of cultural dislocation and the incipient madness which could reside within the most timid personalities. The outcome directly echoes *Repulsion* with a foreign "misfit" failing in a most spectacular manner to adapt to a major European city, but here the tragedy is magnified by having the protagonist go to pieces in the full, unforgiving public view of his neighbours rather than catatonically exiting a confining apartment in the hands of rescuers.

For the next two decades Polanski avoided any overtly supernatural or fantastic subject matter, though his perverse *Bitter Moon* (1992), an intricate narrative of a self-destructive marriage related aboard a cruise ship to an emotionally captive audience, feels thematically in step with his horror films. Its gruesome but tentatively hopeful denouement paved the way for *Death and the Maiden* (1994), an adaptation of the Ariel Dorfman play transformed into an anguished attempt to find solace after a life permanently scarred by violence. Both films involve a trapped listener (Hugh Grant in the former, Ben Kingsley in the latter) caught up in stories told by

10 The character of Jake Gittes (Jack Nicholson) in *Chinatown* shares some peripheral similarities with the other Polanski protagonists as he discovers that nothing he assumed about his surroundings or even himself may actually be true; however, the screenplay by Robert Towne spends most of its time deconstructing the *film noir* genre, somewhat diluting Polanski's artistic instincts but producing a fascinating hybrid all the same.

11 A unique figure in European cinema, Topor also wrote the animated cult favourite *Fantastic Planet* (1973) and appeared as Renfield in Werner Herzog's masterful remake of *Nosferatu* (1979), again with the omnipresent Adjani.

12 Polanski and co-scenarist Gérard Brach collaborated again after *The Tenant* for two more "evil Paris" stories, *Frantic* and *Bitter Moon*; this trilogy makes for an interesting progression of Polanski's treatment of the outsider cast adrift in the City of Lights.

unknown, original manuscript of "The Anjou Wine", a chapter from Alexandre Dumas's *The Three Musketeers*. The discovery sends the book hunter on a globe-hopping trip during which he encounters a variety of characters either reminiscent of Dumas's text or affiliated in a more sinister fashion with *The Nine Gates of the Kingdom of Shadows*, a legendary satanic volume now extant only in three copies. Each copy contains nine similar but slightly variant engravings, the work of the human author (a burned heretic named Aristide Torchia) and Lucifer himself.

During the adaptation process, Polanski and his co-writers eliminated the entire Dumas angle (necessitating the title change as well), condensing and shuffling characters to focus solely on the demonic angle of the story. However, the essential cast of characters is the same: Corso (Johnny Depp), urbane book collector Boris Balkan (Frank Langella), conniving widow Liana Telfor (Lena Olin), lonely Portuguese book collector Victor Fargas (Jack Taylor), and "the Girl" (Polanski's wife, Emmanuelle Seigner), a mysterious, omnipresent beauty revealed to be Satan in human form.[13] From its opening, a wordless sequence in which a prowling camera records a suicide by hanging, plunges directly into the musty volumes adorning a bookcase, and passes through a series of doors hovering in blackness during the opening credits, *The Ninth Gate* functions on many levels at once, all of them potentially deceptive. Our protagonist is immediately portrayed as a compromised, resourceful rascal as he swindles two naïve heirs out of a valuable four-book edition of *Don Quixote*. The literary choice here is no accident; Corso's quest finds him battling many invisible, possibly imaginary forces controlling his fate, and his flawed moral interior but lack of a true evil nature makes him an ideal candidate for seduction. The prosaic evildoing of Corso and Telfor prove to be unworthy amusements to the Girl, who takes a far greater interest in the book hunter's corruption.

Throughout his journey Corso is regaled with stories, beginning with Balkan's speech about the history of *The Nine Gates* and its author. As Balkan admits, even his own copy may be a forgery, and as Corso soon learns, no one should be trusted. However, unlike Polanski's previous subjects who implode or surrender when confronted by the inexplicable, Corso seems only slightly

[13] Balkan in the film is an amalgamation of two characters, his Dumas-reading namesake and the more nefarious Varo Borja. Additionally, Telfor's name in the novel is spelled Taillefer, and "the Girl" nicknames herself Irene Adler, a reference to the only woman who proved worthy enough to tempt Sherlock Holmes in Arthur Conan Doyle's "A Scandal in Bohemia."

possibly insane, suspect narrators (Peter Coyote and Sigourney Weaver). The damage done by the past more than haunts its victims; it consumes them and threatens to destroy any newcomers stepping into its path as well.

For his return to horror, Polanski constructed *The Ninth Gate* (1999) as a streamlined adaptation of Arturo Pérez-Reverte's gothic literary exercise, *El Club Dumas*. The original novel follows the arcane misadventures of Lucas Corso, "a mercenary of the book world", who hunts down rare volumes in the service of rich patrons who prefer to keep their hands clean. A recent suicide exposes a previously

ruffled by his bizarre circumstances; from a compromised and satanic viewpoint, the willingly seduced Corso could in fact be seen as Polanski's first genuine heroic figure in a horror film. "There's nothing more reliable than a man whose loyalty can be bought for hard cash", Balkan observes early in the film, and this potential for temptation makes him the ideal candidate to keep company with Lucifer/the Girl. In one of Polanski's typically fine comic touches, she appears in a hotel lobby reading a paperback copy of How to Win Friends and Influence People, an early tip-off to perceptive viewers about her true nature. Obviously the Girl has a direct hand in the events that transpire throughout the film, but Corso controls his own destiny and makes his own choices. When he finally causes one minor character's death late in the film, the Girl admiringly observes, "I didn't know you had it in you" as she watches the gruesome handiwork. Corso and the Girl also share a significant exchange about semantics in which Corso introduces himself and explains that his name means "run" in Italian, to which she responds, "You don't look like a runner." More aptly, his name also means "course", a meaning echoed when Corso points out the Girl's reading material and asks, "Is this part of your course?" The answer, naturally, is yes.

The wordplay turns up in a more subtle form when Corso meets Baroness Kessler (Barbara Jefford), who claims to have met the devil at an early age ("It was love at first sight") and is now missing part of her left arm. When Corso later insults the Girl in a hotel lobby and accuses her (incorrectly) of stealing a book, she snaps his left arm behind his back to keep him in line. We return again to the issue of translations; in Latin and Italian, the left side of the body is considered to be the corrupt, fallible, and sinister half of the human form, evidenced most directly in the Italian word for "left", "sinistre." The notion of sinister or corrupt influence crops up repeatedly throughout the film, from the three tainted copies of the book (whose illustrations can only be assembled with a missing ninth drawing to become "pure") to Corso's broken spectacles and christening by blood which signify his shift in perception towards a greater allegiance to Satan.

The similarities are striking when looking at The Ninth Gate and its closest companion piece, The Saragossa Manuscript, even beyond the superficially identical subject matter of satanic literary gamesmanship and diabolical secrets concealed in Spain. The widescreen compositions for both films are usually flooded with light, but instead of providing illumination, light here obscures and confuses, allowing the devil to perform trickery in plain view without being noticed. Both films conclude "romantically" with the hero, now converted, retreating from the camera in a burst of bright light towards a decaying, rocky structure to fulfil his destiny and join the forces of darkness. These finales feel both triumphant and enigmatic; a shocking reversal for many viewers who complain that such a resolution is unsatisfying or confused.[14] Our guide through these stories, the rapt audience identification figure who has gone through fire and been transformed by the process, decided to go down the darker road, and ultimately the viewer must decide whether that path is worth following. In fact, there is no other way either film could end. The stories are long, deceptive dances between the devil and the unconverted soul, love stories of the darkest and most dangerous kind.

[14] Perhaps due to Artisan's misconceived heavy metal ad campaign in the U.S., most critics made no attempt to read the film as anything more than another demonic thriller in the vein of such time wasters as End of Days, Lost Souls or Stigmata, all released between the summer of 1999 and the early months of 2000. Even the normally astute Roger Ebert somehow failed to grasp the basics of The Ninth Gate's storyline: "If some of the engravings were indeed drawn by Satan, and if assembling them can evoke the Prince of Darkness, then that would be a threat, right? Or would it be a promise? And what happens at the end - that would be an unspeakably evil outcome, right? But why does it look somehow like a victory? And as for the woman - good or bad? Friend or foe? You tell me" (The Chicago Sun-Times 03 Mar. 2000, local ed.: M6).

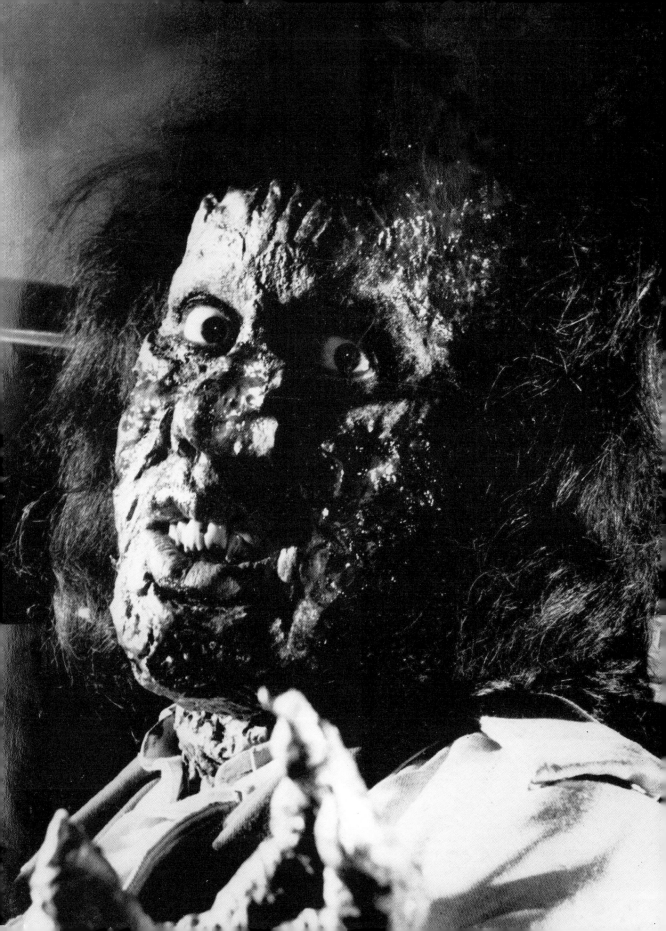

genre histories and studies

The Beast From Bollywood: a history of the Indian horror film

Pete Tombs

The Indian film industry is the biggest in the world. Although production has fallen recently, its output still exceeds 650 full-length features per year. TV set ownership is nowhere near as high as in Europe and the US and cinema is still the main form of entertainment. Every day more than 23 million people go to see films in India. A major hit might be seen by the same people more than a dozen times. Most of these films are two and a half hour marathons, chock full of action, comedy, glamour and music. Pure escapism for an audience looking for a brief respite from the harsh realities of life in a very tough world.

For a star-studded, super production, budgets of Indian movies can match those of Hollywood. However, like all industries, the Indian film business has its bottom feeders. Low budget exploitation movies are a staple product. Popular with the urban poor and in rural areas, these movies feature a higher level of sex and violence than most mainstream releases. Although heavily censored, they are often later loaded with illegal inserts for exhibition in cinemas far from the prying eyes of the authorities.

Some strange plants flower in this steamy hot house of commercial cinema. Threadbare superhero films, jungle epics featuring busty Lady Tarzans in leopard skin bikinis, "curry westerns", violent police dramas and sleazy sex films are all grist to its mill. But maybe the strangest outgrowth of India's poverty row production line was its brief horror boom of the mid 1980s. Indian horror films have all the thrills and chills, guts and gore that we expect in the west; but they have that added something we don't: songs and choreographed dance numbers.

This so-called "Masala" style of moviemaking is the dominant model in the Indian subcontinent. Western audiences, unaccustomed to such a mixture, find these constant shifts of mood a distraction. However, it is worth bearing in mind that at one time even Hollywood movies were like this, with featured dance numbers in crime movies and comic foils popping up in horror flicks. The difference is that in India this "something for everyone" approach has survived while in the West films have developed along genre lines, aimed at specialised audiences.

In India, a film has to at least *attempt* to appeal to everyone. It's a tricky business; one that producers get wrong as often as they get it right. The industry abounds with tales of huge budget mega movies that were resounding flops. One result of this search for the perfect formula is that Indian movies tend to come in waves. When a comedy is a big hit, everyone will try to make comedies, when a love story sets the box office alight, the screens will be awash with romance and so on. It was in this spirit that the horror boom was born. In India, however, the term horror denotes something very specific.

From myths to monsters

Indian cinema has always had a place for mythical monsters and fantastic tales. Although full of scenes of violence and terrifying demons, these stories are part of Indian culture and everyone is familiar with them from childhood. Horror is seen as very much an imported and rather exotic affair. There had been occasional one-off's (for example the 1967 Pakistani film *Zinda Laash*, which was a version of Hammer's

opposite:
Kiran Kumar under heaps of make-up stars as the monster in **Wohi Bhayaanak Raat**.

Dracula), but horror was more or less unknown in Indian cinema before the 1970s. It was the worldwide success of William Friedkin's *The Exorcist* (1973) that sparked the interest of India's movie moguls.

Today, horror movies in India are almost exclusively low budget affairs. There have been few successful star cast horrors. However, in the late 1970s, several mainstream movie makers ventured into the horror field with decidedly mixed results. Raveekant Naigach's *Jadu Tona* (1977) was one of the first of these *Exorcist* clones. Here a man takes revenge on a business rival when his young daughter is possessed by an evil spirit. The film features all the head rolling, vomiting, strange voices and so on, familiar from the original. These kinds of scenes have since become staples of Indian horror movies, tossed randomly into the mix like herbs into the cooking pot.

A couple of years later, in 1979, Rajkumar Kohli directed *Jaani Dushman*, which opens with a scene of pure horror where a man, excited by the sight of a young bride, turns into a hairy, wild eyed monster with long extendible arms. For a few brief minutes all the tricks of the cinematographers trade are employed to create fear and a sense of disorientation: distorting lenses, tilted "Dutch" camera angles, wind machines and an ear-punishing soundtrack of cackling laughter.

The slightly more sober *Gehrayee*, released in 1980, was another *Exorcist* clone. Here a young girl's possession is first of all treated with electro-shock therapy until traditional tantric magic saves the day.

All these films suffered badly from censorship. Both *Jadu Tona* and *Jaani Dushman* were banned by the Government. This served as something of a warning to mainstream producers that they should stay away from such troublesome subject matter. The Indian censor, with a brief to protect filmgoers from explicit sex and Western ideas, would obviously find horror a cause for concern. That was one reason for using *The Exorcist* as a model. The film's story seemed tailor made for Indian tastes. The brave priest fighting an evil, multifaceted demon for the soul of a child was something that resonated with Indian sensibilities. Werewolves, vampires and reanimated corpses, staples of the Western horror film, had never had any place in Indian mythology or in Indian cinemas. Not until the Ramsay Brothers arrived on the scene...

Tulsi and Shyam Ramsay are now recognised as the crowned kings of Indian horror. For thirty years they've ruled the roost. Back in the early 1970s they were just a couple of young guys starting out in the family business. That business happened to be moviemaking.

It is an important aspect of Indian cinema - in fact of Indian business generally - that it is a family run concern. The notion of filmmakers as creative artists seized by the burning need to express their ideas on celluloid is pretty much an alien concept. Movies in India are constructed on the assembly line principal, with different chunks of the film being made separately and the whole thing merged together by a nominal "director." For example, the music is handled by a music director, the dance sequences by a dance master and the fights by an action or "thrills" specialist. The top creators in their field are much in demand, and work on many different productions at the same time. Great originality of concept or execution is not highly valued. A good story with all the right human elements, a star-studded cast and a hit song or two - those are the ingredients that make for movie success in India.

The Ramsay family's involvement in the business began with their father, F.U. Ramsay. He had been a radio manufacturer in Karachi, now in Pakistan. In 1947, following partition of the country, F.U. and family moved to Bombay. In the 1950s the movie business exploded and Bombay was one of the main centres of production. Money, much of it laundered from tax evasion, was flooding into the entertainment industry. Like many other businessmen, F.U. Ramsay viewed show-business as an exciting and effective way to turn a swift profit.

Film is always a risky affair, and the Ramsays had their ups and downs. By the beginning of the 1970s they were feeling the pinch. It was a tough time for the country generally. Political unrest, sectarianism and war with Pakistan were creating a climate of uncertainty that eventually led to the declaration of a national state of emergency in 1975. Cinema was reflecting this mood, with violence, bad language and plot lines featuring previously unthinkable subject matter. Such movies were able to get away with non-star casts and low, low budgets due to their exploitable titles and controversial content.

In 1970, against this background, the Ramsays released *Ek Nanni Munni Ladhki Thi*, a bittersweet drama about a failed

the beast from Bollywood

father who sinks to crime and the daughter who never stops loving him. The film was written and directed by the prestigious, but perhaps past his best, Vishram Bedekar, and three of F.U. Ramsay's seven sons worked on it as assistants.

The film was not a hit and it looked like there were hard times ahead for the family. However while visiting screenings to gauge audience reaction, Ramsay senior noticed an interesting phenomenon. There was one rather minor sequence near the beginning of the film that had audiences glued to the screen. Generally in Indian movie theatres there is quite a lot of moving about, talking and general hubbub. It is only during the songs or in sexy dances that the audience is gripped 100%. The sequence in question was neither of these. The setting was a museum in the middle of the night. A startled cat watches as a mysterious shadow emerges from behind a tree and makes its way towards the locked building. We see the black robed figure glide through the silent corridors of the museum and smash open a glass display case, carrying off the jewelled trophy inside. An alarm is triggered and soon the place is swarming with cops. A clawed hand pulls a power switch, plunging the place into darkness. Torches cut through the gloom. A beam of light picks out a hideous, gargoyle-like face. Suddenly it comes to life and a terrifying creature marches down the museum's grand staircase, impervious to the bullets of the police. They scatter in panic at the sight of this apparently deathless monster.

Of course it is all a scam. The "monster" is actually a clever thief wearing a mask and a bulletproof jacket. Unfortunately, the power of these opening moments is such that the film never really recovers. Audiences went crazy for this sequence, but many of them left after the film's interval when it became obvious that the monster was not going to return.

F.U. Ramsay began to work on a plan to recoup the money he had lost in the movie. If audiences were so keen on this kind of thing, he mused, why not exploit this fact. Make a film with more such sequences. At least five or six of them. In other words, a real, out-and-out horror film.

The result was *Do Gaz Zameen ke Neeche*, written by Kumar Ramsay and directed by the novice pair Tulsi and Shyam Ramsay. The story tells of a murdered man being revived by a chemical accident and coming back to exact his revenge. Like many pioneering works it was not necessarily the best of its kind, but it was effectively the first of its kind. It was also a hit. Consequently it set several precedents that Indian horror films have followed ever since. Firstly, that horror movies are generally low budget affairs. Secondly, that they follow Western models very closely with the "Indian" elements more or less grafted onto a generic plot. Thirdly, that the exploitable elements of horror make it unnecessary to have either great music or star casts; and finally, that they will be most popular with rural audiences and the urban poor and treated as rather a joke by everyone else.

These rules have held fast pretty much up to the present day. Filmmakers who have chosen to ignore them have done so at their peril. Subtlety and originality are not the order of the day here. Indian audiences expect their horror to be direct and upfront. The films must have a monster and the monster must look gruesome. Filmmakers talk about the

above:
Maa Ki Shakti
(aka **Ammoru**).

India

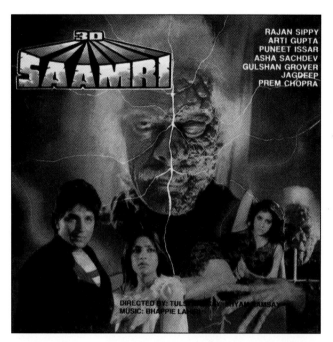

above:
Saamri (1985) was the Ramsay Brothers' follow-up to their smash-hit horror sensation **Purana Mandir** (1984).

concept of a "horror face", meaning that the evil within the creature must be outwardly visible. Due to the lack of special effects available until quite recently, this generally meant that the monster looked like it had a three-day-old pizza stuck to its face. Fangs would have to be real whoppers, at least four or five inches in length, and the monster must always be a lumbering giant. Certain big stunt guys got a lot of work in the late 1980s, when the monster movie vogue was in full flight. An infamous six foot tall Bombay gangster, recently shot by police, revelled in his nickname of "Purana Mandir", taken from the time, 20 years before, when he had featured in the Ramsay Brothers movie of that title, playing a monster.

For the next twenty years, from 1971 to 1991, the Ramsay family concentrated almost exclusively on horror. The basic format remained the same, but they learned how to tweak the component parts just enough to make it work each time. Tulsi and Shyam directed most of the productions (Tulsi on the technical side, Shyam working with the actors), while Kumar Ramsay scripted, Kiran Ramsay was responsible for the sound and Gangu Ramsay the camera. Simple special effects were introduced, largely through stop motion, and Tulsi learned how to create the horror make up that was so essential to Indian genre pics. Over the years they built up an impressive collection of masks, carved idols and stuffed animal heads that

popped up in film after film, giving their work much richer production values that their later rivals. They also acquired a stock company of character actors and comedians who knew exactly what was required of them, and were able to deliver it to order. These factors gave the Ramsays the ability to produce their film quickly and on low budgets which helped contribute to their pre-eminence in the field.

The industry magazines as well as the general public began to notice their names on successive banners and they became a kind of trademark. People talked about "the famous Ramsay touch." For the production line approach of Indian cinema it was perfect: the Ramsays now had their own designer label...

Landmarks in their long filmography include *Aur Kaun?* (1979), which features a female monster, *Ghunghroo Ki Awaz* (1981), a moody ghost story, and *Hotel* (1981), a spectacularly over-the-top precursor of *Poltergeist* (1982), where a hotel is constructed on the site of an old graveyard, causing the angry dead to rise and take their vengeance.

Then in 1984, came the film that really kicked off the Indian horror boom: *Purana Mandir*. The film was a massive success, breaking records at several Bombay cinemas. No Ramsay Brothers film since has been able to match it.

The story, told through flashbacks, concerns a curse visited on female members of a rich middle class family. The family are descended from a line of Rajas who centuries before incurred the wrath of an evil tantric magician. All female members of the family die during childbirth and the current paterfamilias is determined to prevent his daughter marrying so that the curse, and by extension, the family, can be ended.

There were a variety of reasons for the film's success. For one thing, the Ramsays had honed their craft to perfection by this time. They knew exactly how and when to pile on the pressure, when to let up with a comedy interlude and how to keep the audience on the boil with little hints of what was to come. But it was the all-important story here that held the audience's attention. The idea of a young girl unable to have sex and her search for release was one that interested both male and female alike and resonated in all kinds of ways with their experience as young people growing up in 80s India.

At that time, the film business in India was going through one of its cyclical

the beast from Bollywood

periods of uncertainty. Producers, desperate for something to grab hold of, saw the success of *Purana Mandir* as a sign that horror was finally acceptable. Within months, rival productions were being mounted to cash in on the public interest. The Ramsays themselves delivered a kind of sequel, *Saamri* (1985), which had the added gimmick of being shot in 3-D. They also diversified, trying political dramas in *Telephone* (1985) and action/adventure in *Tarkhana* (1986) while Keshu came up with the horror comedy *Khoj* (1989). Their next real innovation, however, was the 1985 production *Veerana* (released in 1988).

Indian horror movies have always taken a strong lead from the West. With the rise of video in the early 1980s, it became possible to see a wider range of Western productions than had previously been possible. *Veerana* was a direct result of this. Its initial inspiration was the 1974 British production *Vampyres*, directed by Spanish-born José Ramon Larraz. Larraz's film tells of a pair of hitchhiking female bloodsuckers who lure passing motorists to their death in an abandoned manor house. The film is as much a sex film as a horror film and was remarkable in its day for the amount of sin and skin that Larraz managed to sneak past the UK censor. *Veerana* takes the same basic plot, but with only one sexy vampire who, it transpires, is possessed by the spirit of an evil witch.

The film is notable for its excessive production design and some very effective make-up, but above all for its numerous sexy scenes, strong even by Ramsay Brothers standards. Other nods to Western horror include an homage to Dario Argento's *Suspiria* (1977), and a direct lift from John Carpenter's *The Thing* (1982).

By the end of the decade the Ramsays were releasing a new movie every six months, and in 1989 it rose to four films a year. To maintain this level of production, other members of the family were venturing into the director's chair. Highlights from this period include Keshu's *Dak Bangla* (1987) and Kiran's *Shaitaani Illaka* (1990).

However, it was back to the familiar Tulsi/Shyam duo for their final film of the 80s, and one of their best. *Bandh Darwaza*, released in 1990, was the Ramsay's version of the Dracula story. Following on from *Veerana*, it features a fair number of sexy scenes and a libidinous king vampire who rises from some very seminal looking slime to do his dirty deeds. Although it was one of their most effective productions, and benefited from a great central performance and gruesome special effects, the film performed only moderately. The problem was not the production itself, but the fact that the market had changed.

In the years since *Purana Mandir* had been a big hit, horror had really come into its own in India. As we have already seen, there had been some big budget attempts to mount horror movies in the late 1970s. However it was the low budget Ramsay format that had been successful and had been most closely imitated in the 1980s. Get a bunch of teens, trap them in a spooky old mansion or empty temple and bring on the ugly monster. A hint of sex, a bunch of songs and a teasing dance number would keep things on the boil. Then finally the evil would be laid to rest in a blaze of fire effects occasioned by the use of the Indian equivalents of the crucifix and holy water: the ancient AUM symbol and the trident of Shiva, the mythical destroyer of the Hindu pantheon.

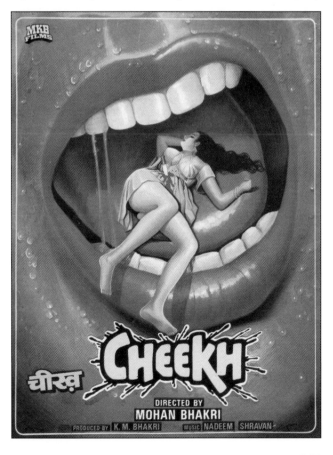

below:
Low-budget producer Mohan Bhakri competed with the big-budget Bollywood horrors by boosting the sex and violence quota in wild Hindi films such as **Cheekh** (1985).

India

right:
More low-budget thrills from Mohan Bhakri in the Westernised shape of **Padosi ki Biwi**.

Variations on this simple formula had been worked by a host of opportunistic producers over the final years of the 1980s. Some were better than others, but all were designed to fill a niche. In India the distributor is king. The country is divided up into six territories, and films are presold for an agreed "minimum guarantee" to each territory. Producers have to produce films that the distributors want to see. Suddenly distributors were asking for horror and were prepared to pay for it. So, naturally enough, horror was what they were given. Almost every month a new horror title was announced Most of these were one-offs, helmed by journeyman directors who would have been as happy in comedy or romance. Some were more interesting, however, and there were even a couple of horror specialists whose success occasionally rivalled that of the Ramsays.

One of the uniting factors with several of the post-Ramsay horror directors is that they had a background in regional filmmaking. These are films made often outside Bombay, and in languages other than Hindi. There are government grants available for the producers of these films, and it is generally a safe bet as they have a guaranteed audience and limited competition from the big producers. Mohan Bhakri, for example, began his career as a maker of films in the Punjabi language back in the 1970s. They were light musical comedies and were extremely successful. By the early 1980s, however, the market for Punjabi films was a difficult one. The state was riven by political violence, and Bhakri looked to the larger Hindi language market for his survival. Aware that he could not compete with the big Bollywood super productions, he decided to give the audience something that they weren't getting from those more conservative crowd pleasers: in other words, sex and violence. His first few Hindi films did just that. *Aparadhi Kaun?* (1982), *Cheekh* (1985) and *Padosi ki Biwi* (1987) were very effective low budget thrillers with several bizarre moments often inspired by Western films. Bhakri is a big movie fan, and his sources are delightfully obscure. For example, *Cheekh* has several scenes inspired by the kinky Curtis Harrington shocker, *Games* (1967).

Sex is another constant element in Bhakri's productions. However he always lightens the tone with healthy doses of comedy, thus avoiding the charge of vulgarity that so often plagues India's low budget mavericks. His earlier films had touched on horror but, following the success of *Purana Mandir*, Bhakri raised the finance for an out-and-out monster movie - *Khooni Mahal* - which was released in 1987 and became his biggest-ever hit. The story is a familiar one. It is the same "bunch of teens in an old manor house chased by a monster" plot that had been used in India dozens of time already. However, it is Bhakri's skilful re-jigging of the basic elements, and his understanding of how to build and maintain tension, that makes the film a standout.

His next film, *Kabrastan* (1988) was another variation on a Western theme. This time it was the Frankenstein story, with a demented doctor who collects body parts from the local graveyard. Here Bhakri tried to limit the risible effects of cheap monster make-up by shooting many scenes from the point of view of the creature. Unfortunately, this only served to confuse the audience, who were never entirely clear what was going on. Another difficult element was the story's setting in a Christian community. The Ramsay Brothers' earlier *Hotel* had used a similar background, and for the same reasons - a reason that highlights one of the difficulties facing Hindi horror filmmakers. Indian custom demands that dead bodies be cremated. This creates a decided problem for a genre of horror that often relies on lumbering, reanimated

the beast from Bollywood

corpses. (That goes some way towards explaining the limited number of vampire films made in India. Coffins for the undead to rise from would be in rather short supply.)

After the experiment of *Kabrastan*, Bhakri returned to the tried and true with *Khooni Murdaa* (1989), a film influenced by the *Nightmare on Elm Street* series in America. The film benefits from a strong performance by veteran bad-guy actor Kiran Kumar. However, it treads a rather over-familiar path. As though to compensate, Bhakri really pulled out all the stops on his next horror project, *Roohani Taaqat* (1991).

The film was produced by a top Punjabi singing star who intended it as a showcase for his talents. Bhakri tried to warn him that a gory horror movie might not be quite the right vehicle for this but, aware of Bhakri's success in the field, the man insisted. The budget was low, which only served to bring to the fore Bhakri's ingenuity and willingness to experiment. *Roohani Taaqat* has many horror sequences and was an ordeal to shoot, but none were more troublesome than the one that shows a skeleton being reanimated by demonic forces. This scene begins with a heart inside the rib cage suddenly pulsing into life. Bhakri set up an elaborate pump system to simulate the beating of the organ. First he tried a goat's heart, but decided that it looked too puny. His assistant then procured a larger water buffalo heart. That was fine until a

above:
More gore from Mohan Bhakri in the special-effects bonanza **Roohani Taaqat** (1991).

passing dog took a fancy to it and ran off with the succulent organ just as they were about to start filming...

Following Bhakri's success, several other refugees from the Punjabi filmmaking community started to look at horror as a possible way into the mainstream. One of the most interesting was Vinod Talwar. Although twenty years younger than Bhakri, he brought to the genre a stronger sense of traditional Indian storytelling, and was less influenced by Western movies and more by comic book imagery.

Again he flirted with horror in his early productions before finally venturing into the world of the supernatural. *Wohi Bhayaanak Raat* (1989) is one of the rare Indian vampire movies. Loosely inspired by Tom Holland's *Fright Night* (1985), it tells of a young student who becomes convinced that his next-door neighbour is a vampire. Kiran Kumar, a versatile character actor who had come to specialise in villains, is very effective as the demonic bloodsucker. The film's most startling sequence occurs when Kumar abducts a young dancer. Stripping her

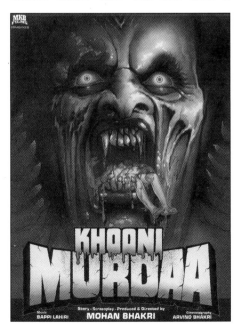

left:
Khooni Murdaa (1989) was influenced by the **Nightmare on Elm Street** series.

above:
Wohi Bhayaanak Raat (1989) was loosely inspired by **Fright Night** (1985).

below:
Vampire horror in **Hatyarin** (1991).

down to her red bikini, he gags her, ties her up and drags her off to his lair. For Hindi horror this was a shocking scene. Astonishingly the censor didn't demand that it be cut.

The film was ambitious, but its limited budget was a source of frustration to Talwar. The lack of special effects meant too many compromises. Many of his ideas had to be abandoned or improvised more or less on the spot. This problem-solving facility was tested to the full by several sequences in his next production, *Hatyarin* (1991). Here the vampire is a beautiful woman, in thrall to an evil tantric magician. She is forced to bring him a certain number of virgin brides to satiate his bloodlust. The horror sequences involve opening graves, animated trees and flying corpses. With no money for expensive computer work, all this had to be done through camerawork, taking us right back to the dawn of special effects and such cinematic pioneers as Georges Méliès. The final climactic battle between good and evil is another *tour de force* of no-budget ingenuity. Many of the scenes had to be acted in reverse, for example, so as to simulate the effect of creeping vines and flying magical ropes. It is to Talwar's credit that these scenes come across as animated comic book panels, versions of the popular poster art so prevalent in India.

By the end of the 1980s, Indian screens were awash with horror. Distributors who had previously been paying a premium price for the films now lowered their offers. Films were being made

the beast from Bollywood

on a budget less than that of a student film in the West. Attracted by the label of "horror", and with little or no interest in the genre, producers were throwing together an ugly faced monster, a few lightning flashes and a bikini clad "scream queen", and calling it a film. Stories were either non-existent or else were lightly "Indianised" versions of Western hits. All the many weaknesses of Indian production methods were magnified in these unlovely and unloved pieces of celluloid.

Filmmakers like the Ramsays, Mohan Bhakri and Vinod Talwar who take their craft seriously soon realised that they would never be able to deliver a professional product for the money that was being offered to them. The Ramsays diversified into children's films (*Ajooba Kudrat Ka*, 1991), crime thrillers (*Inspector Danush*, 1992) and television (*The Zee Horror Show*, 1993 onwards); Mohan Bhakri opened a digital post-production house; and Vinod Talwar moved into family films with *Phool Bani Patthar* (1996).

Horror occupies a difficult place in the Indian film world. A major problem is budget. There just isn't the money available to mount an ambitious production with the kinds of special effects that audiences in the West are used to. One way to increase the budget is to have big stars that draw in audiences. However, big stars do not appear in horror movies, as they think it will alienate their fans. And so there is a circular and self-defeating argument.

The final nail in the coffin for Indian horror came at the dawn of the 90s, with two films that attempted to break the vicious circle of low budget and low ambitions. *Junoon*, directed by Bollywood big shot Mahesh Batt, and *Raat*, from a brash newcomer, Ramgopal Varma, were both released in 1992. Both were flops. *Raat* in particular was criticised for its attempts to rewrite the rulebook on Indian horror movies. Songless, and featuring an abstract soundtrack of electronic noise, the film was a brave attempt to introduce a

above:
Ramgopal Varma's **Raat** (1992).

below:
Vinod Talwar's **Hatyarin** (1991).

above:
Ramgopal Varma's return to the horror genre, **Kaun?** was released in 1999.

In the traditional and less ambitious vein, there has in recent years been a mini-revival of Indian horror films. Young directors and producers, many of them trained in India's burgeoning TV industry, have turned once more to horror as a convenient calling card for their feature film debuts. The last couple of years have seen a proliferation of titles such as *Chudail No. 1* (1999), *The Eyes* (1998), *Murdaa Ghar* (1999), *Ab Kya Hoga* (2001) and *Bhayanaak Raatein* (1999). Alongside old hands such as Kiran Kumar, new starlets like Poonam Dasgupta have popped up to fill the breach left by the departure of 80s scream queens Jamuna and Jasmine. Not content with drawing on Western models, this recent batch of exploitation movies even cannibalises its own heritage. *Murdaa Ghar*, for example, is a shameless copy of Mohan Bhakri's *Khooni Murdaa* that also includes nods to American "neo-stalker" films such as *Scream* (1996) and *I Know What You Did Last Summer* (1997). The new version of *Saamri* (1998) hints at a revival of the Ramsays' 3-D experiment, and *Kabrastan ke Peeche* (2000) uses the Christian background and iconography of both *Kabrastan* and *Hotel*.

The clutzy comics, the bikini-clad vamps, the porridge-faced monsters; all the elements of Hindi horror are alive and well in these cheapo quickies. Budgets however are even lower now than in the bad old days of the early 90s. Quite a few of these films are shot on 16mm and blown up to 35mm for theatrical release. Some have even been shot on Digital video. Special effects are non-existent, and make-up often consists of a joke-shop rubber mask or a pair of plastic fangs. Against this background, it is hard to see how horror will ever be taken seriously in India. But perhaps that is the point. Maybe it never can be.

So who is to blame for this sad state of affairs? Is it the fault of Indian filmmakers, who reduced horror to its few exploitable elements and then continued to exploit them until the barrel ran dry? Or maybe it was the distributors, who offered lower and lower prices. Or perhaps one can blame the audiences themselves, who seem unable to distinguish between trash like *Khooni Dracula* (1992) and a treat like *Raat*.

new style of filmmaking. Unfortunately, when it comes to horror, Indian audiences have no interest in novelty. Indian horror films appeal on a very basic level to an audience who seem to relish the cheap thrills that they dole out. Varma had aimed his film at the urban middle class. Unfortunately, these are exactly the sort of people who refuse to attend Indian horror films to begin with.

A few years later, Varma, who had written, produced and directed *Raat*, went on to fame and fortune with the musical comedy *Rangeela*, the biggest hit of 1995. Buoyed by this success, he returned to horror in 1999 with *Kaun?*, another songless and serious drama. Although it was not a huge hit, the film performed respectably and received festival screenings abroad. Varma's enthusiasm for horror, which he has expressed eloquently in interviews, marks him as something of a unique figure in the Indian film business. The gauntlet he has thrown down, with his low-key and sophisticated approach to horror, has not been picked up by others.

The problem in many ways lies with the term "horror" itself. In India, the word carries so much baggage. To bring up the subject in film circles is almost the same as announcing that you are a half-wit. It just isn't taken seriously. It conjures up images

the beast from Bollywood

of bad acting, lumpy faced monsters, wind machines, and the producer's girlfriend in a bikini. It is the equivalent of the term "Z movie", and carries all the same negative connotations.

"A single thread in a complex tapestry"

To give this argument some perspective, let us go to the other end of the spectrum and take a look at the 1996 movie, *Ammoru* (aka *Maa Ki Shakti*). This Hyderabad-based production, directed by Kodi Ramakrishna and produced by Shyam Prasad Reddy, was the most expensive Telegu language film ever made, and was a hit immediately upon release. The story tells of a simple village girl who falls foul of a black magician who also happens to belong to a family of local landowners. She witnesses him murdering a girl during a magical rite and tells the police. He is arrested and sent to prison. On his release he sets out to ruin the woman's life using his evil powers. This culminates in the death by drowning of the woman's young daughter and the imprisonment and humiliation of her husband.

Just as the woman too is about to become a victim of the evil magician, she calls out in desperation to the village deity. The stone idol comes to life in the guise of Kali, the blue-skinned goddess of death. This terrifying, multi-limbed vision engages in a magical battle with the magician, which ends with her slicing off his head in graphic, blood-spurting detail and then incinerating his corpse. This climax to the film, using excellent digital effects created by Digitalia in London, is one of the best-ever uses of CGI imagery in an Indian film. Gruesome and graphic, it is also highly stylised, like a temple painting come to life.

To explain the film's success, the trade papers had to create a new genre: "mythological/social" is what they called it. But in any other context, it would be horror. And that is the nub of the problem for Indian filmmakers. When asked, they will tell you that there is no tradition of horror in India as there is in Europe and the US, and that is why they draw so much on Western models for inspiration and storylines. In many ways, they are right. India has nurtured no Edgar Allan Poes or Stephen Kings. However, horror is certainly there in the Indian consciousness; it is just sublimated, integrated, one flavor amongst many others, a single thread in a complex tapestry.

Horror, for most Western audiences today, is very much something "out there",

something alien and exotic. It touches on distant folk memories and stories that we only half-remember from childhood. In India, by contrast, it is much harder to exploit those kinds of images precisely because they aren't hidden or lost. They are still very much present in the public's mind as living, contemporary ideas.

In search of something exotic, Indian filmmakers have turned to the West and drawn on our images of horror. Unfortunately it doesn't seem to have worked. It is like trying to dress up as your next door neighbour by taking the clothes left outside for the charity collection. In exactly that way, most Indian horror seems second-hand, threadbare and sadly lacking in contemporary gloss or cultural depth. The truth of the matter is that horror will only really work in Indian movies when it draws on Indian tradition. And maybe that can only happen when that tradition ceases to have meaning, when it becomes almost irrelevant. When it becomes, like folk tales in the West, a distant and exotic memory that requires the stimulus of cinema to bring it back to life.

below:
Contemporary Indian horror, **Ab Kya Hoga** (2001).

In a climate of terror: the Filipino monster movie

Mauro Feria Tumbocon, Jr.

In his 1986 magazine essay, "Where Has All the Horror Gone?", Filipino film critic and scholar Joel David decries the "...scarcity of genuine horror items in contemporary local cinema."[1] He goes on to argue that the sad state of the horror genre exemplifies what has been a general lack of interest in Filipino cinema as a whole.

At the same time that he places the burden on the moviegoer's lack of patronage as the reason for the decline in production, David opines that this period - the 1980s - marks a significant shift from previous decades, notably the 60s which saw a flowering of Filipino horror. However, a tentative survey of Philippine film output from 1927 to 1994 reveals a more or less consistent number of horror movies produced, namely one to two percent of the annual output.[2] No year or decade can claim a significantly greater percentage than any other. This means that over time, Philippine interest in the gothic and in horror has not necessarily diminished.

More than the number and quality of the products, at issue here is the paucity of scholarship on the genre. Except for the short essay by David referred to above, a chapter in Pete Tombs's now-classic *Mondo Macabro*[3] and lengthy reviews of a few films - in particular Mike de Leon's *Itim* (*Black*, aka *The Rites of May*, 1976) and Antonio Jose Perez's *Haplos* (*Caress*, 1982) - there has been little serious inquiry into Philippine horror, either at the formal or thematic levels (though recently Bliss Lim has worked to rectify this situation[4]). Despite the paucity of film prints and video copies currently available, this essay marks a modest attempt to provide a thorough examination of the Filipino horror movie. This is not only to take notice of its formal attributes and the various technical innovations generated through the years, but also to acknowledge the genre's role in reflecting on the national condition; to show that horror in Philippine cinema is as worthy of investigation as the realistic melodrama or the action movie.

Modes of horror in Filipino cinema

Film was introduced in the Philippines at the close of 19th century, but it took another decade for Filipino entrepreneurs to see its potential as a viable business enterprise and begin producing their own movies, notably Jose Nepomuceno - widely considered the Father of Philippine film - with his first feature, *Dalagang Bukid* (*Country Maiden*, 1919). A few silent horror movies were produced during this period: Malayan Movies' *Ang Manananggal* (*The Viscera Sucking Witch*, 1927), *Ang Multo sa Libingan* (*The Ghost in the Cemetery*, 1931), *Mang Tano, Nuno ng mga Aswang* (*Mr. Tano, the Elder of the Witches*, 1932) and *Tianak* (*The Child Monster*, 1932).

Synchronised sound made its auspicious beginning with a horror film, Manila Talkatone's *Ang Aswang* (*The Witch*, 1933), a development which suggests that any technological change in the industry lends itself to the formal dictates of the genre. In the succeeding years, one observes that improvements in other areas of Philippine cinema - sound and film editing, cinematography and design (including make-up, prosthetics and later computer graphics and animation) - all succeed in enhancing the look of the horror film, resulting in a more serious appreciation of the form.

[1] Joel David, "The National Pastime." *Contemporary Philippine Cinema*. Manila: Anvil Publishing, 1990.

[2] Rolfie L. Velasco (ed.), *Philippine Cinema*. Diamond Anniversary Brochure. Manila: Mowelfund, 1994.

[3] Pete Tombs, *Mondo Macabro: Weird & Wonderful Cinema Around the World*. New York: St. Martin's Griffin, 1998: 48-63.

[4] See Bliss Lim, "The Politics of Horror: *The Aswang* (Filipino Viscera-Sucker) in Film," *Asian Cinema* 9.1 (Fall 1997): 81-98; "Monstrous Makers, Bestial Brides: Situating Eddie Romero's B-Horror Films in An Intricate Web of Histories," *Journal of English Studies and Comparative Literature* 1.2 (January 1998): 37-61; and "Spectral Times: The Ghost Film as Historical Allegory," *positions: east asia cultures critique* 9.2 (Fall 2001): 287-329.

opposite:
Mario O'Hara's
Manananggal in Manila.

The Philippines

above:
Celso Ad. Castillo, director of **Kung Bakit Dugo ang Kulay ng Gabi** (aka **Night of the Zombies**).

[5] Kristina Bernadette Cojuangco Aquino is the daughter of Philippine martyr Ninoy Aquino and former President Corazon Cojuangco-Aquino.

[6] Gerardo de Leon is widely considered the master of Philippine cinema, and was the country's second National Artist for Film (an award he won posthumously in 1982).

Filipino horror can be divided into three main categories or subgenres: the ghost/occult film, the *aswang*/witch film and the thriller/slasher movie. The name of each category defines its subject but provides little insight into its specific theme, narrative or visual style. Aside from the fact that they comprise the greatest number produced, given their close affinity to Philippine mythology and folklore the *aswang*/witch films will be given more attention than the others. Furthermore, because the form appears to dominate all historical periods, it may well be considered the typical Filipino horror movie. The other two varieties, while of no less import, may be said to be topical, reflecting the temper of the time. The ghost/occult film, for instance, most of which resemble gothic melodramas with their underlying themes of unrequited love, lust and perversion, was especially common in the 1960s and 70s.

The thriller/slasher movie, on the other hand, appeared most frequently in the mid-1990s. Most of the films in this latter category are based on true-to-life stories and concern themselves with underlying issues of social injustice and abuse of power; practically all of them have poor women as victims and men of wealth and privilege as the murderers/abusers. In Carlo Caparas's *The Myrna Diones Story, Lord Have Mercy* (Golden Lion Films, 1993), for example, Myrna Diones (Kris Aquino, tagged as the "massacre queen" of Philippine cinema after appearing in this picture, *The Vizconde Massacre, God Help Us* [1993] and *The Elsa Castillo Story, The Truth* [*Ang Katotohanan*, 1994][5]) is a disadvantaged village girl who gets abducted (along with her cousins), raped and tortured, then left for dead. But she survives these horrors to recount them and bring the perpetrators - the son of a wealthy congressman and his henchmen - to justice. The popular appeal of these films lay partly on their sensationalistic approach to crime, including the graphic depiction of murder (complete with torture scenes and the mutilation/severing of body parts), but even more on their emotional resonance, as most of the stories remained unsolved at least up to the time of release.

It must be noted that, because of the absence of institutional film preservation in the Philippines, a number of important and worthwhile Filipino horror movies have been lost forever. What is even more tragic, in the case of many existent horror films, video transfers have not yet been made, hence are unavailable for reference. Examples include the following: Gerardo de Leon's *Ibulong Mo Sa Hangin* (*Whisper to the Wind*, AM Productions, 1966),[6] Celso Ad. Castillo's *Kung Bakit Dugo ang Kulay ng Gabi* (*Night of the Zombies*, AA Productions, 1974), *Patayin sa Sindak si Barbara* (*Kill Barbara with Terror*, Rosas Productions, 1974) and *Ang Madugong Daigdig ni Salvacion* (*The Bloody World of Salvacion*, AA Productions, 1975), as well two of what are now regarded as classics of Philippine horror, *4 na Gabi ng Lagim* (*4 Nights of Horror*, 1960) and *Maruja* (1967). Thus, if in what follows some titles are mentioned because of their significance in the history of the genre, I must resort to my personal recollections of the films in question, which are (at best) impressions and/or a few strands of the narrative.

The ghost/occult film

Unlike the Western gothic fiction which deals with what scholars often refer to as extreme periods of anxiety in the present, the Filipino gothic melodrama, i.e., the ghost/occult film, concerns unresolved issues in some remote past, a past that continues to haunt the present. Antonio Jose Perez's *Haplos* (*Caress*, Mirick Films International, 1982) initially confounds the viewer with its overlapping narratives;

in a climate of terror

as a consequence, it suffers from confusing points of view, one reason why it was panned by critics the year it was first screened. Upon further viewing, however, one finds a compelling, richly textured film that succeeds in part due to its lovely star's haunting presence (Rio Locsin as Auring/Aurora) and in part due to Ricardo Lee's skilful writing.

While the film's primary storyline revolves around the attempt of childhood sweethearts Al (Christopher de Leon) and Christy (Vilma Santos) to rekindle their romance after long years of separation, it is the subplot - Al's falling in love with the mysterious woman Aurora, who turns out to be a ghost - which proves to be the more substantial part of the film. Given *Haplos*'s preoccupation with Aurora, a victim of Japanese cruelty and Filipino collaborators during the second world war (she was repeatedly raped and subsequently killed by a band of Japanese soldiers), the film underlines the nation's anguish over that painful experience. In the context of ongoing unrest, in particular the government's military operations against leftist guerrillas in the country, *Haplos* questions the legitimacy of internecine war in the Philippines.

The country's Spanish historic past figures prominently in horror films produced in the 1960s, not for its overt socio-political meaning, but for its romantic setting which allows extensive use of European-style costumes and locations. Once again, the ghost represents the past, with this figure returning to the present and having his or her story recalled in flashback. Armando Garces's *Maruja* (Lea Productions, 1967) is a typical narrative in this respect. Maruja (Susan Roces), daughter of a Spanish landed gentry (her father is Spanish and her mother Filipina), is betrothed to a Spanish military officer named Rodrigo (Eddie Garcia). Unfortunately though, she is in love with Gabriel (Romeo Vasquez), the son of peasant Filipino parents. On the eve of her wedding to Rodrigo, Maruja kills herself by taking poison. One may discern shades of William Shakespeare's *Romeo and Juliet* in the story, but what we have here is actually closer to Philippine national hero Jose Rizal's 1892 novel *Noli Me Tangere* (*Touch Me Not*), as the film's underlying theme of repressed desire relates to Catholic condemnation/ disavowal of earthly lust outside the conventions of marriage.

Upon further examination, however, the film speaks of a transgressive love that is doomed from the start. On account of their different social status - both racial and economic - the love affair between Maruja and Gabriel is unacceptable within the society at large. Their refiguration in the contemporary world, via possession of present-day characters, suggests the need to examine class as an issue that divides society. As a narrative device, possession by spirits succeeds insofar as it accentuates differences of time, place and character. The act of haunting, as cultural scholar Mark Edmundson suggests, shows that life itself is possessed, that the present is in thrall to the past.[7]

7 Mark Edmundson, *Nightmare on Main Street: Angels, Sadomasochism, and the Culture of Gothic*. Cambridge, MA.: Harvard University Press, 1997.

below:
Video cover for **Haplos**.

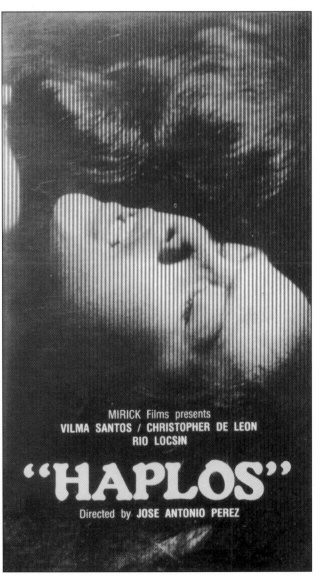

The Philippines

above:
Filming **Gumising Ka, Maruja** (aka **Wake up, Maruja**).

below:
Seance scene from **Itim**.

By cluing in on a possession film's shifts in focus, alterations in tone, colour (there often occurs a switch to monochromes of either blues or reds) and volume, and changes in an actor's movements and gestures, the audience engages not only in the process of storytelling but gains additional understanding of characters' motivations and the director's own choices. Thus, the practical as opposed to merely aesthetic value of such shifts and alterations should not be underestimated.

The latest remake of *Maruja* (Viva Films, 1995; written and directed by Jose Javier Reyes), because it chooses to dismiss possession as a narrative device, fails, devoid of the gothic appeal of the original. On the other hand, Lino Brocka's *Gumising Ka, Maruja* (*Wake up, Maruja*, FPJ Productions, 1978), an apparent update on the original, has sharpened our interest in the title character with its ingenious re-working of the Maruja myth by writer Tony Perez. In this film, Susan Roces (the lead in the first *Maruja*) is Nina Concepcion, a former movie star, now in her middle age, who is planning to make a comeback. Her agent wants her to star in a big picture, the dramatization of a popular folk figure, Maruja. The production company (which Nina owns) decides to shoot the film in the very same house where Maruja grew up, got married and subsequently killed herself. On the eve of the production company's press conference, the ghosts in the house begin to wreak havoc on the unwanted guests from the city. Brocka and Perez's

in a climate of terror

employment of the possession-by-spirits theme has elevated the Maruja narrative to a level whereby it is able to deconstruct the romanticised tragic figure of Maruja herself. By displacing our interest onto the secondary character of Rodrigo - here in the person of Marco (Phillip Salvador), Nina's young lover - as the wronged and betrayed one, *Gumising Ka, Maruja* manages to demystify Maruja in contemporary imagination.

In Mike de Leon's debut feature, *Itim* (*Black*, Cinemanila, 1976), possession by spirits occurs through séance (a common literary device) and becomes a means of uncovering truth. Jun (Tommy Abuel), a photographer, goes home to the province on a Lenten holiday. In his father's abandoned clinic, he finds a film negative; developing it, he discovers a young woman with his father. The young woman turns out to be the sister of another woman Jun has met, who has disappeared.

On the surface, *Itim* engages the viewer with its visual style: a careful attention to detail, riveting camerawork that effectively evokes a sense of dread and fine use of minimal music and silences. It disturbs, however, not because of its anti-patriarchal position (a concern that echoes throughout de Leon's subsequent films) but for its negative attitude towards abortion. Jun's father, now paralysed and confined to a wheelchair, throws himself down the stairs in throes of guilt and remorse after being confronted by his paramour's spirit inhabiting the younger sister (Charo Santos) during a séance.

Until recently, the abortion issue has not been a source of much national controversy in the Philippines - being the only Catholic nation in Asia has made it more difficult for the proponents of abortion to wage a meaningful debate - but popular culture, film in the main, has certainly reinforced the Catholic ideal of preserving life if at all possible. In these films, abortion is viewed as a sin; therefore, those who take away the life of an unborn fetus must be punished.

The *aswang*/witch film

The same theme is explored further in another category of Filipino horror: the *aswang*/witch film. Don Escudero's *Impakto* (*The Devil*, Regal Films, 1996) works on a premise similar to that of de Leon's *Itim*. Dr. Sagrado (Ernie Zarate) has failed in his efforts to become a licensed physician, and so heads off to the province with his wife (Daria Ramirez) to open practice as an abortionist. In an unexplained circumstance, his wife - already advanced in years - bears a child who turns out to be a blood-sucking devil. *Impakto*, through the use of the folkloric figure of the *tiyanak*, ascribes guilt to those who would defy what the film takes to be God's will. Dr. Sagrado, remorseless to the end, faces a slew of vengeful little devils alone in the depths of a forest where he has buried the unborn foetuses, and there he meets his own bloody death.

The *tiyanak* (or little blood-sucking devil) is one of the more common mythical figures in Philippine popular literature, and partly comprises what has become known as the *aswang complex*. In his research on Filipino folklore, Maximo Ramos defines the concept of the *aswang* as a coterie of beliefs about five distinct types of mythical beings: (1) the *mandurugo* or vampire, which sucks the blood of victims like its European

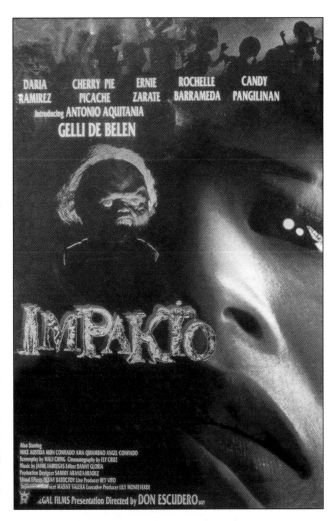

above:
Don Escudero's
Impakto (aka **The Devil**).

above:
Peque Gallaga, maker of **Aswang**.

counterpart; (2) the *manananggal* or self-segmenting viscera sucker, which at night splits its body at the waist after applying a special oil and reciting a chant (the upper portion flies away to hunt, leaving the lower portion behind); (3) the man-eating werebeast, which assumes the appearance of a ferocious cat, pig, dog or bat; (4) the *mangkukulam* or vindictive or evil-eyed witch; and (5) the ghoul, which steals and eats the body of dying persons or the corpses of the newly dead.[8] However, also forming part of the *aswang* complex in the Philippine lower mythology are the following creatures: (6) the *tiyanak*, as discussed above; (7) the *kapre* or tree-inhabiting giant; and (8) the *nuno sa punso* or elf in the mound (also referred to as the "Anthill Dwarf"[9]).

Peque Gallaga and Lore Reyes's *Aswang* (1992), one of the more accomplished and fully-realised Filipino horror features in recent memory, conforms to conventional mythology in the attributes it ascribes to the *manananggal* or self-segmenting viscera sucker. Almost academic to a point, the film presents the ritual, the transformation/self-segmentation and the reconstitution of this creature in stark detail.

Alma Moreno, then-reigning Philippine sex symbol, plays the role of an enigmatic young woman in the village. She barely speaks and appears in only a few scenes (the villagers talk about her whenever she is seen), but her *aswang*-transformation sequence is not to be forgotten. In this sequence, we see Moreno's character perched upon a *nipa*-thatched roof directly above a sleeping pregnant woman (played by Janice de Belen). She is shot against an extremely bright blue sky, her long hair flowing in the wind and her face sporting an anguished cry. Peering through a hole in the roof, when she senses her prey to be asleep she swiftly extends an elongated and tubular tongue, which proceeds to siphon off the viscera of the pregnant woman - including the foetus. It is said that an expectant mother is a choice victim for the *manananggal*, preferring as it does the fresh blood and entrails of an unborn baby or young child.

Of interest in this film is the realistic depiction of the *manananggal*'s mode of behaviour; although stationary, as if suspended by some wiring at the rear, the imagery of Moreno on the roof remains powerful. Later cinematic versions of the *manananggal* display more seamless visual effects work. The extensive use of prosthetics in Gallaga and Reyes's *Ang Madre* (*The Nun*) episode of the omnibus *Shake, Rattle & Roll IV*, Regal Films, 1993), for example, makes possible the showing of actual segmentation of the creature's body into a stationary lower torso and a flying upper part with bat-like wings. While in Don Escudero's *Takot ka ba sa Dilim* (*Are You Afraid of the Dark*, Viva Films, 1996), computer compositing is the technical means used to achieve a more animated *manananggal*, as the creature is actually shown flying in pursuit of her prey, a group of young boys.

Despite a relatively primitive technical method, what sets *Aswang* apart from the rest of the genre is its literate writing (script by Pen Medina and Jerry Sineneng), in which two parallel narratives are tied into a unified whole by the co-directors' astute visual style and sense of humour. Upon reaching home, a young child and her nanny (Aiza Seguerra and Manilyn Reynes) find the girl's mother and all the domestic help brutally murdered by a gang of robbers. Together with the family driver, the pair escapes and finds refuge in a village, now reeling after a series of killings, suspected to be the work of an *aswang*. Eventually, the robbers get wind of the child's whereabouts. In the ensuing chase scene, all of the film's major and minor characters - including Morena's *aswang* / *manananggal*-now-turned-weredog - meet in a hilarious finale as a blurring of the pursued-pursuer demarcation is placed in the fore.

At this point, a slight variation of the *manananggal* character in two Filipino horror films should be mentioned. Common folklore speaks of the *manananggal* as a beautiful woman living a solitary existence in the forest - a figure rarely found in Western mythology. As we have seen, Gallaga and Reyes's *Aswang* portrays this character in traditional folkloric fashion. However, in a later film - Mario O'Hara's *Manananggal in Manila* (MAQ Productions, 1997), written by Floy Quintos - the *manananggal* is a modern woman (Alma Concepcion) who lives in a condominium and works as a successful advertising model. Such a characterisation bears similarities to that of the nun in Gallaga and Reyes's *Ang Madre*, written by Jerry Lopez Sineneng. This atypical character type suggests a fusion of both the Philippine folkloric *manananggal* and the Western gothic figure of the diabolical double. As Mark Edmundson explains, the idea of a second self is that of a horrible

---

[8] Of these different forms, the *mandurugo* is the least commonly reported. Witnesses almost always describe seeing the *aswang* as a *manananggal*, or a werebeast changed into the form of a black cat, a big dog, a savage pig or a strange winged creature. See Maximo D. Ramos, *The Aswang Complex in Philippine Folklore*. Quezon City, Philippines: Phoenix Publishing House, 1990.

[9] For more on the *nuno sa punso*, see: www.pinoystuff.com/ folklore/superstitions/nuno.htm.

above:
The lead character, played by Charo Santos is possessed by the spirit of her elder sister in **Itim**.

other living unrecognised in the world beyond, a figure central to the mode of what he calls "terror gothic" (8). (Note too that the murderer in most thriller/slasher movies is an extension of this notion of a second self.)

Aswang marks one of the high points of Filipino horror and established the tandem of Peque Gallaga and Lore Reyes as major filmmakers in the genre. The six film (to date) omnibus series, *Shake, Rattle & Roll* - three of which (II-IV) they directed as a team, and which happen to be the best in the series - is by far the most successful horror franchise in the history of Philippine cinema. Always exhibited as part of the annual Metro Manila Film Festival in December (the first one in 1984), *Shake, Rattle & Roll* is comprised of three short episodes. Although the distinct stories are separable, they may be related by theme and/or style, if only at the level of the framing of titles. What makes each film in the series interesting, at least those directed by Gallaga and Reyes, is the way the episodes are arranged in sequence, starting with a light but sombre number, followed by a comic one and ending with the most thought-provoking episode of the three.

While the series retells in large part what is already known to mass audiences as folklore - most episodes involve *multo*/ghosts, *kulam*/curses or *aswang*/*manananggal* - its success has allowed Gallaga and Reyes to expand the notion of horror and what is possible in local cinema. Displaying a keen sense of the macabre, they infuse their films with the seriousness of their subjects' mythological past. Nevertheless, an acute awareness of present-day concerns informs their work, affording easier access for their viewers. Furthermore, as remarkable imagists and genre technicians, they provide their films with urgency and importance. Three episodes in *Shake, Rattle & Roll III* and *IV* in particular may be considered watermarks in Philippine horror due to their thematic daring and technical flourish.

Nanay (*Mother*) in *Shake, Rattle & Roll III* (Good Harvest Unlimited, 1992) exemplifies Gallaga and Reyes's tendency to combine their visual skills with attention to a pressing social concern. A simple-minded young student (Manilyn Reynes), on a field trip to a lake, discovers a fellow student dead after catching the eggs of an unknown sea creature. She goes home with

opposite:
Video cover for **Shake, Rattle & Roll IV**, part of the successful series of Filipino anthology horror movies.

her friend's catch only to find a monster in an ice bucket, which promptly attacks her. She loses sight of the monster in the mêlée and we see it hide in the toilet. After a narrative detour showing what usually goes on in a crowded student dormitory, the episode ends with a night of mayhem and gore as the monster makes its final bloody attack on the dorm residents in pursuit of the eggs - her babies. At the core of the narrative is an apocalyptic message of ecological threat: as punishment for destroying nature (in this case, the ecology of a lake), mankind faces death.

Ang Kapitbahay (*The Neighbour*) in *Shake, Rattle & Roll IV* works along similar lines, albeit in a light-hearted, childlike way. In rapid succession and without any warning, little children disappear from the park where they have been playing, until one girl (Aiza Seguerra) sees a monstrous creature emanate from a tree and abduct a child. It turns out to be a *witawit*, a tree creature, who is angered by the cutting down of the trees, their homes. Clearly, *Ang Kapitbahay* addresses its concern to younger viewers. *Nanay*, on the other hand, impresses its more mature audience with technical polish and stylised acting. This episode has effectively expanded the industry's repertoire of visual effects with its imaginative use of prosthetics. When the monster's saliva drops on a human body, for instance, the affected limb dissolves in a gelatinous spill, while the upper part - the face and the chest remain intact - can still be seen talking. How this episode manages to successfully combine the gory and the amusing is to the filmmakers' credit.

Questions about mortality are the focus of *Ate* (*Elder Sister*) in *Shake, Rattle & Roll III*. Based on a script by Lopez Sineneng, this episode provokes its audience to consider the morality of mercy-killing: it may be against the law to kill a human being, but not to bring a dead person back to life. Rosalyn (Janice de Belen), in a fit of guilt decides to visit an elder sister she has not seen for a long time. The sister, Rowena (Gina Alajar), has been confined in a sanatorium for some unknown illness, apparently psychiatric in nature. In the sanatorium - run by a mysterious, devious couple, the doctor (Subas Herrero) and his wife (Armida Siguion-Reyna) - Rosalyn finds her sister devouring ground earth and being totally uncommunicative. Upon further investigation, she discovers that her sister is already dead, and was only brought back to life by the doctor. The only way to keep her at peace is to kill her and bury the body. Gallaga and Reyes, with their own team of writers and technicians (notably Benny Batoctoy for prosthetics), have built a solid body of work that merits more exhaustive study.

Contemporary Filipino horror

What lies ahead for Philippine horror? Already, another Gallaga and Reyes's film, *Sa Piling ng Aswang* (*With the Witch*, MAQ Productions, 1999), has generated interest due to its rational take on the *aswang* mythology. The film is not deconstructive in aim, but instead takes a more clinical approach to understanding the presence of the *aswang* as something that is not so much from another world (the nether-world) as from another subculture. This was already hinted at in previous films, for example O'Hara's *Manananggal in Manila*. In *Sa Piling ng Aswang*, a group of students go on a research trip to study the *aswang* and come face-to-face with their fears, only to discover that the only way to deal with fear is to accept its existence, as well as one other.

Like previous collaborators Don Escudero and Manny Castaneda, new filmmakers have emerged in recent years to follow in the tradition of Gallaga and Reyes with their focus on Philippine folk mythology. Another group of younger filmmakers, including actors Michael de Mesa and Eric Quizon, have made attempts at working in the genre with mixed results. But one stands to be more promising than the rest: Rico Maria Ilarde.

The U.S.-schooled Ilarde's *Ang Babaeng Putik* (*The Earth Woman*, Regal Films, 2000) creates its own mythology borne out of the wastage of the earth. The destructive mirror image of a nurturing mother earth figure, the title character assumes a diabolic double. An aspiring writer seeks the quietude of a provincial house to concentrate on his writing; instead, he finds a woman emerge from a giant plant which he himself has brought to life. The woman becomes a comforter and lover to the writer, but a monstrous creature to the village. After his friend is killed, he is never the same again and leaves the village bruised in spirit.

Ang Babaeng Putik infuses local Philippine cinema with a new energy and vision, though one still somewhat irresolute and uneven. But the very formation of a new mythology for a new audience bodes well for Filipino horror films in years to come.

author's note:
I would like to gratefully acknowledge the support and assistance of the following in the writing of this essay: Roger Garcia, Pio Candelaria for the photographs and Cube Video in South San Francisco for video copies of the films.

genre histories and studies

French Revolution: The Secret History of Gallic Horror Movies

David Kalat

Monsieur Metadier, of the Renoux-Duval Bank, had one true passion: the movies. Every Friday, with all the clockwork regularity one expects from a bank clerk, M. Metadier took himself to the Theatre Gaumont to catch the latest thrilling serial, "Race to the Abyss!" He never missed a show.

And on this particular Friday, like every Friday before it and none afterwards, he left the Gaumont at midnight to catch the train to his suburban home. Scarcely had the train left the station than the two fellow passengers in his compartment leapt to their feet to attack him. Seconds later, they tossed his lifeless carcass from the train like so much garbage.

By a curious coincidence, a petty thief named Moreno just happened to be passing at the precise moment that Metadier's body was thrown from the train. Seeing a golden opportunity, Moreno hid the corpse and assumed the dead man's identity. By Monday morning, M. Metadier's stolen face had been used to defraud the bank of some 300,000 Francs.[1]

This, the attendant dangers of what the French call *cinema*.

Conventional wisdom holds that there is no such beast as the French Horror Film. That something about French filmgoers prevented them from ever developing a taste for such salacious thrills. That while imports, like the output of England's Hammer Studios, may find an appreciative niche audience, the French film industry has never recognised a market for the home-grown product. That to the extent that respectable French filmmakers have deigned to explore the fantastic, they have only ventured as far as science-fiction or poetic fantasies, unwilling to traffic in the lowly and disreputable genre of horror itself. That those rare pull-no-punches, make-no-apologies, full-blooded horror films to come out of France have actually been the work of either marginalised, low-budget indies or foreign directors spending French money. In short, that speaking about the French Horror Film is like discussing the hole of a donut.

All of which may be true to a certain extent, but is by no means the whole truth. While the French film industry has resisted a genuine horror movie tradition the likes of which can be found in England or Italy or Spain, it has nevertheless substantially and extensively influenced the evolution of horror cinema internationally. However, since there is no national film tradition to summarise, each film is basically an island to be discussed on its own. So one cannot easily trace what influence the French horror movie has had on, say, Hollywood, because the question is more what influence each individual film may have had, which of course varies.

The story begins, naturally enough, at the dawn of cinema itself.

Photographing a phantom world

The first ever public film show was held in France in 1895, with a program of shorts made by the Lumière brothers. It set in motion a revolution in public entertainment that launched the cinema as the most popular and important art form of the 20th century. In attendance at the show was a magician named Georges Méliès, who had been performing elaborate conjuring tricks and illusions in his own personal theatre for almost a decade. Méliès was enraptured by the Lumière show, and immediately purchased a movie

[1] From Louis Feuillade's *Les Vampires* serial (1915-16).

opposite: Jean Marais and Josette Day in Jean Cocteau's **La belle et la bête** (aka **Beauty and the Beast**), 1945.

France

right:
Three stills from **Escamotage d'une dame chez Robert-Haudin** (aka **The Vanishing Lady**) (1898) showing the pioneering trickery of Georges Méliès.

projector of his own from the Robert W. Paul Company in London; he had seen the future of illusion-making, and it was on the silver screen.

Together, Lumière and Méliès represent the twin fathers of the cinema. Louis Lumière recognised the commercial prospects of the medium and perfected the technology for its exhibition. Méliès provided the content that audiences flocked towards. In other words, Lumière made it possible to show movies, Méliès made it worthwhile.

Although Lumière's landmark 1895 show included the first fiction film, *L'arroseur arrosé* (*Watering the Gardener*), both his and R.W. Paul's emphasis was on documentary realism. They took their cameras out into the world, photographed what happened, and then projected those visions of reality onto the screen for paying customers. At first, Méliès learned the craft of filmmaking by imitating the Lumière style of cinéma vérité. But within a year, once he had the hang of the device, Méliès pursued a radically different path. Beginning with *Escamotage d'une dame chez Robert-Haudin* (*The Vanishing Lady*, 1898), Méliès began to make the films for which he became internationally famous: trick films. Unfortunately, that term, "trick film", fails to convey the impact of Méliès' innovation. "Trick film" is a term of art for film critics and specialists - these were *special effects blockbusters*. Beautiful women who morph into skeletons and back, spaceships launched into orbit a half-century before the real thing, giant monsters that eat people alive, severed heads that float through fantastic landscapes... Méliès was the first person to realise that cinema's greatest expressive power, and truest claim to art, lies not in rendering the real world on celluloid, but in conjuring up a new world unique to the cinema. The world seen in Méliès's films exists only there, in Méliès' films, an illusion created by the interaction between real objects (actors, sets, lights) with the peculiar properties of the moving picture itself. Méliès made films of events that never happened, events that existed only in the eye of the camera, and in so doing he not only inspired generations of special effects artists in his wake but also laid the groundwork for the development of fantastic cinema.

The modern horror film has its roots in Méliès' so-called trick films, and for more than the obvious reasons. Certainly, the horror film has relied heavily on the shock value of special effects. More importantly, though, the underlying agenda of horror and fantastic cinema is to explore heightened experiences and extreme situations outside the purview of straight realistic drama. The vast majority of films seek a form of representational authenticity, a window on the world, and in striving for realism they follow in the footsteps of Louis Lumière. Horror filmmakers, invoking highly stylised imagery and supernatural situations (whether intended as allegory or merely to shock) owe a debt to Méliès' vision of illusionist cinema. No matter how realistically styled their makers may try to craft them, horror films are not literal representations of the "real world." That is the province of drama. Horror, on the other hand, tends to concern itself with an abstracted, extremist world from which audiences can, perhaps, divine some meaning useful in their everyday lives.

Especially in France but indeed throughout most of the Western world, the mainstream commercial film industry has descended from Lumière's tradition. Perhaps fiction replaced documentary subjects, but nonetheless movies became predominately concerned with photographic and narrative realism. A separate tradition of fantastic films descended from Méliès' sideshow aesthetics, but remained marginalised. Not only were genres like science fiction and horror treated with scepticism or contempt-even Méliès's legacy was considered problematic. More than a few film historians, uncomfortable with the notion of non-representational film, cited as Méliès' greatest contribution to the development of cinema the fact that he was the first to make films longer than the 65 to 80 foot length of the then-standard movie spool. Since the idea of running several spools back-to-back seems with hindsight pretty obvious, the fact that Méliès was making films that ran three or (gasp!) ten minutes long now seems rather trivial compared to the fact the content of those films was so much more iconoclastic and influential, regardless of their length.[2]

The next major figure in the evolution of fantastic film was the great Louis Feuillade. Along with D.W. Griffith, Feuillade is a critical founder of modern cinema, and a major influence on later directors. Born in France in 1874, Feuillade began directing in 1906. He spent several years manufacturing films in the traditional mould before discovering the serial format where he would make his mark. With multi-part serialised pictures like *Fantômas* (1913-14), *Les vampires* (1915-16), *Tih Minh* (1918) and *Barrabas* (1919), Feuillade practically invented the suspense thriller. Feuillade was the premiere director for the Gaumont company, exercising near-total artistic control over his creations. And a prolific creator he was, too: he penned a staggering 800 scripts, directing all but 100 of them.

Feuillade's films are rife with masked superheroes, master criminals, sinister conspiracies, and deceptions and illusions on a grand scale. The convoluted tragedy of M. Metadier described above is typical Feuillade: thrilling, engrossing, entrancing, terrifying and utterly implausible. But the strength of Feuillade's works lie in their juxtaposition of dreamlike fantasy with Lumière-style realism. Feuillade invokes none of Méliès's magic, but concocts a unique magical world all his own. The world of Feuillade *appears* to be our world, corrupted by a pervasive evil from which escape is apparently impossible.

In the 1920s the first wave of French film criticism appeared, the first genuine effort to appreciate film as art. But these critics snubbed the work of Feuillade, one of the most popular and successful directors of the day, precisely because of his success. Feuillade considered himself an entertainer, and judged the worth of his films on the sole basis of how well he kept his audience happy. Critics, seeking intellectual statements from the cinema to justify its artistic ambitions, saw Feuillade as a throwback. "We don't always go to the cinema to study", countered Feuillade, "The public flocks to it to be entertained. I place the public above all else."[3]

Eventually, Feuillade found favour with the critical community. The Surrealists embraced his *Fantômas* serials as an example of pure art, and a later generation of critics hailed his films as masterpieces. Alain Resnais, Georges Franju and Claude Chabrol all cited Feuillade as a major influence on their art, and variously helmed homages to Feuillade's cliff-hanger thrillers. But the tension between the cinema of the fantastic and the artistic pretensions of the French cognoscenti had been well established, and the marginalisation of French fantasy continued.

The fantastic cinema that descended from Méliès and Feuillade took root primarily abroad. It was in places like Germany and the United States that filmmakers began to populate the screen with vampires, monsters, reanimated corpses, mad doctors, evil robots and werewolves. In France, filmmakers, critics and audiences remained uncomfortable with-even antagonistic towards-such lurid pleasures. While no national tradition of gothic horror cinema evolved, iconoclastic and haphazard experiments appeared-shots in the dark, to be sure, but perhaps all the more powerful and effective for their independence.

Consider the case of Jean Epstein's *La chute de la maison Usher* (*The Fall of the House of Usher*, 1928). Throughout the 1920s, avant-garde artist Epstein had collaborated with a young Luis Buñuel to craft a number of visionary masterpieces. In France, Epstein built his reputation on the basis of such progressive arthouse experiments as *La glace à trois faces* (*The Mirror with Three Panels*, 1927). None of

[2] Most of Méliès's works are available on the DVD "Landmarks of Early Film, Volume 2" available from Image Entertainment.

[3] Zagury, F. (1998) "'The Public is my Master': Louis Feuillade and *Les Vampires*." Liner notes, *Les Vampires* (Laserdisc), Image Entertainment.

this page and opposite:
Jean Epstein's
La chute de la maison Usher
(aka **The Fall of the House of Usher**), 1928.

(Margueritte Gance). "There is where she truly lives", he gushes in admiration of the finished painting, unaware of the literal truth of his boast. The painting has sucked Madeleine's soul from her body, leaving a lifeless husk that Roderick reluctantly buries in the family crypt. He fears she is not truly dead, a fear that is unfortunately justified. Soon, Madeleine's cadaver crawls out of the mausoleum to bring holy vengeance down upon her husband's accursed home.

Epstein's *Usher* is a glossy, classy work of art, borne out of its maker's goal of pure aesthetic beauty, yet its content equates that artistic drive with murder and psychic destruction. As an ambivalent statement about the act of artistic creation, it remains a definitive treatment of the theme, far superior to such half-hearted later efforts as E. Elias Merhige's *Shadow of the Vampire* (2001). Furthermore, Epstein's *Usher* has become one of the most highly regarded of the many, many Edgar Allan Poe-inspired films made over the years. With its high-Gothic atmosphere and striking visuals, *Usher* stands as something of a missing link between the excessively stylised Expressionism of the German silents before it (*Das Kabinett des Dr. Caligari*, 1918; *Dr. Mabuse*, 1922; *Nosferatu*, 1922) and the more narrative-driven moodiness of the Universal chillers that followed (*Dracula*, 1931; *Frankenstein*, 1931; *The*

these, though, received any attention outside of France. The only one of Epstein's films to be distributed abroad, much less find commercial success, was a lowly horror film, one obsessed with madness and morbidity.

Epstein took Edgar Allan Poe's "The Fall of the House of Usher" as his principal inspiration, crossbred with a smattering of other Poe tales like "The Oval Portrait" and "Tomb of Ligeia." In Epstein's rendering, Roderick Usher (Jean Debucourt) is a crazed artist, singularly fixated on painting the perfect portrait of his wife Madeleine

the secret history of Gallic horror movies

Old Dark House, 1932). The theatrical success of *La chute de la maison Usher* in America was essential in Hollywood's synthesis of the Gothic horror film.

Following *Usher*'s release, Epstein's career went into rapid decline. The mainline Surrealist movement as organised under André Breton objected to his art-for-art's-sake aesthetic. Epstein belonged to the same avant-garde community that rejected Feuillade as popular trash; with the same breath that the Surrealists hailed Feuillade's *Fantômas* as a work of genius they condemned Epstein's work as hollow pretension. Buñuel, once Epstein's protégé, threw his cards in with Breton's Surrealists and left Epstein to launch his own solo career. Buñuel's first film, *Un chien andalou* (*An Andalusian Dog*, 1928) was nothing less than a reaction against *Usher*, with several shots designed as direct parodies of shots from Epstein's film.[4]

Far from developing any national traditions of filmmaking, the French film scene was devolving into internecine combat, each new movement jockeying for position by rejecting that which came before. One thing the various and sundry movements did share in common, though, was a mistrust of the horror genre, despite its importance and popularity elsewhere.

Fragments of the imagination

In almost anyone else's hands, the subject matter of Abel Gance's *J'accuse* (*I Accuse*, a.k.a. *That They May Live*, 1937) would have made for a crackerjack B-movie, the perfect vehicle for Boris Karloff or Lionel Atwill. In the aftermath of WWI, a mad scientist (Victor Francen), risen from the dead with a piece of shrapnel lodged in his brain and haunted by the ghosts of his fallen comrades in arms, spends the next twenty years holed up in an isolated and moth-eaten lab, obsessed with inventing a device capable of preventing war. His obsession costs him all human happiness, and ultimately drives him over the brink into total insanity. When his inventions are co-opted by war profiteers as Europe re-arms itself for WWII, well what's a mad scientist to do? Of course, bring back the victims of the first combat to horrify the living into playing nice. As the war dead rise from their graves and begin their march, the terrified villagers tie "that crazy inventor" to the stake and burn him alive.

Amazingly, however, when one actually watches *J'accuse*, there is nothing in the experience of the picture itself to suggest that it is a horror film. Far from it, as Gance's treatment of the material elides all gruesome aspects. The result is an overwrought melodrama, one half war picture and one half romance. Gance exploited the horror genre's allegorical storytelling for his own sermonising, but without any desire to simply shock the audience. Gance builds up to his March of the Dead climax for a surprisingly long time, as if the filmmaker was uncertain how to embrace to the inherent supernaturalism of the very idea.

In a touch not dissimilar to Tod Browning's casting of real circus freaks in *Freaks* (1932), Gance cast real WWI veterans as his marching zombies. The effect is devastating. Film scholars like David Skal have long argued that the proliferation of movie monsters after the Great War owed much to the fact that severely disfigured soldiers wounded in combat had been re-assimilated into a society that was simultaneously revulsed by and pitying towards them.[5] In wars past, such injuries would likely have been fatal, but a combination of modern weaponry and modern medicine put on the street large numbers of beings whose human vulnerability and mortality were on constant public display. These were heroes-and victims-but they looked like monsters. Thus were born

[4] Stuart Liebman, Professor of Film Studies at City University of New York. Personal discussions with author, Fall 2000.

[5] Skal, D.J. (1993) *The Monster Show: A Cultural History of Horror*. New York: Penguin Books, 205-206.

above:
Maurice Tourneur's **La main du diable** (aka **The Devil's Hand**, aka **Carnival of Sinners**), 1942.

such sympathetic movie characters as Frankenstein's Monster, the Mummy, the Wolf Man... But the make-up talents of Jack Pierce and Lon Chaney were just imitations; *J'accuse* features the real deal.

Additionally, there are ways in which this film is eerily prescient. Had the picture been made *after* the War, in 1945 or later, critics would surely have seen an allegorical parallel to the development and deployment of the atomic bomb. Like the "crazy inventor" played by Victor Francen, Robert Oppenheimer was a pacifist who found his scientific creations used for military purposes. Moreover, Oppenheimer unleashed forces so horrifying and shameful that they have indeed prevented war - or at least the kind of global conflicts that Gance was immediately concerned with. The destruction of Hiroshima and Nagasaki, like the March of the Dead, had an awesome and awful effect on the world. Yet Gance's allegory was created long before the Manhattan Project got underway, and so few have ever remarked on the atomic age significance of his film.

With elements of *Frankenstein* and *Freaks* in the mix, and a heavy-handed moralising that H.G. Wells would surely have admired, *J'accuse* belongs to the world of horror cinema, but is nevertheless a misfit in that world. Gance was a serious and highly regarded artist, and he dearly wanted his film (a remake of his own 1918 original, which had been written by famous surrealist Blaise Cendrars) to be taken seriously, perhaps to change the world. The 1918 version concluded with the war dead of WWI rising from their graves to punish the survivors; as the world slipped inexorably towards a second World War, Gance felt his message needed to be more forcefully reiterated. *J'accuse* opens with a war-is-hell introductory montage as cruel and hard-hitting as anything until *Saving Private Ryan* (1999), and employs rapid, frequent cutaways to documentary newsreel footage to underscore its authenticity. Like so many in the French film community, Gance did not believe that a horror film could sustain such a serious theme. And so he appropriated aspects of the horror genre to suit his needs, but went no further. Like so many French filmmakers following him, however, Gance did countenance science fiction. His 1930 *La fin du monde* (*The End of the World*, a.k.a. *Paris After Dark*), in which a comet threatens to obliterate the Earth, is a more full-fledged genre picture than *J'accuse*.

For decades thereafter, French filmmakers who deigned to work in fantasy genres generally limited themselves to the more reputable arenas of science fiction and noirish crime thrillers. Horror elements might appear in major works, but genuine horror, as it is commonly known, would be a province only for outsiders.

So it was with Jean Cocteau, one of France's most important directors. As a multiple threat who exercised his many artistic talents in the theater, literature, painting and ballet, Cocteau made films that comprised but a small fraction of his total *oeuvre*, yet are essential works in the history of motion pictures. Cocteau took inspiration from Méliès' trickery to conceive of a poetic cinema. For Cocteau, film was a fundamentally magical experience, where the impossible, the dreamlike and the sublime were vital tools. Yet Cocteau's embrace of the fantastic was tempered by his position as a great national artist; he was part of a movement during the 1920s and 30s to establish a uniquely French cinema.

Thus, a work like Cocteau's *La belle et la bête* (*Beauty and the Beast*, 1945), rife with enchanted castles, monstrous transformations and mystical spells, is a romantic fairy tale rather than a Gothic shocker. Nevertheless, Cocteau's poetic fantasy has a far darker edge than the 1991 Disney cartoon remake, and is filled with magical visions and special effects that are every bit as wondrous as anything accomplished by Disney's technicians a half-century later.

A merchant in the 17th century (Marcel André) intrudes onto the enchanted property of the accursed Beast (Jean Marais), for which the Beast's chosen penalty is death. To save her father, Belle (Josette Day) substitutes herself. The Beast is as stricken by her beauty as she is by his ugliness, and he chooses not to kill her but merely keep her a prisoner. Over time they fall in love, a love that transcends superficial appearances and touches their souls. Belle's love frees the Beast from his curse, and he is restored to human form.

In his role as the tortured Beast, Marais (the 1960s Fantômas) sports some of the most convincing monster make-up the screen has ever seen, which Cocteau himself applied to Marais's face. The intention is to render this Beast as humanly expressive as possible, much like John Chambers's ape make-up designs for *The Planet of the Apes* (1968). The irony of the fable is of course that, with the exception of Belle, the petty and venal human characters are far more monstrous than the noble Beast. The film's message then-monsters are people too-is thoroughly in keeping with the trend towards sympathetic monsters discussed above. One striking parallel between the Beast and the sympathetic monsters of Hollywood can be seen in Lon Chaney Jr.'s Wolf Man character. Through a string of 1940s Universal pictures, the Wolf Man suffered a tragic curse that turned an otherwise decent fellow into a murderous lycanthrope. The Wolf Man desperately wanted to be a normal human being, but never escaped his curse. In appearance and tragic suffering, Marais' Beast and Chaney Jr.'s Wolf Man are very similar, but Cocteau's film ends on an uplifting note, granting the Beast a redemptive release forever denied the world-weary Wolf Man. By contrast, the Wolf Man films follow more in the tradition of *film noir*, with cruel fate and cynical irony the watchwords of the day.

The 1940s also saw the best films of famed low-budget auteur Jacques Tourneur, who worked his adept magic equally well with hard-bitten *noir* (*Out of the Past*, 1947) and stylish psychological horror (*Cat People*, 1942; *I Walked With a Zombie*, 1943). Meanwhile, back in France, Jacques's father Maurice Tourneur helmed a rare attempt at French horror, *La main du diable* (*The Devil's Hand*, a.k.a. *Carnival of Sinners*, 1942).

Taking as its point of departure the horror of compound interest, Tourneur fashioned an eerie fable. The "devil's hand" is a rather creepy severed fist that supposedly brings its owner incredible manual dexterity and skill. Over the centuries it has been the root cause of many men's earthly success - great chefs, swordsmen and entertainers have all enjoyed its power. The catch is to get rid of the damned thing before you die, because the final owner must give his soul to the Devil. And the only method of disposing of the hand is to sell it. At a loss.

Enter one starving artist with poor long-term reasoning skills, and he purchases the dread talisman to become an overnight sensation (like Epstein's *Usher*, *La main du diable* is concerned with the darker side of the artistic impulse). When he does start worrying about the price of eternal damnation, he has to confront the fact that he paid just one penny for the hand, which makes selling it a moot point. The Devil agrees to a bargain, though: the artist can buy back his soul for that same penny, a price that will double daily. So our intrepid but mathematically-challenged hero tries to hang on to his ill-gotten success just as long as he can afford to before the compounded interest overtakes him completely.

Officially the film purports to be an adaptation of a novel by Gérard de Nerval, but there are powerful narrative links to Robert Louis Stevenson's brilliant short story "The Bottle Imp", as well. Stevenson's tale is content with the mechanics of the original set-up: selling the cursed object at a loss before you die. While Stevenson's telling is a marvel of story construction as the hero sells and re-purchases the bottle repeatedly, deflating its price to nothing, the film veers in new directions, concocting instead a sort of infernal Ponzi scheme.

There is much similarity between the directorial styles of the elder and junior Tourneurs: *La main du diable* employs a noirish flashback structure much like Jacques's *Out of the Past*. The film also has several moments of genuine chill, especially as the hand is variously re-severed and sold. Overall, however, *La main du diable* is a misfire. Only sporadically does the horrific mood intrude into what is primarily a tone of whimsy. Pierre Palau del Vitri plays the Devil like a Gallic Elmer Fudd, and Roger Dumas's inappropriately airy and romantic musical score actively undercuts any Gothic atmosphere created by the low-key lighting and expressionistic sets. Whereas *J'accuse* and *La belle et la bête* appropriated horror movie elements for an ulterior purpose, resulting in highly accomplished hybrid creations, *La main du diable* is simply a toothless horror flick. Tourneur lacked the courage of his convictions.

Such a thing could not, could never, be said of Henri-Georges Clouzot. Clouzot's is a dark and cynical cinema, devoid of hope and exclusive of happy endings. Which is unsurprising, since that is an equally apt description of Clouzot himself. "All his work has been surrounded by an air of scandal and affront", writes Roy Armes, "and the shooting of all his films is conducted in an atmosphere of bitterness and recrimination. His own urge to dominate is perhaps reflected in his characters who seek outlets for their lust, hatred, and violence."[6]

It was with his 1943 thriller *Le corbeau* (*The Raven*) that Clouzot established his reputation as a suspense master of the highest order. His twin

[6] Armes, R. (1970) *French Film.* London: Studio Vista Limited, 78.

above:
Georges Franju's **Judex**.

[7] Peary, P. (1998) liner notes, *Diabolique* (DVD), Criterion Collection.

[8] Lowenstein, A. (Summer 1998) "Films Without a Face: Shock Horror in the Cinema of Georges Franju", *Cinema Journal* 37.4, 37.

masterpieces, *Le salaire de la peur* (*The Wages of Fear*, 1953) and *Les diaboliques* (*Diabolique*, 1955), featured sustained sequences of taut suspense such as to make Hitchcock green with envy. Come to think of it, Hitchcock *was* jealous, recognising in Clouzot a formidable competitor. It was largely on the basis of *Les diaboliques*'s international success that Hitchcock began to plan a back-to-basics low budget thriller of his own, a notion that culminated in *Psycho* (1960).[7] Not only do *Psycho* and *Les diaboliques* share many ideas and images in common, but Hitchcock's celebrated refusal to allow latecomers into screenings of *Psycho* already underway was a strategy first employed by Clouzot in the exhibition of *Les diaboliques*. Hitchcock had tried to buy the rights to the novel *Les diaboliques* by Pierre Boileau and Thomas Narcejac, but Clouzot reportedly beat him to the punch by a matter of one month. When the two writers heard of Hitch's interest in their work, they took to writing their novels with Hitchcock's style explicitly in mind. The tactic paid off, and their book *D'entre les morts* was bought by Paramount to form the basis of Hitchcock's *Vertigo* (1958).

Les diaboliques stars Clouzot's lovely wife Vera as Christina Delasalle, headmistress of a rundown boy's school. Her cruel husband (Paul Meurisse) exploits and maltreats both her and the students. Weirdly, Madame Delasalle becomes close friends with her husband's lover (Simone Signoret), who is also one of the school's teachers, because one of the many things they share-apart from the sadistic affections of Monsieur Delasalle-is an utter loathing for the man. They concoct an elaborate plot to murder him, and their "perfect" crime goes off without a hitch, until the evidence starts to mount that their victim has not remained dead…

By a strictly reductionist interpretation of the word "horror", *Les diaboliques* does not quite qualify. In the end, its apparent supernatural plot points prove to have decidedly non-supernatural explanations. But this is splitting hairs. *Les diaboliques*, more than any other French horror picture before it, sets as its program nothing less and nothing more than the terrorisation of its audience. Clouzot pulls none of his punches, never holding back out of some deference to a predetermined ideal of High Art. The result is literally breathtaking.

Scream your face off

"The trouble with Clouzot", groused director Georges Franju, "is that he tries to knock the audience's head off. That's wrong: you should twist it off."[8] And so, Franju set to proving his little thesis. Incorrectly cited on occasion as a New Wave filmmaker, Franju did rise to prominence coincident with the New Wave, and he shared with his New Wave peers a deep admiration for Louis Feuillade. In 1963, Franju even helmed a respectful remake of Feuillade's *Judex* (1916) in homage to the silent era master of thrills. But Franju's greatest achievement, and the film for which he is known today, is *Les yeux sans visage* (*Eyes Without a Face*, also known in English dubbed form as *The Horror Chamber of Dr. Faustus*, 1959).

Les yeux's storyline, by the team of Boileau-Narcejac no less, is a hoary horror movie chestnut: mad doctor Genessier (Pierre Brasseur) grieves that his daughter (Edith Scob) has suffered a disfiguring accident, ruining her once beautiful face. By a lucky coincidence, Genessier is a brilliant plastic surgeon who hopes to restore his daughter's looks by grafting on a face taken from one of Paris's many

the secret history of Gallic horror movies

lovely ladies. Since the graft procedure is experimental (read: it doesn't work), the obsessed doctor begins to accumulate quite a body count of discarded, faceless girls. The more he kills, the closer the police come to catching him.

In strictly narrative terms, there is little that stands out here. The ladykiller scenario reaches back to such B-movie quickies as *Murders in the Rue Morgue* (1932), *Dark Eyes of London* (1939), *The Body Snatcher* (1945) and Edgar G. Ulmer's *Bluebeard* (1944), and would continue to fuel horror flicks in the wake of Franju's hit: Anton Giulio Majano's *Seddok, l'erede di satana* (*Atom Age Vampire*, Italy/France, 1960), Jesus Franco's *Gritos en la noche* (*Cries in the Night*, a.k.a. *The Awful Dr. Orlof*, Spain/France, 1961), Joseph Green's *The Brain That Wouldn't Die* (USA, 1960), and on and on. The imagery of *Les yeux* continues to influence films today, with distinct echoes in *Batman* (1988) and *Face/Off* (1997). Franju's film also belongs to the same tradition as earlier French efforts like *La chute de la maison Usher*, *J'accuse* and *La main du diable* in that it too posits that the act of creation-be it artistic expression or scientific innovation- is intimately interwoven with a parallel act of destruction.

What sets *Les yeux sans visage* apart was Franju's determination to twist the audience's collective head off. Since this is a film about women's faces being surgically removed, and since it came in the aftermath of Clouzot's *Les diaboliques* and England's notoriously bloody *Curse of Frankenstein* (1957), the surgical removal of women's faces would occur *onscreen*. *Les yeux sans visage* was photographed in gorgeous black-and-white (by no less than one of filmdom's finest cinematographers, Eugen Schüfftan), so unlike Hammer's Eastmancolor gore, Franju was able to let his monochrome blood run ink black.

Audiences went wild. At the Edinburgh Film Festival, some viewers actually fainted - prompting Franju to crow undiplomatically, "Now I know why Scotsmen wear skirts."[9] But audiences of any constitution were going to be on the edge of their seats during this sequence, regardless of high-falutin' film-theoretical allegory. What Franju does here is guaranteed to jangle the nerves. Once Genessier and his assistant Louise (Alida Valli) begin the skin-graft procedure, there is no further narrative information left for the scene to convey. There will be no complications to the operation, nor any dialogue between the players. From a strictly *narrative* perspective, there is no remaining dramatic tension to the scene.

Yet there is tension aplenty... it is simply of a non-narrative variety. The audience is primed for the onscreen revelation of the horrible, grisly peeling back of flesh from raw nerves and muscle. If Franju had no intention of showing the face removal-and there is nothing else going on in the scene-then the image would discreetly fade to black. In most horror pictures prior to this, that is exactly what would now happen. Franju, though, is working in a post-Hammer environment. Terence Fisher's Hammer classic *Curse of Frankenstein* included a "shot heard 'round the world", in which Peter Cushing as Dr. Frankenstein casually wiped blood off his hands onto his jacket during an operation. It had been an unprecedented acknowledgment of the essential bloodiness of the action, and opened doors for filmmakers around the world to depict graphic violence.

So Franju keeps the scene going. He's going to show us the blood. But not yet. He is about to substantially raise the bar for onscreen gore, but before doing so, he makes certain that his brief shot - just a few fleeting seconds of celluloid - packs the maximum punch. So he keeps the scene going.

Most of this is just back-and-forth cutting between Genessier and Louise's faces as they go about their gruesome business. There is nothing particularly interesting about these shots. The point is rather the audience's growing awareness of

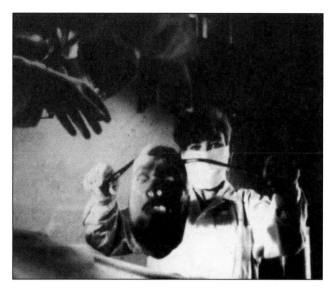

above:
The surgical horror of Georges Franju's **Les yeux sans visage** (aka **Eyes Without a Face**).

[9] Lowenstein, 37-58.

above and opposite:
Les yeux sans visage.

what is *not* being shown. There are three people in the room, but only two are presented to us. These two are involved in an action which is also not yet on screen. The longer the scene continues, the greater the certainty that the next cut *has* to reveal that third person, the central action of the scene, the payoff to the whole business.

But still not yet. Cut after cut, that expectation is defeated-temporarily-only serving to further inflate the expectation for the *next* cut in the sequence...and then the next. So it goes, leaving the audience hanging in suspense until they are ready to explode.

Finally it comes. The showstopper. And, as *L'Express* noted at the time, "the spectators dropped like flies."[10]

Franju had been experimenting with realistic violence and movie gore for some time prior to *Les yeux sans visage*. He got his start in the movie business crafting documentary short subjects. His 1948 short *Le sang des bêtes* (*Blood of the Animals*) was filmed in a slaughterhouse, juxtaposing footage of animals being killed with clips of lovers kissing, or women shopping. The basic ingredients of *Les yeux* were all there: realistic details of shocking horror contrasted with everyday mundanity, and a poet's eye bringing them together with common imagery.

Les yeux sans visage triggered a scandal in the film community in much the same way that Hitchcock's *Psycho* and Michael Powell's *Peeping Tom* (UK, 1960) did: for film critics contemptuous of the tawdry exploitationism of horror, reconciling these major works of horror art from highly respected filmmakers was a real problem. Of course it was a problem that vanished as soon as one accepted horror filmmaking as a valid exercise in itself, that engaging an audience's fear was as legitimate an enterprise as engaging any other emotion-but few critics were willing to do that.

Audiences too faced a problem. In the United States, *Les yeux* was marketed in dubbed form as *The Horror Chamber of Dr. Faustus*, with the face-removal scene tastefully trimmed. The film was shown on a double-bill with *The Manster* (1960), a wild piece of outré storytelling from Japan as lurid as they come. The US promoters naturally played up the exploitation angle on *The Manster*, while carefully positioning *Dr. Faustus* as an "art film":

"*Selected for special showings at the Edinburgh Film Festival*";

"*A ghastly elegance that suggests Tennessee Williams*";

"*Worthy of the great horror classics of our time.*"

Nevertheless, the audience that naturally turned out for such a double feature was not the art-house crowd patronising, say, Truffaut's *The 400 Blows* (1959), but rather a rowdy teenage mob come to see the blood. Whereas French audiences objected to the shocks of the picture, American audiences found the poetry of *Les yeux* slow-going, even dull. Today, critics and audiences around the world hail Franju's film as a masterpiece of horror art, but in 1959 such a concept was seen as oxymoronic, and audiences were polarised in their responses.

Writing for *Les Cahiers du Cinema*, critic Michel Delahaye was so discomfited by the horror-to him a "minor genre"-that he felt compelled to discuss *Les yeux* as a work of *film noir*.[11] Only by reclassifying it as something which he found respectable, falling over himself to justify Franju's trafficking in this lowly plebian style, could Delahaye accept the picture.

Much as French cinema tried to rewrite Méliès' contributions, many important French film histories simply ignore *Les yeux sans visage* altogether, rather than confront its defiantly horrific nature. Several major chronicles of French film exhaustively list all of Franju's works, down to his documentary shorts, except for *Les Yeux*. Others cover it only cursorily, as if it were too trivial to discuss seriously. This, for what was Franju's greatest commercial success.

One of those not ashamed to admit the power of Franju's film was Jesus Franco Manera, who remade the picture in his own idiom countless times over the years: *Gritos en la noche*, *La venganza del Dr. Mabuse* (1970), *Faceless* (1988)... As a Spaniard, Franco's inclusion in a discussion of French horror filmmaking may seem odd, but significant works of Franco's were made with French financing for primarily French audiences.

As a burgeoning cineaste, Franco's sensibilities developed in the darkened theatre of the Cinémathèque Française in Paris. Georges Franju and Henri Langlois were co-founders of the Cinémathèque, and their programming choices were eclectic and eye-opening. The experience was a crucible in which many future filmmaking talents were forged: Truffaut, Godard, Chabrol...

And Jess Franco. A low-budget filmmaker existing on the far periphery of the film industry, obsessively cranking out lurid and often pornographic quickies,

[10] Gay-Lussac, B. (1960) *L'Express* #456.

[11] Hawkins, J. (2000) *Cutting-Edge: Art-Horror and the Horrific Avant-Garde*. Minneapolis: University of Minnesota Press, 73.

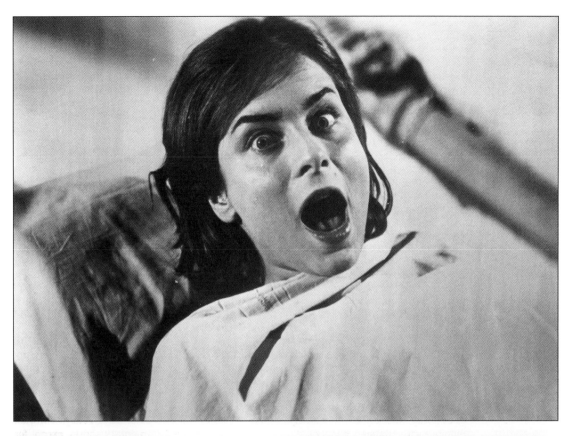

France

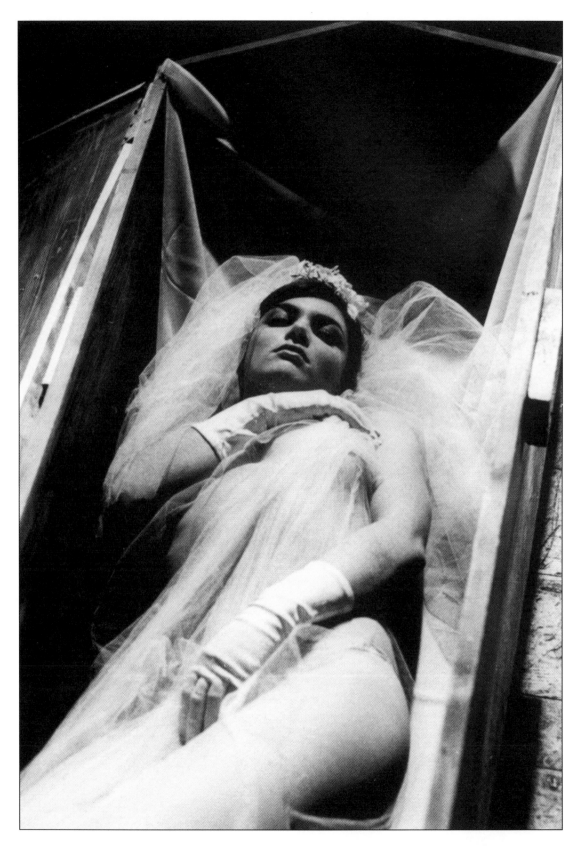

the secret history of Gallic horror movies

above:
Jean Rollin's
Fascination.

opposite:
Rollin's debut feature **Le viol du vampire** (1968).

Franco would never rival the directors of the French New Wave, nor his personal cinematic idols Fritz Lang and Orson Welles. Yet he has won over an impressive base of loyal fans around the world who admire his slapdash eccentricities as the work of a true iconoclast.

Franco already had a handful of remarkably precocious films under his belt in his home country of Spain, but it was *Gritos en la noche* in 1961 that catapulted him to international attention - such as it was. The history of *Gritos* reaches back to 1957, when the father-son team of Marius and Daniel Lesoeur purchased a ramshackle production house called Eurociné. Running against the grain, the Lesoeurs transformed Eurociné into a specialist in horror pictures, despite the apparent prejudice against the genre in France. They cannily noted the popularity of foreign-made chillers, especially those from Hammer, and they observed that the world's first serious critical attention to horror films appeared in the 1960s thanks to the French publication *Midi-Minuit Fantastique*. A readily identifiable niche market clearly existed for such lurid thrills in France, but was being ignored by the major players in the industry. Enter the entrepreneurs.

With *Gritos en la noche*, the Lesoeurs struck low-expectation gold. Both Marius Lesoeur and Jess Franco claim authorship of the script, which is tantamount to arguing over crumbs: *Gritos* is a stroke-for-stroke remount of *Les yeux sans visage*, with even *more* gore (and sex).

Despite its French provenance, *Gritos* is generally regarded as the first Spanish horror movie, thanks to its Spanish director. However, thanks to strict censorship in Spain, the film screened intact in France but heavily edited in Franco's native country. Cash-strapped Eurociné lacked the resources to fully exploit *Gritos*'s popularity. They were able to strike just a handful of prints, so it could only play in a small number of theatres at one time regardless of the potential audience. As a result, it took several years for the picture to turn a profit.[12]

Franco's singular obsessions with erotic horror were exceeded by native Frenchman Jean Rollin's career-long fixation on deeply sexual, hideously gory vampire films, suffused with delicate, dreamy poetry. Equally as marginalised as

[12] Hood, D. & C. Fukuda (2000) "Eurociné, the best little Horror House in France," *Video Watchdog* 63, 24-37.

right:
Brigitte Lahaie's finest role;
Fascination.

13 Lucas, T. (1996) "Versions and Vampires", *Video Watchdog* 31, 28-35.

14 Jean Rollin interviewed by Peter Blumenstock (1996), *Video Watchdog* 31, 36-57. For more on Rollin, visit Marc Morris's website: www.mondoerotico.co.uk. See also Tombs, P. & C. Tohill (1994) *Immoral Tales: European Sex and Horror Movies 1956-1984*. New York: St. Martin's Griffin, 135-76; and the special "Jean Rollin" issue of the online journal *Kinoeye* (2.7, 15 April 2002): www.kinoeye.org/index_02_07.html.

below:
Le viol du vampire.

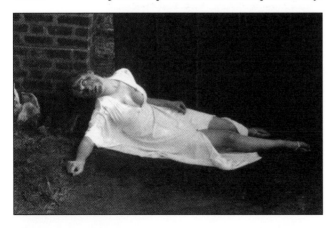

Franco, Rollin also claims a niche audience of committed fans. His pictures are an odd, uncommercial blend of pornography and Gothic horror, entrancing and addictive to the select few.

The low-budget independent film industry in 1970s France was a sex industry. The liberalisation of censorship gradually opened up to hard-core porn, which soon dominated the slates of exploitation producers. Rollin, personally obsessed with his own visions of erotic vampires, cleaved an idiosyncratic path. He did his share of straight sex pictures (as did Franco), and often cast porn stars in his horror epics (since they were used to performing in the nude, whatever their thespian abilities), but he spent most of his producers' money on deeply personal films with little regard for their commercial prospects.

From 1968's *Le viol du vampire* (*Rape of the Vampire*) onwards to the present day, Rollin has exercised what Tim Lucas calls "one of the purest imaginations ever consecrated to the horror genre."[13] Rollin improvised one picture in its entirety- *Requiem pour un vampire* (*Requiem for a Vampire*, 1971)-which was the only one of his films to get a US theatrical release, thanks to sexploitation master Harry Novak who distributed it as *Caged Virgins*. And Rollin's *Les raisins de la mort* (*Grapes of Death*, 1978) was the first notable "gore" film made in France. But of his *oeuvre*, *Fascination* (1979) arguably ranks as Rollin's finest work. An excellent-and of course heavily sexual-psychological thriller, *Fascination* presents a group of rich socialites who indulge in the drinking of bull blood as a cure for anaemia- only to develop an insatiable taboo thirst for the human stuff. They sate this thirst in elaborate ritual gatherings to which they "invite" male victims. Thoughtful, sensual and lushly photographed, *Fascination* is a unique production, and undoubtedly the most accomplished work ever made with a porn-star cast.

Inspired to be a director by a childhood screening of Abel Gance's *Capitaine Fracasse* (1942), Rollin also cites Franju's *Judex* as a major influence; and by extension, a line of influence can be traced all the way back to Feuillade himself. Rollin also took a great deal from his mentor, the surrealist Ado Kyrou. Admits Rollin, however, "You know, there isn't really a French tradition of fantastic cinema. I don't think it can be said that I am a representative of French fantastic culture *per se*."[14]

the secret history of Gallic horror movies

Bloodlust

The emergent dichotomy in French fantastic cinema was clear. On the one hand were the Jess Francos and Jean Rollins, cranking out obsessive and often pornographic exploitation fodder. On the other were the highbrow artists who freely indulged in futurist allegories or bloody crime thrillers but eschewed traditional notions of horror. So we get Claude Chabrol's *Dr. M* (a.k.a. *Club Extinction*, 1990), François Truffaut's *Fahrenheit 451* (1966), Jean-Luc Godard's *Alphaville* (1965), Alain Resnais's *L'année dernière à Marienbad* (*Last Year at Marienbad*, 1961), René Laloux's *La planète sauvage* (*Fantastic Planet*, 1973) and Chris Marker's award-winning 1964 short subject *La jetée* (*The Pier*, remade by Terry Gilliam in 1995 as *Twelve Monkeys*). Science fiction was acceptable to the cinema mainstream, as it dealt with high-minded subject matter, but horror - like pornography - was seen as doing nothing beyond inflaming the baser emotional responses. For this reason, "serious" filmmakers were largely unwilling to follow Franju's example, to make an A-list, reputable horror film.

There were, of course, exceptions to the rule. Two such exceptions - Roger Vadim's *...Et mourir de plaisir* (*...And To Die From Pleasure*, a.k.a. *Blood and Roses*, 1960) and Harry Kümel's *Les lèvres rouges* (*Red Lips*, a.k.a. *Daughters of Darkness*, 1971) - are especially noteworthy. For both films represent modest commercial and critical successes, mindful of the international marketability signalled by the Gothic trendsetters of Hammer. Both are set in the modern day. Both deal with prominent legends of female vampires. Both are fashioned with artistic craftsmanship and sophistication, with a genuine eroticism that does not depend on the sleazy exploitationism of Eurociné. And, it must be noted, neither can claim a purely French lineage.

Vadim came to prominence as a filmmaker in 1956 with *Et Dieu créa la femme* (*And God Created Woman*), starring his then-wife, sex symbol Brigitte Bardot. Later he married another sex symbol, Jane Fonda, and cast her in the pulpy sci-fi extravaganza *Barbarella* (1967), as well as the horror anthology *Histoires extraordinaires* (*Extraordinary Tales*, a.k.a. *Spirits of the Dead*, 1968). Concurrent with *...Et mourir*, Vadim edited a collection of vampire short stories.

His *...Et mourir de plaisir* takes as its departure point J. Sheridan Le Fanu's 1871 novel *Carmilla*. In the pantheon of vampire literature, *Carmilla* occupies a spot second only to Bram Stoker's *Dracula*. Over the years, Le Fanu's tale has inspired such diverse films as Carl Dreyer's *Vampyr* (Germany, 1931), Hammer's *The Vampire Lovers* (UK, 1970) and its sequels, and Vicente Aranda's *La novia ensangrentada* (*The Blood Spattered Bride*, Spain, 1972).

Le Fanu's vampire, Carmilla Karnstein, disguises her identity over the centuries by anagramming the letters of her name into new combinations: Millarca, Mircalla and Carmilla are all different incarnations of the same blood-sucking fiend. Vadim's film introduces us to Carmilla von Karnstein (another of the director's one-time spouses, Annette Vadim), a young woman in 1960s Italy who appears to be the most recent residence of the vampire's being.

Although made a decade beforehand, Vadim's picture plays as a modern-day sequel to Hammer's Karnstein trilogy- *The Vampire Lovers*, *Lust for a Vampire* (1970) and *Twins of Evil* (1971). The influence runs both ways: as much as Vadim mimicked Hammer's style, certainly the 1970s Karnstein films drew inspiration from this one. *Lust for a Vampire*, for example, duplicates one of *...Et mourir*'s more striking visuals, in which blood runs down Carmilla's chest. More importantly, *Lust for a Vampire* shares with Vadim's film the notion that Carmilla's vampiric soul and current physical incarnation are potentially divisible. The present-day Carmilla, in other words, has an independent non-vampiric identity distinctly her own. As such, Carmilla is as much a victim of the vampire as the vampire herself. She is an outcast, a misfit- not a predator.

To aid the sympathetic portrayal of Carmilla, Vadim discreetly places all of the vampire attacks offscreen. What is left is therefore far more chaste and restrained than anything Hammer produced, an elegiac and moody picture rather than one chock-a-block with visceral shocks. *...Et mourir* is a gentle horror movie.

Kümel's *Les lèvres rouges* adapts as its source the legend of a true-life vampire, the so-called "Bloody Countess", Erzsébet Báthory. Born into one of Transylvania's wealthiest and most powerful families in the 16th century, Báthory led a life of astonishing wickedness and sadism. Murderous, ruthless, with a scandalous sex life and a fascination for Black Magic, the Countess killed two of her four husbands and mercilessly tortured her servants. She earned her nickname, though, when she became obsessed with blood. At first it was just a question of biting her victims during torture, to eat their raw flesh and taste their blood. But she soon became fixated on the idea that by bathing in the blood of virgins, she could stop or even reverse the aging process. So, legend has it, in a vain effort to preserve her vanity, the Bloody Countess proceeded to murder some 650 local maidens.

Like her fellow Transylvanian tyrant Vlad the Impaler, the Countess Báthory's infamous crimes led her to be turned into a 20th century movie vampire. Neither Kümel's picture nor Hammer's contemporaneous treatment (*Countess Dracula*, 1970) seem much concerned with dramatising the real Erzsébet, although Hammer's take cleaves much closer to the actual events - no more so than most screen Draculas worry much about the historical Vlad Tepes.

Instead, like Vadim's *...Et mourir*, Kümel stages *Les lèvres rouges* in the modern day. A honeymooning couple find themselves waylaid in the none-too-exciting town of Ostend. As it so happens, hubby Stefan (John Karlen) has a few dark secrets that he has kept from his bride Valerie (Danielle Ouimet), not least of which is the older, domineering homosexual lover back home from whose influence he hopes to flee. Understandably reluctant to introduce the new missus to "Mother", Stefan opts to linger in Ostend. Enter the Countess Báthory (*Marienbad*'s Delphine Seyrig) and her lesbian love slave (Andrea Rau) to wreak a terrible corrupting influence on the young lovers. Stefan wears his darker nature pretty close to the surface, and is easily debauched by the Countess. By far the greater prize is to seduce Valerie as her new acolyte. At the end, Valerie has indeed taken Báthory's place, continuing to tour the world in order to spread her corruption. Interestingly, both *...Et mourir* and *Les lèvres* share the same climax: both pictures conclude by apparently killing off the vampire, only to reveal that her spirit lives on in the body of the heroine. The same device can be found at the end of Michael Almereyda's 1994 vampire film *Nadja* (US).

Clearly a part of the lesbian vampire tradition that was all the rage in 1970s horror cinema, and to which Jean Rollin was single-mindedly dedicated, *Les lèvres rouges* is in all areas of cinematic achievement superior to Hammer's concurrent take on the subject, *Countess Dracula*. Cult film historian Tim Lucas minces no words in declaring Kümel's picture "a genuine artistic triumph."[15] However, the film failed to find the same mainstream reception in France as Vadim's earlier work. The commercial failure of Kümel's follow-up feature *Malpertuis* in 1972 sealed his doom in the industry.[16] Although *Les lèvres rouges* developed a cult following, for many years its only presence in America was in a severely edited form, drastically re-cut by the notorious "film doctor" Fima Noveck. Kümel's original cut did not make it to the US until a home video restoration appeared in 1998.[17]

Despite French financing, neither *...Et mourir* nor *Les lèvres rouges* is a purely French product. *...Et mourir* was shot in English in Italy. *Les lèvres rouges* was shot in English in Belgium by a Belgian director. It would not be until the rise of the duo Jean-Pierre Jeunet and Marc Caro many years later that France could boast of having fully homegrown horror/fantasy filmmakers with mainstream respectability.

Nightmares of the future

Jeunet and Caro cut their teeth as stop-motion animators, making striking short films like 1979's *Le manège* (*The Merry-Go-Round*). After finely honing their unique vision on these short subjects, they transferred that disturbed outlook to full-scale features. On the strength of *Delicatessen* (1991) and *La cité des enfants perdus* (*The City of Lost Children*, 1995), the pair was hailed by critics across the globe as France's answer to Terry Gilliam.

The city of lost children is just that: a fantastical otherworld where an evil mad scientist named Krank (Daniel Emilfork), his family of idiot cloned sons, and an army of one-eyed monsters seek out and kidnap children. A lifetime of cruelty has naturally enough left Krank with a disturbed conscience. Unable to sleep properly, unable to dream, he hopes to steal the brainwaves of innocent babes to give him peaceful, blissful, dreamy nights. Problem is, the experience of being captured and imprisoned leaves the children traumatised, so all that happens is they feed their bad dreams back into Krank's unhappy cranium.

The elaborate, expressionist imagery of *La cité* does indeed invite comparison to

---

[15] Lucas, T. (1998) "Fade Into Red", *Video Watchdog* 44, 20.

[16] Lofficier, J-M and R. Lofficier (2000) *French Science-Fiction, Fantasy, Horror and Pulp Fiction*. Jefferson, N.C.: McFarland & Co., 266.

[17] For more on Kümel and *Les Lèvres Rouges*, see Jenks, C. (1996) "Daughters of Darkness: A Lesbian Vampire Film" in Black, A. (ed), *Necronomicon: The Journal of Horror and Erotic Cinema, Book 1*. London: Creation Books, 22-34. See also Lebbing, M. (2003) "of vampires and the gods of Greece" in Fenton, H. (ed), *Flesh & Blood Compendium*. Surrey: FAB Press, 162-169.

the secret history of Gallic horror movies

Terry Gilliam. The closest analogues in Gilliam's canon, though-*Time Bandits* (1981), or *The Adventures of Baron Munchausen* (1988)-have an ironic attitude, an underlying cynicism that sets them apart from the work of Jeunet and Caro. For all its genuinely nightmarish qualities, *La cité* displays a sense of compassion, of uplifting humanity, of childlike innocence. In short, Jeunet-Caro's film can honestly be described as unique.

Not only did Jeunet-Caro join the big leagues of French film domestically; they proved their mettle abroad as well. Hollywood even invited the pair to helm the fourth instalment of the long-running *Alien* franchise, *Alien: Resurrection* (1997). Jeunet-Caro brought with them their distinctive creative vision, as well as a loyal stable of recurring players, including Dominique Pinon and Ron Perlman. The end result was a happy hybrid, at once an authentic rendering of their French aesthetic, a major studio blockbuster, and a resounding popular success to boot. Warmly received by critics and fans as one of the strongest entries in the *Alien* saga, *Alien: Resurrection* proved that France had at last found its voice in Gothic horror.

Jeunet-Caro's accomplishment is nothing short of remarkable. In France today, some 130 motion pictures are manufactured annually, of which at best ten to fifteen are exported. Few of these receive any significant attention in the world's largest film market, the United States. Even back in France, only about eighty or so manage to get seen. For French filmmakers, exposure is extremely limited, the possibilities for success slim. The French film industry is highly insular and economically desperate. Both *Delicatessen* and *La cité des enfants perdus* performed minor miracles by becoming significant niche market hits outside France. The commercial success of these films in the United States is not despite their gruesome and disturbing content, but because of it. Trading in the lowly genre of horror, as it were, Jeunet-Caro maintained both their artistic integrity and their recognisably French distinctiveness while at the same time earning rare, much-needed profits in foreign markets.

Despite this heady feat, the Jeunet-Caro team have faced some of the same blinkered attitude from the critical establishment that plagued their forerunners in the field of French fantasy filmmaking. In the waning months of 2001,

above:
Roger Vadim's **...Et mourir de plaisir** (aka **Blood and Roses**, 1960).

Jeunet's latest film, *Le fabuleux destin d'Amélie Poulain* (presented stateside under the simpler title *Amélie*) received widespread acclaim and enormous box office success, placing it on the inside track towards a possible foreign-language Oscar. By no means a horror film, *Amélie* nonetheless shares with Jeunet's earlier works many of the same visual motifs, thematic considerations and even recurring cast members- in short, *Amélie* joins the ranks of *Delicatessen*, *La cité des enfants perdus* and *Alien Resurrection* as part of a larger and still-developing body of work. Not that one would glean this from the publicity and promotion of *Amélie*: virtually every review and advertisement in the US touted Jeunet as the auteur behind *Delicatessen* and *La cité des enfants perdus*, carefully and conspicuously eliding any mention of *Alien Resurrection*. Setting aside the obvious slight to Caro's contributions to these films, the glaring omission of what is undeniably Jeunet's most commercially successful and well-known work cannot be an accident.

Just as film historians tried to ignore the presence of *Les yeux sans visage* in Franju's career, conventional wisdom on the conflict assumed that the intended audience for *Amélie* would be unlikely to turn out in such record numbers if they knew it was made by the same Hollywood hack who just cranked out the latest sequel to a big-budget and gore-filled commercial franchise. French art films are expected to be marginalised in the US, their marginalisation and artistic purity being seen as going hand-in-hand. That Jeneut made it onto Hollywood's main stage and had his work seen by millions of happily paying customers around the world chafes with the stereotype of the misunderstood outsider artist. It is hard to maintain street cred as a struggling genius of sadly unrecognised talents when the stars of one's last film have been transformed into action figures for sale at the local Toys'R'Us.

But the revisionist history involved here cuts to the heart of the perceived illegitimacy of horror. Despite his noteworthy achievements, not even Jeneut can earn mainstream critical and commercial acceptance to French horror if *Amélie* fans can't bring themselves to admit the existence of *Alien Resurrection*.

Somewhere along the way, it became a presumption that French film meant (pretentious) art-house fare, and that horror films by dint of appealing to baser emotional reactions were inevitably crass commercial exploitation. These two tenets have all but prevented the French horror film from breaking out of its ghetto. Outside of France, free of this overweening emphasis on film-as-art, directors such as Peter Jackson can find sleazy low-budget creations like *Bad Taste* (1987) breezily promoted as "from the director of *Lord of the Rings*", without a trace of irony; and every time Sam Raimi makes a serious drama, critics dutifully mention his *Evil Dead* films. Hollywood directors can proudly sport horror in their resumes but French art-house makers are expected to remain 'above' that.

For generations, French horror has been a tentative tradition of isolated, often half-hearted, stabs in the dark. Rejected by the critical mainstream, French horror was embraced most fully by outsiders and independents. Few respectable filmmakers dared tinker with the genre. Only *Les yeux sans visage* broke with this tradition, and its notoriety among critics served to dissuade others from following in his footsteps. And as French horror cinema enters the 21st century, the legacy of Franju lingers on.

below:
Les yeux sans visage.

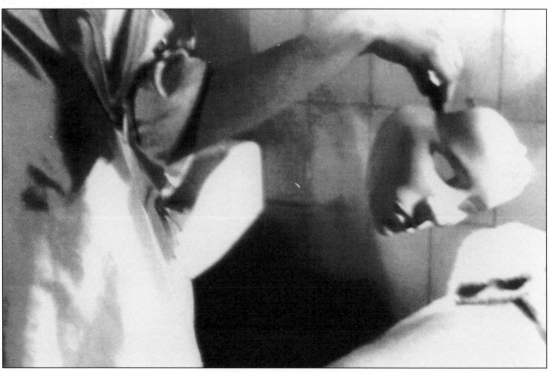

Part Four:
Case Study
- Japanese Horror Cinema

Pain threshhold: the cinema of Takashi Miike 285
- Rob Daniel & Dave Wood; followed by an interview with the director,
"When cynicism becomes art," by Julien Fonfrède

The Japanese horror film series: *Ring* and *Eko Eko Azarak* 295
- Ramie Tateishi

The urban techno-alienation of Sion Sono's *Suicide Club* 305
- Travis Crawford

case study – Japanese horror cinema

Pain threshold:
the cinema of Takashi Miike

Rob Daniel & Dave Wood (article), Julien Fonfrède (interview)

He has been around for over 11 years, with over twenty feature films under his belt, and a similar number of video titles. Why, then, is it only recently Western audiences have discovered the explosive, controversial genius of Takashi Miike?

Since 1999, when he directed *Odishon* (*Audition*) and *Dead or Alive: Hanzaisha* (*Dead or Alive*), the pace has picked up. Western festival screenings of these titles set the touch paper alight, and Miike's name has fast become a byword for an exhilarating, no-holds-barred Japanese cinema, with ideas and stylistic prowess to burn. At the time of writing he has made 17 films, plus one television mini-series since 2000, and shows no signs of fatigue.

Deciding against film school, the iconoclastic Miike became an assistant to revered Japanese director Shohei Imamura on *Zegen* (1987) and *Kuroi Ame* (*Black Rain*, 1989), whose domestic tale of disintegration and trauma foreshadows Miike's films. Currently, Miike is in negotiations to make his first English language film in the UK, a prospect at once tantalising (it would mainline adrenalin into the heart of the country's moribund film industry) and problematic. Can Miike survive the cultural translation, and will the British Board of Film Classification (despite passing *Audition* and *Dead or Alive* uncut) even let him?

Miike began and has largely remained in the Yakuza genre, with *Shinjuku Kuroshakai: Chinese Mafia Senso* (*Shinjuku Triad Society*) in 1995, followed by *Gokudo Sengokushi: Fudo* (*Fudoh: The New Generation*, 1996), *Gokudo Kuroshakai* (*Rainy Dog*, 1997), *Nihon Kuroshakai* (*Ley Lines*, 1999) and then *Dead or Alive*. Twisting the traditional Japanese style of filmmaking with its philosophical and introspective calm, he blends it with an energetic Hong Kong kinetic verve. Busting apart convention and cliché, Miike injects his thrillers with shocking moments of violence, sexual cruelty and perversity on a level rarely seen. All this is done, not with the knowing irony of someone like Quentin Tarantino, but with a humour situated perfectly within the world of each film.

With *Audition*, he changed tack: this dark and disturbing psychological tale of physical and mental abuse blended domestic melodrama with tendon-ripping violence, proving Miike versatile in more than just his cinematic style. In 2001 he would go on to make a film that even he admitted might never get released - *Koroshiya 1* (*Ichi the Killer*) - splattering the screen with all manner of bodily fluids and stirring an uncomfortable frisson of sexual violence into the body-strewn onslaught of the eponymous killer. Screened to dumbfounded audiences at the London Film Festival and at other festivals around the world, it has subsequently been released in a heavily truncated version on Hong Kong DVD. It has now been released in the UK under heavy sanction from the BBFC, which passed the film after noting publicly that it had made cuts to scenes detailing imagery that has *never* (BBFC's emphasis) been permitted in Britain.

Looking in detail at Miike's career work is no easy task. Amazingly prolific, he releases an average of three to four films per year, making it nigh on impossible to keep up with his ongoing output. For this reason we have chosen a small number of titles we believe illustrate the director's unique style. Miike is a visual storyteller, using kinetic editing rhythms and innovative sound designs to trademark his

opposite:
Artwork for the uncut European DVD boxset release of **Ichi the Killer** (1999).

above:
Visitor Q (2001).

films. A near abstract approach to plotting has evolved from early, semi-conventional films such as *Shinjuku Triad Society* or *Fudoh*, to later, surreal works such as *Dead or Alive*, *Audition* and *Visitor Q* (2001). Viewers will be baffled by the story arcs, as Miike subverts traditional storytelling in favour of dropping the audience into a fully formed Yakuza world, where the rules of survival are totally alien. It all makes a kind of sense in the end, but only after a thrilling, baffling walk on the wild side.

Consciously or otherwise, Miike's work seems to have drawn influence from such luminaries of Japanese cinema as Seijun Suzuki, "Beat" Takeshi Kitano and Yasujiro Ozu. Although Miike states that he has not yet seen a Suzuki mind-trip mob flick, this individualistic filmmaker certainly seems like a stylistic Godfather to the director. As with Miike's approach to his Yakuza thrillers, a desire to twist and shape the generic material of *Koroshi No Rakuin* (*Branded to Kill*, 1967) into something wholly original fired Suzuki's imagination. This film's central character can only become aroused when smelling boiled rice, for example, and events such as a hit being thwarted when a butterfly lands on the rifle sight could easily sit in any Miike movie.

Little has been made of the similarities between Miike and Kitano, perhaps because the two are near contemporaries. Both men share a vein of perverse humour and wilfully eccentric storytelling styles. Compare the sombre, introspective vignette structure of *Dead or Alive* with the fractured plotting of *Hana-Bi* (1997), the latter film also shot by Miike's regular cinematographer, Hideo Yamamoto; in each case the story is fragmented so as to strengthen mood and character. Meanwhile, Ozu's legendary use of "non-style" to capture reality is notable in *Audition*, which for an entire hour quietly narrates the simple story of a man embarking upon a tender love affair seven years after the death of his wife. Deliberately slow, lulling those unaware of its later shocks into a warm sense of security, Miike then sucker-punches the audience into witnessing a world turned nightmarish, also echoing Western directors such as Hitchcock, who would gleefully darken his tales with little warning.

Interestingly, Miike never writes his own scripts, frequently working from adaptations: *Fudoh* and *Ichi the Killer* are based on manga, *Audition* derives from a famous novel by Ryu (*Tokyo Decadence*) Murakami and *Visitor Q* is based on an original script by Itaru Era. But the script is merely the first step into Miikeland, with the film being shaped in the editing suite by Miike himself, who calls himself the film's "arranger."

In interviews, Miike has said that for him the script is merely the starting point and that from there, once on set, an improvisation process occurs, with input from the entire crew. Nowhere is this better illustrated than in the now-legendary opening of the original *Dead or Alive*. Famously, Miike threw out the script, condensing twenty establishing scenes into a breathless montage. To the breakneck tempo of a pounding rock soundtrack, a semi-naked woman falls from a high-rise building clutching a bag of cocaine, a

right:
Audition (1999).

Takashi Miike

above:
Fudoh: The New Generation (1996).

Yakuza grabs a shotgun from a passing clown and fires two shots into a parked car, PVC clad girls strip, a mobster snorts the world's longest line of coke (fifteen feet at least), a peroxide bully boy indulges in some rough buggery in a public loo - only to be shivved in the jugular, decorating the wall with crimson modern art - and most incredibly of all, the newly digested contents of a Yakuza boss's stomach are shotgunned into the camera!

As the film slows considerably following this opening volley of imagery, it is not mood setting; and since it only tenuously establishes plot and character, viewers will be scratching their heads long after leaving the cinema. Instead, Miike uses this sequence to provide a commentary on his Yakuza cinema, reminding the audience how visceral it can be. The sensation is akin to reading a long, disturbing sentence missing all of the grammar and most of the verbs.

Miike has likened the frenzied editing of *Dead or Alive*'s opening to the DJ method of scratching vinyl or rapid channel surfing, with a constant audiovisual barrage dazzling the audience's senses and perceptions. Both *Dead or Alive* and *Hyoryuu-Gui* (*City of Lost Souls*, 2000) illustrate this scratching style. *City of Lost Souls* opens with a prison break sequence, again perpetrated to a raucous cacophony of heavy rock rhythms and spliced together with jagged jump cuts. In both films an incredible sense of mood and atmosphere is created visually, but to comprehend the narrative is less easy.

As a counterbalance to Miike's "scratching," the controversial festival favourite *Audition* initially presents a subdued style. Music is used sparsely and the colours are muted and transparent. As the mood of the film shifts into darker territory, however, there is, almost imperceptibly, a boost in painterly cinematic panache, as the screen becomes awash with primary colour schemes: infernal reds, sickly yellows and chilling blues drag the audience into a world they would rather not experience. This range of emotion stems from the considered visual techniques Miike provides each film. Professing a dislike of 35mm with the claim that he does not want his cinema to look first-rate, Miike liberally mixes and matches film stocks and formats. With *Visitor Q* he worked with digital video, using hand held set-ups and long takes to give a sense of "reality TV."

An offshoot of Miike's cinematic verve and style is his cross-fertilisation. What first catches the eye is the mix of Eastern filmmaking styles. The rock 'n' roll cinematics of *Dead or Alive*, *Fudoh*, *Ichi the Killer* and *Shin jingi no hakaba* (*Graveyard of Honor*, 2002) recalls such esteemed Hong Kong filmmakers as John Woo, Ringo Lam and Tsui Hark, with their frenzied bullet ballets and dynamite stylistic bravado moving the action along more swiftly than the eye can see. But Miike plays it more Japanese, exaggerating the violence but focusing on the pain and suffering that accompanies bodily trauma. *Audition* plays like a Hong Kong Category III title as directed by Ozu, schizophrenically sliced down the middle - one half sweet romance, the other half mental and physical evisceration - while the black comedy *Visitor Q* presents a sharply critical view of the patriarchal Japanese family, suggesting that its salvation lies in murder and necrophilia. If the Japanese restraint that Miike so distrusts is to be washed away, only waves of blood will do.

Rooted in too much filth, viscera and the fetid side of human nature to ever be labelled high art, Miike's films thrill the eye and ignite the senses. But he is more than just the master of a three-ring circus. Interwoven into *Dead or Alive* and *City of Lost Souls* is a strong sense of what a cultural and racial mixing bowl Japan has become. *City of Lost Souls* introduces us to a Brazilian protagonist, Mario (Brazilian-Japanese non-actor Teah), rescuing his Chinese girlfriend Kei (Hong Kong actress Michelle Reis) from a prison truck. Returning to Tokyo, the couple become embroiled in an ongoing war between Chinese Triads and Japanese Yakuza. Miike conveys a sense of cultural and geographical displacement by taking his star-crossed lost souls Mario and Kei on a transglobal migration. Throughout the film, Miike creates a paradox with his Triad and Japanese characters who, although geographically more aligned than Mario and Kei, cannot co-exist.

Dead or Alive concerns the ongoing hunt by a cop Jojima (Sho Aikawa) for a gang mob led by the sadistic Ryuichi (Riki Takeuchi). Yakuza and Triad tensions form the basis of this introspective and sombre piece, the summation of a theme first addressed in Miike's feature debut, *Shinjuku Triad Society*. Ryuichi's mob consists of "zanryu koji," children of Japanese descent raised in China after World War II - misfits bereft of an identity. Yet Miike remains characteristically ambivalent about the effects this has on Ryuichi's gang members, as their lack of national pride ensures that no albatross of loyalty hangs around their necks, allowing them to destroy the Shinjuku underworld and control the drug trade from Taiwan with impunity. As shown earlier in *Fudoh*, Miike regards anarchy and uprising against old orders as healthy, and Ryuichi is certainly no more dejected than Jojima,

right:
Audition (1999).

Takashi Miike

the cop on his tail, who accepts $200,000 of mob money for his uncommunicative daughter's life-saving operation.

When discussing the Japanese family, Miike sees an erosion in the patriarchal norm. He states that women are striking out, gaining independent employment, and that men wish for the situation to reverse. *Audition* encapsulates this belief, while the surrealist masterpiece *Visitor Q* would later reach the zenith of familial conflict and disintegration. *Audition*'s protagonist, Aoyoma (Ryo Ishibashi), is unable to meet women in a "traditional" manner, agreeing instead that his video production company - being used to audition girls for a TV programme - would be a good way of finding a partner. Through this he meets the demure, submissive Asami (Eihi Shiina), the model of a Japanese wife, and begins a seemingly idyllic affair which later twists alarmingly into a battle of the sexes. In the final act, as Asami's apparently psychotic nature is revealed, she tortures Aoyoma, claiming that "Men cannot live without women." A loaded remark; with cruel logic Asami may be referring to Aoyoma's spiritual demise after his wife's death, in which case her appalling acts of mutilation are a way of restoring Aoyoma's anima. "The body is dead, but the nerves are awake," she deadpans after shooting him up with tranquilizers.

If Asami is a demented spouse, her psychosis stems from an abusive father figure. But Miike muddies the water further, with ambiguities running rampant through misremembered, hallucinatory flashbacks, alternate takes on earlier scenes and the old "Is it or isn't it a dream?" set-up. It ultimately remains an open question whether Asami's monstrousness is real or fantasy. Encompassing the tensions between all men and women, as well as the male preoccupation with emancipated females, *Audition* is very Japanese in its depiction of social interaction and revenge. But its accomplishments are universal, continuing to advance Miike's family project.

Fudoh, beginning with a shocking scene of infanticide, suggests that while an empire may be built on family shoulders, it can just as easily be toppled because of an uncompromising patriarch. Miike makes it clear that only in a world this perverse could family be destroyed for business. In *Dead or Alive*, the sanctity of the family leads to violence. Ryuichi's younger sibling, whose college education is paid for by his brother's blood money, rebels against everything he holds sacred upon discovering this fact, and, as mentioned above, Jojima is reduced to corruption to pay the large amount of money needed to treat his daughter's possibly fatal illness. She too rebels and shows no gratitude for her father's deeds. Neither of these two men, opposites in every other way, can hold their families together, and it is family that forces them into spectacular confrontation.

"Have you ever done it with your dad?" asks a black-on-white title. *Visitor Q* is lethally uncompromising. A failing TV reporter (Kenichi Endo), attempting to produce a documentary on Japanese youth, pays his daughter for sex. Back at home, the son terrorises the mother with vicious beatings and she finds release in prostitution and heroin addiction. Into this family comes the Visitor (Kazushi Watanabe), and with typical Japanese politeness, they never challenge him for invading their home. Upon discovering his son is being bullied, the father opts to

above:
Fudoh: The New Generation (1996).

above:
Cover of the uncut European DVD release of **Visitor Q** (2001).

make a TV show from it. But when his ex-lover boss scornfully vetoes the idea, he murderously turns on her and the family unity is challenged.

Visitor Q wildly exaggerates Japanese traits of restraint, self-denial and modesty. Irrationally subservient, the mother takes beatings from her son and attends to her family's every need. The father, previously humiliated when a Vox pop turns into rape (as youths insert his microphone into his arse), is plagued by professional self-doubt. The largely unseen daughter shoulders Miike's view of contemporary Japanese youth: inexpressive, prostituting themselves for material gain and embracing a vacuous mass media. The Visitor releases passions that allow these people to function again, as Miike goes for the outer limits of humour. The mother learns to lactate oceans of breast milk, and the father finds empowerment in murder and necrophilia ("The mysteries of life are amazing! Even a corpse can get wet!"), during a prolonged sequence which begins as gross-out comedy only to transform into something shocking, hilarious and remarkable. *Visitor Q* is the pinnacle of Miike's dissection of the family unit, and it will be interesting to see if his other digital video project, *Family*, made a year earlier but still unreleased in the West, lays the groundwork for the extremities depicted here.

What keeps Miike's *oeuvre* from falling into po-faced butchery is his love of dark comedy. Could *Ichi the Killer*, an ultra-ultra-violent tale of a disturbed young man who is fuelled by rape fantasies and goaded into slaughtering high level Yakuza, really work unless it was punctuated by a finely judged humour? For body horror, *Ichi the Killer* is Miike *par excellence*, *Fudoh* and *Dead or Alive* on an apocalyptic coke and speed bender. *Dead or Alive* focused on family disintegration and the loss of national identity, but *Ichi the Killer* is an atrocity exhibition, encapsulated in the young, warped figure of Kakihara (Tadanobu Asano). This ambitious Yakuza, hooked on experiencing the pinnacle of pain, hunts Ichi down to provide it. After torturing a gangster wrongly suspected of slaying an elder, Kakihara hacks off the tip of his tongue as an act of contrition, a toe-curling sequence with a killer comic punchline. The film is obsessed with intimate pain: Kakihara's mouth is cut open into a Joker-like grin and held in place with metal rings; a gangster's moll has her nipples sliced off; another man is suspended by hooks and has his testicles lanced.

Sexual violence is the most problematic area of Miike's work. In his world, sex is a weapon. In *Fudoh*, the father's infanticide is presented as incestuous rape, and male rape is also suggested during *Audition*'s tortuous denouement. Asami sits astride a passive Aoyoma and penetrates him with needles, cooing "Kiri, kiri, kiri" ("deeper, deeper, deeper"). The father in *Visitor Q* is literally raped with his microphone, a neat visual gag implying his professional failure. He is also *maladroit* between the sheets, forever lamenting his "coming too early," and rapes his dead ex-mistress, who gets a posthumous revenge by shitting on him.

Undoubtedly, Miike's films are an acquired taste. Always inventive and increasingly outrageous, his wellspring of inspiration shows no signs of evaporating. *Katakuri-ke no kòfuku* (*The Happiness of the Katakuris*, 2001), a deranged and hilarious murderous musical, proves that he can successfully adapt any genre taking

Takashi Miike

his fancy. In the West, will Miike go the way of Woo, Lam and Hark and be forced to bow to studio interference? Will watered-down Takashi Miike work, or does he need an Asian culture to thrive? With the recent growing interest in Japanese horror cinema in the form of *Battle Royale* (2000) and *Ring* (1998), there is at least some reason to hope that studios will release their panicky grip on this new wave of talent.

When cynicism becomes art: a short interview with Takashi Miike

No longer new or in any sense unknown, Takashi Miike remains one of Japan's hottest filmmakers, following fast on the footsteps of such contemporary Japanese directors as Takeshi Kitano and Kiyoshi Kurosawa. This new master of cinematic mayhem was finally discovered by the West when his *Gokudô sengokushi: Fudô* (*Fudoh: The New Generation*) started touring the international film festival circuit in 1996. He is now seen as one of the most unpredictable auteurs of a new type of Japanese cinema. Many of his films are like sandcastles, where everything is built only in order to be eloquently destroyed, with a style and excess often going beyond previously established limits. In looking over Miike's filmography one can definitely sense the sheer pleasure he gets from making movies, not only because of the sheer number he makes each year (an average of five) but also because of the way his recent work manages to play with its audience. Often, just talking about one of his films is to spoil some of the fun of watching it.

Miike was born in Osaka on 24 August 1960. After finishing his studies at the Yokohama Academy of Broadcasting and Film, he worked as an assistant director for such prominent filmmakers as Shohei Imamura, Kazuo Kuroki and Hideo Onchi. In 1995, he directed his first theatrical release, *Shinjuku kuroshakai: Chinese Mafia sensô* (*Shinjuku Triad Society*), but to this day he also continues to make pictures for television and the prosperous Japanese video market. For the visual innovations and the aggressive pacing that inhabit his work, he is already considered one of the great discoveries of new Japanese cinema. Among his latest and most widely screened releases are *Dead or Alive: Hanzaisha* (*Dead or Alive*, 1999), *Odishon* (*Audition*, 1999) and *Koroshiya 1* (aka *Ichi the Killer*, 2001).

Julien Fonfrède: *There is a strong mix in your films between commercialism and experimentation. Is subverting genres and playing with contradictions something that is consciously in your mind prior to shooting?*

Takashi Miike: Basically, I am not the kind of person who is interested in making films that are simply well done. If you make a genre film the way it's supposed to be made, there are always others who have done it better than you before. If I can't really enjoy myself while making something, there isn't much point in making the films at all. I want do to something different from what other people have done before. I want to get away from conventions. It's also really once I'm on the set that I enjoy experimenting in that way... To see how I can make the whole thing different from what it normally would have become. That's the way I enjoy myself as a filmmaker. And because I am already that kind of person

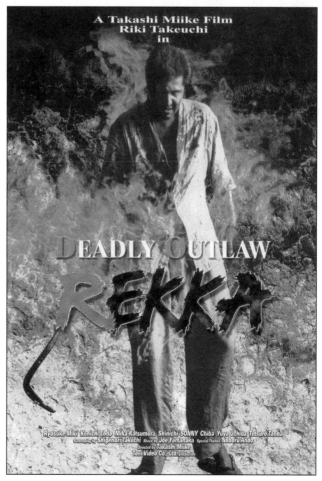

below:
Poster for **Deadly Outlaw: Rekka** (2002).

WORLD PREMIERE!
AGITATOR
10TH RAINDANCE FILM FESTIVAL 23.10.02-01.11.02 WWW.RAINDANCE.CO.UK

TRIADS, YAKUSA, GANG WARFARE, A GIRL AND A MICROPHONE
With Masaya Kato, Naoto Takenaka, Ryosuke Miki, Masatoh Eve

...hippest Japanese film of the year...LA Biz

RAINDANCE OFFICIAL SELECTION
SAT 26 OCT AT 8:45PM CURZON SOHO

above:
The hottest ticket in town.

to begin with, there's sort of a natural development once I'm on the set making the film...

The point of wondering, "What will the critics or the public think of this? Will they accept me or not?" is not of major importance to me. What is more important is that I make films that I feel are right in the circumstances that I am in at a certain moment in time. Whether I am accepted or not is not the main issue. It's like some kind of fate that I make the films that I make. If I think too much about the films, then the fun of making them gets lost. I don't concern myself too much with a dream that I have or an ideal of what kind of movie I would like to make from now on... I make films that I enjoy making at one particular point... And maybe something else develops from there, but that's not the main concern.

JF: But in your films there seems to be a strong sense of thinking about the audience... The whole idea of surprising everyone...

TM: A lot of people are involved in the making of a film. When I make a picture, it goes in a certain direction. But then, on the set, lots of things also start happening depending on everyone's input. Because of all this, things start to develop naturally from there... The audience might be surprised with certain scenes or the ways my films develop, but I think the one who is often the most surprised is me! I'm the one thinking, "What the hell is this? What's happening now?"

If you take *Odishon*, for example... My original point was to give up on all of the horror elements. Usually when I'm on the set, I, myself, am gradually destroying all the plans I had in the beginning. And if nobody stops me, it just goes on and on... It's the same with my way of working with sound. Basically, my approach to making an interesting film is that I need to find feelings and emotions that I have lost. That's the way I work to make the whole experience of directing a film interesting.

JF: Considering all this, I am very curious to know how you work and deal with producers...

TM: (laughs...) They're used to it by now. Most of them now know what kind of person I am. That's why I usually team up with people who allow me to work the way I do. Of course, there are different types of producers and it's not rare that I find myself in the middle of complicated arguments. Anyway, a film that is made without any arguments would probably not be a very interesting film in the end.

JF: How about your producers' reaction when you went to tell them about the ending for Dead or Alive? You would have never gotten away with this in Hollywood, for example. Over there, logic is still very important.

TM: (laughs...) Well, for me the script is only the starting point. From there you use your imagination. The actual film is born from the script... But on the set, there is once again the input of the whole crew. Everybody is bringing ideas... Then it is decided which way the film will eventually go. I think this is probably the only way to make it interesting.

JF: It wasn't the ending that was originally planned...

Takashi Miike

TM: The original idea was that the two protagonists would meet in Taiwan. There would be a shootout there, and you wouldn't have known who won.

JF: Violence in your films is very excessive and often works as some kind of a subtext in itself.

TM: The fact is that everybody has these feelings about violence. Everybody wants to defend or protect his family. That is a very honest reaction. It's our animal instinct. The desire that everybody would live in peace is an illusion. The yearning for violence is very honest. Allowing this to come out is much healthier than trying to suppress it. In my films, people are like monsters or beasts - their violence is extreme, but at least it's honest.

JF: You seem to be one of the few Japanese directors who is interested in mixing the different Asian cultures. Considering that Japanese cinema has always focused essentially on its own culture, this is something I find especially interesting.

TM: The fact is that it's apparent before your eyes, living in Tokyo or Osaka. These cities have really changed in the past several years. They represent a full mix of Asian cultures now... Actually, the Yakuzas are very influenced by foreign cultures these days. Foreigners have entered their world, and now they have to deal with it. It's the same with contemporary Japanese society. If you walk down the streets in Shibuya, there are Iranians trying to sell you stuff... There are all kinds of cultures there, and everywhere else in Tokyo. Films should follow what's really happening...

The fact is that the Japanese nowadays don't really think about what they see. They walk down the streets in Tokyo and are like "Hmmm... There are more foreigners than before, aren't there?" They don't think about it much further than that. They certainly do not make any conclusions about it. It seems like they have lost interest in their own city and their own country. They seem to have become numb. In Hong Kong, for exemple, cinema tends to focus more on what's really happening out in the streets. It tends to reflect much more on contemporary society.

I am actually talking right now about the possibility of making a film in Hong Kong, to be produced by Golden Harvest next year. If I decide to do it, I should have lots of freedom. I want to make something completely crazy.

above:
The authorised Takashi Miike book, first published by FAB Press in 2003.

JF: In the course of your career so far you have worked in almost every genre possible, but you've never made any erotic films; this even though erotica seems to remain a big institution in Japan for new directors.

TM: I think these films are too much of a lie today. They pretend to portray relationships between young people, but the people who conceive the films are usually very old. I don't really like the world of contemporary pink films. Its mind is old. If I was to do something in that genre I am sure it would end up being too grotesque. For me, it's not really interesting, the way the Japanese pink film world is at the moment. All of the stories portrayed in these films are too much like real life. It's not like you watch the films and you say, "Oh... Interesting!"

The Japanese horror film series: *Ring* and *Eko Eko Azarak*

Ramie Tateishi

Beginning in the mid 1990s, Japanese horror cinema underwent a dramatic resurgence that continues to accelerate, with new films being produced at a rate unseen since the mid-to-late sixties. In the year 2000 alone, films such as *Hebi Onna* (*The Snake Woman*), *Odishon* (*Audition*), *Uzumaki* (*Spiral*), *Replay*, *Sakuya* and *Oshikiri* (*The Straw Cutter*), provided a constant flow of cinematic terror, re-establishing the presence of the horror film within the category of the *tokusatsu* ("special effects") genre, which has tended to be dominated by the science fiction and monster films of the Godzilla and Gamera variety. During this resurgence, two of the most popular film series have been the *Ringu* (*Ring*) movies (1998, 1999, 2000), the first two of which were directed by Hideo Nakata, and the *Eko Eko Azarak* films (1995, 1996, 1998), the first two of which were directed by Shimako Sato. *Ring* has inspired an American remake, both have spun off television shows and inspired cult followings, and the influence of both series can also be seen in the style and aesthetic of some of the other films in this Japanese horror renaissance.

The notion of horror constructed in the *Ring* and *Eko Eko Azarak* film series is a horror of the past intruding into the present; a remnant of some distant chaos that emerges to disrupt the stability of the here-and-now not only through its actions, but by its very presence. It is interesting how these two vastly different series deal with the same thematic preoccupation, configured in different ways. The *Ring* films tell the story of Sadako, a spirit who returns seeking vengeance after being entombed in a well forty years earlier. The *Eko Eko Azarak* films focus on the efforts of a powerful young witch to stop ancient forces of evil from manifesting themselves in the present day. To examine this thematic concern in a specifically Japanese context, the critical discourse around tradition and modernity can be applied as a useful model that highlights the tensions and anxieties surrounding the nature of this "horror of the past", and helps to explain why this idea has particular resonance in Japanese horror cinema.

Cultural nostalgia, active destruction

The general approach to Japanese modernity situates its origin at the Meiji Restoration of 1868, which saw the end of the Tokugawa shogunate. As Kevin Doak notes, however, "modernity was defined in a variety of ways (and therefore tended toward obscurity): at times it represented a foreign influence - the West; at other times it referred to the Meiji state and its ideology of 'civilization and enlightenment'; and at still others it referred to the reality of Japanese culture in its only existent (if decadent) form."[1] The transformation of Japanese society on this multitude of levels was rooted in notions of progress and development, which rhetorically signified a break from "tradition" and "the past", as in the "Enlightened Rule" of the Meiji.

One aspect of this modernisation was a restructuring along capitalist lines, which by 1955 had developed into a technological and industrial modernisation; as Kizaemon Ariga notes, "the national reorganization, backed up by industrialization, became a far more important issue" at that point.[2] Considered in terms of the framework of modernity discourse as it relates to the horror film genre, every such step in the

[1] Kevin M. Doak, *Dreams of Difference: The Japan Romantic School and the Crisis of Modernity* (Berkeley: University of California Press, 1994), xvi.

[2] K. Ariga, "Modernisation of Japanese Society," in *Science in Japan* (Washington, D.C.: American Association for the Advancement of Science, 1965), 33.

opposite: Promotional artwork for **Eko Eko Azarak III - Misa the Dark Angel**.

above:
Kwaidan.

[3] Marilyn Ivy, *Discourses of the Vanishing: Modernity, Phantasm, Japan* (Chicago and London: University of Chicago Press, 1995), 10.

[4] *Ibid.*

[5] Gerald Figal, *Civilization and Monsters: Spirits of Modernity in Meiji Japan* (Durham: Duke University Press, 1999), 87.

[6] S. Garon, "Rethinking Modernisation and Modernity in Japanese Studies," *The Journal of Asian Studies* 53.2 (May 1994): 353.

[7] According to Thomas Weisser (personal correspondence with the editor, 10 June 2003), the word "kwaidan" is a bastardised spelling of the Japanese word "kaidan" as transcribed by the British-born writer Lafcadio Hearn (the man who wrote the stories upon which Kobayashi's film was based). The international distributor chose to go with the "w" spelling when the film was released at Cannes in the mid-1960s and the spelling has remained that way since. In Japan, the "w" would not be included.

process of modernisation might be seen as the addition of another "layer" that further distances the past from the present. Industrialisation, particularly in terms of technology, might thus stand as the most "contemporary" of these layers which serve to define the present.

One response to this layering of history is a sort of *cultural nostalgia*: an acknowledgment of what was lost, and an attempt to regain or re-experience it. Marilyn Ivy writes that capitalist development has brought sharply into focus this sort of relationship between the past and the modern. As she puts it, "there is widespread recognition in Japan that the destabilizations of capitalist modernity have decreed the loss of much of the past, a past sometimes troped as 'traditional'."[3] In this type of response, where "Japanese of all generations seek a recognition of continuity that is coterminous with its negation",[4] the movement away from the past is "mourned" - it is not forgotten, but actively remembered; not given up as lost, but sought after.

But there is another, almost completely opposite, type of response available: a repressing of the past in the name of progress and the so-called "modern." This response entails a form of *active destruction*, insofar as it involves a wiping away of the previous foundation in order to construct a new one. What is most interesting about this process is the way in which the elements that characterized the past are (re-) defined as chaotic and/or monstrous, embodying the spirit of primal irrationality that is supposed to have threatened and worked against the new, modern way of thinking. Gerald Figal's examination of Tetsujiro Inoue, an educator responsible for the 1890s discourse on "monsterology", reveals one way in which the conflict between the past and the modern was conceived as a battle against monstrous forces. Inoue worked to reform the Meiji educational system by eliminating all references to folkloric supernatural elements of tradition, such as *tengu* (goblins). According to Figal, "Inoue claimed that his monsterology was a discipline that...attack[ed] obstinate folk beliefs at their roots and that this eradication of superstition (*meishin taiji*) was instrumental for the constitution of a healthy, modern Japanese state."[5] Another instance of this war against the irrational can be seen in the state's attempts to stop the rise of the "new religions" of the 1920s and 1930s. As Sheldon Garon writes, "by creating the category of 'modernity' by which certain sects might be condemned as 'uncivilized', the process of modernisation played a key role in the suppression of the new religions... Like many progressive intellectuals, high-ranking police officials attacked the new religions for 'denying the rationality of modern science' and 'worshiping (sic) superstition and absolute nonsense'."[6] Coded as illogical and chaotic, and thus antithetical to the project of modernisation, such elements were targeted as the embodiments of those qualities that needed to be eliminated in the name of progress. The "modern" and all of its connotations (advanced capitalism, urbanization, industrialization, etc.) can be seen as the top "layer" of history under which lie the traces of the past.

The notion of horror implied in this buried/forgotten past is that the remnants of yesterday may turn vengeful as a consequence of being denied, ignored, or otherwise erased. In sharp contrast to the response of nostalgia described by Ivy, this mode of horror gains its resonance from the position that the past does not simply *rest* beneath the layer of the modern - it actively forces its way through this layer and strikes back at those who buried it. This vengeful quality is what characterizes the past as "monstrous", as it threatens to undo the aura of progress through its destructive acts, as well as through its disruptive presence (functioning as a reminder of a chaotic, pre-modern time).

The idea of the "monstrous past" can be found in many Japanese *kaidan* ("strange tales") and *obake* (ghost) stories. In Masaki Kobayashi's 1964 anthology horror film *Kwaidan*[7] - the most well known Japanese horror movie in the West, along with Kaneto Shindo's *Onibaba*

Ring and Eko Eko Azarak

(released the same year) – two of the "chapters" deal with the consequences of forgetting or burying the past. In one of them, a young lord attempts to put his old life behind him in order to advance socially; in the other, a man forgets the warning of the *yuki onna* (snow woman) to never speak of her after their initial encounter. In both cases, the past is represented as a supernatural force that strikes back in the present: an apparition of the young lord's former lover returns to haunt him in his comfortable new life of status, and the presence of the *yuki onna* is revealed when the man tells the story of his encounter with her, an encounter that happened years ago in a life far removed from his present day. In an interesting variation on the theme of the past-present relationship, it is the man's very remembrance of the *yuki onna* that summons its presence into the here-and-now, but still the encounter with the past is shown to have dire consequences, as the man must confront the wrath of the snow woman after disregarding her warning.

In Japan, the most well known *kaidan* in the cinema is arguably *Yotsuya Kaidan*. There have been at least eight film adaptations of this tale, originally a play written in 1825 by Nanboku Tsuruya. The most highly regarded of these film versions is the one directed in 1959 by Nobuo Nakagawa, a well-known horror director of the 1960s perhaps best known for *Jigoku* (*Hell*, 1960). Nakagawa's version opens with a stylized Kabuki introduction lamenting the sorrow of the story about to unfold, an introduction which invokes notions of tradition in the form of artistic expression. *Yotsuya Kaidan* tells the story of Iuemon Tamiya (Shigeru Amachi), a masterless samurai who murders his wife Oiwa (Kazuko Wakasugi) in order to be with another woman. The connotation of the "modern" can be seen in the special "imported poison" that Iuemon uses to kill Oiwa. Iuemon tells Oiwa to forget about the past and think only of the future as he serves her the poison, words of encouragement that actually reflect his deviousness, particularly in terms of how he perceives his own past (Oiwa) and future (his new bride). The ghost of Oiwa that returns to haunt Iuemon bears a face covered in boils and sores as a result of the poison – physical traces of the specialized, imported "modern" which add another dimension of horror to this remnant of the past. The constant sight of Oiwa's ghost drives Iuemon mad, and in his crazed attempts to slay her (for good this time), he

left:
Kwaidan.

inadvertently kills his new wife and everyone around him. In this story, the vengeance of the past first disrupts the present simply by haunting Iuemon, then moves on to completely destroy it, enacting its role as "monstrous past" as a symbolic representation of Ieumon's conscience, as well as a material force with literal, physically destructive effects in the present. Similar to the Italian *Black Sunday* (1960) directed by Mario Bava, and Chano Urueta's Mexican horror film *The Witch's Mirror* that same year, the ghost acts as a link between past and present, a connection between these time periods that others would prefer to keep separate.

Yotsuya Kaidan is just one in a long line of *kaidan* films, the prime example of Japanese horror cinema throughout the 1960s. Though Kobayashi's *Kwaidan* and

below:
Onibaba.

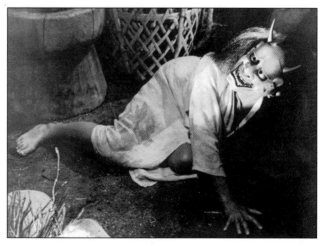

Japan

right:
The true face of horror is finally revealed in **Ring**.

Shindo's *Onibaba* were the only *kaidan* to gain a reputation in the West, Japan in fact produced many such films around this time, most notably Daiei Studio's entire *kaidan* cycle, which included *Kaidan Botandero* and *Kaidan Yukigoro* from 1968 and *Hiroku Kaibyoden* (*The Haunted Castle*, 1969). The most popular films in the Daiei series were Kimiyoshi Yasuda's *Yokai Hyaku Monogatari* (*One Hundred Ghost Stories*) and Yoshiyuki Kuroda's *Yokai Daisenso* (*The Great Ghost War*), both from 1969. Toei Studios, which had previously produced such horror films as *Kaidan Katame no Otoko* and *Kaidan Semushi Otoko* (both from 1965), in the 1970s made the notable "Bloodthirsty" series of films: *Yureiyashiki no Kyofu: Chi O Suu Ningyoo* (*Bloodthirsty Doll* aka *The Vampire Doll*, 1970), *Noroi no Yakata: Chi O Suu Me* (*Bloodthirsty Eyes* aka *Lake of Dracula*, 1971) and *Chi O Suu Bara* (*Bloodthirsty Rose* aka *Evil of Dracula*, 1975), all of which were directed by Michio Yamamoto.

The *Ring* series

In the entire history of Japanese horror cinema, however, no film has ever achieved the popularity of 1998's *Ringu* (*Ring*). Based on a novel by Koji Suzuki, *Ring* stands at the forefront of the horror genre's current resurgence in Japan. Though the film presents a very modern depiction of horror, its thematic preoccupation with the relationship between past and present evokes some lingering aspects of the older *kaidan*. *Ring* thus contains elements of both classic and contemporary horror aesthetics: a film with modern sensibilities that also displays its ties to the lineage of Japanese horror cinema to which it belongs.

below:
Nanako Matsushima as Reiko Asakawa in **Ring**.

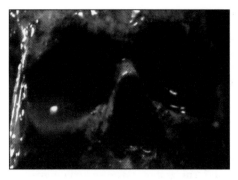

Ring tells the story of Reiko Asakawa (Nanako Matsushima), a female reporter investigating allegations concerning a cursed videotape that causes those who watch it to die a week after viewing. The person who watches the tape apparently receives a mysterious phone call, which marks the beginning of the week-long time limit. The murderer turns out to be the mental/spiritual energy of a dead girl, Sadako Yamamura (Orie Izuno), who was thrown down a well forty years earlier. Reiko ultimately deduces that the only remedy is for the cursed viewer to make a copy of their videotape and give it to someone else, freeing them from the curse by passing it on (somewhat like the notebook in the 1957 Jacques Tourneur film *Curse of the Demon*). Thus, the title *Ring* refers to the ghost's presence in the present day as manifested through the "ring" of the telephone, as well as through the "ring" of cursed videotapes in circulation.

Sadako's manifestations in the present, achieved through these various "rings", are significant because of the ways in which they depict the past emerging into the present via technological means. If technology can be seen to represent the most recent of the "layers" defining history - technological achievement considered as the most advanced stage of modern development - then the notion of horror associated with a ghost from the past is further nuanced by the use of technology as a conduit into the here-and-now. Not only will the past live; it will circulate in the present through the *very technology* that so defines the present. The supernatural presence of Sadako can manifest itself over the phone as well as through photographs, as the faces of those who have been affected by her appear distorted and/or blurry in photos. But it is the VCR in particular that is exemplary of Japan's presence in the technological "modern", with nearly 70% of the videocassette recorders produced worldwide coming from Japan.[8] The use of the VCR/television as Sadako's primary portal into the present day is a unique and distinctly modern touch that further emphasizes the thematic qualities associated with the past and present.

The images seen on the cursed videotape are themselves suggestive of the atmosphere of an old-fashioned *kaidan*: a bright moon filling the sky, a woman in front of a mirror brushing her long black hair.[9] The grainy, black-and-white images take on an enhanced surreal quality as the mirror shifts places on the wall, a space full of floating *kanji* (ideograms) appears, and the bizarre montage closes with a shot of a well. These images are more than just visual signs of the curse of Sadako; they prove to be the key to finding a remedy for the curse, as well. Reiko and her ex-husband Ryuji (Hiroyuki Sanada) scrutinize the images for clues - in effect reading the cursed videotape like a text - in their attempt to solve the mystery of the murders linked to the tape. In particular, they consider the meanings of the *kanji* characters for "volcano", which directs them to the site of the well where Sadako was originally abandoned. These images of the past, which are a source of terror, also constitute their own sort of "salvation" - as they lead Reiko down the well to find Sadako's corpse, the past is finally acknowledged or "remembered."

Ring also explores the relationship between past and present in its initial set-up of the story surrounding the cursed videotape, as two schoolmates - Masami (Hitomi Sato) and Tomoko (Yuko Takeuchi) - are shown discussing the curse. They wonder where the story originated, commenting on the fact that everybody is talking about it. Their fears are exacerbated by the ringing of the phone after Tomoko confesses that she saw the video one week ago. To their great relief, the call turns out to be from one of their friends; shortly afterwards, however, Tomoko is indeed killed by Sadako. This conflation of the reality of the cursed videotape (Sadako's emergence into the present) with urban legend (the questioning of the tape's origin; the widespread stories that develop about it) is developed further as Reiko's investigation proceeds. Scenes consisting of interviews with various people who have heard the story of the cursed videotape reveal how Reiko's job consists primarily of collating and comparing vague rumours, and has little to do with arriving at any definitive conclusions. Except for those who become victims of the curse and so experience it directly, the presence of Sadako in the present is a nebulous one, an urban legend that seems to have originated in some indefinite "past."

The creation of this haunted past is witnessed by Reiko in strange flashbacks that seem to result from her sharing of Ryuji's ability to receive such images. The images come from her contact with an old man who, forty years earlier, revealed the secret of Shizuko (Masako), Sadako's mother, to the press. In the story of the past that unfolds before Reiko's eyes, she sees how Dr. Heihachiro Ikuma (Daisuke Ban), a scientist working on the paranormal, eventually held a public demonstration of his experiments involving Shizuko's psychic powers. The press vigorously denounced the experiments, however, causing Shizuko to react fearfully. Watching her mother from behind a curtain, Sadako killed the first journalist to speak out with a telepathic burst. Shortly thereafter, following Shizuko's death, Dr. Ikuma threw Sadako down a well and sealed it off, thereby removing the last traces of this episode in an action symbolic of the past (represented by the *bakemono* - the "monstrous") being literally buried by the present (in the form of the scientist).

The vengeance of Sadako's ghost can thus be seen as stemming from science's

above:
Nanako Matsushima as Reiko Asakawa in **Ring**.

left:
The wrath of Sadako (**Ring**).

[8] See L. do Rosario, "The Way of All Gadgets," *Far Eastern Economic Review* 156 (25 November 1993): 48.

[9] While this is a common-enough scene, its specific use in a horror film could perhaps be a reference to Kobayashi's *Kwaidan*, in which a ghost's long black hair functions as a story point. It would be worth investigating the question whether Nakata was indeed influenced by Kobayashi's *Kwaidan*, as there are other similarities between the two films at the level of tone and atmosphere.

above:
Hiroyuki Sanada as Ryuji Takayama and Nanako Matsushima as Reiko Asakawa in **Ring**.

opposite:
Poster for **Ring 0**. Rather than being another sequel, **Ring 0: Baasudei** (Birthday) - the third instalment in the **Ring** series - is an ambitious prequel that sheds new light on Sadako's origins and the curse she must bear. Directed by Norio Tsuruta (**Kakashi** [aka **Scarecrow**], 2001) from a screenplay by Hiroshi Takahashi (**Ring 2**), **Ring 0** mixes horror with drama as the young Sadako (Yukie Nakama) joins a Tokyo-based theatre troupe where the play being put on eerily begins to mirror events in the narrative. Then the lead actress is found dead on the stage, and the other cast members complain of strange dreams about a little girl and a well...

right:
A frightening fragment from the cursed videotape in **Ring**.

efforts, first to explain the paranormal, and then to destroy it after it gets labelled "monstrous" by the media. The power of the paranormal, embodied in the telepathic abilities of Shizuko and Sadako, is also linked to primal symbols of nature, thereby strengthening the connection between such power and the uncontrollable chaos that stands as the very antithesis of the "modern." According to the old man, Shizuko used to spend entire days at the seashore, talking to the ocean. This association between Shizuko and the sea takes on greater significance when a typhoon strikes during Reiko and Ryuji's trip to the well, where they travel in the hopes of saving their son Yoichi (Rikiya Otaka), who previously watched the cursed videotape. Sadako's symbol is the volcano, seen as one of the images on the tape - truly a sign of the primordial chaotic. Like the Meiji discourse on monsterology that sought to eliminate the irrational and inexplicable past in favour of progress and the so-called "modern", the attempt made by science to understand and eventually eliminate the "monstrous" in *Ring* is the source of anxiety, even horror.

This idea is developed to an even greater degree in *Ringu 2* (*Ring 2*, 1998), which takes place directly after the events of the first film. The role of the scientist in this story is filled by a group of professors who rationalize the curse of Sadako and much of what took place in *Ring*. In this way, *Ring 2* is itself much like the "modern" in comparison to the inexplicable nature of Sadako's power in the first film. Whereas much of the terror of *Ring* can be attributed to the logic-defying omnipotence of Sadako, the terror in *Ring 2* stems from the fear that scientific explanation of Sadako's power still may not be enough to stop her. With science coded as the "modern" as opposed to the "past" represented by Sadako's supernatural powers, *Ring 2* is a fascinating counterpoint to the original film, advancing the thematic preoccupation with the past and the modern by focusing on the modern response to the past.

The distortion of the faces in photographs is explained as the result of mental energy which affects the exposure of light onto the film. More importantly, the idea first suggested in *Ring* - that Sadako travels along energy waves - is here fleshed out: supernatural power is attributed to the principle of "energy transference." Yoichi, upset with Reiko over a recent series of events, has built up a reserve of anger which, in combination with the presence of Sadako still within him, manifests itself in paranormal abilities. This psychic energy can be absorbed by water, as is verified when Yoichi is told to focus his thoughts on a glass filled with H20, the structure of which changes during an absorbency test. Aware of this principle, one of the scientists hopes to draw Sadako's remaining presence out of Yoichi using a large pool of water as the receptacle. Interestingly, the scientist explains at one point that seawater will not work as well as fresh water, thereby recalling the link between Shizuko and the ocean. His philosophy is summed up in his remark that it is *fear* that kills, and not the cursed videotape - a remark which reflects the idea that what is truly dangerous is the irrational *itself*.

The images on the cursed videotape are now revealed to be various moments seen from Sadako's perspective before she was thrown into the well. The mirror that shifts places on the wall, for example, was telepathically moved by Sadako as she watched her mother brushing her hair. This explanation for the images on the tape, however, is of little consolation to the frightened Mai (Miki Nakatini), Ryuji's assistant, who takes care of Yoichi after Reiko is accidentally killed in an attempt at wresting her afflicted son away from the scientists. The fear that such explanations

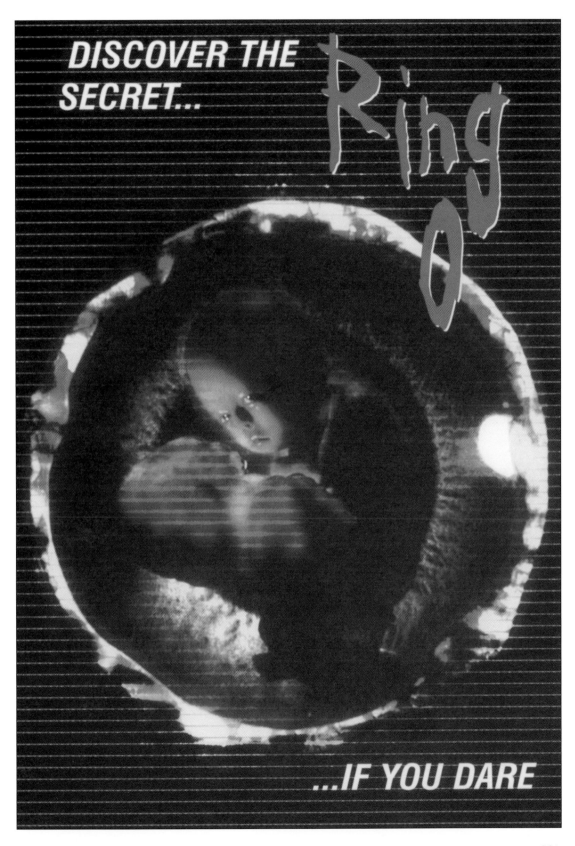

are not sufficient to eliminate the horror generated by the (previously) inexplicable can also be seen in the attempts to construct a model of Sadako's face based on her skull, which has been discovered at the bottom of the well. When the scientists take photographs of their completed model, the flash of the bulb reveals Sadako's real face superimposed over the model. Despite the scientists' knowledge of how mental energy interacts with light, the appearance of this haunting image cannot be prevented.

The most important example of the idea that the chaotic may ultimately overwhelm or transcend any scientific explanation is the experiment to purge Yoichi of his negative energy. The large pool of water that the scientists hope will absorb this energy is instead transformed into a gateway between the real world and the realm of the supernatural. Mai and Yoichi find themselves trapped in this passageway, which looks just like the inside of the well Sadako inhabited for decades. Finally managing to escape, they resurface in the pool of water only to find the lab destroyed as a result of the experiment. Science's effort to do away with the supernatural has led to consequences unimagined - the possibility of becoming lost in the supernatural world itself - revealing the confrontation between past and present to be fraught with terrifying perils heretofore unknown.

The *Eko Eko Azarak* series

Another contemporary Japanese horror film series that deals with issues of the past's disruption of the present is *Eko Eko Azarak*, which recounts the exploits of high school sorceress Misa Kuroi (literally, "Misa Black", played by Kimika Yoshino). Like *Ring*, *Eko Eko Azarak* has spawned a television series and its own cult following, making Misa's face one of the more identifiable signs of the genre in recent years. Based on the Shinichi Koga *manga* (comic) from the 1970s, the *Eko Eko Azarak* film series debuted in 1995, right around the time when a number of *onna senshi* ("female warrior") productions hit the market. Beginning in 1990 with *Lady Battlecop*, an entry in Toei's "V Cinema" series of straight-to-video films emphasizing heavy action (the "V" is for "Violence"), a string of science fiction and superhero-oriented *onna senshi* pictures arrived on the scene. The *Monster Commando* series, *Batoru Garu* (*Battle Girl*, 1992), *Uchu Shojo Keiji Buruma* (*Young Girl Space Detective Bloomer*, 1994), and Go Nagai's infamous *Kekkou Kamen* (*Naked Mask*, 1991-) series all featured strong young female characters who did battle with various types of monsters and villains; the *Eko Eko Azarak* series thus stands as a sort of generic crossover between this strain of *tokusatsu* and the horror film-proper. The monsters and demons that Misa fights are all somehow connected to a clearly pre-modern past. Using her supernatural powers to defend present-day Japan from these threats, Misa represents a "positive" use of the forces of chaos. Her powers (casting spells, reciting incantations, etc.) are rooted in the same ineffable, primeval source as are those of her enemies - powers which defy the "modern" sense of rationality.

In a perhaps not coincidental parallel to the way in which *Ring 2* answers questions which arise concerning Sadako's past, Misa's origins are revealed in the second film in the *Eko Eko Azarak* series. It seems that for at least one hundred years prior to her birth, Misa's powers were foretold in a prophecy. From the time she was a little girl, she was carefully watched; this went on until she reached the age at which her powers began to emerge. *Eko Eko Azarak II: Birth of the Wizard* (1996) establishes that Misa lived the life of a normal teenage girl - surrounded by friends, enjoying parties, and the rest - until the time her powers

came to the fore. Now Kirie (Amina Tominaga), a monster from the century-old Saiga tribe, awakens in the present day to take over Misa's body, desiring her ability to channel supernatural power seemingly without limit.

The film's title sequence shows the extermination of the Saiga clan in 1880, intercut with a shot of a Saiga warrior handing a medallion to a young Misa in the present day. The eventual confrontation between past and present is set up through this opening, which extends into the next scenes of the movie, an archaeological expedition taking place in the here-and-now. A professor and his assistant discover the sarcophagus of a Saiga, who turns out to be Kirie. The professor notes that the Saiga clan existed around the end of the Edo period or the beginning of the Meiji, which would place its origin right at Japan's transition point into the "modern." A tribe in which the use of magic was commonplace, the Saiga exemplifies the link between the pre-modern "past" and the supernatural.

A further link - between the supernatural and the "monstrous" - is made through the explanation of Kirie's vengeance. The Saiga warrior whose job it is to defend Misa in the present day tells her of his love for Kirie when she was a normal Saiga. When Kirie died, he used a form of forbidden magic, Hangon, to bring her back to life; instead, she returned to her body as a monstrous, murderous spirit who exterminated the entire Saiga clan. The past in *Eko Eko Azarak II* is shown to be wholly chaotic, particularly in comparison with Misa's "normal" life in the present. That is, before it gets interrupted by the arrival of Kirie and the Saiga warrior.

The "normality" of the present is most effectively represented in the first and third films of the series, where Misa does battle with evil forces that in some way use high school as a focal point for their entry into the present. This conception of horror works extremely well in a Japanese context, where the generally accepted image of high school is of a place that directly reflects all the connotations of the "modern" - a site where these values are both inculcated and projected. Akio Takahata writes that "historically, since the Meiji Restoration, the country's educational system has been constantly driven by a so-called Catch Up With the West spirit and motivation, in which efficiency and rationalization were

left:
Eko Eko Azarak.

preferred over creativity or individuality."[10] The transmission of the ideals of efficiency and rationalization into high school life is expanded upon by Thomas Rohlen, who describes how schools "teach the segmentation of time into various components... The rhythms and segmentation of the Japanese high school complement very neatly indeed the working order of industry and modern organization."[11] This entire social construction of high school is completely torn apart in the *Eko Eko Azarak* films, where the site of efficiency and rationalization becomes inhabited by those who attempt to summon the forces of chaos and darkness - forces that work against the very ideal of the "modern." (The most immediate comparison that comes to mind in the American context is the popular television series, *Buffy the Vampire Slayer* (1997 -), which also began as a feature-length film (1992). The difference, however, is that *Buffy* plays off the thematic notion that high school is *already* a metaphoric "Hell on Earth"; thus the demonic and monstrous activity centred around this site is an extension of its inherent nature - an extended metaphor. *Buffy*'s mode is hyperbole, while the rhetorical effect of the depiction of high school in *Eko Eko Azarak*, however it may be intended, is one of subversion.)

The first film in the *Eko Eko Azarak* series opens with a quote from Milton's *Paradise Lost* which describes Satan and his devils being cast out from Heaven, thereby referencing one of the most "traditional" sources of evil from the Christian mythos. A series of murders turn out to be the work of Mizuki Kurahashi (Miho Kanno), the class representative, who plans to summon Lucifer to Earth and take on his power. The locations of the various murders form the points of a giant pentagram, at the centre of which lies the high school. The first scene in the film intercuts shots of a Satanic ceremony with those of a woman running down the city streets, fleeing from an unidentifiable

[10] A. Takahata, "Standards vs. Flexibility," The World and I 14.9 (September 1999): 78.

[11] Thomas P. Rohlen, *Japan's High Schools* (Berkeley: University of California Press, 1983), 168.

threat. As in *Birth of the Wizard*, the juxtaposition of scenes which have connotations of the "ancient" with those which connote the "modern" sets up in the viewer the expectation that a confrontation between the two will eventually occur. This strategy extends into one of the first scenes at the high school, where one of the students, interested in magic, details the order of succession of wizards while a number of other students sit around his desk, enthralled. This introduction to what the students are *really* learning about in class reveals how the overturning of the "modern" is already well in place, a notion furthered with the revelation that their teacher, Ms. Shirai (Mio Takaki), is a part of Mizuki's plot.

As this plot approaches fulfilment, the students are trapped inside the school, which has been transformed into a site of chaos by the demonic energy coalescing around the building. Once a locus of normalization, high school has become a place where windows cannot be broken, doors do not lead where they should, and the number of students left alive is magically registered on a chalkboard (erasing and rewriting itself as the students are killed off, one by one). Though Misa is successful in stopping Mizuki, the school is left in ruins - much like the lab at the end of *Ring 2* - these sites of the "modern" bearing the mark of their confrontation with forces that resist the confinement of order.

In *Eko Eko Azarak III: Misa the Dark Angel* (1998), directed by Katsuhito Ueno, Misa (here played by Hinako Saeki, star of the previous year's *Eko Eko Azarak* TV series spin-off) must shut down the high school Drama Club's summer production - actually an effort at creating the perfect "Homunculus", a pure and untainted life-form that will be filled with the souls of human sacrifices. Although the final preparation and actual ritual take place on the grounds of an estate, the rehearsals are conducted at school. In relation to Rohlen's idea of the Japanese high school emphasis on the segmentation of time, it is interesting to note how Hikaru (Yuki Hagiwara), the leader of the Drama Club production, repeatedly voices her concerns about being organized and not wasting time in preparation for the performance. The spirit of the organizational framework of high school is here used *not* for the purpose of getting Japanese youths ready for their entrance into modern society, but for the fulfilment of a project that opposes the very order of the "modern." Amidst a montage of shots featuring the students at work on the production - building and painting scenery, rehearsing dialogue, studying the script - a shot of some of them unrolling a drawing of a giant pentagram is inserted, revealing the presence of the supernatural within the everyday activities of school life. A scene showing a rehearsal changes from innocent to ominous in tone as it begins during the day and ends at night, closing with a long shot of the students standing together by a small light surrounded by darkness, thereby echoing the transformation of the play from innocent school production to ritual of mayhem. In these and other ways, *Eko Eko Azarak III* continues the series' depiction of high school as a realm of the paranormal - something truly horrifying in light of Japan's cultural construction of high school as a paradigmatic site of modernisation.

The nature of the horror depicted in *Ring* and *Eko Eko Azarak* is the disruption of the present by some aspect of the past, an idea that has roots in the heart of classic Japanese horror cinema. In particular, the past which is defined as "monstrous" emerges through elements of society that are symbolic of the "modern" - technology in *Ring*; high school in *Eko Eko Azarak*. It will be very interesting to see how the Japanese horror film continues to develop, both thematically and aesthetically, as the current resurgence epitomised by *Ring* and *Eko Eko Azarak* continues.

right:
Promotional artwork for **Eko Eko Azarak**.

case study – Japanese horror cinema

The urban techno-alienation of Sion Sono's *Suicide Club*

Travis Crawford

No matter what else may be said regarding *Jisatsu Circle* (aka *Suicide Club*, 2002), one has to admit that the film's writer/director Sion Sono certainly knows how to begin a movie (whether or not he knows how to end one would likely prove a more hotly debated topic). Sono's truly bizarre shock-show-*cum*-sociological satire actually manages to grow even stranger as it progresses, but for sheer jaw-dropping visceral impact, it never quite tops its opening sequence (which is not to say that it doesn't try): 54 smiling teenaged schoolgirls stand on the platform of the Shinjuku subway station in Tokyo, clasp hands and then proceed to jump in unison directly into the path of an oncoming train. Crushed heads and severed body parts fill the frame as tsunami-like torrents of blood drench horrified commuters, shortly followed by discontinuous images which would probably even confound viewers who weren't still reeling from the surreal carnage: a gym bag, a computer screen filled with multiplying coloured dots and a televised performance from "Desert," the all-girl pubescent pop star quintet that is, to put it mildly, more than meets the eye. And so begins one of the richest, most complex and inventive entries in Japan's new horror film renaissance - not to mention one of the most mystifying and enigmatic - the extraordinary *Suicide Club*.

Sono's film is a unique piece of work even when judged as an individual entity, but it is all the more singular when viewed in the context of contemporary Japanese genre filmmaking. Although *Suicide Club* shares certain thematic affinities with the school of ethereal, "suggestive" cinematic creep-outs best represented by the work of Hideo Nakata (*Ringu* [*Ring* 1998], *Kaosu* [*Chaos*, 1999], *Honoguari Mizu No Soko Kara* [*Dark Water*, 2002]), Sono's is a more experimental endeavour than those more traditional horror titles. Yet *Suicide Club* is also considerably different in tone from the confrontational, outré exercises in anarchy produced by Japan's reigning doyen of transgressive taboo-busting, Takashi Miike; though both Sono and Miike share a similar affection for heavily stylised bloodshed as a vehicle for audience impact, Sono's film is more cerebral and elegiac than most of Mike's projects. With its elliptical narrative approach and hypnotic rhythms, *Suicide Club* perhaps most resembles the films of Kiyoshi Kurosawa (*Kyua* [*Cure*, 1997], *Kaïro* [*Pulse*, 2001], *Karisuma* [*Charisma*, 1999]) - not least for the way in which both directors survey the potentially cataclysmic effect that technology and the desensitisation of modern life can have on the populace of Japan. But Sono demonstrates a jet-black sense of humour that is largely absent from Kurosawa's filmography, marking *Suicide Club* as *sui generis* cinema indeed.

Suicide's tangled plotline initially unfolds with the clarity of a straightforward mystery thriller, though that changes dramatically as the film evolves. Following the introductory subway suicide spectacular, police are baffled as to the causes behind such an event - particularly when the gym bag that turns up at the scene of the crime winds up containing a chain made of hundreds of strips of human flesh. As Detective Kuroda (Japanese rock icon Ryo Ishibashi, more familiar to Western audiences from his role as the luckless and footloose widower of Takashi Miike's *Odishon* [*Audition*, 1999]) investigates, he is drawn deeper into Tokyo's increasing plague of suicides by a girl calling herself "The Bat," who guides Kuroda to a website which chronicles each of the suicides - before they even happen. As bodies begin plummeting from the sky on a daily basis, the police wonder whether the chipper self-annihilators are cult members, and one girl deals with the suicide of her boyfriend by investigating the teen pop combo Desert (whose hit, "Mail Me!" is omnipresent throughout the film), discovering in the process that the girls aren't quite what they appear to be.

If all of this sounds a bit disjointed, that's not an entirely inaccurate impression: Sono soon abandons the linear narrative structure of a police procedural thriller in favour of the more enigmatic pleasures afforded by a comparatively abstract expressionist interpretation of already challenging themes and labyrinthine scenarios. This disorienting approach intensifies later in the film, though it's worth noting that Sono follows his throat-grabbing, rapid-fire opening with a slow, prolonged hospital suspense sequence involving irrelative characters, already giving his audience fair warning that the story will not unfold in traditional form. Sono's adventurous plotting course ultimately reaches its apex (or nadir, depending on your point of view) during a positively surreal musical number (!) set in an abandoned bowling alley inhabited by a group of pet-stomping glam-rock nihilists who have abducted "The Bat" and her friend - an aggressively outlandish episode which is likely to trigger as many audience walkouts as the cringe-inducing sight of a glassy-eyed mother buoyantly carving into herself with a kitchen utensil (and then there is the matter of Kuroda's genuinely shocking final scene in the film...). But if Sono differs from Miike in many respects, the two share a similar free-form kitchen-sink conceptual approach, one which largely works to an open-minded audience's advantage. Sono may introduce more elements than he is capable of successfully negotiating - and like the recent films of David Lynch, Sono is more interested in introducing and exploring mysteries rather than in actually solving them - but his audacious methods are also richly rewarding.

If *Suicide Club*'s chaotic narrative represents the most potentially critical obstacle to enjoyment for a Western audience, it's safe to say that the film's savage social critique might prove more difficult for the film's native Japanese viewers. Throughout recent years, suicide rates have risen significantly in Japan, an alarming increase which many have linked to the equally dramatic rise in unemployment, though Sono believes the causes run far deeper than that. Although the suicide surge seems to have affected many age groups in Japan, there has also recently been an unnerving escalation in youth crime and violence, a cultural development also explored in *Suicide Club*. In the final months of the year 2000, Japan's Parliament approved the first amendment to the Juvenile Crime Law since 1949, prompted by two infamous crimes earlier that same year: a 17 year-old boy hijacked a bus and stabbed a woman to death, while another boy of the same age beat his mother to death with a baseball bat. Just as public opinion reflected that juvenile crime and violence had suddenly become the most important issue in Japan, Toei Studios released - to much controversy - Kinji Fukasaku's blood-spattered and brilliant teen action opus *Battle Royale* (2000), and shortly thereafter, a trio of Japanese films explored the theme of teen violence within the Japanese school system: Shunji Iwai's fragmented epic of internet chat rooms and pubescent sadism *Riri Shushu no subete* (*All About Lily Chou-Chou*); Akihiko Shiota's muted study of depression *Gaichu* (*Harmful Insect*); and Toyoda Toshiaki's intense manga adaptation *Aoi haru* (*Blue Spring*). *Suicide Club* is closer in spirit to the genre play of the Fukasaku feature than the more serious sociological analysis of the three 2001 productions, but all five films share

below:
After 54 smiling schoolgirls leap under a subway train to their deaths, police find a bag at the subway station with, to put it mildly, grisly contents: small strips of human flesh sewn together in a linking chain.
(courtesy of TLA Releasing)

Sion Sono's Suicide Club

above:
As **Suicide Club** nears its conclusion, another group of schoolgirls approaches the subway platform... *(courtesy of TLA Releasing)*

the same impassioned concern for the future of Japan's youth, and none of them provide easy answers to this current crisis within their country.

Prior to *Suicide Club*, the film's writer/director Sion Sono would have seemed an unlikely candidate for genre movie maverick. Born in Toyokawa on 18 December 1965, Sono first achieved acclaim as a budding teenaged poet, published at the age of 17. He subsequently became interested in filmmaking, creating two award-winning shorts, *I Am Sono Sion* (1985) and *A Man's Flower Road* (1987), before moving into commercial filmmaking with *Jitensha Toiki* (*Bicycle Sighs*, 1990). Sono's previous film work - *Heya* (*The Room*, 1992), *Keiko Desu Kedo* (1997), *Kaze* (*The Wind*, 1998), *Utsushimi* (1999) - has been little seen outside of Japan, though *Suicide Club* will hopefully serve to change that international anonymity. Sono has also continued his interest in poetry, and his recent collaboration with fashion designer Shinichiro Arakawa resulted in the 1999 short film *0cm4*.

Please be warned that the following interview does include discussion of many plot twists within *Suicide Club*, and those who have not yet seen the film may wish to proceed with caution.[*]

Travis Crawford: One of the things I most admired about your film is that there are so many different themes at work within the story. What really started the idea of the film for you?

Sion Sono: The concept for the film originated from my hopeless life in the United States. Two years ago, I lived alone in San Francisco, and it was a horrifying and lonely experience for me. During that time, I worked on the script of *Suicide Club*. The Sion Sono of that time is behind the concept of, and the reason for, the film.

TC: In your director's notes, you speak of "a fundamental darkness spreading in current Japan." Could you discuss this concept further? Why do you feel this condition in Japanese society has arisen recently?

SS: I am not sure if it is really possible to analyse this concept. It can't simply be because of the collapse of the bubble economy, or the expansion of the so-called "peace" - a shallow "peace" - but more because of the entanglement of all of these small details... like leaves which soon apparently grow into a thick forest of darkness.

[*] Special thanks to Tomoko Suzuki at Daiei Co., Ltd. for translation and interview arrangements.

horror cinema across the globe

above:
Be all you can be - kill yourself. Followers of the suicide craze take to the Tokyo streets with placards urging others to take the plunge.
(courtesy of TLA Releasing)

TC: *So why did you elect to approach this very somber theme through the horror genre, as opposed to a more traditionally "serious" dramatic treatment?*

SS: It would have just become too much, if I had made it more serious and dramatic. It makes it difficult to bring people in to see the film if it has too much of an "artistic" taste. I would rather have it easier for the audience to come in to the film, which was the reason I chose to make it a horror film. Though the means of interpretation is different, what is to be expressed through the film is still the same. I wanted to share this anxiety with as many people as possible.

TC: *The film has many sequences of surreal humour, particularly within the opening subway suicide scene. Was there any difficulty in finding a balance between the comical and the disturbing elements of the story?*

SS: Splatter and gore always carry humour within. On the other hand, when it is visually expressed, bloodshed is not so humorous at all. But I wanted to show the blood with as much humour as possible when visualising the reality of suicide. That is why I tried to focus on the splatter effect in all of the suicide scenes. I just like to discuss serious themes with humour.

TC: *And in fact, in your notes, you also mentioned "a cheerful despair where people can die laughing." How has this type of despair evolved in Japan today?*

SS: I have no idea how such a despair evolved in Japan. Like the Kuroda character in the film, I also cannot understand the thoughtlessness of the young people in regards to life and death. I can only "feel" the despair without any specific reason. It is like feeling that the sunset is beautiful. Death penetrates within myself.

TC: *At what point did you realise that you wanted to make the film so shockingly, explicitly gory? Did you ever worry that this use of blood might alienate your audience?*

SS: From the very beginning, I wanted to make this film into a splatter movie. I wanted people to feel anxious and unpleasant, so I never even thought about the possibility of alienating the audience.

Sion Sono's Suicide Club

TC: Speaking of audience alienation, the story of Suicide Club begins as a fairly straightforward mystery/thriller, but soon evolves into something much stranger and more difficult for a general audience. Were you concerned about creating a storyline which would not be simple for many viewers to understand, at least not upon a single viewing?

SS: Yes, I did feel such concern - but I found no other option.

TC: The character of "The Bat" - along with the gang in the bowling alley - are ultimately "red herrings" that don't actually connect to the real causes of the suicide wave, correct?

SS: Yes. But I also think they are very "Japanese." The way that they react is similar to "internet otaku" ("internet freaks").

TC: What drives Kuroda's character to take such a drastic final action, and should the audience have any sympathy for the children who label him "scum" who thinks only of himself?

SS: No, I don't think we need to feel any sympathy towards them. The fact is that Kuroda never even dreamed that his own family was pushed so far to the extent that they would commit suicide, and he was convinced that his family was always safe from such a tragedy. The children just point out that fact, and [that this fact represents] that he is scum who only thinks of himself, and not at all about others.

TC: Let's talk about Desert. What prompted you to introduce a teenage girl pop group as the possible factor behind the wave of suicides? What are your own thoughts on contemporary Japanese youth pop culture?

SS: I thought it was interesting - and also possible - that teenagers like that could be a factor behind the suicides. The fact that such teenagers - or younger, about 12 years old - are actually strong enough to have such hatred towards Japan was to me an angelic beauty. Nowadays, Japan does not have any culture, and this fact *is* suicidal.

TC: The film's stance on Desert is actually rather ambiguous. Are they really instigators of the suicide craze, or are they just a media tool manipulated by those (the children) who are actually behind the suicides?

below:
A defeated Detective Kuroda (Ryo Ishibashi) finds that the tragic Tokyo suicide wave has suddenly hit too close to home. *(courtesy of TLA Releasing)*

above:
Genesis (Rolly), the self-proclaimed "Charles Manson of the information age", serenades his bowling alley captives with a tender little glam-rock ballad of despair.
(courtesy of TLA Releasing)

SS: Right now, I am working on *Suicide Club 2*, and I would like to further discuss this issue in there. How were the high school girls able to join the children? In short, they exist as a media tool, and yet at the same time, as a symbol, just like the Emperor. In *Suicide Club 2*, I want to look further into this issue, and come out with a logical answer - logical like mathematics.

TC: Is Desert a real group in Japan? How were the songs written and the girls assembled?

SS: Desert was created by me for this film. Some of the members are actually training themselves to become real musicians and singers. If I remember her correctly, I believe the girl who played the lead vocal has a theatrical background. The music was composed by Haruko Momoi - her website is www.momoi.com. The lyrics for the song "Puzzle" were created by me. I tried not to make all of the members of Desert so beautiful, because I had in my mind, older pop groups like Bay City Rollers or The Jackson Five.

TC: The ending of your film seems almost apocalyptic, yet it's not without a sense of hope. Do you find the ending of the film optimistic, and what hope do you retain for Japanese youth?

SS: Rather than having a message aimed for numerous youths, I wanted to send a message to a specific individual…or even only to myself. If whether or not my film is "entertainment" is dependent on its having a message aimed at a large audience, then I agree that the ending of the film has rather too much of a "literature" feel. I feel that it was correct for that girl to keep on living. She had her tattoo skinned, which means that she actively chose to live although she was listed on the suicide list. I believe that one has to make up one's own mind whether to live or die, and I expressed this thought through her. It is hard to live in a visionless country like Japan, but I am hoping that strong youngsters like her can find a way to keep on living.

TC: I know that, at the time of this interview, Suicide Club *is about to be released on VHS and DVD right now in Japan, but did it have a theatrical release prior to that? How was the film received in Japan?*

SS: It has already been theatrically released in Japan. There were many kinds of reactions at the release, both for and against the film. It also did quite well. My thought [with *Suicide Club 2*] is to make a film that is a continuation from this to complete the whole film, so that there would be one and only one answer at the end.

TC: Have you seen the other recent Japanese films centred around teen violence and despair - All About Lily Chou-Chou, Harmful Insect, Blue Spring *or even* Battle Royale?

SS: [Of those films mentioned,] I have only seen *Battle Royale*. I think we all came up with quite similar thoughts, so it is not a surprise to see some kind of synchronisation among the films.

TC: Some Western reviewers have compared your film to the work of Takashi Miike (perhaps because of the film's violence and genre subversion), but there are other, simpler comparison points. Like Miike, you feature Ryo Ishibashi in your film. What is he like as an actor?

SS: It is a coincidence. I only saw *Audition* after choosing Ryo Ishibashi for Kuroda, and I did not choose him for his role in *Audition*. I didn't like his role in *Audition*. I think he has an atmosphere to him, which I think is great. Besides being an actor, he is also a rock musician, and I wanted him to give more of that flavour in my film.

TC: And like Kiyoshi Kurosawa's Kaïro, *your film* Suicide Club *also deals with a sense of modern alienation experienced by the "internet generation." What are your own thoughts on the internet?*

SS: The internet is a way of communication which I think is suicidal. Anonymous words or opinions travel around the world. It has a freedom, but at the same time it is very dangerous. It weakens the responsibility and originality of the words. It doesn't have a face at all.

TC: Could you talk a bit about your early career beginnings and your earlier films? Also, you began as a poet, correct?

SS: I am not a very good poet. In most of my previous films, the main character commits suicide, or loses his or her self. But I just realised this similarity after actually making them. There is an English-language page on my homepage (www.sonosion.com), which explains my previous work, so people can check there too.

TC: You also worked briefly in the Adult Video (AV) industry. What was that experience like for you, and what films did you direct?

SS: I only directed one adult movie, and in fact I lost the job of adult movie director after this. As an actor, I was also in one film. In Japan, there is a genre called "pinku eiga" (pink films), and I did direct two films in this genre. I don't really think there was much to experience. The adult movie was called *Nisen Nin No Otoko To Yatta Jyoshid Aisei vs. Anime Otaku No Dotei* [note: the interpreter for this interview translates the above title as "A College Student who Fucked with 2000 Men vs. Anime Otaku's Chastity"). Of course, at the end the chastity was lost!

TC: So in addition to Suicide Club 2, *what other films do you have lined up for the future?*

SS: Other than *Suicide Club 2*, I'm also doing *Hazard* (a true story about a homicide in an S&M club) and *Fuyu No Juryoku* (*Winter Gravity*), a hardboiled story again starring Ryo Ishibashi.

left:
Sion Sono.

notes on contributors

André Barcinski is a journalist based in São Paulo, Brazil. He is the co-author with Ivan Finotti of *Maldito (The Damned)*, the biography of José Mojica Marins, and the co-director (also with Finotti) of *Coffin Joe - The Strange World of José Mojica Marins*, a documentary that won a Special Jury Prize at the 2001 Sundance Film Festival.

Art Black writes extensively on fringe cinema and Asian media. In addition to providing programming for Asian film festivals and writing catalog articles, he has authored historical CD liner notes, served as book consultant and entertainment magazine editor, and written for countless print and internet publications. He contributes a long-running column to *Psychotronic Video* magazine and recently served as senior contributor to the book *Once Upon a Time in China: An Enthusiast's Guide to the Cinema of Hong Kong, Taiwan and the Mainland*.

Travis Crawford is a curator for the Philadelphia Film Festival (www.phillyfests.com), the 2002 edition of which hosted the North American premiere of Sion Sono's *Suicide Club*. His festival programs, New Korean Cinema and Danger After Dark, highlight the best in Asian genre filmmaking, and as a journalist Crawford has written on this subject for such publications as *Film Comment*, *The Village Voice* and *Fangoria*. He is also a regular contributor to *Filmmaker* and *Moviemaker* magazines.

Rob Daniel studied Film at the University of Kent, wrote for *Samhain* magazine, contributed to FAB's book on Dario Argento, *Art of Darkness*, and co-published a book on Argento's *Suspiria*. Currently he is writing for the satellite channel SKY Movies' website, and watching many Japanese films.

Mitch Davis is co-director of International Programming for Montreal's Fantasia Film Festival. He produced Karim Hussain's feature *Subconscious Cruelty* (1999) and wrote/produced/directed the prize-winning short film *Divided Into Zero* (1999) through his production company, Infliction Films. Monthly programmer for Montreal's last living repertory cinema, Cinema du Parc, he has contributed to *Art of Darkness: The Cinema of Dario Argento* (FAB Press), *Ten Years of Terror: British Horror Films of the 1970s* (FAB Press) and a variety of magazines, including *Flesh & Blood*, *Mirror*, *Diabolik* and *Screem*.

David Del Valle has been the Hollywood Correspondent for both *Films and Filming* (UK) and *L'Ecran Fantastique* (France). His articles and interviews have appeared in *Video Watchdog*, *Psychotronic*, *Films in Review*, *Scarlet Street* and many other publications. His definitive interview with Vincent Price appears on DVD: *Vincent Price: The Sinister Image*, from AllDay Entertainment. David currently has a monthly column, Camp David, at the following web address: www.filmsinreview.com.

Jürgen Felix teaches Film Studies at Johannes Gutenberg-University, Mainz. He is the co-editor of the journals *MEDIENwissenschaft* and *AUGEN-BLICK*, and has published books on Woody Allen, the New Canadian Cinema and *The Cinema of Bodies, Art, and Artists on Screen*; forthcoming is a reader on Postmodern Cinema and an introduction to Modern Film Theory.

Julien Fonfrède lives in Montreal where he works as programming director for the Asian Section at the Fantasia Film Festival. He has published a book on Hong Kong cinema and presently teaches East Asian cinema at the University of Montreal. He has also just co-directed the short fiction film *City Without Windows* (2002) and is now co-producing a feature length Canadian fiction film.

Stephen Gladwin is a world horror journalist whose work includes a series of reviews and essays for Midnight Video. His website, "Foreign Screams" (http://pages.cthome.net/puppylove/foreignscreams1.htm), focuses on world horror from Indonesia, Italy, Spain, Hong Kong, the U.S. and beyond.

Ruth Goldberg has an interdisciplinary MA in film history and psychoanalytic theory from the State University of New York. She teaches film studies at SUNY/Empire State College in New York City and at the International School of Film and Television in San Antonio de los Banos, Cuba. Her work has been divided between the fields of horror film and Latin American Cinema. She is currently finishing a book on disembodied hands in film.

Ken Hanke is the author of *Tim Burton: An Unauthorized Biography of the Filmmaker* (Renaissance Books), *A Critical Guide to Horror Film Series* (Garland Publishers), *Charlie Chan at the Movies* (McFarland) and *Ken Russell's Films* (Scarecrow Press). As associate editor of *Scarlet Street* magazine, he has contributed articles on *Bride of Frankenstein*, *Werewolf of London*, etc. His work has also appeared in *Video Watchdog*, *Alternative Cinema*, *Filmfax* and *Films in Review*. Staff movie critic for the *Mountain Xpress*, Ken lives in the Asheville area of North Carolina.

Michael Hoover teaches political science and **Lisa Odham Stokes** teaches humanities at Seminole Community College in Central Florida. They have previously co-authored publications on arts and politics, technoculture and disneyfication. Their writing on Hong Kong cinema has appeared in *Asian Cinema*, *Cinemaya* and *Asian Cult Cinema*. They are the authors of *City on Fire: Hong Kong Cinema* (Verso).

David Kalat is a film historian and promoter of unusual motion pictures. As head of All Day Entertainment, an independent DVD label dedicated to movies that fell through the cracks, he has been involved in several motion picture restoration efforts over the last few years. His other writings include *A Critical History and Filmography of Toho's Godzilla Series* (McFarland) and *Homicide: Life on the Street - The Unofficial Companion* (Renaissance Books), as well as various articles on obscure films and TV that have appeared in *Filmfax*, *G-Fan*, *Midnight Marquee*, *Scarlet Street*, *Video Watchdog*, *Castle of Frankenstein* and other publications.

Pam Keesey is a writer and editor whose first love is monster movies. She is the editor of *Daughters of Darkness* and *Dark Angels*, both collections of lesbian vampire stories, and *Women Who Run with the Werewolves* (all published by Cleis Press). Her fourth book, *Vamps: An Illustrated History of the Femme Fatale* (Cleis Press) explores the development of the image of the female vampire from ancient goddesses through the 1990s. She is also the webmistress of MonsterZine.com, an online horror movie magazine exploring the meaning and significance of horror films in the modern age.

Kim Newman, novelist, critic and broadcaster, is the author of the non-fiction books *Nightmare Movies* (Bloomsbury), *Wild West Movies* (Bloomsbury), *Apocalypse Movies* (Griffin) and *BFI Classics: Cat People*, as well as editor of *The BFI Companion to Horror* (Continuum). His novels include *The Night Mayor*, *Anno Dracula*, *The Quorum* and *Life's Lottery*.

notes on contributors

Gary Needham is completing his PhD in Film Studies at the University of Glasgow Department of Theatre, Film and Television Studies. His dissertation focuses on Italian horror cinema and the *giallo* in particular. He lectures at the University of Glasgow and John Moores University, Liverpool, as well as at the Glasgow Film Theatre. Currently, he is editing (with Dimitris Eleftheriotis) the *Asian Cinemas Reader*.

Kaya Özkaracalar is a PhD candidate and part-time instructor at the Arts, Graphic Design and Architecture Institute of Bilkent University, Ankara. He is founder and editor of *Geceyarısı Sineması*, Turkey's first and only magazine concentrating on horror and exploitation cinema, and has contributed numerous film articles to other magazines and to the weekend supplement of *Radikal* newspaper.

Gary D. Rhodes is a documentary filmmaker who is a faculty member of the University of Oklahoma Department of Film and Video Studies. He is the author of such books as *Lugosi* (McFarland) and *White Zombie: Anatomy of a Horror Film* (McFarland), and editor of *Drive-In Horrors* (McFarland, 2002) and *Silent Snowbird: The Autobiography of Alma Rubens* (McFarland, forthcoming). His documentary film *Lugosi: Hollywood's Dracula* is now available on DVD.

David Robinson is the former film critic of *The Times* (London), an independent film historian and director of the Giornate del Cinema Muto (Pordenone Silent Film Festival). His many publications include *World Cinema 1895-1980* (Eyre Methuen, 1981), *From Peepshow to Palace: The Birth of American Film* (Columbia University Press, 1996) and *Chaplin: His Life and Art* (rev. edition, Penguin, 2001). His special interests are popular entertainment and the pre-history of cinema.

Steven Jay Schneider is a PhD candidate in Philosophy at Harvard University, and in Cinema Studies at New York University's Tisch School of the Arts. He has published widely on the horror genre, and is the author of the forthcoming *Designing Fear: An Aesthetics of Cinematic Horror* (Routledge). He is the editor of *New Hollywood Violence* (Manchester University Press) and *The Horror Film and Psychoanalysis: Freud's Worst Nightmares* (Cambridge University Press), and co-editor of *Underground U.S.A.: Filmmaking Beyond the Hollywood Canon* (Wallflower Press), *Dark Thoughts: Philosophical Reflections on Cinematic Horror* (Scarecrow Press) and *Understanding Film Genres* (McGraw-Hill).

Marcus Stiglegger works as a lecturer at the Institute for Film Studies of the Johannes Gutenberg-University, Mainz, Germany. He has published books on the "Sadiconazista" phenomenon, the films of Abel Ferrara and modern film auteurs. New projects include *Cinema of Extremes: Cultural Studies* and *Ritual and Seduction: Seductive Strategies in Film*; he regularly writes for the German magazines *Filmdienst*, *Splatting Image* and *Testcard*.

Ramie Tateishi received his PhD in Literature from the University of California, San Diego, where he currently works. He has written articles and presented papers on such topics as Hong Kong cinema, Japanese science fiction and Japanese animation.

Nathaniel Thompson is a regular contributor to *Video Watchdog* magazine, maintains the website Mondo Digital (www.mondo-digital.com), and has written liner notes for numerous DVD and CD releases including *Cinema Italiano*, *The Judas Kiss* and *Godmonster of Indian Flats*. He also oversees brand management for horror and cult releases from Image Entertainment, and is editor of the ongoing review journal *DVD Delirium* for FAB Press.

Todd Tjersland is the author of *Sex, Shocks & Sadism! An A-Z Guide to Erotic and Unusual Horror Films from Around the World*. A former columnist for *Cult Movies* and *Guilty Pleasures* magazines, his screen credits include *Faces of Gore* (1999), *Legion of the Night* (1995), *Misled* (1999) and *The Necro Files* (1998). He makes his home in Washington state and is currently the President/CEO of Astaroth Entertainment, a mail order company specializing in "extreme" horror films.

Pete Tombs is the co-author of *Immoral Tales* (St. Martin's Press) and *Mondo Macabro* (St. Martin's Press) and a contributor to *The BFI Companion to Horror*. He has written on various aspects of world cinema for a wide variety of newspapers and magazines in the UK. He is a director of the Mondo Macabro DVD label and has produced two documentary series for UK Channel 4 television. He lives in London.

Donato Totaro has been a film studies lecturer at Concordia University, Canada since 1990, and is a PhD Candidate in Film & Television Studies at Warwick University, UK. His recently submitted dissertation is entitled "Time and the Long Take in *The Magnificent Ambersons*, *Ugetsu* and *Stalker*". He is Editor of the online film journal *Offscreen* (www.offscreen.com), founded in 1997. He has published on recent Asian cinema, the cinema of Andrei Tarkovsky, and the horror genre and is a regular contributor to the US horror magazine *Fangoria*.

Mauro Feria Tumbocon, Jr. has been writing extensively on Philippine cinema for the past two decades in his capacity as film reviewer for various publications in the Philippines and as former member of the Manunuri ng Pelikulang Pilipino (Filipino Film Critics Society). For the past eight years since he migrated to the United States, he has organised the annual Filipino American cine festival and competition in San Francisco. He is founding and present director of the Filipino American cineArts (FACINE), a non-profit community-based media arts organisation which aims to promote and develop Filipino American cinema.

Jan Uhde is Professor of Film Studies at the University of Waterloo, Ontario. His writings include *Latent Images: Film in Singapore* (co-author, Oxford University Press) and *Vision and Persistence: Twenty Years of the Ontario Film Institute* (University of Waterloo Press). He has contributed to periodicals in Canada, the United States, Germany, Holland and the Czech Republic.

Yvonne Ng Uhde is co-author of *Latent Images: Film in Singapore* (Oxford University Press, 2000). She is on the editorial board of *KINEMA: A Journal for Film and Audiovisual Media* and writes the Singapore section of the *Variety International Film Guide*.

Dave Wood studied Film and Art Theory at the University of Kent. He has contributed to the seminal UK horror magazines *Samhain* and *The Darkside*. Specialising in Italian exploitation cinema, he completed an extensive interview with director Sergio Martino in late 2002.

Index

Compiled by Francis Brewster.

Page references in **bold** refer exclusively to illustrations, though pages referenced as text entries may also feature relevant illustrations.

0cm4 (short film) 307
2001 Yonggary see Reptilian
2009 Lost Memories 202
2046 202
24 Frames Per Second (TV series) 85
24 Horas de Sexo Ardente see 24 Hours of Explicit Sex
24 Hours of Explicit Sex 37
2499 antapan krong muang see Dang Bireley and the Young Gangsters
39 Steps, The 117
4 na Gabi ng Lagim 256
4 Nights of Horror see 4 na Gabi ng Lagim
400 Blows, The 274
5 bambole per la luna d'agosto see Five Dolls for an August Moon
6ixtynin9 63
7 Vampires 9
71 Fragmente einer Chronologie des Zufalls 71 Fragments of a Chronology of Chance
71 Fragments of a Chronology of Chance 175, 180
8 1/2 173

A ciascuno il suo (book) see To Each His Own (book)
À Meia-Noite Levarei Sua Alma see At Midnight I Will Take Your Soul
A*P*E 187
Ab Kya Hoga 4, 252, **253**
Abismos de pasion 43
Absurd 169, 176
Abuel, Tommy 259
Accidental Spy, The 202
Accursed Heritage, The see Pusaka Pontianak
Ackerman, Forest J. 7
Adam and Eve 186
Address Unknown 202
Adjani, Isabelle 236, 237, 239
Adventurer's Fate, The 29
Adventures of Baron Munchausen, The 281
Adventures of the Nobleman see Saragossa Manuscript, The
Africa addio 163
Agitator **292**
Agrama, Frank 169
Aguirre, Javier 71
Ahí está el detalle 103
Ahmad, Salmah 129
Ai yu see Prison of Love
Aikawa, Sho 288
Aiqing yu huangjin see Love and Gold
Ajooba Kudrat Ka 251
Akgün, Kadir 215
Akkaya, Aytekin 212
Al tropico del Cancro see Death in Haiti
Alajar, Gina 262
Albertini, Bitto 143
Alcázar, Victor 72
Aldás, Luis **100**
Além, Muito Além do Além (TV series) see Beyond, Far Beyond the Beyond (TV series)
Alemdar, Mehmet 215
Alexandra, Charlotte 233
Ali, A. Bakar 128
Alien: Resurrection 281, 282
All About Lily Chou-Chou 306, 311
Almereyda, Michael 280
Alphaville 279
Alraune (book) 106
Altreiter, Gertrud 176
Alvarez Molina, Jacinto see Naschy, Paul
Alvarez, Pilar 69
Amachi, Shigeru 297
Amélie 281, 282
American Film (magazine) 21
American Horrors: Essays on the Modern American Horrror Film (book) 182
Amin, M. 128
Ammoru **245**, 252
Anak Pontianak 127
And God Created Woman 279
Andalusian Dog, An see chien Andalou, Un
Andrè, Marcel 270
Andrusiac, José 28
Ang Aswang 255
Ang Babaeng Putik 262
Ang Kapitbahay (anthology segment) 262
Ang Katothanan see Elsa Castillo Story: The Truth, The
Ang Madre (anthology segment) 260
Ang Madugong Daigdid ni Salvacion 256
Ang Manananggal 255
Ang Multo sa Libingan 255
Angst **152**, **174**, 175-178, 181, 182
Anin, Kristin 29
année dernière à Marienbad, L' see Last Year at Marienbad
Anthes, Eva 112
Anthropophagous the Beast 169
Anton, Karl 115
Antonioni, Michaelangelo 173
Aoi haru see Blue Spring
Aparadhi Kaun? 248
Apocalipsis canibal see Zombie Creeping Flesh
Apocalypse Now 180
Appaduri, Arjun 51

Aquino, Kris 256
Aquino, Ninoy 256
Arabian Nights (book) 231
Arakawa, Shinichiro 307
Arakon, Aydin 206
Aranda, Vicente 279
Arcane Enchanter, The 170
arcano incantatore, L' see Arcane Enchanter, The
Are You Afraid of the Dark see Takot ka ba sa Dilim
Arenas, Miguel 99, **100**
Arent, Eddi 114, 119, 121
Argento, Claudio 15, 19
Argento, Dario 10, 15, 81, 86, 105, 115, 122, 136, 138, 140, 143, 161, 170, 193, 196, 247
Ariga, Kizaemon 295
Ark of the Sun God, The 212
Armageddon (1997) 45
Armageddon (1998) 185
Armendáriz, Pedro 102
Armengod, Ramón **99**
Armes, Roy 271
Armontel, Roland 235
Armstrong, Michael 75
Armstrong, Robert 101
Arrabal, Fernando 15, 16
arroseur arrosé, L 266
Arslan, Savas 214
Artaud, Antonin 16
Asano, Tadanobu 290
Ashes and Diamonds 231
Asian Cinema (magazine) 255
Assignment Terror 70
Aswang 260, 261
Aswang Complex in Philippine Folklore, The (book) 260
At Midnight I Will Take Your Soul **28**, 29-32, 37
Ataman, Kutlu? 215-217
ataque de los muertos sin ojos, El see Return of the Blind Dead, The
Ate (anthology segment) 262
Atom Age Vampire 273
Attack of the Mayan Mummy 9
Attili, Giorgio 31
Atwill, Lionel 7, 102, **104**, 269
Audition 285-292, 295, 305, 311
aullido del diablo, El see Howl of the Devil
Aur Kaun? 246
Aured, Carlos 72-74
Autumn Begonia 43
Avati, Pupi 143, 170
Avenger, The 115, **116**
Awakening of the Beast 36-37
Awful Dr. Orloff, The 106, 273, 274, 277

Baal, Karin 118, 121, 123
Baclanova, Olga 23
Bad Guy 202
Bad Movie 190
Bad Sleep Well, The 84, 85
Bad Taste 282
Ball, Annie 207
Ballhaus, Michael 177
Balpêtré, Antoine 161
Ban, Daisuke 299
Banchikwang see Foul King, The
Bande des Schreckens, Die see Terrible People, The
Bandh Darwaza 8, 247
Bang Rajan 62
Bangkok Dangerous 62
Banks, Leslie 112, 120
Baoyu lihua see Pear Blossom in the Storm
Barbarella 18, 279
Bardot, Brigitte 279
Bark, Peter 169
Barker, Clive 229
Barking Dogs Never Bite 199
Barrabas (film serial) 267
Bartholomew, David 181
Basic Instinct 46
Bastian, Ilona Agathe 222
Bat, The 95
Báthory, Countess Erzsébet 125, 279, 280
Batman 273
Batoctoy, Benny 262
Batoru Garu see Battle Girl
Batt, Mahesh 251
Battle Girl 302
Battle Royale 291, 306, 311
Batzella, Luigi 212
baúl macabro, El **98**, 99-102
Bava, Lamberto 173
Bava, Mario 9, 10, 86, 105, 136, 143, 161, 162, 170, 173, 297
Bay City Rollers 310
Bazzoni, Luigi 140
Beast and the Magic Sword, The 77
Beast Cops 45, **59**
Beast, The 233-235
Beatles, The 130
Beauty and the Beast (1945) **264**, 270-271
Beauty and the Beast (1991) 270
Bedekar, Vishram 245
Bedlam 8

Bellamy, Florence 233
Belle de jour 108
belle et la bête, La see Beauty and the Beast (1945)
Belmondo, Jean-Paul 120
Bender, Eva 211
Benedetti, Pierre 234
Bennent, Heinz 236
Berber, Adi 118, 120, 121
Beres, Jeff 47
Berger, Kasimir 169
Berger, Katya 169
Berinizi, Lorenzo 233
Berinzini, Jacopo 233
Bernini, Lorenzo 233
bestia uccide a sangue freddo, La see Slaughter Hotel
bestia y la espada mágica, Las see Beast and the Magic Sword, The
bête, La see Beast, The
Beware of a Holy Whore 236
Beyond, Far Beyond the Beyond (TV series) 32
Beyond, The 162, 164-166
Bhakri, Mohan 248, 249, 251, 252
Bhayanaak Raatein 252
Bianchi, Andrea 142, 162, 168
Bicycle Sighs 307
Bido, Antonio 16
Bird with the Crystal Plumage, The 122, **134**, 138, 140, 143
Bissette, Stephen R. 233
Bitter Moon 239
Black Cat, The 7
Black Emanuelle (film series) 143
Black Hole 197
Black Honeymoon 197, 201
Black Rain 285
Black Room, The 102
Black see Itim
Black Sunday 105
Black Sunday see Mask of Satan, The
Black, Andy 280
Blackburn, Kevin B. 127, 128
Blacula 72
Blair Witch Project, The 132
Blanche 233
Blatty, William Peter 213
blaue hand, Die see Creature with a Blue Hand, The
Bloedverwanten see Blood Relations
Blood and Black Lace 136, 142
Blood and Roses 279, 280, **281**
Blood Lust see Dr. Jekyll and His Women
Blood of Pontianak see Sumpah Pontianak
Blood of the Animals see sang des bêtes, Le
Blood Relations 9
Blood Spattered Bride, The 279
Bloodbath of Dr. Jekyll, The see Dr. Jekyll and His Women
Blood-Suckers 9
Bloodthirsty Doll see Vampire Doll, The
Bloodthirsty Eyes see Lake of Dracula
Bloodthirsty Rose see Evil of Dracula
Bloody Beach 185, 197
Bloody Kingdom (short film) 29
Bloody World of Salvation, The see Ang Madugong Daigdid ni Salvacion
Blue Eyes of the Broken Doll 71, **73**, **75**
Blue Spring 306, 311
Bluebeard 273
Blumenstock, Peter 278
Body Snatcher, The 8, 273
Böhme, Herbert 107
Boileau, Pierre 272
Bond, Lillian 84
Bonns, Miguel Iglesias 75
Booze, Boobs and Bucks 43
Bordwell, David 46
Borges, Jorge Luis 139
Borowczyk, Walerian 233-236, 238
Borsche, Dieter 119
Boston Globe (newspaper) 23
Bottle Imp, The (story) 271
Box of Death, The 188
Bozbey, Gönen 215
Brach, Gérard 239
Bracula - The Terror of the Living Death see Orgy of the Dead, The
Brain That Wouldn't Die, The 273
Bram Stoker's Dracula 207
Branded to Kill 286
Brando, Marlon 131, 180
Branice, Ligia 233
Brasseur, Pierre 107, 272
Braun, Pinkas 121
Breakfast at the Manchester Morgue see Let Sleeping Corpses Lie
Breton, André 269
Breve historia del cine mexicano: Primer siglo, 1897-1997 (book) 93
Brice, Pierre 107, **109**
Bride of Chucky 46
Bride of Frankenstein 99, 101
Bride with White Hair, The 83
Bridegroom from a Grave, a 187

Brocka, Lino 258
Brooks, Mel 212
Browning, Tod 7, 23, 24, 93, 99, 100, 121, 206-208, 269
Buck Rogers (serial) 28
Bucket of Blood, A 105
Buenas noches señor monstruo 76
Buffy the Vampire Slayer (TV series) 303
Bulgasari 189
Bullet for the General, A 10
Bunman see Untold Story, The
Buñuel, Luis 19, 23, 43, 108, 235, 267, 269
buque maldito, El see Horror of the Zombies
Burak, Sezgin 211
Burial Ground 164, 168-169
Burke, Frank 143
Busquets, Joaquín **92**
Bustillo Oro, Juan 93, 97, 102
Butler, Ivan 9
Butterfly, The 202
Byung-ki, An 197

Cabinet of Dr. Caligari, The 16, 93, 97, 186, 268
Caged Virgins see Requiem for a Vampire
Cahiers du Cinema, Les (magazine) 274
Caiano, Mario 138
Calla 185
Calles, Plutarco Elías 94, 96, 98
Cameron, James 61
caminante, El 75
Camus, Germán 93, 94, 99, 102
Canby, Vincent 18
Candeias, Ozualdo 33
Canovas, Anne 170
Cantinflas 93, 101, 103
Capara, Carlo 256
Caparrós, Ernesto 86
Cape Fear (1961) 178
Cape Fear (1991) 178
Capitaine Fracasse 278
Capital, Volume 1 (book) 59
Carbon, Julian 43
Cardenas, Goyo 19
Cárdenas, Lázaro 98
Cardona, René **98**, 103
Caress see Haplos
Carmilla (book) 279
carnaval de las bestias, El see Human Beasts
Carnival of Sinners see main du diable, La
Carnivore 188
Caro, Marc 280, 281
Carpenter, John 8, 169, 247
Carpetbaggers, The 186
Carr, Jay 23
Carrel, Dany **1**
Carrie 196
Carrière, Mathieu 236
casa dalle finestre che ridono, La see House with the Windows that Laugh, The
casa del terror, La 9
casa sperduta nel parco, La see House on the Edge of the Park, The
Casas, Benny 81
Cassano, Joseph 229
Castaneda, Manny 262
Castel, Lou 10
Castellari, Enzo Girolami 140
Castillo, Celso Ad. 256
Castle of Blood 105
Cat and the Canary, The (1927) 95, 101
Cat and the Canary, The (1939) 101
Cat O'Nine Tails, The 122, **138**, 140
Cat People 8, 271
Cat's Victims, The 140
Cave of the Living Dead 9
Cemetery Man see Dellamorte Dellamore
Cendrars, Blaise 270
Cérèmonie d'amour see Rites of Love
Cervantes, Augusto de 31
Chabrol, Claude 267, 274, 279
Chace, Daniel 215
Chamber of Horrors see Door with Seven Locks, The (1940)
Chambers, John 270
Chan, Jackie 202, 288
Chan, Peter 62
Chaney Jr., Lon 8, 70, 271
Chaney, Lon 7, 23, 24, 42, 93, 100, 102, 105, 270
Chan-wook, Park 202
Chaos 305
Charisma 305
Chayu Puin 186
Cheekh **247**, 248
Cheuk-to, Li 46
Cheung, Cecilia 202
Cheung, Leslie 43
Chevalier, Maurice 16
Chi O Suu Bara see Evil of Dracula
Chi o Suu Me see Lake of Dracula
Chicago Sun-Times (newspaper) 241
chien Andalou, Un 269
Child Monster, The see Tianak
Chin, Dolphin 57, 58
Chinatown 239
Chinese Ghost Story, A 10, 83

314   fear without frontiers

index

Chinese Torture Chamber Story 53
Chiu-feng, Yune 43
Chi-yeung, Wong 53
Choke Song Chan see *Double Luck*
Chosun Daily (newspaper) 190
Choyonghan kajok see *Quiet Family, The*
Chrisman, Laura 51
Christie, Agatha 130, 143
Chudail No. 1 252
Chung-hee, Park 187, 189
Chungking Express 58
Ch'unhyang-jon 186
Ch'unmong 186
chute de la Maison Usher, La see *Fall of the House of Usher, The (1928)*
Çiğlik 206
Cine East: Hong Kong Cinema Through the Looking Glass (book) 52
Cinema Journal (journal) 272
Cinemaya (magazine) 46
cité des enfants perdus, La see *City of Lost Children, The*
Citizen Kane 98, 173
City of Lost Children, The 280-281
City of Lost Souls 287, 288
City of the Living Dead 162, 164, **165**, 167, 169
City of the Walking Dead see *Nightmare City*
Civilization and Monsters: Spirits of Modernity in Meiji Japan (book) 296
Clapczynski, Stefan 178
Clarens, Carlos 9
Clares, Zulema 82
Clive, Colin 7
Clockwork Orange, A 178
Clouzot, Henri-Georges 271-273
Clouzot, Vera 272
Clover, Carol 52, 140
club Dumas, El (book) 240
Club Extinction see *Dr. M*
Clue of the New Pin, The (book) 123
Cocteau, Jean 16, 170, 270, 271
Coffin Joe see Marins, José Mojica
Cohen, Larry 8
Cojuangco-Aquino, Corazon 256
Cold Eyes of Fear 140
Colonial Discourse and Postcolonial Theory: A Reader (book) 51
coltello di ghiaccio, Il see *Knife of Ice*
Comfort of Strangers, The 81
Comrades: Almost a Love Story 62
comtesse noire, La see *Female Vampire*
Concepcion, Alma 260
Concerto per pistola solista see *Weekend Murders, The*
Concise History of Mexico, A (book) 94
Condition of the Working Class in England, The (book) 54
Contact, The 190, 194
Contes immoraux see *Immoral Tales*
Contreras, Gloria 21
Cop Image 45
Coppola, Francis Ford 180, 207
corbeau, Le see *Raven, The (1943)*
Corman, Roger 8, 105, 109
Cornwell, Patricia 135
Cosa avete fatto a Solange? see *What Have You Done to Solange?*
Così dolce, così perversa see *So Sweet, So Perverse*
Count Dracula's Great Love 71-72
Countess Dracula 280
Country Maiden see *Dalagang Bukid*
Coyote, Peter 240
Craven, Wes 8, 10, 77, 182
Craving, The see *Return of the Wolfman*
Crawford, Joan 24
Crazies, The 75, 161
Crazy Nut, The see *superloco, El*
Creature with a Blue Hand, The **157**
Cries in the Night see *Awful Dr. Orloff, The*
Cries of Terror **70**, 72, **73**, 76, **151**
Crimes of the Black Cat 140
Crimson **80**
Crimson Circle, The **114**, 115
Cronenberg, David 8, 85, 88
Crucible of Terror 105
Cruise, Tom 62
Cry of Apes in a Deserted Valley, The 39-40
Crying Woman, The see *llorona, La*
Cul-de-sac 238
Culpa 84, 87, 88
Cult Movies (book) 18
Cure 305
Curse of Frankenstein, The 8, 273
Curse of the Demon 298
Curse of the Devil 74, 75, **80**
Curse of the Oily Man, The see *Sumpah Orang Minyak*
Curse of the Vampire, The see *Sumpah Pontianak*
Curse of the Yellow Snake, The 122, **123**
Curtis Harrington and the Underground Roots of the Modern Horror Film (book) 233
Curtis, Dan 207
Curtiz, Michael 7
Cushing, Peter 273
Cute Frankenstein see *Sevimli Frankestayn*
Cutting Edge: Art-Horror and the Horrific Avant-Garde (book) 274
Cybulski, Zbigniew 231

da Costa, Augusto 33
Dae-young, Park 199
Dai, Lin 188
Dak Bangla 247
Dalagang Bukid 255
Dalbès, Alberto 71
Dali, Salvador 18
Dalkiran, Biray 216
Dallamano, Massimo 123
dama rossa uccide sette volte, La see *Lady in Red Kills Seven Times, The*
D'Amato, Joe see Massaccesi, Aristide
Dance of the Vampires see *Fearless Vampire Killers, The*
Dang Bireley and the Young Gangsters 61, 63
Dangerous Encounter of the First Kind 46
Dangerous Seductress **228**, 229
Dante, Joe 76
Danvers, Lise 233
Danza macabre see *Castle of Blood*
Dark Carnival: The Secret World of Tod Browning, Hollywood's Master of the Macabre (book) 23
Dark Eyes of London, The 111, 112, 116-120, 273
Dark Thoughts: Philosophic Reflections on Cinematic Horror (book) 105
Dark Water 305
Darkness Visible: A Memoir of Madness (book) 59
Dasgupta, Poonam 252
Daughters of Darkness 9, 279, 280
Dávalos Orozco, Federico 98
David, Joel 255
Dawn of the Dead 161-163, 166, 228
Dawn of the Mummy 164, 169-170, **171**
Day of the Crow, The (book) 135
Day That Doesn't Exist, The 52
Day, Josette **264**, 270
Days of Being Wild 58
De Angelis, Fabrizio 162
de Belen, Janice 260, 262
de Fuentes, Fernando 93, 96
de Leon, Christopher 257
de Leon, Gerardo 256
de Leon, Mike 255, 259
de Mesa, Michael 262
De Nava, Giovanni 165
De Niro, Robert 178
De Rossi, Giannetto 162
De Ruiz, Nick 24
Dead Don't Talk, The see *Ölüler Konusmazki*
Dead Eyes of London 10, 116-121
Dead or Alive 285-292
Dead or Alive: Final 288
Dead or Alive: Hanzaisha see *Dead or Alive*
Dead Speak, The see *Muertos hablan, Los*
Deadly Outlaw: Rekka **291**
Death and the Maiden 239
Death Carries a Cane 140, **144**
Death Cottage, The see *House of Death*
Death in Haiti 143
Death Warrior see *Ölüm Savasğisi*
Debucourt, Jean 268
Decameron, The (book) 231
del Campo, Enrique 96
Delahaye, Michael 274
Delicatessen 280, 281
Dellamorte Dellamore 164, 172-173
Demme, Jonathan 202
démons, Les see *Demons, The*
Demons, The 75
Dendam Pontianak 127-129
Deneuve, Catherine 108, 238
D'entre les morts (book) 272
Deodato, Ruggero 182
Depp, Johnny 240
Dersu Uzala 46
Dery, Mark 56
Despertar da Besta, O see *Awakening of the Beast*
Deutschland bleiche Mutter see *Germany Pale Mother*
Devil Incarnate 39
Devilish Homicide, A 187
Devil's Hand, The see *main du diable, La*
Devil's Possessed, The 74
Devils, The 75
Dewi, Sri 128
Di Leo, Fernando 140
Diabolique (1955) 272, 273
Diabolique (1996) 10
Diaboliques, Les (book) 272
Diaboliques, Les see *Diabolique*
Diegues, Carlos 35
Dika, Vera 182
Discourses of the Vanishing: Modernity, Phantasm, Japan (book) 296
Discreet Charm of the Bourgeoisie, The 235
Ditto 185
Djalil, H. Tjut 126, 220, 222, 227-229
Djinn 131, 132
Dmytryk, Edward 186
Do Gaz Zameen ke Neeche 245
do Rosario, Louise 299
Doak, Kevin M. 295
Doctor K 194
Dol, Shariff 128
D'Olace, Isidro **101**
Doll Maker, The (anthology segment) 34
Dolman 2000 84, 87
Dominguez D., Berta 18
Dominici, Arturo 162
Don Quixote (book) 240
Dong-bin, Kim 194
Don't Open the Window see *Let Sleeping Corpses Lie*
Doo-kwan, Chun 189
Door with Seven Locks, The (1940) 112, 120
Door with Seven Locks, The (1962) **112**, 120-121
Dorfman, Ariel 239
Dos monjes 94, 95, 97-98, 101
Dotulong, Libeth see Menado, Maria
Doty, Alexander 142
Double Luck 61
Douglas, Melvyn 84, 239
Doyle, Arthur Conan 143, 240
Dr Jekyll and Mr Hyde 7
Dr. Butcher M.D. see *Zombi Holocaust*
Dr. Caligari'nin Karisi ve Oglu (short film) 216
Dr. Jekyll and His Women **230**, 235
Dr. Jekyll and the Werewolf see *Dr. Jekyll Versus the Werewolf*
Dr. Jekyll et les femmes see *Dr. Jekyll and His Women*
Dr. Jekyll Versus the Werewolf 10, **68**, 71
Dr. Jekyll y el hombre lobo see *Dr. Jekyll Versus the Werewolf*
Dr. Lamb 47, 52
Dr. M 279
Dr. Mabuse 268
Dr. Mabuse - The Gambler 111
Dr. Mabuse (film series) 107
Dr. Strangelove 167
Dr. Tarr's Torture Dungeon 16
Dr. X 7
Drache, Heinz **112**, 116, 121
Dracula (1931) 7, 11, 23, 93, 96, 99-101, 206, 268
Dracula (1931) (Spanish version) 93-94, 97, 102
Dracula (1958) 207, 244
Dracula (1973) 207
Dracula (book) 279
Dracula in Istanbul see *Drakula Istanbul'da*
Dracula Tan Exarchia 9
Dracula: A Biography of Vlad the Impaler 1431-1476 (book) 207
Dracula's Daughter 7, 96
Dracula's Great Love 9
Dracula's Ring 9
Dragonfly for Each Corpse, A **76**, 144
Drakula Istanbul'da 8, 205-209, **217**
Dreams 125
Dreams of Difference: The Japan Romantic School and the Crisis of Modernity (book) 295
Dreyer, Carl 279
Dry Summer see *Suzuz Yaz*
Due occhi diabolici see *Two Evil Eyes*
Duel 201
Dumas, Alexandre 240
Dumas, Roger 271
Dune (book) 18
Dünyayi Kurtaran Adam 212

...E tu vivrai nel terrore! L'aldilà see *Beyond, The*
Earles, Harry 23
Earth Woman, The see *Ang Babaeng Putik*
Eastman, George see Montefiori, Luigi
Ebert, Roger 241
Ebola Syndrome 45, 54-56, 59, **154**
Eburne, Maude 101
Eck, Johnny 23
Eco, Umberto 135
Economist, The (magazine) 186
Edgar Wallace: The Biography of a Phenomenon (book) 112
Edmundson, Mark 257, 260
Ek Nanni Munni Ladhki Thi 244-245
Eko Eko Azarak 302
Eko Eko Azarak (film series) 295, 302-304
Eko Eko Azarak (TV series) 304
Eko Eko Azarak II: Birth of the Wizard 302-304
Eko Eko Azarak III: Misa the Dark Angel **294**, 304
El Topo 15-18, 23, 85
Elder Sister (anthology segment) see *Ate (anthology segment)*
Elgar, Edward 112
Elias, Luiz 31
Elsa Castillo Story: The Truth, The 256
Elusive Song of the Vampire 9
Emilfork, Daniel 280
Enchanted Monkey, The see *Loetoeng Kasaroeng*
End of Days 241
End of Man, The 28, 37
End of the World, The see *fin du monde, La*
Endo, Kenichi 289
Engels, Friedrich 54-56
Englund, Robert 10
Epstein, Jean 267-269, 271
Era, Itaru 286
Eraserhead 18
Erksan, Metin 213
Erotic Ghost Story 46
Erotic Ghost Story 2 48
Escamotage d'une Dame chez Robert-Haudin 266
Escape Velocity: Cyberculture at the End of the Century (book) 56
Escudero, Don 259, 260, 262
espanto surge de la tumba, El see *Horror Rises from the Tomb*
Espinoza, Leandro 81
Esta Noite Encarnarei no Tue Cadáver see *This Night I Will Possess Your Corpse*
Estella, Ramón A. 127, 128, 130
Estranho Mundo de Zé do Caixão, O (TV series) see *Strange World of Coffin Joe, The (TV series)*
Estranho Mundo de Zé do Caixão, O see *Strange World of Coffin Joe, The*
Et Dieu... créa la femme see *And God Created Woman*
...Et mourir de plaisir see *Blood and Roses*
Eun-hee, Choi 188
Eun-Kyung, Shin 194
Eunuch 186
Everett, Rupert 172
Evil and the Demonic: A New Theory of Monstrous Behavior (book) 166
Evil Dead, The 212, 229, 282
Evil Eye, The see *Girl Who Knew Too Much, The*
Evil of Dracula 298
Ewers, Hanns Heinz 106
Executioners, The **44**, 45
Exorcism 74
Exorcismo Negro **31**, **148**
Exorcismo see *Exorcism*
Exorcist (short film) see *Seytan Kovma (short film)*
Exorcist, The 8, 11, 74, 212-214, 225, 232, 244
express, L' (newspaper) 274
Exterminating Angel, The 235
Eye in the Labyrinth, The **136**, 138, 139
Eye, The 62
Eyeball **139**, 140
Eyeball (magazine) 10
Eyes Without a Face 107, **156**, 226, 272-274, **275**, 277, 282
Eyes, The 252

Fa talai jone see *Tears of the Black Tiger*
Fabricante de Bonecas, O (anthology segment) see *Doll Maker, The (anthology segment)*
Fábulas Pánicas (comic strip) 16
fabuleux destin d'Amélie Poulain, Le see *Amélie*
Face of the Screaming Werewolf 9
Face/Off 273
Faceless 274
Fad (magazine) 24
Fahrenheit 451 279
Failan 202
Falchi, Anna 173
Fall of the House of Usher, The (1928) 267-269, 271, 273
Fall of the House of Usher, The (1960) 8
Fall of the House of Usher, The (story) 109, 268
Fallen Angels 203
Family 290
Fando y Lis 15, 16, 21
fantasma del convento, El 94-98, 100-103
Fantastic Planet 239, 279
Fantômas (film serial) 267, 269
Farrow, Mia 238
Fascination **277**, 278
Fassbinder, Rainer Werner 49, 179, 236
Fear see *Angst*
Fearless Vampire Killers, The 129, 238, 239
Fei taugh mo neuih see *Witch with Flying Head, The*
Fellini Satyricon 16
Fellini, Federico 16, 23, 85, 173
Fellowship of the Frog **110**, 112, **113**, 114, 115
Female Vampire 9
Femme Nikita, La 203
Fenech, Edwige 139
Feng, Yueh 188
Feray, Ayfer 207
Fernández, Esther **98**
Ferrara, Ranieri 165
Ferrer, Mel 168
Ferroni, Giorgio 105, 106, 108, 109
Feuillade, Louis 267, 269, 272, 278
fidélité, La 237
Fifth Cord, The 140, **141**
Figal, Gerald A. 296
Figenli, Yavuz 209
Film 71/72: An Anthology (book) 18
Film Enclyclopedia: Horror (book) 10, 95
Film Quarterly (magazine) 39
fin du monde, La 270
Finis Hominis see *End of Man, The*
Fisher, Terence 10, 273
Five Dolls for an August Moon 143
Flemish Tales (story collection) 105
Florescu, Radu 207
Flower of Evil, A 187
Flowers of Hell 186, 202
Fluch der Gelben Schlange, Der see *Curse of the Yellow Snake, The*
fluch der grunen augen, Der see *Cave of the Living Dead*
Fog, The (short film) see *Sis (short film)*
Fonda, Jane 279
Forced Exposure (magazine) 19
Ford, John 23
Forrest Gump 199
Foul King, The 62, 191
Francen, Victor 269, 270
Franciosa, Anthony 143
Franco, General Francisco 69
Franco, Jesus 9, 10, 75, 81, 83, 84, 86-88, 106, 273, 274, 277-279
Franju, Georges 86, 107, 267, 272-274, 278, 279, 282
Frank, Consuelo **99**, 100
Frankenstein 7, 16, 99-101, 268, 270
Frankenstein Meets the Wolf Man 69, 70
Frankenstein Must Be Destroyed 10

horror cinema across the globe 315

index

Frankenstein's Bloody Terror see Mark of the Wolfman, The
Frantic 239
Freak in the Night 39
Freaks 23, 100, 269, 270
Freda, Riccardo 105, 143, 161, 173
French Film (book) 271
French Science-Fiction, Fantasy, Horror and Pulp Fiction (book) 280
Freund, Karl 7, 99
Fria Jenny (anthology segment) 87
Friday the 13th 181
Friedkin, William 74, 212, 213, 225, 244
Friedman, Milton 56
Friend 202
Fright Night 249
Frisch, Arno 178, 180
frissons des vampires, Le see Sex and the Vampire
Front Page, The 8
Frosch mit der Maske, Der see Fellowship of the Frog
Frumkes, Roy 164
Frye, Dwight 116, 120
Fuchsberger, Joachim 112, 116, 117, 121, 123
Fudoh: The New Generation 285, 286, **287**, 288-291
Fukasaku, Kinji 306
Fulci, Lucio 10, 83, 84, 86, 138, 143, 162, 163, 165, 167, 169, 170, 173, 182
Funny Games 175, 178-182
furia del Hombre Lobo, La see Fury of the Wolfman, The
Furneaux, Yvonne 238
Fury of the Wolfman, The 70

Gabel, Scilla 106, 107, **109**
Gaichu see Harmful Insect
Galeen, Henrik 106
Gallaga, Peque 260-262
Galsworthy, John 112
Games 248
Gance, Abel 269, 270, 278
Gance, Margueritte 268
Garces, Armando 257
Garcia Bogliano, Ramiro 84
Garcia Riera, Emilio 93
Garcia, Eddie 257
Garcia, Juan Antonio 88
Garcia, Luis Alberto 82, **86**
Garon, Sheldon 296
Gate of Hell 186
Gatti rossi in un labirinto di vetro see Eyeball
gatto a nove code, Il see Cat O'Nine Tails, The
gatto dagli occhi di giada, Il see Cat's Victims, The
Gautama Putra, Sisworo 223-226
Gay-Lussac, B. 274
Geceyarisi Sinemasi (magazine) 214
Gehraayee 244
Gein, Ed 175
Gemma, Giuliano 143
George, John 24
Germany Pale Mother 179
Germi, Pietro 175
Gerrard, Charles 101
Ghost 194
Ghost in Love 194
Ghost in the Cemetery, The see Ang Multo sa Libingan
Ghost Taxi 199
Ghunghroo Ki Awaz 246
Giering, Frank 178
Gilliam, Terry 279-281
Gingko Bed, The 190, 191, 193, 202
Giordano, Mariangela **168**, 169
Giornata nera per l'ariete see Fifth Cord, The
giorno della civetta, Il (book) see Day of the Crow, The (book)
Giraud, Jean 18
Girl Who Knew Too Much, The 136, 138, 140, 143
Girolami, Marino 164
glace à trois faces, La 267
Glaessner, Verina 10
Go Tell the Marines 7
Goblin 166
Godard, Jean-Luc 274, 279
Goddess of Mercy 188
Godzilla (1998) 10
Godzilla (1998) 189
Gokudo Kuroshakai see Rainy Dog
Gokudô Sengokushi: Fudô see Fudoh: The New Generation
Goldberg, Ruth 85, 90
Golem, The 93
Good Harvest see Aswang
Goodfellas 66
Goose Alights on the Wintry River, A 40
Goosebumps see Sorum
Gorezone (magazine) 111
Gorilla, The 101
Goto l'isle d'amour see Goto, Island of Love
Goto, Island of Love 233
Gottlieb, Franz Josef 122
Götz, Rudolf 177
Govar, René 70
Gramsci, Antonio 135
gran amor del Conde Drácula, El see Count Dracula's Great Love
gran amor del Conde Drácula, El see Dracula's Great Love
Grand Evil Monster Yonggary see Yongary, Monster from the Deep

Grant, Hugh 239
Grapes of Death 278
Grau, Jorge 73, 162-164
Great Ghost War, The 298
Green Fish 190
Green, Joseph 273
Griffith, D.W. 24, 95, 267
Gritos en la noche see Awful Dr. Orloff, The
Gu wu Xing shi ji see Tales of a Corpse-Ridden Old House
Guerra, Blanca 20
Guinness, Alec 7
Gum gee yuk yip see He's a Woman She's a Man
Gumising Ka, Maruja 258-259
Gûnbay, Altan 209
Gutierrez, Pedro Juan 82, 83
Gynt, Greta 119

Haarmann, Fritz 175
Hadji-Lazaro,François 172
Hagiwara, Yuki 304
Hairy Arm, The (book) 115
Hale, Creighton 101
Hall, Huntz 119
Haller, Magda 97
Halloween 8, 169, 181
Hallucinations of a Deranged Mind **35**
Hamilton, Cicely 112
Hamnett, Brian R. 94
Hampton, Robert see Freda, Riccardo
Han jiang luo yan see Goose Alights on the Wintry River, A
Han, Tian 41
Hana-Bi 286
Handel, George Frideric 41
Haneke, Michael 175, 177-182
Hanging Woman, The 70, 72-73
Happiness of the Katakuris, The 290
Hard-Boiled 45, 48
Hardy, Phil 10, 95
Hark, Tsui 46, 81, 288, 291
Harmful Insect 306, 311
Harpy 185, 197, 201
Harrington, Curtis 248
Harris, Thomas 135
Harta Karun 220
Has, Wojciech 231, 232
Hatyarin 250
Haunted Castle, The 298
Haunted House, The see Maid's Bitter Story, A
Haunting, The 85
Hawkins, Joan 274
Hawks, Howard 8
Hawthorne, Nathaniel 106
Healy, Ted 101
Hearn, Lafcadio 296
Heaven and Earth 131
Hebi Onna see Snake Woman, The
Heider, Karl G. 222, 224
Heilbroner, Robert 59
Hell see Jogoku
Hellraiser 194, 229
Helm, Brigitte 106
Helye guairen see Freak in the Night
Henry: Portrait of a Serial Killer 47, 176
Herbert, Frank 18
herencia macabra, La 99, **100**, 101, 102
Herrero, Subas 262
Hershfield, Joanne 93, 98, 102
Herzog, Werner 212, 239
He's a Woman She's a Man 62
Hexen bis aufs blut gequält see Mark of the Devil
Heya see Room, The
Hidden Treasure see Harta Karun
Hillyer, Lambert 108
Hiroku Kaibyoden see Haunted Castle, The
Histoires extraordinaires see Spirits of the Dead
History of Mexico, The (book) 94
Hitchcock, Alfred 21, 23, 24, 39, 117, 136, 140, 169, 173, 215, 272, 274, 286
Hitler, Adolf 112
Ho-beom, Ra 197
Hoberman, J. 17
Ho-jung, Kim 202
Hole, The 190-191, 201
Holland, Tom 249
Hollywood Gothic: The Tangled Web of Dracula from Novel to Stage to Screen (book) 94
Holofernes 169
Holoubek, Gustow 232
Holy Mountain, The 18, **25**, **146**
Home Alone 76
Hong Kong Cinema: The Extra Dimensions (book) 39
Hong-kyun, Na 197
Honogurai Mizu No Soko Kara see Dark Water
Hooper, Tobe 8, 85
Hoosmann, Al 115
Horror Chamber of Dr. Faustus, The see Eyes Without a Face
Horror Express Train 190
Horror Game Movie, The 197, 201
Horror of the Zombies 168
Horror Rises from the Tomb 72, 74-76
Horror Years, The (book) 9
Horror-wood (webzine) 47
Hotel 246, 248, 252
House by the Cemetery, The 162, 164, 165
House of Death 189
House of Psychotic Women see Blue Eyes of the Broken Doll

House of Wax 105
House on the Edge of the Park, The 182
House with the Windows that Laugh, The 143, 170
Housemaid, The 188
How to Win Friends and Influence People (book) 241
Howard, William K. 122
Howl of the Devil 77, **151**
Howling, The 76
Hu, King 188
Hui, Ann 52
Human Beasts 76, **150**
Human Cobras 143
Human Monster, The see Dark Eyes of London, The
Hummel, Lisbeth 234
Humphries, Reynold 136, 143
Hûn, Agah 213
Hunchback of Notre Dame, The (1923) 7, 100
Hunchback of Notre Dame, The (1939) 16
Hunchback of the Morgue 71, 72
Hungry Snake Woman, The see Snake Queen, The
Hunshi mowang see Devil Incarnate
Hussin, Hamzah 127, 129
Hye-jin, Shim 202
Hyeok-jin, Gweon 187
Hyeon-ho, Shin 186
Hyong-mo, Han 186
Hyon-mok, Yu 186
Hyoryuu-Gui see City of Lost Souls
Hyung-rae, Shim 194
Hyun-jun, Shin 191
Hyun-myung, Kim 196

I Accuse see J'accuse
I Am Sono Sion (short film) 307
I Had My Brother's Wife see Suzuz Yaz
I Know What You Did Last Summer 252
I Spy (TV series) 69
I Walked With a Zombie 8, 163, 271
Ibulong Mo Sa Hangin 256
Ichi the Killer **159**, 202, **284**, 285, 286, 288, 290, 291
Ideology (anthology segment) see Ideology (anthology segment)
Ideology (anthology segment) 34
iguana dalla lingua di fuoco, L' see Iguana with a Tongue of Fire, The
Iguana with a Tongue of Fire, The 143, **144**
Ilarde, Rico Maria 262
Illustrated History of the Horror Film, An (book) 9
Il-sun, Kim 188
Imamura, Shohei 285, 291
Immoral Tales 233
Immoral Tales: European Sex and Horror Movies 1956-1984 (book) 10, 235
immortale, L' 216
Impakto 259
Imperial Leather: Race, Gender, and Sexuality in the Colonial Contest (book) 143
important c'est d'amier, L' see Most Important Thing Is to Love, The
In Search of Dracula 207
Incontro d'amore a Bali 143
Incubo sulla città contaminata see Nightmare City
Indonesian Cinema: Framing the New Order (book) 219
Indonesian Cinema: National Culture on Screen (book) 222
Inferno Carnal **36**
inferno dei morti-viventi see Zombie Creeping Flesh
Inoue, Tetsujiro 296
Inquisición see Inquisition
Inquisition **74**, 75
Insanity 47
Insect Woman, The 188
Insomnia 11
Inspector Danush 251
In-su, Kim 197
Intolerance 95
Invaders from Mars 168
Invisible Man, The 21, 23, 99, 101
Invisible Ray, The 108
Iodo 188
Ishibashi, Ryo 289, 305, **309**, 311
Island of Lost Souls 99, 163
Isle of the Dead 8
Isle, The 185, 198, 202
Ismail, Usmar 220
It! 71
Itim 255, **258**, 259, **261**
It's Alive! 8
Ivy, Marilyn 296
Iwai, Shunji 306
Izuno, Orie 298

Jaani Dushman 244
J'accuse (1918) 270
J'accuse (1937) 269-271, 273
Jack el destripador de Londres see Jack the Ripper of London
Jack the Ripper 10
Jack the Ripper of London 71
Jackson Five, The 310
Jackson, Jalil see Djalil, H. Tjut
Jackson, Neil 163
Jackson, Peter 282
Jacopetti, Gualtiero 163
Jadu Tona 244
Jaka Sembung see Warrior, The

Jamuna 252
Jan Dara 62, **64**, **65**
Jannings, Emil 43
Japan's High Schools (book) 303
Jasmine 252
Jaws 85
Jefford, Barbara 241
Je-gyu, Kang 185, 190, 193, 194, 198
Jenks, Carol 280
jetée, La see Pier, The
Jeunet, Jean-Pierre 280-282
Jian gui see Eye, The
Jiménez, Agustin 97
Jing, Wong 53, 54
Jingling, Hong **42**
Jin-hee, Park 192
Jinn, Ong Lay see Djinn
Jisatsu Circle see Suicide Club
Jitensha Toiki see Bicycle Sighs
Jitnukul, Tanit 62
Jitters, The 10
Ji-woon, Kim 62, 188, 191, 198
Jodorowsky, Adan 19
Jodorowsky, Alejandro 15-24, 83, 85, 236
Jodorowsky, Axel 19, **22**, **146**
Jodorowsky, Teo 21
Jogoku 297
Johnson, Richard 162
Johnson, Tor 120
Joint Security Area 202
Jonathan 217
Jong-chan, Yoon 201
Jong-hak, Baek 196, 199
Jong-il, Kim 188, 189
Joong-hoon, Park 202
Joon-ho, Boog 199
jorobado de la morgue, El see Hunchback of the Morgue
JSA see Joint Security Area
Juan Carlos I 77
Juárez, Jesús 19
Judex (1916) 272
Judex (1963) 272, 278
Judgement Day (short film) 27, 29
Judith of Bethulia 169
Julian, Rupert 42
Jung, Carl Gustav 105
Junoon 251
Jürges, Jürgen 179
Just Do It 199
Jy-hye, Yoon 192

Kabrastan 248, 249, 252
Kabrastan ke Peeche 252
Kader Diyelim (unreleased) 215, 216
Kaidan Botandero 298
Kaidan Katame no Otoko 298
Kaidan Semushi Otoko 298
Kaidan Yukigoro 298
Kaîro see Pulse
Kai-wah, Ng 58
Kakashi see Scarecrow, The
Ka-kui, Ho 53
Kam-fai, Law 47
Kamil, Salleh 128
Kanno, Miho 303
Kaosu see Chaos
Kaptan, Ari 206
Kara Boğa 209-210, 212
Karanlik Sular **214**, 215-217
Kargl, Gerald 175-179, 181, 182
Karisuma see Charisma
Karlatos, Olga 163
Karlen, John 280
Karloff, Boris 7, 8, 28, 70, 102, 108, 269
Kar-wai, Wong 58, 82, 84, 202, 203
Katakuri-ke no kôfuku see Happiness of the Katakuris, The
Kaun? 252
Kaze see Wind, The
Kazikli Voyvoda (book) 206-208
Keiko Desu Kedo 307
Kekkou Kamen (film series) 302
Keller, Sarah 165
Kennedy, Arthur 164
Kenton, Erle C. 163
Kerry, Norman 24
Khoj 247
Khooni Dracula 252
Khooni Mahal 248
Khooni Murdaa 249, 252
Khooni Panja **154**, **155**
Ki-duk, Kim 187, 198, 201, 202
Kier, Udo 235
Ki-hoon, Kim 198
Ki-hyung, Park 192, 193, 198
Kilink Frankestayn'a Karsi 212
Kilink Istanbul'da 211
Kill Barbara with Terror see Patayin sa Sindak si Barbara
Killer Butterfly 188
Killing in Istanbul see Kilink Istanbul'da
Killing Versus Frankenstein see Kilink Frankestayn'a Karsi
King Kong 7, 100, 101, 111
King Kong (1976) 187
King of Kings 69
King, Stephen 8, 253
Kingsley, Ben 239
Kinoeye (journal) 136, 143
Kinski, Klaus 116, 120, 121, **157**, 236
Kirkwood, Burton 94
Kitano, "Beat" Takeshi 286, 291
Ki-woong, Nam 203
Ki-young, Kim 188

316 fear without frontiers

index

Klainer, Sergio 15
Klein, Allen 18
Klein-Rogge, Rudolf 107, 114
Klimovsky, León 70, 72, 75, 144
Kniesek, Werner 175, 178, 182
Knife in the Water 238
Knife of Ice 138
Kobayashi, Masaki 296, 298, 299
Koga, Shinichi 302
Kohli, Rajkumar 244
Koji, Suzuki 194
Kon, Satoshi 144
Kondrat, Tadeusz 232
Kong gu yuan sheng see *Cry of Apes in a Deserted Valley, The*
Koroshi No Rakuin see *Branded to Kill*
Koroshiya 1 see *Ichi the Killer*
Krishnan, Laksamanan 127, 128, 130
Kronos 85
Kubrick, Stanley 167, 178
Kuk-hyung, Kim 197
Kumar, Kiran **154**, **242**, 249, 252
Kümel, Harry 279, 280
Kung Bakit Dugo ang Kulay ng Gabi 256
Kuroda, Yoshiyuki 298
Kuroi Ame see *Black Rain*
Kuroki, Kazuo 291
Kurosawa, Akira 46, 84, 85, 98, 125
Kurosawa, Kiyoshi 291, 305, 311
Kürten, Peter 175, 176
Kurtoğlu, Haluk 215
Kwaidan 296, **297**, 298, 299
Kwang-Chun, Park 191
Kyrou, Ado 278
Kyua see *Cure*
Kyu-ri, Kim 192, 197

LaBine, Jarrod 24
Lady Battlecop 302
Lady in Red Kills Seven Times, The **140**, **142**, 145
Lady Terminator see *Nasty Hunter*
Lahaie, Brigitte **278**
Laila Majnun 127
Lake of Dracula 9, 298
Laloux, René 279
Lam, Bosco 52, 53
Lam, Ringo 288, 291
lama nel corpo, La see *Murder Clinic, The*
Lamar, Adriana **95**
Lane, Margaret 112
Lane, Sirpa 233
Lanetli Kadinlar 215
Lang, Fritz 107, 111, 114, 277
Langella, Frank 240
Langlois, Henri 274
Larraz, José Ramón 247
Last House on the Left, The 8
Last Woman of Shang, The 188
Last Year at Marienbad 279, 280
Latidos de pánico see *Cries of Terror*
Lattuada, Alberto 173
Laughton, Charles 7, 16
Lavia, Gabriele 170
Law, Alex 45
Le Fanu, J. Sheridan 279
Leák Ngakak (book) 220
Leák see *Mystics in Bali*
Leder, Erwin **152**, **174**, 176, **177**, **182**
Lee, Bruce 188
Lee, Christopher 18, 19, 72, 207
Lee, Danny 45, 47, 49, 51, 55
Lee, Norman 112
Lee, Ricardo 257
Legend of the Mountain 188
Legend of the Seven Golden Vampires, The 9
Leni, Paul 7, 105
Lennon, John 17
Lenzi, Umberto 138, 140, 167, 168, 173
Leone, Sergio 163
Leopard Man, The 8
Leper Woman 42
Leroux, Gaston 39-41
Lesoeur, Daniel 277
Lesoeur, Marius 277
Let Sleeping Corpses Lie 73, 162-164
Let's Say It's Fate (unreleased) see *Kader Diyelim (unreleased)*
Leung Chiu-wai, Tony 48
Levin, Ira 238, 239
lèvres rouges, Les see *Daughters of Darkness*
Lewis, Herschell Gordon 226
Lewton, Val 8, 239
Ley Lines 285
libélula para cada muerto, Una see *Dragonfly for Each Corpse, A*
Liberatore, Ugo 143
Licántropo: El asesino de la luna llena see *Licantropus: The Moonlight Murders*
Licantropus: The Moonlight Murders 77
Liebman, Stuart 269
Li-hua, Li 188
Lim, Bliss 255
Linda, Boguslaw 238
Livelihood see *Penghidupan*
Living Dead at the Manchester Morgue, The see *Let Sleeping Corpses Lie*
Lizard in a Woman's Skin, A 138
llorona, La 94-96, 98, 100, 102, 103
Lobo, Jose 31
Lodger, The 7
Loetoeng Kasoroeng 219
Lofficier, Jean-Marc 280
Lofficier, Randy 280
Loke, Ho Ah 128
Lola + Bilidikid 216
Lola + Billy the Kid see *Lola + Bilidikid*
Lomi, Giampaolo 143
López Moctezuma, Juan 16
Lord of the Rings 282
Lorre, Peter 7, 105
Los Angeles Times (newspaper) 16
Loscin, Rio 257
Lost Souls 241
Lothar, Susanne 178, **179**, **181**
Loud, Lance 21
Love and Gold 39
Love Freak, The 39
Lovecraft, H.P. 8, 165
Lovelock, Ray 164
Lowenstein, Adam 272
Lowitz, Siegfried 112
Lucas, Tim 10, 111, 228, 278, 280
Lucchetti, Rubens Francisco 36
lucertola con la pelle di donna, Una see *Lizard in a Woman's Skin, A*
Lugosi, Bela 7-9, 23, 28, 102, 111, 112, 116, 117, 119, 120, 206
Lukschy, Wolfgang 119
Lumière Brothers 265
Lumière, Louis 266, 267
Lunch, Lydia 81
Lupo, Michele 143
Lust for a Vampire 279
Lynch, David 18, 49, 306

M 111
M.D.C. - Maschera di cera see *Wax Mask, The*
Maa Ki Shakti see *Ammoru*
Macabre Legacy, The see *herencia macabra, La*
Macabre Nightmare (anthology segment) 34
Macabre Trunk, The see *baúl macabro, El*
Macbeth 239
MacColl, Catriona 165
Machurrucutu II: Haz lo incorrecto 84
Maciel, David R. 93
Mad Love 10, 99, 101, 105
Mad Monster Party? 76
Madra, Putra 220
Mafeng nil see Leper Woman
Mai, Ching 53
Maid's Bitter Story, A 43
main du diable, La **270**, 271, 273
Mainly on the Plains (TV series episode) 70
Majano, Anton Giulio 273
Makaki, Mio 304
Making Things Perfectly Queer: Interpreting Mass Culture (book) 142
maldición de la bestia, La see *Werewolf and the Yeti, The*
Malkoçoğlu 211
Malkoçoğlu (comic book) 211
Malpertuis 280
Man Sells His Life, A 187
Man Who Saves the World, The see *Dünyayi Kurtaran Adam*
Manananggal in Manila **254**, 260, 262
Manchurian Candidate, The 194
manège, Le (short film) 280
Mang Tano, Nuno ng mga Aswang 255
Man-hui, Lee 186
Manhunter 176
Mann, Micahel 176
Mann, Thomas 16
Manners, David 206
Man's Flower Road, A (short film) 307
Manson Family, The (cult) 239
Manster, The 274
Marais, Jean **264**, 270, 271
marca del Hombre-lobo, La see *Mark of the Wolfman, The*
Marceau, Marcel 16, 21
Marceau, Sophie 237
Mare, Il 185
Margheriti, Antonio 105
Marins, Antonio 27, 36
Marins, José Mojica 9, 10, **26**, 27-37, 81, 83, 84, **148**, **149**, 225
mariscal del infierno, El see *Devil's Possessed, The*
Mariscal, Diana 15
Mark of the Devil 75
Mark of the Vampire 7
Mark of the Wolfman, The 70
Marker, Chris 279
Marriage Trap, The 39
Martin 8
Martin, Frank see Girolami, Marino
Martino, Sergio 135, 138
Martyred, The 186
Maryja (1967) 256, 257
Maryja (1995) 258
Marx, Karl 48, 59
Mary, Mary, Bloody Mary 16
Más fuerte que el deber see *Stronger Than Duty*
Masako 299
maschera del demonio, La see *Black Sunday*
maschera del demonio, La see *Mask of Satan, The*
Mask of Fu Manchu, The 7
Mask of Satan, The 9, 161, 162, 297
Masked Devil see *Maskeli Seytan*
Maskeli Seytan 212
Massaccesi, Aristide 162, 169, 173, 176
Matsushima, Nanako 298, **299**, **300**
Mattei, Bruno 166
McClintock, Anne 143
McNally, Raymond 207
McNaughton, John 47, 176
Medina, Pen 260
Medved, Michael 10
Mekas, Jonas 17
Melford, George 94
Méliès, Georges 9, 250, 265-267, 270, 273
Memento Mori **158**, 185, 195-197, 199, 201
Memento Mori 2 see *Memento Mori*
Memoirs of a Wolf Man (book) 77
Men, Women, and Chain Saws: Gender in the Modern Horror Film (book) 52
Menado, Maria 127-130
Méndez, Fernando 103
Mendik, Xavier 233
Menzies, William Cameron 168
Merhige, E. Elias 268
Merry-Go Round, The see *manège, Le (short film)*
Meu Destino em Tuas Mãos see *My Destiny in Your Hands*
Meurisse, Paul 272
Mexican Cinema: Reflections of a Society, 1896-1980 (book) 94
Mexico (book) 94
Mexico: From Montezuma to NAFTA, Chiapas, and Beyond (book) 98
Mexico's Cinema: A Century of Film and Filmmakers (book) 93
Meyer, Russ 226
Michaëlis, Dario 161
Midi-Minuit Fantastique (magazine) 9, 277
Midnight at Madame Tussaud's 105
Midnight Movies (book) 17
Midnight Song **38**, 40-43
Midnight Song II 42-43
Mid-Nightmare 43
Miike, Takashi 11, 202, 285-293, 305, 306, 311
Mi-jo, Yoon 198
Milano, morte sospetta di una minorenne 135
Milestone, Lewis 117
Mill of the Stone Women **1**, 105-109
Miller, John 229
Mills, Jack see Naschy, Paul
Milne, Tom 10
Milton, John 303
Min, Kim 202
Ming-liang, Tsai 190
Min-sun, Kim 195
Miraglia, Emilio P. 143
Mirror with Three Panels, The see *glace à trois faces, La*
misterio del rostro pálido, El **92**, 99-102
Mistretta, Gaetano 162, 170
Mitchum, Robert 178
Mi-Youn, Lee 192
Mizoguchi, Kenji 125
Modern Germanies (book) 112
Moebius see Giraud, Jean
Mojica, Carmen 27
Mok, Karen 46
Molina, Enrique 69
Molina, Jorge 11, 81-90
Molina, Sergio 77
Molina's Culpa see *Culpa*
Molina's Test (short film) 81-84, **86**, 87-89
momia azteca, La 9
Momoi, Haruko 310
Mondo cane 163
mondo di Yor, Il see *Yor, the Hunter from the Future*
Mondo Macabro: Weird & Wonderful Cinema Around the World (book) 10, 37, 226, 255
Monicelli, Mario 173
Monrak Transistor see *Transistor Love Story*
Monster Commando (film series) 302
Monster of London City, The 122
Monster Show: A Cultural History of Horror, The (book)
monstruos del terror, Los see *Assignment Terror*
Montefiore, Luigi 169
Mora, Carl J. 94
Moreno, Alma 260
Moretti, Nanni 173
Morris, Marc 278
Morrissey, Paul 17
Most Dangerous Game, The 101, 102
Most Important Thing Is to Love, The 236
Mother (anthology segment) see *Nanay (anthology segment)*
Mr. Tano, the Elder of the Witches see *Mang Tano, Nuno ng mga Aswang*
Mr. Vampire (film series) 9
Muertos hablan, Los 99, 101, 102
Mühe, Ulrich 178, **181**
Mukthar, Mehmet 206-208
Mulargia, Edoardo 143
mulino delle donne di pietra, Il see *Mill of the Stone Women*
Müller, Paul 161
Mulvey, Laura 51
Mummy, The 7, 96, 99
Murakami, Ryu 286
Murdaa Ghar 252
Murder By Proxy see *Phantom of Soho, The*
Murder By Television 102
Murder Clinic, The 135
Murder on Diamond Row 122
Murders in the Rue Morgue 7, 99, 100, 102, 273
Murders in the Zoo 101
Murnau, F.W. 125
Musa: The Warrior 202
Musante, Tony 140
Mussolini, Benito 135
My Destiny in Your Hands 29
Myeong-jae, Kim 189
Myers, Mike 56
Myrna Diones Story: Lord Have Mercy, The 256
Mystery of the Ghastly Face, The see *misterio del rostro pálido, El*
Mystery of the Wax Museum 7, **104**, 105
Mystics in Bali 126, 220, **221**, 222, 223, 226, 227, 229
Mythologies of Violence in Postmodern Media (book) 56

Na srebnym globie see *Silver Globe, The*
Nabi see *Butterfly, The*
Nacar, Behçet 209, 210
Nachruf für einen Mörder 175
Nadja 280
Nagai, Go 302
Naigach, Raveekant 244
Nakagawa, Nobuo 297
Nakama, Yukie 300
Nakata, Hideo 194, 295, 299, 305
Nakatini, Miki 300
Naked Killer 46
Naked Mask (film series) see *Kekkou Kamen (film series)*
Name of the Rose, The (book) 135
Nanay (anthology segment) 261-262
Nang Nak **60**, 61-66
Narcejac, Thomas 272
Naschy, Paul 10, 69-80, **151**
Nasty Hunter 227-229
National Geographic (magazine) 125
National Pastime: Contemporary Philippine Cinema, The (book) 255
Nature and Logic of Capitalism, The (book) 59
Necronomicon: The Journal of Horror & Erotic Cinema, Book One (book) 280
Neighbour, The (anthology segment) see *Ang Kapitbahay (anthology segment)*
Neill, Sam 236, **237**
Nepomuceno, Jose 255
Nerval, Gérard de 271
New Tenant 45, 57-59
New York Ripper, The 182
New York Times, The (newspaper) 18
Newman, Kim 11
Next! **137**, 138
Ng, Lawrence 52
Nicholson, Jack 239
Night of Terror 115
Night of the Living Dead 8, 23, 75, 161, 163, 164, 168, 169
Night of the Seagulls, The 168
Night of the Zombies see *Kung Bakit Dugo ang Kulay ng Gabi*
Night of the Zombies see *Zombie Creeping Flesh*
Nightmare City 164, 166-168
Nightmare on Elm Street (film series) 249
Nightmare on Elm Street, A 197
Nightmare on Main Street: Angels, Sadomasochism, and the Culture of Gothic (book) 257
Nightmare see *Horror Game Movie, The*
Nights of Terror see *Burial Ground*
Nights of the Werewolf 70
Nihon Kuroshakai see *Ley Lines*
Nimibutr, Nonzee 11, 61-66
Ninth Gate, The 240-241
Nisen Nin No Otoko To Yatta Jyoshid Aisei vs. Anime Otaku No Dotei 311
Nitya Sumangali 127
No profanar el sueño de los muertos see *Let Sleeping Corpses Lie*
No. 3 190
noche de las gaviotas, La see *Night of the Seagulls, The*
noche de Walpurgis, La see *Werewolf's Shadow*
noche del terror ciego, La see *Tombs of the Blind Dead*
noches del Hombre Lobo, Las see *Nights of the Werewolf*
Noli Me Tangere (book) 257
nome della rosa, Il (book) see *Name of the Rose, The (book)*
Non si deve profanare il sonno dei morti see *Let Sleeping Corpses Lie*
Nonhosonno see *Sleepless*
Noriega, Manuel **98**, 101
Noroi no Yakata: Chi O Suu Me see *Lake of Dracula*
Nosferatu 125, 206, 268
Nosferatu the Vampyre 212, 239
Nostrodamus 102
notti del terrore, Le see *Burial Ground*
Novak, Harry 278
Noveck, Fima 280
novia ensangrentada, La see *Blood Spattered Bride, The*
Novo, Salvador 101
Now You See Love, Now You Don't 45
Nowhere to Hide 202
Nowicki, Jan 232
Noz w wodzie see *Knife in the Water*
Nuda per Satana see *Nude for Satan*
Nude for Satan 212
Nude per l'assassino see *Strip Nude for Your Killer*
Nun, The (anthology segment) see *Ang Madre (anthology segment)*
Nyi Blorong see *Snake Queen, The*

horror cinema across the globe 317

index

Obregón, Alvaro 94
O'Brien, Glenn 17
Obsession (anthology segment) 34
occhi freddi della paura, Gli see *Cold Eyes of Fear*
occhio nel labirinto, L' see *Eye in the Labyrinth, The*
Odishon see *Audition*
Offer, Tonya 229
O'Hara, Mario 260, 262
Oily Man see *Orang Minyak*
Oilyman Strikes Again, The see *Serangan Orang Minyak*
ojos azules de la muñeca rota, Los see *Blue Eyes of the Broken Doll*
Old Dark House, The 81, 84, 269
Olin, Lena 240
Ölüler Konusmazki 212
Ölüm Savasçısı 212
Omar, Latifah 128
Ömer the Tourist in Star Trek see *Turist Ömer Uzay Yolunda*
Onchi, Hideo 291
One Hundred Ghost Stories 298
Onibaba 296, **297**, 298
Ono, Yoko 17
Opera 140
Oppenheimer, Paul 166
Oppenheimer, Robert 270
Oran, Bülent 205, 206, 209
Orang Minyak 127
Ordinary Heroes 52
Orellana, Carlos **103**
Orfei, Liana **107**
orgia de los muertos, La see *Hanging Woman, The*
orgia nocturna de los vampiros, La see *Vampire's Night Orgy*
Orphée 170
orribile segreto del Dottor Hichcock, L' see *Terror of Dr. Hichcock, The*
Ortín, Leopoldo 'Chato' **99**, 101
Ortolani, Riz 170
Oshikiri see *Straw Cutter, The*
Ossessione 136
Ossorio, Amando de 168
Otaka, Rikiya 300
O'Toole, Peter 18, 19
Ouimet, Danielle 280
Out of the Past 271
Oval Portrait, The (story) 268
Owen, Arthur E. 120
Özgüç, Agah 206
Ozu, Yasujiro 286, 288
Pabst, G.W. 111
Padosi ki Biwi 248
Palance, Jack 207
Palau, Pierre 271
Palmerini, Luca M. 162, 170
Pang Brothers 62
Panic Fables (comic strip) see *Fábulas Pánicas* (comic strip)
Paradise Lost (book) 303
Parbpayon Siam (magazine) 61
Pardavé, Joaquin 102
Paris After Dark see *fin du monde, La*
Pasolini, Pier Paolo 173
Passi di danza su una lama di rasoio see *Death Carries a Cane*
Pastor, Rachel 81
Pastore, Sergio 140
Patayin sa Sindak si Barbara 256
Pattison, Barrie 10
Paul, Robert W. 266
Paura nella città dei morti viventi see *City of the Living Dead*
Pear Blossom in the Storm 39
Peary, Danny 18
Peeping Tom 274
Pembalasan Ratu Pantai Selatan see *Nasty Hunter*
Pencil Murders, The 144
Penderecki, Krzysztof 232
Pengabdi Setan **224**, 225
Penghidupan 128
Peón, Ramón 95
People Who Own the Dark, The 75
Pereda, Ramón 95, 99, 102
Pereira dos Santos, Nelson 35
Perez, Antonio Jose 255, 256
Perez, Fernando 83
Perez, Tony 258
Pérez-Reverte, Arturo 240
Perfect Blue 144
Perkawinan Nyi Blorong **222**
Perlman, Ron 281
Person, Luís Sérgio 33
Perver, Canan 213
Perversão **33**, **36**
Pesadelo Macabro (anthology segment) see *Macabre Nightmare* (anthology segment)
Petal, A 190
Petry, Iwona 237, 238
Pflug, Eva 114
Phantasm 225
Phantom Lover, The 43
Phantom of Soho, The 122, **123**
Phantom of the Convent see *fantasma del convento, El*
Phantom of the Opera, The (1925) 7, 42, 93, 100, 102
Phantom of the Opera, The (book) 39
Phantom von Soho, Das see *Phantom of Soho, The*
Phool Bani Patthar 251

Picasso, Pablo 233
Picasso, Paloma 233
Pieczka, Franciszek 233
Pier, The 279
Pierce, Jack 270
Pierro, Marina **230**, 235, 236
P'Imak see *House of Death*
Ping, Hu **38**
Pinon, Dominique 281
Pirandello, Luigi 181
Plague of the Zombies, The 72
Planet Hong Kong: Popular Cinema and the Art of Entertainment (book) 46
Planet of the Apes, The 270
planète sauvage, La see *Fantastic Planet*
Playgirls and the Vampire, The 9
Pleasence, Donald 169
Poe, Edgar Allan 7, 8, 109, 135, 143, 253, 268
Polanski, Roman 49, 129, 238-241
Polselli, Renato 212
Poltergeist 246
Pontianak 9, 126-129
Pontianak (1975) 131
Pontianak Gua Musang 130, **131**
Pontianak Kembali 128, 130
Popiól I diament see *Ashes and Diamonds*
positions: east asia cultures critique (journal) 255
Possession 236-237
Postscript: Essays on Film and the Humanities (magazine) 59, 163, 182
Potloodmoorden, De see *Pencil Murders, The*
Potocki, Count Jan 231
Powell, Michael 274
Pradeaux, Maurizio 140
Preiss, Wolfgang **106**, 107, **108**, 109
Presley, Elvis 69
Price of Doubt, The (unreleased) see *Süphenin Bedeli* (unreleased)
Price, Vincent 8, 105
Prima, Barry 224-226
Prison of Love 39
Psychic, The 143
Psycho 11, 21, 23, 215, 216, 272, 274
Psychology and Alchemy (book) 105
Public Affairs (magazine) 47
Pui, Hui 53
Pulgasari 189
Pulse 305, 311
Purdom, Edmund 169
Pure Blood 9
Pusaka Pontianak 130
Pye, Merrill 23
Pyushchye Krovy see *Blood-Suckers*

Qian Nu You Hun see *Chinese Ghost Story, A*
Qing chang guairen see *Love Freak, The*
Qiu haitang see *Autumn Begonia*
Quartet 237
Quella villa accanto al cimitero see *House by the Cemetery, The*
¿Quien sabe? see *Bullet for the General, A*
Quiet Family, The 62, 191, 199
Quintos, Floy 260
Quionglou hen see *Maid's Bitter Story, A*
Quirk, Robert E. 94, 98
Quizon, Eric 262

Raat 251, 252
Rabal, Francisco 167
Rabenreither, Silvia 177
Rabid 8, **88**
Rächer, Der see *Avenger, The*
ragazza che sapeva troppo, La see *Girl Who Knew Too Much, The*
Raimi, Sam 212, 282
Rainbow Thief, The 18, 19
Raines, Claude 7, 21
Rainy Dog 285
Rais, Gilles de 74
raisins de la mort, La see *Grapes of Death*
Rajhans, B.S. 129
Ramakrishna, Kodi 253
Ramirez, Daria 259
Ramlee, P. 127, 128, 130, 131
Ramos, Maximo D. 259, 260
Ramsay, F.U. 244, 245
Ramsay, Gangu 246
Ramsay, Keshu 247
Ramsay, Kiran 246, 247
Ramsay, Kumar 245, 246
Ramsay, Shyam 244-247
Ramsay, Tulsi 244-247
Rangeela 252
Rao, Balakrishna Narayan 127, 128, 130
Rape of the Vampire see *viol du vampire, Le*
Rappaccini's Daughter (book) 106
Rashomon 98
Ratanaruang, Pen-Ek 62, 63
Rau, Andrea 280
Razak, Abdul 127, 128
Real Fiction 201-202
Rear Window 39
rebelión de las muertas, La see *Vengeance of the Zombies*
Rebellion, Die 175
Rec see *Record, The*
Record, The 197, 198, 201
Red Serpent, The 86
Reddy, Shyam Prasad 253

Reeves, Michael 75
regina dei cannibali, La see *Zombi Holocaust*
Reincarnation of Isabel, The 212
Reinl, Harald 112, 115
Reis, Michelle 288
Rekopis znaleziony w Saragossie see *Saragossa Manuscript, The*
Replay 295
Reptile, The 72
Reptilian 194
Repulsion 196, 238-239
Requiem for a Vampire 278
Requiem pour un vampire see *Requiem for a Vampire*
Resnais, Alain 267, 279
Resurrected Rose 43
retorno de Walpurgis, El see *Curse of the Devil*
retorno del Hombre Lobo, El see *Return of the Wolfman*
Retribution Sight Unseen 52
Return of the Blind Dead, The 168
Return of the Wolfman 75-76
Return to Pontianak **124**, 131-132
Return to Salem's Lot, A 8
Revenge of the Dead see *Zeder: Voices from the Beyond*
Revenge of the Vampire see *Dendam Pontianak*
Reyes, Jose Javier 258
Reyes, Lore 260-262
Reynes, Manilyn 260, 261
Riegel, Karyn 81
Ring (1998) 194, 197, 291, 298-300, 302, 304, 305
Ring (2002) 11
Ring (film series) 295, 298-302
Ring 0 300, **301**
Ring 0: Baasudei 300
Ring 2 194, 300, 302, 304
Ring Virus, The **184**, 194
Ringu 2 see *Ring 2*
Ringu see *Ring* (1998)
Riri Shushu no subete see *All About Lily Chou-Chou*
Rites of Love 236
Rites of May, The see *Itim*
Riti, magie nere e segrete orge nel trecento see *Reincarnation of Isabel, The*
Rivault, Pascale 235
Rizal, Jose 257
Robbe-Grillet, Alain 216
Robinson, Pete 23
Robles, German 10
Robotrix 46
Robson, Mark 8
Roces, Susan 257, 258
Rocha, Glauber 35
Rocky Horror Picture Show, The 81
Roderick, Olga 23
Roel, Marta 96
Rohlen, Thomas P. 303, 304
Roland, Jürgen 115
Rollin, Jean 10, 277-280
Rolly **310**
Román, Leticia 136
Romeo and Juliet (play) 257
Romero, George A. 8, 23, 85, 143, 161-164, 166, 169, 228
Roohani Taaqat 249
Room, The 307
Rosemary's Baby 8, 238, 239
Rosenbaum, Jonathan 17
Rossellini, Roberto 173
Rosset, Edith 177
Rosso sangue see *Absurd*
Rote Kreis, Der see *Crimson Circle, The*
rouge aux lèvres, Le see *Daughters of Darkness*
Ruang talok 69 see *6ixtynin9*
Ruggles, Charlie 101
Run and Kill 47
Russell, Ken 75, 84
Ryan, Edmon 119
Rybczynski, Zbigniew 176

Sa Piling ng Aswang 262
Saamri (1985) **246**, 247
Saamri (1998) 252
Sacramental Melodrama (play) 16
Sade, Marquis de 75
Saint John, Antoine 166
Sakei, Hinako 304
Sakuya 295
salaire de la peur, Le see *Wages of Fear, The*
Salazaar, Abel 93
Salem's Lot 8
Salkind, Alexander 18
Salvador, Phillip 259
Salvati, Sergio 162
Samson vs. the Vampire Women 9
San geng see *Three*
Sanada, Hiroyuki 299, **300**
Sanatorium pod klepsydra see *Sandglass, The*
Sanders-Brahms, Helma 179
Sandglass, The 232-233
Saner, Hulki 213
sang des bêtes, Le 274
Sang-ok, Shin 186, 188, 189, 202
Sangre de vírgenes 9
Sanpasartsupakij, Prince 61
Santa 94
Santa Sangre **14**, 15, 18-24, **146**, **147**
Santo contra las mujeres vampiros, El see *Samson Vs. the Vampire Women*
Santo, Yos 222
Santos, Charo 259, **261**

Santos, Vilma 257
Saragossa Manuscript, The **152**, 231-233, 241
Saragossa Manuscript, The (book) 231
Sarne, Michael 17
Sartsanatieng, Wisit 62
Satan see *Seytan*
Satay, Wahid 129
Sato, Hitomi 299
Savada, Elias 23
Savage Man, Savage Beast 163
Saving Private Ryan 270
Savini, Tom 162
Say Yes 185, **200**, 201, 202
Scandal in Bohemia, A (story) 240
Scardamaglia, Elio 135
Scarecrow, The 300
Scared to Death 100
Scars of Dracula 206
Scary Taxi see *Ghost Taxi*
Schatten see *Warning Shadows*
Schneider, Romy 236
Schneider, Stephen Jay 105, 182, 233
School Killer 9
School Legend 185, 196-197, 201
Schrader, Paul 81
Schreck, Max 206
Schüfftan, Eugen 273
Schulz, Bruno 233
Schulze, Klaus 176
Sciascia, Leonardo 135
Scissors see *Horror Game Movie, The*
Scob, Edith 272
Scorsese, Martin 66
Scott, George C. 168
Scott, Susan 142
Scream 77, 182, 197, 198, 252
Screams in the Night see *Awful Dr. Orloff, The*
Se7en 194, 201
Seal of Dracula, The (book) 10
Secret Tears 198, **199**, 203
Seddok, l'erede di Satana see *Atom Age Vampire*
Seguerra, Aiza 260, 262
Seguin, Louis 23
Sei donne per l'assassino see *Blood and Black Lace*
Seigner, Emmanuelle 240
Sellers, Peter 7
Sen, Krishna 219
Seoul Jesus 190
Serangan Orang Minyak 128, 130-131
Sermet, Özen 209
Serpent's Tale see *Karanlik Sular*
Sesselmann, Sabine **112**, 121
sete vampiras, As see *7 Vampires*
Sette note in nero see *Psychic, The*
Sette scialli di seta gialla see *Crimes of the Black Cat*
Seung-wook, Moon 202
Seven Women Prisoners 186
Seventh Continent, The 175, 180
Severed Heads, The (book) 16
Sevimli Frankestayn 212
Sex and the Vampire 9
Se-yeon, Choi 192
Seyfi, Ali Riza 206-208
Seyrig, Delphine 280
Seytan **153**, **204**, 212-214, 216
Seytan Kovma (short film) 216
Shadow of the Vampire 268
Shafie, Fadzlina Mohamad **124**, 132
Shaitaani Illaka 247
Shake, Rattle & Roll (film series) 261
Shake, Rattle & Roll III 261, 262
Shake, Rattle & Roll IV 260-262, **263**
Shakespeare, William 257
Shaman, The 237-238
Shan, Jin **38**, 41
Shanghai Gesture 84
Sharif, Omar 18, 19, 35
Sharrett, Christopher 56
Shaw Brothers 125, 127, 128
Shaw, Daniel 105
Shaw, George Bernard 112
Sheen, Simon see *Sang-ok, Shin*
Shelley, Mary 7
Shichuan, Zhang 39
Shiina, Eihi 289
Shindo, Kaneto 296, 298
Shining, The 232
Shinjuku Kuroshakai: Chinese Mafia Sensô 11
Shinjuku Triad Society
Shinjuku Triad Society 285, 286, 288, 291
Shiota, Akihiko 306
Shiri **158**, 193, 194, 202
Shivers 8, 88
Shock Theatre (TV series) 111
Shock Waves 10
Shohat, Ella 46
Shrek 56
Si Conat 219
Sidoglio Smithee 84
Siebente Kontinent, Der see *Seventh Continent, The*
Sign of Death, The see *signo de la muerte, El*
Sign of the Four, The (story) 143
signo de la muerte, El 101-103
Signoret, Simone 272
Siguion-Reyna, Armida 262
Silence of the Lambs, The 11
Silver Globe, The 236
Simões, Ilidio 31
Sina do Aventureiro, A see *Adventurer's Fate, The*

318   **fear without frontiers**

index

Sineneng, Jerry Lopez 260, 262
Siodmak, Curt 7
Sis (short film) 216
Siti Zubaidah 128
Siu-Tung, Ching 10, 83
Skal, David J. 23, 94, 269
Skeldon, Ronald 47
Slaughter Hotel 140, **142**, **143**
Sleepless 138
Sloane, Paul 115
Snake Queen, The **156**, **218**, **222**, 223-225
Snake Woman, The 295
So Sweet, So Perverse 135
Soavi, Michele 172, 173
Soler, Julián **101**
Song at Midnight see Midnight Song
Sono, Sion 11, 305-311
sopravvissuti della città morta, I see Ark of the Sun God, The
Sorin, Carlos 84
Sorum 185, 199, 201
Soul Guardians, The 191, 197
Soylent Green 75
Spaghetti Nightmares (book) 162, 170
Spellbound 186
Sphinx, The 102
Spies 111, 114
Spiral 295
Spirits of the Dead 279
Spooky School see School Legend
squartatore di New York, Lo see New York Ripper, The
Squeaker, The see Murder on Diamond Row
Squires, Chris 216
Stam, Robert 46
Star Trek (TV series) 213
Star Wars 212
Star, The (Malasian newspaper) 126
Steele, Barbara 161
Stevenson, R.L. 7
Stevenson, Robert Louis 235, 271
Stiglitz, Hugo 167
Stockwell, Guy 19
Stoker, Bram 7, 206-208, 279
Stoloff, Benjamin 115
Stone, Oliver 131, 179
Strange Case of Dr. Jekyll & Mr. Hyde, The (book) 235
Strange Hostel of Naked Pleasures **29**
Strange World of Coffin Joe, The 33-35
Strange World of Coffin Joe, The (TV series) 32
Strange World of Zé do Caixão, The 27
strano vizio della signora Wardh, Lo see Next!
Straw Cutter, The 295
Strickfaden, Kenneth 101
Stringer, Julian 56
Strip Nude for Your Killer 142
Stroheim, Eric von 16
Stronger Than Duty 93
Styron, William 59
Subspecies (film series) 9
Suchlicki, Jaime 98
Sudarto, Gatot 223
Suharto, General Mohamed 220, 225-228
Suicide Club 305-311
Sukarno, General Achmad 220
Summers, Walter 111
Sumpah Orang Minyak 128, 130, 131
Sumpah Pontianak 127-129
Sundelbolong **225**
Sung-hong, Kim 201
Sun-woo, Jang 190
Sûper Adam Istanbul'da 212
superloco, El 99-102
Superman 18
Superman in Istanbul see Sûper Adam Istanbul'da
Sûphenin Bedeli (unreleased) 215
Suspiria 247
Sutton, Roger 131
Suzuki, Koji 298
Suzuki, Seijun 84, 286
Suzuz Yaz 213
Suzzanna **218**, **222**, 223, 227
Swallows, The 130
Swanson, Gloria 18
Sympathy for Mr. Vengeance 202
Szamanka see Shaman, The

Takahashi, Hiroshi 300
Takahata, Akio 303
Takan: The Golden Medallion see Tarkan: Altin Madalyon
Takeuchi, Riki 288
Takeuchi, Yuko 299
Takot ka ba sa Dilim 260
Tales from the Crypt (comic book) 30
Tales of a Corpse-Ridden Old House 41
Talwar, Vinod 249-251
Tam, Alan 57
Tan, Sooi Beng 129
Tangerine Dream 176
Tapia, Faviola Elenka 20
Tara (anthology segment) see Obsession (anthology segment)
Tarantino, Quentin 285
Tarkan (comic book) **210**, 211
Tarkan: Altin Madalyon **210**, 211
Tarkan: Gûmûs Eğer 211, **217**
Tarkan: The Silver Saddle see Tarkan: Gûmûs Eğer
Tarkhana 247
Tarot of Marseilles (cards) 18
Tarzan and the Jungle Boy 209

Tate, Sharon 238, 239
Taxi Hunter 45
Taygun, Meral 213
Taylor, Jack 240
Teah 288
Tears of the Black Tiger 62
Teenage Hooker Becomes Killing Machine 203
Telephone 247
Tell Me Something 185, 194, 202, 203
Tema, Muzaffer 206
Tenant, The 239, **240**
Tenebrae 136, 143
Teo, Stephen 39, 43
Tepes, Vlad 207-209, 280
Terminator, The 190
Terrible People, The 115
Terror Aboard 115
Terror of Dr. Hitchcock, The 105
Terza ipotesi su un caso di perfetta strategia criminale see Who Killed the Prosecutor and Why?
Testament of Dr. Mabuse, The 114
Testi, Fabio 236
Texas Chain Saw Massacre, The 8
That is the Point see Ahí está el detalle
That They May Live see J'accuse
Thatcher, Margaret 46
Theatre of Death 10
Theatre of Mr. And Mrs. Kabal, The 233
They're Coming to Get You 138
Thi Le, Hiep 131
Thing From Another World, The 8
Thing, The 247
Thirst 9
This Night I Will Possess Your Corpse 31-33, 37, **149**
Thousand on One Nights, The (stories) 130
Three 62
Three Musketeers, The (book) 240
Three Ninjas (film series) 189
Threepenny Opera, The 112
Thrower, Steve 10
Thys, Guy Lee 144
Ti, Le 43
Tian mi mi see Comrades: Almost a Love Story
Tianak 255
Tih Minh (film serial) 267
Time Bandits 281
Timeless, Bottomless, Bad Movie see Bad Movie
Titanic 61, 64, 185, 194
Tixou, Thelma 20, **147**
To Each His Own (book) 135
Todd, Bobby 120
Tohill, Cathal 235
Tokyo Decadence 286
Tomb of Ligeia (story) 268
Tombs of the Blind Dead 168
Tombs, Pete 10, 37, 226, 235, 255
Tominaga, Amina 303
Top Banana Club 45
Topor, Roland 16, 239
Torn Curtain 169
Toshiaki, Toyoda 306
toten augen von London, Die see Dead Eyes of London
Touch Me Not (book) see Noli Me Tangere (book)
Tourneur, Jacques 8, 163, 271, 298
Tourneur, Maurice 105, 271
Tovar, Lupita 93, 94
Towne, Robert 239
Transistor Love Story 62
Treasure Island 7
Trilogia de terror see Trilogy of Terror
Trilogy of Terror 33, 34
Tristana 108
Tropical Animal (book) 82
Trotter, Laura 167
Truffaut, François 274, 279
Truth About Charlie, The 202
Tsuruta, Norio 300
Tsuruya, Nanboku 297
Tun Fatimah 128
Tür mit den 7 Schlössern, Die see Door with Seven Locks, The (1962)
Turist Ömer Uzay Yolunda 213
Turk Filmleri Sözlüğü (book) 206
Tusk 18, 19
Tutti i colori del buio see They're Coming to Get You
Twelve Monkeys 279
Twilight Zone, The (TV series) 202
Twins of Evil 279
Two Evil Eyes 143
Two Monks see Dos monjes

uccello dalle piume di cristallo, L' see Bird with the Crystal Plumage, The
Uchu Shojo Keiji Buruma see Young Girl Space Detective Bloomer
Ueno, Katsuhito 304
Ugetsu monogatari 226
Ulmer, Edgar G. 7, 273
Ulrich, Kurt 115, 116, 121
ultima preda del vampiro, L' see Playgirls and the Vampire, The
Ultime grida dalla savana: La grande caccia see Savage Man, Savage Beast
Último deseo see People Who Own the Dark, The
Uluçay, Ahmet 216
Ünal, Cihan 213
Underdog Rock (CD) 45
Underground Banker, The 45, 52-54
Underground USA: Film-making Beyond the

Hollywood Canon (book) 233
Ungeheuer von London City, Das see Monster of London City, The
Unholy Three, The 7
Unknown, The 24, 100
Unsane see Tenebrae
Unthinking Eurocentrism: Multiculturalism and the Media (book) 46
Untold Story II, The 55
Untold Story, The 45, 48-52, 54, 55, 59
uomo più velenoso del cobra, L' see Human Cobras
Urquijo, Raúl **99**
Urruchúa, Victor 97
Urueta, Chano 101, 297
Useless is Useful (CD) 45
Utsushimi 307
Uygun, Metin 215
Uzumaki see Spiral

Vadim, Annette 279
Vadim, Roger 279, 280
Valdez, Indira 81
Valli, Alida 107, 273
Vampire Bat, The 7, 101
Vampire Doll, The 298
Vampire in Brooklyn, A 8
Vampire Lovers, The 279
Vampire of the Cave, The see Pontianak Gua Musang
Vampire People, The 9
Vampire Returns, The see Pontianak Kembali
Vampire, The 9, 103
Vampire, The see Pontianak
Vampires 8
Vampires in Havana 9
Vampire's Night Orgy 70
Vampires, Les (film serial) 267
vampiri, I 105, 161-162, 169
vampiro, Ee Vampire, The
¡Vampiros en La Habana! see Vampires in Havana
Vampyr 279
Vampyres 247
Van Gogh, Vincent 193
Van Weigen, Pieter 105
Vanilla Sky 11
Vanishing Lady, The see Escamotage d'une Dame chez Robert-Houdin
Vanishing, The (1988) 201
Vanishing, The (1993) 10, 11
Vari, Giuseppe 135
Varma, Ramgopal 251, 252
Vasques, Romeo 257
Veer Kumari 127
Veerana 247
Velasco, Rolfie L. 255
venganza de la momia, La see Vengeance of the Mummy, The
venganza del Dr. Mabuse, La 274
Vengeance of the Mummy, The 73
Vengeance of the Zombies 72, **79**
Vernon, Howard **151**
Vertigo 173, 272
vértigo del crimen, El **151**
Victor, Henry 23
Video Junkie (magazine) 47
Video Watchdog (magazine) 10, 228, 278, 280
Viewing Positions: Ways of Seeing Film (book) 140
Village Voice, The (newspaper) 17
Villarias, Carlos 93, 94, 99, 102
Villatoro, Carlos 96, 97
viol du vampire, Le **276**, 278
Virus see Zombie Creeping Flesh
Viscera Sucking Witch, The see Ang Manananggal
Visconti, Luchino 136, 173
Visitor Q 286-290
Visual and Other Pleasures (book) 51
Vizconde Massacre: God Help Us, The 256
Vohrer, Alfred 116-118, 120, 121
Voivode with the Stakes, The (book) see Kazikli Voyvoda (book)
Vural, Vahdet 215

wachsfigurenkabinett, Das see Waxworks
Wages of Fear, The 272
Wajda, Andrzej 231
Wakasugi, Kazushi 289
Wake up, Maruja see Gumising Ka, Maruja
Wallace, Bryan Edgar 122
Wallace, Edgar 111, 112, 115-117, 119, 120, 122, 123
Waller, Gregory A. 182
Walter, Wilfrid 118
Wang-Magui 187
War of the Worlds, The 85
Warbeck, David 165
Warning Shadows 97
Warren, Jerry 9
Warrior, The 225-226
Watanabe, Kazushi 289
Watering the Gardener see arroseur arrosé, L
Wax Mask, The 105
Waxworks 105
Way, Fay 7
Weaver, Sigourney 240
Weber, Amy 229
Weekend Murders, The 143
Wegener, Paul 106
Weibang, Maxu 39-43
Weisser, Thomas 296
Welles, Orson 18, 88, 97, 173, 277
Wells, H.G. 270

Werewolf and the Yeti, The 74-75
WereWolf of London, The 7
Werewolf's Shadow 70, **71**, 75, **78**
Weston, Armand 169
Whale, James 7, 21, 23, 24, 41-43, 81, 84, 85
What Have You Done to Solange? 123
What? 239
Wheel, The (anthology segment) 62, **67**
While Paris Sleeps 105
Whisper to the Wind see Ibulong Mo Sa Hangin
Whispering Corridors 185, 191-193, 196-198, **202**, 203
White Zombie 7
White, Timothy 129
Who Killed the Prosecutor and Why? 135
Wife and Son of Dr. Caligari, The (short film) see Dr. Caligari'nin Karisi ve Oglu (short film)
Wild One, The 131
Wilde, Oscar 108
Wilder, Billy 83, 84
Willeman, Paul 10
Williams, Linda 140
Williams, Patrick 51
Williams, Tony 59
Wilmington, Michael 16
Wilson, William S. 47
Wind, The 307
Winters, Shelley 239
Wise, Robert 8, 85
Witch with Flying Head, The 126, 220
Witch, The see Ang Aswang
Witch, The see Impakto
Witchfinder General 75
Witch's Mirror, The 297
Witcombe, L.C.E. 255
With the Witch see Sa Piling ng Aswang
Wizard of Darkness (film series) see Eko Eko Azarak (film series)
Wohi Bhayaanak Raat **155**, **242**, 249-250
Wolf Man, The 8
Wolnyoui Han 9
Woman of Fire 82, The 188
Woman of Fire, The 188
Wong Brothers 219
Wong, Anthony 11, **44**, 45-59, 154
Woo, John 45, 48, 288, 291
Woo, Lian Sing 126
Wood, Miles 52
World and I, The (magazine) 303
World Fact Book of Criminal Justice (book) 51
Wray, Fay **104**
Wu-hyeok, Lee 191
Wüstenhagen, Harry 120

Xiaoping, Deng 46
Xinghai, Xian 41, 43

Yalinkiliç, Yavuz 212
Yam, Simon 47, 48, 52
Yamamoto, Hideo 286
Yamamoto, Michio 298
Yasuda, Kimiyoshi 298
Yau, Herman 47-52, 54-57, **154**
Yeban gesheng see Midnight Song
Yeban gesheng xuji see Midnight Song II
Yeh-jin, Park 185
yeux sans visage, Les see Eyes Without a Face
Yiu-kuen, Ng 55
Yo-go-kuei-dam see Whispering Corridors
Yokai Daisenso see Great Ghost War, The
Yokai Hyaku Monagatari see One Hundred Ghost Stories
Yongary, Monster from the Deep 187, 194
Yong-min, Lee 187
Yong-min, Yi 186
Yong-nyeo, Lee 192
Yong-su, Park 192
Yoon-hyun, Chang 194
Yor, the Hunter from the Future 212
Yös, Baris 216
Yoshino, Kimika 302
Yotsuya Kaidan 297
Yotsuya Kaidan (play) 297
You hun see Marriage Trap, The
Young Frankenstein 212
Young Girl Space Detective Bloomer 302
Young-jin, Lee 185
Yu, Ronny 43, 45, 46, 83
Yun-fat, Chow 45, 48
Yungk-yoon, Shin 188
Yureiyashiki no Kyofu: Chi O Suu Ningyoo see Vampire Doll, The

Zagury, Fabrice 267
Zarate, Ernie 259
Zbonek, Edwin 122
Zé do Caixão see Marins, José Mojica
Zedd, Nick 84
Zeder: Voices from the Beyond 164, 170, 172
Zee Horror Show, The (TV series) 251
Zegen 285
Zinda Laash 243
Ziyi, Zhang 202
Zombi 2 see Zombie Flesh-Eaters
Zombi 3 164
Zombi Dawn of the Dead
Zombi Holocaust **160**, 164
Zombie 6: Monster Hunter see Absurd
Zombie Creeping Flesh 164, 166-167, 169
Zombie Flesh-Eaters 162-165
Zulawski, Andrzej 236-238
Zurakowska, Dyanik 70

More Essential Cinema Books from FAB Press

**DVD Delirium
volume 1**

ISBN 1-903254-04-3
UK £14.99 / US $19.99
640pp. 190mm x 135mm

**DVD Delirium
volume 2**

ISBN 1-903254-25-6
UK £14.99 / US $19.99
640pp. 190mm x 135mm

**Agitator: the cinema
of Takashi Miike**

ISBN 1-903254-21-3
UK £16.99 / US $24.99
408pp. 244mm x 171mm

Ten Years of Terror
British Horror Films of the 1970s

ISBN 1-903254-08-6
UK £35.00 / US $49.95
336pp. 300mm x 240mm

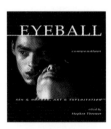

**Eyeball Compendium
1989-2003:
Sex and Horror,
Art and Exploitation**

ISBN 1-903254-17-5
UK £16.99 / US $24.99
384pp. 200mm x 200mm

**Flesh & Blood
Compendium**

ISBN 1-903254-10-8
UK £19.99 / US $29.99
456pp. 246mm x 189mm

**The Haunted World of
Mario Bava**

ISBN 1-903254-05-1
UK £24.99 / US $34.99
352pp. 297mm x 210mm

**Beyond Terror
the films of Lucio Fulci**

ISBN 0-9529260-6-7
UK £24.99 / US $39.99
312pp. 300mm x 240mm

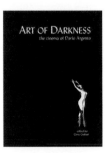

**Art of Darkness
the cinema of Dario Argento**

ISBN 1-903254-14-0
UK £24.99 / US $34.99
320pp. 297mm x 210mm

For further information about these books visit our online store, where we also have a fine selection of excellent DVD and soundtrack CD titles from all over the world!

www.fabpress.com